J. L. Randal

Pre 1971.

PRELATES AND PEOPLE OF THE LAKE COUNTIES

I. THE CHURCH OF ST. NINIAN, BROUGHAM,
from the west bank of the river Eamont, with Cross Fell in the distance.

(Frontispiece)

PRELATES AND PEOPLE

OF THE

LAKE COUNTIES

A History of the Diocese of Carlisle
1133—1933

BY

C. M. L. BOUCH, M.A., Oxon.

*Member of Council of the Cumberland and Westmorland
Antiquarian and Archaeological Society*

KENDAL:
TITUS WILSON AND SON LTD., 28 HIGHGATE
PRINTERS AND PUBLISHERS
—
1948

To

THE RIGHT REVEREND FATHER IN GOD

THOMAS

BY THE PROVIDENCE OF GOD

SIXTY-SECOND LORD BISHOP OF CARLISLE

THIS

HISTORY OF HIS DIOCESE

IS, WITH HIS LORDSHIP'S LEAVE, MOST RESPECTFULLY

DEDICATED

BY

HIS DUTIFUL SERVANT

THE AUTHOR.

" I am convinced that the time has come in our historical writing for a synthesis of local and national history. . . . There are such rich collections of material, both in manuscript and printed in the admirable journals of our local antiquarian societies, from which the conception and portrayal of English history may be deepened and enriched. It is in this direction, I feel, that great progress may be made next in our historical studies; perhaps more than in any other field."

(TUDOR CORNWALL, A. L. ROWSE, p. 10).

" ' Research' is not all that is needed. . . . Rather what is required is zeal, insatiable curiosity, a dogged determination to work at all times and in all places, and then a stern resolve to print the results—even though they seem incomplete, and though there may be a danger of their being superseded on account of later discoveries."

(ON THE WRITING OF HISTORY, Sir Charles Oman, p. 300).

" Being in some measure a stranger to these matters; I have improved my best endeavours to obtain the Justest Light to set these affairs upon their peculiar bottom."

(THE CURATE OF SEATHWAITE TO BISHOP GASTRELL OF CHESTER).

PREFACE.

The words of the distinguished historian, A. L. Rowse, given on the opposite page, stirred me to a decision, long considered but long deferred, of undertaking the work of which this book is the fruit. It has been written in the belief that the Church history of this Border diocese cannot be understood apart from its political and social history. It was not, however, easy to plan the book as the ancient ecclesiastical and civil boundaries of the Lake Counties bore no resemblance to each other. After consideration the best plan seemed to be:

(i) to limit the Church history given under the bishops of Carlisle to affairs within their see, but not to do so with the account of political events or of episodes, such as the Reformation, which could clearly be better treated as a whole;

(ii) to allot four chapters to describing the little that is known of the separate ecclesiastical history of the deaneries added to the diocese in 1856;

(iii) to begin each 'book' with a chapter dealing with the changing economic and social background to the general history.

In these days when every aspect of history has its specialist, there are many pitfalls for the writer whose plan covers so wide a subject as that embraced in this book. I trust that I have not fallen into too many of them—to have avoided all I can hardly hope. Indeed

I fear I may be held guilty of presumption for attempting so ambitious a project. My only excuse is that seeing the need for such a book and loving the history of these counties in which my forebears have dwelt 'time out of mind,' I have tried to fill a gap. I can only hope that many will get as much pleasure from reading the book as I have obtained from writing it. Though it is primarily intended for the general reader, I have given references to the authorities upon which its statements are based in the hope that they may be helpful to students. But the ordinary reader need not concern himself with them; any notes of general interest are placed at the bottom of the page.

Mr. T. Gray of Tullie House has read my manuscript and helped me with his extensive knowledge of books on local subjects; his staff have long suffered under my demands. Mr. J. C. Dickinson of Emmanuel College, Cambridge and Mr. C. R. Hudleston have also read the manuscript and assisted me in other ways. Professor A. Hamilton Thompson has guided me on sundry points and placed at my disposal his unprinted extracts from the archives of the archbishops of York. Mr. W. A. Pantin of Oriel College, Oxford has assisted me with the Middle Ages and in particular with Bishop Merke's life. For help in the section dealing with the modern diocese, I must name Bishop and Mrs. Williams, Bishop Powell, who read through this part of the manuscript, and Canon T. B. A. Saunders. Canon R. A. Davenport, the Rev. S. Young and Miss M. Pickering have assisted me in various ways. The value of a book of this kind is obviously much enhanced if manuscripts hitherto unused have been utilised. That this has been possible is due to the kindness of those who have so willingly allowed me access to their documents; their names will be found on pages 480-2. Particulars of those who have assisted me on special points or have taken or lent me the photographs for the illustrations will also be found in the appropriate places. My wife has designed the coat of arms on the dust cover and helped me with the proofs. To all these, as well as to Mr. C. J. B. Pollitt of Messrs. Titus Wilson and Son and their learned printers, I owe and give my grateful thanks. If by any mischance the name of any one has been omitted, I ask the owner's forgiveness.

C. M. LOWTHER BOUCH.

Clifton Rectory, Penrith,
   Candlemas, 1948.

CONTENTS.

BOOK ONE.

THE MIDDLE AGES.

PAGE

I   The Norman Settlement in Church and State   I

    Appendix I   The oldest parishes in the diocese ..   15

II   The Social Scene in the Middle Ages   ..   17

III   The Thirteenth Century or a Century of Construction   42

IV   The Fourteenth Century or War and Pestilence   63

V   The Decline of the Medieval World and a St. Luke's Summer   107

VI   The Archdeaconry of Richmond (beyond the moors) in the Middle Ages   136

    Appendix   II   Church Extension in the Middle Ages   157

            III   The Heraldry of Bishops and Cathedral in the Middle Ages   166

BOOK TWO.

THE SIXTEENTH CENTURY

I   The Reformation or a Northern Tragedy ..   169

II   The Reign of Queen Elizabeth   196

III   The Diocese of Chester Deaneries (1541-1603)   219

BOOK THREE.

THE STUARTS AND THEIR AFTERMATH (1603-1747)

PAGE

I   The Social Scene in the Seventeenth Century   225

II   The Seventeenth Century:

  i   Under one Crown   244
  ii The Civil War and the Commonwealth   260
  iii Restoration and Revolution   269

III The Episcopate of William Nicolson   ..   289

IV   The Aftermath   313

V   The Diocese of Chester Deaneries   328

     Appendix IV   Church Extension, 1603-1747   ..   337

BOOK FOUR.

THE GEORGIAN WORLD AND THE INDUSTRIAL REVOLUTION (1747-1856)

I   The Social Scene in the Eighteenth Century   339

II   i The Georgian Church and The Age of
        Wesley   357
     ii The Era of Reform   374

III The Diocese of Chester Deaneries   388

     Appendix V   Church Restoration and Building
                 (1747-1856)   396
            VI   Return of churches built or restored
                 at a cost exceeding £500 between
                 1840-1856   401

BOOK FIVE.

THE MODERN DIOCESE OF CARLISLE (1856-1933)

I   The Social Scene   403

II   The Modern Diocese   420

PAGE

Appendix VII List of churches consecrated
1856-69 459

VIII Return of church building and
restoration, exceeding £500,
1856-69 460

IX Return of expenditure on church
restoration under £500, 1840-
72 462

X List of churches consecrated or
licenced, 1869-92 463

XI Return of church building and
restoration exceeding £500
1869-92 465

XII List of churches consecrated or
licenced, 1892-1933 469

XIII Tables shewing value of livings
between 1291 and 1835 with
particulars of appropriated
churches and appropriating
monasteries 470

AUTHORITIES.

' A ' List of books and manuscripts to which
reference is made by abbreviated titles .. 476

' B ' List of manuscripts consulted and the places
where they can be found 480

' C ' List of authorities to which the numbers in
the text refer 483

Index 495

LIST OF ILLUSTRATIONS.

I   The church of St. Ninian, Brougham from the west bank of the river Eamont, with Cross Fell in the distance   Frontispiece

(from a photograph by Mr. P. T. B. Browne)

II   Initial letter of charter of Edward II to the city of Carlisle shewing Sir Andrew de Harcla and the citizens defending it against Robert Bruce in 1315   facing p.   68

(reproduced, by permission of Council, from *Transactions* of the Cumberland and Westmorland Antiquarian and Archaeological Society, Old Series, vi, 319)

III   Kendal Castle in the seventeenth century   facing p.   137

(from a photograph by Miss T. Westerlea of a drawing in the Machell MSS., ii, p. 71, by permission of the dean and chapter of Carlisle)

IV   Sixteenth century carvings on the canons' stalls of Carlisle cathedral   facing p.   213

(from a photograph by the Rev. J. E. Bamber by permission of the dean and chapter)

V   Lady Anne Clifford .. ..   facing p.   271

(from an oil painting at Appleby Castle, by permission of the Lord Hothfield, D.S.O.)

VI   Coniston lake and village ..   facing p.   353

(drawn by J. Smith and published in April, 1792 by R. Blamire, Strand, London, from a photograph by Miss T. Westerlea)

VII   Barrow in Furness in 1874 ..   facing p.   405

(from the ' Graphic ' of 12 September; Mr. J. Melville brought this to my notice)

VIII   Eskdale vicarage at Beckfoot in 1884
                            facing p.   437
        (from the ' Graphic ' of 5 January, from a copy
          supplied by Miss Fair)
        (VII and VIII are reproduced by permission of
          The London Electrotype Agency Ltd.)

  IX   The High Altar, St. John's church,
        Workington   ..   ..   facing p.   456
        (from a photograph by Hyde, Workington, by
          permission of the vicar, Canon J. R. Croft)

Map of the diocese of Carlisle based upon that
  drawn up by the late Canon E. J. Nurse
                            [at end of book]

BOOK I. THE MIDDLE AGES.

CHAPTER I.

THE NORMAN SETTLEMENT IN CHURCH AND STATE.

THE situation which confronted Henry I when he visited Carlisle in 1122 and the reasons which caused him to place the seat of a bishopric there can only be understood in the light of the past history of the district.

After belonging to the kingdom of Strathclyde in the sub-Roman age the Lake Counties fell under Anglian domination in about the early sixth century and became part of the great kingdom of Northumbria. They had no independent existence and there is no sign at this time of the modern county boundaries. In the confusion caused by the Viking invasions the area now known as Cumberland and Westmorland relapsed into a No Man's Land and was at times a part of the Scottish Kingdom. Its history before the Conquest is very obscure and likely to remain so, but it is clear that at the Domesday Survey the whole of the Eden valley and all Cumberland, except a small area round Millom, were not regarded as part of England. Lancashire north of the Sands with the Kent valley and a small piece of south Cumberland were surveyed as part of Yorkshire.

Then in 1092 William Rufus came north to Carlisle with a large army and recovered the town, built the castle and

drove out Dolfin, the Scottish ruler. After his return to
the south the King is said to have sent many English
peasants, with their wives and livestock, to cultivate the
region.

Thus the whole of the district, now embraced by the
diocese of Carlisle, was included in the English Kingdom.
The Lancashire parts of it had been granted some years
before to Roger, son of Roger de Montgomery, commonly
called the Poitevin. He lost them by rebellion though
William Rufus restored them, but it is not an ascertained
fact that Furness and Cartmel were in his possession, 1089-
1102.[1]   Rufus also granted Kendale* and much of south
Westmorland to Ivo Taillebois.[2]   Of the newly annexed
territory it is known that by 1112 Ranulph Meschin was
lord of the lands from Solway to Derwent and of North
Westmorland, with his seat at Appleby. For their
defence against the Scots Ranulph created two baronies:
Liddel, granted to Turgis Brundis, and Burgh by Sands
of which Robert de Trivers became lord.   Ranulph
endeavoured to form a third barony to the north-east of
Carlisle, but his brother William was unable to drive out
the Scotic ruler Gilles, son of Bueth. It is possible that
Ranulph created other baronies and that the grants by
Henry I were confirmatory ones. Then in 1120, by
Ranulph's succession to the earldom of Chester, his
lordship reverted to the king.[3]

This is the background of the situation which Henry
found when he visited Carlisle in 1122, and made two
decisions of far reaching consequence for the future history
of the Border: to revert to William Rufus' policy by
making Carlisle, and not Appleby, where Ranulph Meschin
had established himself, the chief stronghold in the
district, and to found a new see embracing this lately
conquered territory.   It is probable that the king's

---

* Throughout this book *Kendale* is used to denote the barony or parish,
Kendal the town.

motive was not only to provide for the souls of his new subjects but to ensure their sufficient subjection to his rule. The Norman castle and the Norman cathedral would stand reminding all of the power of the Norman king. But there was also an ecclesiastical cause for Henry's action, as he had seen the Scottish bishop of Glasgow, who bore him no allegiance, carrying out episcopal functions in Cumberland. Further this bishop, though ordered by the pope to do so, had refused to recognise the archbishop of York as his provincial. Thus pope, king and archbishop doubtless found little difficulty in agreeing to the establishment of the proposed new see.

The king did not apparently wish to interfere with vested rights or cause more disturbance than necessary. Hence only Cumberland, north of the Derwent, and North Westmorland, i.e. the areas long claimed by Scotland, were placed within the new diocese. The remainder of the modern counties of Cumberland and Westmorland and Lancashire north of the Sands were retained within the diocese of York.

That this decision was made in 1122 seems very probable; it was not, however, brought to fruition till eleven years later, as much preparatory work had to be done, including the provision of a cathedral. The true facts about the founding of Carlisle Cathedral are as difficult to ascertain as those about the creation of the see, in both cases for the same reason—lack of documentary evidence. There had probably been a parish church of St. Mary on the site of the cathedral in 1092. Ancient local tradition gives 1102 as the date of the founding of the Augustinian priory by Henry I. The best modern opinion questions this; it seems possible that a foundation of some kind was started at this time, which made little or no progress until the King's visit of 1122. He was undoubtedly the legal founder of the priory, though tradition also gives a certain Walter the chaplain a definite share in it; possibly the king reaped where the chaplain had sown.[4]

But we miss the significance of Henry's purpose if we think of these events in isolation from others of which they were a part, or if we separate the part from the whole, which was the creation of an Anglo-Norman State in North Western England, where the Conqueror had left his Kingdom without any clearly defined border. This omission his sons rectified. Thus William II's expedition has been truly described as " a turning-point in the history of the North West because it brought this country within the operation of the Norman system of government."[5] This meant very much more than the creation of a new see. In the Church it included the foundation of great monasteries and the building of fine churches; in the State it implied the creation of baronies, with their castles, and the introduction of the manorial system, with the land so divided up as to admit of the Norman administrative machine working. Thus during these years was founded the system that was to last almost unaltered throughout the Middle Ages, and even to survive, in some respects, to the present day.

To deal first with ecclesiastical matters: much of Norman religion expressed itself in the endowment of monasteries. As the Conqueror founded one at Battle, as a token of thanksgiving to God, so his followers, when they received their shares of the new lands, likewise endowed monasteries to the glory of God and for the safety of their souls. They believed in the terrors of Hell and the pains of Purgatory; they also believed that the prayers of the monks could enable them to escape the former and suffer less in the latter. For these hard and warlike Normans really had faith in the value of the monks' prayers. They did not regard them as non-productive members of society. On the contrary they believed them to be most valuable parts of the community. The knight fought, the peasant worked, the monk prayed, each had his contribution to make. Prayer was the end of the monk's life, which centred round the daily offering of the Holy Sacrifice of the Mass and the keeping of the Seven Hours of Prayer. That to the monk was the work of God, and the end and object of his being. The Norman founder really believed this. He was no sentimentalist, he endowed a monastery because he thought the prayers of the monks would give him good value for his money.

The basis of Medieval monasticism was the rule of St. Benedict of Nursia and most of the larger abbeys of England were occupied by monks of this Order. But in these counties only two cells of the great house of St. Mary's, York belonged to them. Following the normal custom of the time, one of the first acts of Ranulph Meschin was to found a small Benedictine priory at Wetheral, between 1106-12; his brother, William, lord of Coupland, followed him with one at St. Bees (R)* soon after 1120.[6]

The end of the eleventh century saw the rise of several new monastic Orders in France. One of these, which its founder believed represented a return to the primitive simplicity of the rule of St. Benedict, settled at Cîteaux in Burgundy. Among its founders was Stephen Harding, an Englishman, but its greatest light was St. Bernard of Clairvaux, one of the most remarkable and Christlike figures in all Christian history and the author of that most beautiful of Medieval hymns *Jesu dulcis memoria*—Jesu the very thought is sweet. Three houses of this Order were founded in these counties. The first, and it subsequently became the most important, was Furness Abbey (R) founded in the Vale of Nightshade in 1127 by Stephen, count of Boulogne and lord of Lancaster, later king of England. Its house had originally, 1123, been

---

* (R) means the monastery so designated was then within the archdeaconry of Richmond and the diocese of York.

situated at Tulketh, near Preston.[7] In 1134 a second
abbey of this Order, an affiliation of Furness, was set up
at Calder, near Egremont, by Ranulph Meschin, son of the
first lord of Coupland. Then, in about 1150, a third
Cistercian abbey was founded at Holm Cultram by Alan,
son of Waldeve, grandson of Gospatric, earl of Northumbria. This was the most important religious house in
Cumberland. The Cistercians loved to build their
monasteries in secluded valleys and places remote from
human habitation. It is not difficult to see, bearing in
mind the undeveloped state of the country eight hundred
years ago, how well the sites chosen fitted into their desire.

This age also saw the rise of communities of clergy,
bound together to live under a common rule, known as
Canons Regular. They soon adopted the Rule of St.
Augustine of Hippo and secured houses in the north at
Hexham, Nostell and Bridlington a few years before the
see of Carlisle was created. They were greatly aided by
Thurstan, archbishop of York, and it was probably on his
suggestion that Henry I founded a house of this Order at
Carlisle, probably in 1122 or 3. (Incidentally does the
cathedral of Carlisle sufficiently emphasise that it is a
royal foundation?). The Augustinian Order must have
been very much in favour with the pious laity at the time
for three other houses were founded in these counties.
In Cumberland Robert de Vaux, lord of Gilsland, in
about 1166,[8] set up a house on the banks of the river
Irthing at Lanercost, in a remote but beautiful situation.
They had two houses in Lancashire north of the Sands.
One at Conishead (R) was originally founded, between
1154-81, by Gamel de Pennington or William de Lancaster II as a hospital for the relief of the " poor decrepid,
indigent, and lepers in the environs of Ulverston."[9] The
other was placed at Cartmel (R) by William Marshall,
afterwards earl of Pembroke, in about 1190.[10] In 1120
the Premonstratensian Order of canons was begun.

About seventy years later a house of this Order was founded at Preston Patrick by Thomas de Workington. Soon afterwards the canons moved to Shap, which became their permanent home.[11]

As can well be imagined this Borderland was not a very suitable place for nuns to settle in; only two nunneries, both of the Benedictine Order, were founded in these counties. A very small one at Seaton (R) near Bootle, was founded by Henry, lord of Millom, in about 1190; the other was at Armathwaite on the Eden. Its founder is unknown, the earliest reference to it is in about 1200.[12]

These monasteries owned much land in these counties including a large amount of what is now called the Lake District, for, as W. G. Collingwood writes, " when early Norman lords had grants of perfectly wild country where the people were so rough that it did not seem likely they would pay them rent, the natural impulse was to give a good piece to the priests."[13] Perhaps the most extensive owners of such lands were the monks of Furness, who received from their founder a very large fraction of Furness not in other recognised control. Evidence, incidentally, of how little was known at that time about the District and how vague was the Norman control over it. Eventually it was agreed, in 1163, that this grant gave the abbey Hawkshead, Satterthwaite and Colton. Then, half a century later, it added to its possessions by the purchase of Borrowdale from Alice, daughter of William Fitz Duncan, and also obtained by exchange a great part of upper Eskdale. Much of our knowledge of early Lake District place names comes from surveys made to ascertain the boundaries of these properties.[14]

Another famous Cistercian house which owned much land in these parts was the great Yorkshire abbey of Fountains. It had acquired, by grant from the afore-said Alice in about 1195, the church, town, and mill of

Crosthwaite with Derwent Island, Watendlath and Langstrath.[15] Yet another Yorkshire Cistercian Abbey, Byland, possessed a considerable amount of land in North Westmorland given them by the Viponts;[16] St. Peter's Hospital, York also owned property in this neighbourhood.[17] To return to local houses; Shap owned a good deal of the fell country to the east of Ullswater,[18] and St. Bees had grants from Ranulph Meschin of the manor of Ennerdale and from Richard de Lucy of the moors above Loweswater; they also had free pasture for their pigs in the Western dales.[19] Lastly, Conishead had a small estate in Langdale.[20]

The management of extensive estates entails responsibilities, so does the upkeep of a great establishment. Thus monks were often of necessity men of business and trade. How this affected them here will be gone into in the section of the next Chapter dealing with local medieval industries.

It is not proposed in this book to go into the details of monastic life. The history of the various houses has been fully described in the Victoria County Histories and elsewhere. But something might be expected of such matters as the effect of the Border wars on local monasticism. It has been felt, however, that this can best be described in the main body of the book rather than in isolation from its context.

Now to turn to more parochial affairs. Owing to the paucity of local records little is known of the spiritual condition of the people at the opening of the eleventh century. It is generally supposed that the presence of pre-Conquest Anglian crosses and ' hogbacks ' shew the existence of an ancient church on or near the place. In some cases—St. Cuthbert's, Carlisle,* St. Martin's, Brampton and St. Ninian's, Brougham[21] a church

---

* Prior Wessington's list of churches where the body of S. Cuthbert rested is now regarded as imaginary (N.S. XXV, 13).

dedication suggests an ancient Christian site.   This is also
true of some of the Irish-Norse names that have survived.[22]
But insufficient evidence remains to enable us to be
certain of the date of our oldest churches; of only two,
Morland, probably, and Over Denton, possibly, can it be
said that any Saxon work may still remain.   Brigham,
c. 1080, and Ormside, late eleventh century, contain some
of the earliest building now surviving in these counties.
These with Kendal, Heversham, Kirkby Lonsdale,
Beetham, Burton and Kirkby Stephen, given by Ivo
Taillebois to St. Mary's York in 1090-7, exhaust the list
of churches of which there is evidence that they existed
before the end of the eleventh century.   In the next one
a very different tale has to be told.

A study of the dates assigned to the oldest parts of our
churches gives some interesting facts.   Of the 94 parish
churches in the ancient diocese: 60 contain architectural
evidence of twelfth century work; 6 shew no such
evidence, and 28 have been destroyed or so much restored
that none of the ancient fabric remains.   Of these 34
churches, monastic chartularies and other records shew
that 21 were in existence during the twelfth and 6 before
the middle of the next century, leaving only 7 of which no
mention can be found before the Taxatio of 1291.[23]   These
latter may have existed earlier, they probably did, but
evidence to prove it has not been found.   In the light of
these figures it can safely be asserted that most of our
ancient churches were in being perhaps well before and
certainly by the end of the twelfth century.   The same is
probably also true of the parishes they served.   But the
most striking fact these statistics prove is that, taking
into account that in 28 churches all architectural evidence
has been destroyed, 9 out of 10 of our older churches were
built or rebuilt during the twelfth century.   Probably
few of the Saxon churches were stone buildings; as late
as in the episcopate of the first bishop a chapel of wattle-
work was built at Trierman.[24]

There is no evidence as to the extent to which these churches served defined parochial areas. Such, of course, had been the practice in most of England for a considerable time. But whether, with its strong Scottish affinities and the effect of the Norse invasions, this was so here we do not know. Perhaps the parochial system, as we know it to-day, did not come into force in the northern parts of these counties until the time of the first bishop. He was probably also the creator of the archdeaconry of Carlisle and of the four ancient rural deaneries; Carlisle (North Cumberland), Allerdale (North-West Cumberland), Cumberland (East Cumberland) and Westmorland.[25]

The monk and cleric to pray; the knight to fight. The defence of this newly acquired Border land, with its strong Scottish sympathies and traditions, must have been in the forefront of Henry's mind when he visited Carlisle and decided to make it the key fortress of his new territory. Ranulph Meschin had already divided the Border lands into baronies, now Henry, while keeping the city of Carlisle and the forest of Cumberland in his own hands, extended the process. In the north he created a small barony of Levington which he granted to Richard de Boivill.[26] While at Greystoke he allowed the English possessor Forne, son of Sigulf, to continue in possession.[27] In Allerdale below Derwent he also recognised the existing owner, Waldeve, son of Gospatric, who had apparently previously enfeoffed Odard de Logis, or the Sheriff, which appointment Henry confirmed.[28] Allerdale above Derwent, or Coupland, was given by the King to William Meschin, brother of Ranulph, who gave the part of it called the Five Towns, or the Honour of Cockermouth, to the above named Waldeve. Before the middle of the century, owing of the failure of issue to Waldeve, this territory, as well as the other part of Allerdale, had passed to William FitzDuncan. He, by his marriage with the only daughter and heiress of William Meschin was already lord of Coupland. Thus the whole of this great fief, stretching from the Wampool, just south of Carlisle, to Millom, was vested in one person.[29]

Henry I kept the two baronies now comprised in the county of Westmorland in their original form, retaining Ranulph Meschin's lordship of Appleby in his own hands and regranting Kendale and much else, after the death of Ivo Taillebois, to Nigel d'Aubigny who in about 1150 granted William de Lancaster a great tract of country including Lonsdale and Kendale. The King, after the expulsion of Roger de Montgomery for rebellion in 1102, incorporated the honour of Lancaster by the inclusion of his estates and those of other banished barons into it.

Having now sketched in the outlines of the Norman settlement in Church and State, it seems best to leave certain other matters to be dealt with in the next chapter and to go on with the story of the first bishop's episcopate.

Athelwold, prior of Nostell, was consecrated on 6 August 1133 by Archbishop Thurstan in York Minster. How far the plans for founding the new see had really progressed seems doubtful because in 1136, after Henry I's death, the pope wrote reminding Stephen of the project for raising " the place of Carlisle to the rank of episcopal dignity " and urging him to supply what was wanting in the original foundation. Presumably a larger endowment was needed. But the pope's letter was somewhat inopportune because Cumberland had passed, by yet another vicissitude of history, from the English to the Scottish King. It is probable that the change was by no means unwelcome to the populace who fought for their new sovereign in the battle of the Standard. David, the Scots King, took up his residence in Carlisle with the intention perhaps of making it his southern capital.

Athelwold appears to have acted under these circumstances with discretion, meeting David at Carlisle in 1138 and attending a Council at Winchester in 1144. Little is

known of the ecclesiastical events of his episcopate.   He
confirmed the grants of Wetheral, with the chapel of
Warwick, St. Michael and St. Lawrence, Appleby, Kirkby
Stephen, Ormside, Morland, Cliburn, Bromfield and
Croglin to the abbey of St. Mary's, York,[30] and of Crosby
Ravensworth to Whitby.[31]   He also witnessed the
so-called foundation charter of the abbey of Holm
Cultram by Prince Henry of Scotland.[32]   One of the most
interesting of the bishop's charters is that in which he
gave his consent to the canons of Carlisle joining the
Order of Arrouaise, a strict congregation of regular canons.
This plan may have had some connection with the visits
of St. Malachy of Armagh to Northern England in 1140
and 1148 ; it was either still born or very short lived.[33]

But death soon caused wonderful changes in the
political and ecclesiastical scene.   Prince Henry of Scotland died in 1152, the next year his father followed him,
to be succeeded by a mere boy.   Then two years later
Stephen died, and Henry of Anjou, whose coronation
Athelwold attended, was able in 1157 to regain from feeble
Scottish hands the territory Stephen had been forced to
cede.   In the same year, on 16 June, the morrow of the
Ascension of our Lord, the bishop died and was buried in
the cloister of Carlisle Priory, which he had built.[34]

Canon Wilson describes Athelwold as pre-eminent
among the prelates who have ruled this diocese; the
present writer must confess that he does not think we
have sufficient evidence to come to any judgment on
the matter.

Evidence of the strength of the new regime was soon
forthcoming since Hubert de Vaux, to whom the king had
given the land—later to become the barony of Gilsland—
which William Meschin had failed to wrest from the
Scotic ruler Gilles, son of Bueth was at last able to do so.
Thus the years 1157-8 can be considered those in which
the English Kingdom on this North Western Border

assumed its final shape and in which the ding dong struggle, lasting over two hundred years, between the English and Scottish crowns for its possession, was definitely settled in favour of the former.   And further they can be considered as the years in which the Norman claim that Carlisle should be an English city, first staked out by William II in 1092, was at last achieved.   The measure of the importance of this prize can be estimated by the time it took to settle the question of its possession.[35]

The English King this time was taking no risks.   We know the matter was now finally settled; he did not.   On the Border the fortifications at Carlisle were strengthened, so were those at Brougham, commanding a ford across the Eamont, at Appleby, protecting another over the Eden, at Brough, guarding the entrance to the pass over Stainmore, and at Kendal.   As for Cumberland work was started on stone castles at Kirkoswald, to protect the Eden valley, and at Cockermouth and Egremont in Coupland.   Our landscape was beginning to assume its familiar form.

In the light of these precautions it is curious to find a long delay in filling the vacant bishopric.   Probably the reasons were financial; the see had no endowment apart from the priory's, which was certainly far from rich. Meanwhile the diocese was in charge of Christian, bishop of Whithern, a suffragan of the archbishop of York, and the archdeacon of Carlisle.   Upon the death of the former in 1186 the king bestirred himself, and the canons of Carlisle were allowed to proceed to election, but the priest chosen, Paulinus de Ledes, declined the honour. There the matter rested until the next reign.

Richard I on his way back from the Holy Land in 1192 landed at Ragusa and made the acquaintance of Bernard, its archbishop.   Whether he came with Richard or independently is unknown, but he was certainly present at King John's coronation in 1199 and remained in constant attendance at court.   So he cannot have been surprised when the pope filled his place.   Ragusa gone, no see in England obtained, was Bernard's position.   But Carlisle was available, though it had few attractions even for a needy archbishop, still Bernard was induced to accept it.   The difficulties, however, were by no means over as the archbishop of York did not relish having another archbishop in his province.   But the pope overcame this by undertaking that Bernard should exercise the episcopal office in the diocese of Carlisle without the use of the archiepiscopal pall and pay reverence and obedience to his metropolitan.   So on 10 January 1204, King John informed the archbishop of his confirmation of this plan and directed the clergy of the diocese of Carlisle to receive Bernard and obey him as their bishop.[36]

In one respect at least the second bishop was better off than the first since there is little doubt that by this time the priory buildings were nearing completion.   In 1130 the Pipe Roll records the payment of £10 to the canons of Carlisle ' for the building of their church '; in 1157, Athelwold was buried in the cloister which he had built; and in the Pipe Roll of 1188 the following occurs " in the work of the great altar and pavement in the church of St. Mary, Carlisle, 26s. 9d., and in the work of the same church 15l. 17s. 9d. . . . and in work of the dormitory of the canons 22l. 19s. 2d."

Thus by the turn of the thirteenth century the work of William II at the end of the eleventh had been finally consummated and Norman ideals in Church and State firmly established, with the various matters at issue, whether these lands were to be part of England or Scotland and whether they were to be within the diocese of Glasgow or York or Carlisle, irrevocably settled.

APPENDIX I.

THE OLDEST PARISHES OF THE DIOCESE.

The following list, taken from the returns for the papal taxation of 1291, may be of interest as shewing the ancient parishes of the diocese. They are grouped under their ancient deaneries.

Carlisle: Crosby on Eden, Denton, Walton, Brampton, Irthington, Farlam, Grinsdale, Hayton, Cumwhitton, Cumrew, Rocliffe, Sebergham, Aikton, Beaumont, Great Orton, Burgh by Sands, Arthuret, Stapleton, Kirklinton, Eston,* Bewcastle, Cambok,* Carlaton,* Castle Carrock, Kirkandrews on Eden, Thursby, Bowness on Solway, Dalston, Wetheral, Carlisle St. Cuthbert, Scaleby, Kirkbampton, Stanwix.

Allerdale: Wigton, Kirkbride, Bromfield, Aspatria, Bolton, Ireby, Uldale, Caldbeck, Crosthwaite, Isel, Bassenthwaite, Torpenhow, Plumbland, Gilcrux, Bridekirk, Cross Canonby, Dearham, Camerton.

Westmorland: Brough under Stainmore, Kirkby Stephen, Ravenstonedale, Musgrave, Crosby Garret, Warcop, Asby, Orton, Ormside, Appleby St. Lawrence, Appleby St. Michael, Morland, Cliburn, Long Marton, Dufton, Kirkby Thore, Newbiggin, Shap, Bampton, Askham, Lowther, Clifton, Brougham, Barton, Crosby Ravensworth.

Cumberland: Edenhall, Kirkland, Ousby, Castle Sowerby, Renwick, Lazonby, Kirkoswald, Croglin, Ainstable, Melmerby, Dacre, Greystoke, Hutton in the Forest, Addingham, Penrith, Skelton, Great Salkeld.

J. R. H. Moorman reckons these returns sometimes only give 87 per cent. of the parishes of the diocese concerned.[37] But a search through the Carlisle registers shews that this was not the case here. All known parishes are included, except Warwick, presumably considered only a chapel,

---

* Decayed during the Middle Ages.

and St. Mary's, Carlisle which was part of the priory. The statement "that the number of parish churches in England was not much different at the time of Domesday Book from what it was in 1800 "[38] is clearly erroneous, as far as this diocese is concerned. Further proof of this can be found in the sections on Church extension.

CHAPTER II.

THE SOCIAL SCENE IN THE MIDDLE AGES.

A QUESTION of much interest to all of us whose forebears dwelt in these counties is how far the ordinary tenor of life was disturbed by the coming of the Normans. Did the substantial freeman of the eleventh century become the lord of the manor in the next one or was he supplanted by a Norman? Were the small freeholders and peasantry depossessed of their land and their place taken by strangers? And did many freemen sink to be bondservants? Alas it is easier to pose these questions than to answer them, for our records are few.

The first point to be noted is that a considerable proportion of the greater tenants, Waldeve of Allerdale, Forne of Greystoke, William de Lancaster of Kendale, and Gospatric of Workington, were of English race. And it may safely be deduced that they would seldom have willingly supplanted one of their own people for a Norman. Our chief reason for believing this, however, is the number of old Norse names found in records such as monastic chartularies, Pipe Rolls and charters. Few local pedigrees can be taken back further than the middle of the twelfth century. They often start with an English name. The opinion stated above is supported by that of W. G. Collingwood. The wording of the tympanum at Pennington church proves that at this time Furness folk talked neither English nor French but Norse;[1] while doubtless Norman kings and lords rewarded their followers and dependents with grants of land, it is probably correct

C

to say that on the whole the existing landowners, both great and small, continued in possession. A striking example of the leniency of Norman rule can be found in the descendants of Bueth, who had kept the king's nominee out of East Cumberland for two generations, continuing to hold substantial property in that neighbourhood.

The introduction of the ordinary Norman manorial system into these parts, except in the more ' civilized ' areas around Carlisle and the upper Eden Valley, was probably a tedious process. In fact, it may be doubted if it ever was introduced in all its severity. Before the Conquest our Viking forebears had spread along the coasts, probably enslaving what remained of the native population, and had settled, each with his small clearing, in the forest. Within each group or district there would be some kind of leader, the heirs of the men who owned the ships that brought the invaders. But it is difficult to believe that they were often either desirous or able to reduce their followers to the level of ordinary bondmen or villeins.

There is no doubt however that such serfs or bondmen existed in these counties. Bongate gives the place where those of the Norman barons of Appleby lived. ' Bondland ' occurs as a place-name in the Wigton barony in the fifteenth century Percy muniments. When Roger de Bello Campo gave lands. in Little Croglin to Wetheral Priory, he included in the gift the services of a villein. William de Croglin went one better and gave them a villein, together with his wife and their offspring and chattels.[2] Such gifts of serfs to monastic bodies were by no means uncommon. Several instances occur in the St. Bees register. The same thing also happened at Furness Abbey.[3]

Apparently much of the land in the episcopal manor of Dalston was once held by servile tenure. A document in the diocesan registry headed " service of ye Bond tenants in Dalston "* though dated 1668 clearly preserves the tradition of customs in the early Middle Ages before these services were commuted for a money payment.

" He shall plow 3 whole dayes wth 3 draughts and shall harrow what he hath plowed, he shall mow wth 8 men for 3 days, he shall sheare wth 2, he shall carry 4 wainloads of hay, and shall have a dinner once a day, he shall pay for carriage 5s. 6d., for commons of the forrest 6s., towards finding a horse to carry some of ye Barony to London 5s., he shall make the 4th part of the Milldambe and Millhouse, and shall carry the fourth part of the Mill stones or timber." All these were redeemed for 21s. 6d. during the lord's pleasure, except the workes of the Mill wth Drawiage of the stones and manure, he shall pay the 13th moulter and pannage† for ten pigs and shall do suit to the Bpp's court at Caldewstones."

The great ambition of the serf must have been to become a free man.   There is a charter of the manumission or free-ing of one, whom he had given to the monks of Calder, by John de Hudleston in 1291.[4] In a charter of Sir Robert Lengleys, granting his bondman a licence to live outside his lands on payment of two shillings a year but reserving to himself his right in all his goods at his death with the power to recall him at the end of the term, we have an instance of how strictly the master enforced his powers.[5] All these instances are of the thirteenth century. But the most illuminating case of all occurs in the manor of Scaleby, where in 1246 there were, in addition to the freeholders, twenty bondmen and six cottars[6], which is clear evidence that in some manors most of the tenants were serfs. That this was so in most parts of England is

* The name of Sir William Dalston as the tenant heads the document. Here we have the case of a man of rank whose ancestors, though themselves free, held land by servile tenure.

† Multure was the contribution paid for grinding at the lord's mill; on the Durham manors, as at Dalston, the serf had to pay one thirteenth (Bennett, 133). Pannage was a fee paid for the privilege of feeding stock in the woods about the village.

undeniable.   As late as 1350 more than half the population were unfree.[7]

But the question of most interest to us in this part of the
country is whether this was also true here.   Rather
striking evidence to the contrary is afforded by the returns
at the inquisition on Baldwin Wake, lord of Liddel, in
1282.   This shews that his tenants consisted of twenty-
four free tenants, two hundred and ninety six free farmers,
with nine neifs and some paupers called selfodes—the two
latter classes are clearly serfs, but as to the rest " there is
hardly, in T. H. B. Graham's words, any direct allusion
in this document to servile tenure."[8]

Here, it is suggested, we have in these free farmers, who
clearly belonged to an intermediate class between free
tenants and serfs, the link between the free communities
of our Viking forebears and the tenants under the
famous local tenure by Border Tenant Right.   Strangely
enough, though much has been written about this,[9] no
effort seems to have been made to discover the actual
conditions and obligations under which land was held by
it in the Middle Ages.   Yet this is a most pertinent
matter for all who are interested in how our forebears
lived seven and eight hundred years ago.

Some account must now be given of the tenure
mentioned.   The matter has been fully investigated by
T. H. B. Graham.[10]   In his opinion this tenure and the
similar one of drenage were both technically servile and
not free tenures, coming under the category of privileged
villeinage.   It is generally accepted that this Border
Tenant Right was a special form of tenure granted to the
men of the northern counties because they had to defend
the country against the Scots.   But if this was really so
similar privileges should surely have been extended to the
folk on the south coast and the Welsh Marches; this does
not seem to have been the case.   Therefore, it is suggested, that this tenure may in fact have had its origin in

more remote causes due to the nature of the Viking settlements.   How extensive this tenure was can only be known when the history of every manor has been investigated.   It certainly applied to the Percy manors in Allerdale, the Gilsland barony and most of Westmorland.[11] One of the most interesting tenures is that of Holm Cultram.   It is generally assumed that copyhold tenancies, which in their origin were pure villeinage, did not confer Border Tenant Right.   But the abbey tenants, whose lands were copyhold, had the right of succession and the liability to " serve the prince on these Borders "— that is Border Tenant Right and duty.[12]   It seems then as if this tenure was not limited, as has been supposed, to customary estates of inheritance, but extended to copyhold.

The essential difference between the former tenure and ordinary copyhold was that the tenant's heir had the right of succession while " the legal feature of base tenure (copyhold) (was) its insecurity."[13]   The land was not conveyed, as in ordinary villein tenure, by surrender and admittance but by indenture entered on the manor roll for registration.

A charter among the Lowther muniments, dated about 1230, which mentions sums due for rent " in lieu of all customary dues," seems to be an early example of this.[14] In the Liddel inquisition and a rental of land in Cliburn Tailbois in 1366 money rent alone is mentioned.[15]   But payments in kind existed as late as about 1525 in Holm Cultram* where eight skeps of meal was the rent of the farm of Dryholm;[16] and about 1584 in Skelsmergh, where hens and capon and two days shearing, in addition to a fixed sum of money, are named.[17]   These work or boon days in the time of sowing and at autumn, generally two or three, are quite common.   There were, of course, other

* I am indebted to the Rev. F. B. Swift for these references to Holm Cultram.

obligations that the tenant had to fulfil. Fines, such as those called a gressum, every ten years in Holm Cultram, or a general fine in the Percy manors on the death of the lord, and a dropping fine, as it was called in the Percy lands, on the decease of the tenant, had to be paid. On the Percy manors the tenants had to grind their corn at the lord's mill as late as 1578.[18] In Westmorland beer had to be bought at the lord's brewery.[19] But these disabilities were very different from the many onerous and uncertain burdens that the peasantry suffered under in most parts of England.

The question whether these customary freeholders were freemen with certain liabilities or serfs with certain advantages remains to be discussed. Shortly, the difference between the classes was that a freeman could leave his village if he wished, could marry whom he desired, that he was, in fact, a freeman, though one with obligations; a serf had no rights, he was simply a chattel of his master's, who could be bought or sold or married at his lord's will. The evidence of the Liddel inquisition shows clearly that most of the men in the barony were free men and not serfs and the presumption is that the same thing was true elsewhere in these counties. What may have happened is that in most places the Norse head man became the lord of the manor and his compatriots became his tenants. But owing to the ancient ties between them he did not as a rule reduce them to serfs, allowing them to continue as the free farmers of the Liddel inquisition.*

One of the differences in the landscape in the Middle Ages and to-day is in the disappearance of the forest of Inglewood.[20] " It may reasonably be doubted whether any other forest in England approached it in size."[21]

* What has been written above must be accepted as of a tentative and exploratory nature. No certain conclusions can be come to until more records are available and more expert exponents of legal subtilties have considered their meaning.

Stretching from the spurs of Crossfell to the sea and from Bowness on Solway to Crosthwaite, it measured about 40 miles east and west and 25 north and south. It is well known how Norman kings, passionately fond of hunting, ordained the Forest Law. It was the fact of subjecting an area to this that constituted a forest, which might, therefore, include land with little timber on it. Wooded land was not as such a forest; it only became so if placed under Forest Law. This point is important because it means that we must not think this large part of Cumberland was thickly covered with giant trees. Nor must we blame the Norman Kings unduly for their action. Indeed it has been said by a student of this matter that " a protracted study of these records tends to the opinion that the establishment of the forests was, in the main, a sound measure, using districts as yet thinly inhabited for the preservation of deer, which formed a valuable food supply, and was used as such."[22] How their commercial possibilities were cared for will be seen later on.

The forests were, of course, primarily used for the preservation of game. In its day Inglewood was famed as a hunting ground that contained every manner of beast that the sportsman could desire. In Henry III's time the hart and hind, buck and doe, the roe, the wild boar and wild sow, and hawks were kept for the king; the right to hunt the hare, fox, wild cat, wolf, badger, otter, marten, squirrel, and all other woodland beasts was the perquisite of the forester in fee. The amount of game in the forest can be gathered from the fact that in this reign 200 harts and the same number of hinds were killed in two successive years, while Edward I, visiting Inglewood in 1279-80, hunted for four days and on the first killed 400 harts and hinds.

The most extraordinary care was taken in protecting the forest. It was illegal to kill a deer, but a man could also be punished for having venison in his possession.   Henry II forbade anyone to have dogs or bows and arrows within the forest, except by warrant.   It was an offence to cut down a tree that might shelter a deer, or to bring forest land into cultivation, or to put up a hut or shelter.   No tanner or bleacher might live within a forest.

But, though the law was harsh, its administration, at least in the time of Edward I, was not so.   The offender on arrest was released if bail was forthcoming, if not he was kept in prison.   On one occasion a man having been detained for three years, owing to the Eyres only being held at this interval, was at once pardoned by the judge; on another two brothers of Hutton in the Forest had killed a hind, before trial one of them broke his leg, so he was only fined 40d. compared to his brother's 20s.   An idea of the usual scale of fines can be seen from the misadventure of the rector of Great Salkeld.   His servant with two greyhounds took a hind on Easter Day.   The parson was, of course, quite innocent and forthwith dismissed the servant.   As however he omitted similarly to dismiss the venison, retaining it at his house, as did William his proctor, rector and proctor were fined 40s. and 10s. respectively.

The rector of Great Salkeld was also archdeacon of Carlisle, which illustrates the fact that all classes seem to have taken a hand in the sport of poaching.   The baron of Wigton and the lady Dyonisia, his wife, stole a hart and a hind with five hind's fawns by night from Plumpton Hay and took them to their house at Blackhall.   Travellers seem to have been especially liable to temptation.   A large company of gentlemen on their return from Carlisle took deer without number.   And the Lady Idonea de Leyburn, while in her forest of Whinfell travelling towards Brougham, allowed her men to loose six greyhounds at a hart which escaped over the Eamont and was killed within the forest.   Even though the animal was sighted

outside it the lady still was liable.   Neither were high
ecclesiastics exempt; the bishop, returning from the
king's court, took a sorrel hart and a hind with his
greyhound in Plumpton.   Lesser mortals did likewise;
poaching incumbents include the rectors of Lowther,
Edenhall, Sowerby and Plumbland; while three servants
of Carlisle Priory allowed their greyhound to course a
hare, and on another occasion (that time they included
the prior's valet) were in the forest, but fled at the sight of
the foresters leaving two greyhounds, one white, one
partly brown and white.   But it was noted that the prior
was not in the district so was blameless.   In any case
the canons did quite well out of the forest as the hides of
all deer found dead in it were their perquisite by leave of
King Henry, their founder; the flesh was also given to
charity, the usual recipients being the hospital of St.
Nicholas, Carlisle.   In some circles it was the custom
apparently to draw on the forest game for festive
occasions: Adam de Langrigg killed a hind which was
eaten at his wedding feast, while the venison of another
was carried to Dacre during William the chaplain's first
mass, he had to find security for 40s.

All these were but amateurs, those of whom it was
said that they " do commonly chase the deer beyond the
Eden by moonlight " must be placed in another category.
For them illicit hunting was not so much a sport as a
profession and a dangerous one too: " one forester shot
him in the thigh with an arrow as he fled, from which he
has died " was the obituary notice of a certain thirteenth
century inhabitant of Skelton.   But what happened to
Ralph of Langwathby and his friends was a more usual
occurrence: " when the foresters appeared Ralph and the
rest ran away leaving one of the dogs behind."   Sometimes other things were left, " two mantles and a bay
horse," for instance, and sometimes there was a battle:
one party " shot at the foresters " . . . and they " by a

sudden onset took from them a fallow greyhound." For
the poacher a last resort always remained and " they fled
to the priory of Wetheral where they were received "
because there was a sanctuary, which must have been
much valued by the fraternity.[23]   Many of the poachers
seem to have been well known to the foresters, so were
their dogs: some of their names Kel, Arthur and Gower
are preserved in the records.

But the forest was very much more than a venue where
the poacher, whether amateur or professional, backed his
skill against the gamekeeper, it was also a place from
which the king drew a substantial income: payments for
wood, for the privilege of turning out swine in the forest,
for fishing in it, and for many other things are entered in
the accounts.   The most interesting of these payments,
however, are those for encroachments and improvements
because these show us the process by which the forest was
slowly but surely brought under cultivation.   Sometimes
the land was sold outright; at others it was only leased.
The process seems to have been a planned and not a
haphazard one.   In Edward I's time a Survey was made
of certain lands which might with advantage be enclosed
and developed.   In this particular case it was decided
not to do so as the rents offered did not justify it.

It is strange how little research has been done by local
historians into the history of the woollen industry.   The
origin of the Herdwick, the well-known fell sheep, can
probably be traced to the time of the Norse invasions and
among the invaders can probably be found the earliest
local shepherds.[24]   But for them the sheep was merely a
source of food and raiment.   The value of its fleece as a
form of merchandise was not realised till the time of the
monks.

Fortunately a document has survived drawn up by or
for Italian wool buyers, probably in about 1315, which

gives valuable information concerning the monks activities.[25] The Italian forms of the names of our local
monasteries are somewhat quaint: Olcholtramo (Holm
Cultram), Chalderea in Choppolanda (Calder), Fornace
in Nortobellanda (Furness), Ciappi in Vestrebellanda
(Shap). As a result of the evidence of this document it is
possible to speak with some certainty of the place of the
local woollen industry in the fourteenth century.

Cistercian monks always placed their monasteries in
secluded and solitary places, also their rule stressed the
importance of manual work. These two facts were
perhaps the chief causes for their interest in sheep which
was given ample scope in these Northern parts by their
ownership of large stretches of Pennine and Lake District
country. They first developed sheep keeping in England
into a trade, which they ran with considerable business
acumen. The document quoted shews that they divided
fleeces into three grades, best, medium, and worst, while
other religious houses sold theirs in bulk, unsorted.
Fountains, with an average of 76 sacks a year, was easily
the chief producer. Unfortunately we do not know what
proportion of these came from their Lake District estates.
Of our local houses, Holm Cultram, 40 and Furness, 30
sacks occupy quite a high place in the lists—of the
Northern abbeys only seven were placed above them in
the amounts they sold. Of houses of other Orders, Shap,
10 a year, and Calder, 4, only sold unsorted fleeces. If
St. Bees went in for sheep rearing their quantities are
included with those of their mother house of St. Mary's,
York.

These lists shew that the best local wool was of quite
high quality. Holm Cultram got 18 marks and Furness
half a mark more for their best fleeces, which compares
favourably with the other prices for Northern wool. The
highest rates—between 28 and 26 marks—obtained on
the Welsh Border and in Lincolnshire. It has generally

been held that local wool was of poor quality. This seems true of Westmorland, but not of Cumberland and Furness.

The high place Holm Cultram held in the lists is interesting, as it does not seem to have been known that this abbey was such an important wool producer; nor that sheep were reared on a large scale on the Solway as well as on the Fells. To further its trade it had houses in the port of Hartlepool, where doubtless the wool was stored while awaiting shipment. In the time of Abbot Gervase (1274-9) it sent 46½ sacks to the market,[26] 31½ of them being of good wool, but the cost of transport must have been heavy as Thirsk or York were the nearest wool markets.

Furness Abbey, though its annual return was less than that of Holm Cultram, was also interested in this industry. Its purchase of Borrowdale, upper Eskdale and Newby-in-Craven in the thirteenth century can only have been for the purpose of sheep walks. The monks were such keen business men that sometimes their activities got them into trouble. The merchants of the Staple at Calais complained, in 1423, that they had tried to evade the customs with a load of wool for Flanders which had been shipped from " le peele de Foddray."[27]

But wool was not only used for export, nor sheep kept only by monks. It was needed for clothes by all; David, a dyer of Carlisle, is mentioned in the reign of King John.[28] As a result of the discovery of the mechanical method of fulling, the thirteenth century saw a movement of the centre of the cloth industry away from the eastern lowlands of England to our northern parts, from the towns to the countryside.[29] Kendal cloth is not mentioned before 1389, when it is stated that " a great part is made of the worst wool within the realm." It is now believed that this local industry had its rise in the enterprise of Westmorland men and was not due, as has often been supposed, to Flemish teachers.[30] But the great developments of loom and spinning wheel only began here when the Kendal clothiers started to increase their trade in the sixteenth century.

The Percy muniments give valuable information about the set up of the industry in West Cumberland in the fifteenth century. Most of the manors round Cockermouth and in the western dales had fulling mills, but in Wigton barony only the capital town had one, from which it can presumably be deduced that these parts were mostly agricultural. There is no evidence that this wool was sold commercially, at any rate by the lord. Individual tenants may have made their own private bargains with travelling buyers. The mills were either let out to a speculator or were reserved for the tenants at so much a head: at Cockermouth, John Richardson, walker, was the farmer for 13s. 4d. in 1439; at Buttermere 2s. 8d. was received from a certain payment called Walking Silver* due by divers tenants in 1483. The industry had its ups and downs. At Whinfell two of the three mills were entirely waste and fallen to the ground in that year, though described as newly built in 1439, despite this a new one was to be put up at Lorton, it cost 2s. Rents varied too: the tenants of Loweswater† paid 28s. for their suit at the fulling mill there in 1439; in 1483, the payment was 21s.[31]

The pastoral world in the Middle Ages was a freer one than the agricultural, largely because in it money rents rather than labour services were the vogue. It was also

* This term was also used in Westmorland (*Rydal*, Armitt, 94). Mark IX³, in Wycliffe's Bible has " a fuller or walker of cloth may not make white," for " no fuller on earth can white them " (A.V.).

† During the Middle Ages, in addition to those mentioned above, fulling, mills are recorded at: Applethwaite (Windermere), Brampton, Carleton, Carlisle, Clifton (C.) Crosthwaite, (W.) Dacre, Egremont, Embleton, Glassonby, Grasmere, Greenriggs, (Mun) Grisdale, Kendal, Millom, Penrith, Sowerby, Staveley, (*E.H.R.* XI 1941, 48); within the manor of Derwentwater, Kirkoswald, within the barony of Liddel (*N.S.* iv, 293; xii, 171-3; xiii, 46); Loughrigg, Troutbeck, and Undermilbeck (*R. of K.*, II, 22, 44, 67).

difficult to apply to it the full rigours of the manorial system since sheep from adjacent manors shared the same pastures and many of the ordinary dues by peasant to lord could not be fulfilled.   Wordsworth was thus making a strictly economic observation when he said that " the voice of freedom was the voice of the mountain."[32]

The tiller of the soil must often have been sadly let and hindered in these parts during the Middle Ages.   With the obstacles—the heath and woodland of the forests, the marshes of the Solway plain, and the fells—nature put in the way, man with his wars and Border raids adding his quota, our forebears must have had little incentive to provide for more than bare necessity.   The men of each hamlet or village, cultivating their strips of the great common field and putting their few beasts on the common land adjoining, would hope to have enough in store to see them through till the next harvest.   As the years went on more and more land was reclaimed.   But, even as late as the first quarter of the seventeenth century, men could die in as rich an agricultural parish as Greystoke of very want of sustenance, if the harvest failed.* · So there is little doubt what conditions were like several centuries before.

This can probably be partly accounted for by the use of the one field system which was prevalent over most of northern Europe and so " was presumably familiar ", in T. H. B. Graham's words, " to Angles and Danes alike at the period when they respectively invaded Celtic Cumberland."[33] To which he adds, as a note, " it is not likely that the Norse settlers in Cumberland interfered with the regulation of the common field, because they were a pastoral rather than an agricultural people, and solitary rather than gregarious in their habits.   I venture therefore to identify the Cumberland mode of cultivation in

* Parish register, burials 1623.

rig and rean with the old English one-field system."
He notes, however, that in the manor of Holm Cultram
the three field system was in use and that some land in
Westmorland was cultivated on the two field one.

The difference between the two latter systems, which
were more usually in vogue in other parts of England, and
the single field one, was that in the former each field was
allowed to lie fallow in turn and thus restored to fertility,
whereas in the latter the one field was kept permanently
under cultivation with the aid of manure.   Also there was
no common right over the cultivated land after it had
been cleared of its crop.   The field was divided into strips,
called dales or riggs, belonging to different tenants, and
separated from each other by unploughed grass ranes or
reans.   To judge from later times, these might be 20 to
40 feet wide and as much as a 1000 feet in length.   Cattle
were put to graze on them to the detriment of the crops.
The amount of land allotted to each husbandman, or
villein ploughman charged with the upkeep of a yoke of
oxen, was thirty acres, not statute acres and not lying
contiguous to one another, so that each man got his share
of good as well as indifferent ground.   Many servile
tenants had less than this, and the better off freemen
more.   At the dissolution of the monasteries a Survey of
Holm Cultram shews that holdings varied from 2 to 73
acres; the average being 12 or 36 statute ones.   Each
tenant had also from 2 to 4 acres in the common field.[34]

Wages were 2d. a day at Skinburness in 1299; coopers
getting 3d.   A few years later crops carried away by the
Scots from Holm Cultram were reckoned at wheat 8s. per
quarter; barley, and beans and peas 6s. 8d. per quarter,
salt 6s.; and salt fish 30s. per hundred.   In 1298 shoeing
for 25 horses cost 9s. 4d. at Holm Cultram; the abbot
paid £3. 6s. 8d. for a palfrey in 1302.   In the middle of the
fifteenth century the bishop's account rolls give some
interesting figures.   He paid 2s. 6d. for a load of hay in
1461, and 2s. for grassing a horse in summer; for having

an acre of land ploughed and harrowed he disbursed 1s. 2d. in 1460, and paid 4d. for two iron hoops for a cart body. In these accounts milk cattle are valued at from 9s. to 10s. each and oxen from 10s. to 12s. 6d.; in 1401-3 the price of lambs was 7¾d., 8d. and 9d. and a hogg (yearling sheep), 1/-; lamb skins were valued at 1s. 0½d. In Henry IV's reign 14 young pigs were priced at 11s. 8d. and hens or ducks at about 1½d. and 3d. each. In 1450 wool was reckoned at 2s. 4d. per stone at Rose Castle.[35]

As can be imagined in counties with so extensive a sea board and so much inland water, both lake and river, fishing has always been one of the chief occupations of the inhabitants. From the earliest times local salmon has been in demand. Henry I endowed the priory of Carlisle with fishing rights in the Eden and Ranulph Meschin did likewise for his foundation at Wetheral. From about 1140 the monks of St. Bees had the sole liberty for making fisheries in the port of Whitehaven, while those of Calder and Fountains had rights in the Derwent. Holm Cultram had extensive privileges: in the Eden at several places, in the Derwent at Seaton, at the mouth of the Ellen, and in the Nith. Conishead Priory had the Leven fishery.[36]

The Percy records throw much light on West Cumberland fisheries in the fifteenth century. In 1439 the fishery of the river Derwent was worth £13. 6s. 8d., and of the Ellen 2s. In Loweswater the fishery of the lake was demised at 2s., Ternemeryn at 1/- and "Kirkebe, in respect of the new stream from Loweswater to Croombok-water," at 6d. In Setmurthy manor the fishery and fishpond of Karell are mentioned; the fishery of Bassen-thwaite lake was valued at 20s. 6d. In Brunholm there was a fishery at Braymyr let at 3s.. The fishing of Buttermere was worth 6s. 8d., Crummock 26s. 8d.,* which

---

* This was let to Peter Johnson in 1439; in 1480 William Pereson, or, as he is called a few lines after, William Pereson Johnson, is the tenant—obviously the first man's son. An instance of how 'son' surnames could be fluid even in the fifteenth century.

was raised to 33s. 4d., with 1/- for an ' elyng.'   Another elyng in the waters of Merron is mentioned under the Five Towns.   The Braithwaite part of the river Derwent was put at 9s. 8d.   In Brackenthwaite an 'elegarth' near the river Cocker is mentioned.   In 1480 in Eskdale the fishery of Brumberwater is named.   There is no mention of fishing in Wastdale.   For this year in Loweswater a fishery of Mosdalebeck is added to that of Ternemeryn and the price raised to 2s. 6d.

In the 1483 accounts the fishery of the Derwent was let at £10. 6s. 8d. to Sir Thomas Curwen and " the said Thomas shall have the punishment (oversight) of all and singular traps both in the said river of Salmon and Kepers for taking them at the forbidden time and of those tributaries of the same river at any season in the case of those obstructing it with nets, kidels, or other con-trivances or engines."   An elyng in the Cocker was let at 6d., and the fishery of the whole of the Ellen at 3s. 4d.   In Setmurthy manor 6s. 10d. was received from the farm of the fishery of Bassenthwaite, and 13s. 8d. from another one at the head of the aforesaid water, and £4 from the farm of the fishery of Wateruse and Karell, together with a fishery in the Brathemyre.   In Buttermere the return was the same as in 1439, except that Crummock was put at 30s. There was a fishery at Egremont worth 5s.   In Eskdale the farm of the fishery of the water of Bromliwater was 1s.

No attempt has been made to elucidate these names; some are obvious, others seem to represent waters that have now disappeared.   But the picture that results both of the value of the various fisheries and of the physical lay out of the West Cumberland lakes at this time is extremely interesting.[37]

The story of the fisheries in other parts of the Lake District is not known in so much detail.   Richard Fleming had a grant of fishing in Coniston in about 1200.   Forty years later the monks of Furness had leave to have a small boat and twenty nets in both Coniston and Windermere. In 1283 the fishing of Grasmere was worth 6d. and Rydal 18d. a year.[38]

Methods differed little from to-day's; hook and net were chiefly used then as now ; fish coops obtained in the upper reaches of the rivers. The width of the free passage allowed to fish in mid-stream was to be wide enough for a sow with her five little pigs; a good instance of the medieval love for strange measures.[39]

Whitehaven coal was certainly known before 1282,[40] but in Canon Wilson's opinion coal was not worked as an industry before the fifteenth century; that John of Dryholme paid 3s. 4d. for trading in sea coal in 1346/7[41] seems to belie this statement. Before 1485 the Dacres worked the mines on Tindal Fell.[42] In West Cumberland in 1439 a coal mine at Great Broughton was farmed at £13. 6s. 8d., and the shaft pillars and the watergate had to be maintained. In 1483 a mine at Sevisyke was worth £4. 13s. 4d. In 1439 the earl of Northumberland paid 53s. 4d. to the abbot of Calder for the farm of his coal mines at Dearham. Many will be thankful for this entry under Loweswater in that year: " and in the decrease of the farm of the coal mine there because it is in the lord's hands for want of a tenant 2s. 6d." In Dean, Robert Brampton had a licence to win sea coal on the lord's soil for his own house, and a mine near Scrogon hegge, worth 6d., is mentioned. In Westward 3s. 4d. was paid in 1483 for the gathering and winning of coals in a stream called Silverbeke.[43]

The value of the quarries of West Cumberland appears to have been fully appreciated. In Dean in 1439, a mine of slate at Wyselholes, worth 6d., and a quarry of slate stone are mentioned. In Papcastle 1s. was received from the farm of a bed of lime. In 1483 under Westward a slate quarry worth 6s. and a small quarry called the Lezestones, 1s., are included, but there was no profit from quarrying a stone called gryndston.[44]

The monks seem to have taken a leading part in almost every industrial activity.   As early as 1153 an iron mine near Egremont was granted to St. Bees.[45]   Soon after Holm Cultram obtained a similar privilege, with a forge, probably at Whinfell.[46]   The Furness monks worked iron mines at several places in their neighbourhood in the thirteenth century, so did the canons of Conishead.[47]   Iron mines are mentioned in the foundation charter of Cartmel Priory.   The copper mines of Newlands, Keswick, have been worked since the reign of Henry III.   Copper and silver mines at Caldbeck are mentioned in 1318.[48]   In the fifteenth century Percy Accounts: in 1454-5 provision is made for wood for working the mines at Rowtanbek and for smelting the ore for lead there; a similar provision for the mines at Coldale is noted.   In 1476/7 the mines of lead and silver ore in Derwent fells were farmed for £6. 13s. 4d. a year, and in 1485 £12 was paid for the farm of the mines of gold, silver, and lead ore belonging to the earl of Northumberland in West Cumberland.[49]

But the most famous local mines were the so-called Silver ones of Carlisle, in reality lead mines and situated at Alston, nearly thirty miles from the city on the far side of the Pennines and in the diocese of Durham. This curious anomaly seems due to it being more convenient for the rent to be collected by officials in Carlisle, hence they came to be reckoned within the county of Cumberland.   They were worked several years before 1133.   At first they were let out to the highest bidder, but eventually the local miners of Alston, as the mine was called from about 1224, ran it themselves for a nominal rent and a proportion of its output in kind.   In the late twelfth century payments were made for lead for the king's houses at Windsor, 55 cartloads to be carried to Caen in Normandy, and 100 for work on the mother church of the Cistercian abbey at Clairvaux.   In about 1359 this interesting local community of miners was superseded by foreign speculators, who, however, did not succeed. During the rest of the Middle Ages little is known about these mines.[50]

In the words of W. T. McIntire: " among the ancient industries of Cumberland none is more interesting than that of the once flourishing manufacture of salt carried on along the shores of the Solway." As in other industries the religious houses were in the forefront of this enterprise, which they began in the twelfth century. Lanercost had salt cotes on Burgh marsh, so did Wetheral, which also had one at Drumburgh. Carlisle Priory also had four in this locality. Holm Cultram, in addition to works in the Abbey district still preserved by the names Sevill Cote, Saltcoats and Raby Cote, had some in Scotland. The monks stored large quantities of salt and carried on an active trade in it, though often hindered by the Scots— in 1325/6 they lost 129 quarters through raids. St Bees had their pans at Whitehaven and in the Duddon estuary. An interesting side light on these activities is afforded by the fact that the tenants of Clifton, Westmorland, paid a boon-service to go to St. Bees yearly to fetch salt.[51]

Perhaps pearl gathering should be added to the list of Coupland industries. Pearls were certainly found in the river Irt and sold to jewellers at the close of the sixteenth century and probably earlier.[52]

In the Middle Ages Carlisle and Appleby were the only towns returning members to parliament, each had two, a privilege Cockermouth shared in 1295, but did not again obtain till 1640. There were a number of market towns before 1300, however. To the north and east of Carlisle: Brampton had its charter in about 1250, and Kirkcambeck in 1251—it is strange to think of this tiny hamlet once being a market town—and to the south, within the area bounded by the Carlisle and Penrith road, the Solway, and the river Derwent, apart from the county capital itself, only Wigton, 1262,[53] Ireby, 1237, and Seaton, 1280,[54] were market towns. Then to the east of this road Kirkoswald, 1201, and Penrith, in 1221/2,[55] had market rights. In the country to the south of the Derwent: Ravenglass, 1208,[56] Cockermouth, 1227, Millom, 1234, Egremont, 1267, had this privilege. In Westmorland, in addition to Appleby, only Kendal, 1189, [57] Kirkby Lonsdale, 1227, Brough *ante* 1281,[58] and Orton, with a charter of the time of Edward I, had it. In Furness and Cartmel, Flookburgh, perhaps in 1278, Ulverston, 1280, Dalton, and Cartmel, or some place in its parish, all had market charters before 1292.[58a] Evidence of how thinly peopled the Lake District* was at this time can be seen from Keswick, 1276,[59] being the only market town within it.

On the whole Society in the Middle Ages was very stable, but from time to time new communities would spring up and a new village or hamlet be founded. Interesting evidence of the extent to which this took place can be seen in the history of the chapelries since the need for a place of worship, where there had been none before, is proof of the settlement or growth of a new community.† We have also evidence of some development in town life. Kendal, as the centre of the Westmorland woollen industry, began to grow in the fourteenth century. Some fresh places also attained the status of market towns— Skinburness, soon to be drowned by the Solway, 1301,[60] Bootle, 1347, Kirkby Stephen, 1351-2, and Flookburgh, 1412,[61]—appear to complete the list. But on the whole there was not much change.

Little information has survived about education in the diocese in the Middle Ages. We know that schools existed

* To illustrate this it may be stated that only three parish churches lay within it—Bampton, Crosthwaite and Bassenthwaite. All the western dales were in St. Bees parish; the southern in Millom or Dalton; the eastern in Kendale, Bampton, Shap, Barton, or Greystoke; the northern in Brigham, Crosthwaite or Bassenthwaite. But in every case, except the three named, the church was in the low lying country outside what is generally called the Lake District.

† See the section on Church extension in the Middle Ages.

because in 1259 injunctions were issued " to parish priests near schools in the cities and castles of the diocese touching their administration to scholars."[62]

The first school mentioned is that of Carlisle in 1188. Other references to it occur in the next two centuries; the last in 1370-1. Then there is a blank. No school is recorded there in the Valor of 1535. Thus, by normal genealogical standards, it cannot be said that the school founded by the Statutes of 1545 has a proved pedigree from that mentioned in 1188.*

There was a school in Penrith at an early date; it was probably of episcopal foundation. A school master was licenced to it in 1340. William Strickland, later bishop of Carlisle, in founding his chantry there in 1395 directed that the priest should teach Church music and grammar. Early in this century the rector of the school at Cockermouth witnesses a deed.[63] No evidence of any other pre-Reformation schools in Cumberland has come to light.

Westmorland was better provided with schools: the senior is Appleby Grammar School. In fact, judged by the interest of its history and the distinction of its sons,† it can surely claim to be the premier scholastic foundation in the diocese. It originated in two chantry bequests of 1286 and 1331; from 1452 various documents prove its continued existence. The Grammar School at Kendal

---

* " There is no historical authority for the tradition that the Carlisle Grammar School was founded by St. Cuthbert. One writer, Symeon of Durham, in the twelfth century, tells us that in 685 Lugubalia, or Luel, was added to the bishopric of Lindisfarne, which had been granted to St. Cuthbert and there " he established a nunnery and founded schools." An earlier writer, Venerable Bede (ob. 735), who, in his life of St. Cuthbert and in his *Ecclesiastical History*, gives many details of the doings of St. Cuthbert at Lugubalia, says nothing of any school. . ." In fact the tradition itself does not seem to date further back than Dr. Hugh Todd in 1698." (Archdeacon Prescott on the *Grammar School at Carlisle* in N.S. xvi, 1-28).

† Of these the most distinguished in the Middle Ages were Thomas Langton, bishop of Winchester and archbishop elect of Canterbury and Christopher Bainbridge, cardinal archbishop of York. For its history see O.S. viii, 404-12; N.S. xxxix, 227-61, and xxvi 150-246 in *passim*.

was founded by Adam Pennyngton, of Boston, Lincolnshire, who, by his will proved 27 July 1527, directed that
the abbot of Risby or " the alderman of Corpus Xt Gild
or some other abbot or Gild " should have the ordering of
his lands for ninety eight years to find " a prest being an
able schole maister, he to kepe and teche a free schole to all
that come in the toune of Kendale where a place is or may
be most convenient for it."*

The school at Brough under Stainmore was founded
in 1506, originally in connection with a chantry. It is
stated that Beetham school was founded by subscription
in 1500,[64] but, as no documents supporting this are forthcoming,† it must be received with caution. There was
certainly a schoolmaster there in 1578.[65]

No evidence of the existence in the Middle Ages of any
schools in Lancashire, North of the Sands has been
discovered. But Cartmel Grammar School was certainly
founded before 1598,[66] when an inventory of its lands was
taken, and may be a late medieval foundation.

During much of the period covered by this survey these
counties were in proximity to a nation with whom England
was at war. How much did this affect the life of ordinary
people? First we must realise that most of the evidence
about this, coming from the English side, would tend to
exaggerate the depredations of the Scottish enemy and
to make the most of the brutalities of which he was
doubtless sometimes guilty. Also much of our evidence
is from returns of, or pleas for remission of, taxation.
The expectant taxpayer was more likely then, as now, to
overestimate the damage to his property than to mini-
mise it.

Excluding the parishes on the Border or along the
Solway, probably the damage done by war to the life of

---

* *Penningtoniana*, Joseph Foster, 62-63. Adam was a grandson of Sir John
Penyngton, ob. 1470. It seems strange that no book on Kendal or its records
gives the exact words of the will endowing the school.

† I am indebted to Mrs. Eaton, headmistress, for inquiring into the matter.

ordinary people was not as great as might be expected. This land, except at the very beginning of our period, was never actually occupied by hostile armies, though, as many of our ancestors probably found out, a friendly one can do harm enough. Edward I waged his wars on enemy soil; but in the weak hands of his son a very different state of affairs came about which resulted in the terrible raids of 1314-22. These no doubt had a disastrous effect on the country side, with, however, one beneficial result— pele towers began to be erected.

These buildings, modelled on the ancient keep with walls from four and a half to ten feet in thickness, still survive in large numbers. They consisted usually of two storeys, an upper one where the lord and his people could retreat and a lower one where the stock of the community could be safely housed. Thus as time went on and means of defence increasd the effect of raiding parties on the countryside lessened. The lord of the manor, with his family and stock generally found safety in his pele tower from anything but a siege, which the raiders were usually in too much of a hurry to undertake. Probably any of his tenants who lived close enough joined him there—it was to his interest to preserve them, while those who lived away from the centre of the demesne got into the woods and waste till the danger was past. In some places, as will be seen below,* the village church was provided with a pele tower to shelter the parishioners.

Thus probably the actual damage of ordinary raids was not very great if warning of the coming enemy reached the village in time for people to take action. If any man foolishly stayed, and resisted, he might be killed but if he escaped to a fortified place or to the waste he would be safe. His hut might be burnt; it was not difficult to replace. The greatest danger of loss was a

* See p. 65.

twofold one: any cattle that there was not time to drive off would inevitably be taken away or killed, and any crops burnt—this was probably the greatest source of ill since if the village community lost its harvest it had little chance of getting through the coming winter.

Apart from such excitements as these the people of a medieval village or town lived a very quiet and self contained life. News from elsewhere must have been infrequent, except for those who lived on or near the few main roads. Life, judged by our standards, was therefore very dull, but for them, with the services of the village church, with the great merry-makings on Holy Days and harvest, with the changing scene that Nature supplied, with the excitements of birth and death, of mating and marriage, it was all they knew. Though they did not perhaps live as full a life as we do now, they probably enjoyed as happy a one, and perhaps when the great call came they were as well or better prepared for it than many to-day. It is as foolish to idealize the conditions under which our forbears lived in the Middle Ages as it is wrong to think of them as existing in circumstances almost akin to brute beasts. Life in those days compared with ours neither resembled a heaven on earth nor a jungle; it was midway between the two as it is to-day, with a slight balance now perhaps in favour of the jungle.

CHAPTER III.

THE THIRTEENTH CENTURY OR A CENTURY OF CONSTRUCTION.

IT is curious how the history of this diocese in the Middle Ages fits itself neatly into centuries, each with its own character. The mark of this one is ordered progress. The ancient differences between England and Scotland, which had long troubled the land, began to be adjusted, though on this horizon there was still a small cloud. The manor of Dalston, the future home of the bishops obtained, the vexed question of the division of the lands of the cathedral between the bishop and the canons settled, the general life of the diocese began to take shape. Then towards the close of the century the cathedral was burnt down and the still small cloud threatened to bring a deluge and so the fair promise ends in the gloom of a northern sky.

Little is known about Bishop Bernard's episcopate. Several of his charters occur in the Wetheral register and there are confirmations of charters by him in those of Lanercost, Holm Cultram, and Whitby. Another of a grant by Anselm de Furness to the House of the Blessed Virgin Mary still has the bishop's seal appended.[1] The see was vacant on 8 July 1214,[2] presumably as a result of his death not long before.

Then there followed another period, this time of four years with no successor appointed, presumably because of the see's poverty as the bishop had no revenue apart from the canons of the cathedral with whom Athelwold had lived, sharing their goods.* The civil disturbances at the end of John's reign brought matters to a crisis. Alexander, the young Scottish monarch, seeing an opportunity to put forward his ancestral claim to Cumberland, laid siege to Carlisle and took both city and castle. His men also attacked the monastery of Holm Cultram and ravaged the whole district. The canons of the cathedral welcomed him, and not only gave him communion, though he was under excommunication, but elected, at his suggestion, a Scotsman to the vacant bishopric. The reaction, after the death of King John, resulted in Alexander withdrawing, in return for absolution, from Carlisle.[3]

One of the first acts therefore of William Marshall, earl of Pembroke, the regent (Henry III was a minor) was to see that the affairs of the cathedral were put on a proper footing. As the result of a complaint, the pope, in July 1217, ordered Gualo, his legate, to place the canons in other churches of their Order, to declare null the attempted election and to distribute the possessions and rents of the church between the bishops and the new canons to be appointed. The division was settled, it was hoped, by an ordinance made by the legate and his commissioners, and confirmed by the pope in April 1221.[4] Unfortunately this award did not give satisfaction or bring peace. Instead, judging by the language of the chronicler of Lanercost, a bitter and sordid dispute ensued during the whole of the episcopate of the new bishop.

This was Hugh, late abbot of the Cistercian abbey of Beaulieu in Hampshire.† Nominated for election by

---

* The fact that the bishop still has the senior stall in the cathedral is probably due to this far off event.

† He had been appointed by King John, but complaints were lodged against him in the general chapter of the order in 1215. He was accused of scandalous neglect of the rule and threatened with deposition, which threat was eventually carried out. He was a favourite of the king's and acted as

Gualo on the pope's orders,[5] he was the first bishop of Carlisle to be elected by the prior and canons.   The royal confirmation was on 1 August 1218, but his consecration, by Archbishop Walter Gray in York Minster, was not until 24 February 1219.[6]

He seems to have been a person of somewhat doubtful reputation, as can be seen from the note below, and it is not easy to assess his work as bishop.   He had a difficult task in carrying out the division of the cathedral endowments between the see and the priory, so it is not surprising to find the Lanercost Chronicler speaking ill of him.   The papal mandate

" to revoke concessions and confirmations made by him and his chapter of churches to sons of living rectors under age, contrary to the decrees of the Lateran Council,"[7]

certainly does not suggest a very conscientious prelate, especially as he had attended the Council.   But Canon Wilson praises his espousal of the interests of the parishioners and more poorly paid clergy, where monasteries had appropriated churches and allowed only a scanty stipend to the chaplain.[8]   The bishop, in accordance with the decision of the Council, refused permission for such appropriations* unless proper provision was made for the appointment of a vicar at a reasonable stipend.

It was in Bishop Hugh's time that mention is first made of a residence for the bishops, apart from the canons.   In

intermediary between him and the pope during Innocent III's interdict. He also, as one of the king's proctors, attended the fourth Lateran Council (*Bishops and Reform*, 1215-1272, M. Gibbs and J. Lang; Moorman, 276).

* Appropriation meant that a monastery which possessed the patronage of a benefice obtained the right to appropriate the endowments, that is use part of them for their own benefit.   The monastery thereby became in fact a perpetual rector.   The disastrous effect of this on parishes in which a vicarage had not been ordained came to a head at the dissolution of the monasteries when many parishes lost all their ancient endowments and sank into perpetual curacies, hence the poverty of some ancient parishes in this diocese.   (See *Vicarages in the Middle Ages*, R. A. R. Hartridge).

1221 he was building a house at Carlisle,[9] and had also just obtained, by the division of the possessions of the priory, a manor house at Linstock. Presumably also needing somewhere to stay when visiting the southern parts of his diocese, he built a house at Fithnenin, near Appleby, and probably called it after his monastery in Hampshire, hence its present name of Bewley.[10]

Bishop Hugh died on 4 June 1223, at the abbey of Ferte in Burgundy, as a result of an accident, while on his return from the Roman Court. The chronicler of Lanercost saw in his death the just judgment of God for the expulsion of the canons and the fraudulent division of their property. But it must be remembered that the bishop had compelled the prior of Lanercost to renounce, in consequence of its being uncanonical, an agreement with Holm Cultram by which the priory obtained the patronage of Burgh church and five marks a year.[11] So perhaps the chronicler was a little biased in his view.

Before an account is given of the next bishop, the story of one who, as related by a Scottish Chronicle, aspired to be bishop must be related. This was Adam de Kendal, abbot of Holm Cultram. He, seeing the bishop —Hugh—to be crippled with age and infirmity, conceived the ambition of gaining the episcopate at an early period. So, alike unmindful of God and his vows, he went to and fro without restraint, and squandered the revenue of the monastery in frequent banquets, sumptuously served, and, as well as by many bribes and much flattery, endeavoured to obtain the friendship and favour of those, both clergy and laity, whose influence might be used in his favour. Thus his house was miserably injured, both spiritually and materially. Perceiving this, certain of the monks conveyed an account of these doings to the superior-general of the Cistercian Order, who caused enquiries to be made, and ended by deposing the abbot in 1223. Throwing himself on the mercy of the chapter, Adam was allowed to take up his abode at Ilekirk, where there was a hermitage belonging to the abbey.   But his worldly ambitions still remained, so, when he heard that the election of a new bishop was about to take place, he bribed a secular priest to go to Carlisle and make enquiries how many of his friends were supporting him.   The man reported that on the day of the election Adam's name was not even mentioned.   At this news the poor man was so upset that before long he lost his reason, and, being possessed of an evil spirit, died a most lamentable death at Holm Cultram as a terrible warning to the ambitious.*

Walter Mauclerk, a prominent civil servant,[12] was elected bishop in August 1223, but as this was done without the royal permission assent was withheld until 27 October.[13]   He was consecrated, sometime between 7 December 1224 and May 1225, at York by Archbishop Walter.

Canon Wilson says of him " the name of Walter Mauclerk will rank among the foremost of the early bishops of Carlisle, who have contributed by their exertions and influence to the endowment of the bishopric."[14]   He might equally truly have said for the position he held in the life of his time and for the example of his piety.

After serving on several embassies he was appointed treasurer of England in 1229 and received this office for life in July 1232.[15]   But he was soon compelled to surrender it.[16]   It is clear that he was one of the party of Hubert de Burgh and when his patron fell Walter Mauclerk shared his fate.   In 1233 he had so serious a quarrel with the king owing, according to the Lanercost chronicler, to the wrong done to the church of Carlisle

---

* *Some records of a Cistercian Abbey*, G. E. Gilbanks, 44-57, where the full details of this fearful warning to those who try unduly to thrust themselves into high places is set out.

that he fled overseas and the diocese was placed under an interdict. By 1235 he was in favour again and once more employed on an embassy. In 1239, he was one of the bishops who took part in the baptism of Prince Edward. Three years later he was the recipient of a gift of a pack of hounds from the king,[17] but despite this mark of favour and his employment on several commissions, he was reproached by him for his lack of zeal, and in 1243 commanded not to interfere in the affairs of State as it was high time he attended to the health of his soul—a hint perhaps that he should retire to his diocese.[18]

During these years he was also an active figure in the civil administration of the county of Cumberland. Sheriff in 1223 and 1225, and custodian of Carlisle castle from 1226 till 1229,[19] he received the custody of the castle and the county of Cumberland for life in 1232.[20] But in 1233 Thomas de Muletone was sheriff, so the bishop must have been dismissed from this office when he was deprived of the treasurership.

Mauclerk does not appear to have been unmindful of the interests of his remote diocese. In June 1226, a papal mandate was issued to enquire and report about the division of the possessions of the church of Carlisle between it and the bishop. The canons seem to have been complaining to the pope about the decision of 1221 and accusing the bishop of usurping the collation of churches in their gift.[21] The dispute lasted all through this episcopate.

The act for which the diocese should most gratefully remember him was that he obtained from the king the grant of the manor and advowson of Dalston by charter dated 26 February 1230; its perambulation by Brian de Insula, Thomas, son of John, and Alan Buche took place on 12 April.[22] Probably a stronghold of some kind was already in existence on the site of Rose Castle. The gain to the bishops of a place of residence further from the

Border than Linstock and sufficiently near Carlisle for them to be in touch with the cathedral and the royal officials at the castle is obvious.   Later holders of the see must often have thanked God for the foresight of Bishop Walter and the generosity of Henry III.   In the same year the bishop purchased the great soke of Horn-castle in Lincolnshire, with its church and dependent chapels, and a few years later conveyed it to his successors in the see of Carlisle.   This was a valuable addition to its assets, yielding about a fourth of its total revenues.   In the stormy years to come, it gave the bishops a place of refuge and quiet, where ordinations could be held when the neighbourhood of Carlisle was ravaged by war.   These two acquisitions did much to put the finances of the see on a secure basis and to give the bishops an income suitable to their position.   They also had an official residence in London, first mentioned in 1238, known as Carlisle Inn, Carlisle House, or Carlisle Place, situated in the Strand, outside Temple Bar, with gardens extending to the Thames.[23]

Now to turn to matters which reveal the mind of Bishop Mauclerk as a religious man of his age.   At one time there seems no doubt that he planned to go on a crusade, probably that of 1248, the seventh, led by St. Louis, the king of France.   But the bishop received a commutation of his vow from the pope by reason of his old age and debility, and instead was required to send warriors according to his means.[24]

He was also a supporter of the greatest religious movement of his time which resulted in the founding of two new religious orders—the friars.   One, the Franciscans, took its ideals and name from St. Francis of Assisi; the other, the Dominicans, from St. Dominic.   They may be described as the Salvation Army of the Middle Ages.   They were bound to poverty, not only as individuals, but corporately as well.   Hence their name of mendicants, but this high ideal was not upheld for long. By 1224 the followers of both these saints had landed in England. Bishop Mauclerk was one of their earliest benefactors, giving them a large plot of ground in Old Jewry, within the City of London, and two mills outside the south gate of Oxford.[25] According to the Chronicle of Lanercost, the Franciscans were settled in Carlisle by August 1233. The Dominicans arrived shortly after, and were established without the walls of the city by 29 September in the same year. There was also a house of Carmelite Friars at Appleby, founded in 1281, and one of Augustinian or Austin friars in Penrith, founded before 1300.[26]

It is pleasant to be able to record an act of consideration by the king towards his old servant in his declining years. In 1244, the keepers of the bishop of Winchester were ordered to take six roes in the warrens of the bishopric and to send two of them to Walter, bishop of Carlisle, "who is ill at Rading" (Reading).[27] On 5 July 1245, the bishop had leave from the king to make a Will. Next year, 13 July, he resigned his see to become a mendicant at Oxford.[28] An act of kindness which throws a light on the bishop's character is recorded in the grant of 17 May 1248 to Roger, cook of Walter, formerly bishop of Carlisle, at the bishop's instance, of 40 shillings out of the chattels of an outlaw.[29] It is nice to think of the bishop, nearing his end, caring for his cook's material welfare. He died on 28 October 1248 " in the religious society of those whom he favoured and endowed before he had embarked on the stormy sea of temporal affairs."[30]

Walter Mauclerk is an interesting person; not only as an eminent man of his time, but as a typical one. He held the highest offices in Church and State; yet he wanted to go on a crusade and died as a simple friar. The writer of the *Flores Historiarum* suggests his reason was remorse, because he owed his bishopric to royal favour, rather than to learning and character.[31]   But his devotion to the scholarly Dominican Order and the little glimpses of his character that are available do not support this view.   Monkish chroniclers are notoriously jealous of those who supported their rivals.   Dwellers in this diocese will remember him for his gift of what was to become Rose Castle, and the world at large perhaps as the man, who, with death near, thought of his cook, and yet, having given all his goods to the poor, had to ask his king to fulfil his wish.

The canons of the cathedral had licence to elect on 1 August 1246.   They chose Sylvester de Everdon.[32] But an entry on the Patent Rolls for 12 September states:

" the prior and convent of Carlisle: inasmuch as Sylvester de Everdon, archdeacon of Chester, would not assent to the election made by them, as it seemed to him to be vicious, have licence to elect again."

Matthew Paris states that he was unwilling to accept the proffered honour, not so much on account of his riches, as of his reluctance to undertake the burden of episcopal office.   At last, under pressure, though he considered himself unworthy, he consented.[33]   The royal assent had been given on 9 November 1246, but the consecration was not till 13 October 1247.   On 18 November, royal payment was authorised of £32. 9s. 10d. for a set of episcopal vestments for the bishop of Salisbury and £37. 9s. 6d. for a like suit for the bishop of Carlisle.[34]

As a result of a papal commission of March 1248, the old dispute about the division of the possessions of the priory was again brought up,[35] and at last final agreement was achieved.[36]

In the last few years relations between England and Scotland had been steadily improving, largely owing to the efforts of Pope Gregory.   We are liable to think of the papacy as valuing England merely as a place that provided benefices and money to meet papal needs that it is well to remember that in those days the pope, as a power above all earthly sovereigns, was also often a power for good. In 1236 he had written to Henry III of England and Alexander of Scotland urging them to come to an agreement, believing that from peace great benefits would accrue to both kingdoms. Next year a meeting between the two kings was held at York in the presence of the papal legate. As a result an agreement was arrived at in 1242, by which Henry handed over to Alexander various manors worth £200, in compensation for the surrender of his alleged hereditary rights to the northern counties and some other claims.

A complaint in 1248 that the ancient laws and customs of the Marches of the two kingdoms were not so well observed as formerly led to an investigation of these in April 1249, and as a result the famous Code, called the Laws of the Marches, was compiled to regulate the intercourse of the inhabitants on the two sides of the Border. The best commentary on the outcome of these efforts is that in 1255 large parts of Carlisle Castle were [in ruins. It should be remembered that the negotiations which led up to this happy result had originated in papal initiative.[37]

It is probable that Bishop Sylvester was not much in his diocese; as an important royal official his place would be with the Court. The only evidences of his being in it are that he witnessed an agreement in 1249 about the bounds of Shap Abbey, the other witnesses of which suggest a local scene; and that he executed two deeds at Bewley in April 1250.[38]

On 13 May 1254, Bishop Sylvester was thrown from his horse, and died of his injuries four days later. It is not known where this happened nor where he was buried.

The canons of Carlisle as usual sent two of their number

to announce the death of the bishop and to ask for a licence to elect.   The king gave them letters patent with

" the royal assent to the election of John, prior of Newburgh, to be elected as bishop and to make restitution of the temporalities, but if they did not elect him to send the person elected to the king."

It seems clear that the latter was not too sure of his ground.   That seems to have been the canons' reading of the situation.   Because they proceeded to elect, not the king's nominee or some prominent royal official, but Master Thomas de Vipont, rector of Greystoke, no doubt a member of the local baronial family of that name—a good illustration of the increasing authority of the Church and the nobility over the Crown.   The royal assent to the election was given on 5 November 1254, and the temporalities restored on 24 December.   His consecration by Walter, bishop of Durham, was on 7 February 1255.   One of the few records of this short episcopate, a licence to Alan de Berwise to build a private chapel there, is dated at Rose, 23 February 1255.   This is the earliest evidence that the bishop was in residence there.   Nothing else of interest is known of this bishop, who died on 25 October 1256.[39]

On his death, Walter, bishop of Durham, successfully pleaded his rights to the sequestration of all the benefices in his diocese belonging to the bishopric of Carlisle, while that see was void.   On other occasions a similar claim was allowed.   The spiritualities of the see during a vacancy belonged to the archbishop of York.[40]   The canons' first choice for the vacancy, Robert de Sancta Agatha, did not consent to the election, so they had licence, 30 December 1256, to elect again.   They chose Robert Chause, archdeacon of Bath.   The royal assent was given on 12 February 1257, and the temporalities restored on 29 September.   His consecration, at Bermondsey by William of Bath and Giles of Salisbury, did

not take place till 14 April 1258. This delay, according
to the Annalist of Dunstable, was because the archbishop
of York made him fair promises and ill returns, and
temporised in confirming his election, with the hope, he
alleges, of obtaining the appointment of a certain Master
John. The bishop designate had to appeal to the pope for
redress.

Robert Chause, unlike the statesman Mauclerk or the
lawyer de Everdon, was first and foremost a diocesan
bishop, not a State official. With him the series of
prelates who resided in the diocese and gave themselves
very largely to the work of local administration may be
said to commence. Judged by the fate of some dioceses
in the Middle Ages, Carlisle was fortunate in this respect.

The most interesting event in this episcopate is the
promulgation of a set of statutes for the diocesan synod.
These are to be found in the second volume of the ancient
episcopal registers between the Acts of the fourteenth
century Bishops Welton and Appleby. As can be seen
from the note below,* their insertion at this point has
caused their true date to be overlooked and their history

---

* Behind the discovery of the true date of these statutes lies a curious
story of human error. Canon Wilson, describing them in *V.C.H.* II, 38-9,
1905, stated that they " probably belong to the great episcopate of Bishop
Halton." But in October 1913, he published an article in *S.H.R.* on
" *Medieval Education at Carlisle* " in which he made several references to
and quotations from a source he called " *Statuta Karleolensia M.S.*,
which he attributed to a diocesan synod of 1259. Nothing was said of
the whereabouts of this MS. The present writer reading the article was
puzzled as to what this document could be. Through the good offices of
Dr. Moorman, he got in touch with Professor C. R. Cheney who suggested that
the MS. referred to was probably the statutes described by Wilson in *V.C.H.*
In which case the canon was correcting his statement by implication, without
actually stating he was doing so. Later a personal investigation of the
episcopal register proved this suggestion to be correct. But not only have
our medieval statutes been misdated, they have also been overlooked—all
modern authorities stating that we had none. Now the wrong is righted and
the truth brought to light. For a description of the statutes the student is
referred to Wilson's accounts and to an article by Professor Cheney in *E.H.R.*,
January 1947, p. 52-7 in which they are placed in their true historical setting
and various erroneous statements about them corrected.

misunderstood. The main body of the statutes, numbered 1-77, are the same as those put forth in the diocese
of Wells shortly before 1258. Similar ones were also in
use in the diocese of York. Bishop Chause was archdeacon of Bath and there seems little doubt that he was
the connecting link between Wells and the North and
that, having introduced them at Carlisle, he passed them
on to his metropolitan.

The statutes entered in the episcopal registers contain
chapters not found in the Wells-York series. Two of
them, on those who obstruct the collection of tithes of
corn and hay and on those who lay hands on ecclesiastical
property, have their counterparts in statutes of Bishop
Kellawe of Durham and Archbishop Greenfield of York
and seem to reflect the unsettled state of society in the
fourteenth century. Another, demanding that priests
of the diocese should be suitably attired at synods and
other gatherings, is similar to one of this archbishop's.
So they probably represent additions made during the
first half of that century. Two chapters—on those who
fail to keep the feasts of St. Cuthbert and reserving the
absolution of perjurers to the bishop—are orginal pro-
ductions and therefore of special interest to us in this
diocese. They may belong either to the earlier or later
series.

Much that is known of the bishop's other activities is
concerned with disputes and law suits. As a result of
one with the abbey of St. Mary's, York in 1266, he had to
surrender his claim to the custody of the priory of
Wetheral, a cell of the abbey, during a vacancy, as well as
the right of visitation and removal of priors. In a
dispute with the king of Scotland he was more fortunate,
as the king failed in an effort to depossess him of the
church of Great Salkeld in 1261.[41] But he lost the
church of Rothbury to King Edward in 1278; the latter
returned it, however, to the canons of Carlisle and Bishop

Irton in 1290.[42]. The most serious lawsuit of all, which began in 1274, was with Michael de Hercla about the ownership of the manor and advowson of Dalston, which had belonged to Michael's ancestor, Hervey, son of Maurice, who had been dispossessed for felony. The manor and advowson had remained in the king's hand for nearly fifty years when he granted them to Bishop Mauclerk in 1230. Michael, passing over this inconvenient fact, claimed as Maurice's heir. The bishop died before judgment was given. His successor thought it wise to buy out de Hercla for £200, which shows what a lawsuit with a powerful opponent cost in the thirteenth century.[43]

The matter next to be related might have been more serious for Bishop Chause than even the loss of Rose. He had excommunicated Richard de Crepping, who succeeded him as sheriff in 1272, at the request of the abbot of Holm Cultram, upon whom the sheriff had made some distresses for debts owing to the Crown. So the sheriff, determining to get his own back, informed the chancellor that the bishop had forbidden his tenants to take the oath of fealty to King Edward, who had just ascended the throne. The bishop, hearing of this, certified the chancellor that the information was false. He had, in fact, requested the sheriff, who was then at Appleby, that he would, either by himself or his deputy, administer the necessary oath.[44]

The chronicler of Lanercost records the bishop's death in these words:

"But in October [1278] Robert de Chalize, bishop of Carlisle died; [he was] eager for the honour of God, philanthropic and ready in urbanity; the world may testify without our assurance how bountiful and liberal he was."[45]

There is a grave slab in Croglin Churchyard with ' In hac tumba jacet Robert' Eps.' upon its bevelled edge, so he may have died and been buried there. He had also a monument in the cathedral which survived the fire of 1292.[46]

The canons were given licence to elect a new bishop on 27 October 1278. They chose William de Rothelfield, dean of York, who renounced the election and died soon after. They then did something that got them into serious trouble. Without petitioning the crown for a new licence, they devolved the right of election to five of their number, who chose Ralph de Irton, prior of Gisburn in Yorkshire, whom they presented to William, archbishop of York for confirmation. He died before he could give this. The chapter of York declined to take any responsibility, and the king, in high indignation that the election had been held without his licence, refused his consent. The convent appealed to the pope, and Prior Irton set off to Rome to support the petition. The pontiff nominated three cardinals to investigate. They reported that the election was void as the choice of the electors was not, in accordance with the usage of the Roman see, pronounced by one of them singly, though they had all unanimously agreeed to it. However, the pope, nominated him to the bishopric, by way of provision,[47] being satisfied as to his character and learning. He was consecrated by the bishop of Tusculum on 25 March 1280, and the temporalities were restored on 10 July. The king accepted the papal provision. So all ended in a satisfactory way for the bishop. But the king did not accept so easily the convent's plea for pardon. It cost them 500 marks, the residue of which was paid on 7 February 1282, to obtain it.[48] Mediæval monarchs were always glad of an excuse for obtaining a little ready money.

All local histories state that the bishop was a member of the Coupland family of Irton of Irton. Professor Tout speaks of " the intensely local character of most of the great religious foundations and notably the Cathedral

Church of Carlisle,"[49] so the accepted tradition may be correct. But there was a family which took its name from another Irton, near Harrogate, who were benefactors to Gisburn Priory, so the question must remain open, until, if ever, further evidence comes to light.[50]

Bishop Irton landed in England on about 30 May 1280 and almost at once began to plan the completion of the cathedral choir. The end of the building depicted on the priory seal, with triple lancet windows, probably shews what this early English east front looked like.[51] To raise money for this he called the clergy together in synod in the following October and demanded of them a tithe of a tenth of their revenues for two years on the basis, not of a nominal, but of a true valuation; chaplains, that is, unbeneficed clergy, as well as incumbents had to pay. The sum demanded of the priory of Lanercost was £24 of new money for one year. So the chronicler has little good to say of him. He was crafty, subtle, and very greedy, using his visitation as a means of wringing contributions from the simple minded clergy of his diocese. One member of the house even burst into Latin verse, which has been translated thus:

> " Poor sheep, bereft of ghostly father;
> Should not be shorn; but pampered rather.
> Poor sheep ! with cares already worn,
> You should be comforted; not shorn.
> But if the shepherd must have wool,
> He should be tender, just and cool.[52]

The picture given is of an imperious, somewhat impulsive person, who, having determined on a certain course of action, would brook no delay. But evidence suggests that he was also an exceedingly able and far sighted man.

There seems little doubt that it was largely owing to his energy that the early English choir of the cathedral, work on which had been started in the middle of the century, was roofed in and completed. The Lanercost chronicler specifically mentions the price of the timbers, glazing and stalls which he had extorted.[53] The choir, as then completed, was probably the same size as it is to-day, except for the short additional bay.

His scheme for a vicarage at Dalston is one of his most interesting projects. He considered the revenue of the rectory to be too large, so in 1285 he prepared a scheme to divide it into three. The new incumbent, with the status of a vicar, was to have £12. 16s.; £15 was to be devoted to the support of the archdeacon of Carlisle; and the third part of £16 was to assist twelve poor scholars in the school of the church of Carlisle, of whom four were to attend Dalston church on Sundays and Festival Days, unless they were hindered by bad weather; this third portion was also charged with the support of an assistant priest to minister in that church. As Canon Wilson truly observes: " one cannot withhold a word of admiration for the administrative ability of the statesman prelate who embraced in one comprehensive scheme such a heterogenous assortment of diocesan agencies."[54] The scheme came to an end in May 1292, after the bishop's death, as the king's consent had not been obtained.[55]

This was not the only instance of the bishop's interest in Dalston. On 6 February 1292, he obtained a licence

" to lead part of the water of the spring of Wellinton, which is within the forest of Englewoode, from the said spring to his mill near the manor of la Rose."[56]

Another example of his administrative ability was his plan for creating a chantry out of the vicarage of Torpen-how. He reserved to himself the advowson and ordained that the vicar should keep in his house and maintain at his own charge three priests and one sub-deacon. The duties of each of them are set out and how the stipend was to be divided arranged. This early attempt at solving the problem of the staffing of the large country parishes by the creation of a college of clergy is most interesting. [57] As will be seen it was imitated in the following centuries on a larger scale at Greystoke and Kirkoswald.

Even more interesting is his legacy to his successors in the see of the furniture of his chapel and house and the farming utensils of his manors. This example, both of foresight and of consideration for others, reveals him in a very different light to that seen by the Lanercost Chronicler. In a charter, dated 14 November 1291, he sets out how a bishop entering upon his see has often found himself exposed to poverty and the need of borrowing money and that instructed by experience he had determined to provide that his successors should have at their disposal 'a chapel' properly equipped with certain books of theology and canon law, and a proper supply of things needful for the cultivation of their manors. The charter then sets out all the property left. The catalogue is given in full by Canon Wilson.[58] A bishop's 'chapel' was a technical term meaning all the furniture and vestments necessary for his carrying out his office. In Canon Wilson's view the trust created in the 'chapel' remains in force to the present day.

In 1291 Pope Nicholas IV imposed a crusading tenth on the clergy. In order that the true value of the ecclesiastical benefices in England might be ascertained, so that this tax could be properly assessed, a new taxation was ordered. Previous ones had understated, so it was alleged, the value of many benefices. Doubtless the clergy complained but posterity is grateful because the returns enable us to know the value of most livings in England at this time. The figures for this diocese and that part of it then included in the archdeaconry of Richmond have been extracted. For this purpose the portions of religious houses and the rectories of livings appropriated to them have been omitted so as to discover

the actual incomes of the parochial clergy. They work
out as follows:—

	Carlisle.	Richmond
		benefices
Value between £0 — 5 a year	12	4
5 — 10	20	9
10 — 20	30	9
20 — 30	11	4
30 — 40	9	2
40 — 50	7	2
50 — 60	3	1

In addition, in Carlisle diocese Greystoke was worth
£120 a year, and in the archdeaconry of Richmond,
Kendal over £123, Brigham £80, and Heversham and
St. Bees £66 each. The yearly average in Carlisle works
out at £17. 11s. and in Richmond £23. 3s.[59] As the
average value of a living in Norwich diocese, more
wealthy than many, was only about £11, the clergy in
this diocese were well off. To illustrate the value of this
income: in 1353 all holders of land to the value of £15 a
year and over were decreed worthy of knighthood, and
a peasant farming 20 acres of ploughland spent about £3
a year upon himself, wife and children.[60] G. G. Coulton
suggests that to get an idea of the meaning of money in
1300, in comparison with 1934, we should multiply by
forty.[61] Thus it can be seen that in those days many
incumbents were among the well-to-do. It should,
however, be remembered that the richer livings were
rectories and in these the stipend was supposed to be
divided into three parts; for the support of the rector,
the upkeep of the church and its services and the relief of
the poor. The social status of the unbeneficed, many of
whom had the care of the parishes of absentee incumbents, can be seen by the fact that 75 per cent. of the

ordinands in Bishop Halton's register had titles of 5 marks (£3. 6s. 8d.) and 25 per cent., 3 marks (£2).

To return to Bishop Irton: he seems to have been very much a man of his diocese. Even when he was employed on national affairs they were of a kind that would naturally be assigned to a Borderer. He was sent with Anthony Bek, bishop of Durham, on the embassy to negotiate with the Scots parliament for the marriage of Edward I's son to Margaret, " the maid of Norway," the infant heiress of the Scottish Crown. On 18 July 1290, the envoys brought the matter to a successful conclusion by the treaty of Brigham. Unfortunately the child died; the throne of Scotland became vacant and the heir in question. The English king claimed the right to settle between the rival claimants. Bishop Irton attended the meeting Edward held to investigate the matter at Norham in May 1291.[62]

The Lanercost Chronicle records his death at Linstock on 1 March 1292 thus:

" For being greatly fatigued by a long journey which he made in deep snow, returning from the parliament in London, he bled himself [on arriving] in the aforesaid episcopate, and when he was liberally refreshing his body, he desired to sleep. In his slumber the vein burst, and before he could be attended to he took leave of human affairs, deluged in blood and deprived of speech."[63]

In writing of the fire which burnt down so much of the city and cathedral on 18 May following, the Chronicler describes Bishop Irton as " a brigand rather than a high priest " and as " that wicked extortioner,"[64] but it is felt that his epitaph is more truly to be found in the works described above than in the malice of a disgruntled monk. It would be nice to think that he was a Cumbrian by birth.

The great fire which destroyed so much of the material progress of the last two centuries in the city and cathedral

of Carlisle and so many of the muniments*[65] recording
that progress must, in the years to come, have often been
felt by the inhabitants as a symbolic one.   Bishop Irton's
place at the end of a century and of a chapter is true in
more than just the formal fact.   The work of the bishop
in the cathedral was destroyed by fire: a bishop who
negotiated the marriage that would have united the
Crowns of England and Scotland: that also was destroyed
—by death, and as a result the folly and ambition of the
English king was to set afoot events that meant that the
land the bishop served was seldom to be free from both
fire and death by violence for some three hundred years.
Truly the end of the episcopate of Bishop Irton is the
end of a chapter, as well as the end of a century of
constructive work.

* The city muniments were undoubtedly lost in the fire. It seems more
doubtful if all the ecclesiastical ones were. Bishop Irton's register was
certainly in existence in 1566 (N.S. xlvi. 176).

CHAPTER IV.

THE FOURTEENTH CENTURY OR WAR AND PESTILENCE.

WAR and Pestilence—because, except for some thirty years in the middle of it, the history of this Border land, during this century, was dominated by futile quarrels with Scotland, while in the middle of the period of comparative peace there were two terrible pestilences and following them, after a period of recuperation, the break in the lawful succession of the monarchy caused by the usurpation of Henry of Bolingbroke, the evils of which were so clearly seen by Bishop Merke. Yet during these years the cathedral choir, with the famous east window, was completed, so despite the folly of men this and other work of the Church went on.

The canons' messengers, who brought news of the death of Bishop Ralph, received the royal licence to elect on 23 March 1292. On 23 April the chapter chose John de Halton,* canon of the cathedral church, as bishop. The king's assent was given on 26 May, and the temporalities restored on 18 June. The bishop, who was consecrated at York on 14 September by Anthony Bek of Durham,[1] was to hold the office for over thirty two years.

---

* The name is usually spelt Halghton in ancient documents, but that adopted by the editor of his register is used here. The place name is not uncommon, so his place of birth cannot be given with any certainty. There is no evidence to connect him with the local family of this name, later seated in Greystoke parish. There was a contemporary family of this name of knightly rank in Northumberland; they used the name John (Northumberland County Hist., X, 393).

Almost at once the new bishop was caught up in the maelstrom of national affairs: he was present at the king's adjudication at Berwick on Tweed in 1292 between the claimants to the Scottish crown by which John Balliol was adjudged the successful competitor. Edward treated him as a puppet and Scotland as a subject land. Balliol goaded to desperation renounced his allegiance and the horrid arbitrament of war became inevitable. In March 1296 the earl of Buchan raided Cumberland,[2] burning Lanercost and assaulting Carlisle. But a land with a divided baronage, many Scottish nobles had estates on this side the Border, could put up little resistance. Then when all seemed over, in a guerilla of genius, William Wallace, the common people found a leader, Scotland a soul and poor Cumberland a scourge. The Scots, after defeating the English at Stirling, carried fire and sword throughout the country, burning the land for thirty leagues round Carlisle.[3] Just before this, 13 October 1297, Bishop Halton had been appointed custodian of Carlisle Castle, and was thus responsible for it from November 1297 to September 1298, when it was more than once besieged. His register contains many interesting entries of his expenses.

But if Cumberland suffered, Cumberland also had glory—of a kind. For Carlisle became the base of the English army in the punitive expedition that Edward organized. His forces assembled there in June 1300, while he stayed at Lanercost. The famous siege of Caerlavrock Castle followed. After its fall, the king returned to Cumberland in September, dividing his time between Holm Cultram, Rose and Carlisle.[4]

The glory, however, had its disadvantages. The bishop in 1301 described how repeated incursions by the Scots had resulted in the destruction and burning of the greater part of his diocese, so that the monasteries were pillaged and the religious men dispersed. Some churches were reduced to ashes and the incumbents forced to beg. Taxation was out of the question, as there was nothing for the tax gatherer to find..[5]

Even churches became fortresses: at Newton Arlosh, built in 1304, the main doorway was only 2 ft. 7 ins. wide and none of the windows, placed 7 ft. from the ground, measured more than 1 ft. in width and 3 ft. 4 ins. in height. Within the church access to the tower was by a small door above which was an opening from which boiling water, or something even more disagreeable, could be thrown down on the unwelcome visitor. Many may regard this as a very unchristian use of a church tower, a view doubtless shared by the Scots intruder. The neighbouring church of Burgh had two towers, each a fortress with walls 6 or 7 ft. thick. At Great Salkeld was another fortified church tower. At Bowness on Solway the rectory was a fortalice, traces of which remained until the last century.[6] It seems probable that the present buildings of Rose were begun at this time.[7] These ecclesiastical fortresses perhaps illustrate better than anything else the condition of the diocese and the mental outlook of the people during this episcopate.

In 1305 Wallace was captured and duly executed as a traitor. Again all seemed over. Then a chance meeting in Dumfries between Robert Bruce, grandson of one of the claimants of 1290, and the Red Comyn, leading to a quarrel in the Greyfriars church there, again changed all, for Comyn was left dead behind the altar. As a hunted outlaw Bruce had no choice but to trust the patriotic section of the Scottish people and revive the Wallace tradition. This time the leader was not an unknown knight but a great noble, who was crowned king in March 1306.

Edward, despite his age, at once set out for the Border, but, being seized with dysentery, had to turn aside to

F

Lanercost at Michaelmas.[8] In March he removed to Linstock Castle,[9] for the parliament at Carlisle, when the ancient city entertained such a throng of great nobles as it had never seen before. The papal legate was also there. On Passion Sunday, 19 March 1307,* after a sermon in praise of peace he, with the bishops who were present, " with lighted candles and ringing bells, terribly excommunicated Robert and his adherents as a perjured man and an unrighteous disturber of the common peace and quiet."[10] But Edward's days were numbered. Having offered up in the cathedral the litter in which he travelled he set out from Caldecotes to Burgh, where he died on 7 July 1307.

His son, Edward II, arrived at Carlisle on 18 July, and " the next day went to Burgh to mourn for his father, with the nobles of the land and prelates of the Church, who were assembled there in great number." He was a very different man from his father, and after a formal expedition over the Border retired to the south. In 1309, the bishop excused his attendance at parliament on account of the distance and the fear of invasion, which came in 1311, when the Scots king stayed three days at Lanercost, " making many of the canons prisoners and doing an infinity of injury."[11] As a result of the lack of royal protection the Border counties had to fend for themselves and buy the Scots off, giving hostages for the greater part of their debt.

The bishop was not in his diocese at this time, but attending the Council of Vienne. He was home again in February 1313, when he was once more ordered by the king to remain in his diocese to defend it against the Scots, and to send a proctor to parliament. In March

* On the following Sunday, probably for the first and last time, Carlisle cathedral was the scene of the making of a bishop. He was Griffin ap Jorwerth, elect of Bangor. The consecrator was Cardinal Peter de Spano (S.S. CLIII 66 note).

he finished his long service as custodian of Carlisle Castle, Andrew de Harcla succeeding him. In 1314, he was again excused from attending parliament as he was needed to guard his diocese, for Edward Bruce had arrived at Rose on 16 April, after invading England by way of Carlisle. He remained for three days, while his soldiers ravaged the countryside, burning many towns and two churches, taking men and women prisoners, and collecting a large number of cattle. But few were killed, except those who made a determined resistance.[12] Things were so bad that the bishop made a private treaty with him on 19 April for the protection of his manors of Rose and Linstock.[13]

One result of the ravages of war was a number of appropriations of rectories by impoverished ecclesiastical bodies. The bishop had licences, between 1301 and 1314, to convert the rectories of Dalston, Rothbury, and Horncastle, and the canons of the cathedral, between 1304 and 1307, for Addingham, with the chapel at Salkeld, Edenhall and Castle Sowerby. Outside the diocese the abbey of St. Mary's, York appropriated the rectories of Kendal in 1302, and Bromfield in 1303; and the prioress and nuns of Rosedale did likewise with Torpenhow in 1312. In every case the reason was the same, " in compensation of the burning of their houses and churches and divers plundering by the Scots."[14]

But greater evils were to follow for, though the royal government was stirred out of its lethargy and a large army collected, the result was Bannockburn. These unfortunate counties soon felt the full force of the victorious Scottish armies which invaded England, at the end of November 1314, and devastated almost all Northumberland; then foraged over Stainmore and burnt Brough and Appleby. From there they turned towards home and passing up the Eden valley, burnt Kirkoswald. The people of Coupland, far away to the south west, such was the terror evoked by their deeds, sent envoys and appeased them by much money. In the following year the king of Scotland tried to capture Carlisle,* besieging it for ten days, but the city, under Sir Andrew de Harcla, beat off his forces. Meanwhile Sir James Douglas, ravaging into Coupland, spoiled the priory church of St. Bees, burnt its manors of Cleator and Stainburn, and attacked the castle and town of Egremont.[15] It was probably during this raid that the beautiful buildings of Calder Priory were devastated so thoroughly that they were never rebuilt on their former scale. No record of such an attack has survived, but the buildings afford evidence that one took place about this time.[16] Next summer, 1316, the Scots got as far as Richmond in Yorkshire, and then turning west plundered their way on to Furness, burning the district. They had never been there before and were delighted, it is recorded, with the abundance of iron which they found.[17] It is curious how Kendal escaped these raids, perhaps there was no good road to it.

The state of the northern counties as a result can be seen by the basis for papal taxation made in 1291 being reduced in 1318, as the clergy simply had not the means to pay. Clerical stipends, largely drawn from glebe lands and tithes, are also evidence of the extent of the destruction of ordinary peoples' means to live and the great raid of 1322 was still to come. The parochial returns are given in Appendix XIII and those for the religious foundations below.† The value of both temporalities and spiritualities in 1291 were £3,171. 5s. 7½d., and in 1318 £480. 19s. for the diocese of Carlisle; and £1,191. 7s. 9d. and £201. 3s. 4d. for the archdeaconry of Richmond.

* It is rather interesting to note that the Chronicle of Lanercost 213, mentions the church of Holy Trinity, apparently just outside Caldewgate. Was there a medieval chapel somewhere near the site of the present city church of this name?

II. INITIAL LETTER OF CHARTER OF EDWARD II TO THE CITY OF CARLISLE shewing Sir Andrew de Harcla and the citizens defending it against the Scots in 1315.

facing p. 68)

When the bishop stated that the Scots had slain men, women, old and young, orphans and widows, burnt nearly all the churches, houses and buildings, driven off their cattle, carried away their treasures, ornaments, and every movable of value, and destroyed the whole country, so that the lands of the bishopric lay uncultivated, the sources of his revenues wasted, and he himself reduced to a state of indigence and want, it is clear that he was not exaggerating.[18]

The mismanagement of the Scots war and the king's reliance on his favourite, Piers Gaveston, caused much discontent, and a strong baronial opposition was formed under the king's cousin, Thomas, earl of Lancaster, to which Bishop Halton and Andrew de Harcla adhered. But, perhaps because of Thomas' dealings with the Scots or because he disapproved of armed rebellion, when events came to a crisis in 1322, the bishop sent his levies to fight on the royal side with de Harcla in the battle at Boroughbridge, in which Earl Thomas was defeated. As a reward de Harcla was created earl of Carlisle and became the most powerful person in the North.

†   FIGURES FOR RELIGIOUS FOUNDATIONS.

DIOCESE OF CARLISLE.

	1291	1318
The bishopric	126. 7. 7	20.
Carlisle	96. 19.	20.
Shap	46. 13. 4	2.
Armathwaite	10.	Waste
Lanercost	74. 12. 6½	Waste
Wetheral	52. 17. 6	4
Holm Cultram	206. 5. 10	40.

ARCHDEACONRY OF RICHMOND.

Cartmel	21. 11. 8	3. 6. 8
Conishead	9.	1. 10.
St. Bees	12. 9. 3	3. 6. 8
Calder	32.	5.
Furness	176.	13. 6. 8
Seton	No return	No return*

* *Taxatio Ecclesiastica*, 320, 333, 329.   These figures also have an interest as shewing the comparative financial position of the different foundations. Holm Cultram it will be noted was then richer than Furness.

Emboldened by this victory the king, collecting his forces, made ready to set out for Scotland by way of Berwick; Robert Bruce, hearing of this, at once set out for England by way of Carlisle. After burning the manor of Rose, plundering Holm Cultram, though his father's body was buried there, and ravaging Allerdale and Coupland, he reached Duddon Sands. He passed over them to Furness where the abbot, wiser in 1322 than in 1315, entertained him, paying ransom that the country round should not be wasted; despite this his men set fire to various places. Next Leven sands were crossed and the lands around Cartmel Priory desolated. Then Kent sands were traversed and Lancaster reached, where another force, under the earl of Moray and Sir James Douglas, joined him. South to Preston went the combined army, some even getting fifteen miles beyond before turning for home. On the way back the Scots rested from their labours at Carlisle and crossed the Border on 24 July. This great raid, occupying three weeks and three days, was over in time for the Scots to be ready for the English king when he set out from Newcastle shortly after 1 August. However, he was soon on English soil again; dysentery and lack of food, the result of incompetence, doing their work. So back came the Scots ; on 30 September they crossed the Solway and lodged five days at Beaumont, wasting the adjacent country. But this time they travelled east sparing these counties, and getting as far as Beverley before turning for home.

Few will blame the earl of Carlisle, after this display of royal powerlessness, for making a private treaty of peace with the Scots king, but Edward did, and de Harcla was condemned as a traitor and executed at Harraby.*

---

* Tradition says that his remains were buried near the Hartley Chapel in Kirkby Stephen Church (N.S. xxvi, 307-11).

However, it has always been an article of faith in Cumberland and Westmorland that he was no traitor, and
endeavoured to save, not to sell, his country. In fact,
in the next year, 1323, a treaty of peace was made between
the two countries on almost identical terms with those for
the acceptance of which the great earl had been condemned. Such was the background of the concluding
years of this episcopate.[19]

We must now consider what had been happening
to Carlisle Cathedral after the fire of 1292, which
destroyed the new early English choir, while leaving its
aisles comparatively unscathed. Indulgences* were
granted in the diocese of Lincoln in 1293 and probably in
York about the same time for the restoration of the
building.[20] According to the architectural evidence some
work was carried out shortly after the fire in repairing
the wall arcade and the lancet windows. The state of
affairs within the monastery, as revealed by Bishop
Halton's visitation of 1300,[21] does not suggest, however,
that much could have been done. The next piece of
evidence is an indulgence granted by Archbishop Greenfield of York for the restoration of Carlisle Cathedral,
dated Rose, 4 March 1307.[22] This states that the fire,
which totally destroyed the cathedral, was caused by the
Scots. If this really was so then there must have been
one, otherwise unrecorded in history, after 1292, as that
was undoubtedly the work of a local incendiary. The
simplest explanation is that our ancestors put down all
evils to the Scots' account, doubtless believing that even
if they had not done the damage with which they were
charged this was not for lack of intention but merely of

---

* An Indulgence was the remission of the whole or part of the punishment
due for sins committed. It was acquired by the performance of certain
specified good works with a disposition of true penitence and the payment of
certain sums of money in commutation of the acts of penance which would
otherwise have been necessary. (See on the whole question *History of the
Papacy*, M. Creighton, 1894, 58-69).

opportunity, so morally, if not factually, these evils could justly be placed to their account. Another matter of interest in this indulgence is " the indication that the choir was still awaiting that work of repair and rebuilding which was to be consummated at some future date."[23] Then in 1318 Archbishop Melton granted yet another indulgence.[24]

Probably then the work of restoration was intermittently carried on during these years (1292-1324).* The grand design of the east window—" unsurpassed by any other in the kingdom, perhaps there is not a window equal to it in the whole world,"[26]—was obviously planned when the work of reconstruction began, but could not have been completed in one generation.

To return to the chronological story of the bishop's life: in November 1322, he pleaded old age, sickness, poverty, and lack of sufficient horses as reasons for not attending the great Council called at Ripon. In February 1324, he was excused from attendance at parliament for the same reason. He continued, however, to work, and in August administered the oath to the Commissioners of Array for the two counties. On 1 November of that year he died at Rose. It has been stated that his body was buried in the north aisle of Carlisle Cathedral;[27] of this there seems to be no real evidence.

His episcopate, only once to be exceeded in length—by Bishop Appleby and then only by four months, covered a most important period in Carlisle's history. His episcopal register is by far the most detailed of the series. But, as Tout observes, a " well kept register tells us nothing as to either the intellectual or moral character of the prelate by whose orders it was kept." So perhaps he was merely a thoroughly competent administrator who lived in momentous days. " A rather commonplace and

* Francis Bond in *Gothic Architecture in England*, 436, dates the capitals representing the seasons in the pier-arcade to about 1310.[25]

conventional, though quite a worthy prelate " is Tout's opinion.[28] On the other hand, Wilson says that " on account of his remarkable individuality (he) may be truly regarded as one of the greatest bishops that has ever adorned the northern see "; R. S. Ferguson agrees and refers to him as " the most distinguished bishop that ever held the see of Carlisle.[29] The present writer believes that the former of these two views is probably nearer the truth. But whatever his gifts may have been Bishop Halton was, at least, a man who faced with terrible difficulties kept the standard of the Church flying in dark and grim days and as such is deserving of honour.

What happened after Bishop Halton's death can best be explained by the following from the Calendar of the Fine Rolls:

" Commission to the king's clerk Robert de Barton reciting that though the late William, archbishop of York confirmed the election celebrated in the church of St. Mary's, Carlisle of the king's clerk William de Ayremynne, canon of York, as bishop of Carlisle, to which the king had given his assent, and the king accepted this confirmation and took the fealty of the said elect bishop and restored to him the temporalities of the see, yet William appearing before the king asserted that he had heard the pope had reserved the said bishopric and preferred Master John de Ros to be pastor of the said church of Carlisle and so the said William could not rely on the said election," 17 April 1325.[30]

Probably it was not long before the king received official confirmation of this as the pope had written to him in March informing him of John de Ross's appointment and tactfully mentioning that he had " Master William written on the tablets of his heart, and will promote him in due place and time."[31] But Master William was well able to look after himself. A little later, being sent to the pope at Avignon to procure for his patron, Robert de Baldok, the chancellor, the see of Norwich, he persuaded him to confer the see on himself instead. A violent quarrel between the two men not unnaturally followed and William was forced to remain for some years in exile abroad; but he was bishop of Norwich.[32]

The whole incident is a striking illustration of the working of the system of papal provision. Between 1317 and 1334, this pope, John XXII, reserved for himself no fewer than eighteen appointments to English sees. In 1328 he asserted a claim to appoint to all vacancies caused by translation.

John de Ross,* was consecrated at Avignon by Bertrand, bishop of Tusculum on 24 February 1325. The temporalities were restored to him on 20 June. An interesting list has survived of the furniture and ornaments of his ' chapel ' of which he acknowledged the receipt on the spiritualities being handed to him. It shows that the trust bequeathed by Bishop Irton was still observed. The ornaments included two sets of vestments for High Mass, a chasuble for daily use, several copes; altar palls, a missal and other books, but not the Bible left by Bishop Irton; one silver gilt chalice and silver cruets; pastoral staff, gemmed mitre, gloves, ring; a thurible and a little book for the confirmation of children. No candlesticks nor candelabra are included, yet there must have been some means for lighting the chapel.[33]

This episcopate was largely occupied with disputes with the prior and convent of the cathedral. Wilson suggests that these were in part due to resentment at the way in which the bishop had been forced on them by the papacy, though they had sent him a laudatory letter on the appointment saying that the announcement of it filled them with ineffable joy. However that joy was short lived. In January 1330, the prior of Durham cited him to answer a complaint of the prior and convent of

* It has been said that he was of the baronial family of Roos of Helmsley. But it seems clear that he was a native of the parish of Ross in Herefordshire (*Duncomb's Hist. of that County*, III, 123).

Carlisle that he had debarred them from the peaceable enjoyment of the fruits of their appropriated churches. Next year the bishop excommunicated the redoubtable John de Kirkby, the prior, for failure to pay the papal tenth granted by the clergy of the diocese. This was followed by a long and bitter dispute between them as to the tithes of the assart lands in Inglewood forest, which, being referred to the secular courts, was still unsettled at the bishop's death.[34]

During this episcopate nothing of any note happened on this Border in the now interminable dispute with Scotland. In 1332, the abbey of Holm Cultram obtained from the Lady Margaret de Wigton the church of Wigton in consideration of their great losses by the perpetual forays of the Scots, so things were evidently just as bad as ever.[35]

Under the year 1332 the chronicler of Lanercost notes:

" in the same year died Master John de Ross, bishop of Carlisle, who was taken away for burial in the south of England, whereof he was a native."

He died at Rose.[36]

The canons of Carlisle had licence to elect on 11 May 1332. Their choice was John de Kirkby,* their prior. The royal assent was given on 8 May (sic) and the temporalities restored on 9 July. The bishop-elect was consecrated on 19 July at South Burton, near Beverley, by William, archbishop of York. Nothing is known of his life before he became prior ; presumably he was just a canon of Carlisle.

We have already met this bellicose, yet exceedingly able prelate in connection with the chapter's disputes with

---

* Fuller (ed. 1840 III, 304) states he was born at either Kirkby Lonsdale or Kirkby Stephen and includes him among the Westmorland worthies. The arms on his seal are three leopards passant regardant (*Durham Misc. MSS.* 1521, 22). This is not the coat of any known Kirkby family. The writer's thanks are due to Canon Greenslade of Durham and to Sir Algar Howard for this information.

Bishop Ross.   He had not long been bishop before he had
another quarrel: On 4 August 1333, Ralph de Nevill and
Geoffrey le Scrope were appointed commissioners to hear
the complaints of John, bishop of Carlisle and Anthony
de Lucy against Ranulph de Dacre and others touching
the dissension between them and to appease the same.[37]
His next step was under the circumstances a wise one;
he had licence, on 9 April 1336, to crenellate or fortify
his dwelling place at ' La Rose.'

Then followed a peaceful occupation.   He was one of a
commission, appointed on 23 March 1337, to fix by
perambulation the bounds between the counties of York
and Westmorland.   This was issued because it had been
shewn in the parliament of Westminster " by the com-
monalties of these counties that disputes frequently
occurred through uncertainty as to these metes and
devises."[38]

This Borderland provided in those days opportunities
for a complete expression of the pugnacious instinct,
thus for some years the bishop was quite happily
employed, so were the Scots.   In September 1337,
Thomas, Lord Wake of Liddell, with the Lords Clifford
and Dacre, together with the bishop of Carlisle and the
men of Cumberland and Westmorland raided into
Teviotdale and Nithsdale.   In October the fighting was
on this side of the Border.   Having burnt the hospital of
St. Nicholas in Carlisle, the Scots paid a visit to Rose
" because they held my lord bishop of Carlisle, who owned
that manor, in the utmost hatred through his having
marched against them in war.   Therefore they destroyed
that place, and everything else on their march with fire."
They then carried the war into Allerdale and Coupland,
escaping across the Border before the Lords Percy and
Nevill could come to the rescue.   In November the Scots
besieged Edinburgh Castle, and the bishop, with Lord
Dacre and the levies of these counties, joined the Eastern
Borderers to relieve it.[39]

For the next few years we hear nothing of the bishop fighting the Scots, probably because he was quite happily occupied at home, where he was having a perfect orgy of rows. The first, with the archdeacon of Carlisle, William de Kendale, began in 1337 and lasted till 1340, when the archdeacon was deprived.* Wilson's sympathies are with the bishop. The dispute was about the archdeacon's right to hold the living of Great Salkeld and to receive the 'third penny,' as the perquisites of chapters and synods. But the real reason for the bishop's action seems to have been that he thought the archdeacon had usurped and meddled in matters that came within his episcopal jurisdiction and was determined to know by what right he claimed the authority he asserted.[40]

In August 1338, the bishop was involved in a dispute with the archbishop's Court at York about the affairs of a John de Skelton, who had a rent charge on the rectory of Kirkland. The bishop, in letters to his provincial, accused the officials of the Court of York of animus against him.[41] He also had a difference with the pope, who threatened him with excommunication, about his alleged non payment of tenths for his Lincolnshire benefices.[42]

Now we come to the most interesting and revealing of this war-like prelate's legal actions. He held a visitation of his diocese in 1338. The evidence suggests that he believed livings had been appropriated by monasteries without episcopal authority, and was determined to make those holding rectories in his diocese prove their rights to them; not, of course, an action likely to increase his popularity in certain circles. In some cases, such as the priory of Carlisle and the abbey of Fountains—appropriators of the church of Crosthwaite—the evidences were produced and amity prevailed. In others, things

---

* It was from this date that the archdeacon declined in status. As will be seen later on, the chancellor of the diocese obtained the position and visitational rights that normally belong to the former and exercised them till recent times.

did not go so smoothly; the great abbey of St. Mary's, York simply ignored the episcopal demand. The bishop thereupon, before December 1338, announced that it had no evidences to prove its titles. In October of the following year, there is a note in his register to the effect that certain persons, not well affected to him, have alleged that he has withdrawn his demands for canonical obedience from the abbot and convent of St. Mary's, York. He states, however, that, while they have the churches of Bromfield and Kirkby Stephen to their own proper uses, they are bound to render him obedience as bishop of the diocese. He accordingly orders his proctor to take the necessary steps to enforce this.

At this time also he was having a kind of " three ball match " with the priory of Wetheral and the abbey of St. Mary's, York, of which the priory was a cell. The monks of the priory appear to have been divided into an anti and pro Kirkby set. The matter in controversy was the right to the advowsons of Wetheral and Warwick to which both the bishop and the abbey laid claim. The former, in October 1338, threatened to excommunicate any who intruded themselves into these churches against his authority. The dispute was still going on in May 1341, when the chapter of York informed the bishop that the prior of Wetheral, having offended, they had sent a mandate to the official of Carlisle inquiring him to cite the prior and his official to appear before the chapter to answer for their contumacy. The matter was eventually carried to the papal court at Rome.

Nearer to home also the bishop did not always find his authority respected. In 1337 at Penrith and in 1341 at Caldewstone, near Carlisle, his officer was assaulted; in both cases he excommunicated the assailants. One of them having died, he ordered the body to be exhumed and cast out of the churchyard, if thought expedient, but left it to his local officer to decide whether or not to take this extreme action.   Afterwards he was induced by Sir Robert Parvyng to relent and absolve the corpse.[43]

The bishop was a member of a royal commission in 1340 appointed to visit the hospital of St. Nicholas, Carlisle, which was reported to be greatly decayed.[44]   In April of the same year he took a little relaxation and got himself into trouble by poaching in Sherewode forest. He took a doe and carried it away, more fortunate than lesser mortals would have been, he received the king's pardon for his offence.[45]

In April and May 1342, he was called upon to settle a difference between the parishioners of St. Mary's, Carlisle and the prior and convent of the cathedral.   The parishioners had petitioned the court of York that a perpetual vicar be appointed, alleging that the canons, to whom the church was appropriated, had neglected the services.   It was only occasionally, they asserted, that the sacrist, to whose department the greater tithes belonged, supplied a priest for their services.   The archbishop's court asked the bishop to inquire into the matter.   He reported that the cathedral church of Carlisle was in a certain sense a parish church; a vicar had never been appointed, but the canons performed the services in a far better manner, for the benefit of the parishioners, than any secular vicar would have done.[46]

We have evidence at this time that despite the troubled state of the Borders men were not unmindful of religious needs.   In 1342, Sir Robert Parvyng, chancellor of Edward III, made proposals for the establishment of a college of clergy at Melmerby, with the rector as master. Sir Robert died in 1343, so the scheme was stillborn. But it is interesting as shewing that the Church was alive to the needs of large country parishes.[47]

On 16 November 1343, letters patent were issued to John, bishop of Carlisle establishing an altar in honour of the Annunciation of the Blessed Virgin Mary in the parish church of Skelton. The two priests of the chantry were to assemble with the parish priest every Sunday and Festival at the High Mass and canonical hours. The bishop granted an indulgence of forty days to those who shall lay hand to the preservation of the rights of the chantry.[48] As Parvyng held the advowson of this parish may we not be seeing his hand in this as well as in the Melmerby scheme?

The bishop was now in employment as a soldier again on the expedition of Henry of Lancaster, earl of Derby, which succeeded in raising the siege of Lochmaben Castle. His other employment in 1343 was probably not so congenial because he was a commissioner, with the bishop of Durham, to treat for peace with Scotland.[49] In the next year he was ordered to assist Edward Balliol, the English puppet king of Scots, who was in command of the English forces in Scotland.[50]

Then the bishop had to deal with a matter we would refer to a sanitary inspector, but in the Middle Ages bishops, as great state officials, had to attend to all kinds of things.

" In the city of Carlisle the air is so corrupted and tainted by dung and manure heaps and so much other filth put in the streets and lanes, and trunks and logs are in the said streets and lanes that the common passage is impeded."

The bishop and Thomas de Lucy are ordered, on 23 April 1345, to see that the mayor and bailiffs improved matters.[51]

The bishop soon had to attend to more serious things than this for a Scots army, said to number 30,000 men under Sir William Douglas, invaded England, burning Penrith and harrying the country around. The bishop, Sir Thomas Lucy, and Robert Ogle of Thursby collected as many men as they could, though it was a small force compared to the enemy's. However stratagem can make up for numbers. During the night, by making unearthly noises, blowing of trumpets, screeching of horns, they made the Scots so alarmed, it is alleged, that they were afraid to eat or sleep. In the fight that ensued the bishop, thrown from his horse, was almost made prisoner, but, by the timely succour of his tenants, regained his saddle and escaped capture. The Scots were routed and fled back to their own country.[52]

Meanwhile the poor had to suffer. His lordship had his sport—doubtless he had got a good bag of Scots and much enjoyment—though his tenants and others were reduced to want to pay for it. On 10 May 1346, and so probably as a result of the raid mentioned above, the king out of compassion remitted the taxes of a tenth and a fifteenth to several manors in the county, including the town of Dalston and the manor of Rose which had been burnt and totally destroyed, with the corn, animals and goods therein, by the hostile incursions of the king's Scottish enemies at the previous Michaelmas, whereby they had nothing to cultivate their lands or to maintain themselves.[53]

The diocese must have been in a deplorable state at this time. From this year to the beginning of the next episcopate even the bishop's register fails. It had been kept all through Bishop Halton's time, despite the fact that the diocese was the scene of incessant war. Now even mediaeval officialdom broke down.

The bishop had been constable of Carlisle Castle from 20 June 1339 and was in office in June 1342 and March 1344. But on 8 September 1345, the castle was committed to Hugh de Moriceby, sheriff of Cumberland, " until the king be fully informed of the dissensions which have arisen between the citizens of Carlisle and the men of the bishop of Carlisle." On 18 October 1345, the castle was committed to Thomas de Lucy.[54] On 14 May 1346, John, bishop of Carlisle was pardoned for all manner of homicides, felonies, etc. committed by him and his men

in " certain debates and dissensions between the bishop
of Carlisle, when keeper of the castle of Carlisle, and the
garrison on the one part and the citizens on the other
part."[55] Evidently the bishop's warlike propensities
had spread to his garrison. Perhaps, there being no
Scots immediately available, they had practised on the
citizens.

The great day of the bishop's life was at hand; at
least it is probable that he looked on it in this light.   The
king of Scots, with a great army, crossed the Border,
ravaging the countryside.   The feudal levy of the North
was got together and the enemy brought to bay on 17
October 1346 at a spot outside Durham, now called
Nevill's Cross.   The bishop fought in the second division
of the English army.   A great victory was won ; and
David of Scotland made prisoner.   The triumph must have
given the bishop peculiar pleasure because it was during
the raid preceding this battle that the Scots " entered
arrogantly into the sanctuary, threw out the vessels of
the temple, plundered the treasury, shattered the bones,
stole the jewels," and destroyed as much as they could of
the priory of Lanercost,[56] a house of the same Order to
which the bishop belonged.   As late as 1409, the priory
had not recovered from the effects of this visit.[57]

In 1347, the bishop was engaged in a lawsuit that has
earned him, as is only right and proper for so doughty a
litigant, immortal fame in the legal world.   The action,
between his lordship and the executors of the late bishop,
concerned the ornaments of his chapel, and decided that
these belonged, not to the estate of a deceased prelate,
but to his successor.   As the ornaments of a parish church
belong to the parish and not to the incumbent so those of
a bishop's chapel belong to the diocese and not to the
diocesan.[58]   This legal decision, accepted by Lord Coke,
still stands.

In 1348, the bishop, in one of his few royal commissions

apart from his work as a Border prelate, had to convey
the Princess Joan, daughter of the king, to her affianced
husband, Alfonso, king of Castile. The bishop contracted
for five marks daily (£3. 6s. 8d.) allowance of board wages,
before setting out on his journey, which was duly paid by
the exchequer.[59]

With the bishop's life drawing to a close, it is pleasant
to record a simple priestly act, very different from the wars
and lawsuits which occupied so much of his time.
Richard, son and heir of Richard de Kirkbride, was " held
under the hand of " John de Kirkby, bishop of Carlisle,
in 1348, in the church of Burgh by Sands.[60]

His register ceased to be kept in 1346, so we have little
evidence as to the ravages of the Black Death in 1348.
Enough information has, however, survived to shew that
these counties did not escape. The imminence of this
great pestilence was announced by a call to prayer by
Archbishop Zouche of York on 28 July 1348. On 15
September in the same year an episcopal order was issued
for the consecration of a parochial grave yard at Windermere. On 3 March 1349, a similar order was given for the
neighbouring chapelry of Grasmere. Both these chapels
were practically independent parish churches with their
own incumbents, but until now their dead had had to be
carried to the distant mother church of Kendal.[61] That
the vicar was willing to forego the jealously guarded right
of burial at this time is suggestive. Another piece of
evidence comes from Cumberland: a chantry had been
founded in 1300 at Bramwra; in 1361, leave was given
to transfer it to Hutton in the Forest, because, owing to
the depreciation in the value of land caused by the scarcity
of tenants and labourers after the great pestilence, the
endowment was not enough to maintain a priest, and the
chapel had been vacant for a long time.[62] But on the
whole the north was less affected than the south. The
evidence of the deaths among the beneficed clergy shew

that in the diocese of York 38.97 per cent. died; in Exeter,
Winchester, and Norwich dioceses 48.8 per cent.; nearly
half the population, if the mortality among the laity was
on the same scale.[63]

Nothing is known about this episcopate after the Black
Death, which in a negative sense is evidence of its effects.
Bishop Kirkby was dead before 3 December 1352.[64]   His
place of burial is unknown.

The bishop's reputation has caused many to think of
him merely as one who liked fighting for its own sake, who
enjoyed a good row, but there was more in him than that.
His quarrels with the abbey of St. Mary's, York, his
archdeacon, and others suggest that the bishop, who had
previously been canon and prior of the cathedral and who
knew therefore what had been going on, knew also that
control had got rather slack in the diocese at the end of
Bishop Halton's episcopate and during that of the ' man
from the south.'   If so, his disputes arose not from a
mere love of a row but from his determination to stand
no nonsense with encroachments on episcopal rights and
privileges.   The true character of the man then is not
that of one who loved fighting for its own sake, but of one
who would fight and perhaps do so with gusto, for what he
believed to be the rights of his see or office.   And with all
his pugnacity, he did his work as a bishop; almost every
year, at least two, and generally three, ordinations were
regularly held, and his register, though less full of local
colour than those of his successors, gives the impression
of a well ordered and cared for diocese.   John Kirkby is
entitled to a high place among our medieval bishops not
only as a famous and redoubtable warrior, an efficient
and capable administrator, but as one of the most
dominant and masterful of the prelates who have ruled
from Rose.

After the death of Bishop Kirkby there followed a
curious incident which could only have happened when

news took a long time to travel. Licence to elect was given on 3 December 1352 and on 10 January the archbishop of York received notification of the royal assent to the election of John de Horncastre. On 22 February, the mandate to Hugh de Louther, the escheator, was issued " to deliver the temporalities of the see to brother John de Horncastre, prior of the house of St. Mary, Carlisle, whose election as bishop has been confirmed by John, archbishop elect and confirmed of York, and who has done fealty to the king." A new page in the episcopal register was started and a writ addressed to him by the king and two nominations to benefices duly entered on it.

Meanwhile on 13 February at Avignon, where the pope had settled because of political trouble, Gilbert de Welton, D.C.L., canon of York, had been appointed bishop of the see of Carlisle, void by the death of John and reserved by Clement VI. On 20 April he was granted a papal licence to hold his canonries and prebends of York and Southwell until next All Saints,[65] and on the following day was consecrated by the pope. By May 1353 news of these happenings reached this country, and on 26 June another mandate was issued to Hugh de Louther to deliver the temporalities.

The new bishop was more fortunate than his predecessors for the last sixty years in finding his diocese at peace, since David of Scotland was shut up in the Tower of London as a result of his capture at Nevill's Cross. Almost the bishop's first act was to issue a mandate summoning his clergy to a synod as he wished to take council and advice from them on arduous business.[66]

There can be little doubt that one of the things discussed was the need for completing the cathedral. We can probably see the result of the synod in the indulgence that the bishop issued in April 1354 so as to encourage people to subscribe the necessary funds. This was repeated in January 1356 and renewed yearly until 1362.[67] What did Bishop Welton do with the money he obtained? The most recent architectural opinion is that the east window was completed and the glass, the upper part of which still remains, inserted before the Black Death of 1348/9. There is no documentary evidence of this in the bishop's register, but nor have we any of the rebuilding after the fire of 1292. The roof is dated by these authorities between 1375 and 1400.* Perhaps Bishop Welton was a collector and not an expender of money, and these funds were subsequently used for the roof. The dislocation of society caused by the pestilences may have made this a slow business and so may account for the delay in continuing the work after 1348/9. But as bequests in the will of John Salkeld, proved 20 January 1359,† suggest that work on the windows was going on at this time, it is just possible that the experts may be in error and the glass of a later date than they suppose.

The bishop's register gives a picture of a hardworking and pastorally minded prelate, who was never absent from Rose for any length of time; with hardly an exception his documents are dated from there. He rarely appears to have attended parliament or provincial councils of the Church in person, but by deputy. He had doubts about the consecration of chapels so, on 25 April 1354, ordered an enquiry into the matter. Two years later he heard that it was doubtful if the church of St. Alban's, Carlisle, where services were regularly performed and where there was a graveyard, had been consecrated. He found this had not been done and accordingly on 12

---

* *Gothic Architecture in England*, F. Bond, in passim and the article by F. C. Eeles in N.S. xxvi, 312-7. The last date in the important note on p. 317 should be 14th, not 18th century. Dr. Eeles has confirmed this fact and in the light of evidence that John of Gaunt is not depicted in the east window (N.S. xlv, 122-5), is quite certain the glass should be dated just before the Black Death. Though what we know of the state of the diocese makes it difficult to believe that it was inserted at that time.

† Item fabrice ecclesie abbathie Karl. cs. Item ad fabricacionem cuiusdam fenestre de novo in cancello ibidem xls.' (Testa Karleol. 20-2).

November 1356 forbade the holding of divine service.[68]
People were afforded better opportunities for worship by
the licencing of chapels in William de Lancaster's house
at Howgill in 1356, in Sir William Lengley's castle of
Highhead and Richard Salkeld's oratory at Corby in 1358;
in the former year a new chapel—recently built near the
castle of Highhead and in the latter one two chapels,
within Sir John de Derwentwater's manors of Derwentwater and Bolton (Westmorland), were also licenced.[68a]
The sick and aged clergy were cared for and so were the
needs of their parishioners; the rectors of Castle Carrock,
smitten with leprosy, and Kirkoswald, worn out by age,
are ordered to accept coadjutors in 1357 and 1361.[68b]

Matrimonial matters also received the bishop's attention: the marriage of William de Stapleton and Alice,
daughter of Richard de Whytefeld, was dissolved in 1360
as it was illegal and fraudulent. But when less than a
month later Alice married John de Gaytescales, the bishop
declared the marriage void. In the same year Emma,
wife of Nicholas de Swayne, was adjudged to have left
her husband for frivolous reasons and ordered to return;
the rector of Greystoke being told to inform her of the
consequences of disobedience. The male was also kept
in order—Christopher de Lancaster was admonished in
1354 to adhere to his wife. And lastly we have a breach
of promise action brought by Godytha, the daughter of
Nicholas de Motherby, against William Whytheved of
Sowerby in 1361; the latter had substituted for the
spurned Godytha one Alice, widow of John de Stokdale.[69]

The maintenance of bridges was held to be a pious act
in the Middle Ages: an indulgence was granted for the
repair of those at Kirkby Thore in 1355, over the Eden,
between Carlisle and Stanwix, in 1356, and at Salkeld in
1360; roads also needed care, so forty days of remitted
penance were promised to all who contributed to the

amendment of a boggy piece of ground at Wragmyre, between Carlisle and Penrith, in 1354.[69a]

Bishop Welton also issued important orders with regard to the archdeacon's visitational powers.[70] Probably he was anxious to insure against the troubles that had taken place in his predecessor's time.

Another instance of his wise administration is to be found in his dealings with the friars about whom there was some friction with the clergy of Carlisle. They complained in 1352 that on Sundays and Festivals during Mass, when a great number of people were present, the friars stirred up tumult by displays of excessive indulgences and plenary remissions, seeking for money and not for the gain of souls. The bishop ordered the parochial clergy not to allow mendicant friars to beg in their churches, unless they carried with them his special licence. He was not, however, unmindful of their needs and granted, for the benefit of those of Penrith who served the chapel at Newton Reigny, an indulgence of forty days to all who should be present when they lighted their candles on Christmas Day, or made them presents because they were very poor.[71]

Bishop Welton though of milder disposition than John de Kirkby also had his private feuds. On 3 June 1356, a commission was appointed to investigate a complaint that while some chattels found at Lynstok were being carried by the servants of the abbot of St. Mary's, York to Wederhale, Roger, vicar of the church of Crosseby, John de Welton and others assembled by order and abetment of the bishop and resisted the bringing of the said chattels and assaulted the servants of the abbot. Further it was alleged that the bishop had unjustly taken and detained these chattels.[72]

There was peace with Scotland during this episcopate. But in a Border land precautions still had to be taken, so on 25 June 1355, the bishop had licence to crenellate his

dwelling place of La Rose.[73] Had Bishop Kirkby been
unable to carry out his licence to the same effect ? Bishop
Welton was one of the Commissioners, appointed in 1356,
to arrange for the release of the king of Scots from his
captivity. In 1359, the bishop and Thomas de Lucy
were nominated wardens of the Western Marches. And
in 1362, the bishop was one of a commission ordered to
enter into a bond of peace and amity with the Scots
King.[74]

None of our local historians seems to have noticed the
remarkable evidence of the effect on these counties of the
second outbreak of the so-called Black Death in 1361-2.
This was, of course, a renewal of the terrible pestilence
of 1348-9. Both are generally regarded as forms of
Bubonic plague. The average number of changes among
the beneficed clergy recorded in the bishop's register for
the years just before and after the plague period are four.
In 1361 there were 3 deaths and 2 resignations in the
first half of the year. Then from October 1361 till 28
October 1362, 6 resignations were recorded, all in the
first 6 months of the period; 16 livings were filled owing
to the death of the previous incumbent—also 2 wills
proved of incumbents to whom no successor was appointed; and 5 livings filled, the reasons for the vacancy
not being given. Assuming half of the unspecified
vacancies were caused by deaths and counting the number
of livings at 90, there is a death roll of over 23 per cent.
of the clergy: Carlisle Deanery 16.6, Allerdale 11.1,
Westmorland 36.0, Cumberland 29.4. After 28 October
the register ceases until 14 August 1363.[75] Of the parts
of the present diocese then in the archdeaconry of
Richmond the evidence is: in the deanery of Coupland
one vacancy filled; in Furness, one; in Kendale, two;
that is, these districts were untouched by the plague.[76]

To turn to the evidence of the wills: during the 3 years
before and the 3 years after 1361-2, 16 were proved at

Carlisle; in the year 1361, 12 up till October but from then till 26 October 1362, 55, including administrations. Some of the evidence is even more significant: 12 wills and administrations were proved on 5 August 1363; 22 from 26 July to 8 August.[77]

Taken together the combined evidence of the vacancies in benefices and of wills and administrations is conclusive of a very severe epidemic. The evidence of locality is also interesting. Professor A. Hamilton Thompson, describing contemporary pestilences in the diocese of York, states: " the general conclusion that the two extremes, mountainous districts on the one hand and marshland on the other, were comparatively immune from pestilence, while normal agricultural country and the lower highlands suffered most heavily is borne out. . ." The evidence both of wills and of benefices is the same here. The areas most affected were the Eden valley and the country north east of Carlisle; though there were exceptions— seven administrations from Thursby were granted on 5 August. But the country bordering on the Solway, both north and south of the Derwent, was unaffected; so apparently was the Fell country.

The last will before the register ceased to be kept was proved on 26 October 1362 and the last benefice filled two days later; then on 18 January following licence is given to elect a new bishop. Can there be any doubt that within a day or so after 28 October the pestilence gripped the household at Rose and that probably the bishop himself died of it?

Further evidence of the extent of the visitation is afforded by the fact that in 1363 the new bishop petitioned the pope that:

" Whereas, on account of the late pestilence, there is a lack of priests in his diocese, he prays for faculty to dispense 40 persons, secular and regular, aged twenty, so that they may be promoted to all holy orders." And " for a faculty to dispense 12 persons of illegitimate birth and 6 others, being sons of priests or illegitimate sons of married men, so that they may be ordained."[78]

Another piece of evidence, probably pointing to the same cause, is that in 1366, 4 out of 14 tenements in Cliburn Tailbois were empty.[79]

Meanwhile we must not forego commending the soul of that worthy man Gilbert de Welton to God. He might be called the 'stay at home bishop.' While it is, as always with medieval prelates, difficult to get behind the official records to see the man, there seems sufficient evidence to justify the assertion that he was a devoted pastor of the souls entrusted to him. He should also be remembered with gratitude for his work in collecting funds for the cathedral.

The licence to elect was issued on 18 January 1363. The order to deliver the temporalities to Thomas, canon of the church of St. Mary's, Carlisle,* whom the pope, after quashing his election to be bishop of that place by the chapter of the said church, had provided to be bishop thereof, is dated 10 August 1363. The king's order contained the statement, now included in all similar documents, that it was issued after the bishop had renounced all words in the pope's bull prejudicial to him and his crown. The consecration was on 18 June 1363 at Avignon, by the pope. This episcopate was to be the longest in the history of the diocese, lasting for thirty years and six months.

The bishop's first known act is that he obtained an indulgence, presumably while overseas, for the cathedral to last for ten years from 1363 to penitents who visited it on the five feasts of the Blessed Virgin or who lent a helping hand to the fabric.[80] It is not easy to be sure

* This was Thomas de Appleby. There was a family of this name, who owned land at Averas Holme on the Eden near Carlisle and also at Strickland Ketel, near Kendal, one of whom, John de Appleby, was made archdeacon of Carlisle and dean of St. Paul's in 1364 by papal provision (n.s. xi, 30-33 and 99).

what work this referred to; probably it was the completion of the roof.

The bishop's register includes more licences for chapels in private houses; more indulgences for the repair of bridges—over the Derwent near Cockermouth in 1366 and the Kent at ' Showemondgate ' (Stramongate) in 1379[81]; more divorces or marriages annulled; also notices showing that episcopal visitation was duly carried out.

But there are matters of greater interest than these routine affairs. The autumn of 1365 was remarkable for violent storms of wind and rain causing so much damage to crops that the bishop ordered special processions with the chanting of the seven penitential psalms, litanies, and other suitable prayers as a form of intercession. Another interesting procession is mentioned in 1372 and again in 1386. In the former year the bishop, on a complaint of the prior and sacrist that some incumbents failed to put in an appearance at the annual homage of the parish priests in the cathedral and so contemptuously broke an old custom, ordered the official of the diocese to proceed against the truants. Apparently during the week after Pentecost the clergy were expected to visit the mother church and to join in the procession, wearing surplices and with the cross carried before them, to the high altar where they made their oblations as a sign of their subjection to the cathedral church. Bishop Appleby evidently attached great importance to this act of homage. It must have been an impressive symbol not only of his authority but also of diocesan unity; an old custom, long disused and forgotten, though not without its lesson even to-day.[82]

Tithes were as unpopular in the fourteenth century as in later ones. The people of Rickardby in 1365 tried so to stack their pease that the tithe was calculated at much too low a figure, and in 1379 those of Aspatria were caught hindering the collectors of tithe sheaves at

Crosbythwaite. Dilapidations were a problem then as they are to-day. In March 1368 the rural dean of Allerdale was ordered to enquire into those of Caldbeck, as the chancel of the church and the rectory had become ruinous through the neglect of the absentee parson. The description of the house and its outbuildings gives a valuable glimpse of the style of a well-to-do incumbent.* In the case of the nave and bell tower of the church of Penrith, which in 1374 was also in bad repair, the blame was laid on the parishioners who were ordered to put matters right under threat of the greater excommunication.[83]

In 1379 the bishop prohibited the holding of fairs and markets on Sundays and festival days in churches and churchyards as they disturbed the devotions of rightly disposed persons. In 1381 a schedule of the value of the livings of the diocese was drawn up; the churches named

---

* The house was surveyed by four parishioners who were ordered to enquire what was deficient and to estimate the cost of repairs. Their report was as follows:—

	£	s.	d.
Chancel	2.	13.	4
Hall ..	2.		
Chief Chamber	—.	13.	4
Guests room ..	10.		
Cook house ..	1.		
Old grainery ..	10.		
Kiln ..	1.		
Long grange	1.		
Great grange	10.		
Cow house ..	—.	6.	8
Wood house ..	—?	13.	4
Guests stable..	—.	6.	8
New Grainery	—.	—.	6
Dove house ..	10.		
Portal	1.		
Fence	1.		
Meadow fence	2.		

£53. 13. 10.*

As the value of the living was £30 per ann. in 1291 and £5 in 1318, this must have been a large bill for the rector to meet, he resigned the living next year. Did he thus avoid paying the dilapidations?

* Folios 202-3.

are the same as in the returns of 1318. The three parish churches—Carlatton, Eston and Cambok, which decayed sometime during the Middle Ages, were then still in existence. One of the minor puzzles of our parochial history is the cause of their disappearance. To end this survey with something that strikes a strange note in modern ears; the bishop threatened disciplinary action in 1385 against the vicar of Bridekirk and the parishioners of Isel[84] because the latter attended Bridekirk church rather than their own.*

An account of this episcopate, in the order of its chief events, must now be given. In 1369 there was another outbreak of the Black Death. The ancient diocese does not seem to have been affected, but the area then within the archdeaconry of Richmond which had escaped in 1361 this time did not do so. The average number of livings filled within it was rather over one a year, but between 8 October 1369 and 9 February 1370, new incumbents were appointed to 5 benefices.[85] As there were only 36 livings in these deaneries this represents almost 14 per cent. This being a plague period, the inference seems reasonably clear.

Taxes had to be paid in the Middle Ages as they are to-day, with the same result as now if prompt payment be not made. So on 4 August 1372 the archbishop and all his suffragans had restitution of their temporalities, which had been inadvertently seized into the king's hands on account of the arrears due to him of the subsidy granted by the clergy for the defence of the realm.[86] Thus in those days the royal prototype of the collector of taxes had a drastic way of dealing with those who took no notice of 'the final demand note.' It is hoped that the fact that they were assured it was done 'inadvertently' lessened the blow.

* He bears witness who says that a much respected and beloved vicar, renowned for his predatory raids upon his neighbours' spiritual vineyards, doubtless counts himself fortunate that this is 1945 and not 1385.

The medieval bishop had, however, pickings on the credit side that his successor to-day has not. On 24 October 1375, the bishop had the wardship of Margaret, daughter and heiress of Nicholas de Layburn, a deaf mute from her birth.[87]

We have already seen how several bishops had to obtain a royal pardon for, as they perhaps put it, inadvertently killing the royal deer. But when the boot was on the other foot it was a different matter. Bishop Appleby was so incensed against poachers in 1374 that he excommunicated those ' sons of iniquity,' who had broken into his park of Rose and taken his deer with dogs, nets, and other engines, so that the deer were totally destroyed.[88]

We next hear of the bishop as a preacher in London. The provincial episcopate must have looked on this as a great opportunity, because (in the words of Bishop Brinton):

" each bishop of England has subjects or parishioners in London, therefore, when he gives instruction there, it is as though he were preaching to his own people and to the other churches of England in addition, so that in effect, by so doing, each of us may apply to himself that word of the apostle (2 Cor. XI, 28) ' that which cometh upon me daily, the care of all the churches ' of England."[89]

Some such thoughts were perhaps in the mind of Bishop Appleby, as before midday on Sunday, 7 March 1378, the feast of Saints Perpetua and Felicitas, he was preaching at St. Paul's Cross, over against the cathedral church, when suddenly a little way off in Westchepe there arose between certain persons of the trade of Goldsmiths and others of the trade of Pepperers no small affray and spread throughout the city.[90] Doubtless his lordship was much disturbed and probably full of complaints of the disorderly state of the metropolis, but if he had known that as a result of this breach of the peace the fact of his having preached would be preserved for the historian to record, his annoyance might have been changed into gratitude.

One of the most important events in this episcopate was the founding of a college of priests at Greystoke. We have already seen how Sir Robert Parvyng made plans for such a college at Melmerby in 1342, but died before his intention could bear fruit. In 1358 Lord William de Greystoke obtained a royal licence for a similar college there. Bishop Welton gave his sanction and all seemed settled, but within a year Lord William died, so this plan also came to nothing. However, his son, Lord Ralph, obtained a new licence in 1374. Again there were difficulties and delays. Some four years later Bishop Appleby appointed a commission to go into the matter; he cannot have been satisfied with the result because in April 1379 another one was named. They reported that the church was served by three chaplains and three clerks, as had been the case heretofore, so that it could not be said that on account of the size of the parish or the fewness of the ministers the parishioners were spiritually neglected—Lord Ralph had claimed that in the absence of the rector the church was badly served and the sick not properly visited—none the less it would be to the greater glory of God if the number of clergy were increased, and that the revenues could sustain a provost and five chaplains at the parish church as well as the chaplains at Watermillock and Threlkeld. But still there was delay and the college was not formally founded till 1382.[91]

The whole scheme is of the greatest interest. In the opinion of many the ideal solution of the efficient working of large country parishes is still to be found in societies of this kind. This proposal also shews that the Church had devout laymen who would put themselves to very considerable trouble so as to ensure that their people had a due and proper supply of clergy to care for their spiritual needs. This college was not a monastic body, with the duty of praying for the souls of the founder and his kin as its primary obligation, but a college of clergy created for the express purpose of saving those of his tenants. We do not know what were the objections to the scheme, but the bishop was clearly determined to have the matter thoroughly investigated.

A prelate in the Middle Ages had all kinds of odd jobs to do. Bishop Appleby was one of a commission appointed on 8 October 1383 to survey a gate and tower upon it, which John Lewyn, maceon, contracted to build in the king's castle of Carlisle and to report any defects therein.[92]

The bishops had always claimed visitational rights over the prior and convent of the cathedral. In 1381 the convent elected William de Dalston, a canon of the house, as prior. The bishop, there being no opposition to this election, decreed that he should be installed. But the prior refused to make the usual declaration of canonical obedience to his lordship and to accept his decision in matters in dispute between the canons, while a party hostile to the prior brought charges of adultery against him. After four years of wrangling, which caused great scandal in the city and diocese, the bishop excommunicated him, and ordered the parish priests of St. Mary's and St. Cuthbert's to publish the sentence at Mass. The city was in an uproar as many of the people took sides with the prior. An armed mob, led by some of the chief citizens, entered the two churches and snatched the bishop's letters from the hands of the officiating priest. His lordship's answer to this outrage on his authority was to threaten to put the city, except the castle and its chapel, under an interdict. The majority of the canons appear to have supported him and implored him to visit the house. He appealed to the archbishop for support, whereupon the prior and his abettors were cited for their disobedience. The matter even got to the ears of the

H

king, who wrote deploring the scandal caused and asking for particulars. At last the prior was persuaded to make the requisite declaration of obedience. Immediately afterwards, on 28 September 1385, he resigned his office.[93]

However, he still remained a canon of the cathedral and still continued to be a nuisance, for on 3 March 1390 a commission was granted—

" upon information from the archbishop of York that when William Dalston, Robert Clifton, and Richard de Euerwyk, canons of Carlisle cathedral, refused to be corrected for certain offences by their prior or the bishop of Carlisle and appealed to him and were by him enjoined to obedience, in accordance with their rule, they, when sent back to the said prior and bishop, gathered some soldiers of the town and castle of Carlisle and forcibly resisted and daily resist the said bishop and prior, and waste the possessions of the house."

to enquire into these matters.[94]

At last the long peace with Scotland had come to an end. In 1380 Carlisle was besieged, but an English army soon relieved it. The effects of the renewal of war on the country side is shewn in the licence granted to the bishop, on 6 September 1380, to appropriate the church of ' Routhebury ' because of the devastation by pestilence and by the Scots of a great part of his lands.[95] The monks of Holm Cultram probably took the wisest course when in 1385 they paid £200 to the earl of Douglas as an indemity for the ransom of their church and lands from destruction.[96] The state of the North Country at this time is shewn by the fact that in May 1385 benefices in the counties of Northumberland, Cumberland and Coupland* were exempted from the payment of the usual tenth, because they " are so devastated by hostile incursions of Scots and the depredations of Englishmen passing through them towards Scotland that they are not capable of paying." Exemptions of a similar kind, with

* The retention of the name of county of Coupland as late as this is interesting.

the county of Westmorland added, continued to be granted for the next thirty-five years.[97]

In 1385 and 1387 Carlisle was again besieged and the country around it ravaged. In the former year a battle with the Scots, under the earl of Douglas, was fought at Hoff, near Appleby. 19 August 1388, was the day of Otterburn; the earl of Douglas was killed, Sir Henry Percy, ' Hotspur,' led captive away. Whoever was the victor, no relief was afforded to this March, as on St. Stephen's day, 26 December, came the terrible raid in which Appleby was almost completely obliterated. So great was the destruction that the ancient borough never recovered its prosperity, though continuing to hold its traditional place as the capital town of Westmorland. Probably at this time Brougham Castle also was destroyed; there is no documentary evidence of this. But the building had been added to by Roger, 5th Lord Clifford; then in 1403 an inquisition reported that it ' is worth nothing because it lieth waste by reason of the destruction by the Scots.'[97a] On 26 May 1389 Thomas, bishop of Carlisle was ordered to certify to the royal exchequer " the names of such places in Cumberland as have been wholly or in part burnt by the king's enemies of Scotland."

Two years later, on Ascension Day 1391, three parts of the city of Carlisle were destroyed by an accidental fire. Houses and buildings to the number of 1500 were damaged in the market place and the three principal streets Castlegate, Ricardgate and Bochardgate. The parish church of St. Cuthbert was also burnt, and the greatest part of the inhabitants removed. To enable them to recover from this blow and from the destruction of all their lands and tenements by the Scots and French the Crown remitted to the citizens the farm of the close of Ellerton in Inglewood forest for four years.[98]

Meanwhile efforts had been made to bring about another

peace between England and Scotland. The bishop was one of the commissioners appointed for this purpose in 1384 and again in 1393, and in the next year was one of those commanded to proclaim on the Borders the articles of a truce concluded with France and Scotland.[99] In 1393-4 he was also employed on a commission appointed to inquire into the liberties of the castle and Honour of Cockermouth.[100]

Little, it will be noticed, is known of the concluding years of this long episcopate. The bishop died on 5 December 1395. No record has survived of his place of burial.

In character Bishop Appleby seems to have been, like his predecessor, a pastoral bishop, but one not unmindful, as his action with regard both to the clerics who did not visit the cathedral and Prior Dalston's rebellion shews, of the dignity of his office. The most important event during his rule was the foundation of the collegiate church at Greystoke. The record of his episcopate need not fear comparison with those of other prelates in this century of notable bishops.

Licence for election was issued on 30 December 1395, and the see filled on 26 January by the translation, by papal provision, of Robert [101] (Reade), bishop of Lismore and Waterford.[102] The temporalities were delivered to him on 30 March 1396. The prior and convent of Carlisle had previously chosen William Strickland, but the pope had refused to consecrate him.[103]

The only thing known about this episcopate is the grant of a licence

" at the supplication of Robert, bishop of Carlisle, for his tenants in Cumberland, in consideration of the great destruction sustained by them from the king's enemies, the Scots, for five years to cut down and fell for their reasonable hearth fuel of housbote and haybote, within the forest of Inglewood, broom, heath, rushes, etc."[104]

He was translated by the pope to the see of Chichester on 5 October 1396.[105]

Thomas Merke, a Benedictine monk of Westminster Abbey, was provided to the see by the pope. The temporalities were restored on 18 March 1397. The date and place of his consecration are unknown; it was before 23 April 1397.

Wilson states truly that "he is perhaps the most famous of all the medieval bishops of Carlisle."[106] Not much is known of his early life; he was probably ordained before he became a monk, which may have been in 1376. He was a student at Oxford 1392-4, when an allowance was allocated to him by the abbey treasurer. In 1395-6 he received a pension of £20 from the abbey.[107]

The bishop was a friend of Richard II, who was a connoisseur. The Evesham Chronicler suggests that the king also spent whole nights in drinking and debauchery with the bishop and others.[108] As Thomas Merke was undoubtedly a scholar, the author of one book, perhaps of more, and spoken of in the highest terms by his university it seems more likely that the bond between them was not in drink but in books.

All his reign the king was in conflict with his uncle, John of Gaunt, duke of Lancaster. So the king had his party, to which the bishop belonged. He accompanied him to Ireland in 1394, and was included in the list of the so called 'courtier bishops.' He was also with him on his second expedition in June 1399.[109] While the king was away, John of Gaunt's son, Henry of Bolingbroke whom he had exiled, landed at Ravenspur in Yorkshire. On his return in August Richard was captured at Flint, the bishop being with him at the time. He remained faithful to the end and was one of his executors, receiving a gold ring worth £20.[110]

We now come to the most famous moment in Thomas Merke's life, and that which has kept his memory bright all down the ages. It was in the parliament of 30 September, when Richard's abdication was received and the crown offered to, and accepted by, Henry of Bolingbroke, that the bishop made, or is said to have made, the speech of which a poet's interpretation is given in the famous lines put into his mouth by Shakespeare in Act IV, Scene I in the play ' *King Richard the Second,*' which contains the words:

> My lord of Hereford* here, whom you call king,
> Is a foul traitor to proud Hereford's king:
> And if you crown him, let me prophesy,—
> The blood of English shall manure the ground,
> And future ages groan for this foul act;

Is it true that any such words, forecasting the evils that were to overtake the country and destroy the Plantagenets, were spoken? The usual view of historians of the last generation was in the negative. " There is no evidence that he raised his voice in his (Richard's) behalf, or uttered anywhere in public the fine sentiments which Shakespeare put into his mouth."[111] But, in fact, the pedigree of this speech has been proved. The original source is the contemporary ' *Traison et Mort de Richard II,*" which Holinshead knew through Hall, and the former is one of the authorities on which Shakespeare is known to have relied.[112] Further, " the probability that Merke had the great courage and loyalty to make such a speech is enhanced by the fact that he alone among the courtier bishops was singled out for punishment."[113] Thus modern writers believe the speech preserves a trustworthy tradition, and is true, as a poet's echo, of one really spoken.[114]

After the speech, Merke was handed over to the abbot of St. Albans, who was ordered, on 28 October, to deliver him to be brought before the king and his council in parliament. Having been heard in his defence, he was

* Bolingbroke was earl of Hereford.

returned to the abbey. He escaped, however, and was in London on 6 December 1399, and later took part in the abortive rising of the earls of Salisbury and Kent. For this he was committed on 10 January 1400 to the more secure custody of the constable of the Tower of London,[115] and was tried and found guilty of conspiring against the king, who wrote to the pope on 15 March asking that he should be degraded and handed over to the secular arm.[116] But nothing further was done about this request, and on 23 June, an order was delivered to the constable to cause Thomas, late bishop of Carlisle, who is imprisoned in the Tower, to be brought to Westminster Abbey and delivered to the abbot, there to abide till further order.[117] On 28 November, " pardon was granted to Thomas Merke, late bishop of Carlisle, who was indicted, with others condemned to death, with having conspired at London and elsewhere to destroy the king. . . The said late bishop asserted he was not guilty and put himself on an inquisition by which he was found guilty."[118]

When he ceased to be bishop of Carlisle is not known; it was before 6 December 1399, as his successor is described in a papal letter of that date as William, elect of Carlisle.[119] But he was not ill treated; he received a manor and forty marks a year for his maintenance.[120] It is generally said that he was translated by the pope to be bishop of Salmas. While it is true that he was provided to this see, which was in Turkey and so had no Christian population, the provision did not hold good because Merke failed to have the letters of translation made out within a certain time in accordance with a certain ordinance of the pope. Therefore on 5 May 1401, some one else was appointed.[121]

On 21 March 1401, he had the royal licence to sue in the Court of Rome for benefices to the value of a 100 marks yearly, bishoprics excepted,[122] and on 5 November to hold them to the value of 300 marks.[123] One of these benefices was the prebend of ' Massam ' in York Minster, as there were proceedings in the King's Bench, it is doubtful if he obtained it.[124] But he was appointed to the vicarage of ' Sturmynstre Marchal ' in the diocese of Salisbury on 19 November 1403.[125] On 31 May 1404 he had a papal indult for ten years to let this vicarage and not to be bound to reside, while engaged in the study of letters at a university or in the service of an ecclesiastical prelate or residing at the Roman Court or in one of his benefices. Copies of this letter were to be sent to the bishops of Chichester and Winchester, implying that he had livings in these dioceses.[126] He had a commission from William of Wykeham, bishop of Winchester, on 10 January 1404 to act as his suffragan and to hold ordinations that year.[127] This bishop died on 27 September 1404, and during the vacancy Thomas Merke had a like commission from the archbishop of Canterbury.[128] On 13 August Thomas had been appointed by the abbot and convent of Westminster to the rectory of Todenham, in the diocese of Worcester.[129]

The most interesting side of his life after he ceased to be bishop of Carlisle is his connexion with the university of Oxford.[130] It is probable that he went there soon after January 1401. Some letters from the university in 1402-3 throw light, not only on his career, but on what Oxford thought of him. The first of these asks the king that a bishop, who was resident in the university and has been teaching and preaching there, might receive assistance in temporal things. Another asks a bishop to give promotion to an Oxford man, a doctor of divinity and himself a bishop, who was lecturing and disputing in the university. Though Thomas Merke is not directly named, there seems no reason to doubt that these letters refer to him. There is another addressed to a cardinal at Rome asking for preferment for a bishop, which will honourably make up for previous injuries, and states that he has most strenuously fought against various errors polluting the Kingdom and particularly against those who bark against the rights and dignities of the Church, and has purged the university of Oxford from errors. There are also two letters addressed to the pope; one, in much the same form as the above, speaks of the bishop being in his destruction of heresies another Augustine, in his morals another Gregory, and in both another Jerome;* the other states that on the fall of Richard II the university had requested the pope that Thomas Merke might be removed from his bishopric, having been induced by the tales of slanderers to believe that his life was execrable, and asked that one, whom they believed would be faithful to Oxford, should be put in his place. This was done but the person appointed was unsatisfactory, so the university asks the pope that he would return Thomas to his former see, for he has long lectured in Oxford and is a great doctor in theology.

He is said to have been at Lucca in May 1408, with his friend William Colchester, abbot of Westminster, and to have signed the appeal of the cardinals gathered there against the pope.[131]   It is certain that he was dead before 13 January 1409, when his living of Todenham was filled.[132]   His friend the abbot did not forget him: on 5 October 1411 when he made arrangements for his own anniversary with the prior of Hurley, he stipulated that memorial should also be made of Thomas Merke.[133]

The local reader must excuse this long account of a bishop, who only held the see for some two years and whose career had nothing to do with it. But it is as Thomas Merke, bishop of Carlisle that he is known to history.   As such he will be remembered " as one of Richard's best and most loyal friends ":[134] a far seeing

---

* In these two letters he is said to have been promoted " ad sedem nul-latem." The authors of the *Oxford Formularies* suggest that, as there was no such see, this is a scholastic witticism and might be rendered the ' see of Nil.' That is, when people found he had, after all, not been translated to Salmas, they said he had been promoted to the ' See of Nil.'

statesman, who alone had the foresight to understand and
the courage to denounce the evils likely to arise from
Henry of Bolingbroke's seizure of the throne; a scholar,
who in the days of his adversity was harboured by his
university; and a man, who suffered loyally for one
friend, his king, and was remembered by another, his
abbot.

CHAPTER V.

THE DECLINE OF THE MEDIEVAL WORLD AND A ST. LUKE'S SUMMER.

THIS chapter is an attempt to give an account of the history of the diocese from 1400 to 1508. Its thinness in parts is acknowledged; but it is at least an effort to do something that has never been done before; even the *Victoria County History* confines itself to a few pages. These years can be divided into three well defined periods: first twenty years of comparatively ordered life and progress; then some fifty of social disorder ; and a third period in which under an increasingly strong central government stable life was resumed and marks of progress in Church affairs can again be recorded. At its end a case of heresy is noted, a portent that the Reformation was at hand.

The circumstances under which William Strickland succeeded to the bishopric are unknown. He is described as " elect of Carlisle " on 6 December 1399 in the papal indult to retain his church of Horncastle for two years.[1] But his consecration, by Richard, archbishop of York, at Cawood Castle, did not take place until 15 August 1400; and the temporalities were not restored until 15 November.

As he was intimately connected with the diocese before becoming its bishop, an account of his earlier career seems desirable. There is no doubt that he was a cadet of the Sizergh family;* his arms, the silver escallops on a black

* The arguments advanced in N.S., xvi, 131, and *Strickland of Sizergh*, H. Hornyold-Strickland, 281, that he was a younger son of Sir Thomas Strickland

field of this family but within a bordure engrailed of the
first as a mark of cadency, prove this. The view that his
coat was without the bordure is an error. There is no
doubt that the bishop married Isabel daughter and
heiress of Thomas and Margaret Warcop and had a
daughter Margaret, whose second husband—her first was
Sir John de Derwentwater—was Sir Robert Lowther.[2]

It has hitherto been assumed that William Strickland,
who is named as a cleric in the will of the hermit of
Lynstock in 1362, was then in major orders.[3]   In fact, he
was ordained sub-deacon in September 1380, and deacon
and priest the following year.[4]   So his wife need not have
died nor his daughter been born before 1362.

With these facts in mind we can reconstruct his early
life. He was probably born about 1340, and was rector
of Stapleton in 1368, when he exchanged livings with the
rector of Ousby. There is no record of his appointment
to the former, so it was probably during the Black Death,
when the registers were not kept. He resigned Ousby
before December 1369. Shortly before this, in September
1368, he had been ordained an acolyte. He was not a
parish priest, however, but an ecclesiastical lawyer; he is
mentioned as a notary public and procurator in 1366.[5]

His name does not occur in local records between
December 1369 and January 1376, when he was nominated by Bishop Appleby as one of his representatives in
parliament. He may have been employed elsewhere as
he is described as ' clericus ' of the diocese of York in
1367.[6]   But in one of the letters from the university of
Oxford to the pope at the time of Thomas Merke's fall,*
the university states " that they asked that one, whom
they believed would be faithful to Oxford, should be put

and Cecilia Wells are now vitiated by the discovery that he was not in major
orders till 1380. Thus he could have married and had legitimate children in
1366. So the omission of his name from Sir Thomas' settlement in that year
shews he was not his son.
* p. 105.

in his place."[7] Was this William Strickland? Taken
in conjunction with the gap of six years mentioned above,
it seems possible that he spent these years as a student at
Oxford.   If this was so, may it not be that his wife died
at the beginning of this gap in his official life? F. W.
Ragg thinks that it was a broken hearted widower who
decided to be ordained;[8] may it not have been that an
able and ambitious man now saw no reason why, if he
took major orders, he should not hold a high place in the
Church?

Perhaps he went to the university, certainly he was
ordained deacon and priest, and was rewarded, sometime
before 7 December 1381, with the valuable living of
Rothbury, Northumberland.[9] But he was still employed
in this diocese. In 1383, he was appointed by Bishop
Appleby to collect the clerical subsidy, when such threats
were used to him in Penrith that he dared not collect it
there.[10] On 5 December 1388, he was presented to the
living of Horncastle by the bishop, who had also appointed him his chaplain and on his death in 1395, the
chapter of Carlisle elected him to succeed, but the pope
refused his approval.[11] In 1396 he had an indult to
choose his own confessor; in 1397, to hold two benefices;
and in 1398, to have a portable altar.[12]

It is, however, more as a builder than an ecclesiastic
that we think of William Strickland to-day. His earliest
operations were at Penrith. In 1386 he had a lease of
thirty-two acres of waste land there and elsewhere, with
the right to construct a fortalice within the town.[13] In
1397 he had a further licence to crenellate his chamber;
and in 1399 another one which states that " at his own
great cost (he) is making a fortalice at Penreth on
the March of Scotland for fortifying that town and the
whole adjacent country; to dig stone in Penreth felles
within the forest of Inglewood in order to complete the
said fortalice."[14] It has been suggested by F. Hudleston

that Strickland's original idea was to build a pele tower with a curtain wall, as a home for himself and an enclosure for his cattle, but later he decided to extend this by putting up a more substantial fortress, which would provide him with a place of residence and the inhabitants of Penrith with a means of protection against the Scots. He thereupon obtained the second licence to get stone from within the royal forest, as this would be more economical than carting it from Stainton, where the earliest stone used in the castle was probably quarried. F. Hudleston's article contains an excellent plan shewing the position of Strickland's original pele and curtain wall.

But his most interesting benefaction to Penrith was the scheme he inaugurated for a proper water supply. Hygenic ideas in the Middle Ages were most elementary, and Strickland's plans shew a mind in advance of his age. The engineering involved also reveals very considerable mechanical ability.[15] His interest in Penrith was not limited to the material needs of the town, he had also a care for its educational ones: in 1395 he founded a chantry, dedicated to St. Andrew, in the parish church, and directed that the priest should teach the children church music and grammar.[16]

Soon after he became bishop he got to work on the episcopal houses: in 1402 he restored the manorial buildings, the chapel and the lord's chamber at Bewley; he also made extensive additions to Rose, including the tower called after him. The rooms in this may have been his private apartments.[17]

The most important of his buildings were those he caused to be erected in Carlisle Cathedral, for which an indulgence was granted on 2 October 1410.[18] According to Dr. Todd he built the tower from the middle to the top, placing in it four large bells, and erected upon it a spire, or pyramid of wood covered with lead. The north

transept was also reconstructed at this time.[19]   Dr. Todd
states that he put in the stalls and tabernacle work in
the choir, also the wooden roof and ceiling of the
chancel, which had remained unfinished since Bishop
Welton's time.*   But he seems to have been mistaken in
this.

The bishop also carried out the ordinary political duties
of a Border prelate.   In September 1401 he was one of
the Commissioners to negotiate peace with Scotland.
Next year, when the Scots invaded Cumberland, committing depredations near Carlisle, he drove them back.
In 1406 he was one of the prelates who signed and sealed
the Act of Succession which settled the Crown on the
Lancastrian line.[20]

After that, except for the indulgence of 1410, nothing
more is known of him.   But he lived on for some years,
dying at Rose on 30 August 1419.   By his will, dated 15
May 1419, he desired to be buried in his cathedral
church;[21] the place is now unknown; it was probably in
the destroyed nave.

The two chief characteristics of Bishop Strickland were
that he was a man of this diocese and one with an
essentially practical mind.   The water of Penrith was
polluted; his response was not to order a litany to be sung
round the town, but to plan for a good stream to be
diverted through it.   The normal duties of chantry
priests were to say Mass for the intention the founder
directed; he ordered that his priest should combine this
with practical service to Penrith by teaching in school.†

---

* *Leland Collectanea*, ed. 1774, I. 346, seems to be the earliest authority for
all this.   Dr. Todd states that this spire or pyramid continued an ornament
of the church for many years, till by reason of its weight it was thought an
oppression to the fabric; and on that account taken down by order of the
chapter some 30 or 40 years before. (*History of the Diocese of Carlisle*, folio
129).   This MS. was written about 1696, so this would be at about the
Restoration.

† The salary, previously paid to the chantry priest, was granted by Queen
Elizabeth to Penrith Grammar School (*N. & B.*, II, 411).

Again, the most economical way to keep the Scots in their place was to put up a strong tower; so the bishop built one at Penrith and another at Rose. He must have liked building them, as he heightened that of Carlisle cathedral and, being a practical man, put four bells in it—they would give out a nice sound, provide a warning if the Scots were near, and tell the people it was church time. But he had something of the artist in him as well because it was under his direction that the canons' stalls were put in, and, being a man of an age that loved colour, he saw that they were painted.* He should surely be ranked among the greater bishops of Carlisle.†

Roger Whelpdale was appointed by papal provision, dated 11 January 1420.[22] The temporalities were restored on 17 March, though he had not yet returned to England, presumably from Rome. He was consecrated in London by Henry, bishop of Winchester. He is said to have been born at or near Greystoke. One of the name, which often occurs in the Penrith district,[23] was master of the college there in the next century.

For us the most interesting thing about him is that he was fellow and later provost of Queen's College, Oxford,[24] which had been founded in 1340 by Robert de Eglesfield, chaplain to Phillipa, queen to Edward III, hence its title. The founder, one of a family that took its name from a place near Cockermouth,‡ was not unmindful of this fact. By the original statutes of the college a preference in the choice of scholars or fellows was given to the founder's kin and to natives of Cumberland and Westmorland. The

* Traces of this can still be seen.
† His grandson, William Lowther was constable of Rose Castle and founded a family, of which a junior branch was at Great Orton until the last century. Through him and his descendants, as well as through the senior Lowther line, a considerable number of people have a minute part of the bishop's blood in their veins to-day.
(A pedigree of these families is in n.s., xxxix, 109, and xl. 60).
‡ An account of the family is given in n.s., xvi, 239-72. The Senhouses of Netherhall, Maryport, are their representatives and as such quarter their arms.

connection thereby established with this diocese has ever since been maintained, not only by the college itself, but by St. Edmund Hall which, though now independent, was for many years linked with it. Thus a large number of men from these counties have been educated at one of these foundations; and many a poor lad has risen to eminence in Church and State thereby. It is unlikely that Bishop Whelpdale was the first Queen's man who was an ecclesiastic of this diocese, though he was, as far as is known, the first bishop, but, as will be seen, by no means the last.

All that is known of this short episcopate is that during it money was raised for the fabric of the cathedral. An indulgence of forty days was granted for this purpose by Bishop Langley of Durham on 4 September 1421. The procurators were Robert and Lawrence de Penreth. Probably funds were still needed to pay for the work on the tower.[25]

Bishop Whelpdale died on 4 February 1423 at Carlisle Place, London. By his will of 25 January he directed that he should be buried in St. Paul's Cathedral; in the porch or some other private place. He also ordained the foundation of a chantry in Carlisle Cathedral, for which he left £200; Masses were to be said for the souls of Sir Thomas Skelton and Mr. John Glaston. Manuscript copies of books written by him still exist in various libraries.[26]

Licence to elect was issued on 5 March 1423, but the pope translated William Barrow, bishop of Bangor, to the vacant see. The temporalities were restored on 16 June.

Little is known about him. He was on the Commission of Peace for Cumberland and Westmorland in 1424, and on two commissions in 1426 and 1428 for raising royal loans.[27] In 1427, he obtained from the Papal Chancery an exemplication, or copy, of letters of Pope Honorius III " which are beginning to be consumed with age." As

I

his dates are 1216-1227 this is further evidence that all the early records of the see were not consumed in the fire of 1292. Two days later the bishop had a papal indult to visit his city and diocese by deputy.[28] He died at Rose on 4 September 1429, and was buried in St. Catherine's chapel in the cathedral.[29]

The next bishop was Marmaduke, son of Ralph, 1st Lord Lumley and Eleanor, his wife, sister of Ralph Neville, 1st earl of Westmorland. The royal assent was given on 5 December 1429, and the temporalities restored on 15 April. The new bishop, who was consecrated the next day at Canterbury by John, archbishop of York, was a person of some academic distinction,* who was to hold the see for over twenty years.

We have evidence of his primary visitation of his diocese in 1431. Few records of medieval visitations in this diocese have survived. They were held at Carlisle, Wigton, Penrith and Appleby, to which the clergy came to make their reports. In the case of the religious houses, the bishop would, of course, visit the convent and monastery itself. The record mentioned—the original is among the Lowther muniments—is a document detailing an award of the bishop in a discord which had arisen between the master with other priests of the collegiate church of Greystoke and Sir Henry Threlkeld about the appointment of a chaplain there. Its chief interest is in the proof that visitations were made in the diocese at this time.[30]

In July 1434 the bishop was on a commission to arrange one of the periodical treaties of peace with the Scots of which no one on the Borders seems to have taken much notice.[31] For in 1438 the king, in response to the petition of the prior and convent of Carlisle " whose possessions have been wasted by war," licenced the

* Chancellor of Cambridge University, 1427; master of Trinity Hall, 1429-43; (Venn).

bishop to grant them the advowson of the church of
Kirkland, assessed at £8;[32] and in 1443 the latter had a
licence to appropriate the church of Caldbeck " in augmentation of his poor estates on the frontier which had
been ruined by burnings and depredations done by the
Scots in time of war."[33]   Six years later, the prior and
convent of Carlisle, " because their possessions were
wasted by invasion of the king's enemies," had a grant of
the royal fishery of Carlisle; they also obtained the
privilege of not finding any night watches by themselves
on the city walls," since it is their duty only to pray for
the good estate of the king and the realm, day and night
nor, save in great necessity, to wear arms."[34]

   The most interesting event in these years is the effort to
raise funds for the fabric of the cathedral about which we
have evidence in a mandate from the archbishop of York,
entered in the register of the archdeacon of Richmond of
20 August 1443 and directed to the clergy of that diocese,
for quaestores to be sent round by the prior and convent
of Carlisle to beg alms for the cathedral church of
Carlisle, for new work of the same.   This mandate was
renewed on 10 December 1445 and during the next
episcopate.[35]

   During these years national affairs were getting into
ever increasing disorder. Bishop Lumley sided with
Henry Beaufort, bishop of Winchester, the chancellor,
in his quarrels with Humphrey, duke of Gloucester. He
was a Trier of Petitions in 1430-1, 1447, 1449, and
Warden of ' le Westmarch ' towards Scotland from 1437
till February 1449. In 1447 he was made lord high
treasurer of England.

   He may have been present at two of the Councils held
at that time in an endeavour to put the Church's affairs
in order.   One of these was the famous Council of Basle,
which he was given permission to attend, with the abbot
of Glastonbury, in 1437, though it is not certain if he

went; the other was that held at Ferrara in the next year when he was again nominated to represent England.

In 1448 the king wished to promote him to the see of London, but the pope thought otherwise. However, in 1450, despite the opposition of the duke of Gloucester, he was translated to Lincoln.

Bishop Lumley was clearly a man of considerable standing in the contemporary political world about whom we would like to know more. He may well have been the ablest of the fifteenth century bishops of this see, but records are so scanty that no judgment of any value can be given. He was dead before 5 December 1450, so his sojourn at Lincoln was very short.[36]

On 14 March following, the escheator was ordered to deliver the temporalities to Nicholas Cloos,* late archdeacon of Colchester, whom the pope had provided. He was consecrated the next day at York House, Westminster, by Archbishop Kemp of York. He had taken part in 1449 in a proclamation of peace between England and Scotland, and in 1451 was on a commission to investigate whether the conservators of the truce between the two countries had been negligent or not.[37]

The only other thing known about his episcopate is that in 1451 he received, with the archbishop, an application from the prior and convent of Carlisle who ' inflamed with the energy of pious devotion ' asked for an indulgence to aid them in procuring a richly decorated statue of the Virgin Mary for their cathedral. They wanted it covered with plates of silver and overlaid with gold, gems, precious stones and many other costly ornaments for the praise of God and the honour of the most glorious Virgin and for provoking the devotion of Christ's faithful people, daily flocking there on pilgrimage.

---

* Venn says of a Flemish family, *D.N.B.* of a Westmorland one. The former seems almost certain to be right. One of the original fellows of King's, 1443, chancellor of Cambridge University, 1450-1 (Venn).

As John Knowblow, parson of Lamplugh, mentions such a statue in the cathedral in his will in 1469 they were presumably successful.[38]

The most interesting thing about this bishop is that he is " supposed to have been the architect "[39] of King's College Chapel, Cambridge. His grant of arms from Henry VI stated that it was given " for the laudable services rendered by him in many diverse ways, both in the works of the building of our College Royal and in other matters."[40] He was translated to Coventry and Lichfield on 30 August 1452.[41]

On the same day the pope provided the see of Carlisle to William Percy—a canon of York, in priest's orders, of a race of earls—with a " dispensation to receive and exercise the rule and administration of the see of Carlisle, notwithstanding his defect of age, he being in his twenty-fifth year."[42] On 11 March in this year a dispensation had been granted to him, " who had completed his twenty-third year, to hold for life any three benefices." He was consecrated, between 16 November and 18 December 1452, in the province of York by Robert of Durham.

He was the son of Henry Percy, 2nd earl of Northumberland, and Eleanor, daughter of Ralph Neville, 1st earl of Westmorland.   Of his birth Fuller observes " as a base child in the point of his father is subject to a shameful, so is the nativity of this prelate as to the place thereof attended with an honourable, uncertainty, whose noble father had so many houses in the northern parts, that his son may be termed a native of North England."[43]   In fact, he was born at Leckonfield, Yorkshire on 7 April 1428, and was educated at Cambridge, being chancellor of the university, 1451-6.[44]

His episcopate covers most of the period of the wars of the Roses. The evil results of Henry IV's usurpation of the throne, foretold by Bishop Merke, came to a head in the days of his grandson, Henry VI. The ablest man of the Royal Family, Richard, duke of York, was a nearer descendant of Edward III than the king. The clash was inevitable. All the great families of these counties: Percies,* Cliffords,† Dacres‡ and Greystokes§ were Lancastrians, though the latter were rather lukewarm ones. It is possible that Bishop Percy's appointment was intended not so much to give the see a bishop as Rose Castle a captain. In the event of trouble it might, in the hands of one on the opposite side, have broken into the Lancastrian core on this West Coast. The translation of Bishop Cloos, so soon after his appointment, and the succession of a man of only twenty-five, belonging to one of the greatest baronial houses, looks rather suspicious.

Though the chief local families were Lancastrians, the Yorkist earl of Warwick, the ' king maker,' had adherents here, especially the Hudlestons of Millom: Sir Richard married Margaret Neville, a base daughter of the earl,‖

* They obtained the position they held on this Western Border through Maud, heiress of the Lucies, lords of Allerdale, who had married, before 15 December 1381, as his second wife, Henry Percy, 1st earl of Northumberland, and dying childless, left her estates to his children by his first marriage on condition that they quartered the Lucy arms, though she had a first cousin of her own blood, William de Melton, living. " Say not the Percy's profit was the Lucy's loss; for what saith the Scripture ' Is it not lawful for me to do what I will with mine own ' " is Fuller's comment (Worthies of England ed. 1840, I. 349). Thus the Percies became lords of all West Cumberland from the Wampool to the Duddon, with the castles of Cockermouth and Egremont.

† They had become the chief family in Westmorland by the marriage, before 1274, of Roger de Clifford with Isabel, daughter and co-heiress of Robert de Vipont, hereditary sheriff of Westmorland, whose family had been granted the barony of Appleby in 1203. They were thus lords of the castles of Appleby, Brougham and Brough. Early in the next century the inheritance of the other coheiress also fell to them.

‡ Originally a family of knights from a Cumberland village of this name, they became great people by a daring act of Ranulph de Dacre, who procured before February 1316, either by abduction or enticement the person and hand of Margaret, heiress of Thomas de Multon, lord of Gilsland and of the castle of Naworth.

§ This barony had passed, in 1305-6, to Ralph Fitz William of Grimthorpe, whose mother was a daughter of the first house of Greystoke.

‖ Through whom many local people have a portion of the ' king maker's ' blood in their veins.

and Sir William, Isabel, daughter of John, marquis of Montagu, his brother. Sir Walter Strickland of Sizergh was another adherent of Warwick's.

One of the evils of the time was the manner in which the gentry made private contracts with great nobles, not of necessity their feudal lords, to serve them in " tyme of paix and werre " as Sir Walter had done in 1448.[45] Entries noting payments made under indentures of this nature are included among the Percy muniments; by 1441 John Lamplough, William Martindale, Nicholas Irton, and John Swyneborne had entered into such engagements; all, except John Lamplough who had died in 1441, were still retained in 1454-5.[46] The gentry followed this example and likewise made their private treaties: Thomas Sandford of Askham retained William of Bradle of Gnyp (Knipe) yoman in 1468, John Clebburn of Banton (Bampton) in 1469, and Henry Walker of Butterwyk Crag and his two sons to " wt hym and hys . . . take parte in pease and were during thaire life and before all oder except y Kyng and Yaire land lorde " in 1470.[47]

It is difficult to blame such men for their actions, since every one had to be ready to defend himself. In about 1435 Robert Crakanthop, justice of the peace, appealed to the chancellor of England " because of great and outrageous riots assemblies gatherings broils and turmoils by people armed like insurgents against the law," but no justice could be obtained because when the court met at Appleby " William de Thornburgh of Meaburn and Henry Threlkeld, Kt. so threatened in life and limb the jury impanelled to enquire, that they through fear of death and mutilation did not venture to be present." No surprise will be felt that Robert was killed at Brampton in 1438.[48] Even a strong castle like Rose was ransacked by marauders in September 1451, and in 1457, its constable, William Lowther, had his home at Hawksdale broken into.[49] The Threlkelds must have been a lawless race at that time. In 1454 John Clybborne complained that one of them with others beseiged his house at Cliburn, shot a thousand arrows into it, and later on captured him on his way to Appleby and put him in prison; and all this was done though he had 'thre justices of the pees ' to help him to defend himself.[50] So, while the great lords paid off their scores by pitched battles, lesser mortals did the same on a scale comparable with their quality. Anyone who could pay an army did so; it might be numbered in thousands as the king maker's, or in ones and twos as Thomas Sandford's.

The bloodshed began with the first battle of St. Alban's, fought in May 1455. Bishop Percy was present at this engagement and his experiences there can hardly have enamoured him of such affrays, for it is recorded that he " was spoiled of all his goods, as well as in horses, jewels, his household, and even his cope, and was left behind alone, only in his rochet, flying on foot as far as Islam " (Isleham).[51]

The war did not spread into these counties for some time. Indeed they were spared the ravages caused by great battles and the passage of large armies and suffered only from the feuds of minor gentry and odd freebooters. That does not mean that the blood of local people was not shed. Probably many young men from these parts in search of adventure in the service of a Percy, a Dacre or a Clifford lord found death instead. At all events it is certain that many a Percy, Dacre and Clifford found it. The mortality among the great families cannot be better illustrated than from the bishop's own relations. His father was slain at St. Albans. Two of his brothers: Thomas, Lord Egremont, who had taken his title from the chief town of the family's Cumbrian barony of Coupland, and Sir Ralph Percy were killed in 1460 and 1463. It was the latter who, just before he died, defending Dunstanborough Castle for his king, uttered the words

" I have saved the bird in my bosom," meaning, it is presumed, " I have followed my conscience to the death."* At Towton the bishop lost a nephew, the 3rd earl of Northumberland, and two first cousins: Ranulph, Lord Dacre, and John, Lord Clifford. His Neville cousins were all, except one, likewise killed off in due course.

After the disastrous Lancastrian defeat at Towton, 1461, the war spread to this diocese, for Margaret, Henry VI's queen, enlisted the help of the Scots. At once Carlisle was involved in a siege, since the castle was held by a Yorkist. However, in June 1461, the bishop's cousin John Neville, marquis of Montagu, relieved the garrison, killing 6000 of the enemy, including Lord Clifford's brother, in the battle.[52] But not apparently before much damage had been done to the city and its suburbs, as the Yorkist King, Edward IV, " in compensation for the immoderate violence and cruelty of the siege," granted the city a new charter, reducing the fee farm rent from £80 to £40 a year.[53] He also granted to the prior and convent £20 yearly " on account of the devastation of their possessions in Carlisle by the rebels, and two tuns of red wine yearly."[54] Meanwhile the castles of the Lancastrians were being subdued: Cockermouth in April 1461,[55] and Naworth, by Lord Montagu, in July.[56]

In the summer of the next year Rose had a distinguished visitor: the earl of Warwick, who held the manor and castle of Penrith and the wardenship of the Western March, staying there during some months for the pacification of the country and the punishment of local Lancastrians. His horses did so much damage to the park, wholly consuming the herbage of ' le Brademedewe,' that the bailiff was unable to account for its issue that year.[57]

---

* *Annals of the House of Percy*; I. 286, *E.B. de Fonblanque*. This is the explanation of the words that so puzzled Chancellor Ferguson (see Cumb. and West. M.Ps., 400).

In those days of terrible blood feuds probably many a hard pressed refugee sought shelter in these sparsely populated lands; Henry VI is said to have done so after the battle of Hexham in 1464. One account has it that he was " frequently concealed in the house of John Machell of Crackenthorpe." There is a room in the hall there known as the king's bedchamber, and a garden, called the king's garden, where he is said to have been hidden, disguised as a labourer. The probability of the truth of this tradition is increased by the fact that John Machell received a pardon from Edward IV in 1466.[58]

Henry is also connected in fact and legend with South West Cumberland. The fact is a bell with a Latin inscription in Lombardic lettering " Henricus Sextus Rex " at Warberthwaite; and the legend that the unfortunate king came on his wanderings to Irton Hall but was refused shelter by its master and slept the night under a great oak, still standing and called the King's oak. In connection with this there is a ghost story:

" the lady in black with white lace, whom members of the family have seen at Irton (the last appearance was about 70 or 80 years ago to the writer's great grandmother), who is said to come out of a cupboard in the corner of the Tower room and go to the window to gaze out, may be the ghost of Margaret Brough-ton, the daughter of another Yorkist house, and the wife of the man who refused the king shelter. The curious part of the story is that the cupboard in question, which always figures promin-ently, marks the obliterated and long forgotten entrance which must have opened on to the original newel stair of the Tower."[59]

Another tradition of Henry's wanderings comes from Muncaster castle, where he is said to have taken refuge with Sir John Pennington and given his host a bowl, still treasured there. It is of greenish glass, enamelled and gilt, and known as the ' Luck of Muncaster '; a king's bedstead is also preserved there.*

* J. G. Lockhart in *Curses, Lucks and Talismans*, 83-94, subjects the legend

While it is acknowledged that stories of this kind may be compared by the sceptical with those of the great company of beds in which Queen Elizabeth is alleged to have slept and considered by the serious student not to be of the nature of true history, yet it is submitted that they often enshrine ancient popular traditions which, though inaccurate in detail, preserve truth in general and that therefore it may be said to be an historical fact that Henry VI did spend sometime wandering in this district after one of his defeats.

Perhaps two more local traditions may be excused. One is of the concealment by his mother, after the death of his father at Towton, of Henry, 10th Lord Clifford, commonly called ' the Shepherd Lord,' in a cottage among the Lake District fells. Wordsworth's " Song at the feast of Brougham Castle " and his " White Doe of Rylstone " give an account of his romantic career. The other is that Sir Thomas Broughton, probably brother of the lady of Irton who turned poor Henry away, himself later became a fugitive, but found in his tenants a mercy his sister denied her king. The story is that taking part in the rising of Lambert Simnel* against Henry VII, he sought refuge, after his defeat, among them at Witherslack, and, living in concealment there for many years, was buried in its chapel.[60]

After having thus wandered—perhaps into the realm of romance, certainly into the days of the Tudors—let us return to sober and contemporary facts. Against such a background of social disorder the reader will not be surprised to be told that but one single act of Bishop Percy's is known : that he leased a tenement in Cardew in 1457.[61] This lease was confirmed by Thomas de

to a critical investigation. On the whole he is sceptical of its truth and suspects much of it originated in the imagination of the 1st Baron Muncaster.

* He had landed with his adherents at the Piel of Foudray in June 1487 and encamped on Swarthmoor, near Ulverston.

Huythuayte, prior of Carlisle, who " erected the bishop's throne in the quire on the back part whereof his name was inscribed."[62] As the arms of Bishop Percy and Richard Neville, earl of Salisbury, beheaded 1460,[63] are on the screen at the entrance to the choir there seems no reason to question the tradition that the tabernacle work above the canons' stalls was also erected at this time. There is little doubt that the appeals for funds issued by the convent during the last episcopate and continued in Bishop Percy's, 7 February 1454, and in Bishop Storey's, 1 May 1472—when the form used was " for the fabric and construction and happy consummation of the new work of the same church "[64]—were also connected with this.

It is possible that this tabernacle work was not the only thing done in the cathedral at this period. Professor Hamilton Thompson, in a letter to the writer, is of opinion that the term ' new work ' implies not a mere addition to furniture or fittings but building. The appeals mentioned covered a period of nearly thirty years, suggesting work on an extensive scale. In the part of the church still standing nothing to correspond with this remains. It is therefore possible that some considerable alteration was made in the destroyed nave. Perhaps, as happened at this time in several northern churches, a great west window was erected. Whether that was so can probably never now be known.

There seems no doubt, however, that the tabernacle work, the choir screen, and the bishop's throne were erected during this episcopate. We can still see the niches where the figures—two angels and a saint for every stall—stood. The carved work, including a group delineating the coronation of Our Lady, under the choir screen still to be seen, with the colour on it still to be distinguished, gives some idea of what the whole looked like in its pristine loveliness.

Bishop Percy died on 26 April 1462.[65] His place of burial is not known. He was only thirty-four years of age. Few can have envied those born into great families in those days. This diocese should remember him and Prior Huythuayte with gratitude when we see the cathedral choir and bear in mind what it must have looked like as they left it for posterity.

John Kyngescote, appointed by papal bull dated 12 July 1462,[66] had received a grant of the temporalities from the king on 16 May, but the mandate for the restitution of the temporalities was dated 20 October; he was consecrated four days later. The chief reason for his appointment was apparently, as stated in the Patent Roll of his nomination, in recompense of £600 due to him from the king's father and the king. The descent from the grim tragedy of Bishop Percy's life to this very business-like reason for filling a bishopric may perhaps be taken as symbolical of the change from the feudal England of the past to the commercial one then coming into being. But while the king got rid of his debt, whether John Kyngescote received his money is more open to question as he died on about 5 November 1463.*

Richard Scrope,† provided by the pope on 1 February 1464,[67] received the temporalities on 5 June and was consecrated on the 24th at York by the bishop of Exeter. As the younger son of Richard, 3rd Lord Scrope of Bolton and his wife Margaret, daughter of Ralph Neville, 1st earl of Westmorland, he was Bishop Percy's first cousin. Four sheets of his register are included in a list of the diocesan muniments compiled for Registrar Joseph Nicolson in 1748-9.[68] This fragment seems to have been seen by Nicolson and Burn as they record the collation of an incumbent to the rectory of Clifton in 1465.[69]

* In December 1463 Archbishop Booth appointed agents to collect the effects of the bishop who had died intestate. (Reg. Booth 360a).

† Chancellor of Cambridge University, 1461-2 (Venn).

The bishop died on 10 May 1468, aged forty-nine. In his will, dated 9 May and proved 31 July 1468 at York,[70] he directed that he should be buried in Carlisle Cathedral before the High Altar.

Edward Storey,* whom the pope provided,[71] had the temporalities restored on 1 September 1468, and was consecrated at St. Stephen's, Westminster by George, archbishop of York.†

He was a member of a committee which met in 1470 to examine Jacquetta, duchess of Bedford (mother of the queen). While the king was at Warwick, she had caused an image of lead to be made in the form of a man at arms, broken in the middle and made fast with wire, which she used—it was alleged—for witchcraft and sorcery. She was acquitted.[72]   She has an interest for us as life tenant of the Richmond fee of the barony of Kendale, granted to her first husband by his father, Henry IV.[73]

From now onwards more information becomes available about the diocese, though the absence of episcopal registers is in some ways irreparable. But some rolls, giving the accounts of the bishop's officials, to some extent make up for their loss. These show that, despite the numerous changes and the disturbances due to Scots and civil wars, the life of the diocese went on; nor do they suggest that anything in the nature of stagnation took place in this century   On the contrary the organisation of the diocese was functioning, well equipped in all departments, with officers not slow in the performance of their duties. The disciplinary powers of the bishop's courts were duly exercised on both clergy and laity, and ample provision made for the religious needs of the

* A Yorkshireman by birth; Chancellor of Cambridge University, 1468-9 and 1471-2 (Venn).

† This was George Neville, brother to the king maker and bishop elect of Exeter at the age of twenty-two, though not consecrated till twenty-five. His natural daughter Alice married Thomas Tunstall of Thurland; their daughters married into the Hudleston and Layton of Dalemain families (N.S. xxviii, 299).

people. The bishops kept a staff of domestic chaplains, passing from one bishop to another and always available to take charge of a parish when the incumbent was ill or died. Licences for non-residence were often issued; of course, the custom of holding livings in plurality was allowed.[74]

Bishop Storey was an active and efficient prelate; he held diocesan synods and visitations according to custom. One was held at Penrith in 1470 when his ' chapel,' or episcopal regalia, was carried by horse from Rose for the occasion.[75] In 1471 he confirmed vicarages for Bampton, Shap and Warcop—the rectories had been granted to the abbey of Shap some centuries before.[76]

In November 1472 Richard, abbot of Melrose, held a visitation of the abbey of Holm Cultram. His directions shew that the priests of the monastery were expected to receive the Holy Eucharist four times a week and those who were not priests twice at least within the space of fifteen days. The study of the Holy Scriptures was ordered to be indefatigably pursued and the abbot directed to procure a man learned in grammar for the instruction of the younger brethren in them.[77]

But the devotional life of religious societies in this Borderland was liable to be sadly let and hindered by the Scots. Whether the two countries were formally at war or informally at peace made little difference to the Borderer. His sport, except for sowing and harvest times, was an all-the-year-round one. So in April 1473, the poor nuns at Armathwaite had to apply to the king for a confirmation of their estates because the buildings of the nunnery had been destroyed by the Scots and the house despoiled of all its goods, and above all its charters, so that they could shew no legal claim to their lands.[78]

In 1474 another element of strife between the two peoples was introduced. The inhabitants of Cumberland constructed a fishgarth or dam in the lower waters of the

Esk, whereby salmon were prevented ascending the river to the detriment of the fishing industry in the upper or Scottish waters. The fishgarth was complained of as a nuisance, and as often as it was removed by the Scots was replaced by the Cumbrians. A commission to investigate was appointed in 1489/90, but the dispute went on for many years.[79] It is all very suggestive of the scene that gave rise to the conversation between Joshua Geddes, the quaker, and the laird of the Lakes of Solway, described by Sir Walter Scott in the sixth chapter of Redgauntlet.

Even before the time of Henry VIII monasteries had been dissolved for various reasons. For instance, in 1477 Edward IV closed the Hospital of St. Nicholas at Carlisle and transferred it, with its lands and property, to the priory of Carlisle. For many years the foundation had been in an unsatisfactory state and a cause of anxiety to the episcopal authorities.[80]

In 1478 Bishop Storey was translated to Chichester. The magnificent cross still standing in the centre of that city was erected by him. He died in 1503. As he was a benefactor to Pembroke College and Michaelhouse, the two foundations with which he was associated at Cambridge, it seems probable that he also remembered this see of which he was bishop for ten years; but if so all record of it has been lost. He seems to have been a worthy and generous man, about whose episcopate we would like to know more.

Richard Bell, whom the pope provided by bull, received his temporalities on 24 April 1478, and was consecrated on 26 April by his predecessor. He was prior of Durham, and carried off a lot of silver plate from there to Carlisle, which his successor at Durham seems to have recovered in due course.[81]

These were years when much church building and decoration took place. The cathedral, of which Thomas

Gudybour was prior, was in the forefront of this movement. The celebrated paintings on the back of the
canons' stalls were executed at this time. One series
shews the life of St. Cuthbert, patron saint of Durham.
The recent discovery of the close resemblance between
these paintings and some miniatures in an illuminated
MS., once belonging to the monastic library at Durham,
forges yet another link between the two places. There
can be no doubt that the artist who painted the scenes
portrayed in Carlisle Cathedral had this Durham MS. in
front of him while he worked. Presumably it was lent
to Carlisle at the request of the bishop.*

The wall painting discovered, but also destroyed, in
1854-5[82] and the screens now in St. Catherine's chapel
were also probably Prior Gudybour's work. Further
he had the roof coloured red and green, on a white
ground; and the choir pillars painted white, diapered
with red roses nearly 12 inches in diameter, with the
letters I.H.C. and J.M. in gold, with subjects of legendary
history on the lower piers. Much of this remained until
the 'restoration' of 1854-5.[83] He also inserted some new
painted glass into the cathedral as the following letter
from Richard III shews:—

"to o[r] welbeloved servant John Crakenthorp, receyvor of our
landes within our countie of Cumberland. We wool and
charge you y[t] of such money as is now in yo handes or next
and furst shall come into y[e] same by vertue of yo[r] office, y[e]
contente and pay unto o[r] trusty and welbeloved in God y[e]
priour of oure monastery of Carlile the some of V[li] which we
have geven towards ye making of a glasse windowe within ye
same o[r] monastery. And thise o[r] lettres shalbe yo[r] warraunt
and discharge in y behalve. Given &c. at Gaynesburgh the
x[th] day of Octobre the first yere of o[r] reigne (1483).

* Two lives of St. Cuthbert ed. by Bertram Colgrave, viii and 32; and
The Burlington Magazine, LXXIII 17-21, where the reproductions from the
two sets of pictures enable the student to compare them. The close connection between them is beyond question. The MS. is in the British Museum
Library (Add. 399 43).

Next year he granted

"the prior and canons of the cathedral church, a great part of the possessions of which had been destroyed by the Scots, two tuns of red wine of Gascony yearly in the port of Kingston on Hull for use in their church, that they might pray for the good estate of the king and his consort Anne, queen of England, and for their souls after death and the souls of the king's progenitors.[84]"

As Richard III only ascended the throne on 26 June 1483, these gifts shew a quick interest in the Border city with which he had been connected during his brother's reign. In 1471 he had received a grant of the lordship and castle of Penrith; in 1474 had been warden of the Western Marches; and in 1475 was made sheriff of Cumberland for life.[85] It was probably during these years that his cognisance of a boar was sculptured on a tower in Carlisle castle, where it still remains. Whatever Richard's sins may have been, we in this Borderland should think of him kindly.

Prior Gudybour also cared for the secular side of the monastery's affairs. He put up the tithe barn, near St. Cuthbert's church,[86] and his initials are in the crypt of the fratry which he rebuilt.

Elsewhere also ecclesiastical building was going on. At Furness some additions and rebuilding of the domestic parts of the abbey took place, and, at the very end of this century or the beginning of the next one, a new tower was commenced at the west end of the nave. As the thickness of its walls far exceeds those of the great tower of Fountains, it is clear that it was planned on a most ambitious scale.[87]

In Westmorland also the same thing was happening: at Shap Abbey a west tower was added early in the sixteenth century. But the most striking evidence of the extent of church building is to be found in the parishes. At Kendal the existing inner and outer aisles and chapels were built in the late fifteenth or early sixteenth century.* Bowness on Windermere was rebuilt, after destruction by fire, in about 1483; and a new chapel erected at Kirkby Lonsdale about three years later. Heversham also had a new chapel and a north aisle put up late in this century, while Kirkby Stephen widened the south one and added a west tower in about 1506. The tower at Brough was built, with much other work, some seven years later and that at Crosby Ravensworth rather earlier. Other churches in which extensive rebuilding occurred about this time or rather later are Beetham, Burton, Morland, Newbiggin, Ormside and Orton.[88]

To return to Bishop Bell: he seems to have kept high state at his installation. Perhaps it was for such ceremonies, so as to give a good social impression to the nobility and gentry, that he needed the silver he had brought with him from Durham. We know that mummers, or wandering players, performed before the company on this occasion, as a note of their payment is contained in the bishop's accounts; also that when the abbot of Holm Cultram came to Rose to receive the episcopal benediction, four clerks from Carlisle, who assisted at the solemnity, departed with a gift of silver We also get a glimpse of high state on another occasion, when Bishop Redman of St. Asaph—he was probably of a younger branch of the Harewood and Levens family— visited the diocese. He was met by Bishop Bell at Penrith in October 1488, a large outlay is noted in the bishop's accounts for the expenses of his lordship and his entourage, and the two cavalcades proceeded to Rose, where the mummers were again commanded and the silver from Durham again perhaps brought out.[89]

During this episcopate a new chapel was built at Rose between 12 November 1487 and 12 April 1489. There

* The church was in a very bad state in about 1450 and money was collected or its repair (N.S. ix, 38-40).

must always have been a chapel of some kind there, but the first mention of it is at Easter 1314, in Bishop Halton's time, when the first known ordination there is recorded.[90] Previously to this ordinations in the episcopal manor are entered in the registers as at Dalston, not Rose—perhaps because the chapel at the castle was too small to hold the number of ordinands usual in those days. The special feature of Bishop Bell's chapel was the roof, which was ceiled with boards and covered with lead, and included a dome. For the building of the chapel boards had been bought from the prior of Carlisle ; others for the ceiling came from Armathwaite. The stone was got from the bishop's own quarry at Shawk; lead came from Bewley and elsewhere. The ornaments included three images which the bishop purchased from York. Another addition that he made to the castle was the tower bearing his initials. Before this, in 1479, he had employed carpenters for several days in repairing the draw bridge. He also spent money on other repair work.[92]

An instance of his consideration for others may be found in his erection of a new pair of gallows in 1487 for, as Canon Wilson puts it, the convenience of his Linstock tenants. But whether this convenience was that they could be hanged by the bishop on the spot without him giving them the needless bother of a walk to Rose, or that they could the more easily and expeditiously hang their neighbours does not appear.[93]

Nothing is known of the remaining years of Bishop Bell's life. He resigned the see on 4 September 1495 and died during the next year at the age of eighty six.[94] To him, as well as to his contemporary Prior Gudybour, the diocese owes a debt of gratitude for what he accomplished and not least for the beautiful brass, for which it may be presumed he left money, which preserves his memory in his cathedral church to this day.

William Senhouse, abbot of St. Mary's, York, was

preferred by papal bull. The temporalities were restored
on 11 December 1495. He was born at Shincliffe, near
Durham. His name is spelt variously Senhouse, Senews,
Senuz, Sever or Siveyer. An endorsement of the papal
bull translating him to Durham describes him as Lord
William Senows, and in a contemporary list of clergy
attending a synod there his name is spelt Senus.[95] This
seems to settle definitely that his name was Senhouse and
not Sever. His exact relationship to the Seascale and
Netherhall family is unknown; that his was a cadet
branch of this family cannot be doubted.

Another of the name, Simon Senhouse, prior of the
cathedral from at least 1505, was his contemporary. The
prior was probably a younger son of one of the Seascale
family.[96] His contribution to the work of building and
beautifying started by his predecessor was the painted
ceiling of the room in the present deanery, called the
prior's room. It is signed in the middle with " Senus
Pryor " and the red rose, the badge of the city, and the
Senhouse popinjay or parrot. The frequency of the
Dacre badge of an escallop shell and staff is a puzzle; no
reason for this is known.[97]

Bishop Senhouse served on an important commission
to arrange for the marriage of the king's daughter,
Margaret Tudor with James IV of Scotland; the marriage
took place in 1502. Their great grandson was to unite
the two crowns and so bring peace to this Borderland.

The only other thing of interest known about the
bishop is that in 1501 he was an arbitrator to a dispute
between his kinsman Thomas Senhouse of Seascale and a
neighbour, William Stanley of Dalegarth. His award is
still preserved at Netherhall.[98] This method of settling
their disputes was often followed by our ancestors in their
saner moments.

In June 1502 William Senhouse, who had retained his
abbotship of St. Mary's, York, was promoted to the

see of Durham. He died in the spring of 1505. His
Durham episcopate was as uneventful as his Carlisle one
appears to have been. He was buried in St. Mary's
Abbey, York.[99]

Roger Layburne was consecrated on 10 or 17 September
1503, and received the temporalities from 15 October on
21 February 1504, but the mandate of restoration was not
granted till 12 November. He was probably one of the
Layburnes of Cunswick, Westmorland, who used the name
Roger. Nothing is known of his episcopate. His will is
dated 17 July 1507. He directed that he should be
buried in St. James' Hospital " near unto Charing Cross,
London."[100]

Between Bishop Layburne's death and his successor's
appointment an incident occurred in the parish of
Brigham which affords an appropriate link between a
chapter dealing with the decline of the medieval world
and one describing the beginning of the Reformation.
The document in question has not been known before and
its discovery throws new light on the early history of
pre-Reformation heresy in the North West.

Nothing has been said of the work of John Wyclif, nor
of the Lollards, because no evidence of their activity in
this part of England has been discovered. But an entry
in the Court rolls of the manor of Derwentfells of 9 May,
23 Henry VII, 1508[101] is suggestive of at least some form
of heretical belief.

" Also they (the jury) say that Issabil Kendal, late of Pardi-
showe in the county of Cumberland, spinster, lives in a
suspicious manner in that she has received no sacraments of the
church in her parish church of Brighame in the county of
Cumberland nor elsewhere as they believe for the space of one
year last past and the said Issabill is of the age of forty years and
able in body but of a perverse opinion as they believe."

This is the only entry in the rolls on the matter. That
a manorial jury of laymen reported someone for erroneous

religious belief is in itself a matter of some interest. But what posterity would like to know is the nature of the ' perverse opinion,' from whence the accused got her views, and whether any other local people shared them.

Professor Hamilton Thompson has advised the writer on this matter and allows him to quote his opinion. He thinks that evidence of the influence of Lollardry in the North of England is rare. The only possible instance, and even that is doubtful, is that of the Austin friar Thomas Richmond which was brought before the York convocation in 1426.[102] " I feel," the professor states, " that the question of Issabill Kendal's religious opinion may be left open, while the suspicion undoubtedly was of heresy. The date seems just a little too early for continental heresy to show its influence in the north; but it is possible that rumours of the growing dissatisfaction with the Church had reached places like Cockermouth with foreign traders, and Pardshaw, of course, as well as Brigham, is close to Cockermouth, and both places would be in touch with local gossip. I think, however, that it is more likely that heresy would enter this way than from the limited area within which at this date Lollardry probably survived." There the matter must rest unless some further evidence should some day come to light.

CHAPTER VI.

THE ARCHDEACONRY OF RICHMOND
(beyond the moors) in the
MIDDLE AGES.

THIS chapter gives the history of the deaneries added to this diocese in 1856. During the Middle Ages they were within the great archdeaconry of Richmond; a relic of the territorial division of north western England before our present counties came into existence. It included parts of Yorkshire, Lancashire, Cumberland and Westmorland, and contained 123 parishes, compared to 93 in the diocese of Carlisle. Its original extent was even greater, as before 1133 it included the area that then became this diocese. In compensation for this loss the archdeacon was granted all the rights of a diocesan bishop, except the spiritual ones. The different parts of the archdeaconry are generally described as on this side of, or beyond, the moors. The parts now in this diocese were in this latter section, and in 1291 were divided into only two deaneries: Lonsdale and Kendale, and Furness, which included Coupland. Subsequently four deaneries are found. The parishes named in 1291,[1] but divided into their later deaneries, are:

Kendale: Kendal, Heversham, Beetham, Burton, Windermere, Grasmere.

Lonsdale: Kirby Lonsdale.

Furness: Cartmel, Ulverston, Pennington, Urswick, Aldingham, Dalton, Kirkby Ireleth.

Coupland: Millom, Whicham, Bootle, Corney, Gosforth, Haile, St. Bees, Irton, Egremont, Lamplugh,

III. KENDAL CASTLE IN THE SEVENTEENTH CENTURY.

This drawing from the Machell MSS.,
reproduced here for the first time, is the earliest known picture of the Castle.

(*facing p*. 137)

Dean, Brigham, Cleator, Beckermet, Harrington, Moresby, Distington, Workington, Ponsonby, Whitbeck, Muncaster.

Arlecdon is not included in this return, it was certainly in existence in 1262, perhaps because it was appropriated to the archdeaconry of Richmond,[2] nor is Warberthwaite, which was a rectory not later than 1220.[3]

There were thus only 37 parishes in an area as large as the ancient diocese of Carlisle with its 93, but chapels especially in the large parishes of Kendale, Brigham, St. Bees, and Dalton were much more numerous. A short account of their history will be found in the section dealing with Church Extension in the Middle Ages. An account of the religious houses has already been given.*

These parts of the archdeaconry contained many places and features of interest to the historically minded. Within them was the highest mountain (Scafell) and the deepest lake (Wastwater) in England; with a parish (Kendale) probably at one time one of the largest in England, with a church exceeded by few in the area it covered. Many would agree that this district could also claim the most beautiful scenery in England.

These deaneries are divided both by political association and by geographical features into three divisions in three counties: Kendale and Kirkby Lonsdale in Westmorland, Furness in Lancashire, and Coupland in Cumberland.

The ecclesiastical parish of Kendale originally included Grasmere and Windermere as well as the nineteen parishes now carved out of it. Its capital town, anciently called Kirkbie in Kendale, though always of importance as the site of the castle of an extensive barony, did not attain to any considerable status until the middle of the fourteenth century, when it became a centre of the woollen trade and steadily increased in prosperity. More

* p. 5-8.

fortunate than other places in these counties it suffered
little, if at all, from Scots raiders. As the prosperity of
the town increased so did the size of its church. Adjoining Kendale to the south are the ancient parishes of
Heversham and Kirkby Lonsdale, each with a noteworthy church.

The history of the Furness district was dominated by
the abbey of that name, its capital being Dalton, with
a church in existence before 1195. It may be exceeded
in antiquity by Urswick, the mother church of Ulverston,
Pennington, and probably also of Aldingham.[4] In the
adjoining district of Cartmel the religious house there and
at Conishead must not be overlooked.

Coupland, which included the great central mass of the
Lake District fells and a good proportion of the lakes, as
well as many delightful valleys, must have been in the
Middle Ages one of the most remote parts of England.
Even to-day much of it, bordered as it is by mountains on
one side and the sea on the other, is somewhat difficult of
access. To the historian it divides itself into four distinct
districts. (a) On its northern boundary, immediately
to the south of the river Derwent, lay the extensive
parish of Brigham, comprising Cockermouth with its
castle—the chief seat of the lords of the barony—and
several beautiful valleys and lakes, with one of the
most interesting churches in Cumberland. (b) To the
west of this parish lay Workington, in medieval times
only a small place, but always of some importance for
its hall, the seat of the Curwens, the oldest of local
families. (c) To the south lay the great parish of St.
Bees, with the Benedictine priory of that name, as
well as the lakes and valleys opening out westwards.
(d) The district to the south of this parish did not
include much of ecclesiastical note except the abbey of
Calder and the very minor priory of Seton. Egremont
with its castle, one of the possessions of the lords of the

barony, and Millom, likewise with a castle and the seat of
the once renowned and still surviving family of Hudleston, were its most important towns.

There seems no reason to doubt that, as far as ordinary
administration was concerned, the affairs of these remote
deaneries were efficiently ordered.   The archdeacon had
his rural deans and a considerable body of officials.   As
to episcopal supervision, it is a very different story.   Our
knowledge, of course, is not complete, but the registers
of the archbishops from 1215 to 1315 are in print and of
those years it is possible to write with some certainty.
During them these deaneries were visited only by Archbishop Wickwane in 1281 and perhaps by le Romeyn in
1294.   But "it may be doubted whether the visitation of
medieval prelates, attended by a large and expensive
household were ever of much spiritual advantage to the
districts affected by them."[5]

As few visitation documents of the diocese of Carlisle
have survived, it may be of interest to describe the
methods adopted by Archbishop Wickwane.   On 29
March 1281 notice was sent to the archdeacon and on
4 April a detailed list of the inquiries to be made followed.
These were: names of churches and their value, of
incumbents and their orders;   number of benefices;
particulars of non-resident clergy, whether beneficed
before or after the Council of Lyons; names of patrons,
details of any pensions payable out of the stipend;
names of appropriated churches and if a vicarage
established, names of churches to be dedicated, and of
intruders into benefices, whether clergy or laity;   all
holders of benefices to appear before him;   those of the
deanery of Kendale and Lonsdale at Burton on 28 April
and those of Amunderness at Kellet on 30 April.   On 13
April all rectors, holding more than one benefice with
cure of souls, were ordered to appear in the church of

Kirkby in Kendale on 26 May and shew their dispensations; likewise all abbots and other heads of religious foundations who held pensions to shew their titles; finally clergy beneficed since the Council of Lyons and not made priests within a year after were to appear to receive censure. On 17 April the archdeacon was asked to furnish similar information about the deanery of Coupland, the clergy of which were summoned to be at Waberthwaite and Muncaster on 19 May.

The archbishop's plans do not seem to have come off, for his itinerary, as given by dated official acts, shews his movements to have been as follows:—April 28 Burton in Kendale, May 2 Cartmel, May 3 Furness and Conishead, May 10 St. Bees, May 12 Burton in Kendale.[6] From this list it looks as if he changed his mind, visiting Coupland deanery on his way from Conishead to St. Bees.

Two other documents in connection with this visitation are the archbishop's corrections of the religious houses of Cartmel and Conishead. Among things ordered are: silence, no talking to women, except by leave of the prior; saddles to be delivered to the prior, and canons not to go out of the cloister without leave, especially for hunting.[7]

Archbishop John le Romeyn gave notice of a visitation on 27 August 1287. The clergy of the deaneries of Furness and Cartmel were to travel to Lancaster, and those of Kendale to Bolton; Coupland is not mentioned. On 20 September the order was revoked.[8]

On 23 February 1294 the archbishop issued another commission for a visitation beyond the moors. The dates were: Lonsdale on 22 March at Kirkby in Lonsdale; Kendale on 24 March at Burton; Amundernesse on 26 March at Lancaster; Furness and Cartmel on 30 March at Dalton; Coupland on 2 April at Egremont. Then on 7 March 1294 notice was given of a visitation of St. Bees priory on 3 April, of Conishead on 29 March, and of

Cartmel on 27 March. But on 21 March these latter were postponed till 6 June.

" It is clear that the archbishop never made these visitations," observes the editor of the register.[9] His grace's itinerary shews, however, that he was at Kendal on 30 March and at Lowther on 1 April.[10] While Bishop Halton's register states he had passed the night of 31 March at Orton, Westmorland, and subsequently stayed with his suffragan at Linstock on his way to Hexham where he was on 4 April.[11]

The next mention made of one in these parts is a commission by Archbishop Greenfield on 13 April 1311, for two of his clergy to visit the remainder of the arch-deaconry of Richmond, the part beyond the moors, which had not been visited by the archbishop by reason of the winter. So on 20 April the vicar general of the archdeacon warned the clergy and laity concerned: the deanery of Lonsdale and Kendale was divided into two parts; at the church of Kirkby in Lonsdale on 4 May and at Kirkby in Kendale on 8 May; Furness and Coupland was likewise divided: Dalton on 14 May, and Egremont on 21 May.[12]

The only evidence, therefore, of physical contact between his grace of York and his poor sheep in these deaneries during the years 1215-1315 is of a passage through them lasting for about a fortnight in 1281 and of a stay of a night at Kendal in 1294. He may have had a suffragan to perform episcopal duties, though there is little evidence of this. In 1281 the bishop of Whithorn had licence to dedicate the chapel at Loweswater.[13] In 1294 the bishop of Carlisle was twice given authority to ordain monks or canons from the religious houses in these deaneries;[14] letters dimissory for this purpose were issued to the bishops of Carlisle in 1298, 1302, 1303; to the bishop of Kildare in 1302, and to any catholic bishop in 1303, 1304, and 1307, and for the rector of Grasmere in

* But he did not do so, see below p. 150, and St. Bees Register, 387-94.

1316.[15] An episcopal blessing was required for the reconciliation of a church or churchyard polluted by the shedding of blood; authority was given to the bishop of Carlisle to do this in the churchyard of Kendal in 1302;[16] and in the chapel of St. Bees in 1309.[17] The only mention of confirmation in these deaneries is a dispensation in 1303 to the bishop of Whithorn from coming to York for three years and leave to confirm and dedicate altars in the diocese.[18]

This is all the evidence that has been found in the archiepiscopal registers for a hundred years of episcopal acts in this area. But Richard, bishop of Sodor, died at Langalyver (Langley) in Coupland in about 1275 on his way from the Council of Lyons, and was buried at Furness. As there was constant communication between West Cumberland and the Isle of Man, of which see the abbey of Furness nominated the bishops, they may have sometimes carried out pontifical duties here.[19] Somewhat later in the century the appointment of Irish bishops and friars, with titular sees as suffragans to the archbishop, became a regular custom but during these years this was not so.[20] When therefore Archbishop Peckham of Canterbury complained in 1280 of " numberless people, grown old in evil days, who had not yet received the grace of confirmation,"[21] his words must have indeed been true of these deaneries.

There is a certain amount of general information about them in the archiepiscopal registers, because during a vacancy the archdeaconry was administered by the archbishop. In Archbishop Gray's register the appropriations of Dalton, Urswick, Kirkby Ireleth, and Millom by Furness Abbey, with the ordination of vicarages, are recorded in 1228. Another appropriation is that of the church of St. Michael of Irton* by the prioress and

---

* This settles the question of its true dedication. *N. & B.* II, 24, gives this as St. Paul.

convent of Seton in the same year.[22] The appropriation
of Kendal church by the abbey of St. Mary's, York was
confirmed by Archbishop Corbridge in 1301[23] and again
by Archbishop Greenfield, with the consent of the chapter
of York, in 1307.[24]

In Archbishop Gray's register there is a record
which takes us back to the customs of early northern
Christianity: proof was produced by William, son of
Thomas de Workington in 1225 that he did not succeed
his father in the rectory of that church, the latter being
only the farmer of it and not the rector. This proof
was necessary because the Church was trying to stamp
out clerical marriage which had been very prevalent and
indeed encouraged in the Celtically influenced Northern
Church.[25]

A Curwen also figures in Archbishop Greenfield's
register: a memorandum, dated 21 September 1309,
stating that Sir Simon Ward, Kt., having confessed
misconduct with Dame Joan Curwen, promised amendment and to avoid all suspected places on pain of paying
£20 to the fabric of the church of York.[26]

It has seemed wise to treat the years 1215 to 1315, for
which the archbishop's registers are in print, as a whole,
and to consider the other evidence available separately.
In Archbishop Melton's time (1317-41) notice of a
visitation by commissaries was sent out on 2 July* 1322.
The dates and places were: deanery of Furness at
Dalton on 14 July; Kendale at Warton on 16 July;
Coupland, divided into two parts: at Bootle on the
same day as Kendale and at St. Bees next day. The
priories of Cartmel and Conishead were to be visited
before 1 August. On 6 September revised notices were
sent out: Dalton and Lancaster on 6 October; Garstang
the next day with Warton and Bootle on the following
one and St. Bees on 9 October.[27]

* The register says 29 September, but Professor Hamilton Thompson
believes this to be the correct date.

Nine years later, 2 September, 1331, a visitation was announced by the archbishop in person, peaceably and quietly, of the whole archdeaconry. He was to begin with the deaneries of Kendale and Lonsdale on Monday 14 October at the chapel of Hornby, and next day be at Whittington, and the following one at the chapel of St. Gregory, in the parish of Burton; then to continue with the deaneries of Furness and Cartmel: Cartmel Priory on Thursday, 17 October, and Conishead Priory and Dalton on the Saturday. There is no mention of where he was to spend the week-end, probably at Furness Abbey. But on Monday, 21 October, he was to recommence work by starting the visitation of the deanery of Coupland at Whitbeck, and the next three days be at Ponsonby, Egremont, and a place not specified.[28]

That a visitation should be held at the chapel of St. Gregory within the parish of Burton is interesting. The chapel must be that at Preston Patrick. Probably the archbishop had stayed the night with the Preston family.* While at the chapel documents were produced to him relating to the chantry in the church at Kendal maintained by the abbot and convent of St. Mary's, York. Founded in 1321, it can probably be identified with that of " Tholde Warke " called Saynte Marye " mentioned in the chantry survey of 1546.[29]

Visitations are not the only things worthy of note in this register. An entry in February 1315 records a commission to the official of the archdeacon to keep the sequestration of the fruits of the church of Bootle vacant by demise. Owing to the constitution *Execrabilis*, one of the pope's pronouncements against pluralism, any one who held more than one living without a papal dispensation was liable to deprivation. Thus this rectory was

---

* An instance of this kind of thing is seen in Carlisle diocese when Bishop Halton held an ordination in the small village church of Clifton in September 1306. (register 1, 268). He was probably staying at Brougham castle.

deemed to be void by the cession of Richard de Insula, who held it as a pluralist without dispensation. In due course both it and Egremont were filled by the pope, but the clerks to whom they were first offered refused them on account of tenuity of revenues and the dangers of war.[30] Later these two churches were collated to William de Feriby and Sir Ralph de Fenton in 1319 and 1320, respectively.*

In March 1323 the abbot and convent of Calder had a confirmation of the appropriation of the churches of St. Leonard of Cleator, and St. John Baptist, Beckermet, with the chapel of St. Bride ' alterius Bechirmet.' This entry proves the name of Cleator's disputed patron Saint,[31] and that St. Bride's, Beckermet was originally a chapel of St. John's, though called a parish in 1262. In Carlisle diocese, Wetheral and Warwick provide a similar illustration of this apparent anomaly.[32]

Licences for non residence in the register include one, on 31 March 1318, to William de Aykeheved, rector of Workington, who had leave of absence from his church for three years for the purpose of study for the sub-diaconate; he was to appoint a vicar. In 1320 this period was prolonged for four years.[33] In 1322 mag. Robert de Corbrig, rector of Egremont, had a similar licence for three years; and in 1324 Henry de Kendal, rector of Whicham and a subdeacon, had one for a year.[34] That two other licences were granted in this period—to William de Cletergh, rector of Haile, for three years and John de Kilnehirst, rector of Bootle, for two in 1332 and 1334—shews how prevalent was this custom.[35]

Letters dimissory were frequently granted; to Thomas of Kirkebi in Kendale in 1318 and to Patrick de Lamplogh

---

* " You will probably note that I do not follow the modern custom of collating people to benefices, but the correct and, in such documents as these invariable custom of collating benefices to their incumbents." Professor A. Hamilton Thompson.

and several monks of Furness in 1320.[36] From this source we get the names of several incumbents: John de Harington, acolyte, rector of Aldingham, 1320, Robert de Warthcopp, rector of Distington, and William de la Chapele, rector of Dean in 1324.[37] Penitentiaries include Thomas, rector of Moresby 1326/7 and Gilbert, vicar of Urswick 1328.[38] Our forbears in the Middle Ages had a great love of exchanges: in March 1334 the register has the collation of the church of Bootle to mag. John de Klynhirst by exchange of the church of Kirkby Underdale with mag. John de Barneby; and in 1337 the institution of Joh. de Etton to the church of Heversham by exchange of the church of Etton with William de Bolton.[39] The only other matter concerning Richmond beyond the moors is letters testificatory of the admission of Hugo de Gayteford to the living of Burton in Kendale in 1301 and his letters of orders.[40] The above are only mentioned here because this register is not in print.

The most interesting local documents in Archbishop Zouche's register are the licences for the consecration of graveyards for the chapels of Windermere and Grasmere in the parish of Kendale. Although presentative benefices, with rectors of their own, both were still dependent upon the mother church for burials. On 15 September 1348, a mandate was directed to two of the archbishop's household clerks ordering them to arrange for the dedication of a churchyard at the parochial chapel of Windermere. And on 3 March 1349 a much more detailed document, in the form of letters patent, was issued licencing the churchyard of the chapel of Grasmere, where a new chapel had recently been dedicated by Zouche's authority, for burial after due consecration. In the petitions for these privileges it was represented that these chapels were sixteen miles from their parish church (as regards Windermere the correct figure is nine), and that a journey through such mountainous country involved great dangers, that in winter conditions were so difficult that Christian burial was often impossible, and that bodies had to be left unburied or deposited carelessly in the woods, streams and lakes.[41]

The next visitation we know of is Archbishop Zouche's, of which notice was issued on 11 October 1347. No schedule of times or places is given, only notices to Cartmel Priory, 7 and 8 November, are entered. Mandates were issued to various commissaries who began to visit at Kendal, but did not proceed.[42]

Then on 15 September following a commission was issued to Hugh, Archbishop of Damascus, to confer minor orders during the visitation, which was to be made by the same commissaries as before, to whom on the same day a commission was also issued. Apparently this was to complete the visitation that ' did not proceed.' The archbishop was also given power to hear confessions and to dedicate the churchyard at Windermere. A special notice for the visitation of St. Bees Priory was issued on 6 October.[43] The most interesting matter that arose from the visitation was an inquiry into the appropriations of various churches by monastic houses. The evidences produced must have satisfied the archbishop as *Dimissio* was granted: 7 November 1348 to the abbot and convent of Furness for the church of Dalton with the chapel of Hawkshead, the church of Urswick, and a moiety of the church of Millom; 10 December to the prior of Conishead for the church of Ulverston with its chapels, and the churches of Pennington, Whitbeck, Ponsonby, and Muncaster with the chapel of Drigg and others; 14 March 1349 the abbot and convent of Calder for the churches of St. Leonard, Cleator and St. John Baptist, Beckermet; and on 3 April to the prior of Conishead—for the church of Haile.[44]

As previously there is little evidence of episcopal supervision in these deaneries. The only instances apart from the archbishop of Damascus of a bishop being in these parts are licences, bishops not named, in January 1343 for the reconciliation of the churchyard of Kirkby in Kendale and the conferring of the first tonsure on clerks of those parts.[45] There is also a commission, 8 January 1351, to this archbishop to give benediction to Robert, abbot of Calder, but probably it was the abbot and not the archbishop who did the travelling. The names[46] of other heads of monastic houses that occur in this register are: William de Lobenham, abbot of Calder, 1347* and Alexander, abbot of Furness, whose obedience was received on 8 December in the same year.[47]

A licence for non residence gives the name of master Thomas de Dalton, rector of Brigham, 1344, but he was dead in July 1349 when master Thomas de Neubolde, priest, was presented by Hugh de Courtnaye, earl of Devon.[48] Among the penitentiaries in these years were master John de Bokham, vicar of Kirkby in Kendale, 1346-8; John Fitch, rector of Aldingham, and William Burton, parish chaplain of Kirkby in Kendale, 1350.[49] Robert de Bethom, rector of the chapel of Windermere, and John Fitch, were commissioners to levy the subsidy granted by the clergy of Kendale and Furness in that year.[50]

The most interesting entry in the registers of Archbishops Thoresby and Alexander Neville is in connection with a visitation to which the prior of St. Bees was summoned on 28 April 1361:

" since then, however, on fuller information we have understood that the monks abiding in the said cell in no wise form a college or convent, nor are they called after the manner of a convent, but the prior is named first and the other monks of the said monastery of St. Mary (York) therein dwelling abide as fellow monks and associates who celebrate divine service in the same place, and this same place of St. Bees has, it is said, at all times

* Both these names are additional to those given in *V.C.H.* II, 177-8.

been called a priory and is immediately founded out of the goods of the said monastery of St. Mary, York, and is altogether subject to their proprietorship."

The summons to the prior and convent was cancelled, and the address to the ' prior et monachi degentes ibidem ' substituted.[51]

There is also a reference, 4 July 1361, to a visitation of the abbey of Calder, which again produced its evidences for the appropriation of the churches named before, with the addition this time to the church of Beckermet of " with the chapel of St. Bride."[52]

There are several dispensations for non residence: John de Strensal, subdeacon 1366-7, master Henry Godbarn 1369-71, master John Bridd 1373-4 and Robert Tynworth 1383, all rectors of Egremont;[53] master Nicholas de Feriby, subdeacon, rector of Heversham 1370; and William de Duresme, deacon, rector of Beetham 1372.[54] It will be noted that three out of the six had not been priested. The mandate for the induction of Henry Hay to the church of Bootle, on exchange for Skirpenbeck, Yorks, was granted in 1366.[55] Two professions of obedience are entered: 1367, John, abbot of Furness, and 1369, Nicholas de Bretby, abbot of Calder.[56] The reader must excuse the inclusion of matters of such minor importance but as these archiepiscopal registers are large manuscript volumes, not generally accessible, it seems worth noting them. Further, as they give all that is known of the history of these deaneries from York documents in these years, they are evidence of their remoteness and isolation.

Archbishop Alexander Neville, consecrated in June 1374, began his second triennial visitation of his diocese in 1377. Unfortunately only a summary of his register has survived; in this the date is 1387, but the former is generally accepted as the true one. The archbishop cited his clergy in the archdeaconry to 39 churches, of which 24 were beyond the moors, they included 5 in Lonsdale, 4 each in Kendale, Furness and Coupland. To judge by the number of churches named as centres it must have been a very thorough affair. The archbishop committed a subsequent visitation in the autumn of 1382 to various deputies.[57]

Except for the commission to William 'episcopus Pharensis' of 23 June 1403 to dedicate and consecrate the chapel of Loweswater in the parish of St. Bees[58] nothing is known until Archbishop Kemp's proposed itinerary for his primary visitation. But he did not reach these deaneries as he abandoned his visitation on account of the bad weather which had imperilled the harvest and thereby prevented clergy and laity going far from home.[59] The archbishop had planned to arrive at Bentham in the deanery of Lonsdale on 6 September 1428 and then to visit the church of Kirkby Lonsdale. From there he was to pass to Kendale in which three days were to be spent: the first at Warton where he proposed to visit Heysham and Burton, the second at Heversham for Beetham and Windermere, and the third at Kendal for that church and Grasmere. Four days being allocated to Amounderness, the archbishop did not expect to reach Furness until 15 September, having spent that day crossing the sands from Kirkham to Conishead Priory, which he was to visit next day. Then he meant to travel to Aldingham, visit Ulverston, Pennington, Dalton and Urswick and spend the night at Cartmel Priory, which he had down for the next day, 18 September; Sunday was to be passed at Furness Abbey, where the abbot and convent were to feed him. On 20 September he was to be at Egremont, in the deanery of Coupland, where Muncaster, Ponsonby, Irton, Lamplugh, Dean, Gosforth, Bootle, Whicham, Millom and Whitbeck were listed for visitation; afterwards the archbishop was to travel on to St. Bees where he was to stay the night. Next day that priory and Calder were to be visited, the latter providing him with food; then he was to go on to Brigham and there visit Workington, Beckermet, Harrington, Moresby, Haile, Waberthwaite, Corney and Distington.[60] Though this visitation never took place, this itinerary is of great interest; some of its geography is of the strangest kind and the plan must have been drawn up by a clerk quite ignorant of the position of some of the localities concerned.

The scheme for the visitation of September 1441 was more sensible. The archbishop, travelling from Lancaster, was to reach Kirkby Lonsdale on 18 September and visit the churches of the deanery. Next day he was to be at Kendal for Windermere, Beetham, Heversham, Burton and Grasmere; and on the following one at Warton for churches now outside this diocese. The night being spent at Cartmel, that priory and Conishead were to be visited during the next two days. The night of 23 September was allocated to Furness Abbey. Sunday 24 September is not named; probably the archbishop proposed to spend it at Furness. Then on Monday, with Dalton as his headquarters, he purposed to visit Hawkshead, Pennington, Kirkby Ireleth, Ulverston, Urswick and Aldingham. After that his grace, who had started at the end of August, was to rest for nearly a month before visiting Coupland deanery which this time was to take four days. On 19 October Dean was the centre for Brigham, Lamplugh, Workington, Arlecdon, Harrington, Moresby and Distington. The night being spent at St. Bees, the next day was to be the priory's turn; then from Egremont the churches of Beckermet, Drigg, Ponsonby, Irton, Gosforth, Cleator, and St. Bees with its chapels were on the list; and lastly the archbishop, who this time was travelling from north to south, was to be at Bootle on 22 October and visit the churches of Muncaster, Whitbeck, Corney, Warberthwaite, Whicham, and

Millom.[61] This time Hawkeshead, Kirkby Ireleth, Arlecdon, Drigg and the St. Bees chapels, omitted in the 1428 schedule, were included. Evidently the archbishop had learned much about this remote part of his diocese in the intervening years.

Fortunately some of the fifteenth century registers of the archdeacons are available.[62] Through them we get glimpses of the life and administration of the Church in this area at a time when the records of the diocese of Carlisle are poor. We see how careful the Church was of the rights of property. The living of Distington being vacant and the patron, William Dykes Esqre., having presented Sir Robert Aspatry, priest, the vicar general of the archdeacon sent a commission on 12 August 1448 to inquire into the patronage. It met in the church there five days later, and the dean of Coupland, Thomas Gosseford, with the assistance of twelve of the local clergy as jurors, investigated the matter. He reported that the living was vacant on 5 August last by the resignation of Robert de Lowther, late rector; that William Dykes Esqre. was the true patron and that William Dykes, late deceased, his father, presented last time. So Sir Robert got his living. The need for this careful investigation is shewn by what had happened at Burton in Kendale some years before: Thomas Horneby had been presented in 1437; then in June 1440, William Trokell was given the living by the king; however, Thomas was still alive and seems to have acted expeditiously, as eight days later William's resignation is noted and Thomas Hornby is re-appointed by the archbishop of York. Something strange must have happened somewhere.

The discipline of the Church is also witnessed, in 1378 Walter de Hoton, rector of Grasmere, had a licence to be absent from his living, so did Nicholas de Feriby, rector of Heversham, but their brothers of Lamplugh, Moresby and Workington playing truant were ordered in 1445 to reside in their benefices. The only other example of anything wrong is a letter from the archbishop to the king in 1455 asking for the arrest of Thomas Gate of Kirkby Lonsdale, chaplain, who had been excommunicated.

Mention of the Church's discipline may be balanced by an instance of her care for her aged servants. When Robert Garnett was appointed on 15 November 1468 to succeed Sir John Bryan in the vicarage of Kirkby Lonsdale it was noted that:

" the archdeacon, also taking consideration for the infirmity and impotence of the said Sir John Bryan, who is now broken down by old age and is deprived of bodily strength so that he cannot labour further in the Lord's vineyard and has no other source of means of support, reserved a yearly pension for him and committed its appointment to the vicar general."

In the institution of William, bishop of Dromore, to the church of Gosforth on 9 December 1465 we probably have an instance of the custom, noted above, of appointing Irish bishops as suffragans to the archbishop for episcopal duties in these remote parts of his diocese

We get instances of Church extension in licences, in 1469, to the inhabitants of Grayrigg in the parish of Kirkby Kendal, for divine service in the chapel there, and in 1467, to Richard Bek of Mikelshawe and William Bateman of Huton for masses in the chapel of St. Mary in the town of Hutton; this is repeated to the dwellers in the hamlets of Old and New Hutton in 1470, when the chapel is described as " newly built in honour of the most high mother of God, Mary."* A chapel in honour of the most blessed Virgin Mary in ' Le Gill ' in the parish of Workington is also mentioned. An Indulgence of forty days was granted in 1454 to all

" who shall visit it, being truly penitent, for the sake of devotion or pilgrimage and shall devoutly say before the image of the said

* The dedication of the chapel of Old Hutton is now said to be St. John the Baptist.

Virgin, for the faithful departed, the Lord's Prayer with the angelic salutation and shall contribute to the fabric of the chapel."

Licences for masses were granted in 1455 to Richard Preston of Preston and Jacobina, his wife in their oratories, within their manors of Preston and Levens; and to Sir Edward Bethum and Joan, his wife in 1463 in their oratory.

In 1430 a commission was granted to the prior of Cartmel for including Alice Skawsely in a certain house for ' Anachoritis ' built next to Kirkby Kendal church. The site of this house is shewn on Speed's plan of Kendal. " Tradition describes (it) as a small beehive hut concealed by fences from the road which encircled it."[63]

In 1432 Richard, abbot of Calder, was commissioned to confer on Margaret, relict of Tho. Lamplogh, armiger, the ring, veil, and mantle of perpetual widowhood; in 1436 the vow of chastity of Alice, relict of Hodgson, once of Cartmel, was noted; in 1458 Robert Egremond, abbot of Cockersand, was commissioned to give the veil to Emmote, relict of Thomas Haryngton, kt.; and in 1467 the prior of Cartmel had to receive the vow of continence and chastity from the honourable and devout woman Dowce, relict of Walter Strickland, Esqre., late of the parish of Kirkby in Kendale, deceased, in order that she may be able the more securely and devoutly to do service to her Maker. These vows do not imply that these women retired into seclusion like an anchorite or nun. In the disordered society of the mid fifteenth century they may often have been used as a safeguard by a well endowed widow against too pressing wooers.

From now nothing is known of the history of these deaneries, except for matters recorded elsewhere in this book, until we come to the lists of clergy given in the subsidy rolls for the years 1523/4 and 1524/5 which throw some interesting light on the staffing of parishes just before the Reformation. In these four deaneries there were 199 clergy: 24 rectors and vicars, 33 curates, 135 chaplains, 4 chantry priests, and 3 canons. Of the 24 incumbents 7 were graduates. A curate was a hired assistant of the incumbent, whether resident or absent, to whom the latter had assigned a cure of souls; a chaplain was a clerk in Holy Orders, who had no such cure* The distribution of the clergy in the various parishes can be seen in the following summary:—

	Rector or Vicar	Curates	Chaplains
Kendal (1)	1	1	45
Cartmel (A) Ulverston (A)	—	1	9
Heversham	1	1	7
Kirkby Ireleth, Kirkby Lonsdale (2)	1	1	4
Beetham	—	1	4
Windermere, Grasmere, Dalton, Urswick, Millom, Gosforth (1)	1	1	3
Lorton	—	1	3
Lamplugh	1	1	2
Brigham (2)	1	—	2
Cockermouth (3) Muncaster (A)	—	1	2
Pennington (1) (A) Hawkshead Whitbeck (A) St. Bees (A)	—	—	2
Aldingham, Bootle, Warberthwaite Egremont, Workington	1	1	1
Corney, Whicham, Distington, Harrington	1	—	1
Burton, Dean, Moresby	1	—	—
Irton (A) Ponsonby (A) Beckermet (A) Haile (A) Cleator (A) Arkyndayl (Ennerdale?) Drigg	—	1	—

(1)—also a canon.   (2)—also a chantry priest.
(3)—also two chantry priests.
(A)—Appropriated.

In the return of 1523 Burton has a curate and four chaplains, Millom and Muncaster each a chantry priest, Whitbeck and St. Bees, each a curate, in addition to the numbers shewn above.

* For a fuller explanation of these terms see *The English Clergy*, A. Hamilton Thompson, 122-3.

The most interesting return is Kendal with its 45 chaplains. It is difficult to see what priestly work they found to do. There were 6 chantries in the church and about 12 chapelries. Even allowing for two priests in some of these there are a considerable number unaccounted for. Presumably the remainder were engaged in some form of semi-lay occupation. Another puzzle is that the extensive parish of St. Bees, which included Eskdale, Wastdale and Loweswater, had only two chaplains to serve it, while in the 1548 list* it had six. Many of these chaplains had very small stipends: more than half received £2 a year or less. There is no evidence in the lists that any of these held more than one post. The average stipend of incumbents, excluding Kendal, was about £13.[64]

It may be felt that this is a somewhat meagre account of the ecclesiastical history of these deaneries for a period of over four centuries. But an historian is limited by the material he can discover or that is discoverable. All that can be pleaded is that an attempt has been made for the first time to gather together what little seems to be known of one of the most remote parts of England. As more records of the diocese of York become available some of the obvious gaps in this account may perhaps be filled in and the history of these deaneries rendered more complete; meanwhile a beginning has been made.

* See below Book II, chapter III.

APPENDIX II.

CHURCH EXTENSION IN THE MIDDLE AGES.*

As our first list of parish churches is that given in the *Taxatio* of Nicholas IV in 1291, little can be written with any certainty of events before that date. Such evidence as we have suggests that until not very long before, parish boundaries were still in a comparatively fluid state. It seems probable that the parishes of Burgh in the north, and Corney in the south, of Cumberland had been founded after the creation of the see.† We have certain evidence that Sebergham had once been a chapel of St. Cuthbert's, Carlisle and Cumrew and Cumwhitton of Hayton,‡ while in Westmorland a place of the importance of Brough was still a chapel of Kirkby Stephen in Bishop Mauclerk's time.§ By 1291 all these places were of full parochial rank. We are probably correct therefore in believing that the number of parish churches in existence at the foundation of the see steadily grew during the years 1133-1291. But between 1291 and the *Valor* of 1535 the only new ones added were Newton Arlosh, Grasmere and Windermere. That a town like Cockermouth, with an important castle, and sending two members to parliament in 1295, was only a parochial chapel throughout the Middle Ages is suggestive of an arrested development. Thus the transition from chapelry to parish seems to have been increasingly difficult, perhaps because of the hardening of vested interests, since the grant of parochial rights to a chapel meant the loss of valuable fees to the incumbent of the mother church. But the hardships inflicted upon the people of such extensive parishes as the ancient ones of Brigham, Dalton, St. Bees, Crosthwaite, Greystoke and above all Kendale, must have been very real indeed.

In the twelfth century these counties were only

---

* This appendix covers the area of the modern, not the ancient diocese.

† *V.C.H.* II, 15-16.   ‡ *Bishop Welton's register*, fo. 19.   § *N. & B.* I, 534.

sparsely inhabited. As marshland was drained, new clearings in the forests granted, land brought into cultivation, and the fells used for sheep raising, new communities grew up. People wonder how folk got to church in the Middle Ages when distances were so great and roads so bad. The answer is that the Church got to them. Wherever a new village or hamlet was created, one of the first things the inhabitants would desire, since people in those days believed in the ministry of the Church, was to have their own chapel. Sometimes the lord of the manor or the grantee of the land would build one: at Thornthwaite, Keswick, Patrick, son of Thomas de Workington having a grant of newly cleared land from Alice de Romeli, built one for his tenants in about 1240.* At Staveley in Kendale, Sir William de Thweng did likewise in about 1338. But all villages were not so fortunate. Probably the erection of the building was not a difficult matter. That the fabric of many parish churches has survived till to-day, but very few ancient chapels, suggests that the latter were only simple structures put up by the people themselves.

The problem for the villagers was not building but endowment since the authorities would not licence a chapel until a stipend had been provided. The inhabitants agreed to contribute a certain amount each year as a charge on their farms and ideally tenants might alter but the charge continued. It was thus, no doubt, that the people of Old Hutton, Kendal, obtained their chapel, newly built in 1470. The charge on their lands was £6. 13s. 4d., probably on the same scale as at Kentmere which was a 1/- for every 6/8 of the lord's rent. In earlier times the amount needed had been less. A canon of Archbishop Islip's (1349-66) fixed it at six marks (£4); Archbishop Sudbury (1375-81) raised it to £5. 6s. 8d.; and later it was increased to £6. 13s. 4d.† Thus it should

* For authorities see lists at end of this Appendix.
† *N. & B.*, I, 232.

be possible to date a chapel's foundation by the amount of its ancient salary, but unfortunately this source of information cannot be relied upon since a small stipend might also be due to farmsteads having decayed. These charges once agreed to were legal, not voluntary, as proved by the lawsuit about Killington Chapel salary in the seventeenth century.* This method of endowment also suffered from the serious disadvantage that while the value of money tended to fall, the salary remained fixed. A stipend providing a living wage in the Middle Ages did not do so in later centuries. Thus chapel incomes often fell rather than rose, giving this diocese in years to come one of its most serious problems.

The history of these chapelries is most interesting. Unfortunately the scope of this volume does not permit of its being treated as fully as it deserves. A list at the end of this appendix gives the medieval ones that have survived to the present day.

These lists are by no means inclusive. There is no doubt that many chapels existed in the Middle Ages of which no record remains. Some perished before the Reformation, others after it. As instances of what sometimes happened to them: the jury of the lordship of Wigton stated, on the 8 October, 23 Henry VII, 1507, that

" the chapel of the Blessed Virgin Mary, Wigton and the hermit's house belonging to the same are ruinous and almost entirely fallen into decay, through the default of Edward Tuffen who gives himself out as the hermit of the same in the country and wrongly and presumptuously spends the gifts of charity bestowed on the said chapel to the grave danger and detriment of that chapel which said chapel is in the gift of the lord and therefore is referred to the Lord's Council; "

and on 7 May, 9 Henry VIII, 1517, there is a further reference to the state of the chapel, " near Wigton," which is still in decay; on 24 October, 15 Henry VIII

* o.s. viii, 93-108.

1523, the jury of Uldale stated that the chapel of the Blessed Virgin Mary there

" which used to be well equipped in books, chalices, vestments, in windows well and decently glazed, in candles. . . is now fallen into decay."*

As illustrations of the statement that the lists in the appendix are by no means inclusive the names of the chapels known in the Holm Cultram district may be cited: St. John's, Skinburness, submerged by the sea soon after 1301—St. John's, Newton Arlosh replaced it—St. Roche, St. Cuthbert, Wolsty, St. Christian, St. Thomas, and perhaps one of St. Laurence;† also those occuring in the manor rolls and bailiff's accounts of the Percy lordships between 1455 and 1524 named; Cockermouth chapel, and chapels of St. Leonard and St. Helen there; chapels of St Leonard, the Blessed Mary Virgin, and St. Mildred at or near Wigton; chapel of the Blessed Virgin Mary at Waverton; the chapel at Uldale already mentioned, and those at Lorton and Borrowdale which have survived till to-day; the chapel of St. Osyth occurs under Papcastle, and the priest of St. Uriel under Braithwaite; the chapels of the Blessed Mary Magdalene at Ranerdale, perhaps Buttermere, and at Brackenthwaite, entered under Loweswater; and the chantry at Keswick.‡ These lists shew clearly how well the medieval Church served these remote hamlets. The intellectual standard of the chaplains was probably not particularly high, but they did bring the people the ministry of the Church. One of the tragedies of the Reformation was that with the break up of the old system most of these chapels were allowed to decay for lack of clergy.

* From manor and lordship rolls (P.M.) under these places and dates.
† *Holm Cultram*, 163-7.
‡ P.M.: manor rolls or bailiffs accounts: 9 Henry VIII, 33 Henry VI (bailiff accts.); ibid. II 51 23 Henry VII, 13-14 Edward IV, 23 Henry VII, ibid.; 22 Henry VII; 15 Henry VIII, 21 Henry VII; 18 Henry VII, 15 Edward IV, and bailiffs accts. 33 Henry VI; 9 Henry VIII.

CHAPELRIES IN CUMBERLAND.

Name	Earliest known date	Mother Parish
Armathwaite	Built anew 1401/2 (N.S. ix, 37)	As the priory of Carlisle claimed rights and liberties within the extra parochial parts of Inglewood Forest these four chapels are held to be within the ancient parish of St Mary's, Carlisle. (N.S. xxiii, 38, xxii, 124, *N. & B. II*, 139).
Hesket in the Forest	1541 but certainly much older (N.S.xxiii 39)	
Langwathby	1302 (S.S.cxli no. 1093)	
Westward	Hermitage of St Hilda 1215; Hildkirk Chapel, 1374 (*H.C.*, 76, 144)	
Threlkeld	c. 1225. (N.S. xxv, 26)	These were chapels within the parish of Greystoke. Only these two are mentioned in the Chantrey Survey (*V.C.H.* II, 208).
Watermillock	Chaplain of 1200-30 (N.S. xxiv, 340)	
Borrowdale	1505. (Manor rolls P.M. roll x, 35)	
St. John's in the Vale	? Site of Hospitallers in 13th century. (N.S. xxiii, 254)	Chapels of Crosthwaite.
Thornthwaite	1554 (O.S. ix, 325)	
Wythburn	c. 1240 (*V.C.H.*, II, 18)	
Keswick	1554. (O.S. ix, 325)	

M

Name	Earliest known date	Mother Parish
Allhallows	Ante 1184 (*St. Bees*, 137) 4 Henry VI, 1425/6, as chapel of All Saints, Ukmanby. (*N. & B.* II, 150)	Aspatria
Bassenthwaite	1471 (*N. & B.* II, 94)	Bassenthwaite
Culgaith	1456, as chapel of All Saints (*N. & B.* II, 446)	Kirkland
Flimby	1123-50 (*H.C.*, 27)	" they reckon y[m]selves in the parish of Holm Cultra," bury at Camerton. (*Miscellany Accounts*, 86)
Newton Arlosh	1304 (*H.C.*, 95) decayed after the Reformation, later refounded	Holm Cultram
High Head or Ivegill	1358 (*N. & B.* II, 319)	Dalston
Newton Reigny	1338, (*N. & B.*, II, 394)	Probably originally in Penrith
Warwick	1131-2 (*Wetheral*, 14-20)	A distinct parish, its church, however, always called a chapel. (*Wetheral*, 15)

CHAPELRIES IN WESTMORLAND.

Name	Earliest known date	Mother Parish
St. Wilfrid's, Brougham	c. 1200 (*L.R.N.W.*, 284)	Brougham
Bolton	Second half of the 12th century (*R.C.H.M.*, 42)	Morland
Milburn		Kirkby Thore
Temple Sowerby	1227/8 (*N. & B.*, I, 270)	

Martindale   1220-47 } (L.R.N.W., 258, 259)
Patterdale   1348   }   } Barton
Mardale   Late medieval remains (R.C.H.M., 206)   Shap
Stainmore   Founded 1506 (N. & B., I, 573) decayed and rebuilt   Brough
on new site, 1608 (N. & B., I, 576)

CHAPELRIES IN COUPLAND.

Ennerdale   1534. No doubt existed earlier (St Bees, 369)
Eskdale   1445 (St. Bees 369)
Loweswater   1125 (St. Bees, 56)   } St. Bees
Nether Wastdale   1535 (Valor Ecc.)
Wastdale Head   1552 (O.S. viii, 197)

Cockermouth   Castle founded about 1221, so chapel in it about
then. (N.S. xi, 130)
Embleton   parochial chapel, 1525 (N.S., xiv, 75)
c. 1210. (St. Bees, 571)
Lorton   Chaplain of, 1198-9 (V.C.H., I, 38)   } Brigham
Buttermere   Under Lorton, perhaps identical with chapel of
Blessed Mary Magdalene at 'Ranerdale,' 23 Henry
VII, 1506-7. (Manor Roll, 12 p. 9 P.M.)

Wythop   1552 (O.S. viii, 198)
Mosser   Chantry chapel, 1547 (V.C.H., II, 56)
Setmurthy   Ante 1225 (N.S. xxv, 26)
Clifton   Ante 1181 (St. Bees, 137)   } Workington
Drigg   About 1170 (St. Bees, 461)   Claimed by Gosforth; ? Muncaster.

CHAPELRIES IN LONSDALE.

Name	Earliest known date	Mother Parish
Barbon, Hutton Roof, Killington	All have architectural remains pointing to a foundation in the Middle Ages (*R.C.H.M.*, 34, 131; N.S. v, 215, and xxxviii, 146)	Kirkby Lonsdale

CHAPELRIES IN CARTMEL AND FURNESS.

Name	Earliest known date	Mother Parish
Cartmel Fell	Founded 1504 (N.S. xii, 285)	Cartmel
Flookburgh	1520 (*V.C.H. Lancs.* VIII, 276)	
Hawkshead	c. 1200 (*ibid.*, 374)	Dalton in Furness
Colton	1530 (*ibid.*, 386)	Hawkshead (*T.* xiv, 311)
Broughton in Furness	1547, but certainly earlier (*ibid.*, 405)	Kirkby Ireleth
Woodland	Pre-Reformation (*ibid.*, 407)	
Lowick	1292 (*ibid.*, 362)	Ulverston
Torver	1538, probably earlier (*ibid.*, 364)	

CHAPELRIES IN KENDALE.

Name	Earliest known date	Mother Parish
Burneside	Possesses a 15th Century bell, which suggests a medieval origin. (*R.C.H.M.*, 220)	Kendale
Crook	14th century bell (*R.C.H.M.*, 72)	do.
Grayrigg	Ante 1469 (*Y.A.J.*, xxx, 133)	do.

Place	Details	District
Hugill or Ings	1546. (*R.K.*, I, 87)	Kendale
Kentmere	1453 (N.S. xxxiv, 195)	do.
Natland	1246, perhaps (*R.K.*, I, 167)	do.
Old Hutton	1467. Newly built 1470 (*V.A.J.*, xxx, 115, 125)	do.
Selside	The Thornborough family had a chapel in their manor house, a 14th century building, which seems to have served for the tenants as well. (*R.C.H.M.*, 243, *N. & B.*, I, 118)	do.
Staveley	Ante 1338. (*Tales of Old Staveley*, McConnel, 8-9)	do.
Underbarrow	1547, *R.K.*, I, 365)	do.
Winster	Font probably medieval which suggests origin at that time. (*R.C.H.M.*, 231)	do.
Ambleside	Perhaps between 1443-94. (*Rydal*, Armitt, 128) Chaplain named 1486 and 1505-6 (*Church of Grasmere*, Armitt, 62)	Grasmere
Troutbeck	1554, presumably of medieval origin (*R.K.*, III, 192)	Windermere
Crosscrake	Temp. Richard I (*Strickland of Sizergh*, Hornyold, 18)	Heversham
Crosthwaite	Probably of medieval origin (*R.C.H.M.*, 90)	Heversham
Preston Patrick	Chapel of St. Gregory, 1331 (*Archbishop Melton's Register*, fo. 454)	Burton

APPENDIX III.

THE HERALDRY OF BISHOPS AND CATHEDRAL IN THE MIDDLE AGES.

The reader will remember the close connection between the bishops and the cathedral in the early days of the see. This is illustrated in their heraldry: the arms of the priory, a black cross on a silver shield, are to-day borne by the bishops with the addition of a mitre. It is noticeable that the episcopal arms are not given by Dugdale as among those he saw in the cathedral, though a coat similar to the priory's, but differenced by a mullet, is included. May it not be that we have evidence here of the days before the method of episcopal differencing became settled?

The families of none of the medieval bishops are known, nor are their arms. In fact the first shield that can be fully blazoned is Bishop Strickland's. Even after his time our knowledge of their coats, bearing in mind the need of cadency marks, is limited.*

All medieval cathedrals were ablaze with heraldry; there is no reason to doubt that this was also true of Carlisle. The arms in the roof, though modern, are probably copies of those anciently there. Medieval shields of Bishop Percy and the earl of Salisbury on the great screen have recently been discovered.† Some remains of the heraldic glass of the medieval cathedral can be seen in the clerestory. We can obtain an idea of the amount that once existed by the list made by Sir William Dugdale at his visitation of Cumberland and Westmorland in 1665. This has never been printed before.

---

* Both the painter of the shields in the Church House and F. J. Field in his *Armorial of Cumberland* have erred in assigning coats to bishops whose families and arms are unknown.

† N.S. xlv, 125-8.

Carlisle

29 March 1665. In the cathedral church of Carlisle carved and painted on the roof of the choir.

1. France and England ancient
2. Edward ye Black Prince
3. Mortimer
4. Percy and Lucy
5. Beauchamp
6. Percy and Lucy.
7. O. a chevron G.[a]
8. Nevill
9. A. a cross S.[b]
10. Percy

In the top windows of the north part of the nave of the church

11. Clifford
12. Percy and Lucy
13. A 3 bars G. over all 3 chaplets of 4 roses G.[c]
14. G. fretty A. a label of 3 points A.[d]
15. G. Seme of cross crosslets and 3 boars heads couped A. a label of 3 points O.[e]
16. A. a cross engrailed G.[f]
17. A. a cross S. charged with a mullet. . .[g]
18. Az. a cross flory A.[h]
19. Az. two bars A. over all a bend checky O. & G.[i]
20. Curwen.
21. Moubray
22. Az. a fesse G. a Canton O. (sic.).[j]

In a certain high window of the north part of the church

23. Mandeville
24. France ancient
25. France and England ancient.

[a] Stafford.
[b] Carlisle Priory.
[c] Greystoke, perhaps, but this differs from their usual coat.
[d] Hudleston, probably.
[e] Swinburne, with a label for difference.
[f] Perhaps a Kirkbride coat, they seem to have varied the colour of their cross.
[g] The arms of the priory, differenced by a mullet.
[h] Edwyn, King of Northumberland; an attributed coat.
[i] William de Leigh; a trick in the visitation of 1615 (Ed. J. Fetherston, Plate 3) makes the bars or.
[j] Not known; colour upon colour !

26.   Edward the Confessor.

27.   Az. a fret. A.[k]

28.   G. 3 bars A. over all 3 chaplets G.[l]

In a high window of the south part

29.   Lowther.

Painted on the wall of the south part of the choir

30.   Skelton and Ratcliffe.

31.   Skelton.

On the highest tower of the castle of Carlisle carved on a building stone

32.   Montague and Nevill.*

[k] Not known among local families, but Harrington used s. fretty arg. As No. 13.

It is interesting to compare Dugdale's list with the shields in the clerestory windows. Those of Richard II and Anne of Bohemia, John of Gaunt,† the Black Prince, Stafford, and three Neville coats are not mentioned by Dugdale. This glass had been laid away in a box until brought out and put in its present position; so it may have been hidden there even in Dugdale's time.‡

This list illustrates the fallacy by which the Roundheads are generally blamed for the destruction of such church ornaments and decorations as survived the Reformation. This heraldic work passed unscathed through both these times only to fall a victim to some other and later vandal.

* *College of Arms MSS.* C. 39 (2) p. 7. The author is much indebted to Garter King of Arms, Sir Algar Howard, K.C.V.O., for supplying a copy of this manuscript.

† For the myth that he is portrayed in the east window see N.S. xlv, 122-5.

‡ O.S. ii, 309.

BOOK II.

THE SIXTEENTH CENTURY.

CHAPTER I.

THE REFORMATION OR A NORTHERN TRAGEDY.

MOST books on English History begin a new chapter with the accession of Henry VII, the first Tudor. But in this one it seems better to make the break between the account of the Middle Ages and the Reformation at the beginning of the episcopate of Bishop Penny, whose tenure of the see commenced a few months before the opening of the reign of Henry VIII, in which the breach with Rome was made.*

In a period such as the Reformation, which affects deeply held convictions, it is almost impossible for any one to be impartial. All a writer can try is to state nothing without documentary authority. That ideal, it is hoped, is upheld in what follows, but an historian is only a fallible mortal.

"The north of England at the beginning of the sixteenth century was the poorest and most backward part of the Kingdom, the part, therefore, which required most attention and care at the hands of a competent ruler. So far Henry (VIII) had not done well by it. He found the north poor, and he robbed it of the only treasure it possessed in the wealth of the abbeys. He found it backward, and he nearly destroyed the only civilising

---

* Professor Trevelyan regards the true date at which the Middle Ages can be said to have ended as a very open question and 1485 as by no means the best year for making the break (*English Social History*, 92-8). There is much to be said for regarding 1569, when the rising of the earls was put down, as the end of the Middle Ages in these counties.

influence at work there, the Church. He found that the people cherished, among many faults, a few rude virtues, truthfulness, personal honour, fidelity to family and friends. He made no serious efforts to reform their faults, but he did his best to eradicate their virtues."[1]

These words are damning; and the effects of the orgy of destruction indulged in by Edward VI's grasping Council were almost as bad. In fact every word in Miss Dodd's survey of the result of Henry's rule is equally true of his son's reign. The Reformation was a Northern tragedy. The evidence for the truth of that statement will be found in the following story. It is not said that the Reformation itself was a tragedy, only that the heartless manner in which it was carried out in the North left the land and people, as its immediate result, poorer in both material and spiritual things than it found them.*

John Penny,[2] bishop of Bangor, translated by the pope by a bull dated 22 September 1508, made his obedience to the archbishop of York on 23 January but did not receive the spiritualities till 29 June 1509,[3] two months after Henry VIII became king.

Little is known of the bishop's activities. During his episcopate two men, an ecclesiastic and a layman stand out. The former was Robert Chamber, abbot of Holm Cultram, who " flourished during the religious revival which preceded the dissolution of the monasteries." Unfortunately little is known about him; though it is clear, from the way in which his days are referred to by witnesses in the legal disputes following the dissolution, that he was remembered as an outstanding personality.

---

* Very similar views were expressed by what Chancellor Ferguson calls ' a thoroughly competent authority,' and are set out in his *Diocesan History*, 129-30.

We have tangible proof of his building activities in the
many fragmentary memorials, with his name, rebus, or
initials on them still scattered about the Holme, and
above all in the porch which he added to the abbey
church on which can still be read " Robertus Chamber
fecit fieri hoc opus A^o D^{ni} M.D. VII." The pedestal for
a statue of Our Lady also remains with his rebus of a
chained bear and the inscription " Lady deyr save Robert
Chamber " on it.[4]

The layman was Thomas, Lord Dacre, who increased
the importance of his family by his abduction of, and
subsequent marriage with, Elizabeth,* daughter and
heiress of Robert, son and heir of Ralph, Lord Greystoke,
by which he added that extensive barony to his possessions. It is as a warrior that most is heard of him during
this episcopate.

In the reign of Henry VII there had been peace on the
Border, in so far as that term could ever be used of the
state of affairs in this troubled land. But in 1513
James IV of Scotland crossed the Eastern Borders, and
Flodden was fought, ' the flowers of the forest ' sung, and
this Border given peace; not so the Scots one. The
English raiders and Lord Dacre had a great time—he
had fought at Flodden with the levies of Gilsland and
intervened at a critical moment of the battle. As a
result the country along the water of Liddell that once
kept four hundred ploughs was so devastated that no man
dwelt there, save only in the towers of Annan steeple and
Woolthorpe. " Such was the contribution to the progress of agriculture that the Lord Warden of the
Western Marches could make four hundred years ago."[5]

In 1516 Lord Dacre joined with Prior Senhouse in the
appeal for funds for the " reedifyeng and building of a

---

* " Thomas Lord Dacre without leave asking, but not without peril to his
person, did take her, married her, and by her had yssue." (Household Books
of Lord William Howard, S.S. lxviii, 391).

new brige of XXI jowelles adionyng the wallis of the forsaid citie (of Carlisle) standing over the river of Eden now byng decayed and a perte of the same fallen down," for which an indulgence had been obtained from the pope.[6]

During these years, under the lead of Cardinal Wolsey, new regulations were drawn up and issued to the monasteries and bishops; and in about 1518 a visitation of the Augustinian houses undertaken: Carlisle Priory was reported to be in a satisfactory condition.[7]   A letter of Bishop Penny's to the cardinal—" from an old man just recovering from a severe illness, unable to take a journey to London "—deplores the obvious vices and errors which were beginning to spread without check through Christendom and wishes Wolsey success in their repression, but this would be a difficult task.[8]

The bishop died in 1520, probably at Leicester, and was buried in the abbey there, where an elaborate tomb and effigy were erected.   This was afterwards moved to St. Margaret's Church, Leicester, where it still remains.[9]

John Kytte[10] archbishop of Armagh, translated by the pope on 12 July 1521, received the temporalities on 11 November.   As he was reluctant to descend in status, the pope gave him the titular archbishopric of Thebes, to enable him to retain his rank.   The last of the statesmen bishops of Carlisle, he had been one of the king's ambassadors on a mission to conclude peace with Spain in 1518, and in 1520 attended Henry VIII and his consort at the Field of the Cloth of Gold.

Kytte was a great friend of Wolsey to whom he owed his bishopric.   The archdeacon of Carlisle at this time, William Byrbanke, who was probably of Cumbrian extraction, was likewise one of the cardinal's adherents.[11] The archdeacon was also a friend of the famous scholar Erasmus.   These men belonged to a group of Churchmen who, recognising the need of reform, desired that it should come from within the Church itself.   With no wish for any violent doctrinal change, they hoped for an increase of learning among the clergy, the reform of monastic morals, the suppression, if need be, of the smaller monasteries and the erection out of their revenues of new bishoprics and educational foundations. However, harsher and less kindly hands were to take the work of reformation in hand.

The bishop lived in troubled days; but was able to continue the work of reconstructing Rose, which Bishop Bell had begun, by building the tower there called by his name, which still bears on its west side his arms and monogram. He also made the castle more like a bishop's home and less like a baron's fortress by dividing the great hall, one part of it becoming a dining room for his lordship and his immediate circle, and by building adjacent to his tower private apartments for himself. He may also have erected the gateway and the buildings about it.[12]

One little action of the bishop shews his concern for the spiritual needs of his flock. In 1523 he wrote to the cardinal beseeching him " to have mercy on many good men, women and children of the parish of Bewcastle within my diocese, who, since before Easter last past, have had neither sacrament nor sacramental that I know of." The parish had presumably been under excommunication.[13]

Some account of the religious activities of Thomas, Lord Dacre must now be given: Influenced probably by the good work done by the priests of the collegiate church at Greystoke, he determined, shortly before December 1523, to found a similar college, with a provost and seven priests, for the parishes of Dacre and ·Kirkoswald. The acreage of the combined parishes was eleven thousand, as there were only " one thowsand howseling people " in it, the foundation was on a generous scale. However, Tudor avarice did not permit the results of the generosity to last for long.[14]

Another action of Lord Dacre provides interesting evidence of the rights of lay supervision claimed by a great baron in a monastic house which his ancestors had founded and also evidence of his interest in the fulfilment of their spiritual vocation by its inmates. As he thought the prior of Lanercost was spending too much time on church building,* he wrote him a letter, dated February 1524, in which among other things he said

" Albeit a parte of my mynde is that for as miche as youe, Maister Prior, being soo often occupied as well in outward warkes and business as buylding . . ., cannot have tymes convenient and space to see to the inwarde parte of yor chirche as to take hede and see the service of God contynually maignteyned, the order of Religion wt the ceremoneys of the same w^tin the Chirche, Closter, Dorto^r and frater observed and kept so weale as nedefull it were."

He then gives directions to the prior so as to ensure that there was no such neglect in future.[15]   Posterity has been apt to think of Lord Dacre merely as an adventurous suitor and Border warrior; it is clear that he was also a man who cared for spiritual things.

This evidence of yet more building activity, taken in conjunction with that at Holme Cultram, noted above, is interesting.   In Carlisle the present north west gate of the abbey precincts was built in 1528 when Christopher Slee was prior; an inscription to that effect was still legible in 1905.[16]   The ancient Church was clearly not dead, at least in good works and devout sons, in this diocese in the years just before the Reformation.

But events were now moving fast towards the destruction of much that the good baron and other christian souls had created with such love and care during some four hundred years.   The formal breach with the past

* It seems probable that the medieval painted west window in Wetheral church, with the Dacre arms in it, may have been one of those put up in the priory at this time, and after the dissolution brought to Corby and thence to Wetheral. (*History of Wetheral*, A. G. Loftie, 22-4).

began with the king's wish to divorce his queen. In this
Bishop Kytte supported his wishes. He also signed the
declaration of the royal supremacy in 1534. In general
the bishop appears to have been a conservative, supporting Edward Lee, archbishop of York, against Cranmer
and the reforming school.[17]

Thomas Cromwell, who had succeeded Wolsey in the
king's favour and become vicar-general in 1535, is said to
have boasted that he would make his master more
wealthy than all the princes of Christendom. So the
clergy perhaps felt a little nervous when a new valuation
of ecclesiastical benefices was at once ordered. A
comparison between it and that of 1291* is interesting.
Working on the same basis as before, these figures for this
diocese, and Richmond beyond the moors result:

Value between		Carlisle benefices	Richmond benefices
£0 – 5 a year		9	0
5 – 10		27	10
10 – 20		24	8
20 – 30		8	4
30 – 40		2	2
40 – 50		3	0
50 – 60		1	0

In addition in Carlisle diocese, Greystoke was valued at
£80 and Kirkoswald at over £73, while in Richmond,
Kendal was worth £92. 5s.[18]

It is noticeable that the total income of the Carlisle
incumbents had dropped from £1616. 17s. 5. to £1201. 16s.
6d. and the number of taxable livings from 93 to 76. To
deal with the second matter first. This drop of 17 can
be accounted for as follows:—3 churches had ceased to
exist, 2 had made no returns, 13 had been wholly appropriated and no vicarages ordained—in all 18, but a new

* p. 60.

parish, Newton Arlosh, had been added, making the total 17. As to the drop in the value of the livings: during these years not only had the 13 wholly appropriated rectories lost all their endowments to a monastic foundation, but a further 12 had also been appropriated, though vicarages had been ordained. The ravages of war had also seriously affected the size of stipends—the Border livings of Arthuret, Kirklinton, Stapleton, and Bewcastle, worth £95. 2. in 1291, were valued at £5. 12. 0. in time of peace in 1535, in time of war nothing. In the Richmond deaneries: the value of the livings had decreased from £810. 13. 6. to £461. 12. 11., and the number of parishes returned from 38 to 25, 13 parishes having been wholly appropriated and 4 more so dealt with, but with vicarages ordained. Thus in Carlisle the average value of livings had dropped from £17. 11. to £15. 16. and in Richmond from £23. 3. to £18. 9., with in addition 13 benefices in each area with no endowment left at all.

At about the same time as this enquiry was going on, another one, as to moral conditions in the monasteries, was taking place. It began in July 1535, and within little more than six months its agents had covered the whole country.[19] The personalities of the two chief visitors are of special interest to us because they were both Cumbrians: one, a Layton of Dalemain;* the other a Leigh† of Frizington. Their characters have been thus portrayed:[20]

"Doctor Richard Layton . . . was a clergyman of that detestable type ' the man's man.' Were he living nowadays he would be seen and heard in the smoking-rooms of clubs, slapping laymen on the back, listening to, if not repeating, the latest risky tale . . . It is to him that nearly all of the immodest tales

---

* Richard Layton was a son of William, and nephew of Bishop Tunstall of Durham (Pedigree in *Cuthbert Tunstall*, C. Sturge).

† Thomas Leigh was brother to William Leigh of Frizington: these Leighs were probably a branch of the Isell family. (N.S. xxv, 137-8, 186).

about the religious are due . . . If ' a man's man ' is a detestable
variety of clergyman, a clever and conceited young don is an
equally hateful type of layman. Such was Dr. Thomas Leigh,
the second in importance among the visitors . . . His intoler-
able arrogance and what one of his colleagues, Dr. ap Rice, called
' his satrapic countenance ' was a cause of offence to everybody,
even to his cousin Dr. Lee of Lichfield."

The results of the work of these and other agents were
collected into a report called the black book or comperta,[21]
and laid before parliament. The propaganda department
had done its work so well that it was received with
horror, and the government had no difficulty in getting a
bill passed suppressing all houses with incomes under £200
a year. Thus all monasteries in the present diocese were
liable to suppression, except the cathedral and Holm
Cultram and Furness Abbeys. Can these reports be relied
on? There is no doubt that they are largely untrue; no
responsible historian now accepts them. The report on
each monastery is much the same, with its lists of names
with alleged sins opposite. To-day it is possible to check
these statements from the many episcopal visitations of
monastic houses that are available.

Thus a reasonably correct idea of their true state can
be obtained from reliable and impartial documents.
They prove all was far from well: light is thrown, for
instance, on the affairs of two of the greatest of the local
houses just before the dissolution. The abbot of Holm
Cultram had died, and in 1531 two of the inmates, Gawyn
Borradale and Matthew Deveys, were candidates for the
post. The latter was chosen; within a year he too died,
after a short illness. Foul play was suggested and the
rejected candidate accused of poisoning the abbot. Since
Borradale was sent to Furness Abbey and confined in a
dungeon there for six months, his brethren must have
been convinced of his guilt. But Thomas Leigh, the
visitor interceded with Cromwell for his release and then,

N

procuring his appointment as abbot, received from him the surrender of the monastery.[22]

At Furness Abbey the abbot was accused in 1530 of having kept back £250 of a royal subsidy he had collected, and of conniving to defeat justice: a murderer, who was his kinsman, had been pardoned owing to his influence. Valuable deeds had been kept from their owners; in 1531 one of the monks, after robbing the dead abbot's bedroom of gold and silver, had, with others, got a smith to break open the chest where the seal was kept and used it to stamp blank parchments, which were utilised to convey the abbey's Yorkshire manors to the earl of Cumberland.[23]

These facts do not suggest a healthy state of affairs. But it must be realised that then, as now, it was the evil doer who obtained prominence. Doubtless there were many virtuous monks who left no memorial. None the less, it is difficult to escape the conclusion that the old fervour had gone and the austerity of the ancient ideal often given place to a desire for comfort and ease. Were things so bad that the only solution was to abolish the whole system? The case for the preservation of at least some monasteries in these northern parts was perhaps put best by Robert Aske, the leader of the Pilgrimage of Grace.

" The abbeys in the (parts of the) North gave great alms to poor men and laudably served God. They were great maintainers of sea walls and dykes; they built bridges and highways; they advanced money to the gentry; brought up their daughters in virtue, and wherever they were situated in mountainous and desert places, they provided horse meat and man's meat to strangers and beggars of corn, whose business led them over the wild northern uplands of Yorkshire, Westmorland or the Bishopric."[24]

But good or bad, the monasteries and friaries all suffered the same fate. The dissolution in these parts commenced on 4 February 1536, when Calder was closed;

Seaton, Cartmel and Conishead followed in the same year; in the next Armathwaite and Furness were suppressed; In 1538 came the turn of Holm Cultram, Wetheral, and St. Bees; in 1539 of Lanercost; in that year also the friars were dispersed.* On 9 January 1540, Carlisle Priory was dissolved—the last prior becoming the guardian of the buildings, and carrying on the services till the new cathedral body was formed. And five days later, Shap was closed.[25]

Shap's dissolution at so late a date is interesting. With an income below £200 a year, it came under the act of 1536. The most probable reason for its survival is its value as an inn. Hospitality, as shewn in Aske's statement, was one of the chief duties of the monasteries. Shap, lying near the high road midway between Kendal and Penrith, must have fulfilled a real need. In those days the journey over this wild stretch of fells must have been a dangerous one. Many travellers doubtless thanked God for the hospitality of the abbey.†

* Their memory is still preserved in Blackfriars Street, and Friars Court in Carlisle, and in the house called the Friarage and the streets named Friar gate and Friar street in Penrith. The name and site of the house at Appleby have completely disappeared.

† The following description of the road in 1634 is doubtless equally true of a century earlier:

' and the next day jorney'd to Kendall (from Penrith) through such wayes, as we hope we neuer shall againe, being no other than climing and stony and nothing but bogs and myres and the tops of those high hills, so as wee were enforc'd to keepe these narrow, loose, stony, base wayes though neuer soe troublesome and dangerous: And marke the mischiefe. If a man marke not his waye very well, and so chance to be out a wea bit the rude, rusticall and ill-bred people, with their gaming and rating, have not will enough to put us in. We could not understand them neyther would they understand us, that had wee not happily lighted on a good old man (hauing lost our way in this dayes trauell upon the fells) we had beene (if not grauell'd) I am sure mir'd and layd up irrecouerably without help or hopes for we had as much adoe, although with his directions, to get off safely, as a tatter'd ship in distresse of weather: it was a hundred to one that wee should soe escape this eminent land danger as this good old man made it plainly and euidently appeare to us: well, through his help (thanks be to God) wee escaped. On wee went for Kendall, desiryng much to be releas'd of those difficult and dangerous wayes, wch for the space of 8 miles trauelling a slow marching pace, wee pass'd ouer nothing but a confus'd mixture of rocks and boggs.' (From the Journal of the Three Norwich Soldiers, Newcastle Tracts, Miscellaneous, M. A. Richardson).

A pathetic picture is often drawn of the fate of the expelled religious. In fact the government was quite generous to them. They can be divided into three classes: (1) abbots or priors: they often got very good pensions, the last prior of St. Bees received one of £40 (in modern values about £1,200 a year);* others like Lancelot Salkeld of Carlisle, who became dean instead of prior, or Gawyn Borradale, who became rector of Holm Cultram, continued to live in the same place with a different title; (2) those who wished to return to the world: they were given pensions in accordance with their length of service: in Holm Cultram these varied from £6 (about £180 a year now) to £2 (£60 now)[26] or they could take a living, generally one in the gift of the dissolved house: Thomas Aglionby, some time a canon of Carlisle, was rector of Bewcastle from 1534 to 1581; (3) those who wished to remain in religion: while the greater houses still remained, they were transferred to another monastery of the same order. But uprooted from their old homes, they were not always sure of a welcome; the abbot of Furness drove away some monks of the suppressed house of his own order at Sawley, who wanted to continue the religious life there.

Wilson asserts that the pensioners had to shew their patents to their paymasters, " as returned convicts are obliged to report themselves to the police."[27] But any society or individual paying a pension requires periodical evidence that the recipient is alive. The Tudor government naturally kept lists of its pensioners. One for Westmorland, dated 6 Edward VI, shews that three pensioners, an ex-canon of Shap and two chantry priests, had died since the last return.[28]

The fate of the monastic churches varied: some like Carlisle, Cartmel, and St. Bees are in constant use to-day, the two latter as parish churches. The naves of Lanercost

* That is pre 1939 values.

and Holm Cultram are also now parochial; in the case of
the former much of the chancel and transepts with the
Dacre tombs still remains.   Extensive ruins of Furness
also stand.   At Carlisle and Lanercost parts of the
monastic buildings also remain in use.

It is sometimes said that monastic lands were given
away to the king's friends.   Some people, like the duke
of Norfolk who rendered valuable service to the Crown
by putting down the Pilgrimage of Grace, were perhaps
rewarded in this way.   Others had to pay for them: Dr.
Thomas Leigh, who had surely earned the king's thanks,
paid £98. 11. 8. a year for the lease of the possessions of
St. Bees, and even then only got it for twenty one years.[29]
Sir Thomas Dacre, the king's servant, was only charged
nine shillings yearly for the lease of Lanercost; when his
son wanted it renewed, however, Edward VI raised the
rent to £55. 17. 7. before giving him a new grant.[30]

Our story must now go back in time to tell of the
Pilgrimage of Grace, which started in October 1536.[31]
If its true meaning is to be understood another event—
the Rebellion of the Earls in 1569—must also be taken into
account.

" The movement which culminated in the Rebellion of the
Earls and their followers was essentially retrograde.   Its aim was
the perpetuation of a system of religion, of government, and of
rural economy, which the mass of the nation had out-grown;
and its failure was necessary to complete the real as opposed to
the nominal union of the English kingdom.   Nevertheless,
recognising that it was well that Elizabeth completed the work of
stamping out Feudalism and bringing the North under control,
which her father had begun, we may still be permitted to regret
the cost."[32]

" The work . . . which her father had begun," that is
both movements had fundamentally the same cause:
the desire of the North to preserve its feudal and catholic
traditions unchanged and the determination of the
monarchy to break them.   The Rising of the Earls must

be described in its chronological place.   But the essential oneness of the two revolts and their importance as a turning point in Northern history has not perhaps been sufficiently emphasised in local histories.

The immediate causes of the Pilgrimage of Grace were the changes in religion introduced by Henry's government and the dissolution of the smaller monasteries.   Its spirit is best expressed in the oath the insurgents administered; it was probably composed by Robert Aske.

" The Oath of the Honourable Men:
  Ye shall not enter this our Pilgrimage of Grace for the Commonwealth but only for the love that ye do bear unto Almighty God his faith, and to Holy Church militant and the maintenance thereof to the preservation of the King's person and his issue, to the purifying of the nobility, and to expulse all villein blood and evil councillors against the Commonwealth from his Grace and his Privy Council of the same.   And that ye shall not enter into our said Pilgrimage for no particular profit to your self, nor to do any displeasure to any private person, but by Counsel of the Commonwealth, nor slay nor murder for no envy, but in your hearts put away all fear and dread, and take afore you the Cross of Christ, and in your hearts His faith, the Restitution of the Church, the suppression of these Heritics and their opinions, by all the holy contents of this book."

This oath gives the aims of the ruling spirits in the rising.   The leader Robert Aske, a barrister, was the younger son of an ancient Yorkshire house, and with him were representatives of most of the great families of the north east.   Two brothers of the earl of Northumberland, the heir of the earl of Westmorland, 5 barons, 23 knights and 27 gentlemen attended the Pilgrims Council at Pontefract.   Conspicuous by their absence were Henry Clifford, earl of Cumberland, a man well hated in his own county and a favourite of the king's, and his neighbour, William, Lord Dacre, who had only just been released from the Tower after a trial for treason and so, perhaps, thought it wise to keep quiet.

While the restoration of the monks—for instance those at Cartmel were put back into their priory—was the chief motive of the insurgents, their religious aims did not stop there. The people of Brough demanded of their vicar that he should pray for the bishop of Rome; those of Kendal that he should " bid the beads* the old way and pray for the pope."[33] And all agreed that heretics and their books be suppressed. Other religious grievances were of a more general, even a more up-to-date, character: the Commons of Westmorland wished to have power to choose their own priest, to remove him, if he misconducted himself, and to turn out the non-resident clergy.

There were also other demands: those at the top of the social scale, and probably others also, wished to get rid of Cromwell and other new men of " villein blood "; those at the bottom to have their agrarian grievances redressed; these were especially strong in Cumberland and Westmorland. During the early sixteenth century much land had been enclosed and sheep farms developed. As a result the lord, becoming more independent, had increased the sum he demanded in fines: the Commons of Kendal complained that where the gressum or fine had been only £2. 13. 4 it was now £40. This state of affairs would obviously be more felt in the pastoral country than in the agricultural lands.

Thus the Pilgrimage was the result of a combined dislike of religious innovations, which the gentry were chiefly concerned to combat, and economic changes against which the Commons rose.

Considering that this was largely a religious movement it is curious how little part the clergy took in it. The archbishop of York seems to have been hostile. Tunstal of Durham fled.[34] Bishop Kytte was not so discreet: " ther is on grett ryott foundon to be doune by the commandment of the byschoppe off Kerlesle,"[35] wrote

* ' Bid the beads,' means at the bidding prayer before the sermon.

Sir Thomas Wharton in August 1537. The parochial clergy were on the whole hostile or at least neutral. Probably there was little love lost between them and the monks, who were naturally more interested. The abbot of Holm Cultram led his tenants to Cockermouth and ordered his monks to take part in a solemn procession, asking for God's blessing on the rising. The abbot of Furness and the prior of Cartmel, more cautious, departed to the safety of the royal camp, but two monks of Furness were imprisoned at Lancaster and several canons of Cartmel executed.[36]

The rising in these counties began with a summons to the Pilgrimage, received in Kendal on 14 October 1536. The contingent from there reached Lancaster on 28 October. On the same day a meeting was called for Stake Green, near Hawkshead. The district of Furness was ablaze with ardour; some 3000 men joined from the fells to the north and east of the abbey. As these were mostly tenants of the monks, it may be considered evidence of their local popularity as landlords. This is borne out from other sources.[37] On the day following the summons to Kendal, the curate of Kirkby Stephen ' did not bid St. Luke's day as a holy day,' which so angered his parishioners that they threatened to kill him. Probably on the same day, Robert Thompson, vicar of Brough, who was a popular preacher and regarded by the people as a prophet, read a summons from the Commons to his flock. The men of the two parishes marched down the Eden: those on one side under Robert Pullen to Penrith, those on the other under Nicholas Musgrave to Lowther. Penrith had already risen and chosen four captains: Anthony Hutton, John Beck, Gilbert Whelpdale, and Thomas Burbeck, who taking the names of Charity, Faith, Poverty, and Pity, wrote letters to the neighbouring gentry summoning them to take the Pilgrim's Oath. In answer Sir Edward Musgrave and

his people from Edenhall came in. On 23 October the
Commons of Caldbeck, Greystoke, Hutton, Skelton, and
Castle Sowerby rose, bringing with them Dr. Towneley,
Richard Bewley and other gentlemen. Sir John Lowther
also came, though his attitude is doubtful: the Commons
certainly thought of him as a friend. Two days later a
big gathering was held at Kitwatling How and the
tenants of the great abbey of Holm Cultram joined up.
At that meeting Dr. Towneley—chancellor of the diocese,
and pluralist vicar of Melmerby, Lazonby, and Dufton[38]—
and the vicars of Castle Sowerby and Edenhall were
instructed to teach the Commons in the Faith. A grim
announcement was also put out that if the other clergy of
the district did not come in they would strike off the heads
of those who had done so. Next day Mass was said at
Penrith, and Robert Thompson, preaching on the Ten
Commandments, shewed how all the present troubles had
arisen from people not following them.

So far the rising had spread without any opposition, but
the attitude of Carlisle still remained undecided. At first
it was neutral; the burgesses sending a message that
though they would not take the oath, they would otherwise be with the Commons. So they set out for the city.
But when Sir Thomas Clifford, son of the earl of Cumberland promised to be their captain, the citizens refused to
admit the rebels, now some 15000 strong, who then
withdrew to Cockermouth, where they were joined by the
abbot of Holm Cultram. From there the Pilgrims
Council ordered Sir John Lowther, who had prudently
retired to Carlisle, the abbot, Dr. Towneley, Richard
Blencow, and Thomas Dalston to go to the city and order
the mayor and townsfolk to take the oath at Burford Oak
on Broadfield.

Meanwhile as a result of negotiations conducted by
Robert Aske, and others on behalf of the Pilgrims, with
the duke of Norfolk, the king's commander, a truce had

been reached. So Sir Christopher Dacre, coming from Carlisle on 3 November with this news, was able to persuade the rebels, though with great reluctance, to accept it and return home. Clarenceux King at Arms proclaimed the royal pardon throughout these counties, beginning at Kendal on 19 December, and ending at Cockermouth a week later. Whether Henry intended to abide by it must be left in doubt. On the east coast the truce was generally kept; on the west there was soon more trouble.

This second rising was preceded by wholesale attacks on tithe barns. Its spirit is best seen in the statement of the Commons of Westmorland to Lord Darcy, one of the Pilgrims leaders, that they would admit no gentlemen to their Council, as they were afraid of them. That is this rising was purely economic and not religious in its motives and demands. Starting at Kirkby Stephen and Appleby, it spread to Penrith and Cockermouth. On 16 February the insurgents, some 6000 in number, again mustered on Broadfield Moor, intending to attack Carlisle. But they were quite leaderless and, having shot off all their arrows at the city, broke and fled when Sir Christopher Dacre unexpectedly appeared with 500 spearmen; that was the end of it—except for the executions: 66 poor men, 45 from Westmorland and 21 from Cumberland, were hung in chains in their villages, and their bodies left for all to gaze upon. But love was not to be gainsaid, even by Henry VIII. The story of the devotion of the widows, preserved in a document entitled " Sayings of certain women concerning the taking down from the gallows and burial of their husbands," is a pathetic one. A single example must suffice:

" Of Percival Hudson's wife: brought her husband to Torpeno churchyard, but the vicar would not suffer him to be buried, so she took him back to the place he had lain, and three days after she and a woman she had hired buried him in Torpeno Church-yard at night."*

So ended the Pilgrimage of Grace and its aftermath, so far as these counties were concerned, but the struggle between the catholic and feudal North and the government in London, with its policy of centralisation, was not yet over. Another outbreak had to come, and more blood had to be shed before the North was finally broken, but over thirty years was to pass before that happened.

Meanwhile Bishop Kytte had died in London on 19 June 1537. He was buried in Stepney parish church, where a stone placed to his memory[39] still remains. He was called the " flatteryng Byshope of Carel " by the earl of Northumberland;[40] perhaps not unreasonably judging by a letter he sent to Wolsey: " though in the extreme parts of the realm, yet on my fidelity, there is no day, but I think of your Grace and not many nights, but I dream of your Grace, written in faith, without flattery."[41] But he had the virtue of loyalty to a patron in adversity: he lent the fallen cardinal some necessities of household furniture when he was " without beds, sheets, table cloths, cups and dishes to eat our meat or to lie in."[42]

Robert Aldrich, or Aldridge, provost of Eton,[43] nominated to the see on 18 July 1537, was consecrated at the Savoy chapel by the bishop of London. The temporalities were restored on 24 August. He retained the provostship of Eton till 1547 though he was requested in 1540 not to linger there, but to return home to his

---

* Those condemned came from the following places: Westmorland: Kirkby Stephen 5, . . . 1, Mallerstang 8, Brough 1, (Temple) Sowerby 4, Stainmore 2, Nateby 1, Soulby 2, Little Musgrave 2, Asby 2, St. Michael, Appleby 8, St. Lawrence, Appleby 3, Bongate 1, King's Meaburn 1, Dufton 1, Smardale 1, Hartley 2,

Cumberland: Penrith 8, (including Sir Edw. Perith, chaplain), Greystoke 1, Newton (Reigny) 2, Cockermouth 2, Brigham 1, Embleton 1, Eaglesfield 1, Pardshaw 1 (this was Percival Hudson buried at Torpenhow), Branthwaite 1, Dearham 1, Talentire 1, Wythop 1.

This list makes 66, but the duke of Norfolk gave the figure at 74. (o.s. xiv, 353-4).

diocese and to remain there, feeding his people both with his preaching and hospitality.[44]

The affect of the Pilgrimage of Grace can probably be seen in Henry's reorganisation of the government of the northern counties—the substitution of the Council of the North as the executive authority, in place of some great feudal lord, and the creation of the diocese of Chester in 1541.

This year also saw the foundation, the charter bearing date 8 May, of the cathedral church of the Holy and Undivided Trinity of Carlisle in place of the priory church of St. Mary. The foundation was on a generous scale, consisting of a dean, 4 canons, 8 minor canons, a deacon and sub-deacon, 4 lay clerks, a master of the choristers, 6 choristers, a teacher of boys to be instructed in grammar, 6 poor men to be maintained at the charge of the church, a verger, 2 sub-sacrists, a porter, who should also be the barber, a butler, who should also be the caterer, a cook and sub-cook: in all 15 clergy, 10 choirmen and boys, a schoolmaster, 7 lay helpers and 6 poor men.[45]

Nearly thirty years have passed since the Scots were mentioned. Now, a new generation having grown up since Flodden and the people beginning to feel in good fettle again, a Scots army invaded Cumberland in the autumn of 1542. The result was the battle of Solway Moss. " Never before had there been a more pitiful defeat. 14000 men were completely vanquished by less than 3000. It was a rout rather than a battle." To add to their troubles the men of Liddesdale, their own compatriots, in order that " they should the more spedely flye . . . toke also their botes from them."[46] Surely to a Scotsman this must have seemed like adding insult to injury.

Meanwhile Henry's appetite for Church lands seems to have increased rather than decreased by the substantial meal of the monastic foundations. Others had been following the example of their royal master which gave a further reason for urgency. So an Act was passed to restrain those who, pretending to be " donors foundors or patrons of . . . colleges frechappelles chauntries hospitalles," had expelled the priests, wardens, or other officers. In order to make certain that they obeyed, the king's 'most lovinge humble and obedient subjects' were asked to enact that all these foundations should be dissolved.[47] Parliament duly agreed on 4 November 1545. One example of how some of his " loving subjects " had tried to get in before their master is shewn by the fate of the chantry of St. Andrew, Penrith, founded by William Strickland. His heir, through his daughter, Sir John Lowther not unreasonably believed that if any one was to get the lands, worth £6 a year with which it had been endowed, he should do so. Thus when the royal commissioners arrived they found that nothing was left to maintain the priest, who received his yearly stipend from Sir John; like master, like man.*

But Henry died before any more was done. During his lifetime Catholicism remained the legal religion. The connection between the papal see and England had been severed; monasticism suppressed; and various abuses which had led, so it was believed, to superstition abolished; beyond that Henry had not gone.

The boy Edward was the new king. His father had provided a Council carefully balanced between those who wished for further changes and those who did not. With the former gaining power, the Reformation proper began with the completion of Henry's plan for robbing the guilds and chantries. Another commission was therefore appointed on 14 February 1548. Its report was on the same

---

* To carry the story further: the Tudors were quite equal to keeping the Lowthers in their place. Queen Elizabeth, in 1564, founded a Grammar School in the town and endowed it with £6 yearly, from the lands of Richard Lowther, Sir John's grandson. (*Miscellany Accounts*, Nicolson, 155 and *V.C.H.* II, 55).

lines as the first one. Here is an example from the
survey of 1546. " The Chaunterie of William Middyltone
in the Parish Churche of Kyrbilonsdaile." Then follows
the list of lands, mostly in Yorkshire, belonging to it,
worth in all £4. 13. 4.

The list of plate and ornaments was:—

" Furst one chales valued	xl s.
One vestemente	x s.
iij olde vestementes	vi s. viii d.
ij alter clothes, ij Corporax	v s.
A Sacringe belle and crewet	
one ' bake ' tabernacle Towelle	
Chiste and j pax	xiij s. iiij d.

Lxxv s."[48]

The prime purpose of the chantries was the celebration
of Mass for the benefit of the souls of those the founder
desired to have remembered. Opinion then, and now,
must differ as to whether this is a desirable thing or not.
But the chantry priest often did more than that: at
Cockermouth he taught ' a grammar schole '; at Hutton
he said the canonical hours with the rector and was
subject to him in all canonical and lawful commands—
this was the almost universal custom; at Torpenhow,
where there were three priests and a sub-deacon, it is
inconceivable that they did not do some parochial work.[49]

More important, for its effect on the working of the
Church, was the dissolution of the collegiate churches.
That at Greystoke staffed a parish of nearly 8 square
miles, in which there were 3000 ' howselinge ' people
(communicants), with a master and 6 priests; and that
at Kirkoswald served that parish and Dacre, with their
1000 communicants, by staff of 8 clergy. The pensions
granted were not ungenerous: the master at Greystoke
received £19 a year and at Kirkoswald £17. 10. 0.; the
other priests £5 each. The result on the religious life of
the parishes concerned must have been disastrous. Greystoke, instead of being served by 7 priests, had 3;·

Kirkoswald and Dacre instead of 8 only 2. The district
chapelry at Mosser,[50] with its chapel and priest, was
absorbed into the parish of Brigham.* Even hospitals
were not spared; that called " le Spytelle " in Wigton
founded and endowed by Henry Percy, earl of Northumberland, as well as similar foundations at Kendal and
Kirkby Lonsdale were closed.[51] The evil results of all
this will be seen later on in the description of the state of
religion and of the people as seen by the Elizabethan
bishops.

But the loving care of Edward's advisers for the souls
of the people was not yet assuaged and their fears of their
being endangered by superstitious practices not yet
removed; or was it perhaps that they were still short of
money? Opinions must differ. But it is certain that,
having deprived the unfortunate people of the services of
many of the clergy, they now turned their energies to
taking the ornaments and furniture of their churches. In
1552, commissioners were ordered to seize all the goods,
plate, jewels and ornaments of the parish churches and
chapels, " leving nevir the less in every parishe churche or
chappell of common resorte two or more challesses or
cupps according to the multitude of the people ". . .
Churches were also entitled to retain " a proper cover for
the communyon table " and a surplice or surplices for the
minister. But all copes, vestments, altar cloths, and
other ornaments, as well as all parcels or pieces of metal,
" except the metal of greatt bell,"[52] were ordered to
be sold to the king's use. The residue of the linen,
ornaments, and implements was to be distributed
freely among the poor. The inventory of church goods
for Cumberland[53] was taken by Sir Thomas Dacre, Sir
Richard Musgrave, Robert Lamplugh, William Pickering,

---

* But appears to have continued in use as it is mentioned in the *Visitation
returns of* 1674 (Chester Diocesan Muniments).

Thomas Salkeld and Anthony Barwis. That for West-morland has been lost.*

Some curious facts arise from a study of the inventories: if they are correct they shew the dreadful poverty of Cumberland churches. According to them Bridekirk possessed no chasuble, nor did Dalston, the bishop's parish church: the former indeed had 2 copes and the latter a cope and 2 tunicles. Skelton had no vestments; nor had Addingham. In Coupland deanery: neither Bootle, Embleton, Nether Wastdale, nor St. John's, Beckermet possessed any, though the first had a cope; Eskdale had 3 vestments but no chalice. The important church of Brigham, which in 1348 had in its chantry chapel alone 7 chasubles, 3 tunicles and a dalmatic,[54] now had a couple each of the first two and none of the last; Egremont, with a large castle within it, had 3 vestments and 2 tunicles, but neither parish possessed a cope. Greystoke was reasonably well off for vestments† but, though it had several altars, had only one pair of candle-sticks; Penrith had none, nor did the cathedral; Kirkoswald, another rich parish had two, but they were of latten, the cheapest material. And none of these churches was in immediate proximity to the Border; it is not surprising to find Stapleton, Arthuret, and Nether Denton possessing only tin chalices: the two former with one vestment each, the latter with none. This explanation cannot account for the poverty of churches as far south as those mentioned.

It is almost unbelievable that these returns were true. A chasuble was an essential part of the celebrant's apparel at Mass: tunicles and copes were by no means so

---

* Only the commissioners names survive: The earl of Cumberland, Sir Walter Strickland, Nicholas Layborne, John Myddleton, Thomas Blynkyn-sopp, and Ambrose Middleton. (*Old Church Plate in Diocese of Carlisle*, ed. Chancellor Ferguson, 313).

† It had two sets of blue ones which suggests that the use of the diocese of Carlisle was either that of Sarum or York.

necessary yet churches had them and not chasubles.
Candlesticks were required to hold candles for lighting
purposes as well as for ceremonial. Of course, in some
cases these may have been of painted wood and not worth
returning. One inevitable deduction from the facts is
that many church ornaments were hidden and not
included in the lists;* another that this was done with the
connivance of the commissioners.

The first Reformed Prayer Book was put forth in 1549,
Bishop Aldrich voting against it in the House of Lords.
The second, and more Protestant one, followed in 1552.
No evidence of local reaction is known, but, judging from
the Pilgrimage of Grace and the concealment of church
ornaments, there seems no reason to doubt that both were
bitterly resented. There is one point in connection with
the English service books which is of some moment: to
what extent did our ancestors understand Cranmer's
classical English? Bishop Robinson writing to Cecil in
1599 says of his clergy " the far greater number is utterly
unlearned, unable to read English truly and distinctly."[55]
Nowadays, though dialects still remain, there is also a
common English tongue. But in the sixteenth century
everyone spoke a dialect. The picture of a local clerk,
who had never been beyond these counties and never
heard another tongue, trying to translate Cranmer's
English to a Cumbrian or Westmerian farmer, never
outside his own district, would be humorous if it was not
pathetic. Much of Cranmer's language must have been
simply meaningless to our local folk.

But there was no open resistance; Henry VIII's
hangings after the Pilgrimage of Grace probably prevented
that. Bishop Aldrich was certainly not in favour of the
changes. He hung on to his office, however, and the
clergy seem to have followed suit, except for Lancelot

* Since this was written I notice Mr. T. H. B. Graham came to the same
conclusion (N.S., XXV, 110).

O

Salkeld, last prior and first dean of Carlisle, who retired on a pension of £40 a year. The evidence of the inventory of 1552 and what happened in Elizabeth's reign suggest that many of the clergy, with the connivance of the bishop and the gentry, just carried on and took no notice of these new fangled notions from London. The state of affairs revealed in Crosthwaite in 1571 can be cited in support of this opinion.*

There is no doubt that the restoration of the " old religion " by Queen Mary was generally welcomed. Fuller accounts for there being no Protestant martyrs† in these counties by the remark that the people were " nuzzled in ignorance and superstition."[56] The late dean was restored and his successor, who had never visited Carlisle, ejected. The incumbents of Ormside, Bridekirk and Bootle[57] were deprived of their livings, the two former because they were married.‡

This diocese must rank Queen Mary among its bene-factors. While one of her donations to it—the restoration of some of the benefices seized by her father—was frustrated by her sister, another—the grant of the advowson of the four prebendal stalls in the cathedral to the bishop—has not been interfered with.[58]

We must also remember the queen's gift to Trinity College, Cambridge, of the valuable advowsons of Kendal, Kirkby Lonsdale, and Heversham. Apparently being concerned, perhaps not unreasonably, as to the health of her father's soul, she desired to make provision for

---

* P. 206.

† While it is true no one was burnt within the diocese, Cumberland had a martyr at this time—one Isabel, wife of John Foster of the parish of St. Bride, Fleet Street, who was burnt 27 January 1556. According to Foxe (*Acts & Monuments*, vii, 748) she " was born in Greystock, in the diocese of Carlisle."

‡ As a comparison it is interesting to note that there were 93 deprivations, mostly for marriage in Essex in this reign; clear evidence of the greater in-fluence of Protestantism in the South. (*Trans. R.H.S.* XXII, 141).

prayers for him.   But her spiritual advisers told her that
it was useless to petition the pope to allow public ones for
this purpose as he would never permit it for one who had
died " so notorious a schismatic."   Presumably the pope
felt either that Henry was so thoroughly damned that
nothing could be done about it, or, that even if something
could be done, he was not going to do it. ⎸ So the queen
instead made this gift to Trinity in his memory.   Rather
a pathetic story that sheds some light on the affectionate
character of a much abused woman.[59]

Meanwhile Bishop Aldrich had died at Horncastle on
5 March 1556, where he was probably buried.   Little is
known of his character; he seems to have been a tolerant
man of scholarly attainments, probably without any very
strong religious convictions.

Owen Oglethorpe, dean of Windsor was consecrated by
Archbishop Heath of York at Cheswick on 15 August
1557.   The temporalities were restored on 28 January.
Then, on 17 November 1558 Mary died, and English
religion was again in the melting pot of Tudor policy.

CHAPTER II.

THE REIGN OF QUEEN ELIZABETH.

FOR a short time after Elizabeth ascended the throne, Mass continued to be said. Then on Christmas Day, when Bishop Oglethorpe was the celebrant, she sent a message ordering him not to elevate the Host, because she did not like the ceremony. He displayed some courage in refusing, and the queen shewed her displeasure by leaving the chapel after the Gospel.

The immediate question was: who should crown her? The archbishop of Canterbury was dead; Heath of York refused; so the responsibility fell to his suffragans: Tunstall of Durham was too old. Oglethorpe alone remained, he agreed to act. Tradition says that on his way south he consecrated the chapel at Watermillock "as appears by a memorandum in an old Bible."* So on 15 January 1559, Elizabeth was crowned with the traditional ceremonial.

By this act the bishop earned for himself a niche in national history. What was his motive? It has been said that he was "a man of no strength of character" who accepted the religious changes "rather than forego the dignity and emoluments of office."[1] Perhaps a more kindly judgment is also a true one, and that he was, like Tunstall, a typical Englishman and a moderate.

As Nicholas Sander reported to Cardinal Morone:

---

* *Survey of the Lakes*, James Clarke, 2nd ed. 1789, 26. But there was certainly a chapel there before this (*V.C.H.*, II, 208), so it may have been only the delayed consecration of an old building.

" the bishop at length undertook the ceremony, after many of the others had been asked in vain, not as a favourer of heresy, but lest, if no one should anoint her, the queen should thereby be enraged, and made more inclined to overthrow religion. Things, moreover, were not yet so desperate, as to prevent many from hoping that she might be turned from her purpose."[2]

But the result was the opposite of what the bishop hoped and on 18 April 1559, by a majority of only three in the House of Lords—Oglethorpe being a dissentient— a new Act of Uniformity was passed, repealing much of the legislation of the previous reign and re-establishing the royal supremacy. Oglethorpe, refusing with the other Marian bishops to take the necessary oath, was deprived on 21 June 1559 and imprisoned. This only meant living with Bishop Grindal of London. As his will is dated 10 November 1559, he was probably already a sick man.[3] He died on 31 December and was buried in the church of St. Dunstan in the West on 2 January.[4] He left money for the endowment of a grammar school at Tadcaster and for the erection of an almshouse there for twelve poor people. We may perhaps feel that the language of Roman piety—" there is no need here to repeat again the testimonies of other writers who have named him amongst the confessors and martyrs "[5]—is somewhat exaggerated. But our unfortunate ancestors, shortly to be delivered over to the persecuting zeal of Bishop Best, must often have cast their minds back to the kindly memory of the last ones of ' the old religion,' under whom there were no martyrs.

By the new Act of Uniformity parliament finally decided that the Reformation was to prevail in England. The new Prayer Book came into force on 24 June, and on the same day letters patent were issued for a royal visitation of the northern province.[6] The government, knowing that the country was in a highly inflammable state, proceeded cautiously. The chief duty of the visitors was to enforce the Prayer Book; the question of taking the oath acknowledging the royal supremacy was not pressed as yet.

The commissioners for the diocese of Carlisle began their visitation of the cathedral on 3 October 1559. After prayers and a sermon by Edwin Sandys,* they commenced their task. The dean, Lancelot Salkeld, who had been the last prior, was the first to subscribe; perhaps somewhat unexpectedly as he had been deprived under Edward VI. The prebendaries and minor canons, except one detained in the country by ill health, also subscribed. The commissioners found everything satisfactory in the capitular body, except that some of the prebendaries had not been in residence, nor kept their quarterly sermons.

Next day the clergy and churchwardens of the deaneries of Carlisle and Allerdale were summoned and two days later those of Cumberland and Westmorland attended at Penrith. At this session the commissioners sequestered the rectory of Longmarton but the incumbent does not seem to have been deprived. The result of the parochial visitation was not, from the government's point of view, so satisfactory as that of the dean and chapter. Nearly a third of the clergy absented themselves and were pronounced contumacious. It is difficult to be certain what these figures imply as some would have genuine causes for absence such as ill health; others as pluralists might only attend for one of their livings.† But even when this is taken into account the figures suggest a number of intentional absentees. The commissioners also had to restore to their benefices the incumbents of Ormside, Bridekirk and Bootle, deprived in the last reign,[7] and

---

* He was of Hawkshead stock. There is a monument to his parents in the church, he founded the grammar school there. He became bishop of Worcester, then of London and finally archbishop of York.

† For instance George Neville, archdeacon of Carlisle, appeared as rector of Great Salkeld at Penrith, and not at Carlisle as rector of Dalston, and so was pronounced contumacious at the latter.

obtain reports from the church wardens on the state of
their parishes. To judge from their returns there was
little wrong; Morland,* Great Salkeld, Shap and Skelton
had no register book, Great Salkeld church was in decay;
Warcop lacked a paraphrase; Skelton and Kirkandrews
had no incumbents. The only reports of breaches of
morality were from Cliburn and Newbiggin.

As all the Marian bishops had died or been deprived,
Elizabeth was left with the problem of filling their places.
The see of Carlisle was first offered to Edwin Sandys; he
refused it, as he told Peter Martyr in a letter in April 1560,
in which he also mentions his work in the northern
visitation in taking down and burning " all images of
every kind."   Having declined it himself he tried
unsuccessfully to get the celebrated Bernard Gilpin to
take it.   So the see remained vacant for nearly two years
before it was accepted by John Best,† who was consecrated at London House by the archbishop of York on
2 March 1561.

So far the government had only demanded of the clergy
adherence to the new Prayer Book and even in that had
been by no means generally successful in the northern
counties.   Early in this year the president of the Council
of the North was ordered to inquire into certain secret
conventicles of recusants.   In May a commission was
appointed, of which the new bishop was a member, to
administer the oath of allegiance to all ecclesiastical
persons, including those who had failed to take it at the
previous visitation, and to certify the result to the royal
courts.   The time had come for a real trial of strength
between the old and new religions.

The bishop, therefore, set out on his first visitation and
found that after three sermons in the cathedral church

* But its register dates from 1538 !

† He was born, according to Hutchinson (II, 630), in the southern part of
Yorkshire of parents of a low station.   There was certainly no family of
visitation rank of this name in the county in 1585.

the common people with much rejoicing affirmed that
they had been deceived. The same thing happened
throughout the county. Everywhere the nobility and
gentry received him with much civility. He was indeed
unable to express his obligation to Lord Wharton and
Lady Musgrave, his daughter, who had entertained him
" for ye Gospell's sake." All was serene, except for one
layman, Lord Dacre, and one body of people: " the
priestes, wicked ympes of antichrist," as the bishop put
it in a letter to the Council, which goes on to describe
them as

" for ye moste parte very ignorante and stubborne, past measure
false and sotle: onlie feare maketh them obedient. Onlie three
absentid themselves in my visitation, and fled because they wolde
not subscribe, of ye which two belonge to my Lord Dacres and
one to ye Earle of Cumberland. Unto which I have assigned
dayes undre danger of deprivation. About XII or XIII churches
in Gylsland, all undre my Lorde Dacre do not appeare, but
bearying themselves upon my Lorde refuse to come in, and at
Stapilton and sondrye of ye other have yet masse openly at
whome my Lorde and his officers wynke, and although they
stand excommunycate, I do no furdre medle with them untill I
have some aide from my lorde president, and ye consaile in ye
northe."

Eventually only Hugh Hodgson, rector of Skelton, and
Robert Thompson, rector of Beaumont, both churches in
the Dacre patronage, refused to accept the new legislation.
The government behaved quite reasonably with these
men. The visitation took place in May, and it was not
until early in August that Hodgson was arrested; even
then he was given another chance at York. He again
refused and was deprived. In the case of Thompson
matters appear to have been delayed still longer, as his
successor was not appointed till 1562. It seems doubtful
if these two men would have acted thus but for the
encouragement of Lord Dacre, a man in Bishop Best's
words, " something too mighty in this country and as it

were a prince." These, with Bishop Oglethorpe, were the only victims in one of the most Catholic parts of the country. It is clear that if the clergy did not accept the new order with alacrity, accept it in the end they did.

The bishop had no sooner got one section of the " wicked ymps of antichrist " in order than he had trouble with another—the cathedral chapter. The dean, a layman, was a perpetual absentee. One cause of episcopal complaint was the way in which the chapter let leases of their property to their own relations for long periods, but more important was their lack of religious zeal and understanding. The bishop complained that " the citie is decaid by theym, and Godes truth sclanderyled." Things, however, began to mend, from his point of view, in 1563, when Barnaby Kirkbride, an ex-monk, died. In a letter to Cecil asking for the place for one Gregory Scott,* a man " well learned and of good zeale and synceritie," the bishop complained that all the rest of the prebendaries were " ignorante preistes or olde unlearned monkes."

But the problem of the laity remained. In 1562 when the bishop wrote to Cecil complaining of the evil influence of the earl of Cumberland and Lord Dacre, so nervous was he of his position that he sent his views in a secret message. He was not alone in this opinion; Edmund Grindal shared it.† Writing to Cecil in 1563 he asked him to be good to the bishop of Carlisle:

"there were marvellous practices to deface him in my lawless country. If the two noblemen of which he complained were touched by the authority of the Privy Council, it would be a terror to the rest."

* He spent his time in refuting Romish errors in abusive verse, " very plainly, not ably and pleasantly." He was rector of Workington 1575-7 (N.S. x, 144) and vicar of St. Michael's, Appleby, 1569-76, as well as chancellor of the diocese (N. & B., I, 342) so at any rate he had ' good zeale ' in feathering his own nest.

† Bishop of London and archbishop of Canterbury; founder of St. Bees School. He was probably born in the parish (O.S. xv, 229).

Our story is working up to the conclusion of the years of open or covert war, which began with the Pilgrimage of Grace in 1536 and reached their climax in the Rising of the Earls in 1569.[8]   For,

" although Henry could destroy the feudal power of the great Border families, he could not uproot ' the olde good-wyll of the people, deepe grafted in their harts, to their nobles and gentlemen,' and in Northumberland at least, ' they knew no other Prince but a Percy.'   In truth the Percies, the Dacres and the Nevilles were lords of the hearts of the North countrymen.   Ever they kept open house, with meat and drink for all who came; they rode always with a noble company of servants, and orderly apparel;   their amusement they sought not in dicing, but in pastimes of hawking and hunting."

So Northern resentment and hostility to the new order in Church and State, though slumbering, was ready to burst out again.

Though the earl of Cumberland is mentioned in Bishop Best's letter, he did not take part in the rising, probably because of his age—he died in January 1570, aged about 72—but the earls of Northumberland and Westmorland and Lord Dacre's heir did.   Their grievances were in part religious;   other causes of their resentment were the centralising policy of the administration and Elizabeth's confidence in the new type of government official like Cecil, rather than in the old feudal lord.   Further the earl of Northumberland had been compelled by a series of petty insults to resign his wardenship of the Marches, and to surrender to the Crown his claims to a copper mine at Newlands.

Then on 16 May 1568 Mary, queen of Scots, fleeing from her rebellious subjects, landed at Workington. Richard Lowther, deputy warden of the Marches, met her next day and conveyed her to Carlisle Castle.   The earl of Northumberland hearing of this claimed, as feudal overlord of Workington, the right to entertain her but

Lowther refused to surrender her, whereupon, as he reported:

'the earl used some rough wordes towards me, adding too that I was too mean a man to have such a charge . . . . and afterwards sent for me to his lodgging and . . . gave me great threatening with many evil wordes and a like language, calling me a varlet."*

Hearing of these matters the queen forbade the earl to interfere and summoned him to court.

Meanwhile the other peer mentioned by Bishop Best, Lord Dacre, had died in 1566; soon after his infant heir was accidentally killed. His uncle, Leonard Dacre, claimed to succeed, but, largely owing to the influence of the duke of Norfolk—stepfather and guardian of the three sisters of the late infant—the barony was adjudged to be in abeyance between them and not to belong to him, though he was the male heir.

So the government was faced with two disgruntled Border lords and a Scottish queen of Roman Catholic faith and great charm. But the rising was not merely caused by the pique of these lords. "England beyond Trent remained an overwhelmingly Catholic country."[9] For ten years the government had to some extent seemed willing to tolerate this. But now special preachers were ordered to travel from place to place; their reception can be gathered from the Spanish Ambassador informing his master that the heretic ministers were arriving in London, having been driven out by the people of the North. In the defence of their ancient faith lord and tenant found a bond of unity—feudal ties and religious fears made strong cement. Thus not only two peers but many gentry and yeomen were in a state of ferment at this time. On the eastern Marches there were also agrarian grievances, especially in Richmondshire, but not on this side, where

---

* *Annals of the House of Percy*, De Fonblanque, II, 17-18. The author observes that these words " form a curious illustration of the arrogance which the great nobles could display towards untitled gentlemen of social position little inferior to their own."

the customs of the Percy Honour of Cockermouth were the model followed.

After much talk and much hesitation, the earls of Northumberland and Westmorland, summoned to Court and fearing arrest, rose in rebellion in November 1569. Their wives seem to have been the real driving force in bringing the issue to a head. Neither peer had any gift of leadership or military experience. On 13 November the insurgents marched on Durham and entering the cathedral threw down the Communion Table, tore up the English Bible and Prayer Book and, having heard Mass, returned to Brancepath; a week later the same thing happened at Ripon. The response to the appeal of the earls had been and continued to be magnificent; next the rebels set out for York to release Mary, but she had been removed to Coventry. They hesitated, the government had time to collect its forces, and all was lost. The earls fled into Scotland, leaving their followers to Tudor mercy, which promptly executed some 800 of them. So all ended well for Queen Elizabeth, Protestantism, and the new gentry. In due course the Scots handed the earls over to their enemies: Thomas Percy was beheaded at York in August 1572; Charles Neville survived, an exile, for many years, dying in Flanders in 1601—the last earl of Westmorland of the ancient line.

Now for the effect of these events on this side of the Pennines: in Westmorland, Lord Wharton, Richard Lowther, and his brother Gerard were among the plotters —an order was issued for the latter's arrest. Fortunately for them their plan for joining the earls was frustrated and no Westmorland name occurs in the list of those attainted. But from Cumberland those of Richard Dacre of Aikton and William Dacre of St. Bees are included. That county, according to Lord Scrope, warden of the Western Marches, writing to Cecil on 30 November, stood in great peril for a few days, it would very likely have entered into rebellion, by means of some tenants of the earl of Northumberland, had not great care been exercised on his part to prevent it—these tenants in the lordship of Cockermouth were capable of mustering a force of 1200 men. At the same time the bishop of Carlisle complained about a conspiracy to kill him and take Carlisle Castle, of which he had charge during the absence of Lord Scrope.

Then, when all seemed over, "that cankered suttill traitor," Leonard Dacre suddenly rose in February 1570. But, though "hys footmen—in the words of Lord Huns-don—gave the prowdyst charge on my shott that I ever saw," defeat followed. Dacre fled to Scotland and thence to Flanders, where he died in 1573; his epitaph describes him as exiled for the sake of his religion.[10]

The failure of the rebellion settled that the two Dacre baronies were to go to the Howards, and the power of the Nevilles and Percies broken. The Marches of the North were no longer to be governed by their ancient rulers, but by royal officials. Twice, in 1536 and in 1569, the Tudors had taught the North a lesson: it did not need another. Thus the defeat of the Rising of the Earls is a turning point in Northern history.

Poor North! but it was inevitable. There could be no abiding peace and progress in this island until a strong central government was established. Our debt to the Tudors is that they did this. Thus few can wish the issue to be other than what it was; many will regret the price that had to be paid to achieve it.

Just after these events, on 22 May 1570, Bishop Best died and was buried in Carlisle Cathedral. The dean, Sir Thomas Smith, once described him as 'that busy bishop of Carlisle' who 'had more tongue than wisdom and goodwill.' It is one of the tragedies of our history that at this critical time its bishop was one of the embittered Marian exiles who came to their dioceses, not as Fathers in God, but as State policemen. He was the first married

holder of the see.   His wife's will, as Elizabeth Beste of
Tonbridge, Kent, widow of John Best, late bishop of
Carlisle is in the Probate office at York.

Richard Barnes,[11] suffragan bishop of Nottingham, was
elected on 25 June 1570; the temporalities were restored
on 26 July.   He was allowed to continue in his office as
chancellor of the cathedral church of York for one year
after his consecration and to hold the rectories of Stocke-
stay and Stonegrave for life, but, if he should obtain the
living of Rombaldkirk, he must resign the former.[12]

The bishop, writing to Cecil on 27 October 1570, told
him that he never came to a place in the land where more
attentive ear was given to the Word than in Carlisle.   He
found the people far more conformable and tractable than
in Yorkshire, and that, if he could receive the aid of the
civil power, he could promise " as faythfull, paynefull
(and if God will) effectual travell as ever poore Bishoppe
did performe within his cure."   The sting was in the
words ' the aid of the civil power'; it was duly given him.
With the authority of the High Commission he was
armed with coercive power sufficient to meet all his
wishes.

So in 1571 he set about a visitation of his diocese.   His
injunctions to the parish of Crosthwaite shew that it still
possessed various " relics and monuments of superstition
and idolatry," including 2 pixes of silver, a silver paxe, a
vestment with a cross of cloth of gold, a copper crosse, 2
chalices of silver, a paire of censures, a holy watter
tankard of brasse, 4 vestments, 3 tunicles, 5 chasubles,
with other vestments and church ornaments[13] The
churchwardens were ordered to sell these and buy " two
fayre large Communion Cups of silver and two fayre potts
or flaggons of tyne for the wyne."   The only other local
list of contemporary ornaments known is that for Carlisle
Cathedral, which shews how lamentably it had been
despoiled.[14]

The Crosthwaite injunctions throw light on the bishop's ideals for public worship. All parishioners of years of discretion and sufficiently instructed in the Christian faith were to communicate at least thrice in the parish church yearly—celebrations were only to be held there, not in the chapels* and the deacons and ministers of the latter were to assist the vicar. Apparently the Prayer Book rubric about confirmation was not considered binding. "A decent perclose of wood wherein the morninge and eveninge prayer shall be read (was) to be placed without the Quear doore." It was to be 12 ft. square and 5 ft. high, with seats and desks. Certain feast days were no longer to be observed and " the saying of divine service publiquely or the gathering together of a concourse of idle people to the church on such forbidden days was prohibited." Lastly it was ordered that " there be no communion celebrated at the burial of the dead, nor for any dead, nor any monethes mynds, anniversaryes or such superstitions used."† Heavy fines and penalties were to be inflicted for any disobedience.

The bishop's visitation of the cathedral on 26 October began with the calling of the roll in the upper chamber of the chapter house. More sermons than had heretofore been preached were ordered. Both adults and children were to receive instruction in the catechism in the parish church. All ministers were to receive the Holy Communion at least eight times a year. This order shews either the inability of the bishop to enforce the Prayer Book or his connivance at the breaking of its rubrics.‡

* This was also the custom at Greystoke in the next century (Parish Register in passim).

† It is worth noting, as evidence of the continuance in Elizabethan days of prayer for the faithful departed, that the grave-slab erected by John Brisco at Penrith to Richard Coldale of Plumpton, who died 27 Dec., 1562, begins and ends with the traditional formula: " Pray for the soul of . ." and " upon whose soul may God have mercy " (History of Penrith Church, D. Scott, 65) and that the inscription on a brass at Morland, dated 1562-3, ends with " on whose soule Jhu have mcy. ame " (o.s., xiii, 149).

‡ The fourth rubric at the end of ' The Communion.'

Apparently even in the reign of Elizabeth a bishop believed that he had authority to put forth an order in contradiction to them.

The bishop seems to have been well satisfied with the results of his visitation because he assured Cecil, on 19 October 1571, that there was no known gentleman or other within his little diocese that openly repined against religion. The only exceptions were the parishes of Arthuret, Kirklinton, Bewcastle and Stapleton, amongst the people of which there was neither fear, faith, virtue, nor knowledge of God, nor regard of any religion at all.

But the parting of the ways had come. The papacy had so far hesitated to take any decisive step against the queen, hoping she might prove amenable. The defeat of the Rising of the Earls and other causes having convinced it to the contrary, the bull of excommunication was published in London on 15 May 1570. Part of the government's answer was to require the clergy to subscribe to the Thirty Nine Articles. During the following years, 1571-6, seven clergy in this diocese were deprived. In some cases the reason is not given, so it cannot be said that every one was caused by a refusal to subscribe, but probably this was so. The incumbents concerned were those of: Dacre, 1571; Melmerby, Crosby Ravensworth,* Asby, 1572; Brougham, Isel, 1575; and Kirklinton, 1576.[15] It is noteworthy that the vicars of Melmerby, Asby, and Kirklinton had all been appointed since 1558, thus their refusal is presumptive evidence that men in favour of the ' old religion ' were still being given benefices. These numbers suggest that there was still a good deal of support for the ancient faith. Owing to livings sinking to curacies, with no appointment entered in the episcopal register, returns for only 73 are available: of these 7, or nearly 10 per cent were, for some reason, deprived in these years.

* He seems to have been restored.

These ejections naturally did not ease the problem of the supply of clergy. Between 1561-8 only 2 deacons and a priest received Holy Orders. But in 1569, 7 deacons and 4 priests were ordained. Bishop Barnes' register shews 70 deacons and 56 priests ordained between 1571-6, which suggests that the Church was beginning to get its house in order. The ordinands were almost invariably men of local birth. Most of them had apparently only been educated at village schools. In some of the lists the ages of the candidates are given, the rule of the ordinand having reached his 23rd year was usually enforced. Sometimes a candidate was admitted to the diaconate one day and to a benefice the next.[16]

The ideals placed before his clergy by Bishop Barnes at his primary visitation of the diocese of Durham at the beginning of 1578, immediately after his translation, probably shew the standard he tried to enforce in this one. The clergy were to learn St. Matthew's Gospel (St. Luke's was set in 1580) in Latin or English. All popish cere-monies, like masses for the dead, non prayer book baptismal rites, and holyday services, were to cease. Popish articles were to be removed, and popish paintings ' perjetted ' over with lime. The Sacrament was to be administered at least once a month—all over fourteen being obliged to partake of it thrice a year; and a catechismal test was imposed on communicants, god parents, and brides and bridegrooms. A yearly examin-ation was to be held in Lent and the clergy were to teach the children weekly and report those parents who would not send them. No fairs were to be held on Sundays, nor taverns to be open during divine service. The clergy were not to keep concubines, nor to frequent taverns or dances.[17]

We can see the other side of the picture from returns of the 1578 visitation of the diocese of Chester.[18] Though these refer to the Richmond deaneries, there is no reason to doubt that similar conditions prevailed in this diocese.

In several places ' relics of popery ' still remained: at Kirkby Lonsdale ' the roode lofte and the walls wherunto the aulter was wyned are not so defaced ' as is appointed; at Skelsmergh Chapel " the altar is defaced but not wholely pulled down "; and at Selside " the altar is not pulled down."

On the whole the church fabrics and parsonages were in a fair state of repair but at Kirkby Lonsdale " the body of the church is in decay in roofe and glass," and at Ponsonby " the glasse windowes in the chancel are in decay." At St. John's Beckermet " the chancel is fallen downe to the grounde and so hath bene these seven yeres "; and at Lorton " the chancell is in very great decay." This was also the case at Brigham and ' hath been these twenty years '; while at Aldingham ' the chancel and parsonage hous be in great decay '. At Egremont they are " in great ruyne and decay in ther person his defaulte," and at Kirkby Ireleth " the vycar kepeth no hous, his lyvinge is so smale.'

Light is thrown on the behaviour of the clergy. At Aldingham " the pson beinge lately admitted is as yet not resyedent but a student at Oxforde "; at Dalton " the vycar kepeth no hospytalyty, the lyvinge is very small," At Egremont " ther pson is not resydent neither doth he make any yearly distrybucion to the poore of the parishe." The same complaint is made at Whitbeck, Lamplugh and Burton. At Kendal " the vycar doth not vysyte sycke being therunto requyred.' The curate of Satter-thwaite " dyd not conscrate at Easter last past.' At Urswick, Torver, and Coniston they want a curate

As to the church services: at Loweswater " they have no servyse but as they provide themselves," and at Hawkshead " they have no svyse upon Wednesdayes and Fridaies, they want a surplesse and the mynister weareth none." At Colton also they had no services on these days, and at Bootle and Dean " no surplesse," though at the latter " they have p'pared money for one." Many places, Gosforth and Millom among others, have had no sermons: at Waberthwaite " they have but had one sermon last yere," while at Haile " they have had no smons these many yeres." At several places " that they have no quarter sermons " is noted. In Windermere and other parishes " they use no perambulation." At Kendal the following return is made: " ther be dyvers chappells in the paryshe wherin ther is no servyce sayd because ther resorteth therunto no company "—no reason is given for this.

As to the furnishing of the churches: several places— Ulverston, " they want a slyr cuppe," and Nether Wastdale—lacked a chalice. At Bootle, they have " no covereinge for the coymon but of lynnen clothe ', at Egremont, ' no covereinge of sylke or buckram for the comn. table." At Corney " the bible (is) not of the largest volume." At Colton " they want a register boke."

Against the somewhat sombre background this chapter gives to the glories of Elizabethan England it is pleasant to rescue from oblivion the name of our first known local antiquary. Edward Threlkeld,* born at Burgh in 1526, was educated at Eton and King's College, Cambridge— what pictures the mind conjures up of this boy from the Solway shore going to school on the banks of the Thames in the reign of the eighth Henry. Archdeacon of Carlisle and rector of Great Salkeld 1568-88, he was also chancellor of Hereford. We know about his interest in our anti- quities because the information he gave in 1574 to the

---

* He was of the Melmerby branch. His father was bailiff of the Dacre barony of Burgh. As Bishop Aldrich was also provost of Eton, he was per- haps responsible for his going there. The MS. mentioned gives a trick of his grandfather's arms—Threlkeld quartering Parvyng. Hence it seems that these Threlkelds got Melmerby through marrying their heiress. (o.s. x 1-47, n.s. xvii 23, xix 61, and Field's Armorial, 206).

unknown author of ' Certain verie rare observations of Cumberland etc.'[19] about the Roman remains on the Wall and at Old Carlisle and Old Penrith constitutes the most valuable part of that manuscript.   At Cambridge he was ' so much admired for his excellent knowledge and eloquence that he was thought to have the help of some good genius.'*

Bishop Barnes was translated to Durham in 1577.   He held that see for 10 years and was only 55 when he died. As there is no evidence that he was a man of any great social influence, he must have been either a very able or a very fortunate one as he was a suffragan bishop at 35, a diocesan three years later, and received the great see of Durham at 45.   It is difficult to tell what kind of man he was; in describing those days of violent religious hates few are impartial.   One writer refers to him as ' a bigot of the first water ' and then misapplies the authority upon which he bases his assertion; another, as " beyond most of his age—as he was early called—learned, affable and generous, if at times over indulgent to offenders."[20]   Let us hope the latter is nearer the truth; it must have been difficult to be a Christian and a bishop in Elizabethan England.

John Meye,[21] archdeacon of the East Riding of Yorks., was elected 12 June 1577, and consecrated at Fulham by the bishop of London on 29 September.   His episcopate lasted for over twenty one years; its importance does not appear to have been commensurate with its length.

Its chief note was the increasing tension between the Romanists and the government.   In 1581 the law making it treason to be reconciled to Rome was passed.   These counties were not lacking in men willing to risk a dreadful death for their faith.   But by this time the tradition of the ' old religion ' had begun to die out.   In 1597 only

* I am grateful to Mr. E. B. Birley for drawing my attention to him.

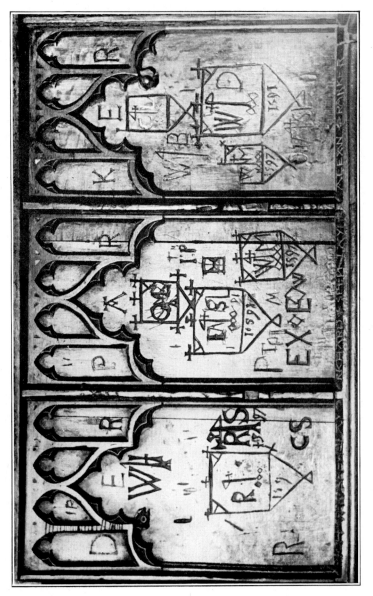

IV. SIXTEENTH CENTURY CARVINGS ON THE CANONS' STALLS OF CARLISLE CATHEDRAL.

(facing p. 213)

four parishes in Cumberland and eight in Westmorland contained any recusants; most of them of some social standing. The diocese produced, however, men believed by their co-religionists to be martyrs for their faith and by the Tudor government traitors to their queen. They were: James Layburn of Cunswick, executed in 1583; John, son of Nicholas Bost of Wellying in the parish of Dufton, executed in 1594; Christopher Robinson of Woodside, near Wigton, who suffered a like fate three or four years later at Carlisle and James Duckett, born at Gilthwaitrigg near Skelsmergh, hanged at Tyburn in 1601.[22] Whatever our views may be of the truth of the faith these men believed, few can, or should, withhold admiration for their constancy even unto death.

It is strange that no one has noticed the curious carvings on the canons' stalls in the cathedral. This may be because they have, until recently, been so covered with dirt as to be undecipherable or that the tradition ascribing them to Jacobite prisoners has been too easily accepted. The carvings, which are often dated and initialled, all have a certain type of sign in common and the initials often correspond with names—Alexander Parker, Christopher and Richard Spenclay, William Monk and William James—written in other places nearby. One carving has the date 1569 on it, the rest either 1591 or 1597. For this reason it was at first thought that they might have been cut by recusants. But it is now certain that they are Merchant Guild marks; thus their significance is civic not religious. They are too rude to be meant for honourable memorials of city dignitaries, yet much time and labour must have been spent on them. The mind is irresistibly called to a vision of a member of the genus boy at work. There seem to be two possibilities: that they were cut by city apprentices sent to the cathedral for catechizing, but according to Bishop Barnes' injunctions this took place in the parish church—the

nave; or that at this time the Grammar school was held
in the choir and that we have here the handiwork of the
scholars. The former suggestion gives a better reason
for the carvings being Merchant Guild marks; the latter
for the place in which they are found.* Whatever the
truth about them may be they are without doubt an
interesting link with the city's past.

The Scots have not been mentioned since, minus ' their
botes,' they hurried north after Solway Moss in 1542.
There was again an outbreak of war in 1556 which was
brought to an end by the treaty of Edinburgh in 1560.
During Elizabeth's reign " there was lasting peace on the
Scottish Border," so writes a great authority.[23] Doubtless officially that was so, but during these years such
famous events as the Raid of the Redeswyre, 1575, and
the rescue of Will of Kinmont from Carlisle Castle, 1595,
took place.   In fact, as far as the actual Borderland was
concerned this was probably in some ways the most disturbed period in its history. " Petty acts of wrong doing
were on the increase; and no man's dwelling was secure
from attack; the days of moss-trooping as an organised
system of robbery had begun."[24] But in most parts of
these counties peace and order reigned.

There is little of interest in Bishop Meye's register.
The supply of ordinands continued to be satisfactory in
quantity, but, judging by Bishop Robinson's report in
1599,† not in quality.   In 1580, the chapel at Matterdale
was granted parochial rights because the inhabitants
stated that:

* There is also a carving with the date 1660 and the initials W. M. and
D. M. adjacent which supports the latter theory. (For the state of the school
at this time see N.S. xvi, 5-8).

Thanks are due to Mr. Farrington, the cathedral verger, who first drew my
attention to these carvings for this and much other help; to the Right Revd.
Monsignor R. Smith; to Mr. J. S. Richardson who first pointed out their true
significance and put forward the apprentice theory; and to Canon W. J. T. P.
Phythian-Adams who suggested the school boy one and also gave other help.

† P. 244.

" from the annoyances of snow or other foul weather in the winter season in that fellish part, they be often very sore troubled with carrying the dead corpses. . . and the infants there born unto burial or christening to their said parish church of Grey-stock."

They had to find and maintain a good and able priest to be resident within the chapelry.[25] The stipend was £4. 5s. a year, perhaps with some land worth £3. 10. 0 a year in addition.[26] The chapels at Newlands,* Maller-stang, and Grisdale, later Mungrisdale, occur for the first time on Saxton's map of 1576. This evidence of Church extension is also borne out by what was happening in the Richmond deaneries in these years.†

The most interesting ecclesiastical document during this episcopate is part of a report of the proceedings of the Court of High Commission in Cumberland between 1575-90.[27] Articles of enquiry were issued to clergy and churchwardens; their replies throw light on the moral and ecclesiastical standards of the time. The curate of Edenhall is ordered " to wear his hose lowse at the knees '; his brothers of Holm Cultram and Laner-cost are presented, the former " for drunkennes and playing at cards and tables at sundrie times "; the latter ' for that he married two cupples of folkes in a prophane place without bannes asking." The church-wardens of Denton " come not to churche neither levie the penalties nor presente the absentee," and those at Irthington are accused because " the churchyard layd common unfenced, the church porche downe, the sur-plesse rent, the Bible rent, no Commandments set upp, and they woulde presente none for not coming to churche." Witchcraft in various forms was evidently prevalent: Anna Harrison, widow, is suspected of it. Anthony Huggen is presented for " medicioning children

* I am indebted to Mr. Clarke of Rowling End Farm for help in dating this chapel.
† Pp. 223-4.

with miniting a hammer as a smith of kynde," Jannet
Huggen as ' a sorcerer and medicioner of children,' and
John Taylor ' for suspect of sorcerie for that he had knyt
in cows taile staves, salt and herbes.'   Other charms are
" burying a quick nowt, and a dog, and quick cock."
Robert Sanderson practised ' medicioning for the worme';
how we are not told, nor what Agnes, wife of John Wyse,
alias Winkan John Wyse, did when she acted as a
" medicioner for the waffe of an ill winde and for the
fayryes " nor the reason why Agnes Watson kept ' a dead
man's scalpe,' Mabell, wyffe of John Browne, was simply
' a witche and taketh mylke from Kye.'

The three following offences look like " relics of
popery ": ' wearing beads,' ' fasting at St. Anthonie's
fast ' and ' ringing a bell at the last floode to provoke
people to prayer ': perhaps William Mester, who was not
only a drunkard but " a rayler against ministers and
wifes," should be put in this category.

We get also some examples of the bishop's attempt to
enforce the Prayer Book rubrics: Alice Thompson who
" will not learn the catechism," and William Forster
" who can't say it," are both presented, so are three
people who " have not receyved thrice this yeare because
they could not saye the Ten Commandments "; they are
ordered to learn them, with the Lord's Prayer and the
Creed, before next Easter.   Was this, and not confirmation, the test for receiving Holy Communion?   We are
left to surmise whether John Dockher, who played ' on
his pipes when the curate was at evening prayer,' or
Jenkin Swan, who cast down his glove in Irthington
church offering to ' fight with any one that would put
furth the hand,' was the more disturbing to the congregation.

As the Elizabethan Church condemned usury as much
as the medieval one it is not surprising to find John
Stricket, who charged George Marshall " 8d. in the weeke

for the lone of 20/-," presented; nearly 200 per cent. was indeed a stiff rate of interest.

Robert Winter, 'a malicious person and beareth evill against his neighbour'; Margaret Gyll, ' that she liveth in disquietness with her husband in banning and scolding '; and Margaret Avery, ' for cursing her father and mother ' were presented. So was Janet Walker, who 'hath had 4 bastards'; she had to do penance in Carlisle market place the next Saturday as well as in her parish church of Lanercost.

These records only shew the seamy side of life and mainly refer to the Border, the least civilised part of the diocese. Doubtless there were plenty of decent Christian folk of whom no record remains, but the picture of the result of a generation of Protestantism is not a particularly bright one. The root of the trouble was that the ancient faith of the people had been destroyed and little put in its place; of the Eastern March it could be stated in 1595 that ' scant three able preachers ' could be found in the whole March; of this one in 1597 that Bewcastle church had been decayed for over 60 years, Lanercost for 3 or 4, and Kirklinton for 20. The first article of the Treaty of Carlisle, signed in May of that year, was that good ministers should be planted at every Border church and the buildings repaired.[28] Perhaps in the southern part of the diocese things were better, but the account given by Bishop Robinson in 1599 hardly encourages such a belief.*

Bishop Meye died at Rose of the plague on 15 February 1598 at eight in the morning and was buried at Carlisle at eight in the evening. He was commemorated on the next day at Dalston.[29] There is little mention of him in the State Papers and he appears to have been something of a nonentity.

* P. 244.

Henry Robinson, provost of Queen's College, Oxford, a native of Carlisle,* was elected 27 May 1598, consecrated at London House by the bishop of London on 23 July, and had his temporalities restored on 5 August.   As his episcopate extended well into the following century, it seems best to treat it as a whole in the next chapter.   On 24 March 1603, Elizabeth died, and James, first of England and sixth of Scotland, reigned in her stead.

---

* According to Hutchinson, II, 630, but Mr. F. H. K. Harrison of Scalescleugh, Carlisle, who descends collaterally from the bishop, states that the family tradition is that he belonged to the yeoman family of Robinson of Nunclose.

CHAPTER III.

THE DIOCESE OF CHESTER DEANERIES, 1541-1603.

THE new see of Chester was created by letters patent of 4 August 1541. It took over in addition to other territory the archdeaconry of Richmond which included Cumberland, south of the Derwent, the parts of Westmorland contained in the barony of Kendale, and the Furness and Cartmel districts of Lancashire. These areas were to remain in it until they were joined to Carlisle in 1856.

The diocese of Chester was at first placed in the province of Canterbury, which thus stretched from Dover to the Derwent. Doubtless some clerk in the south, like many others in those parts even to-day, was ignorant of any geography north of London. Apparently his archiepiscopal master was not so ignorant, or perhaps his grace of York uttered a weighty protest, for in 1542 the new diocese was transferred to the northern province.

The first bishop of Chester was John Bird, whose first episcopal office was also the cause of a strange geographical error. He had been appointed suffragan to the bishop of Llandaff on 15 June 1537, under the title of " bishop of Penreth, in the province of Canterbury." This has often been claimed to be our Penrith, but it has never been in that province; and that a Welsh suffragan bishop would take his title from a place in the province of York and county of Cumberland is inconceivable. The official documents make it quite clear that the Pen . . . in question was one of the ninety places in Wales which have this prefix, probably Pentruth. As always happens in these matters, someone makes a mistake, and everyone repeats it.   In this case the culprit seems to have been Sir Daniel Fleming, who stated in his Description of the county of Cumberland, written in 1671, that Penrith " had the honour of a suffragan Bishop."*

Owing to the paucity of material, it is impossible to give a connected history of these western deaneries during these years, all that can be done is to give a brief account from such records as have survived at York or Chester.

The first of these documents are the returns at Chester for the bishop's visitations of 1548 and 1554. Unfortunately they only contain the names of the clergy and churchwardens and give no further information. The numbers shown below should be compared with those in 1524/5.†

	Number of Clergy.	
Place.	1548.	1554.
Kendale	33	24
Kirkby Lonsdale	11	8
Heversham, Grasmere	9 each	3. 4
Beetham, Ulverston	8 ,,	5. 8
Kirkby Ireleth, Cartmel	7 ,,	3. 4
St. Bees	6(b)	2
Windermere, Burton, Aldingham, Dalton	5 ,,	3. 4. 3. 3
Bootle, Cockermouth	4 ,,	2. 1
Lorton, Millom, Workington	3 ,,	1. 3. 2
Whicham, Corney, Warberthwaite, Gosforth, Brigham, Dean	2 ,,	2 each
Muncaster, Distington, Lamplugh	2 ,,	1 ,,
Whitbeck, Irton, Ponsonby, Beckermet, St. John and St. Bridget, Drigg, Haile, Egremont, Cleator, Moresby, Harrington, Ennerdale (a) Arlecdon, Eskdale, Embleton (a)	1 ,,	1 ,,

(a) Not in 1554.
(b) Includes Loweswater in 1548, not in 1554.

* The question is fully investigated and the documents given in o.s., xv, 303-8.
† P. 155.

The next document that has survived is the record, at
York, of the visitation of 1578.* By far the most
interesting thing in it is a statement setting out the
arrangements made at Kendal for the seating of the
congregation. It is of sufficient interest to be given in
full:

Imprimis. That the Alderman Recorder and such as be called
the Alderman brethren for the tyme beinge of the said Towne or
Borroughe of Kendall shall from henceforth have and occupie
that queare or chappell (called corruptlie in former tyme St.
Sondaie Chapell) latelie removed from the lower parte of the said
churche and new placed on the lefte syde of the middle alley of
the said churche and shall therein sitt and knele to praye and to
heare dyvyne service and sermons (without the lett interruption
or molestation of any other persons or persons) like as theye have
done and used to do by a certain space before this tyme.

Item. That the justices of peace and gentlemen of the said
parishe their wyfes and children shall have their places and seate
in the chapell called the Marquis or Lorde Chappell situate on the
south side of the chancell of the said churche of Kendall there to
praye and heare dyvyne service and that none else except the
said Justices and gentlemen their wifes and children shall sitt or
kneel there to heere dyvyne service nor be permitted thereunto.

Item. That the scolemr and his scollars for their place in the
churche shall onelie have and use the chappell situate on the
north side of the said chancell of the aforesaid church of Kendall
and to the end that the same chapell maye be made more fitt for
the said master and schollars and that the alderman and his
brethren of the said Borroughe of Kendal shall with all convenient hast at their owne privy coste and charges erect and
place formes and seates rounde about the chapell convenient
and seeminge for the place and purpose.

Item. That the organs standinge as yet in the said churche
shall furthwith be solde and the price thereof employed to the use
and reparatyon of the said parishe church of Kendall and that also
that lofte and timber thereof wherein the said organs now standing shall be also presentlie taken downe and removided.

Item. That with all speede after that the alderman and his
brethren of the said boroughe of Kendall shall erecte build and
fitt upp a faire and comelie Lofte in place where the roode lofte

* See also pp. 209-11.

did heretofore stande at their owne privy costs and charges wherein the Justices of peace and gentlemen with wives and childers shall sitt to heare sermons and Dyvyne Service if they will duringe the sermon and service tyme saveinge that it shall and maybe lawfull unto the said alderman and his brethren by fource of thir order and degree to have and take the timber and boords of the Lofte to be taken downe where yet the organs do stand, and the same to employe towarde the new erecting and settinge upp of the Lofte for the said Justices and gentlemen to sitt in at tymes of sermons as afore.

Item. That the ministers Deske where he ministeth to saie Dyvyne service shalbe removid'd to the other syde of the myddle alleye of the said churche, and that a decent forme with a backe shalbe placed on that side of the said alley where the aforesaid Deske now standethe for the said alderman recorder and the alderman his brethren to sitt upon to heare sermons so that the same be done and made at the cost and onelie charge of the said alderman and his brethren provyded also that sufficient wromthe and place be lefte beyond the said forme or seate for the par-rishioners to have accesse and egresse to and from their places and stalls in the said churche.

Item. That the churchwardens of the said churche shall have the use of that stall at the churche doore where they mynded to place the scollers and sitt there themselve if they will or otherwise to place men there as they shall thinke convenyent.

Item. That the whole parish will resolve to provyde and fynde a learned preacher (whereunto they are exhorted) to joyne with the vicar of the said church that by them two they may have everie sondaie in the yeare a sermon to their great cofort and edyfieinge. That the all such stipende and portyons of moneye as were wont to be given to the organ plaier and other unneces-sarie clerks be wholie employed to the stypend of that preacher and the rest to be supplyed by the contribucion of the well disposed pichioners of the said parishe.

That Sir Thomas Boynton Knight is put in trust to see the premesses accomplished and done accordinglie.

The records of archiepiscopal visitations of these deaneries in 1590 and 1595 are also at York. But in neither case did the archbishop get any further west than Kendal or Lancaster, where he 'visited' Kendale, Lonsdale and Furness deaneries. There is no mention of

Coupland in the first and very little about it in the second.   There are a certain number of corrections in the usual forms.*

Archbishop Parker's institution, in 1559, of an order of Readers was partially designed to help in the staffing of chapels.   Their powers were strictly limited; they were not allowed to christen, marry, or celebrate the Holy Communion, nor to preach, but they could take the service of the day, with the litany, and read a homily. Their services were extensively used in the Lake District during the next two centuries.†

There is evidence of a certain amount of Church extension during Elizabeth's reign, and during it the names of several chapels are first noticed.   A commission, appointed by the queen in 1563 to take steps to enforce the new religious regulations in the diocese of Chester, found that church accommodation in certain districts was insufficient as people had to travel too great a distance to their parish church.   In 1568 the queen urged the bishop to take steps to remedy these deficiencies; apparently nothing happened as two years later he was summoned to Hampton Court to explain his inaction.   None the less, this period shows a surprising amount of Church expansion.‡

1556.   Crosthwaite chapel granted parochial rights and consecrated the next year.

1562.   The newly built chapel at Troutbeck licenced and given parochial rights.§

1571.   Langdale and Long Sleddale chapels first mentioned.‖

* 1590 R. VI. A 10, 11, 12; 1594/5 R. VI. A. 13, 14, 15. The former volume contains a notice of a visitation of Carlisle diocese at Appleby, Penrith, Carlisle Cathedral, and Wigton between 2-6 May, 1592, but no returns of its results have been preserved.

† N.S. v, 89-105 for much information about them.

‡ N.S. XX, 97.

§ R.K., III, 208, 192.

‖ Church of Grasmere, Armitt, 62; R.C.H.M. Westmorland, 157, but this is presumptive evidence.

1577. Evidence of chapels at Blawith, Egton cum Newland, Satterthwaite or Graythwaite, Ulpha* and Walney is first afforded by Saxton's map of Lancashire.

1578. Colton chapel consecrated by Archbishop Sandys,† and Hawkshead chapel said to have been granted parochial rights;‡ Witherslack first mentioned in archbishop's visitation§ of this year:‖ also Skelsmergh, but Nicolson and Burn, I, 123, suggests that it may be Pre-Reformation.

1583-6. Between these dates Killington and Firbank chapel was made parochial.

1586. Coniston.   ⎫ granted parochial
1587. Staveley in Windermere. ⎭   rights.¶

---

* At least the chapel named St. John's is presumably Ulpha.

† o.s. xiii, 434.

‡ V.C.H. Lancs., VIII, 374.

§ I must thank the Rev. W. Oliver, Rev. J. S. Purvis and Mr. G. E. Kirk whose joint efforts put me in touch with these valuable, and to us here unknown, Carlisle and Chester diocesan records at York.

‖ 87a.

¶ Bishop of Chester's Register Book, II, 31, 33, 37.

BOOK III.

THE STUARTS AND THEIR AFTERMATH,

1603-1747.

CHAPTER I.

THE SOCIAL SCENE.

THIS Survey should describe the state of these counties in 1603, but owing to the lack of records it will be necessary—if any but the most meagre account is to be given—to interpret this date generously.

In the Middle Ages the three main ingredients of local life were war, agriculture and industry; of these the first two were then predominant. We now witness the gradual elimination of the first, the constancy of the second, and the development, slowly at first but more quickly as the years pass by, of the third.

The development of this Borderland on a peace footing naturally affected the status of our ancient families, but in this the ordinary laws of nature also took a hand. As has already been seen the defeat of the earls in 1569 meant the end of feudalism in the North country. The earls of Northumberland, their work as the guardians of the Border ended, retired to Petworth in Sussex. In 1670 the male line came to an end at the death of the 11th earl. His daughter and sole heiress married the duke of Somerset; by the failure of male issue from this marriage the estates were divided. The Northumberland ones went to her grand-daughter, from whom the present duke descends, while the Cumberland and Sussex ones passed to her daughter, the wife of Sir William Wyndham, from whom they came to Lord Leconfield, the present owner.

Q

The Cliffords, earls of Cumberland only survived into this century for some forty years to end in an heiress, the Lady Anne, the fragrance of whose memory will ever be enshrined in Northern hearts. Her estates passed to her grandsons, the earls of Thanet, from whom they descended to Lord Hothfield, the present owner.

The Dacres, the other famous local family, had already failed in the male line. The duke of Norfolk, ward of the three co-heiresses, married one of them to his heir—her dowry was the barony of Greystoke,* another died young and the third he allied to Lord William Howard;† Naworth castle was her inheritance and from them the present earl of Carlisle descends.

In the seventeenth century Cumberland and Westmorland were the two poorest counties in England; in the assessments for taxation under the Act of 1659-60 the former was rated at £108. a month and the latter at £73. 19. 4. In a previous assessment, 1657, Cumberland had to provide £92. 11. 4. per month or the same as the city of Exeter. Essex was assessed at £3000., the city of London at £4000.[1] Probably the cause of the apparent poverty was the smallness of the population as compared with the acreage of the counties.

The inventories to wills, since they give lists of the deceased's stock, husbandry utensils, and household goods, afford reliable evidence of the individual's financial position. The earliest bundle of these, of the year 1662, which includes some going back to 1649,‡ has been used as the source of the following study.

As a statistical basis the figures given under the letter H. were selected. There are 28 inventories: the average

---

* The Howards of Greystoke descend from a brother of the fifth duke.

† The Howards of Corby descend from Sir Francis, second son of Lord William.

‡ In the Carlisle Probate Registry. The existence of these valuable records seems to be unknown to local historians and genealogists. They are arranged in yearly bundles in alphabetical order.

value of the estates, excluding land and sums owing to the deceased, amounts to £38. 10. Of these 10 are under £20. 8 under £40., 4 under £60. and the same number under £80.; one estate is worth £84., and another £141. It is noticeable that 18 out of the 28 estates, or about 64 per cent., are under £40. This group presumably represents the small tenant-farmers. Counting the estate worth £84. in the £40-80. group, we get about 32 per cent. for this one which is probably that of the more substantial farmers and yeomen. The £141. estate was that of a Carlisle shopkeeper.

The farming community may be interested to have some typical inventories of the stock possessed by their seventeenth century forebears; William Cape of Bassenthwaite halles, estate worth £240. 19. 2., had oxen and kine £32. 10., 5 steers £10., 148 sheep £42. 2. 8., 7 heifers £14. 16. 8., 6 little calves £3. 12. 0., 4 horses and mares £10. 5.; George Birkebeck of Wasdale head, Shap, estate worth £140. 13. 6., had 260 sheep £52., 2 bulls and 12 young beasts £18., 10 kine £28., horses and mares £18.; Thomas Bowman of Hilton Flecan, Askham, estate worth £85. 0. 4., had 2 oxen £6. 6. 8., one stott £2. 13. 4., and two oxe stirkes £3. 6. 8., other 2 stirkes £1. 15. 5., kine £14., 4 calves £1. 14., 3 hogges £6. 6. 8., and old sheep and hoggs £11. 10. 6.; John Hewer of Hawfield, Castle Sowerby, estate worth £64. 2. 4., had 2 oxen £7., 5 young beasts £5., 2 calves and a stirk £1., 5 kine £10., 2 nags and 1 stag £3., 13 sheep £2., and 5 geese, 5 hens, 1 cock and 1 hogg, 10s.; and James Hutchinson, of Asby, estate worth £26. 7. 8. had 80 sheep £14. and one mare £1. 12.

Judging by these inventories spinning at home was not as common as has been supposed: of the 89 names in those from A to D only 13 had spinning wheels or cards in their homes. A few instances of beehives occur: Thomas Bird of Brougham had a hive and Robert Harrison of Appleby 4. The writer of an article on *Home Life in North*

Lonsdale[2] suggests wheeled vehicles were unusual there at this time but these inventories shew they were fairly common: John Fallowfield of Great Strickland and Thomas Lancaster of Fewsdale, among many others, had a cart and wheels.

The usual furniture of a farmstead suggests that bedsteads, with sheets, blankets and pillows, were now in general use. But bedding and bedsteads are often grouped together so it is not easy to say what numbers were normal. Most people, except the very poor, had two or three. They had about the same number of tables and chairs. An ark, a cupboard, and a chest or all three were also common. As can be seen from the illustrations in the *Westmorland* volume of the *Royal Commission on Historical Monuments* the beautiful carved and dated cupboards that are such a well known feature of our oldest farms were mostly built towards the end of this century. Many of these are in houses that must have belonged to the richer yeomen farmers.

Pewter and brass were in general use: Lancelot Addison of Mauldsmeaburn had 'ten platters and one bowle of pewter.' Only the gentry and superior yeomen had silver: William Cape had 'silver spoones' worth £3. Brass candlesticks, though not common, were by no means exceptional; but Will. Bristoe, curate of (Mun) Grisdale has a 'lanthorne.' Table napkins are also not infrequent. A looking glass, or indeed glass of any kind, was apparently only found in gentle houses; Mrs. Elizabeth Atkinson of Carlisle had one. "Curtaines with vallaines and fringe," Jane Dent of Appleby having a pair, were also limited to richer homes. Weapons of sport or war were strangely unusual: John Bracken of Winton had armour valued at a £1; Thomas Todhunter of Penruddock a sword, and Bartholomew Sanderson two guns and other small arms.

The normal value of wearing apparel and riding gear was

between £1 and £2. Of the better off folk, Henry Law of
'Fowgatefoote,' Appleby 'had £10's worth, while John
Barwis of Waverton seems to have carried much of his
property on his person as out of an estate of £59., £20.
was apparel and riding gear. Funeral expenses were
generally about £2. or £3.

Several inventories of richer folk occur; Bridgett, Lady
Fetherstonhaugh had £20. worth of 'apparell.' Her
house had 6 rooms: best chamber, my lady's chamber,
gallery, new parlour, old butterie, and kitchen. What is
strange is that bedsteads occur in all 4 living rooms. And
she must have lived under dreadfully crowded conditions
as her own room contained 3 presses, a cupboard, 2 tables,
3 bedsteads and furniture, a chest, 6 chairs and 4 buffet
stools. Another inventory of this social class is that of
Richard Crackenthorpe of Newbiggin. It shews the Hall
had 18 rooms. The list of furniture and goods is very
interesting. He had 10 folio books, 18 in octavo, and 3
smaller ones in his study, "besides divers other books"
in the house. Someone connected with the establishment must have had definite ideas on furnishing, since
the yellow chamber and the green chamber each had
curtains of the appropriate colour.

But the two most interesting inventories are those of
men below visitation rank. Bartholomew Sanderson, a
shopkeeper of Kirkby Stephen, had goods in his shop
worth £126. 17. 5. His house contained 10 rooms, with
£154. 8. 0. worth of furniture. He had two things; a clock
and a 'paire of virginalls' mentioned in no other inventory. His apparel was worth £20.; his books £2.
Every room in the house, except the hall and the domestic
offices, had a bedstead in it, so the hall must have been the
living room. He had 7 bedsteads, 11 pair of sheets, 8
pair of harden, 20 pillows. His silver was worth £17. 10.;
his pewter £6. 5. On the whole this shopkeeper's home is
the most comfortably furnished of those described in the

inventories. Thomas Addison of Walton* possessed 114 books, worth £18. 3. 0. The value of all his goods was £72, thus his library represented a quarter of the whole; a very proper proportion for a scholar. The books were mostly on scientific subjects, such as navigation, astronomy, and land surveying, but history, philosophy and theology were also included. Sir Thomas Browne's *Pseudodonia*, Sir Francis Bacon's *Concerning the Advancement of Learning*, and Euclid's *Elements* are works still valued that occur. This is an astonishing library to find in a remote place like Walton, close to the Border line. Was he the agent for the Naworth estate?

Several other people, in addition to Richard Crackenthorpe and Thomas Addison, had books: Marian Fallowfield of Penrith had a Bible, Bullinger's Sermons and King James' Acts; Thomas Halton, a citizen of Carlisle, whose inventory has an interesting list of goods and prices, had £3 worth. There are 89 inventories of the letters A to D, of these 12 had books of some sort.

The late sixteenth century and the next one saw much domestic rebuilding by both great nobles and gentry. In Westmorland, Levens was almost entirely rebuilt by Sir James Bellingham (1577-1641), and Sizergh much beautified in Elizabeth's reign by Sir Walter Strickland and his widow. Of lesser houses that of the Browne family at Townend, Troutbeck, was built early in the seventeenth century. The volume mentioned above† can be referred to as evidence of what was taking place in the county in these years.

There is little evidence as to the comparative state of agriculture at this time and in the Middle Ages. New ideas, introduced into other parts of England in the seventeenth century, did not affect these counties till the

* Was he the Thomas Addison, son of Robert of Newleas, Cumberland who matriculated at Queen's, Oxford, 1643, B.A., 1639?

† p. 228.

next one.   The same crops were sown and the same kind of stock kept as in the past.   In many parts the centuries after the Black Death saw land enclosed for pasture.   As sheep required less men to look after them than stock or crops less ' hands ' were needed and so people were ejected from their holdings.   As much of these counties had always been pastoral rather than agricultural this movement had little affect here;   the four northern counties were excluded from Wolsey's enclosure commission of 1517.

Leland in his Itinerary (1535-43) notes the great forest of Inglewood, and the forests of Nicol and Eine (Allerdale or Coupland?)   That he says Carlisle ' stondeth on the forest of Inglewood ' shews how extensive this still was at that date though it is clear from the Survey of the Percy lands of 1578 that much new land had been brought under cultivation since the early Middle Ages.   In the small manor of Dundraw, containing the hamlets of that name, Wheyrigg, and Kelsick, seven holdings are named as improvements and thirteen as on the lord's waste.   The accepted opinion, however, is that general enclosure did not take place here till ' long after the pacification of the Border by the union of the two crowns.'   But the evidence already cited,* of the Pilgrimage of Grace suggests that there may have been more than has been supposed.

The changes in local tenures resulting from the union of the Crowns will be dealt with elsewhere.†   The evidence of the survival of Bond tenancy, shewn in the following extract, seems worthy of record.   The document,[3] with the date 17 September, 1666, headed,

' Words spoken by Sir Wm. Dalston agt ye Bpp's right over his bond tenants.'

contains these words:

' One of Sir Wm Dalston's men, called Laurence Dent, sent by him at a meeting amongst ye Bond tenants told them that in being Bond Tenants they were no better than slaves, or words to that effect.'

* p. 183.   † pp. 247, 250-2.

The inventories, quoted above, shew that by this time farmers were beginning to live above a mere subsistence level. They no longer planted only enough of a crop or kept only enough stock to save them from starvation in the coming winter. They had something over to sell at the market from which they obtained the money needed to buy the furniture they owned. In the pastoral, as opposed to the agricultural districts, this was especially so. The fact that a very high percentage of the older houses of the Westmorland statesmen date from the latter half of this century provides striking evidence of the prosperity of the pastoral world at this time. Perhaps a large proportion of this came from the profits of cottage industries, such as spinning and weaving, rather than from keeping or selling stock.[4]

During these years Carlisle was in a bad way. By the union of the Crowns it fell from an important frontier post to a small market town and cathedral city. The inhabitants, who had probably largely lived on money spent by the garrison, now reduced to twenty men, were much impoverished. In 1617 Bishop Snoden* said that they exercised no arts or trades and had no other means of livelihood except fishing. In 1634 three officers from Norwich who visited the city describe it as ' both for Reuenues, Buildings and Inhabitants and their condition very poore.' They also say:†

' It makes shifte to maintaine a Mayor, distinguish'd by his white staffe, and 12 Aldermen, his brethen, sans Cap of Maintenance but their blew Bonnets wch they are as proud in as our Southerne Citizens in their Beauers. Two of the Aldermen (Sir Rich. Graham and Sir George Dalston) being very worthy Knights doth grace and countenance their Company and poore Citty not a little soe the graue Recorder doth being a Knight also.'

* p. 249.

† Jefferson gives an extract of the Carlisle part of their Journal in his *History of Carlisle* (p. 47) but the copy he took it from—in *Brayley's Graphic Illustrator*—only prints it in a mutilated form which omits the following (he also omits the description of the Shap road given above, p. 179). The whole can be found in *Newcastle Tracts*, Miscellaneous, M. A. Richardson.

In the Heralds Visitation of 1665, five families from Cockermouth, as compared with two from Carlisle and one each from Penrith and Kendal, were of sufficient standing to enter pedigrees. As they presumably attained their position through local trade this is striking evidence of the wealth of the town and suggests that during the first half of this century Cockermouth was the most prosperous commercial centre in Cumberland. Camden, in his Britannia,[5] published 1586-1607, described it as a " mercate town of goode welth . . . built faire enoufh." Bishop Nicolson in 1685, stated that " the houses are built of stone and slated, mostly with blue slate,"[6] while ten years later Carlisle still had " very few stone houses."[7] Presumably Cockermouth had attained its position and its inhabitants their wealth through the wool trade.

These years also saw Whitehaven emerging from a hamlet to a busy seaport.   In 1566 it had only one vessel ' called a pickerde of the Burden of IX Tonnes '*; in 1642 it was a town of 40 or 50 houses, with a chapel; in 1660 it obtained market privileges. Its subsequent rise to prosperity, under the lead of the Lowthers, as a coal mining centre and seaport for the American Colonies was rapid. By 1693, when the chapel of St. Nicholas was consecrated, it had a population of over 2200,[8] and was the sixth port in England. The example of the Lowthers was followed by the Curwens at Workington, which had been granted a charter for a market and fair in 1573. The export of coal began in 1650; thirty years later the colliery was worth £20 a year. In other places in West Cumberland also coal mines were developed during this century. Those at Distington were worked by 1614, and others at Moresby are mentioned in 1680. The collieries at Harrington and Clifton date back to about 1673.   Coal

---

* At this date the names of " the havens and crekes in Cumberland were Bowsteadhill, Skinburnes, Ellnefoot, Workington, Parton, Whitehaven, Ravenglasse, and Powsfoote " (N.S. xxi, 74-80).

was dug for at Weary Hall, Bolton as early as 1567, and mines at Oughterside are named in the will of William Orfeur in 1681.[9]

The iron mines of West Cumberland were also developed during these years. Those at Egremont were certainly worked between 1635 and 1647; in 1676 a mine at Woodend, rented by Thomas Patrickson of Caswell How, Ennerdale, was transferred to John Lamplugh. A letter, of 1694, from William Gilpin of Scaleby to Sir James Lowther, alludes to ' free and plentiful ore at Langaran, near Whitehaven, and that at Frizington and the intended forge at Cleator, for smelting them with pit coal.' At the end of the century, another Patrickson, Richard of Calder Abbey, had considerable litigation about some iron mines at Cleator. In the South West of the county the primeval forests were being turned into fuel. In 1625 there was a forge in Ulpha, worth £300 a year to its Hudleston owners; and from about 1668 they cut down timber on their estates around Millom to the value of £4000, chiefly for forges. The exact whereabouts of the iron mines, which necessitated smelting on such an extensive scale, is unknown.[10]

Thus by the end of the seventeenth century the main outlines of the future development of industrial Cumberland were already foreshadowed.

Mining was also carried on in the Lake District : an early seventeenth century writer speaks of copper mines being worked at Keswick and Newlands, " where likewise black lead is gotten." The Keswick and Coniston Mines were started in Elizabethan times and worked by Germans under royal patronage.[11]

In Westmorland, Kendal, incorporated by a charter of Queen Elizabeth in 1575,[12] had been slowly advancing in prosperity. The woollen trade was regulated and encouraged by her successor in 1609-10 by an Act

" for the encouraging of many poore people in Cumberland and Westmorland, and in the towns of Carptmeale, Hawkeshead, and Broughton to continue their trade of making cogware, Kendals, Carptmeales, and course cottens."[13]

Iron smelting, carried on by the tenants of the abbey in the Furness district in pre-Reformation days but suppressed by Queen Elizabeth, was revived towards the end of this century. Iron works were commenced at Force Forge by William Rawlinson, who died in 1680, and soon after this date those at Cunsey and Backbarrow were founded by the Sandys and Machell families. The Coniston forge was working under Sir Daniel Fleming's direction in 1674/5.[14]

From 1663 the series of *Visitation* and *Correction court books* of this diocese have survived; there are also some of the Chester diocese. These almost unknown documents* are of the greatest interest. They provide lists of Nonconformists, grouped under parishes, records of unbaptized children and clandestine marriages, thus supplying information not found in the parish registers.

These documents shew how controlled was the life of our mid-seventeenth century ancestors. For instance, no one could teach without authority from the bishop. Anthonie Walker was presented at Warcop ' for teachinge schoole w[th]out a Lycence to the p[r]judice and Disadvantage of the psh, w[ch] hindres the building of a schoole,' and Robert Allison at Allhallowes for teaching ' schoole within our pish to the hurt and damage of our Lycensed schoolmaster ' (1674). At Hutton, Isabel Toppin was in trouble as a Quaker for being a midwife and not having a licence, and John Anthony at Wigton ' for practisinge the Art of Chirurgany ' for the same reason (1663). But discipline went further than punishing people for doing things without a licence: at Addingham, Bernard Westmorland was cited ' for being a common and pfane

* The Chester ones at York seem to be quite unknown, even to V.C.H.

curser or swearer' (1663), and at Dalston, Thomas Bell and Elizabeth Winter for evill speech and cursing at the grave or burial of Ann Bell (1671).

In 1699 John Scott of Johnby, Greystoke was presented ' for going to witches and wizards, as is reported by comon fame and his own relacon.' This is interesting as the returns of Bishop Meye's time, though only covering a short period, shew several cases of this.* The only other references to witchcraft noticed in local records of this century occur in a payment " for ye witchfynder " by the Carlisle Corporation in 1649/50[15] and in Bishop Nicolson's diary of 8 August 1684 when he notes " witch of Ainstable clear'd."[16] Our ancestors do then seem to have become rather more civilised in the intervening years. Readers of Hugh Walpole's novel *Rogue Herries* will remember that he devotes a chapter to the killing by her neighbours of the supposed Borrowdale witch in about 1745. The historical facts suggest that he placed in the middle of the eighteenth century an event reflecting the mental outlook of over a century before.

Sabbath breaking was another offence for which the unruly could be punished. ' Spreading manure ' (Bampton, 1663), ' travelling with two loads to Hexham ' (Irthington, 1664), ' scolding the wife of James Grame,' (Kirkandrews upon Esk, 1668), ' entertaining drinkers,' (Morland, 1668), ' carreing corn before 3 o'clock in ye Sunday afternoone,' (Lanercost, 1670), ' selling ale,' (Bromfield, 1670), or just ' quarrelling on ye Sabbath ' (Crosby Ravensworth, 1670), are among the offences that occur in the Carlisle books. The York ones of 1633 supply other instances: Bartholomew Turner of Kendal accused ' of selling flesh openly on the lord's daie in ye forenoone and for giveing evill word to ye Churche,' Geo. Longmire of Troutbeck (W.) ' for leading corne on ye Sunday after sunsett,' and Walter Preston of Dalton

* pp. 215-6.

'for loytering in ye churchyard in service time and being admonished by ye churchwardens wold neither go in nor out.'   At Egremont, Joice, wife of Edmund Grayson, was presented 'for disturbinge Divine service by walk . . .'

A presentment from Hugill (1684 York) of Thomas Collinson 'for making a disturbance in our chappell-yarde by reading of sale notes' reminds us of the ancient custom of crying notices of all kinds after morning service; the stone bench running along the outside of part of Hawkshead church and providing seats for the spectators is a relic of this.   But the cryer was usually —at Helsington and Urswick for instance—the parish clerk.   So probably the cause of the disturbance was the latter's wrath at an encroachment on his rights.[16a]

These presentments shew the games our ancestors played: William Atkinson of West Newton, Bromfield, was accused 'for shooting at Butts' (1664), David Graham and others of Kirkandrews on Esk 'for playing at ninepins' (1672), Thomas Stegdall of St. Mary's, Carlisle 'for suffering cards to be plaid in his house' (1663), Edward Robson and John Barker of Sebergham 'for playing at cards' (1671), Elizabeth Craghill of Brampton 'for keeping a carding house the Sunday before Christmas Day' (1684), William Fallow of Beamont 'for fishing in time of Divine Service' (1672), John Thomson of Ainstable 'for profanacon of the Sabboathe by fishing' (1675), and Thomas Spedding and John Gaskell of Bolton (C) ' for prophaining the Lord's day by playing att football" (1686), were all presented.

Other examples occur in the York books of 1633: 'Anto. Todd of Stirkland Kettle for playing at Shovell board in ye house of Issabell Drinkall widow ye most pte of ye Lord's day'; at Dalton: Jo. Knipe and William Peell ' for bowling upon ye Saboath day in ye afternoone,' John Singleton and Thomas Woodburn ' for playing at pigles* upon Sunday in ye afternoone in time of Divine Service,' and William Fether 'for gardinge in time of Divine service in ye afternoone.' The last example to be given, though not referring to a game, must not be omitted: Tho. Bindlosse, farmer of Kendal, was presented " for drinking and takeing tobacco in ye house of Jo. Warin, Clerke, in evening prair time."†

It seems best, though the record of them occurs in an Elizabethan visitation book, to consider references to handfast marriages at the same time as other instances of irregular unions in the Restoration books.

Such marriages were apparently practised on both sides of the Border.   Scott in *The Monastery*[17] makes the baron of Avenel say

" Catherine is not my wife . . . but she is handfasted with me and that makes her as honest a woman. . . . . When we are handfasted, as we term it, we are man and wife for a year and a day—that space gone by, each may choose another mate, or, at their pleasure, may call the priest to marry them for life."

In such a matter it is impossible to gainsay the authority of Sir Walter that this was the original significance of these marriages on the Scots side of the Border and so presumably on the English one.   But G. Neasham in *North Country Sketches*, dealing mainly with Northumberland and Durham, states:

" at this time (c. 1560) it was customary for young people to plight troth and be ' handfasted ' to each other.   This was regarded as a formal engagement.   If a man refused to keep his promise the woman had her remedy in the Ecclesiastical Court."

He gives instances of this from Durham records.[18]

---

* Wright's *Dictionary of Obsolete and Provincial English* gives to pick as a Lincolnshire word meaning to play at pitch and toss, so this is perhaps the meaning of ' pigle.'   The Lincolnshire and Cumberland dialects have many affinities.

† In describing his visit to Kendal in 1652, George Fox notes that one Cock ' met me in the street, and would have given me a roll of tobacco (for people then were much given to smoking tobacco), I accepted his love, but did not receive the tobacco '. (Fox's Journal, ed. 1827, p. 165).

In the Carlisle book two of these cases occur: from Crosthwaite in 1574 and, three years later, from Westward. At the former, the parties were Janet Fysher and Leonard Bowe.   The presentment says

" Janet allegeth yt about Whitsonday last the said Leonard was handfast to her the said Janett Fysher by worde fitt for yt purpose viz.: heare I Leonard takes ye Janett to my handfast wyef and thereto I plyght the my troth and she taking him by the hand said the lyke worde . . .* and so they kist and this was before a great number of people."

The Westward form, between Agnes Sawcott and Mungo Nicholson, is the same except that the words ' and so lousing their hands ' are inserted and the mention of kissing and the presence of witnesses omitted.

No other evidence of this custom has been noticed in any records of this West Border.   It seems clear that handfast marriage was originally a trial one lasting a year and a day, after which it could become permanent by marriage in church, if the parties desired.   The following record shews that the Reformers tried to turn it into a betrothal by which the parties were bound to marry: in 1574 the churchwardens of Scaleby and Stanwix presented Stephen James and Elena Blaicklocke

" that they being handfast the sayd James hath maried one Jane Alleson of Knells and the said Elena one Chfer Blaichlocke of Ricardby."

Evidence of the Church's success is afforded by the fact that there is no mention of these marriages in the Restoration books.

But instances occur of illegal marriages.   Thomas Hetherington and Margaret Crawe of Lanercost were presented in 1663 for a ' clandestine marriage by a popish priest.'   A good many presentations for irregular marriages are noted at the 1674 Visitation which suggests that determined efforts were being made to put them down.

* Two words unreadable.

To give one example: the curate of Hayton was accused of marrying Richard Graham and Jane Bayty of Arthuret " clandestinely upon the night in his own house." In the York books a case of the same kind is presented from Kirkby Ireleth in 1633; Thomas Askam was accused of " marryinge of a couple without licence about eight of clock in ye night in an unlawfull place."

One of the chief social and religious changes in these years is the growth of nonconformity. Throughout the Reformation there had always been some who adhered to the ' Old Religion.' As time passed others formed Nonconformist groups: Presbyterians, Baptists, Independents, Quakers. Between 1661 and 1673 various severe Acts against them were passed. One of the most valuable parts of the Visitation books are the lists from each parish of those who refused the Communion of the Established Church. Often picturesque details of their behaviour are given. Margaret Marshall of Kirkby Thore was presented in 1663 " for absenting herselfe from the Church and for contemptuous speeches against the same." At Ravenstonedale Edward Johnson insisted ' on putting his hatt on in time of Divine service and being admonished to the contrary did refuse to putt it off,' while William Brummell of Bassenthwaite refused to be catechised ' (1664). At Watermillock, Elizabeth Burton was presented " for making a mocke at our service book ' and Edmund Shepheard ' for saying openly in company that ye masse is read in our church ' (1670). Several cases occur of people burying their dead in an unknown place or in a field. This happened at Great Orton (1663), Brougham (1664), Ravenstonedale (1672), and Bromfield (1674). Cases of people, many of them quakers, refusing to pay their Church assessments are, of course, innumerable.

The Visitation Roll of 1573 for the diocese of Carlisle shews schoolmasters at Penrith, Brough, Appleby,

Barton, Morland, Crosthwaite, Aspatria and Westward. There is no record of one at Carlisle, but Edward Mitchell, ' prebendarie of Carlysle,' who left legacies to the cathedral staff in his will, 22 October 1565, includes " to the two scuyll masters iiis. iiijd. a piece.[19] This is the earliest mention of the school founded by the Henrician statutes. In the Chester deaneries the Visitation of 1578[20] shews schoolmasters at St. Bees, Cockermouth, Lorton, Bootle, Dalton, Ulverston, Barbon, Beetham and Kendal.

In these counties between the Middle Ages and the Restoration schools were founded at Kirkby Stephen 1566, Keswick, 1571, Blencow 1577/8, Urswick 1580, St. Bees 1583, Hawkshead 1585, Kirkby Lonsdale 1591, Stainmore 1594, Dean 1596, Cartmel in existence 1598, Crosby Garret ante 1600, Ireleth 1608, Bridekirk 1609, Bromfield 1612, Old Hutton 1613, Heversham 1619, Dalton 1622, Bampton 1626/7, Addingham 1634, Lowther 1638, Troutbeck 1639, Dendron 1644, Caldbeck 1647, Barton 1650, Hugill or Ings 1650, Burton, 1657, Broughton 1657, Ulverston 1658.[21]

In the light of this list the reader will not be surprised to hear that in the Carlisle Visitation of 1664 the following number of schoolmasters occur in the 4 deaneries: Allerdale 12 out of 27 parishes, Cumberland 10 out of 23, Westmorland 22 out of 32, and Carlisle 18 out of 39. Thus nearly half the parishes and chapelries had a schoolmaster; very often the latter was the incumbent or curate. Unfortunately similar records for the Chester deaneries do not exist. But returns for the beginning of the next century in Bishop Gastrell's *Notitia* shew the following figures: Lonsdale deanery 5 out of 6 parishes or chapelries had a school; Kendal 18 out of 24, Furness 21 out of 27, and Coupland 14 out of 39. It will be noticed that in each return Westmorland has a higher percentage than Cumberland. These figures shew that our ancestors in these counties in the seventeenth century were not quite

R

the wild untutored barbarians that they are often assumed to have been.

The following document from the Lamplugh family papers may end this survey on a not too serious note:

"Deaths taken out of the Register of Lamplugh from Janry. ye i 1658 to Janye ye i 1663

Of a five-bar gate, stag hunting	4
Two duels, first with frying pan and pitchfork	1
Second between a 3 footed stool and a brown jug	1
Kild at Kelton fell races	3
Crost in love	1
Broke his neck robbing a hen roost	1
Took cold sleeping at church	2
Hanged for clipping and coyning	7
Of a sprain in his shoulder saving his dog at Culgate	1
Mrs Lamplugh's cordial water	2
Knockd on ye head with a quart bottle	1
Frighted to death by fairies	4
Of strong October at ye Hall	4
Bewitchd	7
Broke a vein in bawling for a knight of ye shire	1
Old women drownd upon trial for witchcraft	3
Climbing a Crow's nest	1
Led into a horse pond by a will of the wisp	1
Overeat himself at a house warming	1
Died of a fright in an exercise of ye train bands	1
By ye parson's bull	2
Vagrant beggars worried by Esq. Lamplugh's house dog	2
Chokd with eating (barley ?)	4
Old Age	57"

But none of these entries can be found in the Register and the average of burials in the parish at this time is five a year. In S. Taylor's words ' so much for corroborative documentary evidence. There is very little of it and what there is is not favourable to the author of our list of accidents.' Thus this extract cannot be taken at its face value, it is without doubt an ancient document* and must

---

* Mr. Taylor describes the paper as brown with age and the writing as in an early eighteenth century or possibly earlier hand (N.S. xliv, 138-41).

have been compiled with some object.   But whether fact or fiction, it obviously reflects contemporary habits and ideas in one of the most remote parts of England, and so is of interest to-day.   If its compiler was not a faithful transcriber of ancient records, he was certainly some one with a nice sense of humour.

CHAPTER II.

THE SEVENTEENTH CENTURY.

I.

UNDER ONE CROWN.

THE state of this diocese just before the accession of James I can be seen in a letter from Bishop Robinson to Secretary Cecil of 26 December 1599,

" I beseech you not to impute my long silence to neglect of duty. I had to know the certainty of all things before I wrote of them. I find here, more Popish recusants than I thought, yet the number within my diocese is far less than within the barony of Kendal and deanery of Copeland in Cumberland, both belonging to the jurisdiction of Chester."

He then gives the names of some of the chief recusants and goes on—

" Most part of the other gentlemen of the country are sound in religion, and the poorer sort generally willing to hear, but pitifully ignorant of the foundations of Christianity; . . . many of them are without all fear of God, adulterers, thieves, murderers. The chief spring of all this wofulness comes principally of the weakness and carelessness of the ministry. In divers places of the Borders the churches have walls without covering, and they have none to celebrate divine service save certain beggarly runners which come out of Scotland, neither can any men of worth be induced to live there, because their maintenance is withholden, and their lives must be in continual danger.

In the more peaceful parts of the diocese there are some clergymen of very commendable parts, both for knowledge and conscience, but their number is very small. Others there were that might do much good if they had half that delight in discharging their function which they have in idleness, vain pleasures, and worldy cares. The far greater number is utterly unlearned, unable to read English truly and distinctly. One great occasion thereof was the great facility of my predecessor in committing the charge of souls to such as were presented by those who care not how silly the clerk is so long as themselves enjoy the fat of the living.

This is not all; there are divers churches appropriated, and served only with a stipendiary curate; divers chapels of ease served at the charges of the poor people, because their parish church is too far from them. Either must these places be wholly unserved, and so the people grow from ignorance to brutishness, or else such must be tolerated as will be entertained for five marks or £4; the greatest annual stipend that any hath is 20 nobles, towards all charges."[1]

In Wilson's words " this was not the peevish complaint of a partizan like Bishop Best . . . but the sober judgment of an earnest prelate taking a dispassionate survey of his charge and estimating the results of what forty years of the new Church policy had wrought upon the manners and sentiments of the people."[2]

To turn from this depressing picture to records which shew a brighter one. These are the Greystoke registers during the incumbency of Leonard Lowther,* 1597-1609. His career suggests that pluralism was now controlled: previously rector of Great Orton, Bowness on Solway, and Lowther, he always resigned one of his two livings when appointed to a third.

One of his curates kept the register. The rector is generally referred to as ' Mr. Parson '; one entry describes him as " the Right Woorshypfull Mr Leonard Lowther Parson of Graistock." There were four clergy on the staff " Mr Parson dyd mynistre himselfe, and Sr Matthew, Sr Peter, and I did help him."[3] The three latter presumably served the chapels at Watermillock, Matterdale and Mungrisdale. When there was a ' general communion ' the people of the chapelries, accompanied by their curates, attended the parish church.[4] The communicants usually numbered between 450 and 480. As a

* He was a natural brother of Sir Richard Lowther (N.S., xl, 56-9).

sermon was preached and presumably morning prayer and
the litany said, the service must have been a lengthy one.
It is noticeable that though Holy Communion was
celebrated at least three times a year this was not, as the
Prayer Book orders, at Christmas, Easter and Whitsun
but generally in January and August, with an additional
third one; in 1605 in November, in 1609 in April, with the
note ' all the yonge fok dyd recieve.'

Between 1597 and 1609 some twenty sermons are
entered: Christmas Day, the first day in Lent, and St.
Matthew's day, a Wednesday, all occur once as sermon
days. Between 1602 and 1609 ' Mr. Parson' preached at
Watermillock on eight occasions. He was also rector of
Lowther and doubtless did so there as well. His curates
preached very rarely, presumably they read a homily.
' My Lo. Byshope of Carlisle ' preached twice in these
years, and in 1599 " dyd dyne there (at Greystoke castle)
and after evening prayer at church dyd confirme a great
numbre of children." After Lowther's death, the bishop
became rector. In 1610 there were sermons almost every
Sunday. And, what we would call to-day, a preaching
mission seems to have taken place between 23 December
and 1 January, with a sermon every day except two; five
of them by the bishop.

This picture is only fragmentary but it gives a glimpse
of what was doubtless considered a well ordered parish at
work. The reformed Church was, at any rate in some
places, putting its house in order. And it must be
remembered that the authorities had not only to overcome
the confusion caused by the Reformation but to contend
with the disordered state of the Borders.

The union of the Crowns had not produced immediate
peace; the legacy of generations of war still remained.
The state of affairs noticed at the end of the last reign
continued; while King James was on his way to London
he heard of a destructive Scots foray, which reached as far

as Penrith. The raiders were Grahams, of which family the Commissioners appointed in 1605 to bring order into the Borders stated " if the Grahams were not, these parts would be as free from blood and theft as Yorkshire." Eventually the authorities hit upon what they doubtless considered a happy solution—to transport most of the tribe to Northern Ireland. But another family, " that bloodie and theevish clanne of Armstrongs of Whithaughe," still remained.

A famous figure now appears on the scene—Lord William Howard of Naworth who seems to have regarded the catching of Armstrongs as a sport. After an expedition against them in 1607, he wrote to Sir Wilfred Lawson " I was away fishing and I took as many as I could get." Among the ' fish ' landed in this expedition was John Armstrong, otherwise known as " Jock Sowlugs.' Lord William's reputation as the great pacifier of the Borders has been somewhat tarnished by the amount of legend that has grown around it. In Wilson's opinion, however, he stands out in the dry light of authoritative records " as the greatest figure of his time in the civilisation of the Marches."[5] He was also a scholar and an antiquary. His library still remains in the room at the top of the tower at Naworth which he used as a study.*

England and Scotland now having one Crown there seemed no further need of Border Service, so in 1610 he attempted to reduce in status lands held by that service, especially those within the manor of Brampton. The tenants met at Gelt Bridge and bound themselves to resist, with the result that the leaders suffered heavy fines and imprisonment in the Fleet. However, in the end Lord William was not unreasonable and the tenants received long leases of their hereditary lands. This is not the last we will hear of this matter.[6]

---

* *The Lake Counties*, ed. 1932, 131-2. It is difficult to believe, in the light of Wilson's facts, that W. G. Collingwood is correct in denying that he was the great scourge of the moss troopers.

Another famous contemporary figure was John Denton*
of Cardew, the author of the *Accompt*, with whom the
bishop had a lawsuit in 1612-3 about the status of the
manor of Cardew. While nothing can dim Denton's
position as an historian, Wilson's researches have somewhat tarnished his reputation as a man. " It may truly
be said that before his death in 1617, John Denton was a
mischievous influence in Cumberland."[7]   He had been an
agent in the county for the discovery of concealed lands
on behalf of Queen Elizabeth.   This probably originally
necessitated the investigations at the Tower of London
which later on were to lay the foundations of his history.[8]
We also learn from this lawsuit that Denton, as kinsman
to Bishop Robinson, " had the veweing and marshalling
of all his evidences and was trusted to have access unto
them att his pleasure."   So, when it was found during the
preparation of the case that various charters of the
bishop's had been ' lost or embezelled,' Denton was
accused of the theft. Wilson was satisfied that he
vindicated himself; the present writer is not so sure of
this.   But, alas, there is no doubt that the charters were
missing.[9]

These lawsuits were typical of what was happening
throughout these counties.   Our ancestors, no longer
having the Scots upon whom to sublimate their pugnacious
instincts, fell to among themselves by means of interminable and innumerable lawsuits.   Anyone who wishes to
know something of their genius for litigation is recommended to read the story of the Patricksons of Ennerdale
during these years.[10]

The bishop died at Rose on 19 June, 1616, about three
in the afternoon, it is said, of the plague.   He was buried

* *Nicolson and Burn* (II, 284) erroneously call him George and *D.N.B.* has
followed them in this mistake.   Another error is that he was imprisoned in
the Tower of London as a result of this law suit and while thus confined made
his extracts from the royal records kept there.   (*An Accompt*. iii and N.S.
xxxix, 134-5).

in the cathedral about eleven o'clock at night on the same day.[11] The custom of burial at night was common among the gentry at this time. A brass to his memory was set up in Queen's College Chapel and another, almost similar, in the cathedral.[12]

" He was a prelate of great gravity and temperance, very mild in his speech, yet, as one observeth not of so strong a constitution of body as his countenance did promise."[13] He must probably be ranked among the greater bishops of Carlisle; under his rule the devastation caused by the Reformation was still further repaired.

Robert Snoden* was elected by the dean and chapter on 12 September 1616, and consecrated in York Minster on 24 November by Archbishop Matthew, receiving the temporalities on 20 December.[14]

In August 1617 King James visited Carlisle, and the bishop, reporting on the condition of the diocese, stated that:

" 1. The citie of Carlisle is in great ruine, and extreme poverty, partly because the Lieutenant is not there resiant and partly for that ye inhabitants exercise themselves in no Arts or trades, neither have they other meanes of livelyhood besides fishing."

" 2. In the country at large many of the meaner sort, live dispersedly in cottages, or little farmes, scarcely sufficient for their necessary maintenance, whereby idleness, thefts and robberies are occasioned. And according to the nature of the soile, and qualities of the air (like that in Norfolke) the vulgar people are subtill, violent, litigious, and pursuers of endless suites by appeales, to their utter impoverishment, the poor wretches finde admittance of their most unreasonable appeales, both at York and London, for which those higher Courts deserve to be blamed."

3. (Deals with the gentry and is not of much interest).

---

* His name is often spelt Snowden, but his wife signs Snoden so this spelling is used. A letter from her, beautifully written, about the Dalston dispute is in the Diocesan Registry (N.S. xxxix, 133).

" 4.   The state ecclesiastique is hugely weakened not onely by
Impropriations served by poor vicars, and multitudes of
base hirelings, but by compositions contracted in the
troubled time, and now prescribed, yet there are some
show of grave and learned pastors.   And albeit many of
them in their habits and external inconformities seme to
be Puritanes, yet have I not found any of repugnant
opinion to any of our summons or lawes ecclesiastical."

" And though my diocese is not infested with Recusants
so dangerousslye as the Bishoprickes of Duresme and
Chester, yet in my late visitacon some have been presented
and detected to the number of eightie or thereabouts."[15]

This episcopate was much disturbed by a dispute
between the bishop and his tenants at Dalston in 1620,
and especially with his bailiff John Lowther.   The bishop
alleged an " abundance of concealments improvements
and altered tenures that upon search were found."   The
parish was in an uproar; and Mrs. Lowther forced her
way into Mrs. Snoden's boudoir and abused her.   No
doubt Dalston hugely enjoyed itself, but whether the poor
bishop did is another matter.[16]

He died in London on 15 May 1621.   His place
of burial has not been found.

Richard Milburne,[17] bishop of St. David's, born at
Hullerbank near Talkin,[18] succeeded.   The royal assent
was given on 11 September 1621 and the temporalities
restored on 3 October.

The most interesting event during these episcopates was
the king's attempt to raise funds by seizing customary
lands in the Crown manors of Westmorland.   He asserted
that as these lands were held by Border Tenant Right
then, since there was no longer need of men to defend the
Border, there could not now be any legal validity in the
claim to hold land by that Right.   So in 1618/9, a bill in
Chancery was filed against the tenants of the manors in
the Richmond and Marquis fees of the barony of Kendale,
who compromised the action by the payment of £2,700 in
November 1619.

The lords of other manors within the Fees also wanted their bite out of this pie; to them the tenants would not submit. In January 1620 over a hundred of them assembled in Staveley Chapel, instructed an attorney and agreed to meet the expenses out of a common purse. They also preferred a petition to the king to be allowed to retain their custom of tenant right; and got a Bill introduced into the House of Commons for that purpose, in this, however, the Crown apparently forestalled them. Neither Bill made any progress. So the king endeavoured to settle the question by a royal proclamation abolishing this tenure, which Dr. Burn stigmatizes as " one of the most flagrant exertions of despotism that is to be met with in English History."

But the spirit of the Border was not dead. The men of Westmorland were quite prepared to defend their homes against the Scots, whether seated in Edinburgh or London. They commissioned Anthoine Wedtherell, vicar of Kirkby Stephen, to draw up an answering remonstrance in which they complained that the landlords intended

" to pull the skins over their ears, and bray their bones in a mortar: That having peaceably enjoyed their tenements so long, it would be hard that some greedy eagle or devouring vulture should violently pull them out to miseries. The poor bird and weaker cattle are taught and encouraged, for maintenance of their ancient possession, to resist others even to death, though more able and strong, by far than they are. And it was a common saying among them—' If the devil be lord, I'll be tenant '."

Upon this a bill was exhibited against them in the Star Chamber for a libel, and the vicar of Kirkby Stephen charged with the making of it. Eventually the matter was referred to the local Assizes, as the king informed the bishop, stating that he had ordered the judges strictly to enforce the proclamation. The next we know is that the cause came on for hearing in the Star Chamber on 7 November 1623. The defendants' answer was that

" they held their lands and tenements by customary estate of inheritance, descendible from ancestor to heir, by the payment of customary fines, heriots, rents, boons, and Services, and not by Border service, and have pleaded not guilty."

The Court referred the matter to the Chief Justice of the King's Bench and other judges. Their answer, filed on 19 June 1625, decided that Border service was no part of the obligations of these estates but referred again to the Court of Star Chamber the question whether the fines in dispute were fixed, or arbitrary at the will of the lord. The final outcome on this is not known; on the larger issue the tenants had, without doubt, won a decisive victory.[19]

Little is known of this episcopate. After the bishop's death, under 21 January 1625, the following entry occurs in Lord William Howard's Household Books: " to Mr Leonard Milborn* for a coach and 4 horses xxx*li*."[20] Doubtless the sale of his lordship's travelling coach—this means of conveyance had only been introduced into England from the Continent in Elizabeth's reign.

He had died, probably in May 1624; according to Todd at "Rose; lyes buried (as is said) in St. Mary's church yard in Carlisle without any epitaph or grave stone."[21]

Did he die of the plague? 1623/4 was a year of excessive mortality. So much attention has been paid to the great epidemic of 1597/8† that the effects of this later visitation have been overlooked. Apparently a form of typhus fever, it was at its worst in Scotland in the winter of 1622/3, and was caused by a famine comparable to one of the great medieval ones.[22] Evidence of this is afforded by some pathetic entries in the Greystoke burial register for 1623:

---

* The bishop's son; he was vicar of Ousby from 1622 and Skelton from 1623.

† All local histories give the inscription, originally on the north wall of the vestry of Penrith old church, which states that 2500 died at Kendal, 2200 at Richmond, 2266 at Penrith and 1196 at Carlisle. It is generally supposed these figures refer to the deaneries, not the towns, named (o.s. xi, 173).

' a poore hunger sterven beger child '; ' a poore fellowe destitute of all meanes to live '; ' Thomas, son of Richard Bell a pore man, which child dyed for verie want of food and maintenance to live.'

There are nineteen such entries between March and November.   Other parish registers* shew an exceptionally high death rate, suggesting a wide spread epidemic, often worse than the 1597 one.   In many places the number of burials was four or five times above the average.   At Millom the mortality on the second occasion was almost four times as large as on the first; at Watermillock, Newbiggin (St. Edmund), Warcop, Ravenstonedale, Dalston, Bridekirk and St. Bees, double; and at Cartmel, Crosthwaite (W), Brough, and Greystoke, substantially larger than before.   While at Langwathby, Lowther, Crosthwaite (C), Morland, Lamplugh, and Kirkby Lonsdale the numbers were much the same each time, and at Penrith and Edenhall a great deal less at the second visitation.[23]

Richard,[24] 2nd son of John Senhouse of Netherhall was consecrated at York by Archbishop Matthew, receiving the temporalities on 14 October 1624.   Fuller describes him as

" A valiant man in his younger days; and I have heard that in his old age he felt the admonitions of his youthful over violent exercises . . . and became an excellent preacher, his sermons losing no lustre by his good utterance and graceful delivering of them."†

He preached the sermon at Charles I's coronation.   He was killed by a fall from his horse on 6 May 1626.   Nicolson and Burn[25] say that he was buried in the cathedral, but the Dalston register contains an entry of it on 7 May.

Francis White,[26] dean of Carlisle, was consecrated at Durham House on 3 December 1626.

---

* Unfortunately in a good many registers one of the vital years is missing; evidence perhaps of the effect of the plague.

† Fuller's idea of what constituted old age is curious; judging by his dates at Cambridge and those of the 1665 Visitation pedigree, the bishop can hardly have been more than fifty at his death (*Worthies*, ed., 1840, I, 343).

" The service executed by John Cosin, archdeacon of the East Riding in York, the sermon by him preached.   The hymns and psalms sung solemnly by the choice of the king's quire, with those of St. Paul's and Westminster.   The Communion Service, and the consecration, executed by the bishop of Durham.

The Epistle read ⎱   in the King's ⎰ by John Cosin
The Gospel read ⎰   Copes   ⎱ by H. Wickham
                                    archdeacons of York.

The offertory solemnly made by more than twenty persons, bishops, doctors, and other divines of note."[27]

A paper rental of this bishop's was in the Diocesan Registry in 1912.   It gives particulars of the management of the episcopal estates.   At Rose " the constant house-hould, besides worke foulkes and straingers (numbered) about thirty five or thirty six."   The schedule of "fees due att the making of Ministers and Deacons" must make the clergy glad that bishops do not live in such style to-day.*

A copy of the particulars the bishop required at his visitation of the diocese is in the Bodleian Library.   It is entitled " *Articles to be enquired of in the Diocese of Carlisle in the Visitation of the Reverend Father in God, Frances, Bishop of Carlisle.*"   Wilson does not seem to have known of these Articles.

After the visitation the bishop's secretary complained that

" there was never a doctor of divinitie nor advocate, but eleven or twelve licensed preachers, three or four bachelors of Divinity and eight double beneficed men."[28]

This again emphasises the point made by every bishop of the lack of educated clergy, due now more to the poverty of the livings than to the unsettled state of the times.

The visitation articles consist of seventy eight questions.

* There were fifteen officials to be paid, from the archdeacon to the baker, " besides the poser, both att Institution, Ordination & Licencing, maye att examination-demand for his fee ijs. vid. as both Byshop Senhouse warranted his chaplaine and my Lord did me " (Wilson, 147-8; *V.C.H.*, II, 90).

As to the Holy Communion the bishop asked:

" Whether has the blessed sacrament of the Lord's Supper been duely and reuerently administered every moneth, or thrice euery yeere at least, whereof once at Easter to every parishioner of sixteen years and upwards ?" whether it is " deliuered unto or receiued by any of the communicants within your parish that unreuerently sit or stand, or doe not deuoutly and humbly kneele upon their knees ? "

Concerning the ornaments of the Church, the questions include whether the parish has

" a whole Bible of the largest volume of the last translation, the Book of Common Prayer, the two bookes of Homilies and Bishop Jewel's Apologie ? " Whether a Font of Stone " is set up in the ancient usuall place "; " whether there is a conuenient and decent Communion Table with a carpet at time of divine service "; and " a faire linnen cloath at the time of administering the Communion ?"; also whether " is the same Table placed conueniently as it ought, and whether it is so used out of time of diuine service or sermon as is not agreeable to the holy use of it as by sitting on it, or by throwing hats on it, or writing on it, or is it abused to other profaner uses; are the tenne commandments set up on the east end of your church, and whether sentences of Scripture about ? Whether a conuenient seate for your minister to diuine service, together with a comely pulpit set up in a conuenient place with a decent cloth or cushion for the same, whether there is a comely large and fine surplice, a faire Communion cup, a flagon of silver or pewter ? Whether hath any in your parish defaced, or caused to be defaced, any monuments or ornaments in your church " ?

The next section concerns the behaviour of the clergy.

" Whether doth your minister distinctly and reuerently say diuine service upon Sunday and Holidaies and other days appointed to be observed by the Book of Common Prayer, as Wednesdaies, Fridaeies and the eves of every Sunday and Holiday ?" Does he " wear the surplice and dothe he never omit wearing such ?" " Doth he receive the same (the Holy Communion) himself on every day that he administereth to others ?; Doth he never omit the Sign of the Cross in baptism ?; Doth he every ' marry without a ring ?' There are questions asking " Doth he catechise the youth of his parish upon Sundaies and

holidaies, before evening Prayer for halfe an hour or more?"
" Doth he in the Rogation Dayes goe in perambulation of the
circuit of the parish saying and using the Prayers as appointed
by law, according to his duty, thanking God for his blessing and
praying for his grace and favour?"   " If your minister, not being
a preacher, doe every Sunday, when there is no Sermon, reade
some part of the Homilies set forth?"

There is an interesting section about the use of
Confession

" Whether your minister before the several times of the Administration of the Lord's Supper admonish and exhort his parishioners,
if they have their consciences troubled and disquieted to resort
unto him, or some other learned minister, and open his grief, that
he may receive such ghostly councill and comfort as his consience
may be relieved, and by the minister he may receive the benefit
of absolution to the quieting of his conscience and the avoiding
of all scruple.   And if any man confess his secret and hidden
sinnes, being sick or whole, to the minister, for the unburthering
of his conscience, and receiving such spiritual consolation, doth or
hath the said minister at any time revealed or made known to any
person whatsoever any crime or offence so comitted to his
trust and secrecie contrary to the 113 Canon?"

In the part concerning parishioners there is a question
about penance for drunkenness and adultery

" what corporal punishments for any such offences have been
commuted and changed into a pecuniary mulct or summe of
money by an ecclesiastical judge exercising jurisdiction in this
diocese?" and   " Who in your parish doe come to the sermon
only, and not to diuine service; and who doe not reuerently
behave them selves during the time of diuine service, devoutly
kneeling when the general confession of Sinnes, the letany, the
tenne Commandments and all prayers and collects are read and
using all duly and lowly reuerence when the blessed name of the
Lord Jesus is mentioned, and standing up when the articles of
the Beliefe, the Magnificat, Nunc Dimittis, the Te Deum,
Benedictus and Gloria Patri are read, or who doe cover their
heads in the church during the whole time of diuine service,
unless it be of necessitie, in which case they may weare a night
cap . . .?"

Within a year of this visitation, on 9 February 1628,
Bishop White was translated to Norwich.

The see had now had four bishops in twelve years, Barnabie Potter,[29] provost of Queen's College, Oxford, born at Kendal on 11 August 1577, was to occupy the bishopric longer. He was consecrated at Ely House, Holborn, by Archbishop Harsnett of York on 15 March 1629, and received the temporalities on 23 March.

He must have begun his visitation almost at once as the articles were printed in 1629. Wilson refers to it,[30] but does not seem to have seen the original articles[31] as he makes no mention of several interesting questions. The form is much the same as Bishop White's but shorter as this time there were only fifty-five questions, divided into two sections for clergy and laity, instead of seventy-eight. The question as to the use of the surplice is, whether the minister "usually" wears it? He is also asked "whether he has churched any woman after the birth of an illegitimate child without public confession?" (private confession is not referred to, nor is Holy Communion) if he perambulates his parish "as hath been prescribed, and doe use the same without superstition or popish ceremonies"; and if he makes known to the people "what holy days and fasting days are in the following week?"

Some of the questions addressed to the laity are very interesting. The first, the ordinary one about the furniture and ornaments of the church, varies in several respects from Bishop White's: two psalters are added to his requirements, and Bishop Jewel's 'Apology' omitted. The questions as to the font, communion table and pulpit are much the same, but the detailed ones about the possible irreverent use of the table are omitted, so is that about any monument or ornament being defaced. That on the position of the font asks "whether any persons leaving the use thereof doe baptize children in basons or other vessels within the church?"

But the two most interesting questions are:

S

" Whether are there within your said parish any rush bearing, bull baiting, May games, morice dances, marriage offerings, ales or any such like profane pastimes or assemblies on the Sabboth." And

" Whether be there (any) that use to ring the bells super-stitiously upon any abrogated holy days or the evens thereof, and whether is the Passing Bell tolled when any Christian body is sicke and like to dye, as it ought to be; and after the death of any whether there be any superstitious ringing, superstitious burning of candles over the corpse in the day time, after it be light; or praying for the dead at Crosses or places where crosses have been in the way to the church, or any other superstitious use of crosses, with Towels, Palmes, Metwindes,* or other ceremonies of idolatry at Burialls, or superstitiously doe goe on Pilgrimages, or any place dedicated to Our Lady or any Saints or otherwise."†

In these two sets of Visitation Articles the reader will find already in being the main ' platforms ' of two of the schools of the Anglican Church: Bishop White is of the High Church one, Bishop Potter of the Low Church. It is interesting to note how soon the Elizabethan ideal of uniformity had broken down.

The evidence available suggests that the diocese was still in a sorry state. The bishop reported to Archbishop Neile that the wretched stipends of the benefices forced him to admit mean scholars to the diaconate rather than to allow the people to be utterly without Divine Service. He also complained of the supineness of churchwardens

* This word does not occur in either the *Oxford English Dictionary*, nor in the *Dialect Dictionary*.

† Professor Hamilton Thompson, consulted by the writer on the meaning of this passage which he describes as ' extremely interesting ', was kind enough to send this answer

" I am not clear whether ' Towels, Palmes, Metwindes,' etc., are meant to be independent of Crosses, or whether they and the other ceremonies are cited as accompaniments of crosses at funerals. If the second is the case, which I think it is, then it is possible that Towels may mean cloths in which the processional cross was shrouded for the occasion. Palmes suggest palm-crosses which may have been carried by mourners, or it may be that a palm-cross was fastened on the cross or the shroud which covered it. Metwindes, I fear, is quite beyond me; it may be a mispelt form of ' Metwands,' but what use there can have been for yard-measures at such times I cannot say. Nothing else, however, suggests itself."

who never present absentees from church and of magistrates who never punish them.[32]

It seems as if the cathedral was in no better way. The three officers in 1634 described it as

" like a great wild country church, as it appeared outwardly, so it was inwardly neither beautify'd nor adorn'd one whit. The organ and the voices did well agree, the one being like a shrill bag pipe; the other the Scottish tone . . . The communion also was administered and receiv'd in a wild and unreverent manner."[33]

In December 1639, the bishop writing to Secretary Windebank mentions its state

" as soon as I could receive an answer from the dean, I come to give you an account of my care to see His Majesty's royal and religious commands performed for the repairing of the Cathedral Church of Carlisle."[34]

The bishop, discussing how the money can be obtained, refers to the possibility of doing so by means of gifts from the dean and canons, who do not appear to have been over enthusiastic.

He died in London and was buried in St. Paul's, Covent Garden on 6 January 1642.

" His character was most exemplary in every particular, and his household, by his precept and example, so devout that it was called the pious family. Notwithstanding his office, at that time hated by many, he was beloved by all sects, and even those who refused to come to Church were happy with him, because, said they, we would go with him to Heaven."[35]

Fuller says of him:

" he was commonly called the puritannical bishop; and they would say of him in the time of King James, ' that organs would blow him out of the church,' which I do not believe, the rather because he was loving of and skilful in vocal music, and would bear his own part therein. He was a constant preacher, and performer of family duties; of a weak constitution, melancholy, lean, and a hard student."[36]

After this James Usher, the celebrated archbishop of

Armagh held the see, with his Irish one. His letters patent are dated 16 February 1642; but within a year episcopacy had been abolished.

II.

THE CIVIL WAR AND THE COMMONWEALTH.

'The Troubles,'[37] as they have been called by local writers, may be said to have begun in Cumberland in January 1638 when the king ordered the local nobility and gentry to prepare for the defence of that part of the kingdom. In the following year a garrison of 500 men was placed in Carlisle and Sir Nicholas Byron appointed governor. The city's accounts shew how the inhabitants prepared for defence, with corporal Brown's boy as drummer. In 1640 £345 was spent in buying powder and the trained bands of these counties under Sir Philip Musgrave were called out. However in 1641, the danger seeming to pass away, the garrison was disbanded and the arms and munitions of war stored in the Fratry; but not for long.

In August 1642 the king raised his Standard at Nottingham. The local gentry were mostly royalists. In 1643 an attempt was made to take the city by those on the parliamentary side, of whom Sir Wilfred Lawson was the chief—" A Rascall route " Isaac Tullie calls them—but they were driven off by the royalist gentry. In the south at about the same time Lord Molyneux, while besieging Lancaster castle with the Westmorland royalists and others, made a three days raid into Furness,* returning with much plunder. Next, failing to take Lancaster, the royalists suddenly ' stole into ' Thurland castle. In reply Colonel Rigby, early in August, commenced its siege, without interference from a numerous force of royalists at

---

* I have to thank Mr. J. Melville for helping me with the Furness parts of this section.

Kirkby Lonsdale. In south Cumberland Sir William Hudleston, who had been collecting the king's supporters, crossed the Duddon on 28 September, with his Millom men and some from Muncaster under William Pennington. At Kirkby they were joined by a contingent from Furness and Cartmel. The whole force then established themselves at Dalton. News of these events reaching Colonel Rigby, he marched to Ulverston in one day covering thirty miles 'over mountain and through sea and water.' He found his opponents well posted on Lindale close, barring his road. Despite a disparity in numbers, though not in equipment, he at once attacked with complete success, capturing Colonel Hudleston, with several other gentlemen and some 300 of his men.[38]

Next year the crisis of the war in the North turned on the royalist defence of York. To its relief hastened two famous men, Prince Rupert and James Graham, marquis of Montrose. The impetuous prince not waiting for Montrose, Marston Moor resulted. After this disastrous defeat Rupert at first made for Richmond where he was joined by Montrose, who begged him for assistance but getting none, rode by Brough and Appleby,[39] to Carlisle, whence he soon departed on the first of his famous campaigns. Rupert meanwhile had turned south and, after detaching Sir John Mayne into Furness, reached Kirkby Lonsdale on July 18, staying for two days.[40] From there he wrote to Sir John Lowther, the custodian of Brougham castle, who had provisioned it with 'corne and fireinge,' confirming his appointment.[41]

Meanwhile Sir John Mayne had established his headquarters at Dalton. Not far off, in Piel harbour, lay part of the parliamentary fleet, so some of the sailors with local sympathisers set off to drive him out. This second battle for Dalton fought at Newton or Hawcoat reversed the result of the first; the 200 prisoners were sent to the prince at Kirkby Lonsdale. Next Sir John's forces, after burning Northscales on Walney island, settled down at Holker, but by September were compelled by fear of the Scots in Westmorland and Colonel Dodding from Lancaster to retreat, this he successfully accomplished.[42]

Now we must turn back to the north. After the fall of York its governor, Sir Thomas Glemham, retired upon Carlisle, pursued by the Scots under David Leslie. But, after forcing the passage of the Eden at Salkeld—in which engagement Richard Barwise of Ilekirk, a noted Cromwellian, distinguished himself—Leslie returned to the east coast. Sir Thomas, who had been appointed governor of the city, took advantage of this respite to provision it, with the help of the royalist gentry and clergy. Thus the siege did not begin until October. The city was defended with the utmost gallantry by the citizens. When it eventually capitulated, on 25 June, 1645, owing to famine and not to any assault, it was " upon as honourable conditions as any that were given in any surrenders ". The garrison marched out with the honours of war.[43]

The leaders joined the king's army and served under Sir Philip Musgrave. But the battle of Rowton Heath was fatal to the Cumberland contingent: Sir Henry Fletcher and Philip Howard were slain, Musgrave and Sir Thomas Dacre wounded and taken prisoners. But Hudleston Philipson instead rode to relieve his brother, ' Robin the devil ' who was besieged on Long Holme, now Belle Island, Windermere. Next day,* a Sunday, the latter performed his celebrated feat of riding into Kendal church, up one aisle and down the other, in search of some one with whom he desired to do battle. Despite being

---

* This story has been questioned by critics; as it comes from the Westmorland antiquary, Thomas Machell, 1647-98 (MSS. II, fo. 342), there seems no reason for doubting it. His MSS., in five volumes, were used by Nicolson and Burn, and are among the dean and chapter muniments. They deal solely with his own county and come within the same category as Bishop Nicolson's and Dr. Todd's collections.

unhorsed by the guards when he came out, he succeeded in making his escape.[44]

During the siege of Carlisle parliamentarians elsewhere were busy subduing other royalist strongholds. Perhaps even before its investment the Scots had plundered Sir Philip Musgrave's castle at Hartley to the tune of £3000, which sum did not include his loss of stock at Edenhall.[45] In October 1644 the castles of Millom, Naworth and Scaleby were still holding out. The latter did not fall until February 1645.[46] As the will of Nathaniel Warde, vicar of Staindrop, who fell in the siege of Millom, was not proved till April 1645, it seems probable that this castle also held out some time.[47] Nothing more is known of the fate of Naworth.

The second civil war began here in March 1648 with a daring raid by some royalists on Carlisle castle which temporarily regained its possession for the king. By May, Sir Philip Musgrave and Sir Marmaduke Langdale had turned this into a permanent occupation. They then set about raising these counties but met with a rebuff on 13 May in ' the great (parliamentary) victory of Kendale Heath,' losing 300 prisoners. Despite this by the end of the month they had raised 5000 foot and 800 horse.[48] These events caused the despatch to the scene of General Lambert who reached Penrith on 15 June. Next day Colonel Ashton passed through Kirkby Lonsdale and occupied Kendal on his way to join his general.[49] From Penrith Lambert organised a series of attacks on royalist castles. Of the fate of Appleby, we know nothing, except that it fell, but Scaleby, which shared this misfortune, was probably fired. This certainly happened at Greystoke and Rose. So when we read Lady Anne Clifford's statement that in 1649 Brougham was ' verie ruinous and much out of repair ' and Sir Daniel Fleming's assertion that it ' received great damage in the time of the late Rebellion ' there is little doubt when this happened.

Thus in terms of destructiveness the parliamentarians had not passed an unprofitable month.[50]

Then there came another quick change of fortune for, on 8 July, the duke of Hamilton, from Scotland, reached Carlisle, where he placed a garrison of Scots under Sir William Livingstone. Within a week Lambert was falling back towards Stainmore; the duke, following him, captured Appleby. From there Hamilton turned west, marching by way of Orton to Kendal, which he reached on 2 August. After a week's stay, he moved south to Kirkby Lonsdale and Lancashire to meet his fate at Preston.[51] All that remained for the parliamentary forces to do here were ' mopping up operations ' against the few remaining royalist strongholds. Cockermouth castle, besieged for three months by Sir William Hudleston, was relieved by Colonel Ashton on 29 September. On 1 October Carlisle castle was surrendered to Cromwell in person.' He left a garrison, which included two regiments of horse for the purpose of suppressing the moss troopers.[52] Then on 9, or 16* April, Appleby castle was captured by Colonel Ashton. The prisoners who included Sir William Hudleston, who had retired there from Cockermouth, Sir Philip Musgrave, Sir Robert Strickland, Sir Thomas Dacre and 1200 horse, received honourable terms. The leaders were required to go overseas; the rest were sent home.[53]

Next year the king was beheaded and the Commonwealth began. Two years later Charles II, travelling through Cumberland on the way to Worcester, passed by Dalston and Hutton. At the latter Dr. Todd, the rector, waited on him. He described Charles as looking ' very pale and pensive.'[54]

It was after this campaign that Sir Timothy Fetherstonhaugh of Kirkoswald was beheaded at Chester, on 22

---

* The usual date given is the 16th, but *Strickland of Sizergh*, H. Hornyold-Strickland, 116 note, suggests that the former is correct.

October 1651.   His last letters to his wife* are beautiful and pathetic documents.   One quotation will illustrate their spirit:

" As much as you can advise and educate them (his children) in the feare of the Lord and lett them never neglect prayers and private duties.   Settle them in Religion, there are now manie and scarce any good or visable but the olde.   I desire them to Love and still to be helpfull and assisting one to another and so God Almightie will bless and help them, they suckt nothing but virtue from thy wombe and in the presence of God I speak itt thou hast been to me an unparaleld wife and a mother to my children. Though my death be fatall, and some will make itt scandalous, yet posteritie truthe another generation may not call itt soe, nor would have our age have called it so ten years since."[55]

We must see now how these events affected the Church in this diocese.   The date of the ejection of the cathedral dignitaries is uncertain.   They were probably turned out soon after the siege.   The traditional story is that, despite the provision in the terms of capitulation that churches should not be touched, part of the cathedral nave, the chapter house, prebendal residences, with parts of the deanery and cloisters were " in a moment of fanatical fury . . . pulled down, and the materials . . . sacrilegiously used to build a main guard and repair the fortifications of the city."[56]   This tradition cannot in the main be doubted; it descends from Dr. Todd, whose evidence is nearly contemporary.   But there is also evidence that these buildings were already in a bad way. Bishop Snoden in 1617 stated that " the citie of Carlisle is in great ruine, and extreme poverty," and Bishop Potter in 1639 mentioned the king's commands " for the repairing of the Cathedral Church of Carlisle."†   It seems possible therefore that the cathedral and abbey buildings had been allowed to fall into a bad state and that the Scots merely completed what neglect had begun.   Documents suffered as much as persons and buildings, of the

* Bridget, daughter of Thomas Patrickson.
† p. 249 and p. 259.

cathedral muniments Bishop Nicolson records: ' And our very charters (were) sold to make a Taylor's Measures.'* It is noticeable how many of our ecclesiastical records only date from about the Restoration—the Rockcliffe parish registers were certainly purloined by the Scots in 1648—others may have suffered in a similar way.[57]

Fortunately B. Nightingale's researches[58] have made it possible to give fairly definite statistics of the fate of the parochial clergy. In the present diocese, 21 were ejected and in the deaneries of Coupland and Kendale, 10 suffered a like fate; 15 clergy of the diocese and 7 of the 2 deaneries were restored in 1660; 2 of the former had died, the fate of 4 is unknown; of the latter, one had died, and the story of 2 is unknown.

What happened to these ejected clergy? Little evidence is available. Many of them, like Richard Sterne, the future bishop, probably became schoolmasters. In some cases this was in their old parishes where they were thus enabled to give the sacraments from time to time. We get glimpses of them occasionally: Philip Bouch, Cler., an ejected fellow of Oriel College, Oxford† and a Cockermouth man, is found witnessing a Lamplugh family wedding in 1654.[59] Probably one of them had given him shelter. Others were less fortunate. George Buchanan, vicar of Kirkby Lonsdale, suffered " near three years imprisonment."[60] The Commonwealth authorities were not without consideration for the wives and children of these men; they were allowed a fifth of the income of the benefice as sustenance.

After the fall of episcopacy, the control of the parishes was divided between various sects, especially independents

---

* English Historical Library, ed. 1697, pt. II, p. 124. Presumably other missing cathedral muniments, manor rolls, fabric rolls, etc. were destroyed at the same time.

† He had told Cromwell's Commissioners before he was deprived of his fellowship that " I cannot in my conscience performe these things." (*The Registers of the Visitors of the University of Oxford*, 1647-58, ed. M. Burrows, 66).

and presbyterians, until a religious genius appeared and
emptied the churches of all of them. George Fox, ' in a
few years was almost universally accepted as the sovereign
pontiff of Cumberland '—and these words are equally
true of the other two counties—first preached locally at
Firbank in Westmorland, in 1652. After speaking in
Preston Patrick chapel, he ' went to Kendal where a
meeting was appointed in the Town Hall, . . . After the
meeting I staid awhile in the town.' Next he went to
Underbarrow and preached in the chapel there; ' many
of Crook and Underbarrow were convinced that day.'
From Westmorland he passed on to Newton in Cartmel,
then he was at ' Lyndal,' and ' from hence I went to
Ulverstone and so to Swarthmore to Judge Fell's,' where
he met his future wife Margaret Fell. During his stay
he preached in most of the villages of Furness and ' had
very large meetings in Westmorland.'

Next year after preaching at Swarthmore and Arnside,
he was in Cumberland—the first place he names is Bootle
where he preached in ' the steeple-house ' and the next
Millom—tradition affirms that he also stayed at Ash
House, Thwaites.* According to his *Journal* he went
from there direct to Cockermouth and Brigham but the
number of Quakers shewn in the 1684 visitation returns
suggests that he stayed at other places. The next one
he mentions is ' near Colbeck '; then passing to a market
town, ' where I had a meeting at the cross ' (was this
Wigton?), he came to Carlisle. There, after preaching
in the castle and at the market-cross, he says ' I went into
the steeple-house and, after the priest had done, I preached
the truth to the people.' His words, however, caused

---

* It also asserts that his ghost—' a figure in a broad-brimmed hat '—
appears. ' He goes in at a wall upstairs, where there is a walled up staircase,
and comes out down below,' so Mrs. Cross told Miss Fair. I am indebted to
the latter for this and other information about Coupland; also for a description of its history, and a very true one too, as ' a howling wilderness of
blanks.'

such an uproar in the city that the magistrates imprisoned him as 'a blasphemer, an heretic and a seducer.' After his release he continued preaching in these counties.[61]

Fox's success caused such consternation among the independents of the Cockermouth district that they met at Bridekirk in 1654 for a confession of faith ' that they might stand against that deluge of errors that had overflown the country and had shattered to pieces the congregations about Broughton.' Further results of his preaching were movements among his opponents for the increase of church discipline and unity, but all scandalous persons, such as episcopalians, papists and quakers were to be excluded. The moving spirit in these efforts was Richard Gilpin, pastor of Greystoke, a minister of refined and scholarly attainments.[62] But Fox was back again in Cumberland in 1657, travelling from Kendal by Strickland-head where ' most of the gentry of that country being gathered to an horse race, not far off from the meeting, I was moved to go and declare the truth unto them.' This journey included a visit to Gilsland (the district, not the place which did not then exist) Carlisle and the Abbey Holme, and ' a large meeting there is gathered to the Lord.' Next he was at Langlands (near Uldale) for a general meeting ' which was very large; for most of the people had so forsaken the priests that the steeple-houses in some places stood empty.' A meeting at Pardsey Crag followed at which John Wilkinson pastor of Brigham, declared his conversion.

He made another tour of these counties in 1663, when a general meeting was held at Pardsey Crag; he travelled back to Swarthmoor by Keswick and Rydal. That was his last visit to Cumberland but he was at Swarthmoor in 1675-9.[63]

Perhaps the most striking result of Fox's work was its permanence. It is interesting to compare his itinerary with the lists of Quakers in visitation and similar documents and to note that wherever he preached, there, a generation and more afterwards, his followers were still to be found. It is also noticeable that as a general rule they are not found in any great numbers elsewhere—the Penrith and Greystoke districts are the only exceptions observed.[64]

In 1658 Cromwell died; and on 29 May 1660 Charles II entered London. The wheels of fortune had turned; Church and episcopacy were restored. The ejected returned to their livings; their supplanters, to the number of twenty-seven, went out[65]—the remainder presumably agreed with the vicar of Bray.

III.

RESTORATION AND REVOLUTION.

Richard Sterne[65a] was consecrated in Henry VII's chapel, Westminster by Archbishop Frewen of York on 2 December 1660. He had plenty of tasks awaiting him. His diocese was in a pitiable condition: the cathedral nave demolished; the deanery and canons' houses uninhabitable; the remainder of the abbey buildings, except the fratry, pulled down; only one of the capitular body alive; and many livings filled by men, who, even if they conformed outwardly, were but time servers. But Rose though much damaged in the wars, had been partially repaired and lived in by a Cromwellian general.

Among the archiepiscopal records at York is one of a visitation of the diocese of Carlisle—the volume also includes particulars of the Richmond deaneries—undertaken by the chancellor of the archbishop in October 1662. As the document contains lists of incumbents and curates, with particulars of their ordination and careers, it is of considerable interest. It probably represents an attempt on the part of the authorities to check up on the antecedents of the clergy and to insure that they had all received episcopal ordination.

But the bishop held the see for less than four years, so the main work of reconstruction fell upon his successor. He did, however, rebuild the chapel at Rose, which was consecrated on 13 September 1663. Burnet accuses him of " minding chiefly enriching himself." His behaviour there seems to bear this out. Receiving as much money from fines and leases as might have rebuilt the castle, all he did was to refit a few rooms and build some outhouses, leaving his unfortunate successor minus the fines but plus the repairs.[66]   In the diocese the restoration of Church life and discipline began. There is a small slip of paper in the bishop's registry headed: " Given by Mr. Lowther* to ye poor March 22 1664 in consideration of eating of flesh in Lent £1. 6. 8.," with a list of the poor who benefited. The bishop took steps to " afford the rite and benefit of Confirmation by prayer and imposition of hands upon all such people as shall come duely prepared for the receiving of the same."[67]

His efforts must have been sadly hindered by the state of the Borders. The tradition of generations of disorder was not to be lightly overcome and the troubles of the last twenty years had revived the latent spirit of lawlessness. Conditions were so bad that parliament in 1662 passed an Act for the purpose of putting down disorderly and lawless persons, commonly called Moss troopers, who had for many years frequented the counties of Northumberland and Cumberland, and who had increased " since the time of the late unhappy distractions." A crude police force was established to deal with these broken men. The extent of their depredations can be realised from the fact that, not only the Border district, but places so far south as Keswick, Egremont, and Bootle had to be watched.[68]

* John Lowther of Rose.

V.   LADY ANNE CLIFFORD

(*facing p.* 271)

Bishop Sterne was translated to York in 1664. An interesting letter from him to his successor, dated September 1664, giving advice on many matters of diocesan routine, is in the Carlisle registry.[69]

At some point in this history an account must be given of that great lady Anne of Pembroke. This place seems a suitable one, especially as she has been described as a " repairer of breaches and the restorer of paths to dwell in,"[70] the very thing the Church was trying to do. She was Anne, daughter and eventual sole heiress of George Clifford, 3rd earl of Cumberland; Baroness Clifford, Westmorland and Vescy, Lady of the Honour of Skipton in Craven, and High Sheriffess, by inheritance of the county of Westmorland, in right of her father; Countess Dowager of Dorset by her first marriage, and of Pembroke and Montgomery by her second.

She was a devoted adherent of the Church and much attached to its liturgy. It is typical of her that even during the Commonwealth years she refused to communicate, except according to the Prayer Book, and kept, so Bishop Rainbow said, " the rules and forms of sound words prescribed by the Rubrics." She had a chaplain at each of her houses who read to her a daily chapter of the Bible and morning prayers. Her diary abounds in Scriptural references. She was punctilious in taking the Sacrament and often arranged that her whole household also received.

Alluding to her residence at Brougham castle in 1661, she says: " I received the Sacrament there, once at Christmas in the chapel, once at Ninekirks on Easter Day and in July at Brougham chapel which I have recently built." Of the next Easter Day she states " I received the Blessed Sacrament in the church called Ninekirks, this being the first time I came into it, after I had repaired and new built the said church." Elsewhere she says that " it was larger and bigger than it was before and would in

all likelyhood have fallen down, it was soe ruinous, if it
had not bin now repaired by me." The date 1660 with
the initials A.P. are in relief plaster on the east wall of
the church, which still remains almost as she left it. Her
memory is also preserved in Brougham by the Countess's
Pillar which commemorates her last parting from her
mother in 1616 " in memorial whereof she also left an
annuity of four pounds to be distributed to ye poor within
this parish of Brougham, every 2nd day of April for
ever, upon ye stone table here hard by." This laudable
ceremony is still kept up.

In 1655 she caused a great part of Appleby parish
church to be taken down " it being very ruinous and in
great danger of fallinge of itself." She also built there a
vault for her burial. " The whole cost me," she adds,
" about six or seven hundred poundes, being finished the
yeare followinge." Her tomb, with a magnificent display
of Clifford heraldry, is in this church. She also had
Bongate church pulled down and " new builte up
again att my owne charge." But her most enduring
memorial at Appleby must be in the hearts of the old
women who live in the beautiful alms houses she built
there. Perhaps she also repaired the church at Kirkby
Thore, in which the Clifford and Vipont arms are to be
found. Mallerstang had been in decay for some fifty or
sixty years when she decided to restore it. In February
1662, she received an estimate, still in existence, amounting to £46. 15. 6. And in November 1667, she signed a
trust deed settling on the ' Chapell of Mallerstange '
certain lands in Sedbergh which cost her £220, for the
maintenance of a reader to take the " prayers and
Homilies of the Church of England " and " to educate
the children of the Dale . . . in the first beginnings of
reading and writing English." Finally, she set up a
tablet with her initials commemorating what she had
done.

She was on friendly terms with Bishop Rainbow, to whom she presented her portrait which still hangs at Rose. She also gave him one of her famous locks, with her initials " A.P." and the date ' 1673 ' on it which is still used to secure the main door at the castle. She was a great lady, a loyal and devout member of the Church, a benefactor to this diocese, and a true lover of the North Country. She died on 19 March 1676 at Brougham Castle, aged eighty-six years and two months, and was buried in the church of St. Lawrence, Appleby on 14 April.[71]

Edward Rainbow[72] was consecrated by Archbishop Sheldon in Lambeth Palace chapel on 10 July 1664. To him fell the main task of rebuilding the Church in this diocese after the Commonwealth.

On 6 September 1666 he formally visited the cathedral.[73] Dr Todd, describing the state of the abbey at this time says that:

" momentous errors and irregularities have been done or comitted through the ignorance and avarice of the Dean and mandamus Prebendarys in 1660 and since. The ruinous houses of the minor Canons, and other members of the Church were pulled down and they dispersed and sent into the town to live; no new ones built to receive them back into the College. The offices in the Quire were accumulated, the salaries of minor Canons given to laymen, and houses erected and built within (the abbey) and let out on lease to persons of inferior occupations."[74]

The staff then consisted of 36 persons—a dean, 4 prebendaries, 6 minor canons, a master of choristers, 6 choristers, 6 lay singing men, a verger, a subsacrist, 6 almsmen, a gate keeper, a butler and a cook with an assistant. From the visitation it appears that the necessary instruments for the performance of divine service had been provided, with the exception of ornaments, such as copes, which were promised in a short time.* The chapter also reported that " some of the

* But the only old ones the cathedral possesses are the two Pre-Reformation ones mentioned in the Elizabethan inventory. Probably in about 1685, it

T

Church utensils were imbezilled in the late times of usurpation, as the brazen eagle upon which ye Chapters were read."[75]

An interesting account of the standard of worship in the cathedral at the Restoration is given in Thomas Story's *Journal*. He says that when the Apostles creed began all turned their faces towards the east, and when the name of Jesus was mentioned all as one bowed and kneeled towards the altar table, where stood a couple of Common Prayer Books in folio, one at each side and over then painted upon the wall I.H.S.[77] In J. Wilson's words: " the ceremonial in our cathedral was elaborate for a decade or two after the Restoration. The canons were punctilious in posture and attitude during Divine Service; they genuflected in approaching, passing or returning from the altar; they kissed the altar before celebrating. In times of special solemnity they prostrated themselves not only before the altar but also in their stalls." It also appears from old manuscript music books, once belonging to the cathedral, that at this time the Communion Service was sung in full. After 1688, and so presumably before, there were celebrations monthly and at the great festivals.[78] This High Church movement in Carlisle can probably be connected with the contemporary one in Durham under the auspices of its celebrated bishop, John Cosin; the links being found in the deans, Guy Carleton and Thomas Smith, both prebendaries there during his episcopate.

Bishop Rainbow also endeavoured to raise the standard in the parishes. Commissions were issued to the four deaneries: for Carlisle in December 1668, and the remainder in September 1669. The bishop stated in them that it belonged to his pastoral office to see the service of God duly performed; His churches repaired and beautified; and all things therein done in decency and order.

was ordered ' that the two copes be mended and worn by the Epistler and Gospeller."[76]

It was his duty to take notice of what had happened during the long discontinuance of Church government in these late times of war and rebellion.

" The Churches of this our diocese of Carlisle are become very ruinous, the Communion plate and linnen plundered and stollen away, and many disorders committed to ye great dishonour of Almighty God, the scandall and offence of all good Christian people and the breach of the ancient lawes of this land."

The commissioners were instructed to inform themselves

" of all the decayes . . . in any of the said churches, chappells, or in any of their churchyards, houses " . . .; also " to see that the said churches, be provided with plate, pewter, linnen, and other things necessary for the Communion Table, as likewise of bookes, cushions, and other things required for the pulpit and reading desk and other uses; and further to inquire about all temporal concerns of the benefice."[79]

The Visitation Courts and Correction Books[80] give an insight into the state of the diocese at this time.   But as they only contain the presentments of the churchwardens and are not the result of any personal investigation, we cannot be sure how accurately the real state of affairs is depicted.

As to the state of the church fabrics and furniture the general impression resulting is that things were not too bad.   There were, of course, examples of neglect: Castle Carrock:

" the church out of repair, for want of a flagon and chalice for the communion, the two books of homilies, a booke of divine service for the clerke, a cloath for the communion table, a cushion for the pulpit and a register booke " (167 ;).

Camerton:

" the want of a carpet for the communion table, an English Bible of the last translation, the book of canons, the table touching the degrees of marriages, a flaggon, a patten for the bread and wine, a basin to receive the almes and a paper booke wherein to note the names of strange preachers "; (1663).

or Morland:

" the church in very much decay in leads, floore, seats, and windows " (1674).

Many parishes lacked copies of Bishop Jewel's works and a book of Homilies, also the table touching the degrees of marriage. Roccliffe, Dearham, Cross Canonby, Croglin, Plumbland, Castle Carrock, and Scaleby had no register book; Caldbeck and Ireby no ' chist or coffer ' in which to place their books; and Gilcrux, Uldale, Ainstable, no chest with three locks. Long Marton, Stanwix, and St. Cuthbert's, Carlisle lacked glass in their windows. Many chancels, often owing to the neglect of lay impropriators, were in decay: " Thomas Fetherstonhaugh Ar. for not repayring the Chancell or Quire of Walton, he having the tithes." Bromfield, Holm Cultram, and Askham also had chancels in need of repair.

These records supply valuable information on the state of the chapels. In 1670 Great Broughton* chapel " hath for these XXty yeares or more been in much decay and is now ruinous that there is nothing left save some part of ye outward walls standing. It only belongs to ye 2 Broughtons and Ribton." At Thrimby chapel " the seats and pewes within the same are very ruinous and in great decay that none can sit down therein " (1682). Nichol Forest " now in decay " was being repaired in 1678 when Arthur Foster of Ringsfield was presented " for threatening the inhabitants for building their chapel in the same place it was formerly in." In this year two men were accused of " not paying their assessement to the repaire of Wrey Chappell "; and the vicar of Morland " for drawing " the curate of Bolton, " the former curates having alwayes lived at Bolton (it being a corner of the parish) beyond the memory of man." The visitation book of 1682 contains the petition for the consecration of Martindale chapel, but records that the church at Patterdale " is altogether ruinated and fallen to the ground."

* In 1645 Elizabeth, relict of George Lamplough of Dovenbie, left " to the enlarging of the quire of Broughton chapel £5 " (N.S., xxxix, 102-3).

The Correction Court books, as well as Dr. Todd's Histories* which now become a contemporary source, throw light on Post-Restoration clerical life. Though it must be remembered that, as so often happens, it is the scandalous and not the virtuous clergy that we hear about. The very fact that these cases came before the court is evidence of efforts to enforce a higher standard. But first we must describe one of those squabbles which are so typical of the period. The person in question was the chancellor, Roland Nichols.

In Dr. Todd's words:

" in his time† a controversie arose betwixt the then Bishop and the Dean and chapter about his having a seat ascertained to him in the cathedral. The Bishop, with a particular impetus, to shew his authority and to grace his new official, orders him to sit in his own episcopal seat, on the right hand, at the entrance of the Quire. The Chapter, with equal zeal, caused the Door, wch had been set there by the Bishop's order, to be taken down . . . At last to quiet the obstinate and angry Bishop, the dispute was compromised; and this Favorite Chancellor . . . had a seat

---

* There are biographies of Hugh Todd, a native of Blencow, canon of Carlisle and vicar of Penrith, in D.N.B. and in Jefferson's *Leath Ward* (479-81). The latter, after referring to what appears to be the two manuscripts published in the Antiquarian Society's Tract Series, mentions a *History of the Diocese of Carlisle*. Nicolson and Burn (I, iii) also used this work which they describe as a ' large folio manuscript,' ' of which copies are in several hands'.

The present writer has had the privilege of using two of Todd's manuscripts: a *History of the Diocese of Carlisle*, presumably that named above, and a *History of the Bishoprick of Carlisle*, in two folio volumes. A comparison of statements on fo. 129 of the ' Diocese ' with those on II fo. 53 of the ' Bishoprick,' as to when the wooden spire of the cathedral collapsed, suggests that the ' Bishoprick ' was compiled some 20 years after the ' Diocese ' and some 60 after the Restoration i.e. in about 1720. As Dr. Todd lived till 1728 the ' Bishoprick ' represents his mature work and assures him of a more honourable place in the select band of our older historians than has previously been accorded him. The history of these two valuable manuscripts is somewhat obscure. Neither Nicolson and Burn nor Jefferson tell where the ' Diocese ' which they used was located; Wilson (*V.C.H.* II 291) says it ' cannot now be found.' To-day both works are housed in the library of St. Edmund Hall, Oxford. It would be interesting to know how they got there. To F. J. Field (*Armorial of Cumberland*, xiii) must be given the credit of bringing them to our notice, but the present work is the first in which they have been extensively used owing to the courtesy of the principal of The Hall.

† C.M.B. (IX, 13-14) shew this was October 1668.

assigned him, near the middle north door of the Quire, . . .
Within a very few years, the tide of respect, that had run so high
in favour of his official, turned to great displeasure against him,
and the Bishop . . . caused a libell to be preferred against him in
the archbishop's court at York for many grevious corruptions,
and never desisted from the prosecution of him; till he thought
it his interest . . . to resign."[81]

. The chancellor was also rector of Aikton, where there
was more trouble.   At the 1682 visitation it was reported
that

" the chancell is out of repair, soe that the communion table is
defyled with pigeons and dung: that the mansion house is all out
of repair without floor or windows, hearthes or any necessary
furniture for house keeping and that the rector " doth not use to
catechise the young people, nor to have evening prayers, nor read
the communion service at the communion table, nor to observe
holydays . . . nor doth he visitt the sick, or labour to reclaime the
Quakers."

There followed a letter from the bishop complaining
of his ' unparallelled non residence for more than twelve
years,' and requiring him to reside.

A certificate from the churchwardens shews that the
chancellor had obeyed the order and also repaired the
church

" and hath set up therein a faire wainscott pew, and hath bestowed upon the church a faire wainscott pulpitt and is now
making ready a new decent altar table at his owne charge.   He
hath alsoe his parsonage house in good repaire and beautie, the
upper windows all glassed and the lower all ready for glassing.
The Roomes above all flowred with new dayle boards and the
flowrs below all now made and decently habittable."

Another clerk in trouble was Bernard Robinson, vicar
of Torpenhow, who in June 1673

" did personally appear before the said bishop; having been cited
to appear on Friday the 6th of this instant; yet never the lesse
he this day appearing the said Lord Bishop out of respect to his
infirmity and old age to prvent the trouble of another appearance
did then and there psonally object severall crimes and mis-
deamours . . . that he had often neglected his cure and

ministeriall dutyes . . . and that he had at several times behaved himselfe inordinately being given to drunkness and scandalous intemperance . . . and especially his riotous and unlawfull gaming at Penrith." To which " he confessed . . . and is much grieved ana sorry therefore . . whereupon the Bishop, considering his great weakness of mind and his infirmity of old age, did decree him to be suspended . . . for the space of three years next, . . . reserving to himselfe the power of either extending or relaxing this censure. . ."

But the bishop was not always so successful. Jeremiah Nelson, vicar of Stanwix, was accused before him in 1674 " that he was in a Tavern which was an offence against the 75th canon." Upon which he " answered the following words or to ye like effect ' You were also in a Tavern,' to which the bishop said ' you had best accuse me.' And further the Bp. wished him to confesse or declare whether he was in a Tavern. Upon which the vicar answered: ' he would confesse nothing till it was proved, so he forthwith appealed to the archbishop of York and his consistorie."

Another instance of the bishop's disciplinary action occurred at Crosby Ravensworth where the vicar, William Curwen was accused in July 1682 of neglect to have his cure duly served and suffering the vicarage and outhouses to fall into decay. The living was sequestered; a pension of 25s. a month being reserved for the vicar, ' he being aged above ninety years.'

Only one case of public penance is recorded in these visitation records. Robert Ritson of Cross Canonby, who had been found guilty of " severall haynous and notorious crimes of great surrdnes and uncleanns," was " enjoyned to performe his pennance " in the market house at Ireby on 28 January 1668, " where he shall stand for ye space of one full hour bare headed, barefooted and bare legged, apparell'd in white linen after ye manor of such lewd offenders." This was to be repeated in his parish church three days later, and six days afterwards again at the market cross in Carlisle. Later, in 1683-5, several instances of the payment of money, between £2 and £5 in " comutacon," are recorded, presumably in substitution of public penance.

The only matters of liturgical interest are that the curate of Shap was presented in 1670 ' for not usually bidding holydays and observing them,' and his brother of St. Cuthbert's, Carlisle in 1678 ' for yt the sacrament of the Lord's Supper is not administered three times a year.[82]

The bishop was engaged in a lengthy dispute with his predecessor, the archbishop of York, about Rose. Eventually in June 1669, he appealed to the Crown. A committee of inquiry was appointed. The bishop wished the castle, much damaged in the civil war, to be reconstructed on the original lines. But his grace said this would be a costly business; it was better to use what remained of the ancient walls to rebuild the castle in another form. The committee agreed with him and Bishop Rainbow lost his suit, though he was awarded £400 towards rebuilding the chapel. Thus the east and south sides of the castle were sacrificed and the materials used for rebuilding the chapel with two parlours underneath it. At this time also the great staircase, the passage leading to it, and some sleeping chambers were added.[83]

He died at Rose on Wednesday, 26 March 1684 in his seventy-sixth year, and was buried on the Tuesday following in Dalston churchyard under a simple slab of ' plain common freestone ' with a short latin inscription giving his name and date of death.[84]

Never in its history has this diocese had four such rulers in succession as those who occupied the see from the Restoration to the death of Anne. The first of these became archbishop of York, the second was Edward Rainbow, the next Thomas Smith, most munificent of prelates, the fourth William Nicolson, most colourful and

dominating of personalities. In this distinguished com-
pany Bishop Rainbow need not fear comparison.
Chancellor Ferguson has said: " no bishop of the pattern
of the medieval saint has ever adorned the see of Carlisle,
Rainbow was perhaps the nearest approach to one."[85]
At Rose

" four times a day was God publickly called upon by prayers in
that family: twice in the Chappell, which part his lordship's
chaplain performed and twice in the dining room: the latter of
these at six in the morning and nine at night was the usual task
of our right reverent and worthy prelate himself, if not disabled by
sickness. As if he, who was the master of the family, would open
it every morning and lock it every night by the Key of prayer."[86]

Even Dr. Todd calls him ' a pious and worthy prelate.'[87]
A man of a deeper spirituality than William Nicolson,
even if with a somewhat less colourful personality,
Edward Rainbow may well be entitled to rank as the
greatest in the distinguished company named above.

He married Elizabeth,* daughter of Dr. Henry Smith,
master of Magdalene College, Cambridge. A portrait of
the bishop and his wife is at Dalemain; another is in the
hall at Magdalene.

Thomas Smith,[88] dean of Carlisle, was elected by the
chapter on 3 May 1684 and consecrated in York Minster
on St. Peter's day by Archbishop Dolben. The bishop,
son of John Smith, a substantial statesman, was born in
1614 at Whitewall, Asby, Westmorland.†

He will always be remembered for the munificence of
his charity. While dean of Carlisle he restored the
deanery to much the form we know to-day.[89] He also
gave the cathedral an organ and the magnificent set

---

* Her sister married Sir Edward Hasell of Dalemain (Magrath, II, 146).

† Educated at Appleby Grammar School and Queen's College, Oxford,
fellow 1639; during the Commonwealth he was at Hutton in 1656 and at
Cockermouth 1658; canon of Carlisle 1660, of Durham 1661 and dean of
Carlisle 1671.

Thomas Barlow, son of Richard of Orton, Westmorland, provost of Queen's,
Bodley's librarian and bishop of Lincoln, was the bishop's first cousin.

of altar vessels of silver gilt it still uses. As bishop his benefactions continued. At Rose he added a new tower, repaired and beautified several rooms and rebuilt the pigeon-cote which bears the date 1700.[90] In the abbey he purposed to subscribe £100 to the plan for putting up a library;[91] this scheme not maturing he erected the building next to the deanery, apparently as a library and registry combined;[92] many of the books were his gift.[93] His benefactions, amounting in all to £5,226, included gifts to the schools at Asby, Appleby, Carlisle and Dalston; Queen's College received £600, Wren's St Paul's £150, and Durham Cathedral £300.[94]

Charles II had died in 1685, having been admitted on his death-bed into the Roman Catholic Church by Father John Hudleston, second son of Joseph Hudleston of Hutton John.[95] Almost at once the duke of Monmouth made his bid for the throne. After the battle of Sedgemoor, James Burton—who had been concerned in the Rye House Plot and had afterwards been helped to escape by a pious Baptist, Elizabeth Gaunt, daughter of Anthony Fothergill of Brownber, Westmorland—fled to London, where he was concealed. But Burton betrayed those who had befriended him. For her crime—"my fault," she said, "was one which a prince might well have forgiven, I did but relieve a poor family; and lo! I must die for it"—she was burnt at Tyburn in October 1685.[96] Thus the last female to suffer in England in this way was a Westmorland woman.

In the struggle between James and his people these counties, under the leadership of Sir John Lowther of Lowther, were strongly Whig in their sympathies. Despite the royal efforts to influence the elections by removing the lord lieutenants and packing the corporation of Carlisle, the great majority of the justices of the peace, meeting at Penrith in January 1688, refused to carry out the king's wishes.[97]

When James put forth his Declaration of Indulgence suspending the laws against both Roman Catholics and Dissenters, and ordered the clergy to read it from their pulpits, the bishop, writing to Sir Daniel Fleming, said: " As to the reading of the Declaration, I believe it will scarce be read by any in this diocese, for I am resolved to concur with my brethren above in the matter of their late Petition." This was, of course, the famous one presented by Archbishop Sancroft, for which he and his six suffragans were subsequently tried. In another letter Bishop Smith writes of the bishops " however they will have no cause to repent of any thing they have done, the whole nation applauding them for it."[98] He is said to have also written to the seven bishops themselves expressing his sympathy and approval.[99]

These counties were the scene of some exciting events in December 1688. The possession of our ports, facing Ireland, and of Carlisle, the gateway to Scotland, were vital to both sides. The king's hopes of holding them were frustrated by a daring act of Sir John Lowther of Lowther and Andrew Hudleston of Hutton John. The latter, hearing that a ship with arms and ammunition for the Carlisle garrison was at Workington—Henry Curwen was one of the king's supporters—rode over to Lowther to consult Sir John. Hurriedly collecting their friends and tenants these two rode through the night to Workington and, surprising the crew, seized the ship for William of Orange.* Further evidence of popular excitement can

* Wilson omits this incident in V.C.H. II, 298, perhaps he doubted its authenticity. The story first occurs in Nicolson and Burn (ii, 369) in the account of the Hudleston family of Hutton John supplied by Andrew Hudleston, grandson of the man involved. It is supported by documentary evidence on both sides. Letters to and from Sir John Lowther of 12, 15 and 16 December prove conclusively that he seized the arms (R. Com, Hist. MSS. xi Report App. vii, 28 and xiii Report App. vii, 98, 99) and a petition for the place of collector of customs at Whitehaven of May 1690 by Hudleston and his son, in which they claim they " were instrumental in the happy revolution at the hazard of their lives," suggests that they were there (Cal. Treasury Books, ix, 676). It is clear from these documents that the affair took place in

be seen in the fact that even in remote Eskdale the house of Lancelot Porter of Lowholme, a papist, was burnt by the mob.[100]   In Westmorland the militia were called out and marched to Kirkby Lonsdale.   What happened there to the Kendal contingent is told in the words of a popular local ballad:

> " In '88 was Kirkby feight
> When ne'er a man was slain:
> They ate their meat and drank their drink,
> And so went yham again."[101]

The fall of James had important consequences for two Westmorland families.   Among those who accompanied the royal family in its flight were Sir Thomas Strickland of Sizergh and his wife who was one of the governesses to the prince of Wales.[102]   Though Sir Thomas' son subsequently returned to Sizergh their adherence to their ancient faith prevented them taking any part in public life.   With the partial eclipse of one ancient Westmorland family the sun of another arose: Sir John Lowther of Lowther was rewarded for his services by becoming Viscount Lonsdale.   But there are still Stricklands at Sizergh carrying on an honoured name.

For the Church the result of James' deposition was disastrous.   Many, including Archbishop Sancroft and eight other bishops, felt that, having taken the oath of allegiance to one king, they could not do so again while he was alive.   Despite the fact that Archdeacon Nicolson urged the clergy that " a firm allegiance is due to their present Majesties, King William and Queen Mary,"[103] several in these counties joined those, who, refusing the new oath, were deprived.   The names of these men, later called Non-Jurors, were: Thomas Bell, vicar of Askham,

December, and not in October as Nicolson and Burn stated, and that Jackson (o.s. ix, 349-50) was in error in thinking that it was Sir John Lowther of Whitehaven and not Sir John of Lowther who was involved.   The writer is indebted to Mr. F. Hudleston and to Mr. C. R. Hudleston for their help in the above.

John Leigh, vicar of Edenhall and Langwathby; . . . Manton, minister of Crook chapel and Henry Guy, curate of Kendal.[104]

There is an interesting document at York giving the returns of a visitation of this diocese by commissaries of the archbishop in July 1693. It contains full lists of the clergy, parish clerks, schoolmasters, with old and new churchwardens. It is noticeable how high a proportion of the Carlisle deanery churchwardens, 15 out of 38, did not appear. The returns contain the usual presentments; there is nothing in these that is not a duplicate of those already noticed. According to them there was little wrong; only ten churches required any repairs but if all the absentee churchwardens had been there the number might have been added to considerably. The chief interest of the document is in the evidence that such a visitation was made.*

William Nicolson mentioned above, who had been appointed canon of Carlisle and archdeacon by Bishop Rainbow in 1681-2, was involved in two quarrels of some moment in the concluding years of this episcopate.

The first, with Dr. Todd, was concerned with the dean and chapter library, of which the doctor was a joint founder with the bishop and the dean. Dr. Bernard of Oxford, engaged in the compilation of a catalogue of manuscripts in English libraries, wrote to him about this one. The latter in sending him a list included his own histories which he had placed, or intended to place, in the library. Nicolson, in the preface to the first volume of his ' English Historical Library,' violently attacked him, referring to

" Catalogues either drawn thirty years ago or prophetically calculated for about thirty years hence. Of the latter kind is that of a certain Cathedral church, which neither is, nor ever was, furnished with any one single manuscript of the several, in all

* See above p. 223N. and p. 269 for instances of previous ones.

volumes, which 'tis said there to contain: I have some cause to
fear that I shall never live to see such books in that library as are
there mentioned, and I am also afraid that most of 'em (if they
have any being at all) are of that modest complexion which
becomes a private retirement better than an appearance in
public."

Dr. Todd replied in a letter, dated 14 July 1696, to
Archbishop Sharpe of York,[105] to whom the preface had
been addressed

" that he had made four or five small volumes of Collections out
of the Registers and other originals relating to the cathedral and
diocese, and that he thought it not improper to have them inserted
in the Oxford Catalogue, though it was true that only one volume,
in Latin, on the State of the Cathedral, was actually in the
library but the rest were ready bound for it." . . .

Some days after the two protagonists met at Rose.
Todd " complained of being very ill treated," apparently
without getting any satisfaction as he afterwards wrote
a formal letter of remonstrance to his censurer in which he
took the same line as in his letter to the archbishop.   On
the same day Nicolson had written to the primate
restating his accusations.   On 7 August he answered
Todd claiming that what he said was ' punctually true,'
ending with " in short, Brother, if there be scandal given,
you must bear your share of it."[106]

Nicolson was surely in the wrong.   Of course, Todd, by
including manuscripts that were not in the library, was
' punctually ' at fault.   But his action was quite a
sensible one: that they might not be there for a year or so
was of small consequence when the period during which
the catalogue would be used was taken into account.[107]

Towards the end of the century public attention had
been directed by a Royal proclamation to the increase of
coarseness and immorality, so a ' Society for the Reformation of Manners ' was formed.   In 1699 a branch was
established in Carlisle.   The moving spirit was William
Gilpin, son of the celebrated presbyterian rector of

Greystoke in Commonwealth times. As we would view it to-day the objects of the Society were such that all Christian people could unite in its support. Such apparently was the bishop's opinion; he gave it his patronage. His archdeacon thought differently. Thereupon the Chancellor* took the opposite side. With his support the vicar of Brampton set up a branch of the Society there with plans for a weekly lecture, at which the vicar, two neighbouring incumbents, and a dissenting minister were to preside in turn. The archdeacon wrote to the vicar strongly condemning his action: "such societies are not legal ways of procedure." Archdeacon and chancellor were summoned to Rose to answer to the bishop for the strife they were causing. But he was too old and feeble to curb such fiery spirits. An appeal was next carried to the archbishop of York, who avoided the issue. Finally the diocesan drew up a memorandum to be dispersed among his clergy, which on the whole supported the archdeacon's opinions.[108]

The bishop died at Rose on 12 April 1702, aged eighty-seven, and was buried in the cathedral on 17 April before the altar under a plain marble stone with a short Latin inscription.[109] He married† Anna Baddiley, who died in 1698.[110]

---

* Thomas Tullie, who became dean in 1716.

† Did he marry Catherine, widow of Sir Henry Fletcher? (N.S. x, 220, Magrath ii, p. xix-xxi). Letters at Rydal Hall (Nos. 811, 1187 and 1727) certainly suggest that he was in some way related to the Fleming and Fletcher families. The following from Richard Lowther to Monsieur Williamson is even more definite: 'Dr. Smith resides yet with my Ant ffletchr, tis beleiv'd they are married and Sr George Dalston being lately dead, of who he stood in a little awe, tis beleiv'd she will conceall it noe longr' (S.P.D. 18 Sept. 1656). But Sir Daniel Fleming does not mention the marriage in his pedigrees of the Dalston and Fletcher families (his MSS. liber A fo. 15 and 46 and his 'Memoirs,' p. 74); nor does Dugdale in the 1665 visitation. She was buried at Cockermouth as Lady Catherine Fletcher, but, as she may have retained her first husband's name on account of his higher rank, this really proves nothing. Thus, while there is much that suggests such a marriage, it must still remain unproven. I have to thank Mr. C. R. Hudleston, Colonel Haswell and Rev. R. W. Crook for their help on the problem.

His will contained many charitable gifts: his communion plate for the chapel at Rose; £100 to the dean and chapter for the better paying of the salaries of the inferior members of the church and the majority of his books to their library; £500 to the free school at Carlisle; the like sum to the vicar of Penrith and £300 to the vicar of Dalston; Queen's College, Oxford received £500; and £230 was bequeathed for distribution among the poor of the parishes in his diocese, instead of a " publicke and common dole at my funerale."[111]

There is no need to describe his character; his benefactions are his best epitaph. It can truly be said that no other bishop has given so largely to so many different and deserving objects within his diocese. His portrait by T. Stephenson hangs on the great stair at Rose.

CHAPTER III.

THE EPISCOPATE OF WILLIAM NICOLSON.

I. INTRODUCTION.

WILLIAM NICOLSON was elected, as he tells us in his diary,[1] on 13 May 1702; confirmed on 3 June; and consecrated at Lambeth by the archbishop of Canterbury on 14 June. The son of Joseph Nicolson, rector of Great Orton,* by Mary, his wife, fifteenth child of John Brisco of Crofton, he was born at Great Orton on Whitsunday, 3 June 1655,† and educated at Dovenby School[2] and Queen's College, Oxford.‡ Todd gives this account of his early life

" While Batchelor of Arts, Sir J. Williamson, § then secretary of State, sent him at the public expense into Germany. He resided at Leipsic, where he not only gained the knowledge of the modern German Tongue, but also of the ancient Saxon, Gothick, Runic, or Danish languages and became very skilful in all Septentrional Barbarous Antiquities. For want of support and proper remittances being forced to leave Germany he returned to Oxford, . . . When his late Majesty King George did the University of Oxford the honour of a visit; He, with some others,

---

* Later of Plumbland.

† *Diary N.S.* XXXV, 100; Canon Gilbanks in a note in the introduction to the *Registers* states " my oldest parishioner when I asked him said ' of course he was born at Orton—his mother had him in the Porch.' "

‡ He matriculated on 1 July 1670; fellow 1679. Thomas Hearne was, of course, a strong tory and bore Nicolson no good will, so his statement " had good strong parts, but had ye Reputation (and not undeservedly) of a drinking Fellow and boon companion" (Collections I, 187) must be accepted with reserve.

§ Joseph, son of Joseph Williamson, vicar of Bridekirk, was Secretary of State 1674-8. His biography is in *D.N.B.* and *N. & B.* II, 101.

U

was sent to wait on him, in the Road and to Compliment him in his own language. After this, he lived sometimes with Sir Joseph Williamson as his Chaplain. His Reputation and character increasing, Bp. Rainbow, a pious and worthy prelate, invited him to return to his native country; and to encourage him to it, gave him the Archdeaconry, a Prebend and the Vicarage of Torpenhow,* much about the same time. In these mean and remote Promotions, he continued near twenty years; when the Bp. (Dr. Smith) growing very old, and he having some thoughts of succeeding him in the see, he attempted to make himself more known to the world, and Published three small volumes, under the titles of " The English and Scotch Historical Libraries," wherein were several harsh characters and Accounts both of men and things, which he thought fit to suppress or alter in the second edition of the work. These performances were surprising from an unknown Person and generally well received."[3]

II. BISHOP AND ADMINISTRATOR.

William Nicolson was one of a coterie of men, who, as bishops and scholars, were among the ablest that ever ruled over the destinies of the Anglican Church. " By the last decade of the Seventeenth century this most remarkable group was already giving signs of its importance, and of the character of its influence."[4] These men, who included Edmund Gibson, bishop of Lincoln and London, a native of High Knipe, near Bampton,† first made their reputations as historical writers. They were much in favour with the government which needed defenders against attacks on the Revolution Settlement from Tory divines.

* The archdeaconry was given in 1682 and with it the rectory of Salkeld; he had the prebendaryship and vicarage of Torpenhow in 1681; he resigned the latter on accepting Addingham in 1698.

† N. & B. I, 463, and N.S. xviii, 173. Both Nicolson and Gibson were among the leaders in the revival in the study of the Saxon language, which centred at Queen's College, Oxford at this time; the former was the first collegiate lecturer on the subject. A Westmorland man, Edward Thwaites, held a similar office there in 1699; and another John, son of William Smith, rector of Lowther, of St. John's College, Cambridge, belonged to the same school and edited the first critical edition of Bede's Ecclesiastical History. The two last seem to be among our forgotten local worthies (Douglas, 73-81).

Both Dr. Todd and Thomas Hearne affirm that Nicolson was appointed bishop owing to the influence of the Tory Sir Christopher Musgrave, "whose interests he had serv'd in the county elections for members of Parliament."[5] But the real reason is probably shewn in a letter from Edmund Gibson;

" considering upon what terms we were with Scotland, it seemed to be very necessary at that Juncture to place some person of wisdom, interest, and authority upon that frontier, who might have a constant eye upon the counsels of the borders, and power enough within his diocese to assist in an opposition if incursions should be made."[6]

The bishop's diary gives an account of his enthronement. He reached his cathedral city on 14 July 1702, and was met at Wragmire by the choir, the officers of the garrison and others; without the gates were the mayor and aldermen, within a guard of honour, " ye flag out and nine guns fir'd "; at the great gate of the abbey the prebendaries and the choir in their surplices met him and

" carry'd me to the Deanery; Wth an Anthem; lost by ye ringings of ye Bells." After some refreshment the installation took place at Evensong. " The procession began fro the Door of ye Deanery . . .   In ye church, ye Choire made a Lane; thro' wch we pass'd to ye Throne. The Vice-Dean, haveing order'd ye AB's Mandate to be read, Inthron'd me in a pretty long Form . . . Prayers being read as far as ye Anthem I was fetch'd by ye Vice-Dean and Chapter fro ye Throne to ye Bishop's stall; and there in a short form, install'd, . . . After ye Anthem and Remainder of ye prayers, went (in procession as at ye first) to the Chapter House; where I was placed in ye Throne of my predecessors."

The bishop reckoned that the legal fees were not less than £500; his stay in London and travelling expenses took a further £115. The revenues of the see were £775 a year.[7]

As bishop, Nicolson started off with many advantages. A Cumbrian by birth and family, through his mother related to many of the gentle families of these counties, and archdeacon for twenty years—he knew his diocese at the beginning of his episcopate better than many prelates did at the end of theirs.   When the custom of his day is taken into account—a bishop was then expected to attend parliament—he spent a lot of time in his diocese.   Working on the basis of the fourteen and a half years for which the diary affords evidence, he spent approximately two-thirds of them in it; the remainder either in London or travelling; the journey took ten or twelve days.   Whilst at home he lived mostly at Rose, where he entertained freely.

He speedily got to work with a Visitation which he commenced on 7 May 1703, entering his impressions of each church in a book still in existence.[8] Wilson writes of him erring " on the side of pessimism " and of the " musings of a supercilious young prelate " and goes on " if the church was in the deplorable condition described in the journal of his Visitation tour, it must have been in some measure due to his own negligence during the twenty years of his archidiaconate."[9] The present writer's investigation has given a rather different impression. The figures that follow are, of course, only a rough division.   But placing the bishop's reports of the 105 churches of the diocese into 4 categories: (A) 31 he found very little to complain of; (B) 43 were in a tolerably good condition; (C) 21 he regarded as neglected or ill cared for; and (D) 10 were in a really bad state.   Wilson also writes of the " clergy, so severely handled by their young diocesan," but were they?   Again figures tell their tale. In 82 parishes the bishop did not mention the clergy, except very generally; in 18 he wrote words of praise or respect; in 5 of real condemnation.   Such figures hardly support the canon's criticisms.[10]

It must also be remembered that both bishop and clergy had difficulties to contend with over which they had little control.   The journal is full of instances of the lay rectors' neglect of their duties of keeping the chancels in

repair and of the difficulties of dealing with them.   Also
parishes frequently lacked a proper school house; hence
the church was the school and sometimes the altar the
scholars' writing table.   The bishop, and probably the
incumbent also, deplored this, but until someone endowed
a school or the people could afford to build one, they were
helpless.

The best example of how bad a church's condition
could be is Stapleton.

" The Quire here is most intolerably scandalous.   No glass in the
Windows; No Ascent to anything that looks like an Altar; no
Flooring; no Seats.   Under the North Wall bury'd in dirt, we
found an old Grave stone . . .   The parishioners follow the
example of their Parson; and have the Body of the Church in as
nasty a pickle as the Quire.   The Roof is so miserably Shatter'd
and broken, that it cannot be safe sitting under it . . . in stormy
weather.   Not one pane of Glass in any of the Windows; no
Reading Desk; nor did they ever hear that they had a Bell.   The
font is abominable, the seats most scurvily low (and in a word)
everything very wretched . . .   There was no Surplice to be
found . . .   One of 'em told us that sometimes, on an Easter-day,
the Parson had brought a Surplice with him; and Administer'd ye
Sacrament in it; But even that Ordinance (amongst the rest)
was most commonly celebrated without one."

To turn now to the other side; three churches received
the bishop's special praise; Lowther:

" in the fairest condition of any parish church in ye Diocese."

Kirkby Thore:

" the church quire and parsonage house are here in the best repair
of anyone in the diocese "; and

Torpenhow:

" the fairest Inside of any parish-church in ye Diocese."   " The
Quire . . 'tis now in a decent Condition, the Floor good, the
Communion-Table handsomely rail'd in . . .   The Body of the
Church was lately beautify'd upon a Motion made by Mr.
Thomas Addison . . who . . . offer'd to Cover the Middle Isle with
a fair painted canopy of Firs; . . . and ye parishioners, to bring
the rest of the church to somewhat of a Harmony with these new
Improvements, have back'd all the Seats with Wainscot and

floor'd the whole . ... They have also put the Queen's Arms, the Ten Commandments, etc. into neat Frames."

The ideals the bishop aimed at included an altar railed in and placed in a proper position, not crowded round with pews; he noted some altars stood east and west, so it can be presumed north and south was more usual. The walls to be white-washed; a favourite term of praise used by him is " Lightsome," and of disapproval that the walls are dark or dirty; sentences were to be written on them and the queen's arms set up. The font to be in a suitable place and not behind a pillar, as was not uncommon. The seats to be backed and not mere benches. A proper Reading pew for the minister to be placed in the chancel—he disapproved if the pulpit had to serve all purposes. Floors to be paved; he often noted how uneven they were, due to frequent burials; windows to be glazed and opened up and not boarded in.[11]

From his diary we get glimpses also of the bishop's ideals for the clergy. Ordinands had to come up to a definite standard; rejections were frequent:

17 May 1706 " Mr Lowther of Bowness,* endeavouring to surprize me into ye bestowing Deacon's orders upon (one Town of C.C. Cambr) an ignorant rake "; 19 September 1707 " Mr. Stubb and Mr Elbeck (both rejected) for Priests "; 22 December 1709; Mr John Hodgson, Clerk (not in Orders) . . . but cannot turn any one Article of his Creed into Latine "; 27 May 1708 " Mr Perkin, in fresh search of Orders, rejected " and 1 June 1708 " Batchler and Brown (Candidate Deacons) rejected for nonage."

It is clear he took real trouble to see that unfit men were not ordained. He also endeavoured to reform the wrong doer.

28 September 1702 " Mr Moon† came to me . . . After some discourse, wherein he behaved himself too insolently, he promis'd . that he would never, for the future, drink in a public House betwixt Meals, nor in a private one (at any time) to excess; agreeing that if this promise were broken, or that he should ever

---

* Gerard, rector of Bowness, for his chequered career see N.S. xliii, 122-4.

† George Moon, Vicar of Edenhall, 1690-1743.

be prov'd to be guilty (as heretofore) of scandalous swearing, he should be immediately Suspended."

But poor Mr. Moon could not keep it up, for, on 21 October 1707, the bishop notes.

" Mr Moon appear'd, and soberly (under his hand) acknowledg'd himself guilty of ye Articles wherewth he stood Charg'd; begg'd pardon and promis'd an exemplary conduct for ye Future. On this Penance, he was dismiss'd and I pay'd his Fees."

William Nicolson could temper justice with mercy.

We have little evidence as to the extent to which churches were improved as a result of the bishop's activities. The diary of 26 July 1705 has a note that in Greystoke a handsome new font had been set up and the body of the church and ' side-isles ' floored very well. His register contains on 2 November 1714 a seating plan for the newly erected church at Hutton in the Forest— there is no note of its consecration—and the grant of a faculty, 30 August 1717, for the restoration of Hesket church; seats with backs, a gallery and windows to give light to seats below it, new cover for altar and rails before it, are specified

The bishop, as was then the custom, made a visitation of his diocese every three years at the usual four centres; these were the confirmation times. In 1704, as he notes in his diary, 5537 were confirmed. This seems to have been a quite exceptional number. Wilson, after noting it, writes of the total " as incontestable evidence of the influence and zeal of the parochial clergy,"[12] but as there is no evidence in his register that Bishop Smith, who died aged eighty-seven, ever undertook a visitation it is almost certain this great number included many who should have been confirmed years before. Thus its value as evidence is almost negative. Fortunately the bishop gives the number in 1707—1153. In 1710, he only enters the totals at Carlisle, about 120, and Wigton, about 150; these compare with 192 and 181 in 1707. So probably we are safe in believing the figures of 1707 to be about the average, possibly a little on the high side.

III. THE BATTLE OF THE CATHEDRAL STATUTES.

On 10 July 1704, the bishop notes in his diary that he has certain news of the deanery having been given to Dr. Atterbury. For the peace of the diocese it was an unfortunate appointment as these two redoubtable dignitaries had already come to verbal blows about the rights of convocation. A few quotations from one of the bishop's writings illustrates the spirit in which the controversy was conducted:

"to be accosted in such a blustering and surly manner, . . . have raised me above the impotent malice of any such pert and pedling retailer of another man's Collections, as Mr Atterbury has shown himself to be . . . leaving the grosser blunders of his book to the due chastisement of those greater men, with whom he has done me the honour to bespatter me."[13]

These censures, though by modern standards somewhat trenchantly expressed, were not, in the judgment of history, undeserved.[14]

So when Atterbury was appointed dean, the bishop sent the archbishop of York a form of recantation of errors as to the nature of the royal supremacy which he claimed Atterbury held, refusing to give institution unless he signed this document and suggesting that the archbishop should do this. So on 4 September the dean went to Bishopsthorpe. But the archbishop wrote saying that he could not act without authority under the bishop's seal. As the latter refused to give this the doctor set off to Rose. When he arrived, the bishop withdrew his previous form and presented another, which the dean refused to sign. Instead he drew up an answer. Nicolson then seems to have lost his temper, and " in a passion," to quote his opponent's words, " demanded my orders and letters testimonial of my good life and behaviour and said he would examine me as to my learning." Dr. Atterbury then retired to the deanery. The next day the bishop wrote to the secretary of state setting out his position. On the 23rd he had his answer: " Her Majesty expects that there shall be no further delay in giving Institution to Dr. Atterbury." So on 27 September the bishop notes in his diary " This day's post brought ye Queen's convincing Ansr to all my Scruples in a command requireing me to Institute Dr. A. forthwth. I obey." The institution took place next day at Rose.[15]

Thus the bishop had the dean and a canon, Dr. Todd, in the cathedral chapter, with whom he had quarrelled; an offensive alliance seemed inevitable. The bishop in his diary of 25 June 1705 notes that his brother had brought him a copy of an obsolete act of Queen Mary's reign produced by Mr. Dean " wherein 'tis said yt H. 8's new erected colleges . . . have no statutes or Ordinances of any Force or Authority ". It seems best though, so as not to interrupt the story of the great battle that was to ensue, to describe first a small affair Dr. Todd conducted on his own.

On 7 May 1706 the bishop's diary contains the following: " Mr Langhorn in pain for his takeing ye oath of a churchwarden; but encourag'd." Joseph Langhorne was Dr. Todd's curate at Penrith and also master of the Grammar School there. Though he was in deacon's orders, Dr. Todd had nominated him as his churchwarden. The bishop had promised to ordain him priest, but, as he informed the archbishop of York on 23 May, " this voluntary engaging himself in secular business (as I take it to be) stopped my hand." The next day Mr. Langhorne wrote to the bishop stating " I have declared myself to be out of the office of a churchwarden." On 11 June, the bishop sent a monition to Dr. Todd to rectify this irregular choice of a churchwarden by electing another in his room, and also wrote to the curate that, as soon as this was done, he would consider him capable of receiving priest's orders.

On the 13 June the bishop wrote to Dr. Todd of a letter received from him " part of it I take to be slanderous, and, I am sure, it is untrue: as, when you tell me that I have discouraged piety and conformity in your parish; that I threatened Mr. Langhorne with excommunication, and am under suffusions of prejudice." Apparently Dr. Todd's view was that if a clergyman could be a justice of the peace, then he could also be a church-warden; as both were secular offices. It seems clear, though his letter has not been preserved, that the archbishop supported his suffragan. On 17 June the bishop made a further effort for peace by telling Dr. Todd that, as there were already three churchwardens, he would not insist on any new election provided " you and those three certify me that you admit of his (Mr. Lang-horn) declining the office."[16] That is, he made it as easy as possible for Dr. Todd to get himself out of the position he had unwisely taken up. The matter was still reverberating in 1707, when Dr. Todd put forth an " Answer to a Pamphlet entitled, The case of the Curate of Penrith's taking upon him the office of churchwarden . . . In a letter to a Person of Quality."

Now to return to the great battle of the Statutes. To understand the meaning of the entry of 25 June 1705, we must look at the means by which the cathedral was governed. It is one of those described as of the New Foundation, and, by an Act of 1539, Henry VIII had power to make and devise statutes for such under the Great Seal. These were duly promulgated but, and this is the essential point, they were not issued under the Great Seal. The matter was further complicated because various enactments made in the reign of Queen Mary left such statutes without any legal validity. Though powers were given to Queen Elizabeth to put matters right nothing was done and, as far as Carlisle was concerned, nothing had been done since. Therefore it seemed possible that its statutes, by which it had been governed for over a century, had no legal authority. There was no doubt, however, that the charter of 1541 was a legal document. The difference between the two was mainly in the greater power given to the dean, apart from the chapter, in the latter. By it he had the right of making and admitting all inferior officers of the church and of correcting and, if need be, expelling any of them; his consent had to be given to the letting of lands, the granting of leases, and the collation of benefices by the chapter. Rights given to the bishop as visitor by the statutes were not mentioned.

' Dr. Todd was only too willing to act as jackal to the lion,'[17] wrote Dr. Prescott. It is true that Atterbury was a national figure; Todd only a local one. But in all this the present writer believes that it was the former who was the jackal, the latter the lion—Todd was on the spot and was an historian, Atterbury generally non-resident.

We probably see the opening of the campaign in events that occurred in November 1704—within a month or so of the dean's installation. Two of the petty canons had been suspended for ' kicking, boxing and by word abusing each other.' They were re-instated by the vice-dean and chapter. The dean and Dr. Todd protested that this was an infringement of the former's rights to punish all such offences,[18] while the bishop claimed that so gross a misdemeanour should not be punished only by the dean and chapter but that the culprits should be excommunicated. Thus the question of his rights as visitor arose.[19]

Then in June 1705, more trouble occurred. The three prebendaries, who throughout opposed the dean and Dr. Todd, had without the former's consent appointed to the benefice of Castle Sowerby; again the two protested, and

as a result the appointment seems to have lapsed to the
bishop.[20] It was at this time that the dean told the
bishop's brother of his theory about the illegality of the
cathedral statutes.

A year later, further controversy arose over the dean's
refusal to surrender his key of the chapter chest.[21] The
bishop, writing to Chancellor Tullie expressed the opinion
that the chapter could, if the dean continued his obstinacy,
order the lock to be broken. The cause of this trouble
was apparently the dean's refusal to recognise the right
of the chapter to grant leases in his absence.

As a result of all this, the bishop resolved to visit the
cathedral; he issued his monition in August 1707. The
dean at once questioned his right to do this and, claiming
that the ' pretended local statutes,' as he called them
were illegal, refused to give an answer to the Articles of
Enquiry; Dr. Todd also objected. The Visitation,
however, commenced on 25 September, and according to
the latter in the course of it

" the bishop fell into great excesses of passion and used many
approbrious words to the doctor, particularly the following:
Hold thy peace or I'll lay thee by the heels. Thou art a Cockscomb. I tell thee thou art a Cockscomb. Hold thy peace, or I
will have thee turned out by the shoulders which language was
the more surprising, because the doctor did, through the whole
course of the proceeding, behave himself toward the bishop with
the utmost deference and meekness."[22]

Dr. Todd must not be taken as an impartial witness,
though the bishop himself notes in his diary for 21
October:

" Dr. Todd continued his Insolence and was suspended . . .
In some heat on his clamourous behaviour, I happened to call
him a coxcomb; at wch he fired exceedingly, telling me that he
knew not what that word meant. Then, said I, you cannot tell
but what it may be properly enough used."

Then Dr. Todd had recourse to law; and on 22 November, the bishop was served with a rule of the Court of

Common Pleas to shew cause why a prohibition should not be awarded to stay proceedings in the visitation. None the less, on the 24th the bishop continued. He notes in his diary " Dr. Todd appeard, in somewt a more humble manner than heretofore: But refusd to make and subscribe the Form of Submission tendered to him."[23] —this was an acknowledgment of the bishop's right of visitation and of his error in denying it.   Then on the 27th, Dr. Todd still persisting, as the bishop notes, " in his contumacies, he was compelled to pass the severe sentence of Excommunication."

On 6 February 1708 the Court, deciding that the Statutes of Carlisle cathedral were illegal, granted Dr. Todd his prohibition.   But this judgment meant that those of most of the other cathedrals of the New Foundation were in a like way.   Thus the doctor in winning his case ensured his own final defeat, since the cathedrals in question could not be allowed to remain without any valid Statutes.   The best evidence of the serious view of the position taken by those in authority is shewn by the letter the archbishop of Canterbury wrote to his suffragans on 2 February 1708:

" I take it to be a common cause, and of great concern to this Church; which will never be quiet, so long as that evil generation of men, who make it their business to search into little flaws in ancient charters and statutes, and to unfix what laudable custom hath well fixed, meet with any success."[24]

The only way to put matters right was by an Act of Parliament giving legal sanction to the disputed Statutes. This was duly obtained, and the Royal Assent given on 20 March 1708.

On the same day, according to the bishop's diary, Dr. Todd

" declar'd, that he would behave himself dutifully and respectively (sic) to ye Bp of Carlisle . . .   And in Return, ye Bp likewise declar'd, that he would treat Dr Todd with all ye paternal Affection that can be expected from a Bp to one of the members of his Church; and that he will forget and forgive all that has been hitherto taken amiss Amen Amen.''

It is a remarkable comment on the spirit of the time that Edmund Gibson, then bishop of Lincoln, did not approve of this reconciliation, nor with that between the bishop and the dean which also took place.[25].

IV. POLITICIAN AND SOLDIER.

On 18 October 1707 Thomas Hearne described Nicolson as having been once '' firm and staunch to good honest principles, which he has since most shamefully renounced courting ye favour of ye Loggerhead of Lambeth ''[26] (Archbishop Tenison).   But Hearne is not famous for his charity towards his political opponents.   In fact Nicolson's motives for his change were certainly not based upon self interest and so reflect to his honour rather than otherwise.

In the Carlisle election of 1705 he supported the Tory candidate, but by 1708 his views seem to have been altering and he refused to taken any part in the election; by 1710 he had moved right over to the Whigs.   This, however, was the time of that party's fall from power;[27] at the Carlisle election that followed he supported their candidate, and got into sad trouble for doing so.   It was alleged that though a peer of the realm, he had sent a letter to one of the candidates, which was asserted by the Commons to be a breach of privilege, since members of the Upper House were not entitled to interfere in elections to the Lower one.   The bishop, who strongly denied that he ever wrote the words in question, was summoned to the bar of the House and a Vote of Censure passed.[28]

Judging from his diary, the bishop was a regular attender at the House of Lords for three or four months every year.   '' In consequence of the increased authority of parliament, one of the most important duties of the

Hanoverian prelate, according to contemporary esti-
mation, was his attendance upon the sessions of the House
of Lords."[29] This was also true of Queen Anne's time,
so it must not be thought that in being away from his
diocese he was neglecting his duty.

But for the bishop of Carlisle, a watch on the border
was an equally, if not more, important obligation. A
century under one crown had not brought about that
common regard of the two peoples for each other which
had perhaps been anticipated. In fact all that happened
was that the sword was exchanged for the pen, blows by
verbal abuse—international football had not yet come
into being. An example on each side may be quoted: an
Englishman on the Scots in 1708:

" the people are proud, arrogant, vainglorious, boasters, bloody,
barbarous and inhuman butchers.   Couzenance and theft is in
perfection among them.   Their Church services are " blasphemy
as I blush to mention."

The opposite opinion in 1705:

" For England, insolent and proud like Hell
Whose saucie boldness nought but blows can quell,
. . . let another Bannockburn redress
Too long endured affront and grievances."[30]

Thus it can be imagined that proposals to unite the
two parliaments did not meet with an unmixed reception.
During the preliminary negotiations the bishop was
consulted informally by the Commissioners, and sent
reports to his friends in London of the attitude of the
people of his diocese to the plan.[31] In Scotland one
result of the Union was to help forward the Jacobite
cause. The authorities countered by ordering more
active steps to be taken against papists on the Borders
and elsewhere. Nicolson took a leading part in putting
these regulations into effect in his diocese.[32]

Queen Anne died in 1714 and the Hanoverian George
ascended the throne. Next year the son of James II

landed in Scotland to claim the throne of his fathers. On 15 October 1715 the bishop issued a circular letter to his clergy exhorting them to " animate and encourage your respective parishioners in the defence of their Religion, Laws and Liberties."[33]

The local militia called to arms to resist the rebels, assembled at Penrith under the leadership of Lord Lonsdale and the bishop. But, being mostly armed only with scythes, billhooks and pitchforks, though some had swords and muskets of the time of the Civil War, they prudently decamped. It is difficult to blame them though his reverend and gallant lordship did; in this his coachman differed from his master. So a tussle arose between them. However, as his lordship was in the coach and his man on the box, the latter prevailed and the coach also decamped. It was while the bishop, head out of the window, was exhorting his man to stop that the lamentable incident of the loss of his episcopal wig occurred, the tradition of which, with its quaint aftermath, is preserved in the following ' Heroic Ballad.'[*] It describes ' the battle ' and the flight of Lord Lonsdale to Lowther Hall; and then goes on

> The Bishop gain'd his snug retreat,[†]
> Thank'd Heaven he breath'd the air;
> And all his bliss had been complete,
> Had not his head been *bare*.
>
> For, ah ! when on a length of road
> His troubles waxed great,
> The thatch, which hat and wig bestow'd,
> Unkindly left his pate !

---

[*] By Thomas Sanderson: it is entitled ' *Lord Lonsdale's Campaigning—An Heroic Ballad* ' and is printed in *Life and Literary Remains of Thomas Sanderson*, 9-20. There is a note: " The events of the day, as related to the author by one who had a share in its glory, gave rise to the following . . . ." As the author was born in 1759 and brought up at Raughton Head, which adjoins Rose Castle, there seems no reason to question the authenticity of the tradition.

[†] Rose Castle.

Two faithful friends, who near him stood,
Thus spoke without delay:
" We fear, my Lord, you've lost some blood,
As well as wig, this day."

" Why is your furrow'd cheek so wan?
Why trembles all your frame?
With muskets have th'ungodly clan
Ta'en at you deadly aim? "

" I've lost no blood," the Bishop said,
" I've saved my skin from balls;
From cleaving sword I've saved my head,
And reach'd these peaceful walls:

" A hostile tree, with branches rude,
Laid hold of hat and wig,
As trophies for the rebel crowd,
Whose courage waxed big."

" We'll go, we'll go," the friends replied,
" And seek the wig in haste;—
We'll search the road on every side,
Where'er your head has past."

Then with a daring air and mien,
March'd on those trusty men;
Shot, as they went, their glances keen
Through many a bushy glen.

Just as they reach'd a lonely glade,
Where oaks extended round,
They saw a matron, in the shade,
Lie, death like, on the ground.

They rais'd her up—she told a tale
That trembled on her tongue;
Then pointed, with a finger pale,
Where hat and wig were hung.

" That wig," quoth she, " that waves on high,
Upon yon oaken bough,
With foretop pointing to the sky,
Caus'd me to swoon below !

X

" I thought that, though the wig was grey,
  It held a bloody head;
That some religious man this day
  By ruffian hands had bled ! "

The men replied, " Good matron, know
  Yon wig's unstained with blood;
Its owner, safe from ev'ry foe,
  Lies snug in yonder wood."

On this there rose a welcome blast,
  That shook each tree around,
And laid (both) hat and wig in haste
  Soft on the verdant ground.

The men then tied them on a pole,
  E'en with a thong of leather;
And reach'd, though late, the Bishop's hall,
  In spite of wind or weather.

At ev'ry gate, with cudgels rude,
  They knock'd with all their pow'r;
The Bishop cried, " Who knocks so loud,
  At this untimely hour ? "

Quoth they, " We are your friends, and bear
  The hat and wig you lost,
When, liking not their martial air,
  You fled the rebel host.

" If you believe our honest word,
  This wig, your noodle's pride,
Has proved more *fatal* than the sword
  That dangled at your side,

" For by it, in a lonely dell,
  Midst oaks of wond'rous strength,
A hoary-headed matron fell,
  And measur'd out her length ! "

" You joke, you joke," the Bishop said,
  " Ne'er tell so strange a tale:
But, since I've saved both wig and head,
  Go, tap a cask of ale."

They tapp'd a cask right merrily,
Fill'd oft the drinking horn;
They drank, till all the blushing sky
Announc'd th' approach of morn.

" The Bishop gained his snug retreat." But it was
not too safe a one, because one of the rebels, Robert
Patten,[34] former curate of Penrith and son in law of the
late rector of Clifton, whose living he had hoped to get,*
had orders, later countermanded, to capture him. He
was also lucky in that the rebels' plan of seizing his beef
and mutton had been frustrated by the swollen waters of
the Eden.[35]

After the rising had collapsed the bishop was very
active in dealing with the unfortunate prisoners confined
in Carlisle castle. Some letters of his referring to their
trial and imprisonment have survived.[36] Members of
two local families were concerned in the rebellion: one,
James Radcliffe, earl of Derwentwater, for his share in it
suffered on Tower Hill; the other, John Layburne of
Cunswick saved his life, but lost his estates.[37]

We must now describe some events that were perhaps
more religious than political, though in those days it was
often difficult to separate the two.

" When King George acceeded to the crown of Great Brittain,
he was pleased to enquire after his old Oxford acquaintance Mr
Nicolson and finding him promoted to the Bishoprik of Carlisle,
His Majesty immediately bestowed upon him the place and office
of Lord High Almoner of His Household and Court. And, if he
could have been quiet and courtier enough, he had the fairest
prospect of any man living of succeeding to the aged and infirm
bishop of Durham."[38]

The bishop could not be ' quiet and courtier enough '
because he had certain convictions which conflicted with
those of the new king and his policy. George I wished on
political grounds to please the dissenters. In a conversation he had with the bishop soon after his accession, he

* He wrote the history of the rising.

urged that, as they had rendered much service to the
State, they should be rewarded by the repeal of the
Act against occasional conformity.   Nicolson disagreed;
toleration, he said, was a sufficient recompense and " the
security of that is all that the honest men among them
seem to desire now."[39]   Then to make matters worse he
wrote a pamphlet, entitled " a collection of Papers . . .
in a letter to the Bishop of Bangor," attacking this Broad
Church prelate.   The following statement of Dr. Todd's
seems to refer to this:

> " By giving his hand to the Truth of some conversation he had
> in private with a friend about a perplex'd and unintelligible
> sermon preached by the then Bishop of Bangor, . . . wherein his
> old friend Dr White Kenet failed him in his testimony,   he fell
> under some displeasure at Court and his place of Almoner was
> bestowed upon another."[40]

These events are interesting for the light they throw
on Nicolson's religious and political views.   Against
Dissenters he takes the same line as in 1699, when he
objected to Churchmen joining with them in the Society
for the Reformation of Manners.   His opposition to the
bishop of Bangor is also consistent with this attitude.
What is puzzling is that in the latter case he is on the same
side as Dr. Atterbury, whom he had so violently opposed
in the convocation dispute of 1697 and on his appointment
as dean of Carlisle.   One possible explanation is that he
was by religious conviction a High Churchman—this is
borne out by entries in his diary shewing that he kept
the fast days of the Church,[41]—who when he changed his
political views did not alter his religious ones.   To-day
there would be nothing unusual in that, but in the
eighteenth century High Church and Tory views or Low
Church and Whig ones generally went together.   If the
above suggestion is correct, Nicolson shewed an unusual
independence of mind.   What is wholly admirable is his
refusal to buy the approval of the king and the Whig

ministry by altering his religious convictions to suit the
new age.   He would not sell his soul for the bishopric of
Durham.

IV. HISTORIAN.

Thomas Hearne refers to Nicolson as " a proud,
haughty, ignorant, peevish, and huffing writer ";* but
he had little good to say of his political opponents.   The
bishop's historical writings dealt with matters of both
national and local interest.   To the former class belong
the volumes of the " *English Historical Library,*" published between 1696 and 1699; a volume dealing with
Scottish records, 1702, and a fifth one on Ireland, 1724,
completed the series.   These volumes, which supply
information about records available to students, were
more than just lists of these: they contained pertinent
comments on their value, and on the worth of any
books in which they were published.

In 1705 the bishop issued a work of more local interest
entitled " *Leges Marchiarum or Border Laws.*"   The
introductory discourse " of the ancient state of the
Borders " and the following chapters in Nicolson and
Burn's *History* were mostly based on this.   They also
drew very largely on his manuscripts, as they acknowledge
in their preface.   The fruits of the bishop's researches
into local history are contained in four big folio volumes
now in the dean and chapter registry.   A description of
their contents must be given in order that the extent of
the labour involved in their compilation may be realised.
The first of 507 pages mainly contains collections from
national records, such as Patent and Close Rolls, Feet of
Fines, etc., of matters concerning the history of these

* *Remarks and Collections*, IV, 405. Huffing means bullying, storming.
But the bishop himself could be quite reasonably rude: " he is the most
unaccountable and ridiculous Plagiary and Buffoon that ever had his name
upon the title page of any book whatsoever," is how he described a fellow
historian. (English Historical Library, I, ed. 1696, pt. I, 102).

counties; the second of 577 pages is made up of material, generally taken from the episcopal registers, for the history of the parishes of the diocese; the third of 297 pages mostly consists of records of the various religious houses of the diocese and lists of its officers; and the fourth of 472 pages gives the lives of the bishops of the see, with particulars of its revenues. The bishop also compiled the *Miscellany Accounts*, describing the state of the parishes, which have been printed and already referred to.* That much of the matter included in the four folio volumes is now available in print must not detract from the value of his work; rather it makes the modern researcher marvel at his diligence and zeal. One regret that the historian of to-day has is that he recorded nothing of moment about the age immediately preceding his own. An account of the character of the Restoration prelates by a contemporary hand would have been of the greatest interest.

Nicolson must be given a high place among the older local historians. Of these, John Denton, must rank first. Perhaps the second place should be given to Sir Daniel Fleming, whose many manuscript volumes, which include material not available elsewhere, still await proper investigation. Though as a local historian, the bishop may perhaps have to give way to the baronet there is no question of their place in the general field of history. As mentioned above† Nicolson was one of a small group of brilliant men who, as students at Oxford, and later in life, did much for historical research. To his own generation it is probable that he was chiefly thought of as an authority on the Anglo-Saxon language and antiquities. His correspondence shews how throughout his life these studies were among his first concerns, as he wrote in 1705 " I know nothing that hath greater share in my thoughts

* p. 292.
† p. 289-90.

and desires than the promotion of the Septentrional learning."[42]

In addition to this we must remember the great diary that the bishop kept—this shews his interest in the antiquities of his diocese.[43] There is, of course, much more of this than the printed extracts. A transcript of most of it is in Tullie House and fills eighteen large volumes. The bishop was also a competent botanist; a small manuscript volume containing his observations is still treasured at Rose.[44]

V. CONCLUDING YEARS.

As has been seen Nicolson did not shew himself adaptable to the ecclesiastical ideas of the Georgian Court. It was therefore probably with the idea of removing him to a place where he could do no mischief that he was offered the Irish see of Londonderry in 1718, worth over £2400 a year as compared with the £775 of Carlisle. The offer was accepted by the bishop, with the intention it would seem of still living in England. Indeed in a letter to Archbishop Wake he expresses the astonishment and disappointment he felt when the king told him that he expected him to reside in his new diocese.[45] It was not until March 1719 that he preached, on Easter Day, his last sermon in Carlisle Cathedral. After being connected with it for nearly forty years it must indeed have been a sad wrench. His later career need not detain us. On 9 February 1727, he was again translated; this time to the Irish archbishopric of Cashel. But he died suddenly a few days after, on 14 February, and was buried, without any monumental inscription, in Londonderry cathedral.

He married Elizabeth, daughter of John Archer of Oxenholme; by her he had three sons and five daughters; only one of the sons, Joseph Nicolson, chancellor of Lincoln, had issue and in his case only daughters. The

historian Joseph Nicolson of Hawksdale, Dalston was
a son of the bishop's brother John, who was chapter
clerk and registrar of the diocese.[46]   The bishop's will,
dated 30 March 1725, is in print;[47] it contained no
public or charitable bequests.

What kind of man was Bishop Nicolson? A man of
great gifts, " the possessor of an intellect of singular
acuteness,"[48] and of great versatility—Anglo-Saxon
scholar, medievalist, antiquary, botanist, diarist, administrator, politician; lover of a good dinner, and of good
conversation and fond of the sports of his day—hunting
and cock-fighting. A somewhat domineering, imperious,
quick-tempered and, when crossed, quarrelsome person,
with a sharp and caustic tongue. But with another side
to this part of his character; he paid poor Mr. Moon's
fees, when he was in trouble, he met Dr. Todd half-way
and helped him to ' save his face ' when he made himself
absurd over the churchwarden affair; and he entered in
his diary an ' Amen and Amen ' of thanksgiving when the
great Chapter dispute was concluded.

Without doubt, with the possible exception of Bishop
Kirkby, he is the most colourful personality among
the bishops of this diocese. Whether he is the greatest
is more open to question. For to be a great bishop
spirituality is necessary, and William Nicolson does not
seem to have been as much gifted in this respect as was
Edward Rainbow or Harvey Goodwin. While it must be
said therefore that as a bishop he has perhaps to give
place to these two prelates, it can confidently be asserted
that as a man, a personality, he can probably be accounted
the greatest who has ever ruled from Rose.

CHAPTER IV.

THE AFTERMATH,
1718-1747.

SAMUEL BRADFORD[1] was consecrated at Lambeth by Archbishop Wake on 1 June 1718. ' The Northern gentry were generally much adverse to him when he first went to Carlisle on account of his opposition to Atterbury. But he won their respect and esteem.' Hearne describes him as 'a most sad, dull, vile wretch,' which merely means that he was a whig.[2]

His register contains little of interest; he held a yearly ordination, two in 1721 and a visitation in the summer of 1719 about which he wrote to the archbishop:

' I made my visitation at the four usual places that I might as soon as possible acquaint myself with the state of my diocese. I have hitherto met with all due respect from the clergy, which I hope to preserve by a faithful discharge of my duty amongst them. I did not confirm during my visitation as believing it could not be done in so orderly and decent a manner as I desired; but have promised to go through the diocese again, as far as I am able, to confirm a few parishes at a time, such as can most easily be got together."

This he did in 1721,

' appointing one or two days in a week for that purpose that it might be done more regularly and with greater ease both to myself and the people.'[3]

During this episcopate Penrith church was rebuilt—the application for the faculty is dated 2 December 1720— and was consecrated by Bishop Nicolson on 17 March 1722. The order of the service is fully set out in the bishop's register.

A letter of his son's gives a pleasant picture of life at Rose at this time

" we rise about 6, breakfast and study till 11, dress and to prayers in our chappell; walk in ye gardens, dine, chat and drink tea, read an hour or two: at 4 to chapell; after yt walk or ride or visit a neighbour and drink a glass of ale, or fish or some such country amusement till 8; then sup: to prayers at 9 à la mode de Benet; then to bed those that please . . . We keep 2 publick days in the week, Mondays and Thursdays, when we expect company to dinner and seldom are disappointed."[4]

He was translated to Rochester in 1723, and died in 1731, being buried in Westminster Abbey, of which he was dean.

John Waugh,[5] dean of Gloucester, elected on 23 August 1723 and consecrated at Lambeth by Archbishop Wake, was the son of John Waugh of Scattergate, Appleby, yeoman.[6]   Considering he was a Whig, Thomas Hearne is quite polite: " he was looked upon when of Oxford and in other places, as a tolerable good preacher but hath no reputation for learning "; elsewhere he describes him as " a plain popular preacher and a great tutor."[7]

His register only contains ordinary routine matter,* except for a certificate in 1725 that the church of Crosby Garrett is now in a good state of repair, and an order, dated 30 June 1726

' as a result of a personal view and examination made by us 21 of this inst. June, to the minister and churchwardens of Kirk Levington to provide by 10 August next a carpet, linen cloth, challice, patten, rails for the Communion Table, new decent reading desk, pulpit and clerk's desk and place for hanging of the bells; also the floor to be made plain and even; seats and pews repaired and mended; and arrears for building the gallery to be levied."

This shews that little had been done to improve things

* A faculty of Sept. 1726 for a gallery in Kirkby Stephen church states that " in former times (it had) an organ wch has long been taken down and demolished." (Reg. p. 639).

since Bishop Nicolson's visit in 1703. It is obvious that Waugh had heard about it and as a result went to see for himself. That no other entries of this kind are included in the register suggests that this state of things was by now unusual.

He died in Queen's Square, Westminster, 29 October 1734, and was buried under the Communion Table at St. Peter's, Cornhill. His portrait by John Vanderbank was engraved by Faber. He is said to have married Elizabeth, whose surname was probably Simpson and whose brother lived at Sebergham.[8] Thomas Hearne has it that he " fell in league with a widow, the relict of one Mr. Fiddes (the son of old Mr. Fiddes, minister of Brightwell.)"[9]

John Waugh was the last of a series of local men of yeoman ancestry, all educated at Queen's College, Oxford, who were bishops of Carlisle. His predecessors in this were Bishops Robinson, Potter, and Smith; Nicolson was also at Queen's but of higher social status.

The new bishop, George, fifth son of Sir Daniel Fleming of Rydal was born on 10 June 1667, and sent to St. Edmund Hall, Oxford.

A series of letters[10] that passed between father and son, throwing light on the characters of the two men and the habits and ideas of the age, covers his Oxford life. We will start with one written on the eve of his proposed ordination on which Sir Daniel had determined. George, himself, was not so anxious for this, indeed he wrote on 21 September 1692 of his " natural avertion " to it. None the less he went

" according to custom to My Ld of Oxford's chaplain to be examined by him where I met to my sorrow and indignation much other entertainment than I either expected or I hope deserved; which I was frustrated of my so good intention." So, alas, he was " debarred holy orders . . for as yet I never heard of any that after one repulse ever made a second effort."

However, Sir Daniel was not convinced by this alleged precedent and wrote on 29 November

" when sons pretend Inate aversions (I cannot tell what) against their own good and their Father's desires, it often happens that such sons may live to repent it and see ye vanity of their own wandering Projects and Designes . . .   I see no reason that the caprich of a chaplain should debarr them (who are well affected to the King and Church) from Preferment."

On the 27 January, Sir Daniel returned to the attack

" Ye Study of Divinity is ye most honourable and that it would, in all probability prove the best for your Soul Body and Estate."

Can we wonder that the young man surrendered, and told his father

" I am sorry I should be so long in such a cloud, as not to see my own interest and what is more my duty, but being now Sr myself, I cannot but admire my own ill behaviour, and your clemency; my undutifulness and your most paternal affection."

Thus all was well, and on 27 May 1694 George Fleming was ordained deacon, and on 3 June priest, by Bishop Smith in Rose Castle Chapel.   His reward was not long in coming: on 26 March 1695 he was presented by the bishop, a relative, with the living of Aspatria.

However, as the study of divinity was very important and Oxford more pleasant for a well to do young man than Aspatria, George continued his studies; a curate sufficed for his parish.   Before long he had another idea, writing to his father in October 1695 that he was thinking of accepting the place of a chaplain to the East India fleet,

" ye stipend indeed is but small, being £40 p. Ann. but there are so many advantages as have very well rewarded my predecessors journeys, particularly the last who brought £3000 home with him."

Sir Daniel's answer shewed shrewd common sense

" I believe ye Bishop will not give you leave to be so long absentee; and have a care of loseing ye substance in catching at ye shadow."

In fact, George had already realised this and written to his father telling him so.

Thus he continued at Oxford; but on 7 May 1696 Sir Daniel wrote

" I hear that my Lord Bishop is not well pleased that you come not down according to your promis unto his Lordship."

However, on 30 June, he is able to say

" My Lord is willing that you shall continue at Oxford longer, so as you study Divinity, and fit yourselfe for ye serveing of your cure in person, according to your Duty."

By January 1697 Sir Daniel was again getting annoyed:

" the Bishop, your parishioners, and I will then expect you, and I've hope you'l not then fail us all. I doubt not but that it will prove for your Health, Wealth and Reputation . . . and I shall consent to your keeping a curate."

He was evidently thoroughly alarmed by this because, on 8 February, Dr. Mill, principal of St. Edmund Hall wrote to Sir Daniel

" He's far from Loitering here for his pleasure . . . He made his Profession entirely his business . . . My Lord has very few such men as he is in his Diocese. A man of singular and every way exemplary sobriety and conduct; great prudence and Discretion."

Sir Daniel wisely forwarded this to the bishop, who promptly gave his consent to his remaining at Oxford.

On 25 October 1697 Dr. Mill could report the end of his studies " the onely fault he has (and 'tis a very good one) his great bashfulness and modesty. I wish he had a little more Assurance." Even then Aspatria did not see him much—on 11 March 1698, Sir Daniel wrote to Dr. Mill " All this last sharp winter I have detained my son here . . . He hath made some visits to Rose Castle and Aspatria." Then on 9 June he could tell his father that the bishop " was so very kind as to make me a proffer to live with him in ye Quality of his chaplaine." In March 1701 the rector of Caldbeck died leaving that living and a canonry vacant; the bishop offered George Fleming his choice, he decided on the latter, which he held till 1727. In 1703 he became vicar of Stanwix and Kirkland, and resigned Aspatria. Two years later he vacated the former on being made archdeacon of Carlisle and rector of Great Salkeld; he held these till 1734. He resigned Kirkland in 1717, but soon made up for it by obtaining Ousby, which he kept till 1735. Then in 1727 he exchanged his canonry of Carlisle for the deanery, still retaining the archdeaconry. In 1729 he was given the family living of Grasmere, which he held till 1733, when he resigned it for his son, who also succeeded him in the archdeaconry.

Then he rounded off his career in the diocese by becoming its bishop. He was consecrated at Lambeth by Edmund Gibson, bishop of London, on 19 January 1735. A year later his brother, who had been created a baronet in 1705, died and the bishop succeeded to the title and the family estates.

His register mostly consists of routine matters. During his episcopate we have evidence of the work of Queen Anne's Bounty. In 1704, the queen had announced her intention of giving up for the benefit of the Church the revenue from first fruits and tenths. In 1706 and 1707 all livings below £50 were discharged from these payments. By 1713 the governors began distributing the income for the benefit of poorer livings. The method they adopted, by ballot, was a bad one as one parish could have several augmentations, each of £200, while others, perhaps more deserving, had none. There were two returns from this diocese: on 12 December 1707 in Bishop Nicolson's time of all rectories and vicarages under £50 a year and on 26 January 1739 in this episcopate of all curacies (which meant perpetual curacies and chapelries) under £30. Combining the two together, we get the following results:

Yearly value	Rectories & Vicarages	Perpetual curacies	Chapelries	Total
£0 — £5	—	4	5	9
5 — 10	4	8	11	23
10 — 20	6	3	4	13
20 — 30	5	8	4	17
30 — 40	10	—	—	10
40 — 50	12	—	—	12

In one parish, Kirkandrews on Esk and one chapelry, Nichol Forest, all record of any endowment had been lost. The lowest stipends were: vicarages, Shap £6; perpetual curacies, Flimby, £2. 4. 0.; and chapelries, Newlands, £2. 11s. 7.[11] The income of the bishop was £775 a year.

One of Q. A. B's. rules was that any chapelry receiving an augmentation became automatically a perpetual curacy and so had to be held by a priest. Thus the bishop's register contains many instances of readers who had previously served these chapelries being ordained; in fact, the ' order ' soon ceased to exist.

The most spectacular event of this episcopate was the Jacobite rising of 1745. On 25 July Prince Charles Edward Stuart, grandson of James II, landed in Scotland. His defeat of Sir John Cope at Preston Pans on 20 September left the path to the Border open. By 7 November the ' Rash Adventurer,' as he was called by the tactful, had arrived at Stonegarthside, within a few miles of Carlisle. On the 9th his mounted troops surveyed the city from Stanwix Bank. But, hearing that General Wade was about to advance to its relief from Newcastle, the Highlanders turned east to engage him. The attack not materialising, they came back to Carlisle. On the afternoon of 13 November the city was surrounded; two days later it surrendered and the gateway to England was open.

Why Carlisle gave in so easily has caused much speculation among historians; one has said the garrison and people were Jacobites at heart;[12] another that they were cowards;[13] and a third that the behaviour of the militia, who were chiefly to blame, could only be attributed to a want of morale and discipline.[14].

To discover the truth let us look at the situation within the city: the garrison consisted of about 80 old soldiers, invalids, ' very old and infirm,' and seven companies of militia made up of 287 men from Cumberland and 249 from Westmorland—in all 536. In the nominal roll of these men notes as to their arms are recorded and contain such entries as " no sword, gun bad, wants a bayonet, quite incomplete "; hardly one appears to have been properly equipped. There was also a company, 61 men, of light horse,* and a pressed body from the city, ' mostly poor labouring people,' with no pay. The circuit of the castle walls, of about 700 yards, needed some 600 men for defence. Those of the city, longer still, were described as " very low, and might have been scaled with great ease and very weak, might easily have been thrown down." The governor had " a very severe fit of gout, and (was) still very lame and full of pain when the Rebels came before Carlisle." He had applied for 500 men, due from Ireland, but was told that " Carlisle was not, nor could be, of consequence enough to put the Government to the charge of sending an express on purpose "; that this had been said was known to the militia officers and so presumably to the townsfolk. General Wade, when asked to come to the relief, replied that he intended to move his troops to Lancashire to meet the rebels there.[15]

Can the local militia then be blamed if they failed to see why they should die for a government that had not sent, and refused to send, enough troops to garrison the city, whose fortifications they had neglected and whose defence they pronounced to be of so little consequence as not to be

* I am indebted to Miss Elsas for the information as to the strength of the militia. The figures are taken from the *Lieutenancy records of the County— Militia muster roll for* 1745, pp. 1-8. Previously the traditional figure for the strength of the Militia was about 700 men.

worth an express letter? They felt presumably that under the circumstances the best thing they could do was not to try to hold an indefensible city but go home and protect their own wives and children. Thus, while we must deplore their lack of disciplinary sense, we can commend their fund of commonsense.

So Charles Edward, preceded by a hundred pipers, entered Carlisle. During their short stay his troops appear to have behaved well. The only loss of ecclesiastical property was the parish registers of Stanwix.* This forbearance shews considerable restraint because the clergy, led by the chancellor John Waugh, had taken an active part in the defence of the city. The cathedral tower had been used as an observation post with two clergy stationed on it with ' a large spying glass.' When the Highlanders came before Carlisle these clerics acted as aides-de-camps to the governor and also took their share of watching on the ramparts by night.[16]

The story of the prince's advance to Derby does not concern us. A glimpse of the attitude of the countryside is obtained from an entry in the Heversham parish books of 1/- spent for hiding the communion plate as his army passed by and of 5/- for ringing the bells when it was defeated.[17]

The retreat commenced on 6 December. An advance guard, consisting of about a hundred hussars, reached Kendal on Saturday the 14th. After a slight skirmish in the town, in which some people were killed, the cavalry went on to Eamont bridge, but, seeing Penrith beacon on fire, returned to Shap. Meanwhile, a rumour having arisen that the Highlanders had been defeated, the country people took up arms. Thus, when the hussars set out the next day to make another attempt to get to Scotland, the result was not inappropriately called in a contemporary letter ' the Sunday Hunting.'

Divine service must indeed have been somewhat

* See note on p. 327.

disturbed in many villages that Sunday morning. The duke of Perth and the hussars travelled up the Eden valley by Cliburn, Temple Sowerby, where they crossed the river, and Culgaith to Langwathby Moor. But there they found the men of Penrith and others. So, pursued by the locals, back went the gallant duke and his hussars to Culgaith and then, by Newbiggin Moor, Kirkby Thore, and Bolton, where they re-crossed the river, through Morland, Newby and Reagill, to Shap and Orton, where they refreshed themselves before rejoining their main body at Kendal.

The next day, Monday, 16 December, the whole army, plundering the country-side as it went, continued its retreat. The main body reached Shap that evening and Penrith on the following one, but the artillery train lagged a day behind. The pursuing English army, under the duke of Cumberland, advancing along the main road, across Brougham Common and through Lowther park, tried to get to Eamont bridge before the artillery. So the Highlanders had to turn and fight; a brief skirmish on Thrimby hill and a more considerable one at Clifton* followed. The latter was in fact a small battle, with the Highlanders lining the enclosures at the south end of the village and the English troops attempting to drive them out. The burials of eleven dragoons are recorded in the parish registers. By this stand the prince's men saved their artillery. To commemorate this ' victory ' the duke of Portland presented Penrith church with fifty guineas with which two chandeliers were bought.[18]

On 19th December the prince reached Carlisle; he only stayed a short time and then departed north, leaving four hundred men in the castle to retard the pursuit. But by 30 December all resistance had ceased. Carlisle had stood the last of its many sieges and Englishmen and

---

* The skirmish at Clifton occupies an important place in chapter LIX of Sir Walter Scott's novel *Waverley*.

Scotsmen fought before its walls the last of their many battles.

Judged by his behaviour the duke of Cumberland,* despite his title, appears to have shared with many other Englishmen the delusion that Carlisle is Scottish soil. The prisoners were kept in the cathedral, in the nave, or St. Mary's church, not the choir. The result can best be understood from letters Prebendary Wilson wrote to Dr. Waugh—27 January 1746.

" You may imagine better than I can describe the condition the Rebs. left the Parish church in, for yt. was their prison : I was given to understand the damage it suffered wd. be made good, but upon enquiry no further power was given than to the cleansing and washing of it. This proves of little use, for the flags being old, spungy, and ill laid, the earth under them is corrupted and till that is removed the Cathedral church will not be sweet, nor will it be safe to have service in it. The pews in the parish church are most of them broke to pieces. If you can obtain a power to have this done, and the pews repar'd, you'll merit the thanks of the body."

14 February,

" the burning of sulphur and tar had that effect that we had service in the Cathedral on Sunday last."

3 April,

" Church work at Carlisle, you know goes slowly forward. It is but a few days since I got an estimate from workmen of the expence we must be at to put the Church in the repair it was before it was made a prison. If it fall wholly upon us, we need not, I think, be much dismayed, as thirty pounds will defray all."[19]

The cathedral not only suffered by being made a prison, it nearly lost its bells. Again we quote from the same correspondence.

* Strangely enough there is no mention of the events of the '45 in the Corporation Order books. No meeting took place between 30 September 1745 and 25 March 1746. At the latter a resolution was passed that the Corporation should wait on the duke without the gates, with " their Ensigns of Honour, the Aldermen and Council in their Robes and that Aldm. Pattinson, Deputy Mayor, doth entertain the Duke after the Best manner he can at the expense of the Corpn." (Book VI, p. 192).

9 January:

" A demand made by Major Balfour, in the Duke's name, of the bells of our Cathedral, as a perquisite to the train of artillery, was a surprise upon the members of the Chapter here, and very ill relished by them.   Mr Birket Mr Head and myself waited on the Duke to desire his protection, alledging that the bells were the property of the Dean and Chapter, and given to them in their Charter; that the Chapter was not conscious of any behaviour in themselves but such as became dutiful and loyal subjects; that the town had not any right in them.   The answer given us was that the Duke would not interfere in it : that if it was a perquisite to a train we could say nothing against it.   A moderate composition, I believe, would pacify the claimant; but I'm firmly resolved at present, as are my two brethren, not to submit to any. Is this the reward for all our toil ?   If the Major takes them down, which he still threatens, I doubt not the Lord Chief Justice will oblige him to replace them."

on 20 January:

" Mr. Balfour has left the town without pressing the thing further I imagine we shall hear no more from him, and that he is ashamed of the length he has gone.   He has reason to be so, for it was a scandalous, unprecedented, and illegal demand, and this he ought to be made sensible of."[20]

It was sometime, however, before the bells were used again, for in April 1747, Mr. Wardale wrote to Dr. Waugh " I think we have nothing new in Carlisle worth your hearing but the chimes, which began yesterday (the Duke's birthday), and go very well."[21]   Now there is a local tradition that because the cathedral bells welcomed the ' Rash Adventurer ' when he entered Carlisle, an order was given for them not to be rung again for a hundred years.   The above statement is evidence that this tradition is wrong; further no such order is mentioned by any of Dr. Waugh's correspondents.   It is inconceivable that if one had been given he would not have been told of it.   Yet a tradition of this kind is rarely devoid of any foundation.   May it not be that for some reason the bells did cease for a time—the words " which began yesterday " support this view—and that popular theory invented the traditional reason to account for this stoppage. Then, when later on the bells could not be rung for fear of damage to the tower, the old tradition of the order was revived as a popular explanation of their silence.[22]

Now an account must be given of one called by some at this time bishop of Carlisle. " In the devoted band which joined the Prince at Manchester in 1745 may be found more high-minded gentlemen than the Reverend Thomas Coppock, but not many of a more lively and interesting character." The truth about his life has recently been investigated.[23] Previously too much credence has been placed upon the " Life " and " Forged Speech,"* both published soon after his death, but now known to be full of inaccuracies, and in fact " malignant slanders."

He was born in 1719 at Manchester, where his father was a tailor. Educated at the Grammar School, he obtained a school exhibition and entered Brasenose College, Oxford, in 1739, taking his B.A. in 1742. After that there is a gap in our knowledge. Something went wrong, but what it was is unknown as he disappears from view until December 1744, when he is back again at Manchester, seeking ordination. But, presumably because of what had taken place in the past two years, none of the Manchester clergy would sign the necessary Testimonial. He therefore forged one with two signatures attached to it and then obtained a genuine third one. With his Testimonials in order he betook himself to London and there achieved his purpose, being ordained deacon by the bishop of Exeter in December 1744, with a title as curate of Snave, Kent. Before long news of the forged Testimonial seems to have reached the authorities, as in

* This has a certain interest because it has a false imprint—Carlisle printed by Thomas Harris—there was no printing press in the city until about 1770 (o.s. xiv. 17-8).

September 1745, a new curate is licensed to Snave, and Thomas Coppock is found once more at Manchester.

So it is not surprising that when the prince reached that city, he found him a ready recruit. Marching as chaplain of the Manchester Regiment to Derby, he was in the retreat to Carlisle. There, left behind with his regiment in the castle, he was captured.

One of those marked out by the government for punishment, he made pathetic efforts to avoid the gallows—he was only twenty-seven. His last letter to the archbishop of Canterbury asking for his intercession ends " I'm Your Grace's most unfortunate, most unhappy, most miserable, and most dejected son," but all in vain. On St. Luke's Day 1746, he was drawn on a new sledge from the castle to Harraby, and there duly hanged. It is difficult to read the account of his life without feeling that he was a man of considerable parts, who with greater good fortune might have achieved a more honourable niche in history than fate has accorded him.

There is, of course, no truth in the story that he was appointed by Charles Edward to the see of Carlisle. That the prince would have conferred a bishopric, not in fact vacant, on a young man in deacon's orders and of doubtful antecedents, is unbelievable. There is no doubt that his enemies said this, and that the " Forged Speech " was entitled " *Genuine dying speech of Parson Coppoch, pretended Bishop of Carlisle.*" But there is no factual support for the story which, though occasionally contradicted, has travelled down the centuries. Perhaps Coppock did hope for such preferment: he was clever and ambitious, the only English clergyman to join the prince, and Bishop Fleming was an old man. The truth may be that the title was a nickname given by the troops and accepted by Coppock in a spirit of hopeful anticipation.

During these critical months the bishop's health was not good. But he stuck to his post at Rose, which the

Highlanders visited on 15 November, when the well-known incident of the gift of the white cockade to the baby, later Lady Clerk, took place.[24]   He was consulted by Dr. Waugh on various occasions and attended a meeting held at Carlisle in connection with the defence of the city.   Nor does he seemed to have been prevented from carrying out his usual episcopal duties as he preached at Allonby and was living at Rose just before the Highlanders returned.[25]

The bishop died there on 2 July 1747 and was buried in the cathedral, where there is a marble monument.[26]

In the obituary notice that appeared in the *Gentleman's Magazine*,[27] it was stated that ' by his death Society had lost one of its most valuable members and the Church of England one of its chiefest ornaments; and that he had been in the habit of punctually joining with his family ' four times a day in the publick devotions of the church.'

His register, with its regular list of two or three ordinations a year, suggests a worthy and conscientious prelate.   He married Catherine, daughter of Robert Jefferson of Carlisle and left issue.

Note from p. 321.

After the above was in page proof it was found that the Stanwix registers cannot have been destroyed, as stated in Mounsey " Carlisle in 1745 " p. 64, as they are intact from 1661.   Nor can this refer to any earlier volume as Bishop Nicolson noted in 1703 that they only began in that year.   (Miscellany Accounts, p. 105).   The statement quoted by Mounsey was made by the vicar of the parish, Dr. Waugh.   How he came to make such a mistake must remain a mystery.   Perhaps the registers were hidden by some one for safety; then, this being forgotten, it was assumed that they had been destroyed. Later, when they were recovered, they were duly brought up to date, but with no thought for the snare left for the poor historian who accepted the contemporary evidence of the vicar on such a simple matter of fact.

CHAPTER V.

THE DIOCESE OF CHESTER DEANERIES.
1603-1747.

THE only records at York or Chester of the Church in the western deaneries between 1603 and the Restoration are the two volumes at York of the commissioners' Visitation of 1633.* They supply much interesting information.† At Arlecdon, St. Bride's Beckermet, and Flookburgh the floors were not paved nor flagged. St. Bees' "chancel (is) in decay for that the roof is fallen downe and is likely to ruinate the steeple of the church"; Burton in Kendale "is not flagged nor coated but very disorderly." At Hawkshead "Ye South side of their church is in decay." Harrington "is not beautified," nor is Corney "with sentences of Scripture."

Other churches lack some of the required ornaments: Brigham: "they want a booke of homilies, a poor man's box and a table of the degrees of marriage." Arlecdon "have noe potte of pewter for ye coṁon" and St. Bride's "no standing potte of pewter for the wine." At Burton the 'cupp is very meane, not worth 30s.,' Selside "lack a pewter platter for ye bread," nor have they a "decent cover for ye communion table, have onely a lining cloth," and Ennerdale want "A cover of silk or stuff for the Coṁon." At Kendal "ye names of those that are marryed buryed and baptized are not all registered." At Cartmel "one of ye belles is not in tune but is putt to castinge."

* R. VI. A 23 B 4.
† Some of which has already been used in the chapter on the social scene.

The curate of Cockermouth was in trouble for " not reading praier on the eves of Sundaies and holidaies nor on Wednesdaies and Frydaies, except in Lent, and sometimes sayeth psalmes after the lessones instead of the hymnes appointed . . . he hath sometimes read praires without a surplesse and omitted to catechise the youth upon Sondaies and holidaies." At Dean much the same complaint as to the omission in reading " praires " is made. At Burneside the curate is presented for ' not tolling a bell to give warning to praires ' and for " omitting to weare the surplesse sometimes." The curate at Coniston also did not read prayers on Wednesdays and Fridays and his brother at Ponsonby sang " psalmes instead of Te Deum." Further he taught " schoole in the church," which likewise happened at Cartmel Fell chapel and Staveley. At Coniston two people were presented " for puttinge a stall upp in ye churche."

The vicar of Kirkby Ireleth was reported " four pte of his Vicaridge house in decay and in ruine and for not making his pte of his churchyard wall," and the incumbent of Bootle for " suffering the parsonage house to be in decay."

From the York books of 1669 and 1684* we learn that at Eskdale the churchyard wall was in decay and Brigham wanted a book of canons (1669). In 1684 Ponsonby lacked locks for its chest, had no book of homilies, ' nor a surplice decent to be worne '; at Blawith the chapelyard had been incroached upon and at Aldingham they had no book of canons nor table of degrees. At Pennington a presentment was made against ' our predecessors, churchwardens for two years successively contrary to the 89th and 90th canons.' In the accusation against James Wilson of Kendal (1684) ' for detaining a portion of three pounds p. ann. given to the free schoole of Heversham ' we have an illustration of the fate that often befell

* R. VI. A. 28. 29; R. VI. A. 34.

charitable bequests in those days. At Old Hutton the curate was accused of 'neglicence in not reading divine service on several Sundays ' (1684) and at Arlecdon he had not received any ' stipend being £5 p. an. and two years and a halfe unpaid.' There are the usual cases of breaches of Sunday observance and of people doing things without a licence. By far the most interesting point in the returns is the evidence of the hold nonconformity had in these deaneries. At Colton chapel the churchwardens were presented for allowing two of them to expound and preach in the chapel; at Selside it was not known whether the curate was in orders or not (1669). As has been noted above* there were many Quakers in these deaneries, almost every parish had some: in 1684, Brigham had 36, Dean 26, Loweswater 20; Kendal 45, Hugill 22, Heversham 28; Kirkby Lonsdale 27; most of the Furness presentments are simply 'not coming to church ' with no details but small places like Cartmel Fell had 16 and Lindale 18.

From now onwards the Chester records are more numerous and increasingly complete visitations lists are in existence. The only one containing any presentments is that of 1677, but there is nothing in it of special interest.

In 1674 the bishop was at Cartmel for Furness and Coupland on 30 June and at Kendal on 2 July for that deanery and Kirkby Lonsdale, but three years later the Coupland people had to go to Kendal, and those of Furness to Ulverston. In 1691, another method was tried—Furness and part of Coupland at Cartmel and the rest of Coupland with Kendale at Kendal. But in 1698 and 1709 arrangements become more reasonable: Kendale deanery at Kendal, Furness at Cartmel, and Coupland at Whitehaven, though other plans were adopted in 1701 and 1712—southern Coupland at Cartmel and northern at Kendal and Cockermouth. Four years later, Coupland

* p. 269.

presentments were taken at Cockermouth and White-haven. Then in 1737 (intervening returns, except part of 1725, seem to be missing) the plan of 1698 and 1709 was returned to and became for the rest of this period the accepted one. The records from which these details are taken contain little of interest except for the names of the clergy of the various parishes and chapelries. The Visitations were held either in May, June, or July. The bishop usually allowed himself three days between the deaneries. In 1716 for instance he was at Cockermouth on 1 June, Whitehaven on the 4th, Cartmel on the 7th, and Kendal on the 9th.

There is some interesting evidence about Kendal church in the years after the Restoration. In 1670 a deep hole was dug in church for ' burying ye bones '; six years before a man had been paid for varnishing a new censer for Church use. It seems probable that these two facts are related as presumably the incense was used as a means of fumigation. Ancient churches, with frequent interments within their walls, must have often been sadly in need of such. None the less it is noteworthy to find the people of Kendal so intelligent as to use incense for this purpose.

The High Church revival at Carlisle in these days has already been mentioned;* a kindred movement appears to have taken place at Kendal. In 1675/6 the Communion Table was enlarged and railed in for the exclusion of dogs; fine green cloth with a silk fringe was bought for a table cloth. The table frame and the communion rails were painted the same colour, and the Lord's Prayer and Creed embellished on a green framed canvas. Then in 1684 the church was ' beautified ' with texts in the usual way and quaint devices in green, yellow, and black painted upon the whitewash; the font and pulpit were

* p. 274.

also painted green. Next year and in 1686 much of the building was reflagged.*

During the years 1603-1747 much church building and repairing was going on as can be seen from the lists in Appendix IV. Thus, while we have little evidence of episcopal activity in these deaneries, we have much proof of parochial zeal since the directing energy for all this building must have come from the people themselves and not from the bishop in far away Chester.

BISHOP GASTRELL'S NOTITIA.

From time to time in this book Gastrell's *Notitia* has been noted as a reference.† Some account must now be given of this work: Francis Gastrell became bishop of Chester in 1714. He seems almost immediately to have started collecting materials for a parochial history of his vast diocese. While of the greatest interest as almost the only source of information for the history of many small chapelries, it suffers by comparison with Bishop Nicolson's contemporary survey in being wholly based on written returns, not on personal visitation. As a result it lacks the human touch of the *Miscellany Accounts*, and suffers from the omission of any description of church buildings. The method followed is simple. The pages of the book, a large folio volume, are divided into two, each parish or chapelry occupying a couple of them with the four columns devoted to accounts of (1) the stipend and patronage, (2) parochial history, (3) schools, (4) charities. *The Notitia* seems to have been seen by Nicolson and Burn and used by them in their history. The sources relied on are the Chester diocesan registers, various records at York, returns sent in answer to a questionnaire from Dr.

---

* o.s. xvi, 169-171.

† The Lancashire part of *The Notitia* was printed many years ago by the Chetham Society, but in fact so mauled by the transcriber that it is sometimes hard to trace the original in it, as any one who will look at this can see.

William Stratford,* and other returns which seem to be missing. The parishes are arranged under their rural deaneries, in alphabetical order, each with its chapelries, if any, in the like order.

A summary of stipends from figures given may be of interest

Yearly value	rectories and vicarages	perpetual curacies	parochial chapelries	other chapelries	Total
£0 — £5	—	1	10	6	17
5 — 10	1	8	20	10	39
10 — 20	4	2	2	1	9
20 — 30	4	1	1	—	6
30 — 40	3	—	1	—	4
40 — 50	5	—	—	—	5
50 — 75	6	—	2	—	8
75 — 100	1	—	—	—	1
100 — 200	3	1	—	—	4
Totals	27	13	36	17	93

These figures speak for themselves and illustrate, even when the difference in the relative value of money is allowed for, the poverty of many of the parochial clergy before Queen Anne's Bounty began its beneficent work. It will be noted that 56 out of 93 livings were worth less than £10 a year.

Fortunately many of the returns upon which the bishop drew have survived. Some of the answers to the question how the church assessment was raised are noteworthy, Kendal:

" soon after the visitation, commonly on St Peter's day, there is a meeting in our parish church of all the church and chapel wardens and as many of the parishioners as shall think fit to appear (public notice of which is always given in the parish church and

* Called the Benefactor in an article about his life and gifts in N.s. xxvi, 63-76. He gave large sums to augment poor livings. During his life he is said to have given £1000 for this purpose here and elsewhere. By his will our parishes received over £3000. In addition he gave communion plate to Egremont, Ulpha and perhaps to St. Nicholas, Whitehaven.

all the chapels upon the Sunday immediately before) at which
meeting they joyntly consider of an assessment by the pound
sufficient to keep the church in good repair and defray such other
charges as may be incumbent upon 'em for the year, which
assessment the church and chapel wardens of each place, with the
advice and assistance of some of the principal inhabitants, do
charge upon every Estate according to the value of it, and is
collected by each warden within his respective division.   There
are three other days vizt ye 18th of October, ye 27th of December,
and on Easter Tuesday upon which the church and chapel wardens
are by Custom obliged to appear, and for that reason they call 'em
peremptory Days; they then consult further about the Repairs of
the church, bring in their several assessments, and see the money
duly applied."

Broughton:

" We have a particular custom of making church Lays, or
assessmts by the Quindam, as they call it, whereby the leasewhole
estates if worth, for instance, ten shillings per annum, pay as much
to the Repairs of the church as an Estate of thirty pounds per
annum.   They give this reason for it; that every one hath equal
Liberty and priviledge and probability of Improvement of Divine
Service, sermons, sacraments and Sacramentals."

Cockermouth:

" We have four men call'd Proctors which collects of every
Inhabitant at Eastr three halfpence which they call com'unicant
money but neither provides bread nor wine with it . . . if any
body above ye age of 16 years refuse to pay their dues (as they
call it) they get a conviction before ye Justices of ye Peace and
make them pay unreasonable charges.   They will not receive
their dues sent by any Quaker unless they will carry such fees
themselves but get them convicted."

St. Bees:

" Our way of assessing to the necessary repairs of our church is
by couples and half couples, which is done the Tuesday in
Whitsun week by the church Wardens Foremen of the four and
twenty, and of as many of that Number as appear, which Assessment is afterwards mitigated on St John's Day according to
Equity, and with Respect to the abilities of every Parishioner.
This is the Custom, the ancient and immemorial Custom, of the
parish of St Bees.   The assessments laid for the Repairs of the
Parish Church are collected by the four Churchwardens and paid

on St Mark's Day to the Churchwardens and Foreman of the four and twenty at which time the Parish accounts are stated, and afterwards registered in a fair hand."

Then some interesting answers were given to the question whether there was any remarkable custom in the parish. St. Bees:

" twelve pence is paid for the Head of every fox, and for the Head of every Brock or Badger; four pence for the Head of every Raven, and as much for the Head of every Eagle; whereby the Assessments to the Repairs of the Parish church are very much lessen'd more especially in the mountainous parts of the parish."

Loweswater:

" We have one remarkable custom within ye Parish touching ye small sallary Belonging ye Church viz 4l. 11s. 6d. wch is ye yearly Intrst of 55l, or thereabouts, Stock wch has been made up among ye Inhabitants ymselves, there being nothing given by ye Impropriators of ye Tythes to ye church; and ye sd Stock goes in every Quartr of ye Parish by Turn, and is Lodged by equall Proportions in ye hands of ye Twelve Sydemen for ye year, that is, three in every Quarter of ye Parish, According to ye Turn of ye Estate, changing every year, and for wch Stock of 55l they pay 20d p. pound to ye Curate and always have done so time out of mind, as doth appear by ye ancient church Books, being always reckoned a parochiall duty incumbent upon their Estates, or ye possessor thereof."

Millom:

" we have an ancient custom of laying out church tax by ye name of cullsale* wch is six pounds six shillings throughout ye whole parish. A cull sale is two pounds two shillings in Ulpha; one pound four shillings and four pence Above Millom, seventeen shillings and threepence Below Millom; sixteen shillings and one penny Chapel Suken; and one pound six shillings and four pence Thwaits; wch makes up ye sum of six pounds six shillings, a whole Cull sale."

The returns also give particulars of the parish clerk's fees. These are generally 2d from every household in the

---

* " Cull, an animal drafted from the flock, as being inferior or too old for breeding, usually fattened for the market " (*New English Dictionary*, J. A. H. Murray). Hence this word for the collection of Church dues is presumably a survival of the days when these were given in kind.

parish, though there are some variations on this: at
Urswick he received 4d from every married couple and 2d.
from every widower or widow; at Workington it was 3d.
and 1½d. respectively. He also received fees for marriages; at St. Bees 2d. for one by banns and 1/- for one by
licence; at Brigham the rate was 3d. and 6d. He also
had a fee at burials: at St. Bees it was 4d. for every grave
in the churchyard and 6d. for one in the church, with
another 6d. for replacing " the Flaggs upon the Graves
after they are settled." At Distington he had a fee, 2d.,
at a churching and at Kirkby Lonsdale, where " he hath
6d. for every Baptisme," the 2d. he received from every
house was called ' Smoke money.'

The only mention of confirmation in these returns is
from the incumbent of Dalton who states that ' in the
afternone (he) reads an Homilie or Catechiseth the youth
and fitts them for Confirmation.' We have evidence
from elsewhere that the sacrament was administered.
Sir Daniel Fleming of Rydal in his *Memoirs** tells us
that his children were confirmed at Kendal in 1671, 1674
and 1677; one was aged 12, two 14 and another 19. The
Pennington registers mention children going from there
to Cartmel for confirmation in 1712 and 1725. But it is
difficult to see how those from the more remote places,
especially in Coupland, can ever have got to the bishop.
There is nothing to suggest that he stayed anywhere en
route for the purpose.

* p. 75.

APPENDIX IV.

CHURCH EXTENSION AND RESTORATION
1603-1747.

In the following lists, the letter ' A ' denotes that this is the first time any record of the chapel mentioned has been found—it may, of course, have been in existence some time before; while ' N ' means that its building or consecration can be placed with reasonable certainty in the year named. The other chapels or churches mentioned were rebuilt at the date given.*

DIOCESE OF CARLISLE.†

Swindale (A) probably bt. early 17th century (V).   Stainmore bt. on new site and c. 1608 (IV).   Arthuret bt. 1609 (IV).   Martindale rb. 1633 (V).   Kirkandrews on Esk (N) bt. 1635 (VII).   1st vicar instituted 1637 (I).   Great Broughton (A) mentioned 1645 (XI).   St. Ninian and St. Wilfrid, Brougham rb. 1658-60 (IV).   Mallerstang rb. 1663 (IV).   Soulby (N) c. 1663 (I). Lowther Hall chapel (N) c. 1666 (I).   Armathwaite rb. 1668 (IV). Raughton Head c. 1678 (VI).   Nichol Forest (A) rb. 1678 (II and VIII).   Wreay rt. 1678 (II).   Thrimby rb. 1681 (IV).   High Head or Ivegill rb. 1682 (IX).   Camerton rb. 1694 (X).

Hutton-in-the-Forest newly erected 1714 (I).   Hesket-in-the-Forest rt. 1717 (I).   Langwathby rb. 1718 (X).   Penrith rb. 1720-2 and c. 1722 (I).   Holm Cultram rt. 1724 (I).   Skelton rb. 1724 (I).   Bampton rb. 1726-8 (I and V).   Nichol Forest rb. 1726 (VIII).   Swindale l. 1728 (I).   Renwick rb. 1733 (II and IV).   Mardale rt. 1737 (I).   Ravenstonedale rb. 1738-44 (V). Lanercost rt. 1739-40 (III).   Wreay c. 1739 (I).   Wythburn rb. 1740 (X).   Grinsdale rt. 1740 (X).   Allonby (N) c. 1745 (I).

* bt. = built.   rb. = rebuilt.   rt. = restored.   c. = consecrated.   l = licenced.
† I. *Carlisle Episcopal Registers.*   II. Carlisle Visitation Books.   III. Chancellor Waugh's Notes.   IV. *N. & B.*   V. *R.C. H.M. Westmorland.*

CHESTER DEANERIES.*

Burneside rb. 1602 (I).   Colton rb. before 1603 (VII).   Ireleth (N) bt. 1608, at first as a school.   Staveley in Cartmel (A) reader there 1618 (III).   Rampside (N) said to have been built 1621 (III).   Lindale (A) reader there 1627, but probably pre-Reformation (III).   Middleton (N) c. 1635 (I).   Whitehaven chapel (A) mentioned 1642 (VIII).   Dendron (N) bt. 1644 (I).   Seathwaite (A) in parliamentary survey of 1650 (III).   Witherslack † c. 1671 (I).   Satterthwaite rb. about 1675 (I).   Firbank (A) curate of, mentioned 1691 (VI).   St. Nicholas Whitehaven c. 1693 (I). Old Hutton rb. 1699 (I).

Selside bt. 1707 and c. 1709 (I and II).   Grayrigg rb. 1708 (V). Cockermouth (a) licence to build new chapel 1709 (I and II). Longsleddale rb. 1712 (IV).   Holy Trinity Whitehaven (N) c. 1715 (I and II).   Finsthwaite (N) c. 1725 (II).   Thwaites (N) c. 1725 (II).   Natland rb. about 1735 (V).   New Hutton bt. 1739 (V).   Firbank rb. 1742 (IV).   Hugill or Ings bt. 1743 (IV). Rusland (N) c. 1745 (II).   Field Broughton (N) bt. 1731 and c. 1745 (II).   Helsington (N) bt. 1726 (IV) and c. 1745 (II).

VI. Miscellany Accounts, Bishop Nicolson.   VII. o.s. viii, 292.   VIII. *Ibid.*, 303.   IX. *Ibid.*, ix, 247.   X.   *Ibid.*, xxiii, 206-71.   XI. *Ibid.*, xxxix, 103.

* I. *Bishop Gastrell's Notitia* and original returns.   II. *Chester Episcopal Registers*, IV and V.   III. *V.C.H. Lanc.*, viii.   IV.   *R.C. H.M. Westmorland*. V.   *N. & B.*   VI. *R. of K.*, III, 305.   VII. o.s. xiii, 434.   VIII. *Ibid.*, III, 351.

(a) a plan of the chapel is annexed to the licence, *Chester Episcopal Register* (IV, 98-100).

† Witherslack should have been placed among the Pre-Reformation chapels. The ' priest at the chapel of Our Lady on ye . . in ye Widderslakke ' is mentioned in 1542. (Wills and Inventories of the Archdeaconry of Richmond, Surtees Society, xxvi, 27).

BOOK IV.

THE GEORGIAN WORLD
AND THE INDUSTRIAL REVOLUTION,
1747-1856.

CHAPTER I.

THE SOCIAL SCENE IN THE EIGHTEENTH
CENTURY.

HITHERTO this book has been planned in the belief that within this Border diocese the history of Church and State are such that one can not be understood apart from the other. But henceforth these counties have very little political, though they have still much social, history. Thus its future chapters, other than those devoted to the Social Scene, will be largely confined to ecclesiastical events, while those allocated to that Scene will be proportionately increased.

Previous surveys of social conditions have told of a reasonably stable society; now an ever changing world will be described, yet, as always in England, the essential structure of Church and State remains unaltered. In these years, of the three ingredients to our history—war, agriculture and industry—the second remains constant, the last occupies an ever larger place in our economy and the first disappears. But the discovery and subsequent development of the Lake District ensures that a third ingredient still has its place.

The last of the bundles of inventories (1737) shew that so far there had been little change in the relative numbers of the various property groups and that prices also were much the same. Thomas Hobson of Gilcrux, clerk, had £5 worth of books; Joseph Shaw of Mallerstang owned a silver watch, value £1, some silver spoons and a 'seeing glass,' 2/6. No one had weapons. Lancelot Rawes of Barugh, Orton (W) had 6 cows and 4 heifers £20, 54 ewes and a ram at 5/- each, 45 geld sheep at 4/-, and 37 wether sheep at 3/6; wool £5 and clock £2. 10. Black cattle are named in 8 inventories; John Share of Blunderfield, Kirkoswald, had 8 valued at £8. 8., his 2 mares were worth £2 each. John Hunter of Milburn had 3 cows £3. 15; 8 heifers and steers £5. 19; mare and stagg £2; 80 sheep £16, and corn £11 and hay £3, while Mary Finkle of Thornthwaite, Crosthwaite, had only a cow and heifer £2. 17. and a horse, 15/-. John Taylor of How-berry, Kirklinton, had, with stock, 12 bushels of oats threshed £2 and 6 pecks of bigg 7/6, with pease and hay at 13/-.

So far local agriculturalists had been much behind the rest of the country in the introduction of new ideas and methods; now change was in the air.[1] Philip Howard of Corby introduced clover into Cumberland in 1752 and turnips three years later; about this time wheat was also first cultivated here. As evidence of our backwardness it may be mentioned that the two former had been introduced into England as early as 1645. By this method, as winter food was provided for cattle, it was no longer necessary to slaughter all stock except the few kept for breeding purposes. As late as 1793 turnips were not a common crop in Westmorland. Neither peas, beans, clover, nor rye grass were commonly cultivated in that county. By the end of the eighteenth century potatoes were grown by almost every farmer both for home use and market. Oats and barley, the most important cereals, provided bread for the inhabitants.

The cattle were mostly a small breed of long horns, with

a few Galloways. No one seems to have paid any attention to improving stock. Dairy farming was important in both counties. In Westmorland, in comparison with its size, many more milch cows were kept than was usual elsewhere. The produce of the dairy formed a large proportion of the farmer's profit; local butter was sold in the London market. The sheep were mostly Herdwicks, Blackfaced and Silverdale. In Westmorland the wool was sold either to Kendal manufacturers or to those at Bradford and other places in the West Riding.

The extent of the commons is shewn by the fact that in 1793 only about a quarter of the total acreage in Westmorland was cultivated, while in Cumberland 150,000 acres of common were considered to be improvable. Enclosure on a considerable scale began in 1763; in Cumberland just under 40,000 and in Westmorland rather over 10,000 acres of waste lands were so dealt with between that date and 1800. As a result of the passing of a general enclosure Act in 1801 this process increased. A Cumbrian, William Blamire, was the chief official concerned with this.

Towards the end of the century perhaps the greatest figure in local agricultural history appears on the scene. John Christian (1756-1828), who on his marriage in 1782 to Isabella, daughter and sole heiress of Henry Curwen of Workington, took that name in addition to his own, has been called 'the father of Cumbrian farming.' Having travelled widely at home and abroad he brought an enlightened mind and wide experience to bear upon the problems of local agriculture. It was through his activities that short-horn cattle were introduced and the advisability of penning sheep on turnip land realised. As he resided for part of the year on Belle Island, Windermere, Westmorland also benefitted from his experience. He was succeeded in his work as a pioneer agriculturalist

by Sir James Graham of Netherby (1792-1861), who
devoted his energies chiefly to devising improved systems
of land drainage, so necessary in our damp climate.   He
has been described as " the most illustrious parliamentary
figure that the county of Cumberland has ever produced."[2]
His example and methods as an agriculturalist were
followed in Westmorland by Lord Lonsdale.

While all this was for the benefit of local agriculture and
the larger landowners it spelt ruin for many statesmen,
either small freeholders or tenants with the right of
inheritance, who had not the means to compete with these
new methods.   Though they received their portion of the
enclosed common land this did not compensate them for
the loss of their ancient rights, as each allotment needed
new drains, hedging and ditching, so the small owner,
unable to face this expenditure, was often tempted or
compelled to sell his share to those with the necessary
capital.   In the Fell country, where the enclosure of
fields by the stone walls we see to-day had taken place
long before, this did not apply.

Statesmen both in the low country and the fells also
suffered by the invention of the ' spinning jenny,' since
by concentrating spinning in factories it deprived them of
a means by which their wives and children had for
generations contributed to the family income.   This was
probably also the reason for the statesmen's " misguided
burdening of their land with portions for big families
which, with fallen prices, it could not carry," noted by
Professor Clapham[3] as the chief cause of their decline,
because the widow and unmarried daughters, no longer
being able to earn their own living at home, had to be
provided for out of the estate.   In the early years of the
eighteenth century almost every cottage had its hand
looms with all the family participating in the work: the
small hamlet of Oulton had over 50; in Wigton there
were 11 textile establishments.   Some country people

grew their own flax and prepared it in all its stages.   Over 3000 pairs of knitted hose were sold every week at Kendal market.   Almost every farm in the limestone area had its small kiln.   A special straw was grown for Penrith's flourishing trade in straw hats.   At one time every considerable village had a tannery—Cockermouth had 7 and Egremont 4.   Most villages had their breweries, flour mills, saw mills, and bobbin mills; almost all these small industries have disappeared.

Thus it was towards the middle and end of the period covered by this survey that the owners of many small estates, whose forebears had farmed their lands for generations, passed away.   Wordsworth notes[4] that between 1770 and 1820 the number of freehold statesmen was halved and the size of their holdings doubled.   A study of parish registers of the period gives the same impression.   Names, familiar ever since they began, disappear; lands farmed for generations by the same families know them no more.   Their fields swallowed up in some great estate, their farmsteads occupied by a tenant or allowed to fall into ruin, they went to swell the population of an industrial town.   For the social historian this is one of the most important and tragic events of these years.

Some information of housing conditions in the countryside at this time has fortunately come down to us.   One writer states, in 1794, that " the houses in general in our villages are still thatched and built of mud or clay "* but another one says this " applies, if it applies at all, only to the Northern and Eastern extremities of the County."[5] Fortunately the notes in Hutchinson's *Cumberland*, which contain much valuable information as to conditions at this time, enable us to check up on these rather

* Hutchinson (II, 515), gives an interesting account of how these clay houses were built, neighbours assisting, in a day or two. " They generally ground with stone about a yard high and a house thus built will stand (it is said) 150-200 years."

contradictory statements. They shew that, except for villages on the Border and west of Carlisle, houses were by now built of brick and covered with blue slates. If they were whitened over they must have looked charming—at least outside. No such authority is available for Westmorland, but the evidence cited in the last social survey suggests that in this respect this county was in advance of Cumberland.

To turn from village homes to village schools, the demands of space preclude the names of those founded since the Restoration being given but the summarised figures for 1660 to 1800 are:

Cumberland,	endowed grammar schools	19
	non classical schools	25
Westmorland,	endowed grammar schools	23
	non classical schools	5

This list only includes endowed schools;[6] we have little evidence as to the number of private ones, but some is provided by Jonathan Boucher* in his autobiography. Dealing with only one small area, in the middle of the eighteenth century, he mentions schools at Blencogo, Crookdake, and Allonby in the parish of Bromfield, as well as the endowed school at the latter. Others he names in this neighbourhood were: Raughton Head, Wigton with a headmaster and an usher, Aikton, Aspatria, St. Rouk's (Abbey Town) and Westward. As half of these were unendowed schools there were obviously a considerable number of them. At Crookdake the master, going from house to house for his victuals, had a salary of £8 a year. Boucher, at the age of sixteen and a half, was asked to teach 32 boys at 10s. each in 1754, apparently at Wigton; this he considered a very good offer.[7]

To pass now to the world of commerce: in the mid-seventeenth century Cockermouth had been the most

---

* He was the son of John Bouch of Blencogo. There is a monument to his memory in the chancel of Bromfield church (N.S. xxvii, 117-51).

thriving business town in Cumberland; by the middle of this one its place had been taken by Whitehaven.   Defoe in 1724-6 says:

" Whitehaven (has) grown up from a small place to be very considerable by the coal trade, which is increased so considerably of late, that it is now the most eminent port in England for shipping off coals, except Newcastle and Sunderland . . . 'tis frequent in time of war, or upon the ordinary occasion of cross winds, to have two hundred sail of ships at a time go from this place to Dublin, loaden with coals."[8]

To-day when we think of Whitehaven we think of coal; but at one time its name also reminded people of tobacco. In 1739-40 nearly four and a half million pounds passed through it as a result of an extensive trade with Virginia; its decline was due to competition from Glasgow.[9]

A writer in the *Gentleman's Magazine* of 1748 described the place as

" a thriving and well built town; it exceeds Carlisle in extent about 1/3 but is thrice as populous " and " the vast supply of coals in this neighbourhood has raised this port from a fishing town to be next after Bristol and Liverpool on the west sea, and the roads leading to it are equal to the best turn pikes about London and every day improving."[10]

Other evidence of the prosperity of the town is that it had its own newspaper ' *The Whitehaven Weekly Courant* ' as early as 1736, while Carlisle had to wait till 1798 before the first number of ' *The Carlisle Journal* ' appeared.[11]

Bishop Creighton, a native of Carlisle, begins the last chapter of his history of the Border city with the words

" the dramatic period of the history of Carlisle is now ended, and it only remains to tell how the dirty and dispirited town of 2,500 inhabitants which existed in 1747 has passed into the neat and prosperous town of to-day."[12]

This he attributes initially to the opening up of the military road to Newcastle, 1751-8.   The first important commercial venture, the effort of a firm of Hamburg merchants to establish a woollen factory, failed; nor was

another effort by the Hodgson family more fortunate.
But in 1761 a calico printing business was successfully
established by Scott, Lamb, & Co. Soon afterwards
Messrs. Ferguson started their works;[13] other commercial
undertakings followed. By the turn of the century the
city's population, over 10,000, is evidence of its increasing
prosperity.

During these years Workington continued to grow in
wealth. Described in 1748 ' as a town of pretty trade,
above 50 vessels belong to it,'[14] its chief support was the
export of coals from the Curwen pits to Ireland. Also
ships up to 600 tons were built and the accessories thereto
manufactured. Both the Lowthers and the Curwens were
interested in the salmon fishing in the Derwent.[15] But its
prosperity had declined by 1842 when ' the general
depression felt by the town ' is mentioned; the number
of vessels belonging to the port had fallen from 160 in
1790 to 95.[16]

The most important development on the west coast was
the building of a harbour, by an Act of 1748/9, at the
hamlet of Ellenborough by the Senhouse family; it was
called Maryport in compliment to the founder's wife.
As at Workington the export of coal and ship building
were the chief occupations of its inhabitants. Submerged
by later building, delightful old houses from its early days,
reminiscent of the good taste of our Georgian ancestors,
still remain.

The opening of Maryport harbour was the result of the
development of the coal industry north of the Derwent:
Henry Curwen obtained a lease of the colliery at Seaton in
1722, next year Sir James Lowther started mining at
Dearham; and the Dykes family, at Gilcrux, and Mr.
Senhouse, at Ellenborough, both had small pits in 1740.
In the Greysouthen township work began anterior to
1750 and at Broughton, by Mr. Senhouse and others, in
1755. No further developments of any note occurred

until the extension of mining operations to Flimby and Birkby in 1781.

In South Cumberland and North Lancashire also these years saw an increase in industrialism. A smelting furnace was started at Duddon Bridge in 1737. The Backbarrow Iron Company, which began operations in Millom in 1716, commenced exporting from Barrow in 1745. Two years later the Bigland dock on the Leven was named and the Newland forge commenced. In 1782 the company which worked it made Barrow their principal shipping port.

The Industrial Revolution, which is generally considered to have begun at about the last date, had comparatively little immediate affect on life in these counties. More pits were sunk at Whitehaven and Workington between 1781 and 1820, but the only new area opened up was Cleator Moor in 1802. The census of 1801 tells the same tale; of the towns affected by the industrial changes: Carlisle had a population of 9521, Whitehaven 8742, Workington 5716, Maryport about 3000, Harrington 1357, Hensingham and Seaton under 600, and the remainder under 400. But after the turn of the century there was more development; mines were started at Aspatria in 1822 and at Dovenby in 1830.[17]

In West Cumberland an iron ore mine at Crowgarth, Cleator Moor, was leased in 1753. But, as it was said in 1816 that the mine there was ' not much worked till the year 1784 ' and that the one at Bigrigg, Egremont, had ' not worked for many years,' little seems to have been done. This is borne out by statistics shewing that the population of Cleator and Egremont in 1688 and 1801 were 330, 362 and 1410, 1515 respectively—evidence that there was not much industrial development in these years.[18]

Most of these areas being on the coast, the problem of transport was a comparatively simple one; which

probably accounts for the badness of our roads. The
only ones shewn on John Ogilby's road map, 1675, are
those from Kendal to Carlisle, by Shap, and from
Egremont, through Whitehaven and Workington, by
Cockermouth and Bothel to Carlisle—the two being
linked by a road from Cockermouth to Keswick, Ambleside and Kendal. The Newcastle to Carlisle road crossed
the Eden at Corby and then went through Castle Carrock.
It seems doubtful if there was any road open to wheeled
traffic throughout the year. Goods were mostly carried
by pack-horse; Nicolson and Burn say that 354 passed
through Kendal weekly.[19]

The first attempt to improve matters arose from the
way in which the state of the roads had hindered the
efforts of the king's troops in 1745; hence the building of
the present road from Newcastle to Carlisle in 1751-8.[20]
From these years the series of Turnpike roads began.
As a result travel became much easier: stage waggons
from London to Kendal, in place of packhorses, began in
1757. A post-chaise was first kept in Kendal in 1754;[21]
they were not introduced into Carlisle until 1759.[22] A
' Flying Machine ' was on the Kendal to Carlisle road in
1763, presumably connecting up with the coach of the
same name that travelled from London to Manchester.
In 1773 a service from London to Carlisle, by Boroughbridge, was started.[23] Thus Penrith, also the junction
of the road to Whitehaven, became ' perhaps the greatest
thoroughfare in the north of England.'[24] With the
' discovery ' of the Lakes it also became the place at
which many, like the poet Gray, stayed on their way to or
from Ullswater and Keswick.

It is probably true to say that the building of the
Turnpikes and the general improvement in travelling
conditions that resulted were as important for the social
life of the North West as the centralizing policy of the
Tudors had been for its political life. As the latter had

broken down one form of separation from the rest of the
kingdom; so the former was now to break down another.
The only exception was Coupland, south of Egremont,*
beyond which the Turnpike did not run as late as 1816.[25]

The chief result, apart from the economic ones, of the
improvement in the roads was that the beauties of these
counties began to be discovered by the outside world.
Even before this, seaside holidays in them had started
to be popular.   Allonby was described in 1748 as 'grown
from a petty village to have a kind of market, especially
in the summer . . . and has a considerable concourse for
bathing in the sea.'[26]   A writer on North country life in
the eighteenth century states 'another sign of social
change was the rise of seaside resorts, notably Scar-
borough and Allonby.   By the 1770's the latter was a
favourite resort of English and Scottish gentry, complete
with bathing machines and the like.   The season lasted
until the end of September."[27]   In the genealogy of
such places Allonby then must rank quite high.   It still
retains much of its old world charm, having wisely left
modern development to its rival at Silloth.

Our eighteenth century ancestors had great faith in
'drinking the waters.'   These counties possessed two
spas: the better known was at Shaws on the banks of the
Irthing whose medicinal properties had been recognised
for a long time.   Nicolson and Burn write of invalids
"who resort hither in great numbers in the summer
months."[28]   The poet Burns in his Border tour, 1787,
mentions "Wardrue, the celebrated Spa, where we

* As evidence of the primitive conditions that prevailed there, Miss Fair
tells me of a tradition that 'early in the 19th century the postman walked
with mails from Ulverston to Whitehaven returning the next day with the
mails to Ulverston.   It is said this continued for several years; it is 44 miles
each way.'   But this story can be 'capped' by one from Parson and
White's *History and Directory of Cumb. and West.* 1829 p. 199 of a native
of Corney, who "aged 81 lately walked to Ulverston, where he played on
the violin all night and walked home next day by way of Dalton, a
distance of 50 miles, without enjoying 'a blink o' rest."

slept."[29]   But its chief claim to fame is that Sir Walter
Scott, after staying in the Lake District, met his future
wife in the summer of 1797, "at the then peaceful and
sequestered little watering place of Gilsland." He
probably used material his observant eye gathered during
this stay in *St. Ronan's Well*.[30]   During the concluding
years of the Georgian era Gilsland (it acquired this name
in about 1770 or soon after) was thus a place of some
popularity: in Sir Walter's day it boasted a ball room
and both Hutchinson and Lysons mention its good
accommodation and boarding houses.[31]   Of the other spa
—in the parish of Crosby Ravensworth—Nicolson and
Burn state that there "was discovered some few years ago
a spaw water now known by the name of Shap Well, to
which in the summer season is a considerable resort."[32]
But it was evidently no rival to the fashionable Gilsland—
accommodation for visitors was meagre until William,
earl of Lonsdale caused a good hotel to be built in about
1825-30.

It may seem presumptuous to claim to have anything
new to tell about the history of that much written up
area—the Lake District.   But the author believes that
something can be added to W. G. Collingwood's story of
what may be called its ' discovery.'[33]

G. M. Trevelyan, describing it as it was in the reign of
Queen Anne, states "the dales were just beginning to
take on their brief perfection of rural loveliness ordered
but not disciplined, in contrast with the mountain
magnificence above and around." He compares this
with their appearance "choked, tangled, swampy, and
featureless" in the previous centuries.[34]   An interesting
commentary on this last statement is that the ancient
roads lay much higher up the fellside than those we are
familiar with to-day.   For instance the road from
Grasmere to Ambleside ran behind Rydal Mount, along
the side of Nab Scar.   The sites of ancient smithies on the

sides of fells is further evidence of how our ancestors avoided the valleys.[35]

Visitors were few; such as there were complained of the local bread as " exceedingly black, coarse, and harsh " and " the houses as ' sad little huts ' of unmortared stone, more fit for cattle than for men.   Already ' here and there was a house plastered ' and sometimes ' the oat clap bread ' was cleverly baked and delicious."[36]   Fish from the lakes, especially char-pie, was much in demand, even in London.[37]

But on the whole the outside world knew little of a part now so famous.   When, in 1724-6, Daniel Defoe made his tour he described Westmorland as ' a county eminent only for being the wildest, most barren and frightful of any that I have passed through,' with its west side bounded ' by a chain of almost impassable mountains, which in the language of the country, are called Fells and these are called the Furness Fells.'   Around him were ' impassable hills whose tops (were) covered with snow . . . but notwithstanding this aspect of the hills, when having passed and descending the frightful mountains,' on his way from Kendal, he found the country ' pleasant rich and fruitful.'[38]   In Defoe's account not a word is said about the lakes; either he did not know of their existence or he considered his public would not be interested in them.

By the middle of the century taste was changing; the pages of the *Gentleman's Magazine* shew the polite world taking notice of the life and scenery of these hitherto almost unknown parts.   An interesting letter to its Editor in August 1749 describes the writer's* visit to the black lead mines on Honister.   After describing his progress up Borrowdale to Seathwaite he goes on

---

* His name was George Smith, he generally signs G. S.   A short account of his life and writings is given in N.S. xviii, 49-50.

" The scene that now presented itself was the most frightful
that can be conceived; we had a mountain to climb for above
700 yards, in a direction so nearly perpendicular that we were in
doubt whether we should attempt it . . . the whole mountain is
called Unnisterre or, as I suppose, Finisterre, for such it appears
to be; myself and only one more of our company determined to
climb this second precipice, and in about another hour we gained
the summit.   The scene was terrifying, not an herb was to be
seen but wild savine, growing in the interstices of the naked
rocks; the horrid projection of vast promontories; the vicinity
of the clouds, the thunder of the explosions in the slate quarries,
the dreadful solitude, the distance of the plain below, and the
mountains heaped on mountains that were piled around us,
desolate and waste, like the ruins of a world which we only had
survived, excited such ideas of horror as are not to be expressed.
We turned from this fearful prospect afraid even of ourselves,
and bidding an everlasting farewell to so perilous an elevation,
we descended to our companions."[39]

In this year there is also a description of ' a surprising
inundation in the valley of St. John's near Keswick.'
Derwentwater is called Keswick water both in this and
the previous account; was this because the earls of
Derwentwater, having been involved in the '15 and '45,
the use of its ancient name was taboo?   In 1754 there is a
description of another dreadful storm in St. John's and of
our local weather conditions ending with ' I am persuaded
you are always colder at London in winter than we.'   No
more is recorded of this district till 1761 when a letter
is printed from someone who had stayed in one of the
Lake District valleys.   The account begins with the
usual horrific description of terrifying precipices, etc. but
ends with a charming picture of rural life.[40]

Now we come to the fateful year 1769, when the poet
Thomas Gray planned his tour of the lakes and staying at
Keswick made his great resolve.   Despite the awe
inspiring beauties and the terrifying dangers of the wild
mountains he determined to adventure himself into the
valley before him.   As a sensible precaution he took his

VI. CONISTON LAKE AND VILLAGE IN 1792.
From a drawing by T. Smith.

(facing p. 353)

landlord as a guide, and, on 28 October, ' a heavenly day,'
he set out to explore the dread prospect.   The reality
came up to, if indeed it did not surpass, the promise.
" The place reminds me," he wrote afterwards,

" of those passes in the Alps where the guides tell you to move
with speed and say nothing, lest the agitation of the air should
loosen the snows above and bring down a mass that would
overwhelm a caravan.   I took their council here and hastened on
in silence."   But after reaching Seathwaite he found that " all
further access is here barred to prying mortals, only there is a
little path winding over the fells, and for some weeks in the
year passable to the dalesmen, but the mountains know well that
these innocent people will not reveal the mysteries of their
ancient kingdom, ' the reign of *Chaos* and *Old Night* ': only I
learned that this dreadful road, divided again, leads one branch
to Ravenglass, and the other to Hawkshead."[41]

So the first guide to the Lakes came to be written.
This then seems a suitable place to consider the sequence
of events in their discovery.   First there had been the
period, to about 1750, when the outside world knew little
about them.   Next the stage, from then to 1769, during
which visitors to the easily accessible lakes—the Windermere group, Ullswater, Thirlmere, and the Keswick lakes,
probably also Coniston, were not infrequent.

But of the remainder of the Lake District very little
had been seen by the outside world.   John Wesley seems
to have been the only person known to have passed
through it.*   A study of maps provides some startling
evidence of the extent of popular ignorance.   To take that
' drawn and engraved ' for Nicolson and Burn's County
History as an example.   It gives the lakes mentioned
more or less correctly, but the western ones are hopelessly
out of scale.   In place of Ennerdale there is a lake called
Broadwater, which is placed nearer to Cockermouth than
Loweswater.   Where Buttermere and Crummock should
be three small lakes are shewn.   Wastdale is given a

* p. 370.

2A

shape like the letter L reversed, with the head facing due north and Eskdale shewn with a considerable lake in it. The only mountain named in the Scafell group is ' Hardknot Mtn.' And, most surprising of all, a coach road is given running south east out of Whitehaven, which crossing Ennerdale proceeded to Wastdale head, where it turned south and passing to the east of ' Hardknot Mtn.' and ' Wrynose Mtn.' reached Ambleside. At least that is where the coach and four got to on paper; where it would have got to in reality the reader can imagine if he has ever walked over any of this route or possesses a modern map of it.

Could anything illustrate better the general ignorance of the geography of much of the Lake District than that such a map could be printed as late as 1777? In fact Donald had published a much more correct one in 1770 but Nicolson and Burn cannot have known of its existence. But this strange story of error is not finished yet: T. West in his *Guide* gives a list of the chief Lake District mountains. As late as his 1799 edition he heads this with Crossfell, 3390, followed by Helvellyn, Skiddaw and Saddleback; no mountain in the central Scafell-Gable group is mentioned. It was not until the 1813 edition that he revised this list giving the mountains in their true order, though even then Gable was omitted.* Thus it can be said that the geography of the lakes and dales of West Cumberland was not known till the end of the eighteenth century† and the correct heights of the highest mountain group in England, the Scafell range, not discovered till the beginning of the next one.

---

* Lysons', *Cumberland*, 1816, print the same list as West giving as their authority the trigonometrical survey of 1811.

† " William Gilpin may be said to have ' discovered ' Crummock and Buttermere in 1772." (N.S. xliii, 94). But George Smith's map in the *Gentleman's Magazine* of 1751 (xxi opp. p. 201) shews that he knew their correct positions so he was really their ' discoverer.' But the Scafell group can only be properly seen from much further south.

The reasons are not far to seek.   It is only from south west Cumberland, then almost unknown, that this range can be clearly seen from the ground—the eighteenth century tourist did not indulge in fell walking.   Also it will be remembered that Gray, told by the dalesmen the absurd story that Styhead was only passable for some weeks in the year, states " these innocent people will not reveal the mysteries of their ancient Kingdom "—that is the local people did not want strangers wandering into those parts.   Why this was so is doubtless because "until the younger Pitt reduced the high duties, the scale on which smuggling was carried on was prodigious."[42] Readers of ' Guy Mannering ' will remember the important part Sir Walter Scott makes the Solway smugglers play in that novel.   There is no doubt that an illicit trade was carried on on a large scale between France and the Plantations and England, through Ireland and the Isle of Man all along the Cumberland coast.   A by-product of the ' Forty five ' was that many of the smugglers exchanged goods with the Highlanders for weapons, to the discomfiture of the Revenue Officers.[43]   There is a tradition that one of the smugglers named Moses had a secret hiding place for whisky near the top of Gable.[44] So the dales folk had good reasons for discouraging too inquisitive strangers.   Thus it is really not difficult to understand why so little was known about the heights of this central group of Lake Mountains.

Tourists then mostly stayed on the ground: Jos. Budworth, author of a *Fortnight's Ramble to the Lakes*, 1792, who had climbed Helvellyn, Skiddaw, Old Man and Langdale Pikes, is the only one of the many writing about the Lakes in those days who shews the least interest in fell walking.   The first recorded outsider who ascended Scafell appears to have been S. T. Coleridge, who did so in August 1802.[45]   Even in 1811 the proper names for the two parts of the mountain were not known;

the surveyors calling them ' high point ' and ' low point.'
But Jonathan Otley in 1823 mentions that ' shepherds
best acquainted with the mountain ' called the deep
chasm ' Mickledoor ' and the two parts Scafell and The
Pike.[46]   By this time the rambler must have become a
more common phenomenon; and the discovery of the
Lake District may be said to have been completed when
on 7 October 1818, William Wordsworth made an
excursion to the top of Scafell.[47]

CHAPTER II.

I. THE GEORGIAN CHURCH AND THE AGE OF JOHN WESLEY.

RICHARD OSBALDESTON[1] was consecrated at Lambeth by the bishop of Rochester on 4 October 1747.

The outstanding man in the diocese at this time was John, eldest son of Bishop Waugh, who had married a daughter of the dean, Thomas Tullie, who resigned the chancellorship in favour of his prospective son-in-law. For the active part he took in the '45 Waugh was rewarded with the deanery of Worcester. But he retained the chancellorship and died in 1765 in possession of both pieces of preferment, as well as the second stall in Carlisle cathedral and the vicarages of Caldbeck and Stanwix, to all of which he had been preferred by his father in 1727 when he was about twenty four.

We know about his influence largely because of the survival of his copy of Bishop Nicolson's *Miscellany Account* in which he entered notes about the state of the churches during his years of office.* These appear to have been based upon answers to the searching set of questions he drafted for the bishop's primary visitation in 1747 and from his own periodical visitation. They thus afford interesting evidence of the functioning of the chancellorship in the middle of the eighteenth century.

* The whereabouts of the original manuscript is unknown. It, or a copy of it, was undoubtedly used by Chancellor Ferguson for his *Diocesan History of Carlisle*. A copy of it, which he bound up in an interleaved copy of Nicolson's *Miscellany*, is now in the Jackson Library at Tullie House, where it has been all these years without anyone realising what it was. Wilson makes no mention of it in *V.C.H.*

The picture of the diocese can be compared with Bishop Nicolson's survey of fifty years before.

The following are some typical examples:

Shap:[2]

" I don't know now of any schools taught in this or any other parish church, in most of the chapels schools are taught, they being most of them partly founded for that purpose, but in the churches I have taken much pains to prevent its being done."

Cliburn:

" This want of (Communion) Rails has been very frequent. I never saw it anywhere but at Cumwhitton where they are now provided and I think in most, if not all, places in the Diocese. I have lately found some without but I think I shall soon get all done."

Bongate, Appleby:

" The chancel is now whitened. There are some few Drops in the roof, which is all leaded that they can't find out.

Edenhall:

" The church handsomely fitted up, all wants whitening and sentences which is promised shall be done immediately."

Kirkbampton:

" Wants boards to kneel upon."

Burgh-by-Sands:

" New seated and in very good order, only no backs to the seats in the church.   The chanc. Inc. much crowded even to the rails— the seats next the rails take down when there is a sacrament. Two loose Forms very indecently placed within the rails for the singers which thrust the Communion Table into a corner, I ordered them to be removed forthwith."

Holm Cultram:

" They new roofed with Large (*sic*) the large middle Isle and took away the side Isles and part of the chancel end and made the whole one good building . . . but tho' it stands high (is) strangely damp."

Some churches afford evidence of real neglect: Melmerby: " all the other seats broke and very bad; the walls want cleaning and ornaments, the Books bad and imperfect," and Barton, " the roof of the church bad. The Chancel and Isles very bad; a very imperfect Bible and no paten or plate." Sometimes this was due to the neglect of the lay impropriators of the rectory. They were also indifferent clergy: the curate of Hesket was 'necessitous, idle and indecent'; he had a large family and an income of £22 a year. The chancellor specially praises the people of Ravenstonedale who had rebuilt their church in which, however, they

" were much oppressed and opposed . . . by the late Governor Lowther . . .* but they shewed the most noble spirit for years that ever I saw and got through their good with unanimity and to perfection."

At Renwick he

" was surprised with a neat clean new built little church, all lately done at the expense of the poor inhabitants, who are, as they told me, but 24 in number. The chancel and all things about the church very well and the people willing to do anything required of them."

A priest Waugh delighted to honour was George Braithwaite, curate of St. Mary's, Carlisle and minor canon:

" by the best account I could ever get from him he was admitted a singing boy at the Restoration or within a year after. He was advanced from that to a singing man, till made a minor canon. He has been now (1747) 68 years a Reading minor canon in June last, and 87 years, or thereabouts, a member of the church of Carlisle. Did his Duty constantly till within this few years that his sight failed him, when the rest of the minor canons voluntarily undertook to do his Duty for him in the Cathl. and to assist him in his parish, in which he still performs the offices of Christenings, Weddings and Burials, and may live many years. He has very seldom been a day absent from the church.†

* Robert Lowther of Maulds Meaburn, governor of Barbadoes.
† He was buried at St. Mary's on 16 December 1753 " aged 110." But this figure and that of 87 years given above do not stand up to the test of investigation. He occurs in the first post Restoration list of choristers in the *Dean and Chapter Minute Books* of 1668, being third on the list. He is head boy 1669-1675; lay clerk 1675; petty canon 1679; deacon 1680; priest 1681; curate of St. Mary's 1685. So he would be born in about 1657 and probably entered the choir in 1665-6. He would then have served 82-3 years in 1747, and be aged 96 at his death. That he was born 1643 is inconceivable.

Waugh gives some interesting side lights on parsonages. In the best circles tiles were replacing thatch; at least this was so at his own house at Stanwix, though, judging from his remark about Gilcrux " the house is but ordinary, a low thatched house " this would seem to be unusual. From the number of new houses built the standard cannot previously have been very high. Even in a good living like Bolton the upstairs was reached by a ladder, and at Kirkbride the vicarage, though very neat and comfortable, " was only built of clay." In some of his comments the chancellor shews an hygenic sense: the vicarage of Plumbland was ' in a wretched, low damp and unhealthy situation '; that at Uldale in " a damp situation," and at Greystoke there was " a very good house, but very damp."

His notes bring out clearly the great prevalence of pluralism. Under Bromfield he states " but here no vicar having resided for above 46 years things cannot be supposed to be as good as they should be." Out of just over 100 parishes included in the survey, 34 were held by pluralists and these among the richest. Three of the prebendaries of Carlisle also held livings, worth respectively £123, £120-30 and £240 a year, and the archdeacon had Great Salkeld, £70, and Greystoke, £300. Aikton, £160-70, was joined to Barton £60-70. A Whitehaven incumbent had Clifton, £60, as a country house no doubt. A fellow of All Souls held Edenhall, £55. At Ireby the chancellor noted that the vicar keeps a curate " and between them the parish is very well taken care of." The possible fate of the curates, who kept places warm for pluralists, is illustrated by that of Mr. Lazonby at Wetheral, who, " on Mr. Gilbanks succeeding and coming to reside, was left with a large family quite destitute."*

Waugh gives the incomes of the benefices. Though

* He eventually became curate of Ainstable.

there had been a definite advance in many cases on the previous figures,* especially of the poorer livings, the additions do not justify a further summary, except one of those of over £50 a year, not hitherto given.

Yearly value.	Number of livings.
£50-£75	20
75-100	13
100-125	4
125-150	4
150-175	4
180	1
300	1

In July 1753, the bishop made a visitation of his cathedral.[3] His questions and the dean and chapter's answers include:

" Is divine service every day morning and evening duly and orderly celebrated according to the manner and custom of St. Paul's Cathedral in London? " *Answer*: " Not according to St. Paul's, London, which the mean qualifications of our lay singers will not suffer." " Of what use is the wall that separates the nave or west part of the church from the Cross Isle, if it can be taken away with convenience, why is it suffered to continue to deface the beauty of the church? " *Answer*: " The wall is for the warmth of the congregation and cannot be taken away without inconvenience." The answer to questions about their attendance at the services is: " the dean and one of the canons have leave of absence from His Majesty; the other canons say that they are generally resident according to the Statutes and never absent any length of time or all together . . . that they think they keep residence better than it was ever kept before in this church."

After his visitation the bishop ordered:

" the roof lately ruinous now repaired, but to be looked to, walls to be plaistered, whitened, and made clean, floor to be well paved, windows well glazed; the wall separating the nave or St. Maries Church from the Cross Isle to be taken away, . . . moveable benches or seats Reading Desk, Communion Table, and Pulpit

* p. 319.

(to) be placed in the part called St. Maries Church . . . all within two years."*

It is noticeable that eight years after the destruction caused in 1745 St. Mary's had not yet been made good.

In 1752 the dean entered a caveat against the admission of Henry Richardson to the living of St. Cuthbert's, Carlisle, objecting to him as having acted a very wrong part, as curate of Penrith, when the rebels were there in 1745. He lost his case and a mandamus was issued ordering the bishop to admit and licence Mr. Richardson, which he duly did.[4]

The bishop was translated to London in 1762. He seems to have been above the average of Georgian prelates, and, from his monitions about the cathedral, a man of taste with a real zeal for its welfare.

Charles Lyttleton[5] was consecrated in Whitehall Chapel by Archbishop Drummond of York on 21 March 1762. The beginning of his episcopate was occupied by a wrangle with his predecessor over dilapidations at Rose and the state of the port, 'sour as verjuice,' he had bought from him. He made considerable improvements at the castle, repairing Strickland's Tower which cost him, as his register records, £636. 3., while he only received £317. 5. from timber sold.[6]

The cathedral at this time was in need of repair. According to Nicolson and Burn

" the roof was elegantly vaulted with wood . . . but this failing by length of time, together with the lead roof, the dean and chapter some few years ago new laid the roof; and the ceiling being totally ruined and destroyed, they in the year 1764 contracted for a stucco groined ceiling, and for cleaning and whitening the whole church."[7]

* " In 1813 the nave of the church, heretofore a blank space, but used for parochial purposes, was fitted up with neatness and elegance, separated from the internal part of the cathedral, and made a more commodious place of worship for the parish of St. Mary." (*Cathedral Guide Book*, 1816). But how could " a blank space be used for parochial purposes ? " Does this really refer

The bishop gave £100 for this purpose, but, alas, he also recommended his nephew as the architect. This was Thomas Pitt, created Lord Camelford in 1784. His skill in Gothic architecture was recognised by Horace Walpole.[8] He was "a man of high honour, character, and charm."[9] But away went the beautiful and unique medieval oak ceiling of the choir, the medieval bishop's throne, the ancient screens behind the high altar, and the parclose ones between the columns of the choir arcades—we can see what they were like by those around St. Catherine's Chapel to-day—to be replaced by what Billings in 1840 called ' the present barbarous masses of Gothic woodwork."[10] Fortunately the ancient choir stalls were spared.*

The bishop died in London on 22 December 1768. " He was a gentleman of extensive learning and particularly in matters of antiquity . . . (and) of a noble, generous and humane disposition, a friend to all mankind and never had an enemy."[11] He was a fellow of the Royal Society and president of the Society of Antiquaries.

Edmund Law,† consecrated in Whitehall Chapel on 24 February 1769 by Archbishop Drummond of York, occupied this see for over eighteen years. He seems to have visited the diocese and held an ordination each year

to the erection of galleries in 1813-14? " Separated from the internal part of the Cathedral." Was the wall taken down as ordered in 1753 and restored in 1813? (N.S. xxxix, 48).

* An account of this " restoration " and of the ultimate fate of the " barbarous masses," some of which are now in St. Mary's, Carlisle, can be found in N.S. xvii, 78 and xxxix, 50.

† Son of Edmund Law, curate of Staveley in Cartmel and Patience Langbaine of Kendal (N.S. xviii, 170-3, and xix, 151-6); born at Cartmel 1703; educated there and at Kendal; sizar at St. John's College, Cambridge, 1720; fellow of Christ's, 1726-7. When he became bishop he was master of a college (Peterhouse), university librarian, archdeacon, prebendary of Lichfield, Lincoln and Durham (Venn). He had previously been archdeacon of Carlisle and rector of Great Salkeld, and rector of Greystoke. The latter he retained till his death, serving it by a curate who was also rector of Lazonby, though he usually lived at Greystoke—a curious example of pluralism within pluralism.

usually in August, though in 1773 it was at Cambridge; in 1775, 1778-9 however there is no record of one. The only entry in his register of any interest is the licencing for Divine Service of the church of Kirkandrews on Esk in August 1780; it was to last " until such time as by the favour of the Almighty we shall be enabled to consecrate the said church." " His intellectual power was universally acknowledged, and he was accounted one of the best metaphysicians of his age." He was the author of several learned books.[12] He died at Rose on 14 August 1787 and was buried in the cathedral where there is a monument to his memory. His wife was Mary, daughter of John Christian of Ewanrigg. One of his sons, Edward Law, became Lord Chief Justice and first Baron Ellenborough in 1802.

An account must now be given of William Paley, whose clerical career affords a good example of eighteenth century pluralism. He was made vicar of Musgrave, worth £80 a year, in 1775. Next year he resigned his fellowship at Christ's College, Cambridge to reside on his benefice where he tried farming some of his land, but ' almost invariably lost.' Towards the end of this year he became vicar of Dalston, £90 a year, and in the next one of Appleby, £200. He thereupon resigned Musgrave —he used to spend six months at each living. In 1780 he was made a prebendary of Carlisle, £400, and two years later archdeacon and rector of Great Salkeld, £120. In 1785 he became chancellor, at least £100 a year, and in 1792 added the vicarage of Addingham, £140, to his preferments. Next year exchanging Dalston for Stanwix, £140, and, asked his reasons for this move, he replied: " Why, Sir, I had two or three reasons for taking Stanwix in exchange; first, it saved me double housekeeping, as Stanwix was within a twenty minutes walk of my house in Carlisle; secondly, it was £50 a year more in value; and thirdly, I began to find my stock of sermons coming over again too fast." In 1794 he obtained a prebend in St. Paul's, about £100 a year, but soon after did better with the sub-deanery of Lincoln, £700; in return the bishop of Lincoln was allowed the disposal of the doctor's Carlisle prebend. In the following year Paley got the rectory of Bishop-Wearmouth, Durham, £1200; the donor being allowed to dispose of the livings of Stanwix and Adding-ham. The archdeacon was so pleased with the rectory house at Bishop-Wearmouth that, deciding to reside there permanently, he resigned his chancellorship of Carlisle, but retained the archdeaconry till 1804.

He was the author of many books, including the famous *Evidences of Christianity*, *The Clergyman's Companion in Visiting the Sick*, which passed through many editions and *The Young Christian instructed in Reading, etc.*, for use in schools. In some correspondence about this book in 1792, he mentions that Sunday schools were first set up in Carlisle about seven years ago.[13]

The ' wire pulling ' that took place after the death of Bishop Law is interesting as showing the way in which episcopal vacancies were then filled. The first name put forward was that of Dr. Richard Watson, to whom the duke of Norfolk wrote from Greystoke offering his good services. But he replied that he had ' no wish whatever respecting the see of Carlisle.'*

Next a famous local, or indeed national, character appears on the scene: Sir James Lowther, 1st earl of Lonsdale (1736-1802),† a ' man of immense wealth and

---

* *Anecdotes of the Life of Richard Watson*, I, 304-7. He was born at Heversham, and was made bishop of Llandaff in 1782; he held it till 1816, living most of the time at Windermere. See Sykes, for a more kindly state-ment of his career than is usually given.

† That he was ' Galloping Jimmy,' and not ' Farthing Jimmy ' is proved by squibs with such titles as ' Memoirs of Galloping Jemmy, alias The Tyrant of the North, alias the earl of Toadstool.' The reason for the nickname is shewn in a letter from Lowther, of Sept. 1771, from Sir William Lowther to Henry Lowther, rector of Aikton: ' We arrived about eight oclock and Sir James came in an hour after, who had only set out from London the morning before, he is a

political influence, whose violence, arrogance, despotism
and caprice rose almost to the point of madness ';[14] such
is the judgment of history.   But it must be remembered
that many of the stories about him have come from his
political opponents.*   It is probable that a very different
judgment will result when his private correspondence is
made public; his letters to his mother and sisters reveal
him as a man of strong family affections.   The clue to his
character, and the tragedy of his life, seems to lie in the
possession of almost unlimited wealth, with the absence of
some of those precious things, a happy marriage and a
' quiver full ' of children, that no wealth can purchase.
But whatever his faults, or his sorrows, he was certainly a
personality and the dominant figure in these counties for
half a century.   The first person he put forward was
Dr. William Lowther, rector of Lowther and Aikton (of
the Colby Leathes branch of the family), whom Dr.
Watson believed to be wholly unfitted for such a dignity;
he declined the offer.   The earl then suggested Dr. B.
Grisdale, a minor canon at the cathedral and master of
the grammar school.   Pitt, the prime minister, mentioned
this recommendation to the archbishop of Canterbury.
But the earl was told

" that no encouragement could be given to such a project; that
a man of much more respectable pretensions must be thought of,

most expeditious traveller.' ' Farthing Jimmy,' was of course, his cousin,
Sir James Lowther of Whitehaven.
    William Lowther, mentioned above, was rector of Swillington, Yorks.;
and of Cartmel, 1741-68.   More generous than most pluralists, he gave
' the profits ' of the latter to his curate, Mr. Walker, and eventually
resigned the living in his favour.   Sir William was father of William, 2nd
earl of Lonsdale (N.S. xlii, 89-91).   For Henry Lowther see N.S. xliii, 124-6.
    * Evidence of this seems to be afforded by the following letter of April 1768
between the same correspondents:
    " I am sorry to hear Sir James has met with so much difficulty in his election;
I know nothing but what I see in the Publick Papers, but I hope those statements are far from being true, as Sir James' enemies have been very industrious
in filling the papers weekly with their own accounts.   I think it is a great pity
they have never been contradicted, as strangers know nothing but what they
see in the prints, they are generally by this means led to believe things are much
worse on Sir James' side than what I really hope and believe they are."

(The letters quoted above are from the Lowther muniments)

if his lordship was anxious to recommend to the vacant see with success. This was at first taken angrily, but Mr. Pitt was firm; and Dr. Grisdale was withdrawn. Some other fancies from the same quarter occasioned further delay; till it was signified that it was high time that the vacancy was filled forthwith. This brought from his lordship a full recommendation of Dr. Douglas, which was acceded to."[15]

The latter, a canon of St. Paul's, was at Southampton, so Lord Lonsdale rode there, and, as the canon relates:

" I was sent for to the George Inn on Wednesday night, 19 September, to a gentleman who had just arrived; and I found his lordship. He soon opened his business with me and after a pretty long conversation, in no part of which he hinted any expectation of return but such as gratitude must require, I accepted;[16] . . ."

John Douglas[17] was consecrated in Whitehall Chapel by Archbishop Markham of York on 17 November 1787. He followed the contemporary custom of spending the summer months in his diocese and holding a yearly ordination. In his register the stipends of curates are mentioned for the first time: £20 seems to have been about the average. He made considerable improvements at Rose, where, among other things, he renewed the great staircase. He also built a new Register Office in which to keep the records and had the Journals and Court Books of the manor of Dalston rebound.[18] He was translated to the see of Salisbury in 1791. " He was exemplary in his life and beloved by many, but the greatest religious movement of his day was beyond his ken and not known to his philosophy."[19]

It is generally said that, apart from the period immediately following the Reformation, the Church was in a worse condition during the half century that has just been reviewed than at any other period in its history. It is difficult to know how true this was of these counties. The reader will have seen what little is known of the activities of the bishops: that they were men of eminence and intellectual power is beyond question; but that they

shewed any, except the most perfunctory, interest in
their flock in this diocese is doubtful. Among the
parochial clergy the greatest evil was pluralism. In its
eighteenth century form it was not, as it is to-day, a
method of giving incumbents a living wage and sufficient
work but simply a means whereby the rich became richer
and the poor remained poor. The spiritual needs of a
parish were never considered—pluralities could be three
hundred miles apart.* Many men continued unbeneficed
all their days with the likelihood of destitution in old age
or infirmity.[20]   Robert Robson, born at Sebergham of
yeoman stock and educated at Queen's, Oxford, had to
wait thirty three years before he got a living—in the next
generation the family had acquired influence so his nephew
obtained a prebendaryship and two other benefices within
ten years.†   The possible fate of those who failed in the
quest has been seen in that of Mr. Lazonby of Wetheral.‡
As to the standard of Church life in the parishes, we have
little to judge by but Chancellor Waugh's survey, just
before this period, does not suggest stagnation; nor does
the record of church building and restoration given in
Appendices IV and V.

Despite these abuses the middle years of this century
saw two great and allied spiritual movements within the
Church. One of these, usually called the Evangelical
Revival, will be discussed later on; here that associated
with the name of John Wesley will be described. "However Churchmen may deplore some of his acts and the

* p. 380.

† *The Oldest London Bookshop*, G. Smith and F. Benger, p. 21, 24, 34-5, 52.
Robert Robson's brother James was the owner of this shop (now Ellis, New
Bond St.), 1759-1806, and the book contains, p. 77-141, an interesting series of
family letters which illustrate the substantial position held by the better off
Cumberland yeoman in those days. Amongst the correspondence are some
letters from Isaac Denton, the bishop's registrar, one of which, p. 80-1, states:
" For ye parsons in our country live intolerably long, I cannot help thinking
they live out of spite for their successors: for a great many of them indulge
themselves so much that they cou'd not I am sure hold out such a number of
years if they had not stamina as strong as old Parr."

‡ p. 360.

general tendency of his teaching, John Wesley must always stand out in English Church history as the greatest religious figure of the eighteenth century."[21] He was, of course, a Churchman and, claiming to be one to his last days, wished his followers to be and act likewise.

Wesley preached in these counties for the first time in July 1748, when he was at Nenthead and Alston, and for the last one, at the age of eighty six, in June 1790 at Carlisle.* In the intervening years he visited or passed through them twenty six times, usually at intervals of two to three years; on all but two occasions he included Whitehaven in his itinerary.

Like all previous travellers, he found West Cumberland difficult of access. On his first visit to Whitehaven, September 1749, he journeyed from the east coast. Two years later he came from the south, by Ambleside, and then 'over more than Welsh mountains.' Next year, after preaching at Clifton near Penrith, his Journal shews he was at Lorton—so he probably followed the road from Penrith to Keswick and then over Whinlatter. In 1757 he again came from Ambleside and 'got over the mountains safe.' Two years later approaching from Lancashire he tried yet another route, in his own words:

' At Lancaster we were informed, it was too late to cross the sands. However, we resolved to make the trial; we passed the seven-mile sand without difficulty, and reached Fluckborough about sunset . . . setting out early, we came to Bottle, about twenty-four measured miles from Fluckborough, soon after eight, having crossed the Millam-sand without either guide or difficulty. Here we were informed that we could not pass at Ravenglass before one or two o clock; whereas, had we gone on (as we afterwards found) we might have passed immediately. About eleven we were directed to a ford near Manchester-Hall (Muncaster) which they said we might cross at noon. When we came thither they told us we could not cross; so we sat still till about one: we then found we could have crossed at noon.

* I have to thank Mr. T. H. Bainbridge for loaning me the MS. of his article on ' John Wesley in Cumberland,' to be published in *Trans.* xlvii. He has also helped me in the agricultural sections of this book.

However we reached Whitehaven before night. But I have taken my leave of the sand road . . . especially as you have all the way to do with a generation of liars, who detain all strangers as long as they can, either for their own gain or their neighbours. I can advise no stranger to go this way: he may go round by Kendal and Keswick often in less time, always with less expense and far less trial of his patience."

But the reader, remembering what has been told above about smuggling, will perhaps feel that there was more in all this than met the preacher's eye.

By 1761 he must have forgotten his own advice about the Kendal-Keswick road because he records, in April 1761, that, after sleeping at a ' little quiet house a few miles beyond Kendal':

" We were soon lost in the mountains; but in an hour we found a cottage and a good woman who bade her son ' take the galloway and guide them to the fell foot.'   There we met a poor man . . . He piloted us over the next mountain, the like to which I never beheld either in Wales or Germany.   As we were climbing the third, a man over took us who was going the same road; so he accompanied us till we were in a plain level way which in three hours brought us to Whitehaven."

What route was he following? Probably that from Ambleside, by Wrynose and Hardknott, to Eskdale, then, either from the Wool Pack Inn or Boot, over Burnmoor, with Scafell on his right, down to Wastdale and thence by Black Sail pass into Ennerdale; where he would soon be on ' a plain level way to Whitehaven.' If this was the route—and it is difficult to see any other to agree with the given data—then Wesley was the first person to travel through the central Lakeland passes and leave an account of his journey behind.*

* In a note to the Standard Edition of the Journal, iv. p. 448n, it is surmised that he followed the Keswick route, but that would not take him over three mountains.   According to this note Mr. Chris. Graham of Kendal suggests the way named by Hardknott to Boot and then down Eskdale; here again there is no ' mountain the like to which I have never beheld ' etc.   The only other possible alternative appears to be the Esk Hause route; that he followed this seems almost incredible.   I have to thank Dr. L. F. Church for lending me this volume.

He was also the first visitor to shew an appreciation of our mountain scenery. As has been noted above, for the eighteenth century the charm of the Lake District lay in its lakes, not in its fells, mountains were things of horror and terror, not of beauty. But Wesley found God ' nowhere more present than in the mountains of Cumberland,' when he preached at Lorton, and could describe a ride from Whitehaven to Keswick as ' solemn and delightful '; at Seaton (Workington) he found ' the greenest turf in the country.'

At first he always made his journeys on horseback, but by 1772 he also used a chaise on occasion. He generally went to Scotland by crossing the Solway Firth at Bowness. His energy was indeed astounding. On his first visit to Whitehaven, setting out from Hindley Hill on the east of the Pennines, he rode there in one day. On the next one he preached in the market-place; then held a meeting of those he had touched. At five on the following morning he again spoke in the market-place and at three in the afternoon at Hensingham, and was back at Whitehaven for services at six and eight. The next day was a Sunday,'

' I began examining them one by one. At eight I preached at the Gins . . . Between one and two I preached again at Hensingham . . Thence I hastened to church; and in the midst of the service I felt a sudden stroke: immediately a shivering ran through me and in a few minutes I was in a fever . . But when I came from church, hearing there was a vast congregation in the market-place I could not send them away empty and while I was speaking to them God remembered me and strengthened me.'

On the Monday he preached twice and again on Tuesday morning; then, at two in the afternoon, set out for Hindley Hill where he had promised to speak on Wednesday evening. He seems to have rested at Keswick, but was off again at three-thirty and, after travelling all day, preached as arranged in the evening. Thursday was set

apart for fasting and prayer. Next day he was off again
for Whitehaven, which he reached, after travelling over
Hartside and spending the night at Gamblesby, on
Saturday afternoon. On the Sunday he preached in the
Gins at eight, at Hensingham at two, and at Whitehaven
at five; he also attended church for Morning and Evening
Prayer and the ' Lord's Supper.'

After Whitehaven, Cockermouth seems to have been
his favourite place; he visited it nineteen times. When
he preached there on a Sunday in April 1761 at five in the
evening he noted, ' Even the genteel hearers were decent;
many of the rest seemed deeply affected. The people of
the town have never been uncivil. Surely they will not
always be unfruitful.' But when, in May 1780, he
preached at eight in the morning it was ' to the poor only;
the rich could not rise so soon.' He visited the town for
the last time on 2 June 1788. ' I had never such a season
there before; the glory of the Lord seemed to fill the
house and the people trembled before him.'

Though he had passed through the city before this,
Wesley did not preach in Carlisle until April 1770 when he
noted that ' it was here a day of small things; the Society
consisting but of fifteen members.' In 1788 ' the preach-
ing-house, begun three or four years ago, is now completely finished. It is neat, lightsome and cheerful.
But it was very ill able to contain the congregation.'
Carlisle had the privilege of being the last place in these
counties to be visited by the great evangelist, on 2 June
1790, when his Journal contains the entry: ' the work a
little increases here; a small handful of people stand firm
and those that opposed are broken in pieces. Our house
would not near contain the congregation and the word of
God was with power.'

He first preached at Kendal in April 1753 when
' I was a little disgusted at their manner of coming in and
sitting down, without any pretence to any previous prayer or

ejaculation; as well as at their sitting during the hymn which indeed not one (though they knew the tune) sung with me. But it was far otherwise after the sermon; for God spake in his word. At the second hymn every person stood up and most of them sang very audibly.'

When he next preached there, 1764, he complained that there were ' seceders and disputers of every kind ' and four years later wrote ' I once more cast my bread upon the waters and left the event to God.' He never preached there again.

Wigton was another place where all did not go well. On his first visit in May 1757, he described it as ' a neat well built-town,' but in 1761 noted

' I was a good deal moved at the exquisite self sufficiency which was visible in the countenance, air, and whole deportment of a considerable part of them. This constrained me to use a very uncommon plainness of speech. They bore it well.'

None the less Wigton only saw him once more, in 1776. Nor was he very complimentary about Appleby which he describes as ' a county town worthy of Ireland, containing at least five and twenty houses.' But of Lorton ' a little village lying in a green fruitful valley, surrounded by high mountains, the sides of which are covered with grass and woods and the bottom watered by two small rivers,' he must have carried away more pleasant memories. He preached there thrice; and on the first occasion, May 1752, found ' a very large and serious congregation.'

Similar thoughts he must have had of a farmer's house near Brough when, at noon in June 1768, ' the sun was hot enough but some shady trees covered both me and most of the congregation. A little bird perched on one of them and sung without intermission from the beginning of the service unto the end.'

On the whole the student of his Journal is constrained to agree with Canon Wilson that: ' the preaching of

John Wesley in Cumberland was not attended with the enthusiasm and wholesale conversions which marked the progress of George Fox a century before.'[22]   He seems to have passed through so many places—Ambleside, Keswick and Penrith, for instance—so frequently and yet preached there so infrequently; he was at Workington and Ulverston but once; Kendal he left alone in disgust. Only at Whitehaven, Cockermouth and Carlisle does he seem to have met with a reasonable measure of success. It was only after his death that his manifold labours for his Master bore fruit in the rapid growth of his ideals, the results of which are to-day apparent to all.[23]

II.
THE ERA OF REFORM.

Though it was not for another generation that the reform of the Church's administration and endowments took place, it seems right to begin the period covered by the above heading with the episcopate of Edward Venables Vernon,* consecrated at Whitehall on 6 November 1791 by Archbishop Markham of York, because not only has it been said of him that he was ' the first of a series of bishops . . . who lived at Rose Castle, made it their home, bound up with their dearest family interests and did not reckon it as a mere summer residence,'[25] but in the next year Isaac Milner began, as dean of Carlisle, his work as leader of the Evangelical Revival in this diocese.

This movement, keeping as it did within the parochial system, does not appear to have spread to this diocese until now.   The dean, though he spent most of his time at Cambridge—he was president of Queens' College—exercised a great influence from the pulpits of the cathedral and St. Cuthbert's.

* He was born in 1757,[24] son of George 1st Lord Vernon by his 3rd wife Martha, only sister of the 1st earl Harcourt; he married Anne sister of G. G. Leveson Gower, 1st duke of Sutherland.

' When it was known that the dean was to preach in the cathedral, I have seen the aisle and every part of it so thronged, that a person might have walked upon the heads of the crowd. An hour before the service began people had taken their seats and by the time the sermon began the congregation used to number, so it is said, several thousands.'[26]

More will be heard about the dean's activities when the story of the next episcopates is told, for ' the seed sown by this eminent man took root downward and bore fruit upward. The principles of which Dean Milner was the champion are stamped broad and visible on the ecclesiastical life of the nineteenth century in the diocese of Carlisle.'[27]

Of Bishop Vernon himself we know little beyond what appears in his official acts. His register shows that at the beginning of his episcopate he generally held two ordinations a year at Rose, but in later years the number was often three or four; in 1800 they were held in February, June, September and December. It also contains a petition by Humphrey Senhouse of Maryport which throws light on contemporary standards of clerical behaviour. It resulted in the deprivation, in 1794, of the vicar of the chapel there because he

' hath been addicted to gross habitual and excessive Drunkenness; hath at divers times been drunk whilst performing divine service in the chapel aforesaid; hath in the said chapel and elsewhere uttered indecent, impious and profane expressions; and hath at sundry times refused to perform the duty belonging to the curacy of the said chapel.'

The register also provides evidence of the stipends paid to assistant curates: seven men got £20 a year; one £25; three, £30; four, £40; one £50 and one as much as £63. The last instance of £20 being paid is in 1800; after that date, £40 appears to be the recognised minimum. This seems about the average elsewhere.[28] Sometimes curacies were combined with schoolmasterships, or more than one curacy held—a morning service being taken at one church, an afternoon one at the other.

Bishop Vernon more than bore his share in beautifying Rose; one of the garden walks is still called ' Lady Anne's walk ' after his wife, ' a very high dame ' as she appeared to her neighbours at Dalston.[29]   The bishop's ten children were all born at Rose, ' where he lived in a charming simplicity.'[30]   In the autumn of 1796 the work included, with some repairs, making a new way into the library by cutting a passage through the middle of the outer wall, between the Constable and Bell Towers which was 9 ft. 6 in. thick.   The bishop also excavated the basement of the latter tower, ' which before was for upwards of 15 feet from the ground a solid mass of stone and earth,' and converted it into a small dressing room.   During the last four episcopates, including this one, £4133. 19. 2. was spent on improving Rose of which £3048. 7. was recovered by the sale of timber.[31]

Bishop Vernon was translated to York in 1807; he was archbishop forty years.*   ' For sixteen years he (had) administered the affairs of the see of Carlisle with good sense and discretion, spending more than the whole income of the see upon the wants of the diocese.[32]

Samuel Goodenough[33] was consecrated in Whitehall chapel on 13 March 1808 by his predecessor.   In the beginning of the bishop's register there is a note: " the archbishop's option† was the rectory of Rothbury whereof the Revnd. Dr. Watson is the present rector "; other entries of this kind also occur.   It must have been an

---

* In 1830 on the death of Earl Harcourt, the estates of that family descending to him, he added that name to his own.   His great grandson Lewis was created Viscount Harcourt in 1917.

† " Every bishop (whether created or translated) is bound immediately after confirmation to make a legal conveyance to the archbishop of the next avoidance of one such dignity or benefice belonging to his see, as the said archbishop shall chuse and name; which is therefore commonly called an Option " (Codex Juris Ecclesiastici Anglicani, ed. 1713, E. Gibson i, 133).   I am indebted to Dr. N. Sykes for this reference.

exciting gamble on his grace's part: he would consider the value of each living in the new prelate's patronage; weigh the ages of the incumbents and perhaps the state of their health; and then back his winner in this queer race with death or promotion. At the other end, did the holder of the option know; and if so, what were his thoughts? For he had also to make his guess— whether the promotion for which the archbishop considered him ripe was earthly or heavenly.

During most of this episcopate Dean Milner—he lived till 1820—continued to dominate the city and its neighbourhood. The dean and Bishop Vernon seem to have ' hit it off,' but in Bishop Goodenough's time there were clashes between these two men of strong convictions, though these did not impair their personal friendship.[34] The first was about the church school at Carlisle, founded on Dr. Bell's or the National System and long known as the Central School.* In March 1812, the bishop wrote to the dean "that if I have anything to do with the plan, that plan must be to educate for the inculcating of the doctrines, and for the adopting of the principles of the Established Church." In another letter he insisted that the children should learn the catechism, be instructed in the liturgy and attend the Church on Sundays. But the dean wished to allow the children of Nonconformists to attend; in the end the bishop prevailed. Whether we agree with him in this or not, all surely will join in admiring him in his zeal for this school which he attended every Thursday and Saturday, riding over from Rose for the purpose.[35]

In September 1813 the dean presided at the first meeting of the Carlisle Auxiliary to the British and Foreign Bible Society—a work in which Churchmen and Dissenters combined—again the bishop differed and stood aloof. He

---

* It was on the Sally port, and remained in use until replaced by John Fawcett's school on the West Walls.

took the same course, and so did the cathedral chapter and most of the more influential people in the city, when a branch of the Church Missionary Society was formed in Carlisle in 1817. Another famous Church Society, that for Promoting Christian Knowledge, had had a branch within the diocese for three years. In 1819 the Clergy Widows and Orphans Fund was started. The Church of England and the diocese of Carlisle, as we know them to-day, were beginning to take shape.

Bishop Goodenough's register shews that he held a yearly ordination, generally in July. The stipend of newly ordained curates was at first about £30 a year. Later it rose to £60, £70, or even £120, which the curate of Bowness was given in 1814—as late as 1819 his brother of Borrowdale only had £30. Most of these men would be priests in charge for absentee pluralists and the worth of the benefice would probably fix the stipend of the curate, since the absentee had to make some ' profit ' out of it.

The bishop was found dead in his bed at Worthing, where he had removed after a severe fit of illness, on Sunday 12 August 1827; he was buried in the North Cloister of Westminster Abbey six days later. His portrait is in the hall of Christ Church, Oxford. He married Elizabeth, daughter of James Ford, M.D., physician to Queen Charlotte. Among his descendants are some who have risen to eminence in Church and State, especially Admiral Sir William Goodenough, G.C.B. R. S. Ferguson, writing in 1889, says:

" Tradition still lingers in Carlisle of the stately presence and commanding figure of Dr. Goodenough, as he appeared for the first time in his cathedral, and of the Spartan discipline he maintained among his numerous progeny . . . It should be recorded that he was the last bishop of Carlisle to wear a wig and Milner the last dean."[36]

He was an eminent botanist and the first person to cultivate seakale.[37] The author has received an account of him from Mrs. Williams, wife of Bishop Williams, whose grandmother was Bishop Goodenough's grand-daughter:[38]

" as a small child I used to hear stories of the severe old bishop. How he drove behind four horses in the family coach to London once a year, my little grandmother sitting between him and Mrs. Goodenough, holding the bishop's wig-box on her knees. In it were three wigs known as Highty, Tighty and Scrub; the first for London and State occasions; the second for official appearances in Carlisle; and Scrub for home wear."

The *Carlisle Patriot* of 24 August 1827 has the following note which illustrates the tone adopted towards the filling of episcopal vacancies in those days.

" The bishopric of Carlisle is giving our ricketty Cabinet some trouble. Lord Lansdown wants to promote Dr. Maltby* a keen Whig prosody grinder. Lord Gooderich inclines to Dr. Goodenough of Westminster.† We feel no little curiosity as to the decision, for we wish to know which party is really our master. One report we have heard, which we give for the laughter of our readers, Lord Holland it is said proposed—Sydney Smith ! ! ! the jester of the Edinburgh Review."‡

But the new bishop was Hugh Percy,§ elected on 8 October 1827.

Change was in the air—in 1832 the Reform Bill was passed—and three years later *The Report of the Commissioners appointed by His Majesty to inquire into the Ecclesiastical Revenues of England and Wales* presented to parliament.

It must be realised that no reorganisation of the Church's revenues had ever taken place—there had been

---

* Subsequently bishop of Chichester and Durham.

† Son of the bishop, later dean of Wells.

‡ The famous wit and canon of St. Paul's.

§ Son of Algernon Percy, 2nd son of Hugh, 1st duke of Northumberland, who had been created earl of Beverley in 1800. Having taken Holy Orders, he married a daughter of the archbishop of Canterbury and was provided with the livings of Bishopsbourne, about £1500 a year, and Ivy church, about £460, to begin with. Next, at the age of 26, he became in 1810, chancellor and canon of Exeter; then in 1812 chancellor of Salisbury, over £3,000 a year; and in 1816 canon of St. Paul's, about £1800 a year, and of Canterbury. In 1822, there followed the archdeaconry of Canterbury, in 1825 the deanery and in the same year the bishopric of Rochester, with the expectation, if not the promise, of early promotion. (*Letters of George IV*, III, 12 September 1827).

spoliation at the Reformation, but little reorganisation.
During the course of centuries the value of some livings
and offices had greatly increased, while others remained
almost stable; as a result bishoprics varied between
Durham £19,066 a year, and Rochester, £1,459; and
livings between Doddington, Ely, £7,781 and three in
Norwich diocese worth under £10 a year. The size of the
populations of dioceses and parishes equally varied: the
bishop of Lincoln shepherded 1249 parishes, his brother of
Rochester 94; the parish of St. Anne's, Manchester had a
population of over 270,000.

Pluralism was rampant: the bishop of Carlisle remained
chancellor of Salisbury and a prebendary of St. Paul's.
The vicar of Addingham was also incumbent of Hampton
Wick, Middlesex; a minor canon was vicar of St.
Mary's, Carlisle and rector of Talbenny, Pembrokeshire;
the vicar of Ormside was perpetual curate of Hensingham and chaplain of Chatham Dockyard. The extent of
the evil is shewn by the fact that out of 128 livings in this
diocese and 112 in the Chester deaneries, 56 and 33
respectively were held by pluralists.

The statistics that follow have been taken from the
Report; detailed figures are given in Appendix xiii.

Stipend		Carlisle Diocese	Chester deaneries	Total
	Under £50	4	6	10
Between	£50 – 75	23	30	53
,,	£75 – 100	25	33	58
,,	£100 – 150	25	23	48
,,	£150 – 200	18	7	25
,,	£200 – 300	15	7	22
,,	£300 – 400	10	2	12
,,	£500 – 600	4	2	6
,,	£600 – 700	2	—	2
,,	£900 –1000	1	1	2
,,	£1000 –1100	—	1	1
Totals		127	112	239

Greystoke, Penrith and Torpenhow made no return, and Great Salkeld was attached to the archdeaconry. Whellan, in 1860, makes them worth about £700, £200, £305 and £380 a year respectively.[39] The best commentary perhaps on the figures for this diocese is that the average stipend in England and Wales was £285, in Carlisle, £175. Only Sodor and Man, £157, and St. David's, £137, had a lower average; the only other diocese with a return under £250 was York, £242.

The commissioners also received returns about benefice houses; the following is a summary of these:

	Fit for Residence	None	Unfit for residence	Total
Carlisle	84	13	31	128*
Chester	49	53	10	112
Totals	133	66	41	240

It is noticeable, both in stipends and housing, that parishes in the diocese of Chester were in a worse way than those in Carlisle. This may have been partly due to lack of episcopal supervision, but mainly it was because the former included parishes of great size, with chapelries which had never possessed any proper endowments and in most cases had only recently been promoted to parochial status.

The first result of the report was the formation in 1836 of a body of Ecclesiastical Commissioners. One of their earliest tasks was to reduce many of the large stipends to a reasonable level by which they acquired a considerable sum of free money. This was not to be used for building new churches, a charge upon the diocese or parish concerned, but for the endowment of new parishes and the increase of stipends in old ones. The outcome of their efforts was soon seen by his lordship's stipend being

* In this return Great Salkeld was included, the other three livings were not.

raised to £4500 a year. Before long the parochial clergy
began to benefit; between 1841 and 1844 the following
augmentations were authorised for livings in public
patronage.

Population	Stipend raised to
above 2000	£150 a year
below 2000 and above 1000	£120 ,,
,, 1000 ,, 500	£100 ,,
,, 500	£80 ,,

These schemes affected twenty five parishes in this
diocese. In 1845 the plan, familiar to-day, of meeting a
benefaction by the grant of a like sum as a means of
benefice augmentation is found at work.* In 1844 a
scheme for the appointment of honorary canons in the
cathedral is recorded in the bishop's register.

In 1849 Archibald Campbell Tait, headmaster of Rugby
became dean of Carlisle—he was later to be bishop of
London and archbishop of Canterbury. The cathedral
was in a bad way at this time: the dean noted in his diary
of the day after his installation " with much dismay "
that though it was Sunday and the Feast of the Epiphany,
there were only nine or ten communicants. His attempts
to raise the standard met with opposition. There was
difficulty too about the establishment of an afternoon
sermon on Sundays, although the dean was willing to take
the entire responsibility of it upon himself.[40] Two years
later an Act of Parliament was passed to ' facilitate the
management and improvement of episcopal and capitular
estates.' Within a year the chapters of Carlisle and
York had agreed to transfer their estates to the Ecclesiastical Commissioners, though at the former, where there
was strong opposition in the chapter, the dean had
difficulty in forcing the matter through.[41] Another
Commission, appointed in the following year to inquire

* These figures and dates are taken from Bishop Percy's register, where the
names of the parishes concerned can be found.

into the state of cathedral churches, sent out question-
naires. Bishop Percy in one of his answers objected to
the idea of permanent residence for the canons. The
present plan " has not suffered the cathedral clergy to be
unworking outside the cathedral, nor the parochial clergy
to be an inferior class to them, it has secured equality.
When the cathedral clergy cease to be parochial also,
another order will be raised in the Church." The returns
shew that there were two daily choral services, with two
sermons on Sunday; the Holy Communion was celebrated
monthly and on great festivals.[42]

The most important local outcome of these investigations was the revelation of the dilapidated state of the
fabric. As a result the commissioners ordered £15,000 to
be expended, out of the capitular estates, on its restoration
—the returns shew that £4,480 had been spent on repairs
in the past fourteen years.[43] Thus came about the great
restoration, or should it be ' restoration,' by their
architect, Ewan Christian, in the years 1853-6. On two
points most people would put inverted commas to-day;
one is the washing out of the fifteenth century paintings
on the pillars;[44] the other the substitution of imitation
thirteenth century windows in the chancel for the
perpendicular ones that had been placed there to give
light to the high altar. This needless change roused the
ire of E. A. Freeman, the historian.[45] But on the whole
the work was well done; one piece of real restoration was
the removal of the plaster ceiling put up in 1764. Fortunately enough of the original roof, " this unique
specimen of a waggon-headed ceiling,"[46] remained to
allow a faithful restoration to be made. The original
colour scheme—red and green upon white—was not
adhered to, the present one of blue, ornamented with
golden stars, being substituted. Another important
alteration was the erection of the present south door as
the chief entrance. The west end, as we see it to-day, is

also Mr. Christian's work.   It must have been at this
time that the heraldic glass referred to above (p. 168)
was inserted in the clerestory windows.   The statement
that one of the shields was the Black Prince's seems to
be an error; a closer view of it shews a label ermine,
the differencing mark of John of Gaunt.

Some account must now be given of John Fawcett who,
as vicar of St. Cuthbert's, Carlisle from 1800-1851, carried
on the leadership of the Evangelical party after the death
of Dean Milner.   He not only continued his work by his
interest in the cause of the Church Missionary Society
and The British and Foreign Bible Society, but also as
an acceptable preacher.   The building of Upperby Church
was largely due to his zeal; he was also one of the founders of the Cumberland Infirmary.   He lived in a large
house in Botchergate, with an inscription in Hebrew
over the door—'The gift of my people'.   His name was
memorialised until this century by the Church school on
West walls known locally as Fawcett's.   This establishment was staffed by an able body of teachers, and few
schools in the country of elementary status were more
successful.   At his death he was accorded a public funeral
and was buried in St. Cuthbert's churchyard; a 'programme ' of the funeral hangs in the church; there is also
a more permanent monument in the chancel.*

Meanwhile Bishop Percy was not idle; as can be seen
from Appendices V and VI, in this small diocese 13 new
churches or chapels were built and 18 old ones rebuilt,
wholly or in part, during his episcopate.   These totals
only include those entered in his register.   New diocesan
organisations started included a Clergy-Aid Society in
1838 and an Education Society in 1855.   The first
district committee of the Society for the Propagation of

---

* I am indebted to Canon H. B. Wilson, the present vicar of St. Cuthbert's,
for this material.   Mr. Fawcett was also for a time headmaster of Carlisle
Grammar School and vicar of Scaleby.

the Gospel was formed at Kirkby Stephen in 1835. The Society had, of course, received support from individuals within the diocese before that date—Bishop Nicolson became a member in 1703—but on a very small scale; in 1825 there were only four subscribers; Penrith had a collection and a sermon.*

It is perhaps as the first president of the Cumberland Infirmary that Bishop Percy is remembered by many to-day. The building was completed in 1830, but owing to a lawsuit not opened till 1842. A writer in the *Carlisle Patriot* on 9 February 1856 stated that " the Infirmary, which received a high share of his attention, bounty, and care, is a noble result of his unwearied perseverance as our columns have frequently shewn."

In the years 1829-31 he carried through extensive alterations at Rose, which completely changed the appearance of the fabric. The incongruous mixture of architectural styles, caused by successive bishops having introduced their own ideas, gave way to a uniform plan under a scheme prepared by the Quaker architect Thomas Rickman. Inside the magnificent oak staircase ornamented by the bishop's arms, the famous Chinese wall paper, and the carved mantel-pieces in the drawing room were erected.[47] A charming series of pencil sketches by Mrs. Williams' grand-mother, Mrs. Wybergh, shew the castle as it was before these changes. One of the most delightful of these, of the chapel, disproves Wilson's belief that an east window was introduced by Bishop Sterne. Presumably this was put in by Bishop Percy, who is also said to have brought the carved panels of the stalls from Lambeth Chapel. These drawings shew that the canon was also mistaken in believing that Kite's Tower was the front of the castle till this rebuilding; sketch III shews it in 1826 where it is to-day.[48] To complete his plans the bishop employed Sir Joseph Paxton

* I am indebted to Mrs. Landers, S.P.G. archivist, for this information.

to lay out the gardens.   In all he is said to have spent
£40,000 on these improvements, of which £10,000 was
borrowed from the see.[49]   Despite all this the castle must
have been an uncomfortable place to live in.   " There
was no heating apparatus in the days of Percy and not
a single curtain throughout the house.   The upper bed-
rooms had not even shutters."[50]

During this episcopate Rose nearly had to stand yet
another siege because as a duke's grandson the bishop was
suspected by the Chartists.   Bricks were thrown at him
in Carlisle and his effigy burnt.   A threat that Rose was to
be attacked was taken so seriously that muskets, concealed in packing cases labelled hardware, were brought
into the castle and sentinels placed on the Carlisle road to
give warning.   But in the end all that happened was some
rioting in Dalston.[51]

Bishop Percy died suddenly at Rose on 5 February
1856* at the age of seventy two, after an episcopate of
over twenty eight years, the longest since that of Bishop
Appleby, and was buried in Dalston churchyard on 12
February.   According to a statement in the *Carlisle
Patriot* of 16 February he wished to be buried beside his
second wife in Carlisle Cathedral, but the home secretary,
refused to allow the vault to be opened.   He married
firstly, in 1808, Mary, eldest daughter of Charles Manners
Sutton, archbishop of Canterbury, by whom he had a
numerous family; and, secondly, Mary, daughter of Vice-
Admiral Sir William Hope Johnstone.   The bishop's
eldest son Algernon Charles Percy married Emily,
daughter of Reginald Heber, bishop of Calcutta, and
added that name to his own; his heirs still exist in the
male line.   A ward in the Cumberland Infirmary is named

---

* Dean Tait states that he was intending to go to London, when he had the
faint from which he never recovered, to renew the leases of his stall in St.
Paul's, and meant to distribute the fines of some £60,000 amongst the poorest
livings in Cumberland (*George Moore*, Smiles, 484).

after Bishop Percy; there is also a mural monument in the cathedral.

An obituary notice in the *Carlisle Patriot* of 9 February 1856 states:

His manner was polished and courteous, but far removed from familiarity. Few of the clergy were admitted to his society, most of them only met him on public occasions, yet no one had reason to complain of a mere want of polite reception. His punctuality was proverbial; his attention to any public business he undertook was highly exemplary. In some things he may have been deemed hard to deal with and dictatorial, especially by those who did not know him well and had not studied his manner. . . He was an example of what a parish priest ought to be. He frequently officiated most unostentatiously for the neighbouring Clergy when necessarily absent . . . and even within a few days of his death visited the sick in the parish of Dalston and in the absence of the vicar had administered the Sacrament to the old and infirm. He was of the High Church, but no Tractarian and set not his affection on mediaeval frippery; he stood aloof from that and equally so from the disorganised portion of the Church, who descend so low in the case of discipline as to be indistinguishable from dissenters. Take him all in all, it may be long, perhaps, ere we find in his situation a better man."

Miss Ellen Goodwin describes him as

" a great farmer; he was reputed the best judge of a horse in all the district and Sunday afternoons were usually spent looking round his farm and giving an opinion on any neighbours' horses which were being bought or sold. He used to drive his own four horses all the way to London and to say there was no such hill as ' Rose Brow ' in all the distance. Old Johnny Fawkes, who had been a stable boy under Percy, he never called him anything else, was never tired of telling of old times. It was very striking to find how Bishop Percy lived in the hearts and memories of those who knew him; we heard comparatively little of the sayings or doings of either Bishop Villiers or Waldegrave."[52]

CHAPTER III.

THE DIOCESE OF CHESTER DEANERIES.
1747-1856.

DURING the opening years of this period visitations were held every five or six years, generally at Kendal, Cartmel and Whitehaven. Many of the returns only contain lists of names. In 1778, Beilby Porteous, who had been consecrated the year previously, substituted Ulverston for Cartmel. Coupland deanery is not included in the general return but in a copy of Bishop Gastrell's *Notitia* in the Chester Dean and Chapter Library information is given about it, from a return of 1779, so it may have been visited in that year.

From the 1778 returns we learn that the vicar of Kirkby Lonsdale resided and had a resident curate at £30 a year. Holy Communion was celebrated eight times a year, with communicants as follows: 10 August 1777, 29; 12 October, 42; Advent, 48; Christmas, 81; 1st Sunday in Lent, 1778, 16; Good Friday, 62; Easter, 64; Whitsunday, 27. There were two services on Sunday, with one sermon; and the children were catechised between Easter and Whitsunday. At Barbon the curate mentions one man " who was first Protestant, then Quaker, next Methodist. What he is now, we will not pretend to say. But this it is evident that name and appearance with him constitute religion." There were two Sunday services, with one sermon; at Christmas, etc., " the inhabitants frequent the mother Church to partake of the Lord's Supper "; the children were catechised after Easter. These services seem to be the normal, but in some places the afternoon service was only held in the summer. Holy Communion was generally celebrated four times a year. At Kendal there were morning and afternoon Sunday services, with daily prayer at 11 o'clock. The catechism was taught every Sunday and on Wednesdays and Fridays during Lent. Holy Communion was celebrated monthly and at Christmas, Easter and Whitsun; Palm Sunday, Good Friday and Trinity Sunday; the communicants averaged a 100, with double that number at Easter. At St. George's there was also a sacrament Sunday monthly, average 15 communicants; Burneside had 40 at Easter and 30 on three other days.

From 1778 to 1811 the visitation took place every five years. 1789 is the next return that gives any details. Amid a mass of routine answers a certain amount of interesting matter can be gleaned from it. At Hawkshead " prayers are said every festival and on every Monday (being a market day) thr. ye year "; and at Pennington they " were usually read also every Friday morning till about two years ago they were declined for want of a congregation." At Cockermouth prayers were read every Wednesday and Friday and all Holidays; ' The Eucharist ' was celebrated once a month; there were 200 communicants at Easter and between 60 and 70 at other times. At St. Nicholas, Whitehaven prayers were read every day in the week and Holy Communion celebrated monthly. At Holy Trinity there were prayers three days a week and Holy Communion monthly with 200 communicants at Easter and at other times between 30 and 70. At Workington there were two services on Sundays and one sermon, prayers were read on Wednesdays and Fridays in Lent and daily in Passion week; and on State occasions and all holidays ' but on these last the congregations are thin.'

The returns from some of the incumbents contain interesting and even curious remarks. Cockermouth:

' The stipend payable out of the tithes of the parish has been withheld by the improp., Lord Lonsdale,* so that in fact the church has now no endowment. Can your lordship get this matter rectified? Since the death of the late incumbent in the year 1768 no successor has been appointed by the patron, ought not some steps to be taken to fill up the vacancy?' Joseph Gilbanks, offic. minister.'†

Rusland:

" I have neither expounded the Church Catechism myself nor used any printed exposition of it. And I have reason to believe that should I attempt anything of the kind, it would not be acceptable to my congregation; no such thing having been practised in this country for a long time."

St. John's, Beckermet:

" I do not reside upon my Cure, I reside upon a very respectable curacy in Wiltshire, and I have been regularly here once a year."

Setmurthy:

" there is but one who can be said to absent himself from public worship. The reason which he assigns is that he cannot bear the cold which he has found in the chapel. He is of the low rank."

Dean:

" during forty years constant residence and due attendance on our annual visitation of the commissary of our archdeacon of Richmond, we have not once been favoured with the presence of that our ecclesiastical officer and but deputies and sub-deputies have only some times supplied his place."

The account of the destruction of the old parish church at Workington and the building of the new one is interesting.

" The church was then very small and incommodious and indecent, but I formed a scheme for pulling it down and rebuilding it by voluntary Subscriptions, finding it could not be effected by any other means and after various attempts and by indefatigable perseverance prevailed upon the bulk of the principal Inhabitants to enter into a proper agreement for the purpose;

---

* For his character see p. 365-6 above.

† But the appeal was unsuccessful; no incumbent was appointed until 1795. *Addition to p.* 163 *above*: the chapel had burial, and therefore parochial, rights in 1361. The dedication was then to St. Mary. (*Testa. Karl.* p. 32).

and though an opposition was made to it by a few wch. engaged us in a suit at Chester and afterwards upon an appeal at York for ten years, a Decree was obtained in favour of it and the Church and Chancel was rebuilt in 1772."

The returns of 1804 and 1811 are mostly brief replies to definite questions. But some light is thrown on life in the Lake District chapelries. In 1804 at Buttermere banns of marriage are never published and "the ministration of public baptism of infants etc. is not always performed in the chapel on account of distance and the rigours of winter." Prayers are read twice a Sunday "except a little in the depth of winter, when there is no evening service"; Holy Communion is celebrated twice a year with between eleven and fifteen communicants. The same applied to Ennerdale and Eskdale where in the depth of winter "there is no Service done in the afternoons, owing to the snows and stormy weather." In 1811 it is recorded of Wastdale Head Chapel that "no burials are at it." They had to go twenty miles distant to the mother church of St. Bees for interments. St. Bees had a celebration at 7 o'clock in the morning of Easter Day.

How the bishop of Chester administered these deaneries we do not know—occasionally another bishop's services were used: In 1715 William Nicolson consecrated Holy Trinity, Whitehaven, in 1753 Bishop Osbaldeston St. James' Whitehaven; and Dr. Watson, bishop of Llandaff, who lived at Windermere, had licence to consecrate the churches of Egton and Newland in 1791 and of New Hutton five years later. Such licences are exceptional. Judging from the dates in the episcopal registers—it is noteworthy that almost invariably churches were consecrated in the summer—the bishop generally performed these functions himself. On other matters, however, we have really no evidence. Presumably the bishop at his visitation confirmed those presented but the distances must have precluded many from coming. It was not till

1821 that any regular mention of Confirmation occurs in the visitation records.   There is ample evidence, as can be seen in Appendix V, of active Church life in the number of new churches erected or of old ones rebuilt or restored during these years.   Of the latter the most important was Kendal.   In 1848 the architect had said that it is

" difficult to describe the wretched condition of the fabric. Centuries of neglect or injudicious repair have resulted in leaking roofs, walls green with mouldering damp, columns more than their diameter out of the perpendicular and tottering to their fall . . . a tout-ensemble presenting about as melancholy a spectacle of neglect, ruin, and irreverence as imagination could conceive."

But little was done for two years, then, in 1850, the master of Trinity College, Cambridge, the patrons of the living, visited the town, and, seeing the terrible state of the building, induced the college authorities to take in hand the restoration of the chancel.   The east wall was pulled down and a new window, of less width than the medieval one, inserted.   The chancel was also extended into the nave one bay further west, and a new roof, raised to the original height, put on.   The parishioners, doubtless stimulated by this example, commenced work on the remainder of the building.   The rest of the roof was taken up to the same level as in the chancel; the fourteenth century west porch demolished and replaced by the present structure; and the floor lowered between nine inches and three feet to its original level.   Other alterations included the removal of the old square pews and their replacement by low open benches and the insertion of six stained glass windows.   As a result when the building was re-opened for public worship on 3 June 1852, the congregation " must have felt it difficult to believe that they were worshipping, indeed, in the same church."   Doubtless all this was necessary, but the best comment on it is " the church has been too drastically restored to retain much architectural interest."*

This is a pathetically brief account of nearly a hundred years of Church life but where records are absent the historian is helpless. Perhaps in the future some other writer may be more successful. In 1856, on the death of Bishop Percy, the ancient association of these deaneries with the archdeaconry of Richmond came to an end and they were joined to the diocese of Carlisle.

Before we take final leave of them, however, an account must be given of a once famous institution that flourished in their midst—the Theological College at St. Bees. Though Archbishop Cranmer had hoped that in every cathedral provision would be made for the training of men for Holy Orders little was done until the beginning of the eighteenth century when the bishops of Salisbury and Sodor and Man planned to establish colleges in their dioceses for this purpose. In both cases the project failed to achieve any lasting result. In 1804, the bishop of St. David's made another attempt, however, lack of funds held up his plans. But two years later George Henry Law, youngest son of Bishop Law of Carlisle and bishop of Chester, founded such an institution at St. Bees. It can thus be acclaimed as the first Theological College to achieve success.

The idea of the founder was to provide " for the better instruction of those candidates for Holy Orders who were unable to obtain a University education." It owed much to the munificence of William, 2nd earl of Lonsdale, who endowed it with the vicarage of St. Bees and rebuilt the choir of the ruined priory church for its use as a lecture room and library. Wordsworth refers to it in his poem on St. Bees in words that perhaps do not represent him at his best.

---

* o.s. xvi. 182-7, R.C.H.M. Westmorland, 119.

On 9 February 1856 the *Carlisle Patriot*, describing the restoration of the church, mentions that there were a hundred students at the college:

" previous to admission (they must be) well versed in the Classics as the course of study does not exceed two years.   In this period the standard divinity works are diligently studied, and such principles inculcated as are likely to form faithfull ministers of the gospel."

A local guide of 1870 stated that the foundation " supplies more candidates for Orders in England and Wales than any other theological college; the average number of students is from 80 to 90." According to ' *The College Calendar* of 1882 there were two terms in the year; January to April and August to November, the fees being £10 a term. Each student was expected to provide himself with a house or rooms—the expense of board and lodging was estimated at between 18/- and 24/- a week. The services were morning prayer daily at 9 a.m., but on Holy days and Wednesdays and Fridays in Lent at 11, with evening prayer on Fridays at 7-30. On Sundays there was a celebration at 8 a.m., in addition to morning and evening prayer. By then its decline was beginning: *The Calendar* of 1890 mentions some 60 students in residence the previous year—in 1846-8 there were 120. The falling off may have been partly due to the demand for a higher standard for ordinands but was probably chiefly caused by the college's lack of buildings, which made it impossible for it to provide any form of corporate life. It ceased to exist in about 1894.*

A. G. Bradley, while gathering material for his *Highways and Byways in the Lake District*, visited St. Bees to see the college:

" I had all my life been familiar with the name of St. Bees as a prolific nursery of north country parsons, and as the best known

---

* The above is based on *Dictionary of English Church History*, Ollard and Crosse, 588-9; Whellan 429-30; and The College Calendars.

perhaps of all those gateways to the Anglican ministry, which are somewhat indiviously known as ' back doors '."

He gives an amusing description of his efforts to find it. His first inquiry of a ' tired-looking individual ' as to the way to the college was met with the answer ' T' College ! Thear's nae college here.' He then asked a " trustworthy looking matron "; again the response was " There's no college here, sir." So he wondered whether he had really got to the right place. But to the question " is this St. Bees? " a small urchin answered ' aye.' He therefore tried the station-master " Would you be kind enough to direct me to the college? " to which the answer was " the grammar school, I suppose you mean. sir." Further questions about " an establishment here, that has been turning out parsons with blue hoods* by the hundred since a long time before you and I were born," elicited no satisfactory reply. At last, however, a knowing porter was found and from him the news obtained " that the college had collapsed some three years previously."

It seems strange indeed that a foundation that endured so long should have left so little impression on the minds of the people in whose midst it had once flourished.†

---

* The hood was in fact at first half red and half white silk and then of black stuff lined with puce.

† The college is, in a sense, even to-day fulfilling its purpose; since the income from Elizabeth Nicholson's foundation, " for preparing young men for the ministry," founded in 1882, and from the college exhibition fund, is now assisting the training of the ordination candidates of this diocese.

APPENDIX V.
CHURCH RESTORATION AND BUILDING.
1747-1856.

Date	DIOCESE OF CARLISLE.		CHESTER DEANERIES.	
	Ancient church or chapel.	New church.	Ancient church or chapel.	New church.
1749	Uldale rb. abt. 1749 (G)			
1753				St. James' Whitehaven c. (A)
1755				St. George's, Kendal c. (B) Mansergh c. (B)
1756	Mungrisdale rb. (C)			
1757			Hutton Roof rb. (D)	
1758	Culgaith c. (A)			
1763		Maryport c. (A)		
1767		Plumpton c. (A)		
1768	Kirkland rb. (C)			
1770	Temple Sowerby rb. (D)			
1772			Workington rb. (above p. 390-1)	
1773			Crosscrake rb. (D)	
1776			Mosser c. (B) Dendron c. (B)	
1777	Threlkeld rb. (C)			

Year			
1778	St. Cuthbert's, Carlisle rb. (C)		
1780	Hayton rb. (C)		
	Kirkandrews-on-Esk l. (A)		
1784	Dufton rb. (D)		
1785	Westward rb. (C)	Irton rb. (C)	
1788	Wigton rb. (C)		
1789	Brampton c. (A)		
1790		Gosforth rb. (C)	Hensingham bt. (C)
1791		Egton c. (B)	
1792	Bewcastle rb. (C)	Setmurthy rb. (C)	
1794	Flimby rb. (C)	New Hutton c. (B)	
1796	Camerton rb. (C)	Thwaites rb. (C)	
1807		St. John's, Beckermet rb. (C)	
1810		Ambleside rb. (C)	
1811		Hensingham c. (B)	
1813		Embleton rb. (C)	
1814	Thrimby c. (A)		
1815		Barbon rb. (D)	
1816	Nichol Forest c. (A)		
1819		Coniston rb. (F)	
1823		Moresby rb. (E)	St. Johns', Workington c. (B)
1825			Haverthwaite c. (B)
			Rydal c. (B)

Date	DIOCESE OF CARLISLE. Ancient church or chapel.	New church.	CHESTER DEANERIES. Ancient church or chapel.	New church.
1827			Pennington c. (B) Burneside c. (B)	
1828	Brampton, enlarged (A) Castle Carrock rb. (C)			
1829			Arlecdon c. (B) New Hutton c. (B) Lindale c. (B) Loweswater c. (B)	
1830	Stapleton c. (A)	Christ Church, Carlisle c. (A)		
1831	Uldale rb. (C)	Holy Trinity, Carlisle c. (A)		
1832	Askham rb. (C) Thornthwaite c. (A)			Holy Trinity, Ulverston c. (B)
1833				Casterton c. (B)
1836				Levens c. (B)
1837				Brathay c. (B) St. Thomas', Kendal c. (B) Milnthorpe c. (B)
1838	Maryport c. (A)	St. John's, Keswick c. (A)	Selside rb. (D) Grayrigg c. (B)	
1839	Height (Rosley) c. (A) Houghton c. (A)			Holme, Burton c. (B)

1840			
1841			Ponsonby rb. (C)
			Buttermere rb. (C)
			St. George's, Kendal c. (H)
1842	Stanwix c. (A)		
	Wreay c. (A)		
1843	Newlands rb. (C)		
1844	Stainmore c. (A)		St. Bridget's, Beckermet c. (B)
1845	Borrowdale rb. (C)	Holme Eden c. (A)	
1846	Renwick c. (A)	Upperby c. (A)	
	Thursby c. (A)		
	Musgrave c. (A)		
	Allonby c. (A)		
	Kirklinton c. (A)		
	St. John's-in-the-Vale rb. (C)		
	Clifton, Penrith, chancel re-built (D & H)		
1847	Ireby c. (A)		Christ Church, Whitehaven c. (B)
1848	Aspatria c. (A)		Applethwaite (Windermere) l. (B)

| | DIOCESE OF CARLISLE. | | CHESTER DEANERIES. | |
Date	Ancient church or chapel.	New church.	Ancient church or chapel.	New church.
1849	Newton Arlosh c. (A) Rocliffe (c) (A)	St. Paul's, Holm Cultram (Silloth) c. (A) St. Cuthbert's, Holm Cultram c. (A)		
1850		Christ Church, Penrith c. (A)	Drigg c. (B)	
1853	Thornthwaite c. (A)	Talkin Chapel bt. (E)	Preston Patrick c. (B) Walney rb. (F)	Grange c. (B)
1854	Patterdale c. (A)	Gilsland c. (A)	Cockermouth c. (B) Thwaites c. (B)	Bardsea c. (B)
1855	Crosby-on-Eden c. (A)	Scotby c. (A)	Ambleside c. (B)	

(A) = Carlisle Episcopal Registers.
(B) = Chester Episcopal Registers.
(C) = n.s. xxiii, 206-76.
(D) = R.C.H.M. Westmorland.
(E) = Carlisle Diocesan Deed Book.
(F) = V.C.H. Lancs. viii.

(G) = Chancellor Waugh's notes.
(H) = History of Cumberland and Westmorland, W. Whellan
bt = built.
c = consecrated.
l = licenced.
rb = rebuilt.

APPENDIX VI.

Return of churches built or restored at a cost exceeding £500 between 1840-1856.*

	New building.	Restoration.
Ambleside	9000	
Aspatria	3000	
Bardsea	2000	
Beckermet; St. Bridget's	2700	
Brougham: St. Wilfrid's Chapel		1000
Burton		2944
Cockermouth	6670	
Crosby-on-Eden	2000	
Crosthwaite, Keswick		4000
Dufton		700
Drigg	1500	
Gilsland	1000	
Grange-over-Sands	2892	
Grasmere		680
Greystoke		2183
Holme St. Cuthbert	800	
Holme Eden	1512	
Houghton	1692	
Ireby	564	
Irthington	989	
Kendal		12000
Kirkby Stephen		7586
Kirklinton	1600	
Lanercost		4400
Musgrave		550
Newbiggin		800
Newton Arlosh	800	
Patterdale	1800	
Penrith, Christ Church	2700	
Ponsonby		1680

* This return is taken from a Parliamentary paper printed by Bishop Goodwin (as an appendix to his Charge of 1875) which covers the years 1840 to 1872. These figures, giving particulars of the years before 1856, have been extracted from it. The remainder of the figures, as well as a further return for 1872-1892 (House of Lords *Journals* vol. 124, p. 382), is given in appendices viii and xi. The latter return has been published by the Stationary Office. In the original returns shillings and pence are sometimes given; these have been omitted here.

	New building.	Restoration.
Preston Patrick	1500	
Rocliffe*	1700	
Silloth, St. Paul	835	
Scotby	1600	
Stanwix	3100	
Thornthwaite: Braithwaite		915
Thwaites		1677
Upperby	1000	
Walney	800	
Warcop		1800
Windermere, St. Mary's	1460	
Wreay		3000

* The spelling of this name adopted here is that used by N. & B. and the Diocesan Calendar. The more usual form to-day is Rockcliffe. But it is clear that the name was originally the red, not the rock, cliffe. Hence the spelling used here seems the right one.

BOOK V.

THE MODERN DIOCESE OF CARLISLE.
1856-1933.

CHAPTER I.

THE SOCIAL SCENE.

THE chief differences in the state of these counties at the last survey and at the opening of this one were caused by the building of railways and the rapid growth of the industrial town of Barrow-in-Furness. Those two events are symbolical of the alteration between the England of the Georges and that which we know to-day.

Indeed, the first railway—from Carlisle to Newcastle—had been authorised within one year of Bishop Percy's consecration. The next, between Carlisle and Maryport, opened in 1846, was eventually carried down the west coast to Barrow, thus at last opening up the hitherto most isolated parts of Cumberland and Lancashire. In the same year through communication between Carlisle and London, by Lancaster, was established. Two years later the lines between Carlisle and Edinburgh and Carlisle and Glasgow were in operation. That from Carlisle to Silloth was opened in 1856. The last major one to be constructed, the old Midland line by the Eden valley, was not used for passenger traffic until as late as 1876.[1]

All these lines ran through Carlisle; thus the coming of the railways enabled the ancient city to regain its old position as ths leading town of the North West. But anyone who studies the pictures of old Carlisle, and then walks along that pathetic fragment, the west walls, may perhaps wonder if after all the city did not sell its soul

for " a mess of pottage," or more accurately for a mess of
railway lines.   However it certainly increased much in
prosperity: by 1851 its population had reached 26,310 and
by 1900 43,480 while Whitehaven, almost as populous as
Carlisle in 1801 had only 14,190 inhabitants in 1851 and
19,324 in 1900.

Apart from Aspatria and Flimby—where the figures
for the years 1801, 1851 and 1900 were, 327, 1123, 2885,
and 273, 555 and 2482 respectively—there was little
change in the ratio of increase in the coal mining areas.
Most places were one and a half times or twice as large in
1851 as in 1801 and twice or thrice as big in 1900 as in
1851.   But in the iron ore districts the discovery of the
Bessemer process in about 1856 caused an increased
demand for Cumberland Haematite and the coming of the
railways gave the necessary facilities for meeting it.
The result can be seen in the census returns.

	1801	1851	1900
Arlecdon ⎱	354	643	1632
Frizington ⎰			3709
Cleator Moor	362	1779	8120
Egremont ⎱	1515	2049	⎱3599
Bigrigg ⎰			⎰2162
Millom	589	980	9182
Workington	5716	6280	26143

It will be noticed that in the fifty years 1851-1900
Workington, at the former date only half as populous as
Whitehaven, had by the latter passed its neighbour and
become the second biggest town in Cumberland, largely as
a result of the building of extensive steel works.   In the
other places named, all on the edge of the western Lake
District valleys, a similar growth took place.   Eskdale
only just escaped, several veins of ore being discovered in
it and worked from 1872 to 1883; since then mercifully
nothing further has been done.[2]

It is interesting to note that in Professor Trevelyan's

VII. BARROW IN FURNESS IN 1874.

(facing p. 405)

opinion³ the greatest development in the Industrial
Revolution in the reign of George III was in the pro-
duction of iron—its result can be seen in the Black
Country of the West Midlands. In these counties the
discoveries of the earlier period caused comparatively
little change. Coal and iron mines there had been for
over a century; they increased in number but not to
such an extent as to cause any noticeable alteration in the
appearance of the countryside. Now, as the figures
quoted above shew and as the eye of the traveller can see,
the aspect of parts of the beautiful Solway shore was
changed in a generation by the sudden increase of the
local iron ore industry.

In the Furness district iron mines were discovered at
Askam in 1851 and those at Lindal developed. Then in
1859 the Haematite Iron and Steel works at Barrow were
constructed and in 1888 the Naval Armaments Company
established. The latter was absorbed by the Vickers
Maxim Company in 1897 and Barrow became famous as a
place where great warships were built. Many people
seem to think that the town ' sprang up in a night.' But
in 1836 it was described as " the principal port of Furness
for the exportation of iron ore and also visited for sea
bathing." It was still quite a small place; in 1851 the
population of Dalton and Barrow together was only just
over 4,500; ten years later this had nearly doubled and
presumably most of the increase came from Barrow. In
1871 when Barrow's population was counted separately,
this was 18,500; by 1881 it had reached 60,000. So the
really rapid growth of the town took place between these
years. It received its charter of incorporation in 1867.
The town is very well laid out and extremely healthy.⁴

In the last chapter on the Social Scene the revolutionary
effect of the Turnpike road on the lives of our ancestors
was considered; in this one not only must results from
the invention of the railway be noted but also those from

the motor car. From this latter, Carlisle, on the main road to Scotland, also benefited since all road traffic on the west side of England had to pass through it. Other towns, chiefly Penrith and Kendal also gained, especially the latter which was not on the main railway line. In both places hotels, neglected since the days of the stage coach, regained their prosperity. But for many of the smaller market towns the result has been very different. While people were limited to the pony trap and railway, the small town of the neighbourhood kept its traditional place; for the lads and lasses around, it was the weekly metropolis of pleasure. Now the journey by 'bus, car or motor-bike to one of the bigger towns became a simple matter. Thus larger places gained and smaller ones suffered. Perhaps it should also be noted that the luxurious cinemas in the bigger towns provided yet another incentive for pleasure seekers to visit them.

The car also affected the lay-out of towns. Previously people had to live within a distance of their work circumscribed by the locomotory powers of horse or railway, now motor cars and 'buses greatly increased these limits. So these years saw our towns both spreading along the main roads in so-called ribbon development and throwing out new suburbs by the erection of houses built by local councils in replacement of the slums which had been such a disgrace to Victorian England. For the Church these schemes created problems which must be obvious to all.

Now, having moved from town to suburb, let us go further afield to consider the fate of agriculture during these years. It, as well as industry, benefited from the coming of the railway. In April 1838 two wholesale egg merchants at Kendal market bought up all the eggs at 4½d. per dozen, and taking them in carts to Carlisle, put them on the railway for Newcastle for shipment to London. In September 1847 a fortnightly cattle fair was started at Kendal, followed two years later by one at Milnthorpe station to provide fat cattle for Manchester. Penrith was another centre for these fortnightly fairs. All towns, however, did not benefit; Wigton market, noted for its corn and other produce, suffered from the farmers of the Abbey Holme sending their surplus on the Silloth railway to Carlisle.

Drainage and the system of feeding sheep on turnips, combined with the introduction of superior breeds and crosses, led to the number of sheep being little short of what the commons had maintained. Cattle breeding also developed; Shorthorns became the prevalent stock, and the neighbourhood of Penrith pre-eminent for its number of high-bred ones.

Then from 1875 came a series of bad harvests and in 1879 the most famous of all wet summers. At the same time Europe was faced with a great influx of American wheat. Only Great Britain and Belgium did not put on a tariff, so the country was flooded with cheap imported wheat and its agriculture slowly ruined. But in 1880 it was said that not " a district in England could be selected where farmers and landlords have been so little ' hit ' by the prevailing agricultural depression of the last few years as the counties of Cumberland and Westmorland." There was no lack of enquiries for farms and never before had those who occupied mountain land been in a more flourishing state. Depression made itself felt, however, a year later and by 1892-3 was acute. In Cumberland land declined in value 12.6 per cent., and in Westmorland by 13.4 per cent.; the corresponding figure for England and Wales was 23.4 per cent.[5] This state of affairs continued until the war years 1914-18, when the country once more found its farmers were valuable members of society.

" The year 1870 was a turning point in educational and therefore in social history "[6]—in it the Act setting up Board Schools was passed and school attendance, until the age of thirteen, made compulsory, with State control over teachers and schools much extended. This Act was the first serious attempt by the government to grapple with the problem of national education. Previously, except for £20,000 a year distributed by the Educational Committee of the Privy Council, the money needed for buildings, staff and equipment had to be provided by voluntary subscribers.

It is astonishing what had been achieved by these means. A study of the data given by Whellan in his History of these counties, published in 1860, shews that by then most parishes and many hamlets had schools. The majority were Church ones, with the incumbent as ' governor,' in 1874 there were at least 254 of these in the diocese. There were also many others: some founded by a dissenting body such as the Friends; others for the poor—ragged schools they were called—some set up by firms for the children of their work people; or, and in the villages this was often so, set up either by some benefactor or by the community as a whole for the education of its young.

In his Pastoral Letter in 1870 Bishop Goodwin paid a striking tribute to the educational level reached in the diocese.

" I apprehend that if this diocese had been an average sample of England, the elementary Education Act would not have been passed, I do not mean to assert that the condition of elementary education throughout the diocese is all that can be wished; far from it; but still so much has been done and there is such goodwill in the diocese to do more, that it would have been quite possible to bring up, in the course of a few years, educational appliances to educational need."

These views are supported by some words of Bishop Ware who, referring in 1890 to the continuous improvement in educational facilities, said:

"no doubt it was more needed in the south of England than here in the north where there was a larger number of old endowed schools. In fact, as regards the north west of England, I doubt whether the changes of modern legislation . . . . may not have made it more difficult for the poor man's clever son to rise in the world than it was then."[6a]

It is not easy to reconcile these opinions with Professor Clapham's statement that " it was the Cumberland statesmen and small farmers of the sixties who had been most reluctant to let their children go to school; they were too useful on the farm."[7] The Act of 1870 only applied to elementary schools. Full time education, after the age covered by the Act, was still generally limited to that provided by the ancient endowed grammar schools. But our ancestors of a century ago were a self reliant race. All the larger towns had Mechanics Institutes, each with its library and its course of lectures, the prototype of the modern night school. These Institutes, started in Scotland in 1823, had spread into England, largely owing to the energy of a man of Cumberland stock, Henry 1st Lord Brougham (1778-1868). Those in these counties, with date of foundation, were: Carlisle 1824, lapsed and restarted 1833; Kendal 1824; Penrith 1830; Maryport 1844; Whitehaven 1845; Workington 1849; Wigton 1850; and Barrow ante 1860. Some towns—Carlisle had seven established between 1846-57—also had working men's reading rooms. We must not therefore think that Englishmen in those days were necessarily either illiterate or lacking in zeal for knowledge because it was not provided for them by the State.[8]

Further evidence of this zeal can be seen in the foundation in the next generation of a number of Scientific and Literary Societies which organised lectures for their members. Sometimes a course was planned with an examination at the end. In 1876 a Cumberland (Westmorland was added to the title in 1884) Association for the Advancement of Literature and Science was founded to which the various local bodies were affiliated. It issued a yearly volume of Transactions; the last in 1891-2.

State aid was extended to secondary schools by the Education Act of 1902. Of the many ancient grammar schools mentioned in earlier surveys, few have survived to rank as secondary schools to-day. Of those now recognised by the Board of Education in Cumberland: Carlisle, Keswick, Penrith and St. Bees date back to Elizabethan times or earlier; Nelson and Thomlinson Schools, Wigton and Samuel King's School, Alston represent older foundations, while Carlisle and County High School, and Brampton, Cockermouth, Millom, Whitehaven, and Workington County Secondary Schools are of more recent date. Westmorland, well endowed with grammar schools in the past and escaping industrialism in the present, has only had to provide one new school—Kendal Girls High School—to meet modern needs. Of its ancient grammar schools still surviving as such Appleby, Kendal, Kirkby Stephen, Kirkby Lonsdale and Heversham have been named in previous surveys, while Windermere, 1665, and Kelsick (Ambleside) 1721, are of later date. In North Lancashire, Ulverston Grammar School is the only old foundation surviving. There are modern secondary schools for boys and girls at Barrow. In the diocese there are also denominational secondary schools at Casterton (Anglican), Wigton (Friends) and Barrow (Roman Catholic).*

We left the Lake District fully discovered and William Wordsworth on the top of Scafell. After the opening up of new lands settlers often follow; this was so here for, as W. G. Collingwood writes in describing what he calls the Romantic settlement, " these good people, like the

---

* I have to thank G. B. Brown (Cumberland), H. C. A. Wimberley (Westmorland), and A. E. Womersley (Lancashire) for the statistics upon which this paragraph is based.

Vikings, first came on raids and then as immigrants."[9] In fact the two movements of discovery and settlement, which for convenience of arrangement have been kept separate, overlapped.

Keswick, as a place where people went to live for other reasons than earning a livelihood, has a far longer history than any other of the well known Lake District towns. The first great regattas were held on Bassenthwaite Lake in 1780 and on Derwentwater in the following years.[10] As a Cumbrian shepherd cannot be imagined organising a regatta, as a means of passing the time, it can safely be asserted that by this date Keswick and its neighbourhood had a considerable "residential" population. Some interesting letters, written five years later by a friend from Keswick to Miss Martha Irton of Irton, give a vivid picture of contemporary Lake District life. It is clear, from the names mentioned in them, that the residents in Keswick and its neighbourhood at that time were mainly of local stocks.[11]

It was not till the turn of the century that the real 'invasion' began, probably receiving its impetus from the writings of the so called Lake poets. Wordsworth, already famous, came to live at Dove Cottage, Grasmere in 1799 and the following year Coleridge settled at Keswick, where he was joined three years later by Southey. In 1834 de Quincey published his *Reminiscences of the Lake Poets* in which he described the daily life of his three famous neighbours and their coterie. Their story, and that of the many who followed them, has been often told and need not be repeated here.

By 1856 the next stage in the story of "the invasion" had begun—the settlement in the Lake District, not of poets and writers and their distinguished friends, but of ordinary men and women, who set up house in Keswick or Windermere in the same spirit as people in the south settled at Brighton or Bournemouth. Two books, one

published in 1855,[12] the other in 1864,[13] give a good picture
of the district at this time.   Miss Martineau's account of
Windermere is of great interest.   Originally the lake
village was named Bowness;   then in about 1846 the
railway company, ending their line at a hamlet called
Applethwaite, called their station Windermere, after the
Lake.   Soon there grew up around the station and running
down to Bowness, a small town, likewise called Windermere, of which it could still be said in 1855 that " the
new buildings (and all are new) are of the dark grey stone
of the region," and, Miss Martineau adds " for the most
part of a medieval style of architecture."

Behind that remark lies a story, for the moving spirit
in all this was the Rev. J. A. Addison, who " had a
passion for ecclesiastical architecture."   He was Warden
of St. Mary's College (the building itself was called St.
Mary's Abbey), a school designed to afford " a cheap and
thorough education, on sound Church principles."   It
really was a college, with a warden, subwarden, and
fellows, and a distinguished list of patrons from among
' the nobility and gentry,' with two bishops, a chancellor,
and two rural deans as well.   Pupils were divided
financially into two classes;   the sons of the clergy, who
paid 30 guineas a year, or even less, and those of the laity
who paid 50.   Not only were these ' young gentlemen '
taught classics and the usual curriculum, but also
fortification—we can almost hear in the air the thunder
of the charge of the Light Brigade—and still more, the
pupils were to be seen about the place " in a college garb
of the olden time."[14]   In its original form the college
failed, but the ideals behind it are of interest because in
them we can see the influence of William Sewell, founder
of Radley, and Nathaniel Woodard, creator of the group
of schools bearing his name.   Presumably Addison had
neither the capacity nor the capital to carry out his
ambitious plans.   If all had gone well Windermere might

to-day be the home of a great public school; a curious and almost forgotten chapter in its history.

Mr. Addison was also minister of the proprietary chapel of St. Mary's, Windermere; at least this seems implied by the following note in the *Carlisle Patriot* of 9 February 1856: " our readers are aware that the sale of this church has lately been effected by the assignees of the Rev. J. Addison to the township of Applethwaite." The church is first mentioned in a licence from the bishop of Chester of 27 September 1848, which describes it as the new church at Birthwaite in the township of Applethwaite which " has been erected." The licence was renewed at various dates, but its consecration did not take place till 8 August 1856[15]—presumably the delay was caused by its uncertain status.

Windermere was clearly beginning to flourish: there were " villas on either side the road on the way to Bowness," and the pedestrian would " pass rows of lodging-houses," and at the " port of Windermere " see the new steamboats on the lake.[16] Miss Martineau's book gives a Directory, with the occupations of the inhabitants. Thus we can get a picture of the settlement of the " invaders," and of the " progress " of the different places. The big centres of population, in terms of people marked " Esqr." in the Directory, were Windermere and Bowness, 40 such names, Ambleside, 27, Keswick 14 and Hawkshead, 10. In the number of lodging-houses the order is the same, except that Hawkshead had none. So in 1855 Windermere and Bowness were the most favoured resorts, for both the well to do resident and the tourist. Considering Keswick's long history, it is strange that for the former class Ambleside was twice as popular; as regards lodging houses, the disproportion was not so great. Of other well known places in the district: Grasmere, Coniston and Patterdale each had a few residents, but only eight lodging houses among them.

The impression given by this Directory, that the ordinary tourists' Lake District was limited to the three centres of Windermere and Bowness, Ambleside, and Keswick, is borne out by Mrs. Lynn Linton, the author of the other book mentioned. Writing of the Western lakes and valleys, she describes the walk round Loweswater as " not often taken, because so few people ever care to stay at any of these lakes," by which she means also Buttermere and Crummock. Ennerdale she calls " the least known, and, at the present time, the least likely to be visited of all the lakes."[17]

A difference between the two books is that, while both assume that most of the district will be visited on horseback or by coach, Miss Martineau in 1855 is much more definite on the perils of the high fells than Mrs. Lynn Linton in 1864. The former, for instance, in mentioning the ascent of Skiddaw by ladies on ponies, says " there must be a guide . . . once for all let us say, in all earnestness and with the most deliberate decision, that no kind of tourist should ever cross the higher passes, or ascend the moutains without a guide."[18] The latter, however, makes no mention of guides. She even relates climbing Scafell in June to see the sunrise.[19] What did she wear? It is difficult to associate the normal dress of a ' Victorian lady ' with the ascent of Scafell. She also gives details of quite a number of mountain walks; but she does describe Styhead as " terrifying—in certain aspects literally terrifying."[20] Thus it seems that fell walking, beloved by so many to-day, had become prevalent between those two dates.

About this time too, with the charms of Wastdale beginning to be appreciated, the well known " auld Willie Ritson " started to cater for tourists. But climbing in the Lake District, in the real sense of the word, does not seem to have become popular till about the eighties, though the Pillar rock had been ascended by a tourist as early as 1848 and again in 1850. Judging, however, by the reminiscences of " old Wastdalians "— " we who had the luck to be there in those early days " in the *Journal of the Fell and Rock Climbing Club*— another generation was to pass before such feats became popular and Wastdale Head the " Mecca " of the climber.[21]

In conclusion something must be said of two mechanical devices: the bicycle and the motor car. Of the former, A. G. Bradley could write, in *Highways and Byways in the Lake District*, " since the advent, however, of the blessed cycle."[22] And what a paradise for the cyclist must Lakeland have been in those days, while he still had the road to himself without any other mechanical contrivance to torment him.*

The effect of the motor car on the Lake District was two fold: since by it visitors were now enabled to reach it more easily, and by charabanc day trips were made possible for the workers in the great industrial towns of Yorkshire and Lancashire. It also meant the opening up and settlement of the incomers in the hitherto inaccessible western valleys—places previously the habitat only of farmers and shepherds becoming the holiday homes of archbishops and prelates, heads of colleges and regius professors, headmasters and other notable folk. So to-day while the aristocracy of wealth is still to be found in Windermere and Keswick, that of intellect is more likely to be discovered in Buttermere or Eskdale.

Probably the historian of the future will say that the most important developments in Lake District history in these years were the growth of the idea of National Parks, with a National Trust to preserve them, and the movement that brought about the foundation of youth

---

* ' A bicycle archdeacon ' was hinted at in 1891 (Diocesan Magazine, 11) and H. E. Campbell, archdeacon of Furness in 1905, used one in visiting his country churches.

hostels in many of the valleys. These inter-related movements really had their source in the realisation of the value to body and soul of that most economical, and yet most enjoyable of pleasures, fell walking and to the determination of kindly and far-seeing folk that some places, by being kept inviolate from their enemies, should be preserved for pedestrians.

In a book in which its *Transactions* have been so extensively used—in very truth it could not have been written without them—some account must be given of the activities of the Cumberland and Westmorland Antiquarian and Archaeological Society, which was founded on 11 September 1866. Throughout its long history it has been its good fortune to have men with the requisite gifts of leadership and scholarship ever ready to further its work. The first of these was the Rev. James Simpson, vicar of Kirkby Stephen, who was born at Lyth, Westmorland. As chairman of Council, editor, and from 1882 president, he did much to ensure the survival of the then infant Society.[23] In 1868 R. S., or Chancellor, Ferguson succeeded him as editor, and in 1870 the first volume of its *Transactions* was published by Titus Wilson of Kendal.

The chancellor's first paper in them (with Mr. C. J. Ferguson) was printed in 1868. Three years later he published *Early Cumberland and Westmorland Friends* and *Cumberland and Westmorland M.P's.* Then in 1873 he resumed his articles in the *Transactions*; between that year and 1900 he published over a hundred of these, he also edited six volumes in the *Extra Series* and five in the *Tract Series* of the Society's publications, and published *A History of the diocese of Carlisle* (1889) and histories of *Cumberland* (1890) and *Westmorland* (1894). Even this does not exhaust this extraordinary man's productivity; he was also editor of the *Cumberland* volume in the *Victoria County History* Series, to which he contributed the article on Early Man. Further, papers and reports to the Society of Antiquaries, letters to newspapers as well as other miscellaneous writings and lectures also came from him. And this vast flow of work was not the result of browsing in comfort in a well stocked library but arose from the study of original sources and unprinted manuscripts or from the excavation of unexplored remains. Surely we cannot be in error in according him a foremost place among local historians and antiquarians.

After the chancellor probably the most eminent local antiquary at this time was William Jackson of St. Bees. Though he did not print very much—he contributed some twenty articles to the *Transactions*—he was a great compiler of pedigrees, who pursued the ramifications of a family's descent with almost bewildering zeal. He was also an assiduous collector of books, prints, autographs, etc., relating to these counties, which, with the manuscripts containing his pedigrees, he bequeathed in 1890 to the proposed new library at Carlisle.

The years we are considering may indeed be called the heyday of the amateur historian. The sources of local history were almost untapped, the field of archaeology ungleaned. Above all in the secure and leisured life of Victorian England there were many who had not only the zeal and knowledge but also opportunity for research and study. Thus the chancellor, though he towered above his contemporaries, was not a lone figure. During these years membership of the Society steadily increased: a list of names was first printed in Volume III (1877-8); it showed an original membership of 49 men which had increased to 198 men and 33 women at the date of publication. In the last volume edited by the chancellor, XVI (1900), the number of members was given as 420.

Upon Ferguson's death in 1900 Henry Ware, bishop of Barrow-in-Furness, became president of the Society and W. G. Collingwood, editor of the *Transactions*. The

Society was indeed fortunate in its third editor, who was
to hold that position alone until 1920, and jointly with his
son, R. G. Collingwood, until 1925. He brought the
Society's yearly volume up to a new standard, both in
text and illustrations, with a cover designed by himself
and, above all, an index which he also compiled. In
addition to six historical novels, depicting life in our
district, he wrote more than sixty articles for the
Transactions, on much varied subjects, including the two
very important inventories of local historical remains.
His *Lake Counties* and *Lake District History* are local
classics, so is his monumental *Northumbrian Crosses*; he
also edited three of the volumes published under the
Society's auspices.   Other places which benefited from
his work include the neighbouring county societies of
Yorkshire and Dumfriesshire.

Dr. Ware was succeeded in the presidency by T. H.
Hodgson (1909-15) who with his gifted wife had been for
many years the chief local member on the Cumberland
Excavation Committee. On his resignation, Professor
F. J. Haverfield, a scholar of Roman antiquities with an
international reputation, was elected. After his death
in 1919 the editor, W. G. Collingwood, became president;
in which office he was followed by his son, another Roman
scholar of great repute.   He was also editor, with T. H. B.
Graham and W. T. McIntire, for the years 1926-34.   The
standard of the work of these men, with that of F. G.
Simpson, on the Roman remains in our district invites
comparison with the best of a similar kind in this or any
other country and has indeed earned the Society an
international reputation.   In a diocesan history it seems
right that the names of H. Brierley and Colonel J. F.
Haswell, who have between them transcribed over
thirty volumes in the Society's parish register section,
should be mentioned.

Canon James Wilson, vicar of Dalston, who succeeded

Chancellor Ferguson in the editorship of the *Cumberland Victoria County History*, must rank for his work on these volumes among the more eminent of our local historians. What has already been said about the *Transactions* is equally true of the editor's contributions to these volumes—if they had not been written the present writer's work could not have been accomplished. Wilson's own contributions were the articles on the Ecclesiastical history, the monastic houses, and the Political history. He also wrote a history of *Rose Castle,* and edited the *Chartulary of St. Bees.* He contributed some thirty articles to the *Transactions*, but an unfortunate difference of opinion with the editor over the publication of Gospatric's Charter caused him to send much of his later work elsewhere.

For the historically minded another outstanding event of these years is the opening, on 8 November 1893, of Tullie House, Carlisle. The building, menaced with destruction, was saved by Chancellor Ferguson and his brother and purchased by public subscription for presentation to the Corporation of Carlisle, which at a cost of over £20,000 added two wings and cleared the site of outbuildings, leaving, however, the original house, with its pleasant garden, intact. Within it are contained not only the Public Library and a Museum, with a large collection of local antiquities including many Roman and Medieval remains, but the Bibliotheca Jacksoniana, consisting of a collection of books and manuscripts dealing with the history of these counties, the nucleus of which was the bequest, already mentioned, of William Jackson, to the city of Carlisle.

CHAPTER II.

THE MODERN DIOCESE.

O N the death of Bishop Percy the ancient diocese of
Carlisle passed away. The Commissioners had
included in their report of 1836 a recommendation

" that the Sees of Carlisle and Sodor and Man be united, and that
the diocese consist of the present diocese of Carlisle, of those parts
of Cumberland and Westmorland which are now in the diocese
of Chester, of the deanery of Furness and Cartmel in the county
of Lancaster, of the parish of Aldeston now in the diocese of
Durham and of the Isle of Man."*

The two latter suggestions were not carried out. The
remainder of the scheme duly became law by an Order in
Council of 10 August 1847, with a proviso that it was not
to come into effect without Bishop Percy's consent which
was not given. The area now added to the diocese was
still divided into its four medieval deaneries of Coupland,
Kendale, Furness and Cartmel, and Lonsdale, having
respectively 46, 33, 37 and 8 parishes or parochial
chapelries; an addition of 124 parishes to the 142 already
in it.[1]

Henry Montagu Villiers† was consecrated on 13 April
1856 in Whitehall Chapel by Archbishop Musgrave of
York.[2] Owing to the shortness of his episcopate, he had

---

* The provision for the island's transfer was made without the knowledge
of the bishop, William Ward, who was then almost blind. He at once set to
work to save his see, and his efforts hastened his end. The provision was
repealed in 1838, immediately after his death. (Dict. of English Ch. History,
Ollard and Crosse, 348).

† George Moore used all his influence to obtain the see for Dr. Tait, the
dean. It was during this vacancy that he lost five of his daughters from

little chance of getting to grips with the problems of his diocese. But the appointment of an archdeacon of Westmorland in May 1856 and the division of the diocese into eighteen rural deaneries in January 1858 made a start with the necessary replanning. One thing that must be deplored is that when the ancient deanery of Coupland was divided into three, its title was dropped. Its name, which went back to a time before the county of Cumberland was formed, had only survived in that of the deanery which had thus a peculiarly historical significance. Is it too much to hope that some day it will be revived?

The bishop was a strong Evangelical and a disciplinarian. In 1857 the incumbent of Wythop was suspended because the duties of the cure were inadequately performed and the incumbents of Newton Arlosh and Eskdale forbidden to exercise their functions for several years on a charge of habitual drunkenness. Next year the rector of Great Orton, found guilty of simony, was deprived of his living; the patron losing his turn.[3]

George Moore, the Cumberland philanthropist, said of the bishop: " his powers of preaching are great.* I think him the most large-hearted Christian gentleman I ever knew. He is also very honest and straight-forward in his opinions." He also refers to his great interest in education.† Mr. Moore also mentions getting a letter from him: " To my astonishment I find . . . that he has

scarlet fever—the window in the north transept of the cathedral is their memorial. It is supposed that it was largely because of this loss that he was offered, at the suggestion of Queen Victoria, the see of London (*Archibald Campbell Tait*, Davidson and Benham, 187). He was succeeded as dean by Francis Close, " whose character had preceded him to Carlisle as a violent Low Churchman, and whose appointment caused a stir among the clergy of the diocese, who were for the most part of the High Church party." (*Memorials of Dean Close*, 28). Villiers was the 5th son of the Hon. George Villiers. When his brother became 8th earl of Clarendon he was raised to the rank of an earl's son.

* He " especially appealed as a preacher to the poor. No minister in London was more popular than Villiers." (*D.N.B.*).

† George Moore shared this interest. The George Moore Educational Trust was founded in his memory.

in his diocese 11 livings under £50 a year; 9 under £60; 16 under £70; 26 under £80; 21 under £90; 35 under £100; that is 118 clergymen with an average income of £83 a year." He held a meeting to ventilate this matter and sending the money raised to the bishop, received this answer: " in two cases during this present week your present has enabled me to help poor clergy; and I do believe that I have carried essential comfort to homes which I really could not have done without your kind assistance. I cannot help letting you share the pleasure."[4]

On 24 August 1860, Dr. Villiers was translated to Durham.* He died on 9 August 1861.† He married Amelia Maria, eldest daughter of William Hulton of Hulton Park, Lancashire. One of his sons, of the same name, was vicar of St. Paul's, Knightsbridge, London and a well known High Churchman.[5] Perhaps the best tribute to his memory is to be found in the words of George Moore quoted above.

Samuel Waldegrave,‡[6] was consecrated on 11 November 1860 in York Minster by Archbishop Longley and others. His Charges at his three Visitations, 1861-4-7, give a good picture of the state of the diocese. In the first the bishop stressed the need of more support for ' Foreign Missions.' Out of 267 parishes, 57 gave £614. 11. 5. to S.P.G., and

* S. Baring-Gould in *The Church Revival*, p. 183, states that he gave the living of Houghton le Skerne, worth £1,300 a year, to his son-in-law named Cheese. " This provoked a cartoon in *Punch*. A poor needy parson is shewn by a table, whereon stands a Stilton Cheese, and the bishop is decanting over it a bottle of port, labelled £1300, and saying: ' I am exceedingly sorry, dear brother in the church, but you see I have not a drop for you, I have poured it all into my Cheese ' " . . . " it is said that this cartoon so wounded Bishop Villiers that it led to his death." Was it this action that Bishop Waldegrave was thinking of when he said " true it is that his warm affections may at times have betrayed him into actions of doubtful expediency? " (*Primary Visitation* of 1861).

† " Our contemporary the *Carlisle Patriot*, possibly by the aid of some spirit rapping medium, announced the death of the Right Reverend Prelate 4 or 5 hours before it took place." (*Carlisle Journal*, 13 August 1861).

‡ He was the second son of William, 8th earl Waldegrave.

116 £1151. 6. 4. to C.M.S. In February 1862, the bishop
founded the 'Church and Parsonage Building and
Benefice Association.'* At his second Visitation he was
able to report that £4,638. 9. 7 had been subscribed and 9
new churches and 16 new parsonages built and 13 livings
augmented. But there were still 47 villages without a
church; 51 livings with no parsonage and 96 benefices
under £100 a year and 64 under £150. Of the clergy
ordained since 1860, 22 were University men, 26 had been
to a theological college and 12 had been to neither. Of
the 33 university men ordained by Bishop Villiers only 10
remained, of the 22 literates only 3; the rest had gone
south in search of better pay. 50 parishes had no
parochial collections, " or if so only to meet some such
local want as the purchase of a harmonium." The
third visitation gives further statistics shewing the
poverty of the clergy.

The following letters (in the Hudleston MSS.) from the
Bishop to A. F. Hudleston, who had just succeeded to the
Fleming lands, are of interest for the light they throw on
the former's character and ideals. The first, of 29
April 1861, explains itself.

" You will, I trust, not deem me intrusive if I venture to
express to you the interest I feel in the recent dealings of our God
with you. To succeed to property is at all times a matter for
serious reflection on the responsibilities which that property
involves. You have already proved in the possession of another
heritage that you appreciate and would endeavour to discharge
these responsibilities. May grace be continued and encreased to
you—so that the owner of Rydal may be even better known than
the owner of Hutton John as the helper and succourer of all who
are engaged whether at home or abroad in carrying the Truth as
it is in Jesus to the doors of the sinners for whom He died. But
I cannot forget that Rydal brings with it the responsibility of
patronage. May you be helped so to exercise that patronage as
to be the honoured instrument of causing the lake of Windermere
to share the privileges which once belonged to the lake of Galilee,

* Now called the Carlisle Diocesan Church Extension Society.

the privileges of hearing the Gospel preached to the poor by those whom we may truly call Christ's representatives—for where a faithful minister of His comes there He comes himself.

Pardon me, dear Sir, so nearly a stranger for thus writing—but I feel constrained to do so—nor shall I write alone I will, God helping me, pray for you."

The remaining letters shew the circumstances under which C. D. Bell became vicar of Ambleside in July 1861.

4 June 1861.

" I think it right to tell you, in confidence, that a most serious charge—that of open drunkenness—has been brought against the incumbent of Ambleside.   I have given him a few days to consider and consult whether he had better quietly retire and cut short all proceedings by resignation or abide the result of a commission . . ."

18 June

" The good people of Ambleside are like a flock of sheep; signing a memorial in favour of . . .   But universal experience is that such memorials are of little value.   We must act as we feel to be for the best—for the people and place and, if our gracious God guide us as I trust he will, they will soon acknowledge that we have done rightly.   The more I hear of Mr. Bell, the more satisfied I am that if he take it he will prove the right man."

28 June

" I am much concerned to say that (the late vicar) seems resolved to stay on at Ambleside in the house which has hitherto been occupied by the incumbent of that place. . .   The owner of that house is, I gather from his letters, much disappointed at the post having been conferred on Mr Bell instead of on . . .   Can you suggest any plan by which Mr Bell may be provided with a temporary home so that he may have an opportunity of making himself known at Ambleside.   When once that has been accomplished the good people, if any there be, who now wish to frighten him away, will be ashamed of themselves for what they have attempted to do."

Dr. Waldegrave's " rule was on strictly evangelical lines, and the clergy who differed from him in opinions or practices were resolutely discountenanced."[7] He objected to harvest festivals:

" to introduce choral services, and as it would seem surpliced processions into our mountain valleys, is, to say the least, an innovation. To do so in direct contravention of the well known opinions and wishes of the bishop, to whom you have sworn obedience, is something more. If that choral service is accompanied by any peculiar ceremonies, even in a modified degree, of harvest celebrations such as have recently occupied so much public attention, the matter is still worse."

So wrote the bishop to the vicar of Woodland, sending a copy to a neighbour of the incumbent with the request that he would make the contents known and prevent all whom he could influence from attending the service.[8] But " there were few churches in his diocese where he did not preach, either on a Sunday or weekday. He would now and then spend a week in going from place to place, preaching in one of his churches each succeeding evening."[9] During his episcopate 34 new churches were consecrated,* some 30 others restored; 36 new parsonages were erected and the same number of benefices increased in value. The Church Extension Society raised £15,955 to help these works. The bishop increased the number of Confirmation Services and held them in more places than had hitherto been the custom. In 1862 he confirmed 3970 candidates at 25 places in the archdeaconry of Westmorland; in 1863 in the Carlisle archdeaconry the figures were 2968 and 30 respectively. He started the Diocesan Calendar in 1867; it has continued ever since.[10]

He supported Lord Shaftesbury in his efforts to legislate against ritualism. " The revival of Tractarianism, in a new and more popular guise, alarmed him profoundly and it is well known that apprehension, lest the revival of Catholicism should make headway in his own diocese, harassed his mind to a degree which was possible only in the case of a very sensitive and conscientious man."[11] He spoke in the House of Lords

* Appendices vii and viii.

against judicial and corporate officials being allowed to
wear their insignia of office in places of worship of any
denomination; vigorously opposed all attempts to relax
the law of Sunday Observance; voted against the
disestablishment of the Irish Church;[12] and with six
other English bishops absented himself, on principle,
from the first Lambeth Conference in 1867.[13]

He was taken seriously ill in the winter of 1868-9. In
February 1869 a commission was granted to Bishop
David Anderson, previously bishop of Rupertsland, to
perform episcopal functions in the diocese and in March
this was extended to " all acts belonging to the office of
bishop of Carlisle."[14] Dr. Waldegrave died at Rose on
1 October 1869 and was buried in the cathedral churchyard; an altar tomb with a recumbent effigy in white
marble was erected in the south aisle of the cathedral.
He married Jane Ann, daughter of Francis Pym of the
Hasells, Bedfordshire and had issue. Several incidental
tributes reveal his character. " After Villiers was
succeeded by good Bishop Waldegrave, I overheard the
incumbents of two churches speaking of the characteristics
of the two bishops; "with Bishop Waldegrave," said
Mr. Marshall, " I feel that I am in the company of a
friend; but in the presence of Villiers I felt frozen."[15]
" Bishop Villiers and Bishop Waldegrave," wrote Mr.
James Cropper of Ellergreen, " were both excellent
leaders, and the latter so earnest and so sanctified, if I
may use the term."[16]

Here a pause must be made for the story of a remarkable man and a great spiritual movement. Francis Close,
dean of Carlisle, had previously been vicar of Cheltenham
where his ministry was so much blessed that he is said
to have received more than 1500 pairs of embroidered
slippers from his female admirers.

The book, from which the above statement is taken[17] is
entitled *Memorials of Dean Close*, edited by " one who

knew him." The writer, a low Church man like the dean, brings out fully his great powers as a preacher, his extensive charity, his noble work for the Cumberland Infirmary and the high place he held in the life of the city and in the hearts of many of its inhabitants.* [18] Yet, running through the book is another note as when the author writes of "that self will by which Francis Close was often impelled to domineer and lord it over others, while he could bear no restraint nor interference with himself."

An example of this was seen soon after he became dean for, in 1858, he quarrelled with the precentor, who had altered an anthem without his authority; a lawsuit resulted in the dean's defeat. *The Times* made somewhat caustic comment on what it calls his "rather sharp work" concluding with "he evidently now believes in the Divine authority of Deans. Obey those who have the rule over you—and remember that the Dean has the rule over you, and that I am the Dean."[19]

The Times once referred to him as "the Pope of Cheltenham." Like often has an antipathy to like, so Dean Close hated, with a bitterness exceeding all his other hates, that other pope, who dwelt at Rome. But what is so curious is that he could condemn the "popery (that) in every form, political, civil, ecclesiastical, has ever been, and is still, the deadly and destructive enemy of civil and religious liberty,"[20] and yet be the chief agent in sending to prison a poor lecturer named Holyoake who publicly proclaimed his disbelief in God, for exercising that same liberty.[21]

No one could wax more eloquent on "those two lovely twins civil and religious liberty" or preach more movingly on the "thesis that Popery is destructive of Civil and

* "For his earnest eloquence as a preacher and his unwearing advocacy of Church expansion, temperahce, foreign missions, and other philanthropic agencies, he deserves a grateful recognition."

Religious Liberty " than the dean,[22] but when Charles Bradlaugh asked for liberty to affirm instead of taking the usual oath, then the dean had indeed much to say about that " blaspheming infidel,"

> " if those fools, as Scripture called them, who said in their hearts ' there is no God,' said it only in their hearts, they did not wish to meddle with them. Let them have their own liberty; let them choose their own path to perdition; but if their wicked lips spoke the same—if they write, and print and circulate the same—if they flash it in the face of Christian people—if they blast and pollute them with stuff of the most degrading kind—religious liberty ceased to be liberty in that case, and the Christian religion could not tolerate it,"[23]

yet these words were uttered by the same lips that said " despotism is Popery—Liberty is Protestantism."[24] To the dean liberty apparently only meant liberty to agree with Francis Close, all else was licence.*   Narrow indeed was the path to be trod if the wrath of this decanal " Mr. Barrett of Wimpole Street " was to be avoided and the bounds of his charity not over passed. Even then it is a little surprising to find the Salvation Army one of the subjects of his castigation. " I have no doubt," he wrote to the *Record* in July 1882, " that the movement originated in a desire to do good, but Satan has prevailed to make it a great organ of mischief."[25]

Some of his statements are indeed remarkable, for, as the author of the " *Memorials* " said, " when he rode his persecuting hobby he was not exact in his sayings." " Between drink and tobacco the whole country reels to and fro like a drunken man " is almost humorous. So, in its ludicrous overstatement, is " there is not a greater curse in Europe than the British racecourse." Most people at least hope that there has been some progress

---

* This attitude seems to have been characteristic of ' eminent Victorians.' Dr. Arnold " believed in toleration, too, within limits; that is to say, in the toleration of those with whom he agreed. ' I would give James Mill as much opportunity for advocating his opinion,' he said, ' as is consistent with a voyage to Botany Bay.' " (*Eminent Victorians*, Lytton Strachey, new ed., 191).

between the time of the Judges and the present day; not so Dean Close " if the government of Victoria was not the same as the government of Joshua it was nearly so." But the most astounding statement of all is perhaps this: " the more a man is advanced in human knowledge, the more is he opposed to religion and the more deadly enemy is he to the truth of God."[26]

Wilson describes Close as belonging " to the straitest sect of militant Protestantism."[27] But some deeper explanation is needed to explain the extraordinary vehemence of his language and the wide range of his hates. The clue perhaps lies in that strange statement quoted above identifying the government of Queen Victoria with that of Joshua, since it suggests that to the dean the days of the Judges were the time when human rule most nearly approached his ideal. That is, as the deity of the dean's golden age smote, it is alleged, the Amorite, the Canaanite, the Hittite, the Perizzite, the Hivite and the Jebusite, so his servant of Victorian days likewise smote Papists, High Churchmen, drinkers of alcohol, smokers, Salvationists and atheists. But the result, alas, was often the exact opposite to that intended. " The vehemence of his denunciation served to propagate the principles he condemned."[28] The moral is obvious, temperance in language is as necessary a virtue as temperance in the use of alcohol or tobacco.

It is pleasant to turn from the negative and denunciatory Old Testament Protestantism of Dean Close to a great piece of evangelistic work which, though it has cast its influence on men and women from all over the world, owed its inauguration to a priest of this diocese and takes its name from a place within it.

The Keswick Convention,[29] was begun in 1875 by Canon Harford-Battersby, vicar of St. John's, Keswick. Passing through a remarkable spiritual change at an Oxford Conference, he was moved to start something of a similar

kind in his own parish.   In this he was helped by Robert
Wilson, of Broughton Grange, near Cockermouth, a
member of the Society of Friends.   At first it met with
some hostility not from High Churchmen but from certain
evangelical stalwarts.   " Most of them had bad tempers
and when they were assured that God could give victory
over their bad tempers, they angrily cried " sinless
perfection."[30]   But the opposition faded away before the
evidence of the Divine blessing in the fruits of holiness
and the converts to missionary labours that resulted from
the early meetings.   The first convention was attended
by some 400 people; as years passed the numbers
averaged about 5000.

" The fundamental aim and object of the Keswick Convention
from its commencement was the promotion of holiness and not the
development of new Christian enterprises.   Character, and not
service, was the aim held closely before all who spoke and heard
at those meetings.   What we were intended to be, and not what
we were called to do, was the prominent thought in the whole
Convention.   We did not profess to meet in order to develop the
fullest Christian activities, but to develop the highest possible
Christian character."[31]

The next bishop was Harvey Goodwin, dean of Ely.
The speed with which the see was filled is remarkable.
Bishop Waldegrave died on 1 October 1869; on the 10th
Mr. Gladstone wrote to his proposed successor, who was
consecrated on 29 November in York Minster by Archbishop Thomson and publicly enthroned on 15 December.
Before Bishop Waldegrave's time this ceremony had
generally been done by proxy; he insisted upon being
personally enthroned but the public were not admitted.

The new bishop, the son and grandson of a solicitor,
came from a different social stratum to his predecessors.
He was also of a different type of Churchmanship.   Even
before his nomination fears of a change had been expressed; George Moore had written to the prime minister
mentioning them.   Mr James Cropper, writing after

Bishop Goodwin's death, states that he had heard that a bishop of ' the Percy Type ' was to be appointed and feared the result.[32]

I. ADMINISTRATOR.

" His chief work for the diocese of Carlisle was not the starting of new machinery. But it fell to the lot of the bishop to be, what he was once described by the bishop of London as being in regard to the Church House Scheme, the fly wheel to harmonise, steady and unify the machine."[33] But Bishop Goodwin did start much new machinery in the diocese.

His first important step was the formation of a diocesan conference; its first meeting was held in the Fratry in August 1870. It then embraced a goodly number of ex-officio members, both clerical and lay, with three clergy, one the rural dean and three laymen from each deanery. At the same time ruridecanal chapter meetings were inaugurated. The conference met yearly in Carlisle for two days; and very lively discussions they had. The ruridecanal meetings also had their subjects, generally three in number, to debate.

Bishop Goodwin was a great believer in the value of the written word. At Christmas a pastoral letter was sent to all the clergy surveying the work of the past year: confirmations, how they were to be conducted, the position and value of lay readers, the place of the diocesan conference and ruridecanal meeting, the movement for elementary education, behaviour in church, singing in church, the practice of family prayer, a plan for an album of photographs of churches and for a day of missionary supplication—were among the many matters he wrote about.

Once every three years a visitation of the diocese was held and a Charge to clergy and churchwardens put forth and printed. That of 1872* was divided into three sections: I. matters arising out of replies to Visitation Articles which the bishop had sent out: (*a*) difficulty with regard to burial of non-conformists, (*b*) frequency of administration of the sacrament of the Lord's Supper, (*c*) average number of communicants, (*d*) young persons confirmed coming to Holy Communion, (*e*) preparation of young parishioners for Holy Communion, (*f*) parishioners joining in Church Service, (*g*) Collections of hymns used, (*h*) maintenance of fabric and services, (*i*) average attendance at day schools and sunday schools, (*j*) Foreign and Home Missions, (*k*) use of new Tables of Lessons, (*l*) use of surplice, (*m*) celebration of Ascension Day: II. Points connected with diocesan arrangements: (*a*) Diocesan Conference and organisation, (*b*) Church Extension Society, (*c*) Elementary Education; III. Matters of Public interest: (*a*) The Bennett Judgment, (*b*) the Athanasian creed; IV. Conclusion: V. Appendix and notes. The whole takes up 72 pages of print. The Charge to the dean and chapter at the visitation of the cathedral, the first to be held since 1753, was equally

* The following statistics from this volume are of some interest:

(1) Methods of Parochial Finance.

Expenses defrayed by Church Rate	in	43	parishes
,, Voluntary Church Rate		44	,,
,, Offertory		41	,,
,, Endowment or fund		11	,,
,, House to House collections ..		13	,,
,, Pew Rents		14	,,
,, Clergyman and friends		6	,,
,, Offertory, combined with rate or collection		30	,,
,, Voluntary subscriptions and Collection		67	,,

(2) Missionary Societies supported.

S.P.G.	in	15	parishes
C.M.S.	,,	29	,,
A.C.S.	,,	3	,,
C.P.A.S.	,,	2	,,
Bible Society	,,	4	,,
Sermons and meetings for various Societies	,,	113	,,
Nothing is reported as being done	,,	108	,,

thorough: the statutes under which the foundation was governed were reviewed and the lack of residences for the minor canons noted, so also was the fact that they took occasional duty outside the cathedral; the anomaly of lay clerks filling the part of deacon and sub-deacon was investigated; the need for moral and religious instruction of the choristers was stressed, and the state of the cathedral school considered satisfactory; the oath that the ' poor men ' of the foundation had to take was examined, likewise the way the duties of the precentor and sacrist were carried out; the value of a personal visitation by the chapter of their lands and the care of the cathedral library was also mentioned. The whole occupied 20 pages.

The bishop held seven visitations of the diocese and four of the cathedral during his episcopate. These did not consist merely of the clergy and churchwardens having to listen to the bishop's Charge but included a conference, both clergy and laity being invited to join in the discussion.

The bishop's methods of arranging Confirmations may be seen by taking the years 1880-3 as examples. In 1880 they were held in the archdeaconry of Carlisle, between February and April and in September, at 47 different churches at 11 a.m. or 3 p.m. 1881 was a visitation year, so there was no confirmation tour, but services were held in most of the large towns. In 1882 the archdeaconry of Westmorland had its turn during March and August, and services took place at 36 different centres at the same times as in 1881, except that one was as late as 4 p.m. In 1883 it was Carlisle's turn again, but the bishop expressed his willingness to have a service at any town in the other archdeaconry.[34]

In 1870 the number of rural deaneries was increased to twenty, but in 1882 reduced to nineteen.[35] A more important piece of reorganisation was the creation of a

2F

new archdeaconry of Furness in 1884; it included that
district and the southern part of Coupland. At the same
time some parishes from the deanery of Keswick were
transferred from the archdeaconry of Carlisle to that of
Westmorland.[86] In 1887 a layman, R. S. Ferguson, was
appointed to succeed Chancellor Burton* and the right
of visitation restored to the archdeacons.[37]

Two years later the bishop nominated his son-in-law,
Canon Ware as his suffragan. Behind this appointment
lies a strange story. In 1888 the bishop of Ripon
wished to have a suffragan in his diocese. Being
limited in the choice of a title by the Act of Henry
VIII, authorising such assistant bishops, he chose Penrith, being unaware that the town named was probably
Pentruth in Wales.† So Bishop Goodwin procured the
passing of " the Suffragan Nomination Act," which
enabled titles for such prelates to be taken from places
other than those named by Henry VIII; thus the bishop
suffragan of Penrith was able to change his title, choosing
Richmond in his own diocese. Meanwhile the bishop of
Carlisle seems to have reflected that there was something
to be gained by an ageing diocesan with an unwieldly
diocese having one for himself. So the modern town of
Barrow in Furness gave a title to a bishop and the see of
Carlisle had its first suffragan.[38]

While some of the chief diocesan organisations had been
started before Bishop Goodwin's episcopate, many can be
dated from his time. Of those of a devotional or more
moral nature, the Church of England Temperance Society
was started in the diocese in 1874,[39] the Girls' Friendly
Society and the Diocesan Sunday School Union in 1878,[40]
and an Association for Preventive and Rescue work in
1883. In his Pastoral Letter of 1870 the bishop expressed

---

* For the story of how the chancellor had usurped the archdeacon's functions
see V.C.H. ii 119-20 and Charge of 1887.
    † p. 219.

his willingness to licence lay readers, many of whom are now so invaluable to the clergy in their work.[41] In 1875 a Clerical Training Fund was formed to assist men preparing for Holy Orders.[42] One of the great events of Bishop Goodwin's day was Diocesan Sunday, first observed in 1878; upon it every parish was asked to have a collection which was given in turn to various diocesan societies.[43] The bishop was keenly interested in overseas missions, almost every year his pastoral letter contained some reference to them: in 1873 a Missionary Students' Fund was started and an Annual Day of Prayer for Missionary Work first kept.[44] A Diocesan Magazine was started in 1890, its purpose was very much that of the Diocesan Gazette to-day.[45]

But the really great new work of this episcopate was in church building; its record is indeed astounding. The bishop claimed in his Charge in 1890 that during the twenty one years of his episcopate 67 churches had been built, rebuilt, or restored in the archdeaconry of Carlisle, 42 in that of Westmorland and 27 in that of Furness; in all 136. These figures agree with the list in the official returns printed in Appendix XI. But the return only dates from 1873, whereas this episcopate began in 1869. The bishop's register shews that between 1869-73 a further 16 new churches or chapels were built and old ones rebuilt or restored; it also gives the names of some half dozen chapels built and not included in the official return. The total number therefore was at least 158. The official records give the cost of building at £139,803. 14. 7 and of restoration at £169,507. 4. 4, adding £41,334. 2. 10 for the extra churches we get £350,645. 1. 9, as the grand total. But the bishop was still not satisfied; almost his last piece of diocesan business was to attend a meeting to consider the need for mission rooms and more church accommodation.[46]

One of the new churches was St. Mary's, Carlisle,

consecrated in 1870: St. Mary's was the mother parish of the city;* its church, however, had always been the cathedral nave. Now the parishioners were evicted; though the dean and chapter built them this new church within the abbey precincts. So the opportunity was missed of rebuilding the nave and thus solving the problem of space that necessitated the removal of the parish congregation by restoring the mother church to its original size. Many cathedrals to-day have a nave altar with its appointments. But in Carlisle this custom would have existed with an unbroken tradition of over eight centuries behind it.

Another memorable event in Church extension was the consecration of four churches, dedicated to the four evangelists, at Barrow in Furness on 22 November 1879. They were only meant to be temporary buildings, permanent structures were expected soon to be erected but, except in one case, this has not happened.†

II. SHEPHERD.

A. THE CLERGY.

Rawnsley, describing the state of the diocese when Bishop Goodwin came to it, paints a sombre picture of the morals and educational standard of the clergy. Indeed the bishop in 1889 mentioned " a famous article on them that appeared in a Review years ago, based upon truth but spiced to suit the public taste." It was said

---

* *Nicolson and Burn* (II, 246), state that St. Cuthbert's is " the first and more ancient " of the parish churches of Carlisle, but until the Commonwealth the mayor and corporation had their pew in St. Mary's (o.s. vii, 315); the city's ancient fair time was the feast of the Assumption of Our Lady and fifteen days after (N. & B., II, 240); and the fourteenth century seal of the corporation had the Blessed Virgin as its central figure. These three facts taken together shew, it is believed conclusively, that the patron saint of the city was Our Lady, the Blessed Virgin Mary, and her church the principal one within it.

† St. John's was rebuilt as one of the octo-centenary churches.

VIII. ESKDALE VICARAGE IN 1884.

A nineteenth century relic of the days before the age of Reform.

" that there is one great and unpleasant difficulty in the diocese and that is the prevalence of intemperance among the clergy. Many of them are not graduates of any university and in consequence lack general culture and refinement . . . there yet remained the old complete separation between the so-called country gentry and the clergy. The latter were too poor to buy books; they possessed no means of going beyond the bounds of their parishes, except on foot, or by a possible lift in a market cart. The clergymen were still thrown upon the farm for social intercourse."[47]

How far was this true?   With regard to the educational standard of the clergy exact statistics can be given.   In 1868, 56.1 per cent. were university graduates, 6.4 had been to a theological college and 37.5 had no stated educational qualification.[48]   Therefore the assertion that the local clergy " were generally unlearned and little above the farmers" is obviously an exaggeration.   Considering the zealousness of Bishop Goodwin's predecessors and the amount of church building and restoration that took place,* it is difficult to believe that the clergy's moral and professional standards were really so indifferent.   In those days even at Oxford and Cambridge strange survivals of Georgian eccentricity lingered on into the era of Victorian respectability; doubtless the same thing happened sometimes in the remote valleys of the Lake District.

Bishop Goodwin's methods of dealing with these problems were very practical.   In 1890, he claimed that whereas in 1869 the average stipend was £206, in 1883 it had risen to £250, dropping, however, to £238 in 1889. Since 1869, 78 parsonage houses had been built, rebuilt, or improved.†   Opportunities of the clergy meeting

---

* As the Church Extension Society was not founded till 1864, most of this must have been done by the incumbents and their parishioners unaided.

† His Charge in 1890 contains these prophetic words " I confess that if I have any anxious feeling concerning parsonages, it is rather with respect to their excellence and their beauty, and the expense of living in them implied by these qualities, than to the cases in which they are wanting.   Much as one delights in the thought of the clergy being housed in a manner befitting their

each other for mutual discussion were provided by the ruri-decanal chapters and meetings. But above all there must have been the feeling—and no one who reads his pastoral letters at Christmas can doubt it—that in the bishop the clergy had a friend. A charming illustration of this is afforded in his Pastoral Letter of 1886:[49] he was very short sighted, he mentioned this fact on his first coming into the diocese and asked that if he passed people without recognising them it should be attributed to his infirmity not to unkindness or caprice. Apparently some, forgetting this, had been offended, so he mentions the matter again and begs " to make petition to the clergy now, as I did then, not to take offence, when as I can assure them on the word of an honest man, no offence is intended." The bishop's care for his clergy also shewed itself in his appeal to the laity in 1888 for a fund to enable the poorer ones to take a holiday. Thus the " Harvey Goodwin Rest Fund " was started. Evidence of the bishop's popularity is afforded by the fact that even before the scheme was made public £2500, out of the £3000 he asked for, had been provided.

B. Church Life.

The various Charges and Pastoral Letters issued by the bishop shew clearly the great interest he took in the due observance of the rites and ceremonies of the Church. In his Charge to the dean and chapter in 1890, the bishop mentioned that some years ago " I thought it would be an impressive solemnity if each bishop should upon one

---

habits and their recognised social position, I cannot but feel that in some cases a large house, built in an ornamental style, may become a heavy burden upon a slender income. I would wish that in not a few instances the purse of the incumbent, rather than the glory of the architect, had been manifestly the first consideration. But it is no use to cry over shed milk, and it is equally useless to grieve over expensive parsonages already erected; nevertheless I should like to put it on record, in case the next generation of clergy should feel themselves hardly used, that a warning voice was uttered by myself upon more occasions than one, and I may add generally uttered in vain." (p. 11).

great day of the year—say Whit Sunday, a festival so connected with the thought of baptism in early times—administer the Holy Sacrament of Baptism in his cathedral church to such children as should be brought to him to be baptized."[50] His directions about Confirmation shew the great importance he attached to its reverent administration: candidates were to be confirmed two at a time, an innovation in this diocese, as this method would " bring each individual candidate into more intimate and personal contact with him who ministered the ordinance."[51] These directions were revised in 1885 and again in 1887.[52]

The connection between this service and the reception of the Holy Communion was stressed.[53] The bishop continuously emphasised the importance* of this sacrament. While he did not disguise the fact that his ideal was the due observance of the scriptural and apostolic custom of a celebration every Lord's Day, for the present, however " monthly celebrations appears to me to be the least that we ought to tolerate."[54] In 1884 the bishop was able to write of the list giving statistics as to the frequency of celebrations that " it at least shows that the scandal of quarterly communions is very nearly obliterated," but he adds " I wish I could say as much of the scandal connected with neglect of the Lord's Table on the part of the parishioners."[55]

The bishop held strong views about kneeling. In his Pastoral Letter of 1870 he wrote that people " seem to me to be sadly defective in the matter of kneeling; the habit

---

* Statistics of celebrations of Holy Communion from the bishop's charges:

	1872		1881		1890	
Weekly and oftener	in 10 churches	in	22 churches	in	57 churches	
More than monthly	,, 19	,,	,, 47	,,	,, 56	,,
Monthly, and Great Festivals ..	,, 71	,,	,, 120	,,	,, 158	,,
Monthly	,, 66	,,	,, 54	,,		
Six to ten times a year	,, 62	,,	,, 37	,,		
Three to five times ,,	,, 47	,,				

of sitting during the most solemn confession of sins is so inexcusably bad." He intimated that he would decline to consecrate new churches where kneeling arrangements had not been properly made.[56]   In his Charge in 1872 he again refers to the matter, giving information where hassocks, then apparently something of a rarity, could be obtained.

He had always been interested in Church music. In this Charge he also asked for particulars of the hymnal used, of the nature of the instrument employed to accompany the singing,* and whether the people joined heartily in the service.[57]   In his Pastoral Letter of 1870 he stated that " the singing in most of the churches is not such as it should be " and recommended the formation of Church Choral Societies.[58]   To give further encouragement he got distinguished musicians to lecture and arranged for the subject of the place of Church music to be a matter for discussion at the Diocesan Conference.[59]

The bishop emphasized the importance of Ascension Day: " I have thought that this subject was worthy of a place amongst my Visitation Articles," he said in his Charge of 1872.[60]   By the end of his episcopate he was able to note a considerable improvement.

It was probably during this episcopate that Harvest Festivals became common. It will be remembered that Bishop Waldegrave disapproved of them, but Bishop Goodwin, in his Pastoral Letter of 1875, gave them his blessing.[61]

	* Hymns used			Instruments used		
Ancient and Modern in	103 parishes			Organ in	93 churches	
S.P.C.K.	„	45	„	Harmonium in	171	„
Kemble	„	28	„	Barrel organ in	3	„
Mercer	„	19	„	No instrument in	15	„
Marshall	„	10	„			
Tate and Brady	„	5	„			
Local	„	3	„			
Various	„	52	„			
None	„	6	„			

A Pastoral Staff was presented to Bishop Goodwin for his use and that of his successors in the see by the Lord Lieutenant of Cumberland, on behalf of the subscribers, at the Church Congress held at Carlisle, on 30 September 1884. The staff, now kept in the cathedral, was based upon that depicted in Bishop Robinson's brass and a similar motto was inscribed on it: Corrigendo, sustinendo, vigilando, dirigendo.[62]

This diocese was little affected by the Oxford movement during these years. The brethren of the Holy Cross opened an Oratory in Caldewgate, in the parish of Holy Trinity, Carlisle in 1873. From the description of the furniture of the chapel and of the opening services, the ceremonial was of a kind that would excite no comment to-day—then it aroused the wrath of Dean Close; the bishop, however, refused to interfere.[63] This year also saw some trouble about ceremonial at Wetheral. In reply to the churchwardens' complaint against certain ritualistic innovations, the bishop pronounced floral decorations harmless, candles for light and brightness at the evening service not unfitting, chanting the psalms the only reasonable way of reciting them, surplices for the choir the right thing.[64] Then, in December 1873, the churchwardens wrote to the rector telling him they would not suffer the introduction of any ornaments without a faculty. He defied them by placing vases with flowers on the reredos and otherwise decorating the church. When the churchwardens removed these ' ornaments,' the rector summoned them before the consistory court. After four hearings, judgment was given in his favour and the churchwardens admonished.[65] The only other trouble in the diocese was at St. George's, Barrow in 1878. The ritual practices complained of were such as would cause no comment now.[66]

The adherents of the Oxford Movement emphasized the value of sacramental confession. In July 1873, the bishop preached a sermon on what he 'conceived to be sober Church of England views on the subject.' The fury of Dean Close " found vent in a series of comminations which are read with astonishment to-day." One of them included the statement " such an absolution cannot and ought not to be indicated; our Church does not require it of us; and even if she did, we are not bound to a slavish subserviency to every minute sentiment which may be detected in her as erroneous, nor to any ceremony which may be proved unscriptural." The bishop called this " a very dangerous admission " and went on " who has a right to say that any particular sentiment is minute, or any particular ceremony unscriptural?[67]

The bishop was probably an adherent of this movement in his Cambridge days, but as bishop claimed that he belonged to no party in the Church.[68] At the same time the things he emphasised—the importance of the Holy Communion, the place of Ascension Day, the value of good music and the virtues of reverence—were those the followers of the Oxford Movement stressed.

III. EDUCATIONALIST.

Within a year of his becoming bishop, Harvey Goodwin was faced with the problems set for those controlling Church schools by the Education Act of 1870.* He immediately set about strengthening diocesan educational methods. In his first Pastoral Letter[69] he mentioned statistics he had obtained and a special fund he had started to enable parishes to put their schools in order; he also referred to the need for inspectors in religious knowledge. In his next letter[70] he said that as the method of inspection by rural deans and their assistant inspectors had not given general satisfaction, a paid inspector was to be appointed, with Canon Prescott having the supervision of Church schools as his special task.

* p. 408.

Most of the bishop's other Pastoral Letters contain references to Church schools and education. He often included the diocesan inspector's report or a summary of it: in 1872, 200 schools were inspected; in 1874, 230; by 1882, 320 were under the inspector's care; and in 1890 the total had risen to 338.

During this episcopate, largely owing to the influence of the bishop, the ancient Dean and Chapter School became Carlisle Grammar School. First mooted in 1875, the scheme was finally approved, by Order in Council, in 1880. The Ecclesiastical Commissioners granted £10,000, as an addition to the endowment of the school and a further sum of £5000 towards the cost of new buildings, a sum equal to the latter one was to be raised by local contributions. The new school was opened by the bishop, who was, ex officio, a governor, in 1883. At the same time a Cathedral Choir School was formed, with a minor canon as headmaster, for the education of the choristers.[71]

IV. Scholar.

It is typical of the bishop, as of all truly ' big men,' that he was a man of many interests. At Cambridge he took his degree, as second wrangler, in mathematics. While at the university he was keenly interested in church architecture and was one of the small group who formed themselves into ' The Ecclesiological Society.' When he became dean of Ely he had a chance of putting his ideas into practice. " The result bears striking testimony to his knowledge, skill and aptitude." He was also a member of the Royal Archaeological Institute and presided at meetings held in Carlisle in 1882 and at Edinburgh in 1891, when he read a paper on the treatment of ancient buildings which " became a classical authority on the subject, quoted far and wide."[72] Further evidence on the breadth of his scholarship is shewn by his article on " The Roman Wall."[73] When he was described as ' a sound and well informed archaeologist,' these words were not merely complimentary.[74]

It can therefore be appreciated that he was not just a figure head as vice-president of the Cumberland and Westmorland Antiquarian and Archaeological Society. It may be mentioned, as illustrating the interest that the clergy of that time shewed in local antiquities, that two of the five conveners of the first meeting were in Orders,[75] and when the first list of its members was issued in the 1877 volume, 53 of the 198 subscribers were clergymen and 8 out of the 34 articles in the volume were contributed by clerics. Though the bishop never wrote for the Society, " he frequently brought his powerful influence to bear upon our projects, particularly that of cataloguing and describing the Church Plate of the Diocese and of publishing Bishop Nicolson's ' Miscellany Accounts '."[76]

Mention should also be made here of the bishop's habit of having his yearly Pastoral Letters, his Visitation Charges, with reports of the meetings of the Diocesan Conference and other materials printed, and later bound up in a series of volumes—there are seven of them— entitled Carliolensia. These are not only of great value in illustrating his methods of work, but supply much material for the history of the diocese during his episcopate. Another idea of the bishop's was the compilation of a diocesan album to be kept at Rose, containing photographs or sketches of his churches, with, if possible, some historical notes. He first mentioned it in his Pastoral Letter of 1872 and referred to it again in 1889.

In 1877 the bishop promoted a scheme for circulating in every parish a history of its finances. Each incumbent was to draw up an account of the source of its endowments. A committee of experts was appointed to advise him.[77] This plan making slow progress, the bishop, in 1885, urged the parochial clergy " that you should investigate for yourself the history of your own parish with regard to ecclesiastical matters, and especially with regard to its endowments."[78] Four years later in praising a history of the rural deanery of Gosforth, he stated "I shall be glad when a similar history has been produced from every deanery; and we might then perhaps bring the histories together in the form of a diocesan volume."[79]

The change the bishop made in his signature arose largely from his interest in the history of the see. Previously to 1890, he had signed 'Carlisle'; in his Christmas Pastoral of that year he announced that in future he would use the form 'Carliol,'* "the ancient form in this case recommends itself to my mind just because it is ancient; it marks the antiquity of the see; it reminds us that we date from Henry I."[80]

The bishop was a considerable author. In addition to the seven volumes of Carleolensia already mentioned, he issued, between 1845 and 1862, five volumes of parish sermons and published other theological works.[81] It is rather strange that *The Times*, reviewing Rawnsley's 'Life,'[82] describes it as being "somewhat less interesting than might be expected because the bishop's life . . . left little room for literary record." In fact the exact opposite is true, except as regards private and official letters; he seems to have been a very succinct correspondent.

V. Extra Diocesan Activities.

Bishop Goodwin often preached in the metropolis: at Westminster Abbey, St. Paul's Cathedral or elsewhere. He preached in the Abbey at the funeral of Charles Darwin and at Newcastle-on-Tyne before the British Association. No Church Congress programme during

---

* With his usual thoroughness the bishop had investigated how previous holders of the see had signed: Nicolson, Bradford, Waugh, Douglas, Vernon, Goodenough used the ancient form; Fleming, Osbaldiston, Lyttleton, Law, Percy, Villiers, Waldegrave the modern one (49).

these years was complete without his name among its
lecturers or speakers.   Early in his episcopate he leased a
house in the west end of London where he commonly
resided for three months in the year.   He was on the
committee of many societies and regarded it as part of his
duty to attend the meetings, considering that he had a
duty to the Church as a whole as well as to the diocese over
which he presided.   Of these outside responsibilities two
deserve mention: the Royal Commission on cathedrals of
which he was chairman, its sittings lasted from 1879 to
1885, and the building of the Church House at Westminster, as the Church's memorial of Queen Victoria's 1887
Jubilee.   It was at Bishop Goodwin's suggestion that the
memorial took this form[83] and it was largely due to his
work that the scheme was brought to a happy conclusion.

VI. Last Days.

The bishop had been suffering from heart trouble for
some time, but carried on with his duties in the usual way.
But while staying with the archbishop of York at
Bishopsthorpe, he was seized with a bad attack and died
within two days, on 25 November 1891.   He was buried
at Crosthwaite, Keswick on 28 November; a recumbent
effigy, designed by H. Thornycroft, was placed in the
cathedral in his memory.   He married Ellen, daughter of
George King of Bebington House, Cheshire in 1845 and
had issue.

Was Harvey Goodwin the greatest bishop who ever
ruled from Rose?   The reader is reminded of what was
said when the character of William Nicolson was under
consideration.*   There the palm was left to be divided
between Edward Rainbow and Harvey Goodwin.   Without going into the question further it can at least be
confidently said that the latter was the greatest among
those who have been bishops of the modern diocese.   He

* p. 312.

was truly its creator. Inheriting a diocese, recently formed and covering an area embracing three counties that was indeed only a diocese in theory, he left one that was a diocese in fact. He was once described as ' the strongest bishop on the bench '[84] and that in days when the episcopal standard was indeed high. Thus it is perhaps surprising that he was never translated—a study of the names of those who held the greater sees in these years lessens the surprise.

So we take leave of Harvey Goodwin; a great administrator and organiser both in this diocese and in the Church beyond it; a true shepherd of the souls entrusted to him who tried to instil into them a deeper knowledge of the realities of the spiritual life and a greater reverence for the Church, her sacraments and ceremonies; a true friend to his clergy for whose material, as well as spiritual betterment he cared much; a scholar who, whether as mathematician, ecclesiologist, antiquary or theologian, shewed a real understanding of his subject; but above all the creator of the modern diocese of Carlisle and a true man of God, who was humble enough to say to those whom he had unwittingly passed by " I can assure them on the word of an honest man no offence is intended."[85]

The election of John Wareing Bardsley, bishop of Sodor and Man since 1887, was confirmed on 26 February 1892. Bishop Goodwin had so effectively laid the foundations upon which the modern diocese has since been carried on that few events that an historian records took place during the next episcopates. The tasks of the bishops were the unspectacular ones of fulfilling essential episcopal functions; of seeing that the machinery of the diocese ran smoothly; and of providing such new places of worship as were required—twelve churches or chapels were built or rebuilt in this episcopate.* But each had his own distinctive contribution to make. In 1893

* See Appendix XII.

Bishop Bardsley started the Diocesan Trust and Finance Association, out of which evolved the Board of Finance.

The son of a poor man, he had himself also known comparative poverty, having married on £150 a year. At his primary Visitation in 1894, he suggested the creation of a Sustentation Fund with the object of increasing the value of poor livings by annual grants. In his next Charge he announced, as a commemoration of the Diamond Jubilee, the inauguration of the Queen Victoria Carlisle Diocesan Retiring Pension Fund*—by his third visitation, in 1900, the scheme was already working and three pensions awarded. At the Diocesan Conference of 1901, he brought forward a plan for raising the 131 livings below £200 a year to that sum. A committee of laymen was appointed to deal with the matter; the report, for which Viscount Cross was largely responsible, was presented at the next year's conference. Thus the Laymen's Fund for the Permanent Augmentation of Benefice Endowments was founded. These efforts to help the poorer clergy are those by which Bishop Bardsley both should be, and would have liked to be, remembered.

Two other new ventures were begun in this episcopate: the Diocesan Mission for the Deaf and Dumb in 1894 and the licencing of a Church Army Van in 1895.

The bishop and his wife were simple homely people—whenever they stayed, as then often happened, with one of the clergy, and two bedroom candles were provided, they always blew out one of them so as to avoid undue extravagance. Another kindly habit was to invite the younger clergy and their wives to spend a few days at Rose.

In 1898 the bishop had an attack of ptomaine poisoning, while on holiday in Egypt, and never fully recovered. He died at Rose on 14 September 1904 and was buried at

---

* Now administered by the Pensions Committee.

Raughton Head.* He married, in 1862, Elizabeth, daughter of the Rev. Benjamin Powell of Wigan and sister of Sir F. S. Powell, Bart., and by her had issue. Bishop Bardsley was not a great bishop, but he was, which is perhaps of more honour, a holy and humble Christian and a devout Evangelical.

" His unaffected manner and amiable and genial character made him a favourite with the clergy and the laity, who both trusted and respected him . . . Few men of his position have excited so little criticism or have gained such universal goodwill, and none has been more sincerely regretted."[86]

John William Diggle† was consecrated on 2 February 1905 in York Minster by Archbishop Maclagan. He added two more to the long list of diocesan organisations: the Missionary Council, established in 1907, to bring home to every Churchman the duty of supporting overseas missions; and the Church House, founded in 1909, to provide rooms where small meetings could be held and the clergy and others meet in social intercourse. During his episcopate eleven churches or chapels were consecrated.‡

The bishop§ is chiefly remembered as a great preacher and orator; whenever he was announced to preach or speak, his fame had gone before him and the place was full to the doors with an expectant crowd, for, in addition to his gift of ready speech, he had also the boon of ready tears—as can be imagined the populace found the combination of oratory and weeping irresistible. In the early years of his episcopate his energy as a preacher was

---

* C. W. Bardsley, rector of Ulverston and author of *A Dictionary of English and Welsh Surnames*, was his brother.

† " I was born a poor unfriended boy. I attended a national school in the village in which I lived." So he said at his enthronement. After holding various curacies and livings, he became canon of Carlisle and archdeacon of Westmorland, 1892, rector of Birmingham 1901, archdeacon 1903.

‡ Appendix XII.

§ I am indebted to Mr. E. Williams of Carlisle for help in the following account.

2G

tremendous; he was in demand everywhere and everywhere he went.   As he once remarked: " Rose Castle is a
place where I occasionally lodge."   Some of his sermons
are still remembered, especially one in the cathedral on
the death of Edward VII.   He had a happy flair for
publicity; he once received an anonymous letter saying:

" I am glad you are going for a holiday, for now I shall be able
to read something in the newspaper, beside the speeches of the
bishop of Carlisle."

Some people accused him of playing to the gallery and
liking to be in the limelight.   The truth would seem to be
that knowing what the public was interested in, he
talked about it.   His speeches and sermons were therefore
always topical, so they were ' good copy.'   But it was
hardly fair to blame him for speaking about what
interested people; that he did so is merely evidence that
he was in touch with the life of his time.

He was a broad Churchman—at times so broad that he
appeared to some to cease to be a Churchman.   He
desired to embrace all Christians in a universal Church
based upon Baptism and the Bible: the former to be the
sole condition for the reception of the Holy Communion;
the latter the only basis for teaching in schools, both
National and Church ones.   At times Church people
found his views a little difficult to understand, especially
his attitude to the Education Bill of 1902.   While the
Church was trying to save its schools, the bishop did
nothing to help.   Though we may question the rightness
of his views, we cannot but admire his courage in taking
a line that alienated many of his friends and supporters.

He was on very friendly terms with Nonconformists—
he objected to their use of the term Free Churchmen,
declaring that the Established Church was equally or even
more free—and believed in the interchange of pulpits.
He was also a great supporter of Reunion, though by this
he meant only Reunion with Nonconformity; the greater
question of that of all Christendom was beyond his ken.

In many things he was apt to take an independent view. He was not a teetotaller and objected to mere children being encouraged to take pledges that they could not understand. Nor was he a Sabbatarian: he once said that if people had first attended church in the morning, he favoured their being allowed to enjoy pastimes on the village green; these should, however, be held in a different atmosphere to every day games and be conducted so as to bring the classes together. His was by no means a stereotyped mind; nor was he simply a party man with a party label, he was himself with his own beliefs and his own ideas and what he conscientiously held to be true he practised and taught without fear or favour.

He died at Rose on 24 March 1920, after a long and very painful illness, borne with an exemplary fortitude and courage which aroused admiration in all who beheld it. He was buried at Crosthwaite, Keswick, on 29 March, after a service in the cathedral. He married twice, in 1874, Cicely Jane, daughter of Peter Butterfield of Broughton, Manchester, and in 1884, Edith, daughter of G. W. Moss of Aigburth, Liverpool. He left issue by both wives.

Bishop Diggle, inheriting a well organised diocese in an age when society was stable and little fresh planning was required, lived through the troubled years of a great war, when little in that respect could be carried out. His task, which he fulfilled admirably, was to perform the ordinary duties of the episcopal office. It was above all " his outspoken frankness of thought and his sympathy with all classes that won for him the title of ' the people's bishop '."[87] He was the author of several theological works and of a life of Bishop Fraser of Manchester. He was a keen fisherman, a hobby he shared with Archdeacon Prescott and Canon Wilson.

An account must now be given of two priests of outstanding ability. John Eustace Prescott, archdeacon of

Carlisle, 1883, and chancellor 1900, was without doubt, after the death of Bishop Goodwin, the most forceful personality at diocesan headquarters.   In the cathedral chapter his word was law; in the diocese his authority, wielded through the chancellorship, was equally supreme in many matters. He was a rich man and a generous benefactor to the cathedral: one of his gifts, the present font with its magnificent cover, cost over £700; on another, the stained glass in the window over the south door—he spent over £1,000.

As chancellor, Dr. Prescott ruled without fear or favour: the countess of Derby's wish to place a statuette of her infant son within the sanctuary of Witherslack church was rejected.   About an application for a grave space at Millom, he said " he was sorry that this application was supported by an argument which applied to a rich man and did not apply to a poor one." He discouraged unsightly glass globes or imitation flowers in churchyards and the inscription " To the glory of God " on memorial tablets, which were only examples of human vanity.[88]

But to those who appeared before him he would sometimes be caustic or even rude.   He was also an extreme partisan in his dislike of anything that in his opinion savoured of ' advanced churchmanship '; thus applicants to his court did not always receive justice.   Matters came to a crisis in 1916 over the faculty for a second altar in St. John's Windermere.   Prescott, determined that there should not be any in this diocese, though he admitted they were legal refused the application.   Such strong feeling, however, was aroused that even the chancellor was somewhat intimidated, and when soon after another application—from St. John's, Keswick— came before the court, he allowed it.[89]   Some three years later his refusal to authorise a window in St. Paul's church, Carlisle picturing the crucifixion led to a successful appeal to the Provincial Court of York.[90] It is said that he never recovered from this blow; though he continued to sit, apparently in good form, as at the last court he ever held, he likened the proposed war memorial of Orton, Westmorland, to a tea caddy.[91]

His real claim, however, to our remembrance is neither as a man of unusually dominating personality, nor as a chancellor liable to confuse his personal idiosyncrasies with the law of the land, but as an historian. His edition of the *Register of the Priory of Wetherhal*, with its invaluable notes is one of the prime sources for our early history. He also published *The Statutes of Carlisle Cathedral* and *Visitation in the Ancient Diocese of Carlisle.* For the *Transactions* of the Society he printed two important papers. We should also remember his gift to the diocese of his library, now in the Church House.

Hardwicke Drummond Rawnsley* was the author of a considerable amount of poetry, of a biography of Bishop Goodwin and of a series of books on the Lake District. He was also a strenuous opposer of any desecration of its beauties: plans for railways from Braithwaite to Buttermere, up Ennerdale, or from Windermere to Ambleside were among the projects he resisted. As years pass by he may well be chiefly remembered as one of the founders of the National Trust in 1894.† Canon T. B. A. Saunders, with an abler pen than the present writer's, has supplied the following account of him. " Of course, he was unique, a baffling personality. Whether he charmed or piqued one the more, hard to say. At his best he was indescribably delightful as a raconteur and as a host. Despite his broad, muscular, deepchested, mariner-like, hirsute figure, there was somewhere a touch

---

* Vicar of Wray, Ambleside, 1878, and Crosthwaite, 1883-1917; canon of Carlisle, 1909, chaplain to the king 1912. He married firstly Edith Fletcher and secondly Eleanor Simpson, the author of the Grasmere plays and of a biography of her husband.

† See *The Lake District and the National Trust*, Bruce Thompson.

of the feminine, in his light melodious voice, in the poise
of his head, the wave of his hands.

His energy was unbelievable.   It was almost a lust of
perpetual motion.   Yet there must have been long spells
of sedentary energy too, for his writing was prodigious in
bulk and much of it was delightful.   It was the fashion
to smile a little at his poetry.   But nobody could afford
to gibe at his grip of nature, and his genius for painting in
words the fells of the Lake Country according to the
season of the year.

When he made professional excursions into theology,
he was, of course, off his beat.   The fruits were sometimes
grotesque.   Yet he escaped the snare of intolerance which
besets the more expert ecclesiastic, and if he scarcely
knew what he believed about dogmatics, at least we were
sure that he desired beneficence and good feeling to rule
the world; not that his tongue lacked bite, but he was
preserved from dull rancour by his gift of fun.

Nor was he capable of serious history, for he possessed
no faculty of solid verification.   To him a hypothesis
passed without effort into certainty.   Not that he was
conscious of romancing in the sense that he would invent a
story to fit his purpose.   It was just the not uncommon
want of sound training in the principles of evidence.   If
he had given himself to " Greats " instead of to Natural
Science at Balliol, his genius for handling history and
archaeology with almost a fairy touch would have gained
the value of a surer accuracy.

His method of working a parish was peculiar.   He was
constantly away from it running hither and thither to
innumerable committees, and often in London.   But he
spent money generously on curate and lay-reader and
kept a sharp eye on their parochial diligence.   He was
entirely uninterested in such things as ritual and always
celebrated at the North End, though he was in no sense an
Evangelical, but really what might be called a very mild

Modernist. His reading in church was quite admirable. He was a great draw to tourists at Crosthwaite, not for his theology but for the charm of his voice and the cultivated presentation of attractive religious and ethical ideals.

As a member of the cathedral staff he filled a niche which is rarely occupied—a man of culture, means, and such dignity as a canonry still affords; an ecclesiastic who was not stuffy; a man of the world who was an idealist; a man of letters who was also a man of deeds; a charming acquaintance who never bored; a man of some fame who could be treated like a fellow-undergraduate with chaff; a preacher who was never pompous; a sinner against conventions whose vagaries were atoned for by gracefulness and quick remorse for unintended offence."

To return to the story of the bishops: Henry Herbert Williams, principal of St. Edmund Hall, Oxford, was consecrated in York Minster on 24 August 1920 by Archbishop Lang. Probably never before has the cathedral had a chapter of such note as during the early years of this episcopate. The dean was Hastings Rashdall, ' historian, philosopher, theologian ' and a scholar of European fame. Of the canons: H. N. Bate was later dean of York; O. C. Quick, later regius professor of divinity and canon of Christ Church, Oxford, and F. W. Matheson, later warden of Trinity College, Glenalmond, and dean of Carlisle. But from the diocesan point of view the most important person at headquarters was H. E. Campbell, who had succeeded Dr. Prescott as archdeacon of Carlisle and chancellor. Having held incumbencies in several parts of the diocese, no one was better fitted to introduce the new bishop to his work.

Another member of the chapter, T. B. A. Saunders, did much to increase the devotional atmosphere of the cathedral by furnishing, with his wife, St. Catherine's chapel, which had long been used as a clergy vestry, and by erecting an altar in the north choir aisle in her memory.

During these years the mural tablets were cleaned and candlesticks placed on the High Altar.   Another memorial gift was the strengthening of the walls of the tower, by Mrs. Rashdall in memory of her husband, so that the bells could be rung.   In 1927 a silver processional cross was presented to the cathedral by the bishop and Mrs. Williams on the occasion of their silver wedding.   Then, at the very end of our period, a Society of Friends of the cathedral was formed;   among its projects are plans for the provision of proper vestries and the rebuilding of the nave.

As this episcopate may be said to represent a continuance of the Goodwin tradition it seems right that during it a cope and mitre should have been added to the ornaments of the bishop's ' chapel,' to which an episcopal staff had been given in Bishop Goodwin's time.   Another valuable gift was that of a smaller pastoral staff, for use outside the cathedral.   Both the latter and the processional cross, mentioned above, were made by the Keswick School of Art.

A movement to make the interior of our churches more comely was assisted by the formation of an Advisory Committee.   As a result many chancels are now ordered as the Prayer Book directs and side chapels have ceased to be a rarity.   Perhaps the most remarkable piece of restoration carried out has been that at St. John's Workington, where a barnlike structure has been converted by an enthusiastic vicar and congregation into a thing of beauty.   As instances of the restoration of small Lakeland churches, Buttermere and Nether Wastdale may be cited;   and as an example of the same kind of thing in a rather larger building, the restoration of Millom parish church must not be overlooked.   An interesting attempt to improve the interior of a rather dark church in an industrial town can be seen in the painting of the stone reredos of St. George's Barrow.

IX. THE HIGH ALTAR OF ST. JOHN'S CHURCH, WORKINGTON.

(*facing p.* 456)

These years witnessed a great increase in the place of the Eucharist in the worship of the Church. The cathedral now has a daily celebration with a sung one on Sundays and Saints days; and the celebrant is vested in accordance with the rubrics. In many parish churches also the Lord's Service is now the principal one on Sunday mornings with the usual accompaniments of a simple ceremonial.

Despite all this, it is probable that posterity will not regard any of these as the most important event that took place in these years, for in 1919 the so-called Enabling Act was passed by which the Diocesan and Ruridecanal Conference and Parochial Church Council were given legal form, though in this diocese they had functioned ever since Bishop Goodwin's time. Their work here was much furthered by the assistance of a notable band of laymen.

This episcopate saw a certain amount of reorganisation of diocesan headquarters. Previously both the bishop and his suffragan had lived in the north of the diocese, now the latter was given a living in, as well as a title from, Furness. At the same time the cathedral canonries began to be attached to various spheres of diocesan work. In this see of widely scattered communities, the motor car much simplified the problems of diocesan administration. Rose, with its amenities for the visitor added to by the installation of electric light and central heating, also became more accessible to the clergy and others, with the result that the castle was increasingly used for conferences of different kinds. The work of the Council for Social and Moral Welfare, formed in 1926 in place of the Association for Preventive and Rescue work, was furthered by the institution of a 'Women's Offering' service held at various centres. The intellectual life of the clergy was cared for by a series of 'Way of Renewal' meetings, as well as by a yearly conference of the Central Society for Sacred Study held at Rose.

The year 1933 was celebrated as the octocentenary of the foundation of the diocese. The archdeacon of Carlisle, D. F. Campbell, son of the chancellor, was responsible for most of the arrangements, which included an exhibition in the Fratry of ecclesiastical ornaments lent by various churches in the diocese. The archdeacon was tragically killed in a car accident during the year— the furniture in the chancel of the new church of St. Barnabas, Carlisle was given in his memory. This was one of three churches—the others were at Barrow and Whitehaven—built to commemorate the octocentenary. During the year a series of services were held in the chief towns of the diocese culminating in a great act of thanksgiving in the cathedral attended by representatives of every parish. A number of pilgrimages from the parishes, including a large one from Barrow, to the mother church at Carlisle also took place.

And now, having finished my task, I have but to add a prayer that God will continue in the future, as in the past, to guide and sustain his Church in this diocese; and a hope that when its nonocentenary comes someone less unworthy of the honour—though perhaps he will not love it more—will perfect and continue this history.

Sunday within the octave of All Saints, being the eve of All Souls, 1947.

APPENDIX VII.

List of Churches consecrated, 1856-69.*

Old parish or chapel.	New parish or chapel.
1856	Murton
	Applethwaite (St. Mary, Windermere)
	Great Broughton
1857 Irton	West Newton
1858 Ennerdale	
Langdale	
1859 Gosforth	Skirwith
1860 Farlam	
1861 North Stainmore	St. George, Barrow-in-Furness
	Trinity Chapel, Borrowdale
	Low Wray
1862	Blawith
1865 Staveley, Kendal	Waverton
Irelèth	St. Stephen, Carlisle
Woodland	Christ Church, Cockermouth
	Allithwaite
1866 Asby	All Hallows, Kendal
Lazonby	Arnside
Ulverston	
Wythop	
1867 Nicholforest	Midgeholme
	St. John, Carlisle
	St. James, Carlisle
	Hayton, Aspatria
1868	Frizington
	Highhead or Ivegill
	Pooley Bridge
	Lupton
	Gamblesby
1869 Uldale	St. James, Barrow
Walton	Sawrey

* These are all taken from the Bishop's Register.

APPENDIX VIII.

Return of Church Building and Restoration, exceeding £500,* 1856-1869.

	New building	Restoration
(Addingham) Gamblesby	1075	
Aikton		650
Ainstable		100
Allhallows		734
Allithwaite	3000	
Appleby St. Lawrence		1391
(Arlecdon) Frizington	3000	
Arnside	1063	
Arthuret		1830
Asby	3000	
Aspatria		125
Barrow-in-Furness:		
St. George	13000	
St. James	13000	
(Barton) Pooley Bridge	891	
Bassenthwaite		1600
St. Bees		4750
Beetham		3300
Blawith	1501	
Borrowdale		730
Grange	510	
Bolton, Cumberland		980
Brathay		930
Brigham		2840
Bromfield		1640
Broughton, Great	1100	
Broughton-in-Furness		2500
Burneside		850
Carlisle:		
The cathedral		21610
St. Cuthbert		560
St. James	4457	
St. John	5187	
St. Stephen	8000	
Holy Trinity		1050
Cartmel		5248
Casterton	641	
Cleator		1500

	New building	Restoration
Cockermouth (Christ Church)	4000	
Crosby Ravensworth		5211
Crosscrake		500
Dacre		1600
Dalton-in-Furness		2490
Egton-cum-Newland	200	1250
Ennerdale	800	
Farlam	2000	
Finsthwaite	2200	
Firbank	500	100
Gosforth		790
Grayrigg		950
Hawkshead		2660
Hayton, Aspatria	1500	
Heversham		5407
Holme	750	90
Hutton-in-the-Forest		580
Ireleth	2044	
Irton	4000	
Ivegill and High Head	3121	150
Kendal:		
All Hallows	1314	
St. Thomas		671
Keswick		1060
Killington		500
Kirkby Lonsdale		9415
Lupton	643	
Kirkby Thore		550
Kirklinton		86
Kirkoswald		1500
Lamplugh		1868
Langdale	1900	870
Lazonby	2800	
Lindale		870
Low Wray	3500	
Lowther		1235
Melmerby	1200	
Muncaster	2538	
Murton-with-Hilton	611	
Nicholforest	2000	
Ousby		509
Penrith		1942

	New building	Restoration
Plumbland		2726
Preston Patrick		300
Raughtonhead		108
Rusland		900
Satterthwaite		563
Sawrey	2300	
Scaleby		1053
Scotby		100
Seathwaite	750	
Skirwith	2700	
Stainmore	800	
Staveley, Kendal	1890	
Troutbeck		580
Uldale	3100	
Ulverston		8000
Underbarrow	1800	
Upperby		189
Walton	2000	
Warwick		1093
Waverton	895	
Westnewton	1500	
Wetheral		573
Whitehaven:		
Holy Trinity		1100
St. James		1726
Windermere:		
St. Martin		7100
St. Mary		1700
Woodland	1007	
Workington		2043
Wythop	750	

* See note to Appendix VI.

APPENDIX IX.

Return of expenditure on Church restoration under £500, 1840-1872.*

Addingham	220	Levens	222
Allonby	300	Lorton	120
Appleby, St. Michael's	236	Mardale	135
Arlecdon	200	Maryport	400
Armathwaite	200	Matterdale	130

Bampton	86	Millom	180
Barton	334	Morland	100
Bewcastle	32	Natland	329
Beaumont	window	Newlands	200
Bolton, W.	307	Newton Reigny	355
Broughton, Field	Vestry etc:	Orton, Great	371
Camerton	140	Plumpton	25
Carlisle, Christ Church	365	Renwick	496
Castle Sowerby	201	Rydal	254
Cliburn	120	Salkeld, Great	229
Clifton (W.)	300	Sebergham	50
Crosby Garrett	205	Selside	48
Culgaith	260	Setmurthy	382
Cumwhitton	200	Skelton	105
Dean	374	Soulby	240
Embleton	150	St. John's in the Vale	286
Eskdale	18	Threlkeld	80
Flimby	396	Torver	200
Gilcrux	46	Urswick	400
Grinsdale	12	Watermillock	30
Helsington	480	Whicham	440
Hensingham	447	Wigton	325
Hugill or Ings	67	Wythburn	328
Hutton Roof	150		
Kendal, St. George's	200		
Kentmere	460		
Kirkbampton	389		
Kirkbride	107		

* This is part of the return noted in Appendix VI. In this case it has not been possible to extract the figures, so the full return is given here No similar return was made for the years 1872-92.

APPENDIX X.

List of Churches consecrated or licenced 1869-1892.

	Old parish or chapel	New parish or chapel
1869		Gaitsgill
		Cotehill
1870	St. Mary, Carlisle	Blackford
	Bridekirk	St. Paul, Carlisle
	Nether Denton	
1871	Skelsmergh	Great Strickland
		Newbarns, Barrow

	Old parish or chapel	New parish or chapel
		Christ Church, Silloth
1872	Ainstable	Cumdivock
		Cleator Moor
		Christ Church, Maryport
1873	Old Hutton	Dalton-in-Furness (l) (iron church)
		Welton
1874	Finsthwaite	Osmotherley
1875	Seathwaite	Lindal (l) (iron church)
	Winster	St. Jude, Ulverston (iron church) (l)
	Crosscrake	The Hill, Millom (l)
1876	Grange	Eamont Bridge (l) (iron church)
		Hethersgill
1877	Crosthwaite, Kendal* (l)	St. George's, Millom
1878	Croglin	Hawes, Bassenthwaite
	Brampton	
	St. John, Beckermet	
1879		Barrow:
		St. John
		St. Luke
		St. Mark
		St. Matthew
1880	Mansergh	Tebay
		Bigrigg
1881		Seascale (iron church) (l)
1882	Martindale	
1883	St. Nicholas, Whitehaven*	Seaton
		Swarthmoor
1884	Watermillock	St. Saviour, Penrith (l)
	Torver*	
1885	Lowick* (l)	
	Kirkcambeck	
1886	Distington	All Hallows, Penrith (l)
		Netherton (l)
		Kirkland, Lamplugh (l)
		St. Perran, Roose*
		Lindal with Marton
1887	Crook	St. John, Windermere

	Old parish or chapel	New parish or chapel
1888		Dunnerdale (l)
1889		Westfield, Workington (l)
1890		Seascale
		Eskdale Green
		Botcherby (l)
1891	Mosser	Kirksanton
		Haverigg

* Not in the episcopal register, but inserted on reliable evidence. It is rather strange but there is no evidence of the consecration of St. Nicholas, Whitehaven, either at Chester in 1693 or Carlisle in 1883. The first record, for which I am indebted to Mr. J. Melville, of St. Perran's, Roose is on a Barrow street map of 1886.

l = licence.

APPENDIX XI.

Return of Church building and restoration exceeding £500* 1869-1892.

	New building	Restoration
Ainstable	1500	
Allonby		509
Appleby, St. Michael's		3300
Arnside		545
Bampton		2023
Barrow:		
St. George	3000	
St. Matthew	1300	
St. Mark	1250	
St. Luke	1250	
St. John	1472	
Newbarns	2050	
Bassenthwaite		1000
St. John's Chapel	5000	
Beckermet, John the Baptist	2866	
Beetham		5233
Beaumont		700
Blackford	1160	
Bootle		3300
Borrowdale		730
Bowness-on-Solway		2562
Brampton	8643	204
Brathay		1320

	New building	Restoration
Bridekirk	5100	
Brigham		850
Brough		2084
Broughton-in-Furness		4200
Dunnerdale	600	
Burgh-by-Sands		700
Burneside		5000
Caldbeck		500
Camerton		
Seaton	2052	
Carlisle:		
St. Mary	6157	
St. Paul	3700	
Holy Trinity		886
St. Cuthbert		1633
Botcherby	520	280
Cartmel		3500
Casterton		800
Castle Carrock		750
Castle Sowerby		509
Cleator Moor	9000	
Cliburn		700
Cockermouth, Christ Church		1450
Colton		900
Cotehill	1316	
Corney		517
Croglin		900
Crook	1800	
Crosby Ravensworth		10000
Cross Canonby		900
Crosscrake	4136	235
Crosthwaite (W)	6723	
Cumdivock	900	
Cumrew		2300
Dacre		1700
Dalston		2000
Dalton	13603	
St. Margaret's (iron church)	1000	
Dearham		1300
Netherton	5000	
Denton, Nether	1652	

	New building	Restoration
Distington	6000	
Egremont		7000
Bigrigg	2600	
Embleton		800
Eskdale		1000
St. Begh's Chapel	2000	
Finsthwaite	4170	
Gosforth		380
Seascale	4100	
Grasmere		600
Greystoke		800
Haile		826
Harrington		1900
Hawkshead		3237
Hayton		1150
Heversham		1385
Holm Cultram		1500
Hugill or Ings		1324
Hutton Old	1250	
Hutton Roof		2685
Irton		1500
Isell		950
Kendal, St. George		1506
Keswick	3265	
Kirkbampton		670
Kirkby Ireleth		2750
Kirkby Stephen		7376
Kirkoswald		1400
Lanercost		
Hethersgill	1631	
Lindal and Marton	4166	
Long Marton		2555
Low Wray		1000
Loweswater		1200
Lowick	1856	
Mansergh	2500	
Maryport		2516
Christ Church	2000	
Middleton	1350	
Millom		220
Hill chapel	575	

	New building	Restoration
Kirksanton	1000	
St. George	11470	
Haverigg	1522	
Milnthorpe		2214
Moresby		1825
Mosser	1000	
Muncaster		3106
Newton Reigny		750
Ormside		781
Orton, Great		527
Orton		2500
Penrith, St. Andrew		3037
Allhallows	650	
St. Saviour	300	
Ponsonby		1800
Preston Patrick		1576
Rocliffe		800
Raughton Head		727
Gaitsgill	1365	
Rydal		1407
St. Bees		1646
Salkeld, Great		748
Satterthwaite		600
Sawrey		682
Seathwaite		1005
Silloth, St. Paul		700
Christ Church	4410	
Skelsmergh	1400	837
Skelton		570
Strickland, Great	1000	
Tebay	1975	
Temple Sowerby	1188	
Thornthwaite		220
Braithwaite	510	
Torpenhow		1120
Torver	1400	
Ulverston, Holy Trinity		2685
Osmotherley	1462	
Stainton	500	
Watermillock	2781	
Welton	970	50
Westward		600

	New building	Restoration
Wetheral		2307
Whitbeck		834
Whitehaven, St. James		865
St. Nicholas	10092	
Wigton		1228
Windermere, St. John	4796	
St. Mary		6728
Winster	1525	
Witherslack		542
Workington, St Michael		7185

* See note to Appendix VI.

APPENDIX XII.

List of Churches consecrated or licenced 1892—1933.

	Old parish or chapel	New parish or chapel
1892		Newbiggin-on-Lune
1893	Barbon	West Seaton
1894		Field Broughton
1898		Grizebeck
1899	Allhallows	St. Barnabas, Carlisle (l)
1900	Flookburgh	St. Barnabas, Dalton (l)
		Braithwaite
1901		St. Aidan, Carlisle
		Penruddock
1905		Broughton Moor
1906		Netherton
1908	Plumpton	Grasslot (l)
1910	Natland	
1911	Walney	St. Margaret, Dalton
1913	Hensingham	Calthwaite
1915	Satterthwaite	
1916		Corney (iron church)
1931		St. Peter, Kingmoor
1932		Currock church hall (l)
1933	St. Paul, Grange (chancel)	
1935	St. John, Barrow in Furness*	
1936	St. Barnabas, Carlisle*	
1937	St. Peter, Whitehaven*	

* These are the three octocentenary churches which, though consecrated outside this period, seem therefore to lie within it.

APPENDIX XIII.

Tables shewing value of livings between 1291 and 1835 with particulars of appropriated churches and appropriating monasteries.

These lists give the stipend of benefices in:

1291, from the returns of the Taxatio of Pope Nicholas IV.

1318, from the revised figures put forth for the northern counties in that year.

1535, from the Valor Ecclesiasticus of Henry VIII.

18th century, from statistics in the Carlisle episcopal registers, Chancellor Waugh's survey, and Bishop Gastrell's Notitia.

1835, from the returns published by the Ecclesiastical Commission.

In the tables below the capital letters in italics give, in conjunction with the list of abbreviations, the ecclesiastical body to which the rectory was given. If the letter occurs in column I then all the subsequent figures apply to the vicarage only. If they appear in another column, column IV, for instance, then the previous figures give the whole rectory but the sum in columns IV V, VI only those of the vicarage. Where a small a, not in italics, occurs it means that the living was wholly appropriated, and no vicarage ordained, hence at the Reformation all the endowment was lost and the living sank to a curacy, to become a perpetual one in the eighteenth century.

Table of Abbreviations:

nt, not taxed; nr, no return; w, waste; a, appropriated; pc, perpetual curacy; x, in time of war nil; *Arch, archdeacon of Richmond*; *Ar, Armathwaite Nunnery*; *B, Bishopric of Carlisle*; *C, Carlisle Priory*; *Cal, Calder Abbey*; *Car, Cartmel Priory*; *Con, Conishead Priory*; *D & C Y, Dean and Chapter of York*; *Fo, Fountains Abbey*; *Fur, Furness Abbey*; *G, Gisburn Priory*; *HC, Holm Cultram Abbey*; *Hex, Hexham Priory*; *J, Jedburgh Abbey*; *K, Kirkoswald Collegiate church*; *L, Lanercost Priory*; *Q, Queen's College, Oxford*; *R, Rosedale Nunnery*; *St B, St. Bees Priory*; *Sta, Staindrop Collegiate church*; *S, Shap Abbey*; *Se, Seaton Nunnery*; *Wa, Wartre Priory*; *Wat, Watton Priory*; *Wh, Whitby Abbey*; *Y, St. Mary's Abbey, York*; *&,* in the following parishes the episcopal registers (Halton III 183-9) shew different figures to those given in the Taxatio viz. Sebergham £1. 2. o, Aikton £4. 8. o, Thursby £2. 4. o, Bowness £4. 8. o, Wetheral £1. 2. o.

	£ s. d.	£ s. d.	£ s. d.	£ 18th cent.	£
DEANERY OF CARLISLE	1291	1318	1535		1835
Aikton	19 4	4 &	4 13	165	546
Arthuret J	30	w	1 2 x	170	687
Beaumont	10	nt	8 1 6	18	nr
Bewcastle	19	w	2 x	60	81
Bowness on Solway	30	4 &	21 13 9	125	393
Brampton L	8	nt	7 15 4	90	466
Burgh by Sands HC	9	nt	5 1 9	13	91
Cambok	8	w	—	—	—
Carlisle					
St Cuthbert C	17 1 4	5	a	7	124 pc
St. Mary C	nr	nr	a	7	179 pc
Carlatton	6 13 4	w	—	—	—
Castle Carrock	6 10	nt	5 12	50	159
Crosby on Eden B	4 5	nt	3 11 4	27	90
Cumrew	4 10	nt	a C	10	81 pc
Cumwhitton	8 14	nt	a C	10	102 pc
Dalston B	12 16	5	8 18 2	85	201
Denton	nt	nt	4 5 5	16	196
Eston	4 6 8	w	—	—	—
Farlam	nt	w	a L	4	98 pc
Grinsdale	3 4	nt	a L	2	108 pc
Hayton	14 10	nt	a C	9	123 pc
Irthington L	10	w	6 1 5	30	222
Kirkandrews on Eden	nt	nt	3 11 5	9	249
Kirkbampton	18 10	nr	14 17 10	45	100
Kirklinton	42	w	1 1 x	60	98
Lanercost	—	—	—	16	107 pc
Orton, Great	8	nt	9	80	370
Rocliffe	10 13 4	nt	a C	20	73 pc
Scaleby	10	nt	7 1 0	18	107
Sebergham	5	1 &	a C	19	139 pc
Stanwix B & C	8 10	n.t.	9	90	264
Stapleton	4 2	w	1 9 x	24	98
Thursby	20	2 &	11 10 4 C	40	160
Walton	50	w	a L	6	131 pc
Wetheral Y	32	1 &	10	52	108 pc
DEANERY OF ALLERDALE					
Aspatria C	6 13 4	1 6 8	10 4 0	75	249
Bassenthwaite	9	1 6 8	a J	22	123 pc
Bolton	18	8 6 8	19 18 2	90	512
Bridekirk G	13 6 8	2	10 8 6	50	137

	1291			1318			1535			18th cent.	1835
	£	s.	d.	£	s.	d.	£	s.	d.	£	£
Bromfield	53	6	8	17	6	8	19	11	1 Y	80	270
Caldbeck	30			5			45	13	6	150	436
Camerton	20			5			a		C	15	95 pc
Cross Canonby	15			4			a		C	25	76 pc
Crosthwaite *Fo*	20			4			50	8	1	120	312
Dearham *G*	4	13	4		nt		4	10	2	15	85
Gilcrux *Cal*	4	13	4		nt		5	14	1	22	71
Holm Cultram	—			—			—			44	140
Ireby	20			4			a		C	25	64 pc
Isel *Hex*	6				nt		8	13	1	nr	157
Kirkbride	6			2			5			50	230
Plumbland	18			4			20	14	8	140	371
Torpenhow *R*	16			3			20	11	6	125	nr
Uldale	18			5			17	18	0	60	151
Wigton	36			13	3	4	17	19	9 *HC*	50	120

DEANERY OF CUMBERLAND

	1291			1318			1535			18th cent.	1835
Addingham	40			10			9	4	6 C	100	253
Ainstable *Ar*	5	4	8		nt		8	8	2	35	225
Castle Sowerby	40	11	8	8			17	10	3 C	50	98
Croglin	9	15	4		nt		8			60	223
Dacre r	50			13	6	8				K	
v	9	2	8				8			14	89
Edenhall	24	1	4	6	13	4	17	12	C	50	178
Greystoke	120			20			80	7	8	300	nr
Hutton-in-the Forest	4	2	4	2			18	10	1	39	123
Kirkland	40			8			8	10	C	63	221
Kirkoswald	48	1	5	5			73	14	10	8 K	95
Lazonby *L*	7	6	8	1			13	1	2	70	551
Melmerby	13	13	4	2			12	11	4	65	172
Ousby	11	19		2			13	13		30	353
Penrith *B*	9	6	8	2			11	10	1	96	nr
Renwick	9	11	4		nt		a *Hex*, or *Y*			4	92 pc
Salkeld	12			2			22	10	8	70	345
Skelton	30			6	13	4	43	2	7	140	294

DEANERY OF WESTMORLAND

	1291			1318			1535			18th cent.	1835
Appleby:											
St Lawrence *Y*	10				nt		9	5	1	85	306
St. Michael *Y*	13	6	8	1			20	12	9	40	175
Asby	20			3			23	13	4	95	205
Askham	17	3	10	2			4	13	8 *Wa*	31	156
Bampton	13	6	8	2			7	1	4 *S*	8	101
Barton	40			10			11	1	*Wa*	75	130

	1291			1318			1535			18th cent.	1835
	£	s.	d.	£	s.	d.	£	s.	d.	£	£
Brough under Stainmore	30			6	13	4	6	18	7 Q	150	492
Brougham	13	6	8	2			16	10	7	50	290
Cliburn	13	6	8	3	6	8	9	1	4	40	188
Clifton	10			1			8	3	4	60	150
Crosby Garrett	24			3	6	8	9	14	4	60	107
Crosby Ravens- worth *Wh*	5				nt		7	13	4	35	150
Dufton	13	6	8	2			19	0	6	44	172
Kirkby Stephen *Y*	26	13	4	5			48	19	2	140	356
Kirkby Thore	40			5			37	17	8	155	959
Long Marton	20			4			21	15	5	—	673
Lowther	35			5			25	7	2	125	283
Morland *Y*	26	13	4	4			11	18		70	177
Musgrave	13	6	8	1			16	8	10	48	149
Newbiggin		nt			nt		4	10	4	22	113
Ormside	13	6	8	2			15	9	4	40	166
Orton *Con*	10				nt		16	17	4	—	192
Ravenstonedale	6	10	6	2			a		*Wat*	21	110 pc
Shap	20			2	13	4	8	15	7 S	6	73
Warcop	35			3	6	8	9	5	1 S	45	194

ARCHDEACONRY OF RICHMOND.
  DEANERIES OF COUPLAND AND FURNESS.

	1291			1318			1535			18th cent.	1835
Aldingham	53	6	8	10			39	18	11	200	1093
Arlecdon		nr			nr		a		*arch*	10	94 pc
Beckermet St. Bridget } St. John }	7			1			a		*Cal*	7 / 7	87 pc / 57 pc
Bootle	20			2			19	17	2	70	525
Brigham	80			20			20	15	11 *Sta*	44	190
Cartmel	46	13	4	8			a		*Car*	100	113 pc
Cleator	4	13	4		nt		a		*Cal*	6	77 pc
Corney	8				nt		9	17	1	22	140
Dalton *Fur*	10				nt		17	6	8	19	113
Dean	22	13	4	5			19	3	1	74	318
Distington	6	13	4		nt		7	0	11	68	301
Egremont	12			3	6	8	7	12		45	249
Gosforth	20			4			17	14	7	35	140
Haile	6	13	4	2			a		*Con*	11	82 pc
Harrington	6	13	4		nt		7	7	3	37	250
Irton	4	13	4		nt		a		*Se*	4	96 pc
Kirkby Ireleth *D & C Y*	6	13	4		nt		5	6	8	13	125
Lamplugh	23	6	8	3	6	8	10	4	6	71	256
Millom *Fur*	6	13	4		nt		8	5	4	26	189

	1291			1318			1535			18th cent.	1835
	£	s.	d.	£	s.	d.	£	s.	d.	£	£
Moresby	4	13	4		nt		6	2	2	23	105
Muncaster	10				nt		a		Con	10	97 pc
Pennington	5	6	8		nt		a		Con	10	141
Ponsonby	4	6	8		nt		a		Con	9	113 pc
St. Bees	66	13	4	10			a		St.B	12	103 pc
Ulverston	12			5			a		Con	28	149 pc
Urswick *Fur*	5				nt		7	17	4	20	86
Waberthwaite	nr			nr			3	11	8	18	131
Whicham	10	13	4	2	13	4	8	14	11	49	243
Whitbeck	10				nt		a		Con	9	76 pc
Workington	33	6	8	10			23	4	11	100	966

DEANERIES OF KIRKBY LONSDALE AND KENDALE.

	1291			1318			1535			18th cent.	1835
Beetham	30			10			13	7	4 Y	13	159
Burton	40			13	6	8	15	17	0 Y	31	199
Grasmere	16			3	6	8	18	11	4	80	109
Heversham	66	13	4	20			36	13	4 Y	60	516
Kendal	123	6	10	13	6	8 Y	92	5		100	285
Kirkby Lonsdale	16			3	6	8	25	15	2	49	250
Y											
Windermere	10			2	13	4	24	6	8	71	253

CHAPELRIES IN THE ANCIENT DIOCESE OF CARLISLE.

	Ancient stipend			18th century			1835
	£	s.	d.	£	s.	d.	£
Allhallows	5			8	10		80
Armathwaite	—			5	10		50
Bolton, Penrith	—			8			61
Borrowdale	3	5		3	5		62
Culgaith	3	5	8	6	0	8	75
Flimby	—			2	4		82
Hesket in the Forest	—			29	19		97
High Head or Ivegill	—			13			46
Langwathby	—						held with Edenhall
Mallerstang	—			8			64
Mardale	2	15		2	15		76
Martindale	—			9	15	7	43
Matterdale	6			6	4	9	54
Milburn	—			25			85
Mungrisdale	6	0	9	8	14	11	57
Newlands	2	11	7	2	11	7	51
Newton Reigny	—			21	12	7	51
Nichol Forest	—			lost			132
Patterdale	—			9			57
Raughton Head	3			10	10		63
St. John in the Vale	3	7	11	24	17	6	63

	Ancient stipend £ s. d.	18th century £ s. d.	1835 £
Soulby	—	20	78
Stainmore	—	18	119
Swindale	—	9	56
Temple Sowerby	1	25	96
Thornthwaite	2 16 8	2 16 8	59
Threlkeld	8 16 6	8 2 6	53
Thrimby	—	10	53
Warwick	—	—	held with Wetheral
Watermillock	6 11 4	7 1 10	55
Westward	—	23 10	99
Wreay	—	14 0 8	86
Wythburn	3 16 10	3 16 10	82

CHAPELRIES WITHIN THE ARCHDEACONRY OF RICHMOND DEANERIES.

	Ancient stipend	18th century	1835
Ambleside	8	10	80
Barbon	2 10	3 1 6	66
Blawith	4	4	59
Burneside	5 14	13 5 8	109
Buttermere	1	1	56
Cartmel Fell	1 10	8 10 2	67
Clifton, Workington	3	ruinous	89
Cockermouth	—	34 13 4	132
Colton	13 6 8	18 16 8	84
Coniston	3 19 10	3 19 10	100
Crook	3 8	7 3	57
Crosscrake	—	ruinous	89
Crosthwaite	6	13	113
Drigg	—	5 6 8	88
Embleton	5 6	8 5	54
Ennerdale	4 13 4	4 13 4	84
Eskdale	5	9	66
Firbank	2 13 4	4 8 4	68
Flookburgh	—	9 12	121
Grayrigg	6 13 4	6 13 4	84
Hawkshead	20	42	110
Hugill or Ings	2 6	6 10	59
Hutton, Old	4 17 10	9 17 10	98
Hutton Roof	4	2 10	70
Ireleth	3	3	63
Kentmere	6	8 6	70
Killington	9 6 8	8 10	75
Langdale	5 15 6	5 15 6	71
Lindale	3 17 6	5 8	71
Longsleddale	5	9 5	69
Lorton	5	7	49
Loweswater	—	4 11	76
Lowick	4	9	92
Middleton	—	8	100

	Ancient stipend			18th century			1835
	£	s.	d.	£	s.	d.	£
Natland		15		ruinous			96
Preston Patrick	3	6	8	3	6	8	78
Rampside	8	3	4	8	13	4	75
Satterthwaite	2			6			71
Seathwaite	3	12	6	3	18	9	60
Selside	4			8	5		94
Setmurthy	2			2			54
Staveley, Cartmel	2	4	9	6	3	6	108
Staveley Kendal	6	13	4	7	3	4	80
Torver	5	1	0	7	1	0	59
Troutbeck	4	12	3	9	12	3	43
Ulpha	3	6	8	5			49
Underbarrow	5	12	6	9	1	6	92
Walney	9	14		9	14		94
Wastdale Head	3			3			49
Wastdale, Nether	5			5			66
Winster	3	17		5	1		61
Witherslack	5	13	8	31	1	8	93
Woodland	7			7			68
Wythop	2	2		2	7		51

AUTHORITIES.

These lists must not be taken for a full bibliography of local historical sources; they only give books quoted, not books consulted.

' A ' shews books and manuscripts to which reference is made by abbreviated titles.

' B ' gives manuscripts consulted and the places where they can be found. But those in private ownership are not accessible without leave.

' C ' is a list of the authorities to which the numbers in the text refer.

A

Abbey, C. J.: The English Church and its bishops, 1700-1800, 1887.

A.J.: Archaeological Journal.

Armitt, M. L.: Rydal, ed. by W. F. Rawnsley, 1916.

Bennett, H. S.: Life on the English Manor, 1938.

B.A. and R.A.: Bailiffs and Receivers Accounts, see under MSS.

C. & T.: Castles and Towers of Cumberland and Westmorland, J. F. Curwen, 1913.

C.B.P.: Calendar of Border Papers.

C.Ch.R.: Calendar of Charter Rolls.

C.Cl.R.: Calendar of Close Rolls.

C.F.R.: Calendar of Fine Rolls.

C.I.P.M.'s.: Calendar of Inquisitions post mortem.

C.L.R.: Calendar of Liberate Rolls.

C.Pap.L.: Calendar of Papal Letters.

C.Pap.P.: Calendar of Papal Petitions.

C.P.R.: Calendar of Patent Rolls.

C.S.D.: Calendar of Scottish Documents.

C.S.P.: Calendar of State Papers, Domestic.

C.D.H.: Carlisle Diocesan History, R. S. Ferguson, 1889.

Charge: Bishop Goodwin's Charges can be found in the seven volumes entitled Carliolensia. They also contain his Pastoral Letters and Reports of the Diocesan Conferences of his episcopate.

Cl: Economic History of Modern Britain, J. H. Clapham, 1930-8.

Close, F.: The Footsteps of Error, 1863.

C.M.B.: Minute Books of Dean and Chapter of Carlisle, see MSS.

Cowper, H. S.: Hawkshead, 1899.

C.P.: The Complete Peerage, ed. V. Gibbs and others, 1910-45.

Cumberland: History of, R. S. Ferguson, 1890.

C.V.B. (*Y*): Diocese of Chester Visitation Books at York, see under MSS.

C. and W. M.P.'s: Cumberland and Westmorland M.P.'s, 1660-1867, R. S. Ferguson, 1871.

D. and B.: Archibald Campbell Tait, R. Davidson and W. Benham, 1891.

D.N.B.: Dictionary of National Biography.

Douglas, D. C.: English Scholars, 1939.

E.H.R.: English Historical Review.

E.S.H.: English Social History, G. M. Trevelyan, 1944.

Fleming, S. H. *le*: Manuscripts of, Hist. MSS. Comm. xii Report.

Foster, J.: Alumni Oxeniensis, 1891.

Fuller, T.: Worthies of England, ed. 1840.

Gastrell, Bishop F.: Notitia, see under MSS.

G.M.: Gentleman's Magazine.

Halton: The Register of Bishop John de Halton, ed. W. N. Thompson, 1906-13.

Hearne, T.: Remarks and Collections, i-viii, 1884-1907.

H.C.: The Register and Records of Holm Cultram, F. Grainger and W. G. Collingwood, 1929.

H.: The History of the county of Cumberland, W. Hutchinson, 1794.

L.D.H.: Lake District History, W. G. Collingwood, 1925.

L.: Chronicle of Lanercost, ed. Sir H. Maxwell, 1913.

L.R. of N.W.: Later Records of North Westmorland, J. F. Curwen, 1932.

L. and P. H. VIII: Letters and Papers of the reign of Henry VIII, ed. J. S. Brewer, 1862-.

Lunt, W. E.: Financial Relations of the Papacy with England to 1327, W. E. Lunt, 1939.

Lysons, D. and S.: Cumberland, 1816.

Magrath, J. R.: The Flemings in Oxford, 1903-24.

Mem.: Memorials of Dean Close, edited by one who knew him.

Milner, M.: Life of Isaac Milner, 2nd ed.

M.A.: Miscellany Accounts of the Diocese of Carlisle, William Nicolson, ed. by R. S. Ferguson, 1877.

Moorman, J. R. H.: Church Life in England in the 13th century, 1945.

Mounsey, G. G.: Occupation of Carlisle in 1745 by Prince Charles Edward Stuart, 1846.

Nightingale, B.: The Ejected of 1662 in Cumberland and Westmorland, 1911.

N. L.: Letters on various subjects to and from William Nicolson, ed. by J. Nichols, 1809.

N. & B.: History of Westmorland and Cumberland, J. Nicolson and R. Burn, 1777.

O.S. and N.S.: Transactions of the Cumberland and Westmorland Antiquarian and Archaeological Society: Old Series, 1866-1900, New Series, 1901-46.

P.L.: Bishop Goodwin's Pastoral Letters, see under Charge.

Pearce, E. H.: The Monks of Westminster, 1916.

Prescott, J. E.: Statutes of the cathedral church of Carlisle, 1879.

R.: Harvey Goodwin, Bishop of Carlisle, H. D. Rawnsley, 1896.

R.K.: Records of Kendale, ed. W. Farrer and J. F. Curwen, 1923-6.

R.O.W.: Records of Old Westminsters.

Report: Reports of Diocesan Conference, see under Charge.

R.C.H.M.: An Inventory of the Historical Monuments in Westmorland, Royal Commission on Historical Monuments, 1936.

R.H.S.: Transactions of the Royal Historical Society.

S.H.R.: Scottish Historical Review.

St. B.: Register of St. Bees, ed. by J. Wilson, Surtees Soc., cxxvi, 1915.

Steel, A.: Richard II, 1941.

Strickland: Strickland of Sizergh, H. Hornyold-Strickland, 1928.

S.S. ii: Wills and Inventories of the Northern Counties, Surtees Soc., 1835.

S.S. vi: The Charters of the Priory of Finchale, Surtees Soc., 1837.

S.S. ix: Hist. Dunelm Scriptores Tres., Surtees Soc., 1839.

S.S. lvi: Register of Archbishop Walter Gray, Surtees Soc., 1872.

S.S. lxviii: Household Books of Lord William Howard, Surtees Soc., 1877.

S.S. cxiv: Register of Archbishop William Wickwaine, Surtees Soc., 1907.

S.S. cxxvii: Miscellanea ii (Documents relating to Visitations of the Diocese and Province of York) Surtees Soc., 1916.

S.S. cxxiii, cxxviii: Register of Archbishop John le Romeyn, Surtees Soc., 1913-7.

S.S. cxxxviii, cxli: Register of Archbishop Thomas Corbridge, Surtees Soc., 1925-8.

S.S. cxlv, cxlix, cli, clii, cliii: Register of Archbishop William Greenfield, Surtees Soc., 1931-8.

Sykes, N.: Church and State in England in the xviii century, 1934.

Testa. Ebor.: Testamenta Eboracensia, iii, Surtees Soc., xliv, 1864.

Testa. Karl.: Testamenta Karleolensia, ed. R. S. Ferguson, 1893.

Todd, H.: History of the Bishopric of Carlisle, see under MSS.

Tough, D. L. W.: The last days of a frontier, 1928.

Tout, T. F.: Chapters in Medieval Administrative History, 1920-33.

West, T.: Antiquities of Furness, 1774.

Westmorland: History of, R. S. Ferguson, 1894.

Wetheral: Register of, J. E. Prescott, 1897.

Whellan, W.: The History and Topography of the counties of Cumberland and Westmorland, 1860.

White, F. D.: Lives of the Elizabethan Bishops of the Anglican Church, 1898.

W.: Rose Castle, J. Wilson, 1912.

Wood, A.: Athenae Oxonienses, 1813.

Wylie, J. H.: History of England under Henry IV, 1884-98.

Venn, J. and J. A.: Alumni Cantabrigiensis, 1924-

V.C.H.: Victoria County History of Cumberland.

V.C.H. Durham: Victoria County History of Durham.

V.C.H. Hants.: Victoria County History of Hampshire.

V.C.H. Lancs.: Victoria County History of Lancashire.

Y.A.J.: Yorkshire Archaeological Journal.

B

Manuscript	Where deposited	The author's thanks are due to
Carlisle diocesan muniments		
Episcopal registers 1292-1385 and 1561-1933	Carlisle diocesan registry	The bishop and the registrar
Visitation and correction court books 1573-7, 1663-86		
Miscellaneous 17th century documents		
Registrar J. Nicolson's record book		
Diocesan Deed Book		
Dean and chapter minute books, 1663-1704,	The dean and chapter registry	The dean
Machell manuscripts,		
Nicolson manuscripts		
Chancellor Waugh's survey of the diocese c. 1747	Jackson library, Tullie House, Carlisle	The curator
Dr. Todd's Histories of the Bishopric and of the Diocese	St. Edmund Hall, Oxford	The principal
Chester diocesan muniments		
Episcopal act books 1541-1856	Chester diocesan registry	The bishop and the registrar
Visitation books, 1548-1856		
Bishop Gastrell's Notitia		
Miscellaneous 17th century documents		

York diocesan muniments		
Episcopal registers of Archbishops Melton, Zouche, Thoresby, A. Neville and W. Booth	York diocesan registry	Professor A. Hamilton Thompson
Visitation books:		
Chester diocese, 1578-1684		
Carlisle diocese, 1662 and 1693		The archbishop and the registrar
Durham diocesan muniments		
Episcopal register of Bishop Langley	Durham diocesan and dean and chapter registry	Professor A. Hamilton Thompson
Miscellaneous MSS. 1521-2		Canon Greenslade
Lieutenancy records of the Cumberland militia	Cumberland county record office Carlisle	Clerk to the Cumberland County Council
Corporation of Carlisle order books, 1745-6	Town clerk's office, Carlisle	The town clerk of Carlisle
Inventories to wills, 1665 and 1737	Carlisle probate registry	The registrar and officials
Bailiffs and receivers accounts and manor rolls of the earl of Northumberland's estates in west Cumberland, Henry VI to Henry VIII	Cockermouth castle	Lord Leconfield and his agent
Survey of these estates in 1578 (copy)	Jackson library, Tullie House, Carlisle	The curator

Manuscript	Where deposited	The author's thanks are due to:
Sir Daniel Fleming's manuscripts	Lowther estate office	The Earl of Lonsdale and Viscount Lowther
Lowther muniments		
Hudleston manuscripts	Hutton John	F. Hudleston and C. R. Hudleston
College of Arms MS. c. 39	Heralds College	Garter King at Arms
Holm Cultram rental, c. 1525	The parish chest	The vicar and Rev. F. B. Swift
Exchequer T R miscellaneous books, 61 and 149	Public Record Office	Rev. W. Oliver
Miss E. Goodwin's MS. book	In possession of Bishop and Mrs. Williams	Bishop and Mrs. Williams

C.

BOOK I.

CHAPTER I.

p. 2   [1] *Lancashire Pipe Rolls and Early Charters*, W. Farrer, x-xi.   [2] *R.K.* I ix.   [3] *V.C.H.* II 240-1.   [4] These questions are discussed by J. C. Dickinson in N.S. xlv 134-43; see also for a description of the Norman Cathedral N.S. xxxvii 56-66.   [5] *R.C.H.M.* liv.   [6] Cumberland Monasteries are described in *V.C.H.* II 131-210, from which the dates have been taken.

p. 6   [7] *The Coucher Book of Furness*, Cheetham Society; *Antiquities of Furness*, T. West; *Annales Furnesienses*, T. A. Beck; O.S. xvi 221-302, W. H. St. John Hope; and *V.C.H. Lancs.* II and VIII.   [8] N.S. xlii 186.   [9] *V.C.H. Lancs.* II 140, West 185; *Religious Houses of Medieval England*, D. Knowles, 83.   [10] N.S. xlv 51.   [11] *R.K.* II 298; *N. & B. I*, 470.   [12] *V.C.H.* II 190-2.   [13] *L.D.H.* 64.   [14] *L.D.H.* 65-6.

p. 8   [15] N.S. xxi 159, 172, and *Fountains Chartulary*, W. T. Lancaster, in passim.   [16] N.S. ix 252-70.   [17] N.S. ix 236-51.   [18] *Monasticon*, Dugdale, VI 869.   [19] *St. B.* 39, 57, 40.   [20] *L.D.H.* 72.   [21] *St. Ninian and the Origins of the Christian Church in Scotland*, W. D. Simpson, in passim.   [22] O.S. xv, 288-302.   [23] If any one wishes to check these figures he must work through N.S. xxiii 206-76 and *R.C.H.M.* and compare the results with evidence from the local Monastic Chartularies, certain articles in the *Trans.* and *N. & B.*   [24] *V.C.H.* II 17.   [25] *V.C.H.* II 16, 13, 117, 121.

p. 10   [26] *V.C.H. I* 421, N.S. xii 59 and xxviii 46.   [27] *V.C.H. I* 421, II 241. *The Ancestor* VI 121-34.   [28] *V.C.H.* I 421, *St. B.* 492, N.S. xv 63-75, and xxix 81-90.   [29] N.S. xxix 69-80 and xxxii 28-37.   [30] *Wetheral* 45.   [31] *Historical MSS. Com. XIth Report* 319.   [32] *H.C.* 91.   [33] N.S. xlv 141-2.   [34] W. 5.   [35] *V.C.H.* I 13.   [36] *V.C.H.* II 19-22.   [37] Moorman 4-5.   [38] *The English Parish Church*, A. R. Powys, 19.

CHAPTER II.

p. 17   [1] *L.D.H.* 78, 135.   [2] *Wetheral* 280, 261.   [3] *St. B.* 241, 424, 445.   [4] *Ibid.* 565.   [5] N.S. xx 90, xi 280.   [6] *C.S.D.* I 313.   [7] Bennett. 277.   [8] *C.S.D.* II 63, N.S. xiii 51.   [9] N.S. xxvi 318-36, *Westmorland* 125-39.

p. 20   [10] N.S. xxv 86-96, xxviii 78-95, xxx 44-54.   [11] *Brief, Leconfield v. Joliffe* i and 46-7 (P.M.), *Westmorland* 125-39.   [12] *H.C.* 168.   [13] *Med. Village*, Coulton, 122.   [14] N.S. xii 339.   [15] N.S. xiii 45-51, xxviii 239-49.   [16] MSS. in possession of the vicar of Holm Cultram and Mrs. T. Ostle.   [17] *R.K.* I 257-8.   [18] List of penal orders at the end of the survey of 1578. (P.M.).   [19] Armitt, 403-27, 69.

p. 22   [20] This section is based on articles by F. H. M. Parker in N.S. v-vii, ix-xii.   [21] N.S. v 35.   [22] N.S. xii 1.   [23] *Wetheral* xxiii.   [24] O.S. xv 1-8.   [25] *The Growth of English Industry and Commerce during the Early and Middle Ages*, W. Cunningham, 4th ed. 628-41, *Thoresby*

Society Miscellanea, 1-21. [26] *H.C.* 43-96. [27] *L.D.H.* 114. [28] *The History and Antiquities of the Exchequer*, T. Madox, 278. [29] *E.H.R.* XI 48. [30] N.S. xxii 85-9. [31] *B. and R.A.* (P.M.). [32] *The Wool Trade in English Med. History*, E. Power, 6-8.

p. 30 [33] N.S. x 133, see further vii 42-53, viii 340-51, x 118-34, xiii 1-30. [34] N.S. x 131-3, viii 18, xxx 52-3, ix 28. [35] N.S. ix, 120-46. [36] *L.D.H.* 116, *H.C.* 2, 22, 26, 57; *V.C.H. Lancs.* VIII 352. [37] *B. and R.A.* (P.M.). [38] *Memoirs of Sir Daniel Fleming*, Porter and Collingwood, 14-5, *L.D.H.* 116, *Armitt* 270-3. [39] *V.C.H.* II 332-5.

p. 34 [40] *St. B.* 207. [41] N.S. ix 37. [42] *V.C.H.* II 342. [43] *B. and R.A.* (P.M.). [44] *Ibid.* [45] *St. B.* 70. [46] *H.C.* 21-2. [47] *The Early Iron Industry of Furness*, A. Fell, 1-22 and 69. [48] *V.C.H.* II 242-3. [49] *B. and R. A.* (P.M.). [50] *V.C.H.* II 338-40, O.S. viii 21-8, N.S. xlv 22-33.

p. 36 [51] N.S. xlii 1-8. [52] N.S. xli 41-4. [53] All dates, unless otherwise stated, from the Gazetteer in *The Lake Counties*, W. G. Collingwood. [54] *St. B.* xxv. [55] *History of Penrith*, Ewanian, 58. [56] N.S. xxi 237. [57] *R.K.* I 2. [58] N.S. xlvi 228. [58a] *V.C.H. Lancs.*, VIII 275, 278, 350, 286*n*, 313, 257, 259. [59] N.S. iv 289. [60] *H.C.* 95. [61] O.S. xvi 41. [62] *S.H.R.* XLI 42, and this book 53. [63] *S.H.R.* XLI 42. [64] *Schools Inquiry Com.* XIX, 325. *N. & B.* I 573-5 and 222. [65] *Y.V.B.*, R VI A 7. [66] *Annals of Cartmel*, J. Stockdale, 37.

CHAPTER III.

The dates of election, consecration, etc. are taken from the *Handbook of British Chronology*, and the *Calendar of Patent Rolls* of the appropriate years, unless otherwise stated.

p. 42 [1] *Wetheral* 492-508. [2] *Ibid.* 497. [3] *V.C.H.* II 246. [4] *C. Pap. L.* 1198-1304, 48, 81-2. [5] *N. & B.* II 252. [6] *V.C.H. Hants.* I 141. [7] *C Pap. L.* 1198-1304, 78, 91. [8] *V.C.H.* II 153. [9] *Rot. Lit. Claus.* I 463, 480. [10] W. 10. [11] *H.C.* 5.

p. 46 [12] Biography in *D.N.B.* [13] *D.N.B.* [14] *V.C.H.* II 24. [15] *C. Ch. R.* I 165. [16] Tout I 220. [17] *C. Cl. R.* 1237-42, 443. [18] Last two paras. based on *V.C.H.* I 25 and *D.N.B.* [19] *C. Lib. R.* 2, 44, 59, 90. [20] *C. Ch. R.* 1226-57, 165. [21] *C. Pap. L.*, 1198-1304, 112. [22] *C. Ch. R.* 1226-57, 115 and *C. Cl. R.* 1227-31, 391. [23] W. 14-17. [24] Lunt, 430 [25] *N. & B.* II 254. [26] *V.C.H.* II 194-9. [27] *C. Lib. R.* 1240-5, 236. [28] *N. & B.* II 255-6 and *Hist. of University of Oxford*, Maxwell Lyte, 27. [29] *C. Lib. R.* 1245-51, 182. [30] *V.C.H.* II 26. [31] *D.N.B.*

p. 50 [32] Biography in *D.N.B.* [33] *V.C.H.* II 26. [34] *C. Lib. R.* 1245-51, 152. [35] *C. Pap. L.* 1198-1304, 256. [36] *V.C.H.* II 24, 124-6. [37] *V.C.H.* II 247-9. [38] N.S. xiv 57, iii 240. [39] *Wetheral* 319, 61. [40] *V.C.H.* II 27-8. [41] *V.C.H.* II 29. [42] *C. Ch. R.* 1257-1300, 356. [43] W. 31, 35, 203-5. [44] *N. & B.* II 258. [45] 16-17. [46] O.S. vii 262, N.S. xx 34.

p. 56 [47] *N. & B.* II 259-60, *V.C.H.* II 29-30. [48] *C.P.R.* 1281-92, 10. [49] *Halton* I ii. [50] N.S. xli 115-6. [51] Illustration in O.S. vii 330. [52] 23-4, *V.C.H.* II 30-1. [53] 88. [54] N.S. xxii 3-5, 18-22, cf. xvi 3. [55] *C. Cl. R.* 1288-96, 263. [56] *C.P.R.* 1281-92, 475. [57] *N. & B.* II 125-6 and *Halton* I 323. [58] W. 111-2. [59] *Taxatio Ecclesiastica* 318-328. [60] *Medieval Panorama*, G. G. Coulton, 165. [61] *The meaning of Medieval Moneys*, G. G. Coulton, 5. [62] *D.N.B.* [63] 86-7. [64] 88-9. [65] N.S. xlvi, 174-81.

CHAPTER IV.

The dates of election, consecration, etc. are taken from the *Handbook of British Chronology*, and the *Calendar of Patent Rolls* of the appropriate years, unless otherwise stated.

p. 63 [1] The account of this episcopate is based on Professor Tout's introduction to his register, except where otherwise stated. [2] *L.* 115. [3] W. 39. [4] *V.C.H.* II 250. [5] *Halton* I 168. [6] *V.C.H.* II 257. [7] N.S. xxviii 398. [8] *L.* 179. [9] *C.P.R.* 1301-7, 479-502. [10] *Carlisle,* Creighton, 53.

p. 66 [11] *L.* 183, 197. [12] *L.* 205. [13] W. 41. [14] *C.P.R.* 1292-1301, 569, 1301-7, 20, 149, 241, 321, 516, 1307-13, 434, 1313-7, 186. [15] *L.* 210-1 213-5, and Leland, *Collectanea*, ed. 1770, 24. [16] O.S. viii 489-90, ix 233. [17] *L.* 216-7. [18] *V.C.H.* II 33. [19] *V.C.H.* II 260-3 and *L.* 240-6.

p. 71 [20] *S.S.* Vol. cxxiii, p. xix, 5. [21] *Halton* I 119-22. [22] *S.S.* Vol. cliii, 64-5. [23] *Ibid.* p. xlii (Professor A. Hamilton Thompson). [24] O.S. I 32. [25] For a description of them see O.S. II 280-96. [26] *Carlisle Cathedral*, C. K. Eley, 46. [27] *Halton*, xxvii. [28] *Halton*, xliii. [29] *V.C.H.* II 42, private letter in possession of Mrs. Williams.

p. 73 [30] 1319-27, 343. [31] *C. Pap. L.* 1305-42, 468. [32] Tout, 307-8. [33] W. 113-5. [34] *N. & B.* II 264, *V.C.H.* II 42, 145. [35] *V.C.H.* II 164. [36] *N. & B.* II 264.

p. 76 [37] *C.P.R.* 1330-4, 499. [38] *C.P.R.* 1334-8, 245, 445. [39] *L.* 306-8. [40] *V.C.H.* II 118-9. [41] *N. & B.* II 443. [42] *N. & B.* II 265, *V.C.H.* II 42. [43] *Reg.* 382, 414, 385, 399, 380, 422, 427, *V.C.H.* II 42, 185. [44] *Studies in Church Life in England under Edward III*, Wood Legh 42, 52, 57. [45] *C.P.R.* 1338-40, 445. [46] *V.C.H.* II 136-7. [47] *V.C.H.* II 204-5, N.S. xix 30, 61. [48] *C.P.R.* 1343-5, 146-7. [49] *D.N.B.* [50] *D.N.B.* [51] *C.P.R.* 1342-5, 507-8.

p. 81 [52] W. 45. [53] *C. Cl. R.* 1346-9, 30. [54] *C.F.R.* 1337-47, 140, 334, 363, 438, 441. [55] *C.P.R.* 1345-8, 83. [56] *L.* 332. [57] O.S. i, 138. [58] W. 115. [59] *N. & B.* II 265-6. [60] *C. of I.P.M's.* XII 367. [61] *A.J.* LXXI 102, *Y.A.J.* XXV 170. [62] *V.C.H.* II 35-6. [63] *Medieval Panorama*, Coulton, 496. [64] *C.P.R.* 1350-3, 366.

p. 85 [65] *C. Pap. L.* 1342-62, 482, 610, 513. [66] *Register*, 1 & 10. [67] *Ibid.* 162, 178, 65, 86, 117. [68] *Ibid.* 5, 27-8. [68a] 30, 52, 47. [68b] 43, 86. [69] *Ibid.* 68, 72, 115, 76. [69a] 118, 120, 71, 112. (The folios are out of their order in the register). [70] *V.C.H.* II 119. [71] *V.C.H.* II 197-8. [72] *C.P.R.* 1354-8, 443. [73] *Ibid.* 342. [74] *N. & B.* II 267. [75] *Bishop Welton's Register* under these dates. [76] *A.J.* LXXI 146-7. (Professor A. Hamilton Thompson). [77] *Testa. Karl.* in passim. [78] *C. Pap. P.* 1342-1419, 437. [79] N.S. xxviii 246-7.

p. 91 [80] *C. Pap. P.* 1342-1419, 437. [81] *Register*, 154, 311. [82] *V.C.H.* II 135. [83] *Register* 145, 318, 263. [84] *Ibid.* 313, 340, 357. [85] *Y.A.J.* XXV 173-5. [86] *C.P.R.* 1370-4, 190. [87] *C.P.R.* 1374-7, 244. [88] W. 173. [89] *Preaching in Medieval England*, G. R. Owst, 209. [90] *Memorials of London*, H. T. Riley, 415.

p. 96 [91] *V.C.H.* II 204-6. [92] *C.P.R.* 1381-5, 353. [93] *V.C.H.* II 134, 146. [94] *C.P.R.* 1388-92, 218. [95] *C.P.R.* 1377-81, 558, but see page 67. [96] *V.C.H.* II 166. [97] *C.F.R.* 1383-91, 95, and in passim. [97a] N.S. xxii 153-4. [98] *C.P.R.* 1388-92, 60, 430, 446. [99] *N. & B.* II 269.

p. 100 [100] *C.P.R.* 1391-6, 358, 524. [101] Biography in *D.N.B.* [102] *C. Pap. L.* 1362-1404, 539. [103] *N. & B.* II 269. [104] *C.P.R.* 1396-9, 5.

[105] *C. Pap. L.* 1362-1404, 535.   [106] *V.C.H.* II 43.   [107] Pearce 116.
[108] Wylie I 2.   [109] Steel 7, 220, 261.   [110] *N. & B.* II 270.   [111] *A History of the English Church in the 14th and 15th Centuries*, W. W. Capes, 157.   [112] *14th Century Studies*, M. V. Clarke, 88.   [113] Steel 282.
[114] See also *Bulletin of the John Rylands Library*, XIV 153-5.

p. 103   [115] *C. Cl. R.* Henry IV, I. 28-34, Wylie, I 91-9.   [116] *Proceedings of the Privy Council*, I 116.   [117] *C. Cl. R.* Henry IV I 167.   [118] *C.P.R.* 1399-1401, 385.   [119] *C. Pap. L.* 1396-1404, 317.   [120] *Political History of England*, 1377-1485, C. Oman, 160.   [121] *C. Pap. L.* 1396-1404, 395.
[122] *C.P.R.* 1399-1401, 450.   [123] *C.P.R.* 1401-5, 6.   [124] *Letters of the Reign of Henry IV*, Rolls Series, 66.   [125] *C.P.R.* 1401-5, 315.
[126] *C. Pap. L.* 1396-1404, 619.   [127] *William of Wykeham's Register*, Hants. Record Society.   [128] *Canterbury Administration*, Churchill, I 233-4.   [129] Todd, *Bishoprick*, I 165.   [130] This section is based on *Oxford Formularies, Oxford Historical Society*, N.S. IV ed. H. E. Salter, W. A. Pantin and H. G. Richardson.   [131] Wylie III 349-51.   [132] *N. & B.* II 270.   [133] Pearce 116.   [134] Steel 296.

CHAPTER V.

The dates of election, consecration, etc. are taken from the *Handbook of British Chronology*, and the *Calendar of Patent Rolls* of the appropriate years, unless otherwise stated.

p. 107   [1] *C. Pap. L.* 1396-1404, 317.   [2] N.S. xvi 129-30.   [3] *Testa. Karl.* 44.
[4] *Bishop Appleby's Register* 281.   [5] *Ibid.* 232, 240, 269, 152.   [6] *Ibid.* 240, 294, 204.   [7] This book p. 105.   [8] N.S. xvi 130.   [9] *Northumberland County History* xiv, 319.   [10] Strickland, 282.   [11] *N. & B.* II 269.
[12] *C. Pap. L.* 1396-1404, 48, 66, 141.   [13] *C.P.R.* 1386-9, 237.   [14] *C.P.R.* 1396-9, 66, 480.

p. 110   [15] N.S. vii 281-91, xviii 174-88, xxx 13-26, the latter is Mr. Hudleston's article.   [16] *N. & B.* ii 410, *Valor Ecclesiasticus* 290.   [17] W. 10, 74.
[18] *C. Pap. L.* 1404-15, 220.   [19] N.S. xxxvii 64.   [20] Strickland, 283-4.
[21] *Test. Ebor.* iii 60-1.   [22] *C. Pap. L.* 1417-31, 157.   [23] A pedigree of the family is in N.S. xliii 31-49.   [24] *The Queen's College Oxford*, J. R. Magrath, I 134.   [25] *MS. Register* fo. iiib, Professor A. Hamilton Thompson has kindly supplied this record.   [26] *Test. Ebor.* iii 65-8, and Magrath op.cit.   [27] *C.P.R.* 1422-9, 561, 571, 356, 482.   [28] *C. Pap. L.* 1417-31, 564, 563.   [29] *N. & B.* II 273.   [30] *V.C.H.* II 206.   [31] *D.N.B.*

p. 115   [32] *C.P.R.* 1436-41, 185.   [33] *C.P.R.* 1441-6, 183. This appropriation never took place.   [34] *C.P.R.* 1446-52, 228.   [35] *Y.A.J.* xxx, 79, 99.
[36] *C.P.R.* 1436-41, 88, and 1446-52, 230, 407, and *D.N.B.*   [37] *D.N.B.*
[38] *V.C.H.* II 139.   [39] Venn.   [40] *D.N.B.*   [41] *N. & B.* ii 274.   [42] *C. Pap. L.* 1417-31, 600, 109, 608.   [43] Fuller iii 409.   [44] Venn.   [45] Strickland 59.   [46] *R.A.* 21 *and* 33 *Henry VI (P.M.)*.   [47] N.S. xxi 188-9.
[48] N.S. x 489-93, 430.   [49] W. 161-2.   [50] N.S. x 429.   [51] *Camden Society N.S.* xxviii 152.

p. 121   [52] *Paston Letters*, ed. Gairdner, ii 13.   [53] *Royal Charters of Carlisle*, ed. R. S. Ferguson, 53-5.   [54] *C.P.R.* 1461-7, 87.   [55] *Paston Letters*, ed. Gairdner, ii 7.   [56] *Letters and Papers of Henry VI*, 779.   [57] W. 47.
[58] *History of England*, Lingard, ed. 1883, iv 151, N.S. xxxiii 119.
[59] N.S. xli 84, Rev. S. Taylor.   [60] West 210.   [61] *Lowther Castle muniments*.   [62] *N. & B.* ii 303.   [63] N.S. xlv 125-8.   [64] *Y.A.J.*, xxx 110, 137.   [65] W. 47 quoting *bishops accounts rolls*.

p. 125   [66] *Le Neve's Fasti*, Hardy's ed., 329.   [67] *C. Pap. L.* 1458-71, 226. [68] In a volume in the diocesan registry, Carlisle.   [69] i 415.   [70] Venn, *Test. Ebor.* iii 169.   [71] *C. Pap. L.* 1458-71, 226.   [72] *Rolls of Parliament* vi 232.   [73] *N. & B.* 39, *R.K.* i 48.   [74] *V.C.H.* ii 44.   [75] W. 111. [76] *N. & B.* II 275.   [77] *V.C.H.* II 165.   [78] *V.C.H.* II 191.   [79] *V.C.H.* II 264.   [80] *V.C.H.* II 202.   [81] *S.S.* vi p. xxviii-xxxi.

p. 129   [82] N.S. viii 234, with an illustration.   [83] O.S. xv 14, *A.J.* xvi 374. [84] *V.C.H.* ii 148.   [85] *Ibid.* 267-8.   [86] *Ibid.* 148.   [87] O.S. xvi 231, 251. [88] Dates taken from *RCHM*.   [89] W. 25, 151, and *The Redmans of Levens and Harewood*, W. Greenwood, 119-123.   [90] *Halton* ii.   [92] W. 125, 118, 214-8, 86.   [93] W. 9.   [94] *S.S.* vi p. xxviii-xxxi.   [95] *S.S.* ix p. cccxcvii, cccciv.   [96] O.S. xii, 255.   [97] N.S. vii 191, with illustration [98] *O.S.* xii 255.   [99] *D.N.B.*, *V.C.H. Durham* ii 28.   [100] *N. & B.* II 277. [101] *P.M.*   [102] Wilkins, *Concilia* iii 487-91.

CHAPTER VI.

p. 136   [1] *Taxatio Ecclesiastica* 227-8.   [2] Gastrell's *Notitia*, under Arlecdon. [3] *St. B.* 304.   [4] *V.C.H. Lancs.* VIII 315, 336.   [5] *S.S.* cxlix p. xi. [6] *S.S.* cxiv, 116-9, 345.   [7] *Ibid.* 148-50.   [8] *S.S.* cxxiii 337.   [9] *Ibid*, 349-50.   [10] *S.S.* cxxviii 201.   [11] *Halton* I 6.   [12] *S.S.* clii 214-5. [13] *S.S.* cxiv No. 386.   [14] *S.S.* cxxiii No. 1003, 1008.   [15] *S.S.* cxxviii No. 242, *S.S.* cxxxviii No. 790, 789, 794, 799, *S.S.* clii No. 2086, *S.S.* cliii p. 278 note.   [16] *S.S.* cxxxviii No. 791.   [17] *S.S.* clii No. 2505. [18] *S.S.* cxli No. 1098.   [19] *St. B.* p. xxxi, 112 note, and N.S. xliii, 1-19. [20] *S.S.* cxli, p. xxii.   [21] *Medieval Panorama*, G. G. Coulton, 190.

p. 143   [22] *S.S.* lvi 50, 23, 160-2, 18.   [23] *S.S.* cxxxviii No. 788.   [24] *S.S.* clii No. 2091.   [25] *S.S.* lvi No. ix, p. xxvii-xxx, N.S. x 136-7.   [26] *S.S.* cxlv 212-3.   [27] *fo.* 446-7.   [28] *fo.* 454.   [29] O.S. xvi 161, N.S. viii 133.   [30] *fo.* 442-4, *C. Pap. L.* 1305-42, 179.   [31] N.S. xxv 20.   [32] *St. B.* 131, *Wetheral* 15, 46.   [33] *fo.* 442, 445.   [34] *fo.* 448-9.   [35] *fo.* 454, 456. [36] *fo.* 443, 445.   [37] *fo.* 445, 449.   [38] *fo.* 450.   [39] *fo.* 456-7.   [40] *fo.* 445-6.

p. 147   [41] *Historical Essays in Honour of James Tait*, Some letters from the Register of William Zouche, archbishop of York, Professor A. Hamilton Thompson, 332-3, 339-42.   [42] *fo.* 69b.   [43] *fo.* 71.   [44] *fo.* 71b, 72b, 73, 74.   [45] *fo.* 65.   [46] *fo.* 79.   [47] *fo.* 70.   [48] *fo.* 67, 75.   [49] *fo.* 67b, 77b, [50] *fo.* 78b.

p. 149   [51] *fo.* 290b.   [52] *fo.* 289.   [53] *fo.* 291b-2b, 293-4, and *A. Neville fo.* 86, 88b.   [54] *fo.* 293b,   [55] *fo.* 218b.   [56] *fo.* 293b.   [57] *Y.A.J.* xxv 184. [58] *Reg. Scrope fo.* 149.   [59] *S.S.* cxxvii, 144.   [60] *Ibid.* 207-10.   [61] *Ibid.* 278-80.   [62] In *Y.A.J.* xxv 129-229 for the years 1361-99 & 1419-41; and xxx 1-143 for 1443-73.   [63] *The Hermits and Anchorites of England*, R. M. Clay, 79.   [64] *Exchequer T. R. Miscellaneous Books*, Nos. 61, 149.

BOOK II.
CHAPTER I.

p. 170   [1] *The Pilgrimage of Grace*, M. H. and R. Dodds, ii 227.   [2] Biography in Venn.   [3] *N. & B.* II 277, D.N.B.   [4] *V.C.H.* II 169.   [5] *V.C.H.* II 269. [6] *MSS. of S. H. le Fleming*, Hist. MSS. Com. xii Report, App. Part vii 6.   [7] *Chapters of the Augustinian Canons*, H. E. Salter, 131-43. [8] *L. and P. H. VIII* iii 77.   [9] O.S. xiii 59.   [10] Biography in *D.N.B.* [11] *V.C.H.* ii 47, O.S. xv 35-42.   [12] W. 85-6.   [13] *L. and P. H. VIII*, iii, 34.   [14] *V.C.H.* II 208-10.   [15] *V.C.H.* II 156.   [16] *V.C.H.* II 149.

p. 175 [17] *D.N.B.* [18] *Valor Ecclesiasticus. Henry VIII*, the net figures are given. [19] General authority for this section is *English Monks and the Suppression of the Monasteries*, G. Baskerville. [20] 125-6. [21] Those for Cumb. and West. are printed in o.s. iv, 83-90. [22] *Some Records of a Cistercian abbey*, G. E. Gilbanks, 91. [23] *V.C.H. Lancs.* II 123. [24] *Political History of England*, 1485-1547, H. A. L. Fisher, 406. [25] Dates from *V.C.H. Cumb. and Lancs.*, and for Shap *N. & B.* I 476. [26] *H.C.* 157. [27] *V.C.H.* II 53. [28] o.s. xiii 368-73. [29] *St. B.* 598. [30] *N. & B.* II 501.

p. 181 [31] The following section is based on *The Pilgrimage of Grace*, 1536-7, M. H. and R. Dodds, mostly from i, 216-25, 369-72, and ii 114-20. and o.s. xiv 335-70. [32] *Trans. R.H.S.*, N.S. xx 201. [33] *R.K.* i 80. [34] *Cuthbert Tunstal*, C. Sturge, 153. [35] *C.D.H.* 113. [36] *V.C.H. Lancs.* II 129, 147. [37] *Ibid.* II 43, 122-4. [38] *V.C.H.* II 51. [39] *N. & B.* II 278-9 for inscription. [40] *Life of Wolsey*, Cavendish, ed. Singer, 463· [41] *L. & P. H. VIII* iv 1117. [42] *Life of Wolsey* op. cit. 225, 257-8.

p. 187 [43] Biography in *D.N.B. and Venn.* [44] *Proceedings of the Privy Council*, VII 88. [45] Prescott, 23-4. [46] *V.C.H.* II 274-6; o.s. viii 257-62; and N.S. xii 41-3. [47] N.S. viii 124-5. [48] N.S. viii 127. [49] *V.C.H.* II 36, 55 [50] *V.C.H.* II 58, 207, 210. [51] *H.* II 478, N.S. xxvii, 58; *R.K.* i 87. [52] o.s. viii 189. [53] *Ibid.* 186-204. [54] o.s. iv 164, 173-77. [55] *C.S.P. Dom.*, 1598-1601, 363. [56] Fuller I 341. [57] o.s. xvi, 215; *C.S.P. Dom.* Elizabeth, X 147, 149. [58] o.s. xv 21-6; *V.C.H.* II 59-60. [59] o.s. xvi 163.

CHAPTER II.

p. 196 [1] *D.N.B.* [2] *Extinction of the Ancient Hierarchy*, G. E. Phillips, 60-1. [3] *op. cit.* 140-4. [4] *The parish register.* [5] Phillips, op. cit. 144. [6] The account of this reign is generally based on *V.C.H.* II 60-88. [7] *History of the Church of England*, R. W. Dixon, V 151. [8] This section is based on R. R. Reid's article in *Trans. R.H.S.*, N.S., xx, 171-203. [9] *Reign of Elizabeth*, J. B. Black, 104. [10] o.s. iv 411-3; *V.C.H.* II 277-8. Annals of the House of Percy, E. B. de Fonblanque, II, 580.

p. 206 [11] Biography in *D.N.B.* and Foster. [12] *N. & B.* II 283. [13] *V.C.H.* II 79-80, N.S. xlv 42-4, where it is given in full. [14] Prescott, 106. [15] *Episcopal Register* and *N. & B.* II 381, 442, I 496, 507, 392, II 98, 463. [16] *Bishop's Register*, in passim. [17] Tough, quoting from the *Ecclesiastical Proceedings of Bishop Barnes*, 13-28 and 29-46. [18] *C.V.B.* (Y) 1578, Chester, R. VI A. 7.

p. 212 [19] *Newcastle Tracts, Miscellaneous*, M. A. Richardson, No. I. [20] White, 184-5, *D.N.B.* [21] Biography in Venn. [22] o.s. x 131, *D.N.B.* [23] *History of England*, G. M. Trevelyan, 358. [24] *V.C.H.* II, 279-80. [25] *Register*, fo. 110. [26] *N. & B.* II 372. [27] *Gillesland*, Anon. but G. G. Mounsey, 75-7. The present whereabouts of the original is unknown. [28] *C.B.P.* II 171, 613, 622. [29] *N. & B.* II 284.

BOOK III.
CHAPTER I.

p. 225 [1] N.S. xiv 162. [2] o.s. xi 371. [3] In the Diocesan Registry. [4] N.S· xliii 177-9 and *R.C.H.M.*, plates 19-23. [5] ed. 1610, 767-8. [6] Quoted in *Wordsworth's Birthplace*, J. Bolton, 20. [7] *Through England on a side-saddle*, C. Fiennes, 169. [8] o.s. iii 351 and Lyson's, 23.

p. 234 [9] *V.C.H.* II 348-83 and o.s. iii 305. [10] o.s. v 191, N.S. xxv 157, 165; *Gilpin Memoirs*, ed. W. Jackson, 38; *Cleator and Cleator Moor*, C. Caine, 203; N.S. xxiv 224 and will of William Hudleston, 1625, P.P.R. [11] *The Theatre of the Empire of Great Britain*, J. Speed, 1611, 87; *L.D.H.* 123. [12] *The Boke of Recorde of the Burgh of Kirkby Kendal*, ed. R. S. Ferguson, 274-305. [13] *R.K.* iii 58-9. [14] Cowper, 282-91; and West, xxxiii-v. [15] *Royal Charters of the city of Carlisle*, ed. R. S. Ferguson, 326. [16] N.S. i 16. [16a] N.S. xiv 306, viii 116, vi 198.

p. 238 [17] Chapter xxv. [18] p. 191-3. [19] *S.S.* ii 229. [20] *C.V.B.*(Y) 1578, R. vi *A*. 7. [21] *Schools Inquiry Commission, vol.* xix *Northern Division*, 159-293, 295-465; *V.C.H. Lancs.* viii and *Bishop Gastrell's Notitia*, in passim; Cowper, 463-504; *Annals of Cartmel*, J. Stockdale, 37.

CHAPTER II.

p. 244 [1] *C.S.P. Dom.* 1598-1601, 362-3. [2] *V.C.H.* II 76. [3] 18 Jan. 1606. [4] 17 Nov. 1605. [5] *V.C.H.* II 282-4. [6] *S.S.* lxviii, 413, 425-7; *V.C.H.* II 285. [7] *S.H.R.* VIII 5-21. [8] N.S. xvi 55. [9] See also article in N.S. xlvi. [10] N.S. xxv 128-243. [11] *Dalston Registers*, ed. J. Wilson. [12] *N. & B.* II 284. [13] Wood II 857.

p. 249 [14] Biography in Venn. [15] *C.D.H.* 131-3. [16] W. 219-31; N.S. xxxix 122-3, 133-4. [17] Biography in Venn. [18] o.s. iv 441. [19] *N. & B.* I 51-9; *Westmorland* 129-37. [20] *S.S.* lxviii 56. [21] i 178. [22] *Social England*, ed. H. D. Traill, iv 156. [23] Parish Registers named and o.s. xi 158-86.

p. 253 [24] Biography in Venn. [25] ii 286. [26] Biography in *D.N.B.* and Venn. [27] John Cosin, *Works.*, i 85. [28] *V.C.H.* II 90. [29] Biography in *D.N.B.* [30] *V.C.H.* II 90-1. [31] *Articles to be enquired of in the Diocesan Visitation of the Right Reverend Father in God Barnabie (by the providence of God) Lord Bishop of Carlisle*, 1629. [32] *C.D.H.* 133. [33] *Ibid.*, 134. [34] *C.S.P. Dom.*, 1639, 478. [35] Fuller, iii 306. [36] Wood, iii 23.

p. 260 [37] General authorities: *V.C.H.* II 286-91; o.s. vii 48-53, xi 104-16; *A Narrative of the Siege of Carlisle* 1644 *and* 1645, Isaac Tullie. [38] West lii-iii. [39] *Montrose*, John Buchan, 75-6. [40] *E.H.R.* vol. xiii. [41] *Hist. MSS. Com.* xiii Report p. 89. [42] *Slingsby's Diary*, ed. 1836. p. 123-9. [43] See above No. 37. [44] *V.C.H.* II 289; *N. & B.* I 185-6. [45] *Life of Sir P. Musgrave*, G. Burton, 8-9. [46] *C. and T.* 467-8. [47] *Allerdale above Derwent*, S. Jefferson, 161; Warde's Will at Durham. [48] *V.C.H.* II 288-9; *Kirkbie Kendale*, J. F. Curwen, 12-3. [49] *C. and T.* 474.

p. 264 [50] *C. and T.* 78, 236, 205, 231; N.S. xxii 155. [51] *V.C.H.* II 290; *C. and T.* 477. [52] N.S. xxiv 217; *C. and T.* 478. [53] *Strickland of Sizergh*, H. Hornyold, 116 and note. [54] *Leath Ward*, S. Jefferson, 425. [55] N.S. xiv 207-12. [56] *V.C.H.* II 93.

p. 266 [57] *V.C.H.* II 93. [58] *The Ejected of* 1662 *in Cumb. and West.*, B. Nightingale, in passim. [59] N.S. xxxviii 124. [60] N.S. xxix 181. [61] *V.C.H.* II 95; *Fox's Journal*, ed. 1827, I 163-71, 199-207; *C.V.B.*(Y), 1684, R. vi, *A*. 34. [62] *V.C.H.* II, 95-6. [63] *Journal*, i 400, ii 26-7, 197, 216, 267, 275. [64] *C.V.B.*(Y), op. cit.; *Chancellor Waugh's Survey*, see MSS. [65] Nightingale, op. cit. i 80-1.

p. 269 [65a] Biography in Venn and *D.N.B.* [66] W. 91. [67] *Register*, 257-8. [68] *V.C.H.* II, 293-4. [69] Among a bundle of 17th cent. documents.

[70] From her *Funeral Sermon* preached by Bishop Rainbow.　[71] This section is based on *Lady Anne Clifford*, G. C. Williamson, in passim.

p. 273　[72] Biography in *D.N.B.*, Venn, and *R.O.W.*　[73] *S.H.R.* XVI, 132-40, J. Wilson, throws light on post Restoration Chapter affairs.　[74] Todd I, 273-4.　[75] *Register* Rainbow, 400-1 and *C.M.B.* VIII, 468.　[76] o.s. VIII, 233-6.　[77] *ed.* 1747, 3-4.　[78] *Round Carlisle Cross*, J. W. Brown, 51, 42, 50, 52.　[79] *Register* Rainbow, 460-1.　[80] In the care of the diocesan registrar.

p. 278　[81] Todd, I, 296-8.　[82] All the above from *Court and Correction Books* under the dates quoted.　[83] W. 92-5, 238-44.　[84] *N. & B.* II, 291.　[85] *C.D.H.* 206.　[86] *Life of Edward Rainbow*, Anon, 69-70.　[87] Todd, i, 183.

p. 281　[88] The account of his early life from Magrath II, p. xvi-xx.　[89] N.S. vii, 200.　[90] W. 97.　[91] N.S. xxiv, 12-6.　[92] *N. & B.* II, 293.　[93] o.s. ii, 312-36.　[94] *N. & B.* II, 293.　[95] *N. & B.* II, 376.　[96] Macauley's *History of England*, ed. 1898, II, 151, and *The Fothergills of Raven-stonedale*, C. Thornton and F. McLaughlin, 13.　[97] *V.C.H.* II, 295-8.　[98] le Fleming, 210-1.　[99] Abbey I, 159.

p. 284　[100] le Fleming, 231 and N.S. xiv, 102.　[101] *V.C.H.* II, 297.　[102] *Strickland of Sizergh*, H. Hornyold, 135-49.　[103] *N.L.* I, 6, 12.　[104] *The Non-Jurors*, Canon Overton, alphabetical list; *The later Non-Jurors*, H. Broxap, 36, 46, 51.　[105] *N.L.* I, 43-6.　[106] *Ibid.* 47, 51.　[107] o.s. ii, 314-21; iv, 1-12.　[108] *N.L.* I, 146-7; C.D.H., 158-61.　[109] *N. & B.* II, 293.　[110] Magrath II, p. xxi.　[111] Will in o.s., iv, 6.

CHAPTER III.

p. 289　[1] Printed in N.S. i-v, xxxv.　[2] M.A. 84.　[3] i, 183.　[4] Douglas, 266.　[5] Todd I, 184; Hearne I, 187.　[6] Sykes, 72.　[7] *Ibid.*, 150.　[8] *Miscellany Accounts of the Diocese of Carlisle*, ed. R. S. Ferguson, 1877.　[9] *V.C.H.* II, 102-3.　[10] *The Articles of the Visitations of 1703 and 1710* are in the British Museum Library.　[11] *M.A.* in passim.　[12] *V.C.H.* II, 104.

p. 296　[13] *N.L.* I, 229-30.　[14] Douglas, 263-4.　[15] *N.L.* I, 267-86, and *Diary*.　[16] *N.L.* I, 308-20.　[17] Prescott, 7. This with Todd's account in I, 266-72 are the main authorities.　[18] *C.M.B.* X, 14, 49.　[19] *Diary*, 30 Nov. 1704.　[20] N.S. iii, 15, 16, 33.　[21] *N.L.* I, 322.　[22] Prescott, 10.　[23] It is given in *N.L.* II, 362.　[24] *N. & B.* II, 295.　[25] *Diary*, 25 March, 1708.

p. 302　[26] Hearne, II, 62.　[27] *E.H.R.*, 1935, 436-8.　[28] *M.P's.*, 93-4, *Diary*, 14 March, 1711.　[29] Sykes, 47.　[30] *England under Queen Anne*, G. M. Trevelyan, II, 176-7.　[31] Sykes, 72.　[32] *V.C.H.* II, 104, 299.　[33] *N.L.* II, 432.　[34] *Diary*, 15 Nov., 1707.　[35] W. 56-7.　[36] *Original Letters*, Sir H. Ellis, 1st series III, 357-96.　[37] o.s. x, 138.　[38] Todd, I, 184.　[39] Abbey, 106.　[40] Todd, I, 185.　[41] N.S. i, 13; iii, 2; iv, 57; v, 23.

p. 311　[42] *N.L.* II, 650.　[43] N.S. ii, 183; iii, 20-1; iv, 8, 9, 69; v, 18; xxxv, 128.　[44] *The Bulletin of the Institute of Historical Research*, IX, p. 198 gives a list of Nicolson's MSS. in the British Museum and Bodleian Libraries and in that of Ch. Ch. Oxford.　[45] N.S. v, 17.　[46] Pedigree in N.S. i, 49.　[47] In o.s., iv, 9.　[48] *Reign of Queen Anne*, J. H. Burton, ii, 320.

CHAPTER IV.

p. 313 [1] Biography in Venn and *D.N.B.* [2] Abbey, 34, and Hearne VIII, 126.
[3] Sykes, 122. [4] W., 157. [5] Biography in Foster. [6] o.s. xiii, 440-8.
[7] Hearne, viii, 126, I, 216. [8] o.s. xiii, 440, pedigree. [9] Hearne, I, 216.
[10] Magrath III, in passim. [11] *Nicolson's register*, 155-6, and *Fleming's Register*, 67.

p. 319 [12] Mounsey, 99. [13] *Carlisle*, Creighton, 176, 178-9. [14] *V.C.H.* II, 303.
[15] Mounsey, 72, 80, 79, 95-6, 88. [16] *Ibid.*, 64, 74-5. [17] n.s. xxv, 51,
[18] o.s. x, 186-228; n.s. i, 167-70; xviii 209-10; *Westmorland*, 257-79.
[19] Mounsey, 186, 194, 193, 218. [20] *Ibid.*, 173-4, 180-1. [21] *Ibid.*, 269.
[22] For a history of the bells see o.s. viii, 135-65. [23] *Trans. of Lancashire and Cheshire Antiquarian Society*, xl, 45-75. [24] o.s. viii, 237-44;
and W. 58-9. [25] Mounsey, 22, 72, 122, 195. [26] *N. & B.*, II, 298.
[27] xvii, 324-6.

BOOK IV.

CHAPTER I.

p. 340 [1] The section that follows is based on n.s. xlii, 56-66, xliii, 87-95, and
xliv, 81-92; see also n.s. ix, 120-46 and xliii, 175-97. [2] *V.C.H.* II, 312.
[3] *Cl.* I, 104. [4] *E.S.H.*, 375. [5] n.s. xxvii, 147-8. [6] *Schools Inquiry Commission*, vol. XIX, Northern Division, 159-293 and 295-465.
[7] *Reminiscences of an American Loyalist*, Jonathan Boucher, 8-16.

p. 345 [8] *A Tour through England and Wales*, Every Man's ed., 273.
[9] *Economica*, June, 1929, xxvi, 192-6. [10] *G.M.* XVIII, 3-5. [11] o.s.
xiv, 30, 18. [12] p. 189. [13] *History of Carlisle*, S. Jefferson, 86-90.
[14] *G.M.* xviii, 3-5. [15] Lysons', 172-5. [16] *Allerdale above Derwent*, S.
Jefferson, 258-9. [17] *V.C.H.* II, 366-79; *V.C.H. Lancs.* VIII, 277,
304, 358, 348; *The Millom District*, F. Warriner, 48. [18] *Cleator and Cleator Moor*, C. Caine, 207; Lysons', xxxviii-xxxix and cxxiv.

p. 348 [19] n.s. xviii, 33 and *N. & B.* I, 66. [20] *V.C.H.* II, 308; n.s. ii, 274-81.
The commissioners original minute book is at Tullie House. [21] *Westmorland*, 175. [22] H. II, 663. [23] *History of Penrith*, Ewanian, 179.
[24] *Survey of the Lakes*, J. Clarke, ed. 1787, 15. [25] Lysons', cx. [26] *G.M.*
XVIII, 292. [27] *History*, n.s. xxv, 123. [28] ii, 505. [29] *Complete Works of Robert Burns*, Gebbie, ed., ii, 302. [30] *Life of Sir Walter Scott*, J. G. Lockhart, ed. 1837, 265-6. [31] H. i, 63; Lysons', 133.
[32] i, 481.

p. 350 [33] *L.D.H.*, 155-71. [34] *E.S.H.*, 302-3. [35] n.s. xxviii, 274-5. [36] *E.S.H.*
302-3. [37] Armitt, 292-3. [38] *A Tour through England and Wales*,
Everyman's ed., 270-1. [39] *G.M.* XXI, 51-3. [40] *G.M.* XXI, 200;
XXIV, 464-5; XXXI, 72-3. [41] *Journal of a Tour through the Lakes*,
ed. 1803, 20-1. [42] *History of England*, W. E. H. Lecky ed. 1902, V 296.
[43] n.s. xlv, 18-20. [44] n.s., iv, 352. [45] *Journal of the Fell and Rock Climbing Club*, iii (1914), 69. [46] *A Concise description of the English Lakes*, 1st ed., 48. [47] *Journals of Dorothy Wordsworth*, ed. E. de Selincourt, I, 425.

CHAPTER II.

p. 357 [1] Biography in Venn. [2] Owing to the form in which the MS. has survived no clearer reference can be given. [3] *Register*, 186-210.

[4] Prescott, 12-3 and *Register*, 235. [5] Biography in *D.N.B.* [6] W., 98-100, 245-57 for the correspondence in full and *Register*, 1-2. [7] ii, 249. [8] *D.N.B.* [9] *C.P.* II, 504. [10] *Carlisle Cathedral*, R. W. Billings, 6. [11] *N. & B.* II, 299.

p. 364 [12] *D.N.B.* and Abbey, 246-51. [13] *Memoirs of Archdeacon Paley*, G. W. Meadley, in passim. [14] *C.P.* VIII, 134 quoting Lecky. [15] Sykes, 404; Sir James Lowther and the earl of Lonsdale are the same person. [16] Sykes quoting his *autobiography*. [17] Biography in *D.N.B.* and Foster. [18] W. 101. [19] Abbey, 262-3. [20] Sykes, 191-206. [21] *History of the Church of England*, H. O. Wakeman, ed. 1914, 437. [22] *V.C.H.* II, 106. [23] *The Journal of the Rev. John Wesley*, Everyman's Edition, in passim.

p. 374 [24] Biography in *D.N.B.* and *R.O.W.* [25] *C.D.H.* 173. [26] Milner, 130, 59, 291. [27] *V.C.H.* II, 110. [28] Sykes, 207-9. [29] W. 108. [30] *C.D.H.* 173. [31] W. 75-6, 101-3 and *Register*, 287-94. [32] *D.N.B.* [33] *D.N.B.* and *R.O.W.* [34] Milner, 196. [35] *Ibid.*, 276-8, 285. [36] *C.D.H.*, 187. [37] *R.O.W.* [38] N.S. xxviii, 399.

p. 381 [39] 544, 604, 256, 621. [40] *D. and B.*, I, 149-55. [41] *Ibid.*, 176-7. [42] *First Report*, published in 1854, 586-8 and 9-10. [43] *Ibid.*, 9-10. [44] O.S. xv, 14; N.S. viii, 234. [45] O.S. vi, 499, 501. [46] *Carlisle Cathedral*, C. K. Eley, 44. [47] W., 103-4. [48] W. 128-31; they are reproduced in N.S. xxviii, opp. p. 398. [49] W., 105-8. [50] From an MS. containing reminiscences of Rose Castle by Miss Ellen Goodwin, in possession of Bishop and Mrs. Williams. [51] W. 60. [52] See Reference 50.

BOOK V.
CHAPTER I.

p. 403 [1] *Cumberland*, 279-82. [2] *V.C.H.* II, 385-99. [3] *History of England*. 605. [4] *V. C. H. Lancs.* VIII, 306-7, 314, and II, 339-75. [5] N.S. xliv, 81-92. [6] *E.S.H.* 580. [6a] *Trans. Cumb. and West. Association for the advancement of Literature and Science*, XV, 94. [7] *Cl.* III, 105. [8] *Bishop Goodwin's Pastoral Letters*; *E.S.H.* and Whellan, in passim.

p. 411 [9] *L.D.H.*, 165. [10] *Ibid.*, 167. [11] N.S. xliii, 96-116. [12] *A Complete Guide to the English Lakes*, H. Martineau. [13] *The Lake Country*, E. Lynn Linton. [14] 8-9. [15] *Episcopal Registers of Chester and Carlisle* under these dates. [16] 8-9. [17] 189 and 227. [18] 93. [19] 208-14. [20] 202. [21] *The Journal*, in passim. [22] 262. [23] N.S. xxiii, 1-6.

CHAPTER II.

p. 420 [1] *V.C.H.* II, 111-2. [2] Biography of Villiers in *D.N.B.* [3] *Register*. [4] *George Moore*, S. Smiles, 158-9, 195, 249-50. [5] *D.N.B.* [6] Biography in *D.N.B.* [7] *D.N.B.* [8] *The Church Revival*, S. Baring Gould, 184. [9] Obituary Notice in *Diocesan Calendar*, 1870. [10] *Ibid.* and *Charges* of these years. [11] *Carlisle Patriot*, 8 October, 1869. [12] *D.N.B.* [13] *D. and B.* I, 378. [14] *Registers*. [15] *Mem.* 30. [16] *R.* 355.

p. 426 [17] *Mem.* 9. [18] *Ibid.* [19] *Mem.* 37-43. [20] Close, 34. [21] *Mem.*, 11-20. [22] Close, 344, 350. [23] *Mem.* 67-8. [24] Close, 353. [25] *Mem.* 108. [26] *Mem.* 68, 74, 37, 67, 16. [27] *V.C.H.* II, 114. [28] *Ibid.* [29] *The Keswick Convention*, C. F. Harford, in passim, and the Rev. L. Ashby. [30] Private information. [31] *The Keswick Convention*, C. F. Harford, 77.

p. 431 [32] *R.* 355. [33] R. 347. [34] From the bishop's *Pastoral Letters* and *Charges* of the years named. [35] *V.C.H.* II, 123-4. [36] *V.C.H.* II, 120-1 [37] *V.C.H.* II, 118-9 and *Charge* of 1887. [38] *Report*, 1888, p. 21 and 1889, p. 12; *P.L.*, 1888, p. 7 and 1889, p. 3-7; *V.C.H.* II, 40. [39] *P.L.* 1874, p. 22. [40] *Report*, 1878, p. 58 and *Diocesan Calendar*, 1926. [41] p. 9. [42] *Charge*, 1875, p. 59. [43] *P.L.*, 1877, p. 27 and *Report*, 1878 p. 17. [44] *P.L.*, 1873, p. 27. [45] *Report*, 1890, p. 37. *P.L.*, 1889, p. 19. [46] *R.* 326.

p. 437 [47] *R.*, 133-5. [48] *Diocesan Calendar* of 1868. [49] p. 29. [50] p. 11. [51] *P.L.*, 1870, p. 4-7 and 1872, p. 15. [52] *P.L.*, 1885, p. 26-7 and 1887, p. 31-2. [53] *Charge*, 1872, p. 11-2. [54] *Charge*, 1872, p. 8-9. [55] *P.L.*, 1884, p. 12. [56] p. 39. [57] p. 14. [58] p. 39. [59] *Report*, 1875, p. 46, 1877, p. 55-63. [60] p. 17. [61] p. 23.

p. 441 [62] *P.L.*, 1884, p. 4-5 and *R.* 237. [63] *Carlisle Journal*, 10-31 Jan. 1873; *Secret History of the Oxford Movement*, W. Walsh, 66-8; and *R.* 178-9. [64] *R.*, 178-9. [65] Transcript of shorthand notes in Jackson Library. [66] *V.C.H.* II, 114. [67] *V.C.H.* II, 114-5; *P.L.*, 1873, p. 7-8. [68] *Report*. 1874, p. 71. [69] *P.L.*, 1870, p. 20. [70] *P.L.*, 1871, p. 17. [71] *R.* 230-2; N.S. xvi, 17-9. [72] O.S. xii, 168-9.

p. 444 [73] *Murray's Magazine*, II, 822. [74] O.S., xii, 167. [75] N.S. xxxiii, 1. [76] O.S. xii, 169. [77] *C.D.H.*, 199-200. [78] *P.L.*, 1885, p. 13. [79] *P.L.*, 1889, p. 21. [80] *P.L.*, 1890, p. 28. [81] A full list is given in *P.L.*, 1889, p. 35. [82] 3 Jan., 1896. [83] *R.* 361. [84] *The Times*, 3 Jan., 1896. [85] *P.L.*, 1886, p. 29.

p. 449 [86] *Carlisle Journal*, 16 Sept., 1904. [87] N.S. xx, 259. [88] *Carlisle Patriot*, 31 July 1908, and 31 May, 26 July 1907. [89] *Cumberland News*, 26 Feb., and 8 April 1916. [90] *Ibid.*, 10 Aug. and 22 Nov. 1918. [91] *Carlisle Journal*, Dec. 1919.

INDEX.

Note: Where there are entries immediately after the place name and others after church or chapel, as at Ambleside; the former refers to notices of secular affairs, the latter of religious ones in general and not only to the church fabric.

Abbreviations: c. = century.
(2) = two references on same
   page.
appropr. = appropriation.

Cumb., West. = Cumberland, Westmorland.
n = note.

Addingham, 15, 67, 192, 235, 241, 462, 472; vicar of 290n, 364, 365, 380.
Addison, Lancelot, 228; J. A., 412-3; Robert, 230n; Thomas, 230, 293.
Aglionby, Thomas, 180.
Agriculture, 30-2, 227-8, 230-2, 340-3, 406-7; see enclosures, prices, statesmen.
Aikton, 15, 204, 278, 344, 360, 365n, 366, 460, 471.
Ainstable, 15, 236, 237, 276, 360n, 460, 464, 465, 472.
Aldingham, 136, 138, 146, 148, 150, 151, 155, 210 (2), 220, 329, 473.
Aldrich, Bishop, 187, 193-5, 211n.
Allerdale, above and below Derwent, baronies of, 10, 17, 70, 76, 118n, 225; forest of, 231.
Allhallows, 162, 235, 460, 469, 474.
Allison, Jane, 239; Robert, 235.
Allithwaite, 459, 460.
Allonby, 327, 337, 344, 349, 399, 462, 465.
Alms giving, 423, 432n.
Alston, 35-6, 369, 410, 420.
Ambleside, 348, 350, 354, 369 (2), 370, 374, 410, 543; chapel of, 165, 397, 400, 401, 475; growth of, 413-4; vicar of, 424.
Anchorite, 154.
Anderson, Bishop, 426.
Anthony, John, 235.
Appleby, 18, 36, 37, 114, 227, 228, 229, 261, 314, 373; barony, 2, 11, 118n, 226; St. Lawrence, 12, 15, 272, 273, 364, 460, 472; St. Michael, 12, 15 201n 272 358, 462, 465, 472; castle, 13, 118n, 263, 264; grammar school, 38, 240, 281, 282, 410; friars at, 49, 179n; Scots and, 67, 99; and Pilgrimage of Grace, 186, 187n; Lady Anne Clifford and, 272; alms houses, 272.

Bishop, 53, 72, 91-100, 108-9, 386; John de, 91n.
Appropriations, 44, 175-6, 471-4.
Archer, Elizabeth, 311; John, 311.
Arlecdon, 137, 151, 152, 220, 328 (2), 330, 398, 404, 462, 473.
Armathwaite, 132, 161, 337, 462, 474.
   Nunnery, 7, 69n, 127, 179, 472.
Armstrong, family of, 247; John, 247.
Arnside, 267, 459, 460, 465.
Arrouaise, Order of, 12.
Arthuret, 15, 176, 192, 208, 240, 337, 460, 471.
Asby, 15, 187n, 208, 227, 281, 282, 459, 460, 472.
Ascension Day, 432, 440.
Ashton, Colonel, 263-4.
Askham (West.), 15, 119, 227, 276, 284, 398, 472.
   (Lancs.), 405.
   Thomas, 240.
Aske, Robert, 178, 182, 185.
Aspatria, 15, 92, 399, 401, 404, 460, 471; chapelry of, 162; school, 241, 344; vicar, 316-8; coal mines, 347.
   Robert, 152.
Assistant Curate Society, 432n.
Athelwold, Bishop, 10, 11-2, 42.
Atkinson, Elizabeth, 228; William, 237.
Atterbury, Francis, 296-302, 308, 313.
Averas Holme, 91n.
Avery, Margaret, 217.
Aykeheved, William de, 145.
Ayremynne, William de, 73-4.

Backbarrow, 235, 347.
Baddiley, Anna, 287.
Bainbridge, Archbishop, 38n.
Balfour, Major, 324.
Bampton, 15, 37n, 119, 127, 236, 241, 290, 337, 463, 465, 472.

Baptism, 83, 257, 336, 391, 438-9.
Barbon, 164, 241, 388, 397, 469, 475.
Bardsea, 400, 401.
Bardsley, Bishop, 447-9; C. W., 449n; Elizabeth, 449.
Barker, John, 237.
Barlow, Bishop, 281; Richard, 281.
Barneby, John de, 146.
Barnes, Bishop, 206-9, 212.
Baronies, 2, 12, 118n, 171, 225-6.
Barrow, Bishop, 113-4.
Barrow-in-Furness, 347 (2), 409, 410; bishop of, 417, 434; churches, St. George, 441, 456, 459, 460, 465; St. James, 459, 460; St. John, St. Luke, St. Mark, St. Matthew, 436, 464, 465, 469; St. Paul, 463, 465; St. Perran, 464, 465n; growth, 403 (2), 405.
Barton, 15, 37n, 163, 241 (2), 358, 360, 463, 472.
  Robert de, 73.
Barugh, 340.
Barwise, 52.
  Alan de, 52; Anthony, 192; John, 229; Richard, 262.
Bassenthwaite, 15, 37n, 162, 227, 240, 460, 464, 465, 471; Lake, 32-3, 411.
Bate, H. N., 455.
Bateman, William, 153.
Bayty, Jane, 240.
Beamont, 15, 70, 200, 237, 463, 465, 471.
Beck, John, 184.
Beckermet, St. Bridget's, 145, 149, 220, 328 (2), 399, 401, 473; St. John's, 137, 145, 147, 149, 151 (2), 155, 192, 210, 220, 390, 397, 464, 465, 473.
Beetham, 9, 39, 131, 136, 149, 150, 151, 155, 220, 241, 460, 465, 474.
  Sir Edward, 154; Joan, 154; Robert de, 148.
Bek, Bishop Anthony, 61, 63; Richard, 153.
Bell, Ann, 236; C. D., 424; Richard, 253; Thomas, 236, 253, 284.
  Bishop, 128-32.
Bellingham, Sir James, 230.
Benefices, exchanges, 146.
  houses, dilapidations, 93; state, 210, 278, 329, 360; size, 437-8n; numbers 381, 423, 425, 437.
  numbers, 15-6, 93-4, 136-7, 175-6.
  patronage, 152.
  stipends, 60-1, 68, 156, 175-6, 318-9, 330, 333, 361, 380-2, 422, 423, 425, 437, 448.
  poverty, 210, 258, 386n, 422, 423.
Bernard, Bishop, 13-4, 42.
Best, Bishop 197, 199-206, 245; Elizabeth, 206.

Bewcastle, 15, 173, 176, 180, 208, 217, 397, 463, 471.
Bewley, 132; castle, 45, 51, 110.
  Richard, 185.
Bible, 127, 211, 215, 255, 359.
Bicycle, 415.
Bigland dock, 347.
Bigrigg, 347, 404, 464, 467.
Bindlosse, Thomas, 238.
Bird, Bishop, 219; Thomas, 227.
Birkbeck, George, 227.
Birkby, 347.
Birkett, Edward, 324.
Black Death, 83-4, 86, 89-91, 94.
Black Sail pass, 370.
Blackford, 463, 465.
Blackhall, 24.
Blacklead mines, 351.
Blacklock, Christopher, 239; Elena, 239.
Blamire, William, 341.
Blawith, 224, 329, 459, 460, 475.
Blencogo, 344, 344n.
Blencow, 241, 277n.
  Richard, 185.
Blenkinsop, Thomas, 192.
Blunderfield, 340.
Bokham, John de, 148.
Bolton (Cumb.), 15, 234, 237, 360, 460, 471.
  (West.), 87, 162, 276, 322, 463, 474.
  William de, 146.
Bond Tenants or villiens, 18-22, 31, 231.
Books in 17th c., 229-30, 340.
Boot, 370, 370n.
Booth, Archbishop, 125.
Bootle, 7, 37, 136, 143, 150, 151, 192, 211, 267, 270, 369, 465, 473; clergy, 144-5, 146, 149, 155, 194, 198, 220, 329; school, 241.
Border Tenant Right, 20-2, 247, 250-2.
Borders, state of, 171, 214, 217, 246-7, 270, 291, 303.
Borrowdale, 7, 28, 236, 351, 378 chapel, 160, 161, 399, 460, 465, 474; T. Gray's walk up, 352-3.
  Gawyn, 177, 180.
Bost, John, 213; Nicholas, 213.
Botcherby, 465, 466.
Bothel, 348.
Bouch (Buche), Alan, 47; John, 344n; Philip, 266.
Boucher, Jonathan, 344.
Bowe, Leonard, 239.
Bowman, Thomas, 227.
Bowness-on-Solway, 15, 64, 245, 294, 371, 378, 465, 471.
Bowstead Hill, 233n.
Boynton, Sir Thomas, 222.
Bracken, John, 228.

Brackenthwaite, 33, 160.
Bradford, Bishop, 313-4.
Bradle, William of, 119.
Braithwaite, 33, 160, 402, 453, 468, 469.
George, 359.
Bramery, 83.
Brampton, 15, 29n, 36, 119, 237; church of, 8, 397, 398, 464, 465, 471; manor , 247; vicar, 287; school, 410.
Robert, 34.
Branthwaite, 187n.
Brathay, 398, 460, 465.
Braythemyre (Braymyre), 32, 33.
Bretby, Nicholas de, 149.
Bridd, John, 149.
Bridekirk, 15, 94, 192, 194, 198, 241, 253, 268, 289n, 463, 466, 471.
Bridges, maintenance of, 87, 92, 171-2.
Brierley, Henry, 418.
Brigham, church, 9, 60, 134, 137, 138, 151 (2), 192, 210, 328, 329, 330, 336, 460, 466, 473; parish 37n, 157, 187n, 191, 267; chapelries, 137, 163; clergy, of, 148, 155, 220, 268.
Brisco, John, 207n, 289; Mary, 289.
Bristoe, Will., 228.
B. & F. Bible Society, 377, 384, 432n.
Broadfield moor, 185, 186.
Broadwater, 353.
Bromfield, 15, 236, 237, 240, 360; church, 12, 67, 78, 276, 344n, 460, 472; school, 241, 344.
Bromliwater, 33.
Brough-under-Stainmore, 37, 67, 253, 261, 373; castle, 13, 118n; church, 15, 131, 157, 163, 466, 473; school, 39, 240; Pilgrimage of Grace at, 183-4, 187n; vicar, 184, 185.
Brougham, 24, 227, 240, 322; St. Ninian, 8, 15, 162, 208, 271-2, 337, 473; St. Wilfred, 162, 271, 337, 401; castle, 13, 99, 118n, 123, 144n, 261, 263, 271, 273; Lady Anne Clifford and, 271-2.
1st Lord, 409.
Broughton-in-Furness, 164, 235, 241, 334, 460, 466.
Great, 34, 268, 276, 337, 346, 430, 459, 460.
Moor, 469.
Margaret, 122; Sir Thomas, 123
Brown, of Troutbeck, 130; John, 216; Mabel, 216.
Brownber, 282.
Brumberwater, 33.
Brummell, William, 240.
Brunholm, 32.
Bryan, John, 153.
Buchanan, George, 266.

Burbeck, Thomas, 184.
Burgh-by-Sands, 2, 15, 36, 66, 157, 211; church 45, 65, 83, 358, 466, 471.
Burneside, 165, 329, 338, 389, 398, 460, 466, 475.
Burnmoor, 370.
Burns, Robert, 349.
Burton, 9, 131, 136, 139, 140, 144, 150, 151, 164, 241, 328 (2), 401, 474; clergy of, 146, 152, 155, 210, 220; Chancellor, 434.
Elizabeth, 240; James, 282; William, 148.
Buttermere, 29, 160, 163, 391, 399, 415, 453, 456, 475; Lake, 32-3, 353, 354n, 414.
Butterwyk crag, 119.
Byland Abbey, 8.
Byrbanke, William, 172.
Byron, Sir Nicholas, 260.

Caldbeck, 15, 185, 267; mines at, 35; rectory, 93; church, 115, 276, 466, 472; rector, 317-8, 357.
Caldcotes, 66.
Calder Abbey, 6, 19, 138, 234; industries of, 27, 32, 34; and Scots, 68; income, 69n; approp. churches, 145, 147, 149, 472, 473; abbot, 148, 149, 154; visitations, 149, 151; dissolution, 178.
Caldewstone, 19, 78.
Calthwaite, 469.
Camerton, 15, 162, 275, 337, 397, 463, 466, 472.
Campbell, D. F., 458; H. E. 415n, 455.
Cape, William, 227, 228.
Cardew, 123, 248.
Carlatton, 15, 94, 471.
Carleton, 29; Guy, 274.
Carlisle, archdeacon, 13, 24, 58, 88, 360; status, 77, 434n; archdeaconry, 10, 381, 434.
bishopric of, endowments, 13, 42-5, 47-8, 50, 69n, 98, 115, 291, 381-2; vacancies, 13-4, 42, 365, 379; account rolls (15th c.), 31, 126; sequestration, 52; 'chapel,' 59, 74, 82, 127, 441, 456; mistaken elections, 73, 85; registrar, 125, 312, 368n; heraldry, 166; patronage, 194; fees on appointment, 291; pretended bishop, 326; signature, 445; approp. churches, 471, 472.
Carlisle cathedral and priory, 25, 73, 128, 161, 223n, 311; the abbey 265, 269, 273, 291; altars, 14, 126, 455-6; appropriated churches, 67, 114-5, 471, 472;

Carlisle cathedral and priory—*contd.*
bells, 112, 323-5, 456; brasses, 132, 249; building, 14, 57–8, 71-2, 85-6, 91-2, 110-1, 115, 124; canons, 194, 269, 360, 361, and see prior and convent; chapels, 113, 114, 129, 363, 455; chapter house, 207, 265, 291; cloisters, 12, 14, 265; dean and chapter, 201, 269, 277; 324; deanery, 133, 265, 269, 281, 291; destruction (1292), 61-2, 71, 114; (1645), 265-6, 269; dissolution (Henry VIII), 177-81; dormitory, 14; east window, 72, 86n, 168n; Edward I at, 66; endowments, 13, 69n;
episcopal burials in, 12, 72, 111, 114, 126, 205, 217, 249, 253, 287, 327, 364, 386, 426; consecration, 66; enthronement, 291, 430; throne, 124, 363;
foundation of (Henry I), 3, 6, (Henry VIII), 188; fratry, 130, 260, 269, 431; fisheries, 32; friends of, 456; gate, 174, 291; glass, 86n, 129, 166-8, 384, 421n, 452; heraldry, 124, 166-8, 384; high church movement in, 274; honorary canons, 382; indulgences, 71-2, 85, 91, 113, 116, 124; library, 282, 285-6, 288, 433; minor canons, 299, 359, 427, 433; monuments, 56, 327, 364, 387, 426, 446; muniments, 266; nave, 124, 214, 265, 269, 323, 361, 362n, 436 and see St. Mary's; organ, 281; ornaments, 116-7, 192, 206, 273, 282, 441, 452, 456; paintings, 124, 129, 383; pilgrimages to, 91-2, 116, 458;
prior and convent of, and Bishop Appleby, 97-8, and Bishop Ross, 74-5, and episcopal elections, 43, 52, 56, and St. Mary's, 79;
prisoners, 323; restorations, 129, 362-3, 383-4, 460; Richard III and, 129-30; roof, 86, 111, 129, 166, 362-3, 383; salt cotes, 36; school, 58, 433, 443, see Carlisle Grammar School; Scots and, 67, 114-5, 121; screens, 124, 129, 166, 363; services, 259, 274, 361, 375, 382, 383, 457; south door, 383; staff, 188, 273, 288; stalls, 111-2, 124, 129, 213-4; state in 17th c. 259; statutes, 296-302, 433; tithe barn, 130; tower, 110-1, 113, 321; visitations, 71, 77, 97, 172, 198, 201, 273, 300, 361-2, 432-3.
city and citizens of, 36, 114, 283, 386, 409 (2); Norman kings and, 1-2, 10, 13; Scots and, 11, 43, 64, 66-8, 70, 76, 98-9, 214; fortifications, 13, 265, 320; medieval industries, 28, 29n; friars at, 49, 179n; burnings, 61-2, 99; Edward I at, 66; sanitation, 80; Bishop Kirkby and, 81-2; Eden Bridge, 87, 172; fishery, 115; charter, 121; Wars of Roses, 121; Pilgrimage of Grace, 185-6; merchant guild marks, 213-4; market cross, place, 99, 217, 267, 280; townsfolk of, 227, 228, 230; state (17th c.), 231, 232-3; mayor and aldermen, 232, 291, 323n; corporation, 236, 282, 323n, 436n; James I at, 249; civil war, 260-4; George Fox at, 267-8; Parliamentary elections, 302; in 1745, 319-21, 322-5, 326, 327; printing press, 325n, 345; state (18th c.), 345-6, 348; state (19th c.), 347, 403-4, 406-7; Wesley at, 369, 372, 374; church schools at, 377, 384.
city churches and parishes of, St. Mary, 3, 16, 161, 237, 252, 323, 361-2, 363n, 435-6, 463, 466, 471; clergy, 79, 97, 359, 380; St. Cuthbert, 8, 15, 99, 157, 276, 374, 397, 436n, 460, 466, 471; clergy, 97, 280, 362, 384; Holy Trinity, 68n, 398, 441, 460, 466; St. Alban, 86; Christ Church, 398, 463; St. Stephen, 459, 460; St. James, 459, 460; St. John, 459, 460; St. Paul, 452, 463, 466; St. Barnabas, 458, 469 (2); St. Aidan, 469; St. Herbert, 469.
castle, 1, 98, 130, 168, 205; captures of, 43, 263, 322, 326; governors, 47, 64, 67, 81, 205, 260, 320; state, 51, 97, 320; prisoners in, 202, 214, 307, 326.
chancellor of, 77n, 357 (2), 434n.
diocese of (ancient) foundation, 3-4, 11; deaneries, 10, 252n, 285, 471-3; synodical statutes, 53-4; muniments, 62, 113-4, 125, 248; liturgical use, 192n;
visitations, the archbishop or his officers, 223n, 269-70, 285; the bishop, 77-8, 92, 114, 127, 199-200, 206-8, 254-8, 274-5, 292-4, 313, 357; commissioners, 197-9.
visitation and correction court books, 238-9, 240-1, 275-80; octocentenary of, 458, 469n.
(modern) creation of, 420; archdeaconries, 421, 434; rural deaneries, 421, 433; visitations, 422-3, 431-2, 433, 448;

diocesan conference, 431, 432, 440, 448; ruri-decanal conferences, 431; suffragan bishop, 434, 457

diocesan, Advisory committee, 456; Association for preventive and Rescue Work, 434; Board of Finance, 448; Calendar, 425; Church Army van, 448; Church House, 166n, 449; Church Extension Society, 423n, 425, 432, 437n; Church and parsonage building and benefice association, 423; Clergy Aid Society, 384; Clergy widows and orphans fund, 378; Clerical training fund, 435; Council for social and moral welfare, 457; Education Society, 384; Gazette, 435; Harvey Goodwin rest fund, 438; Laymen's fund, 448; Magazine, 435; Missionary Council 449, Day of prayer, 431, 435, Students fund, 435; Mission for the deaf and dumb, 448; Retiring pension fund, 448; Sunday, 435; Sunday school union, 434; Trust and Finance association, 448.

Grammar school, 38, 214, 241, 282, 288, 366, 384n, 410, 443, see cathedral school.

High school, 410.

House, 48, 113.

Journal, 345.

Museum (Tullie House), 311, 419.

Cartmel, 2, 37, 235, 253, 261; church and parish, 136, 328, 336, 460; clergy, 155, 220, 366n, 330, 331, 388; chapelries, 164; priory, 6, 70, 138, 154; mines of, 35; income, 69n; visitations, 140, 141, 143, 144, 147; dissolution, 179-80; and Pilgrimage of Grace, 183-4; approp. churches, 473; school, 39, 241, 363n.

Fell, 164, 329, 330, 475.

Casterton, 398, 460, 466; school, 410.

Castle Carrock, 15, 87, 275, 276, 348, 398, 466, 471; Sowerby, 15, 25, 29n, 67, 87, 185, 227, 299, 463, 466, 472.

Caswell How, 234.

Catechism, The, 207, 209, 216, 255, 278, 329, 336, 377, 388-9, 390.

Ceremonial (Church), 192n, 256, 258, 274, 441, 457.

Chamber, Abbot, 170-1.

Chantries, 58, 79-80, 83, 110, 113, 144, 160, 188-91.

Chapele, William de la, 146.

Chapels, chapelries, 37, 83, 86-7, 137; foundation, 87, 157-9; domestic, 87, 92, 154; endowments, 158-9, 318-9, 333, 335; numbers, 159-60; services, 210-1, 329, 388-91; state, 210-1, 245, 276, 328; schools in, 329, 358; see Church extension.

Chause, Bishop Robert, 52-6.

Chester, bishop of, 330-1, 391; diocese of, 188, 219, 244, 250, 380-1, 420; see Richmond, archdeaconry of.

Christian, Ewan, 383-4; John, 364, and see Curwen; Mary, 364.

Church, assessments, 240, 276, 333-5, discipline and morals, middle ages, 87, 143, 152-3; 16th c., 209, 215-7; 17th c., 235-8, 256, 278-80; 18th c., 292-5, 299, 359, 368n, 375; 19th c., 421, 424, 437; see excommunication and penance.

extension, 16, 153, 214-5, 223-4, 384, 425, 435-6, 437, 447, 449, see chapels and appendices.

High and Low in 17th c., 258.

High, 274, 308, 331-2, 387, 421n, 430-1; see ceremonial.

Missionery Society, 378, 384, 423, 432n.

Music, 432, 440.

of England Temperance Society, 434.

Pastoral Aid Society, 432n.

services, 210, 278, 329-30, 388-9, 394; see baptism, etc.

Churches, fortified, 65; markets in, 93, 329; decayed, 94; spoliation of, 191-4; schools in, 213-4, 293, 329, 358; beautifying of, 293, 331-2, 456; burials in, 331, 336; chapels in, 452, 456.

state, 16th c., 206-7, 210-1, 215, 244; 17th c., 275-6, 278, 328; 18th c., 292-5, 314, 358-9.

ornaments, 17th c., 255, 257, 275, 328, 331; 18th c., 314, 358-9; 20th c., 452-3.

wardens, presentments of, 215-7, and see visitations; curate as, 297-8; two years as, 329.

yards, markets of, 93, 237; reconciliation of, 142, 148; neglect of, 215, 329; misuse of, 236-7; ornaments of, 452.

Cleator, 68, 137, 145, 147, 151, 155, 220, 234, 347, 460, 473.

Moor, 347 (2), 404, 464, 466.

William de, 145.

Clergy, deprivation of, 194, 200-1, 208, 266, 269, 284-5; discipline and morals, see Church; numbers, 154-6, 209, 220; pensions, 87, 153, 279; quality, 209, 214, 244, 250, 254, 258, 423, 437.

Clerk, Lady, 327.

Cliburn, 12, 15, 21, 91, 120, 199, 322, 358, 463, 466, 473.
John, 119, 120.
Clifford, arms of, 167; Lady Anne, 226, 263, 271-3; 3rd Lord, 76; 5th Lord, 99; 9th Lord, 121; 10th Lord, 123; Roger de, 118n; Sir Thomas, 185.
Clifton (Cumb.), 29n, 163, 233, 475.
  (West.), 15, 36, 125, 144n, 307, 322, 360, 369, 399, 463, 473.
  Robert, 98.
Cloos, Bishop, 116-8.
Close, Francis, 421n, 426-9, 441, 442.
Coaches, travelling, 252, 348, 371, 379.
Coal mines, 34, 233-4, 345-7, 404-5.
Cocker, fishery of, 33.
Cockermouth, 36, 37, 92, 138, 266, 281n, 287n, 348; Honour of, 10, 100, 204-5; castle, 13, 118n, 121, 163, 264; industries, 29, 233, 343, 344; school, 38, 190, 241, 410; and Pilgrimage of Grace, 184-7; state, 17th c., 233; George Fox at, 267, 268; Wesley at, 372, 374.
  Chapel, church, 157, 334, 338, 400, 401, 475; clergy, 155, 190, 220, 389-90; chapels, 160; origin, 163, 390n; services, 329, 389; Christ Church, 459, 461, 466.
Colby Leathes, 366.
Coldale, 35; Richard, 207n.
Coleridge, S. T., 355, 411.
Collingwood, R. G., 418; W. G., 417-8.
Collinson, Thomas, 237.
Colton, 7, 164, 211 (2), 224, 330, 338, 466, 475.
Communion, see Holy.
Confession, auricular, 256, 257, 441-2.
Confirmation, 246; in middle ages, 142; Elizabethan bishops and, 209, 216; c. 1660, 270; 18th c., 295, 313, 336; 19th c., 391-2, 425, 431, 433, 439.
Conishead Priory, 6, 8, 138, 147, 150, 151; industries, 32, 35; income, 69n; visitations, 140, 143, 144; dissolution, 179; approp. churches, 473, 474.
Coniston, 413; chapel, 210, 224, 329 (2), 397, 475; mines, 234, 235; Lake, 33-4, 353; Old Man, 355.
Copper mines, 35, 234.
Coppock, Thomas, 325-6.
Corbridge, Robert de, 145.
Corby, 87, 340, 348.
Corney, 136, 151 (2), 155, 157, 211, 220, 328, 349n, 466, 469, 473.
Cosin, Bishop, 254, 274.
Costumes, 228-9.

Cotehill, 463, 466.
Council of the North, 188.
Coupland, 138-9, 163, 231; deanery, 421; roads, 349.
Crackenthorpe Hall, 122.
  John, 129; Richard, 229, 230; Robert, 119.
Craghill, Elizabeth, 237.
Crawe, Margaret, 239.
Creighton, Bishop, 345.
Crepping, Richard de, 55.
Crofton, 289.
Croglin, 12, 15, 55, 276, 464, 466, 472.
  Little, 18.
  William de, 18.
Crook, 165, 267, 285, 464, 466, 475.
Crookdake, 344 (2).
Cropper, James, 426, 430.
Crosby-on-Eden, 15, 88, 400, 401, 471.
Crosby Garret, 15, 241, 314, 463, 473.
Crosby Ravensworth, 12, 15, 131, 208, 236, 279, 350, 461, 466, 473.
Crosbythwaite, 93.
Cross, Viscount, 448.
Cross Canonby, 15, 279, 466, 472.
Crosscrake, 164, 396, 461, 464, 466, 475.
Crossfell, 354.
Crosthwaite (Cumb.), 8, 15, 37, 157, 239, 340; church, 77, 401, 453n, 455, 472; chapelries, 161; ornaments, 206-7; school, 241; episcopal burials, 446, 451.
  (West.), 29n, 164, 223, 253, 464, 466, 475.
Crowgarth, 347.
Crummockwater, 32-3, 353, 354n, 414.
Culgaith, 162, 242, 322, 396, 463, 474.
Cullsale, 335.
Cumberland, duke of, 322-4; earl of, 1st, 178, 182, 185; 2nd, 192n, 200-2; 3rd, 271.
  Infirmary, 384, 385, 386, 427.
  and West. Antiquarian & Arch. Society, 416-8, 444.
  and West. Association for the Advancement of Literature and Learning, 409-10.
  V.C.H. of, 416-7, 419.
Cumdivock, 464, 466.
Cumrew, 15, 157, 466, 471.
Cumwhitton, 15, 157, 358, 463, 471.
Cunsey, 235.
Cunswick, 134, 213, 307.
Curates, assistant, in middle ages, 155; stipends of, 330, 359, 367, 375, 378, 388; fate of in 18th c., 360, 368.
Curwen, arms of, 167; family of, 138, 233, 346; Henry, 283, 341, 346; Isabella, 341; Dame Joan, 143; John Christian, 341; Sir

Thomas, 33; William, 279; see de Workington.

Dacre, 15, 25, 29n, 173, 190-1, 208, 461, 466, 472.
  family of, 34, 133.
  arms of, 174n; 1st Lord, 76, 118n, 121; 2nd Lord, 171, 173-4; 3rd Lord, 182, 200-1; 4th Lord, 201; 5th Lord, 203.
  Sir Christopher, 186; Leonard, 202-3, 205; Margaret, 118n; Richard, 204; Sir Thomas, 181, 191, 262, 264; William, 204.
Dalegarth, 133.
Dalemain, 126n, 176, 281.
Dalston, church, 58, 132, 192, 217, 280, 386, 466, 471; parish, 15, 162, 236, 253, 264, 282, 312, 376, 386, 387; barony, manor, 18-9, 47, 58, 81, 231, 367; lawsuits about, 55, 249n, 250; advowson, 58, 67; vicar, 198n, 288, 364, 418.
  Sir George, 232, 287n; Thomas, 185; Sir William, 19, 231; William, 97.
Dalton-in-Furness, 37 (2), 136, 157, 349n, 405; church, 138, 142, 147, 461, 464, 466, 473; chapel-ries, 137, 164; clergy of, 155, 210, 220, 336; townsfolk, 236, 237 (2); school, 241 (2); in civil war, 261 (2); St. Margaret, 466, 469; St. Barnabas, 469; Thomas de, 148.
Deaf and dumb, 95, 448.
Dean, 34, 137, 146, 150, 151, 155, 211, 220, 241, 329, 330, 390, 463, 473.
Dearham, 15, 34, 187n, 276, 346, 466, 472.
Defoe, Daniel, 345, 351.
Dendron, 241, 338, 396.
Dent, Laurence, 231; Jane, 228.
Denton, Over, 9.
  Nether, 15, 192, 215, 463, 466, 471.
  Isaac, 368n; John, 248, 310.
Derwent Fells, manor of, 29n, 35, 134-5.
  river, 32, 33, 92, 346.
  water, manor of, 87.
  Lake, 352, 411.
  James Radcliffe, 3rd earl of, 307, 352.
  Sir John de, 87, 108.
Deveys, Matthew, 177.
Dialect, the local, 17, 193, 238, 245.
Diggle, Bishop, 449-51; C. J., 451; Edith, 451.
Distington, 137, 146, 151 (2), 155, 152, 220, 233, 336, 464, 467, 473.
Docker, John, 216.

Dodding, Colonel, 262.
Domesday Survey, 1, 16.
Douglas, Bishop, 367; James, 2nd earl of, 98-9; Sir James, 68, 70; Sir William, 80.
Dovenby, 276n, 289, 347.
Drigg, 147, 151, 152, 155, 163, 220, 400, 401, 457.
Drinkall, Isabel, 237.
Drumburgh, 36.
Drunkenness, 215, 216, 279, 294-5, 375, 421, 424, 437.
Dryholm, 21.
  John of, 34.
Duckett, James, 213.
Duddon, estuary, 36; sands, 70, 261; bridge, 347.
Duddon, estuary, 36; sands, 70, 261; bridge, 347.
Dufton, 15, 185, 187n, 213, 397, 401, 473.
Dundraw, 231.
Dunnerdale, 465, 466.
Durham, bishops of, 52, 134, 212, 274, 307; cathedral, 204, 274; diocese, 54, 238, 250; plate, 128; monastic library, 129.
Duresme, William de, 149.
Dykes, family of, 346; William, 152.

Eaglesfield, 187n.
  Robert de, 112.
Eamont Bridge, 321, 322, 464.
Earls, Rising of, 169n, 181, 202-5, 208.
Ecclesiastical Commission, 379-83, 470-6.
Edenhall, 15, 25, 67, 253, 263, 358, 472; vicar of, 185, 215, 285, 294-5, 360.
Eden Valley, 1, 18, 67, 90, 322, 403.
Education, 421, 432, 450, and see schools.
Egremont, 29n, 37, 138-9, 237, 270, 343, 347, 404; castle, 13, 68, 118n; fishery, 33; iron mines, 35, 234, 347; church, 136, 140, 141, 144, 150, 151, 192, 211, 333n, 467, 473; clergy, 145 (2), 149, 155, 210, 220; roads to, 348, 349.
  Robert, 154; Thomas Percy, Lord, 120.
Egton, 224, 391, 397, 461.
Ellen fishery, 32, 33.
Ellenborough, 346 (2).
Ellenfoot, 233n.
Ellergreen, 426.
Ellerton, 99.
Embleton, 29n, 163, 187n, 192, 220, 397, 463, 467, 475.
Enabling Act, 457.
Enclosures, 183, 231, 341.

Ennerdale, 8, 155, 163, 220, 234, 248, 328, 354, 370, 391, 453, 459, 461, 475; Lake, 353, 414.
Esk, fishery of, 128.
Eskdale, 156 220, 284, 354, 370, 404, 415; Furness Abbey and, 7, 28; fishery, 33; chapel, 163, 192, 329, 391, 421, 463, 467, 475; St. Bega's chapel, 465, 467; Esk Hause, 370n.
Eston, 15, 94, 471.
Etton, John de, 146.
Euerwyk, Richard de, 98.
Evangelical Revival, 368, 374-5, 384, 421, 424.
Everdon, Bishop de, 50-1.
Ewanrigg, 364.
Excommunication, 43, 55, 66, 75, 77, 93, 95, 97, 173, 200, 208, 299.,

Fairs, Sunday, 93, 209.
Fallow, William, 237.
Fallowfield, John, 238; Marian, 230.
Farlam, 15, 459, 461, 471.
Fawcett, John, 384.
Fawcett's school, 377n, 384.
Fawkes, J., 387.
Fell, Judge, 267; Margaret, 267; and Rock Climbing Club, 415. Walking, 355, 414, 416.
Fenton, Ralph de, 145.
Ferguson, C. J., 416; R. S., 416-7, 419, 434; Messrs. 346.
Feriby, Nicholas de, 149, 152; William de, 145.
Fether, William, 238.
Fetherstonhaugh, Lady Bridget, 229, 265; Sir Timothy, 264-5; Thomas, 276.
Fewsdale, 228.
Fiddes, Mr., 315.
Field Broughton, 338, 463, 469.
Finkle, Mary, 340.
Finsthwaite, 338, 461, 464, 467.
Firbank, 224, 267, 338 (2), 461, 475.
Fisher, Janet, 239.
Fisheries, 32-4, 127-8.
Fitch, John, 148.
Fithnenin, 45.
Fleming, 423; Bishop, 315-8, 326-7; Sir Daniel, 220, 235, 263, 283, 287n, 310, 315-7, 336; Richard 33.
Fletcher, Lady Catherine, 287n; Sir Henry, 262, 287n.
Flimby, 162, 319, 347, 397, 404, 463, 474.
Flookburgh, 37 (2), 164, 328, 369, 469, 475.
Force Forge, 235.
Forster, William 216.
Foster, Arthur, 276; Isabel, 194n; John, 194n.
Fothergill, Anthony, 282; Elizabeth, 282.

Fountains Abbey, 7, 27, 32, 77, 130, 472.
Fowgatefoot, 229.
Fox, George, 238n, 267-9, 374.
Friars, 48-9, 88, 179.
Friends, Society of, 235, 240, 267-9, 278, 330, 334, 385, 388, 408, 410, 430.
Frizington, 176, 234, 404, 459, 460.
Fulling mills, 29.
Funerals, difficulties of, 146-7, 215, 391; expenses of, 229, 336; irregular, 240; customs at, 207, 258.
Furness, District of, 137, 138, 235, 330, 351, 405; Norman Settlement, 2, 7; dialect, 17; Scots raids, 68, 70; and Pilgrimage of Grace, 184; in Civil wars, 260-2.
    Abbey, 5, 7, 18, 42, 140, 144, 146, 150, 151; industries, 27-8, 33, 35; income, 69n; abbot, 70, 148, 149; tower, 130; and the Isle of Man, 142; appropr. churches, 142, 147, 473, 474; dissolution, 177-81.
    Archdeaconry of, 415n, 434.
    Anselm de, 42.
Furniture and furnishings, 228-9.

Gaitsgill, 463, 468.
Gamblesby, 372, 459, 460.
Games and sports, 215, 237-8, 242, 268.
Garnett, Robert, 153.
Gaskell, John, 237.
Gastrell, Bishop, his Notitia, 241, 332-6, 388, 470-6.
Gate, Thomas, 153.
Gaunt, Elizabeth, 282.
Gayteford, Hugh de, 146.
Gaytescales, John de, 87.
Gelt Bridge, 247.
Ghost story, 122, 267.
Gibson, Bishop Edmund, 290, 291, 300, 318.
Gilbanks, Canon, 289n; G. E., 46n; Joseph, 390; Mr. 360.
Gilcrux, 15, 276, 340, 346, 360, 463, 472.
Gilpin, Bernard, 199; Richard, 268; William, 234, 286, 354n.
Gilsland, barony of, 6, 12, 21, 118n, 226; district of, 171, 200, 268; spa, 349-50; church, 400, 401.
Gilthwaitrigg, 213.
G.F.S., 434.
Gisburn Priory, 56-7, 471, 472.
Glassonby, 29n.
Glaston, John, 113.
Glemham, Sir Thomas, 262.
Godbarn, Henry, 149.
Goodenough, Bishop, 376-9; Elizabeth, 378-9; Sir William, 378; Dr., 379.

Goodwin, Bishop, 401n, 453; visitations, 431-3; diocesan organisation, 431, 433-4; suffragan bishop, 434; diocesan societies, 434-5; church building, 435-6; the clergy, 436-8; church services, 433, 438-40; confession, 441-2; education, 408, 442-3; local history, 444-5; character, 446-7.
Ellen, 387, 446.
Gosforth, 136, 150, 151, 153, 155, 163, 211, 220, 397, 445, 459, 461, 467, 473.
Thomas, 152.
Graham, family of, 247; Chris, 370n; David, 237; Sir James, 342; James, 236; Sir Richard, 232; Richard, 240; T. H. B., 418; see Montrose, earl of.
Grange, in Borrowdale, 459, 460, 464; over-Sands, 400, 401, 469.
Grasmere, chapel of, 83, 136, 137, 146, 150, 151, 157, 165, 401, 467, 474; clergy of, 141, 152, 155, 220, 318; Lake, fishery, 34; parish of, 29n, 350, 411, 413; Plays, 453n.
Grasslot, 469.
Gray, Thomas, 352-3, 355.
Gray, Archbishop Walter, 44, 142-3.
Grayrigg, 153, 165, 338, 398, 461, 475.
Grayson, Edmund, 237; Joyce, 237.
Graythwaite, 224.
Great Gable, 354, 355.
Greenfield, Archbishop, 54, 71, 141, 143.
Greenriggs, 29n.
Greysouthen, 346.
Greystoke, 30, 63n, 112, 194n, 236; barony, 10, 17, 118n, 171, 226; church and parish of, 15, 37, 60, 157, 175, 192, 207, 245-6, 295, 381, 401, 467, 472; rector, 52, 87, 268, 287, 360, 363n; college, 59, 96-7, 100, 114, 173, 190; chapelries, 161; and Pilgrimage of Grace, 185, 187n; castle, 213, 246, 263, 365; plague at, 252-3; Family of, arms of, 167; 1st Lord, 118n; 4th Lord, 96; 5th Lord, 96; 7th Lord, 171; Elizabeth, 171; Robert, 171.
Grindal, Archbishop, 197, 201.
Grinsdale, 15, 337, 463, 471.
Grisdale, B., 366-7.
Grizebeck, 469.
Gudybour, Prior, 128-30, 132.
Guy, Henry, 285.
Gyll, Margaret, 217.

Haile, 136, 145, 147, 151, 155, 211, 220, 467, 473.

Halton, Bishop de, 53, 61, 63-73, 81, 84, 132, 141, 144n; Thomas, 230.
Harcla, Andrew de, 67, 68, 69, 70-1; Michael de, 55.
Harbours in Cumb., 233n.
Hardknot, 354, 370, 370n.
Harford-Battersby, Canon, 429.
Harraby, 70, 326.
Harrington, 137, 151 (2), 155, 220, 233, 328, 347, 467, 473.
family of, arms of, 168; Emmote, 154; John de, 146; Sir Thomas, 154.
Harrison, Anna, 215; Robert, 227.
Hartley, 187n, 263.
Hartside, 372.
Harvest Festivals, 424-5, 440.
Hasell, Sir Edward, 281.
Haswell, J. F., 418.
Haverfield, F. J., 418.
Haverigg, 465, 468.
Haverthwaite, 397.
Hawcoat, 261.
Hawfield, 227.
Hawksdale, 119, 312.
Hawkshead, 7, 184, 198n, 235, 353; church, 147, 151, 152, 155, 164, 210, 224, 237, 328, 389, 461, 467, 475; school, 198n, 241; growth of, 413.
Hay, Henry, 149.
Hayton (Carlisle), 15, 157, 240, 397, 467, 471.
(Aspatria), 459, 461.
Head, Erasmus, 324.
Helsington, 237, 338, 463.
Helvellyn, 354, 355.
Henry VI, 117, 121, 122-3.
Hensingham, 347, 371 (2), 372, 380, 397 (2), 463, 469.
Heraldry, 75n, 107-8, 117, 124, 133, 166-8, 211n, 384.
Heresy, 134-5.
Hermits, 108, 154.
Hesket-in-the-Forest, 161, 295, 337, 359, 474.
Hetherington, Thomas, 239.
Hethersgill, 464, 467.
Heversham, 330; church, 60, 131, 136, 138, 150, 151, 155, 164, 220, 365n, 461, 467, 474; patronage of, 9, 194; rector, 146, 149, 152; school, 241, 329, 410; in the '45, 321.
Hexham Priory, 472.
Hewer, John, 227.
High Commission, court of, 206, 215-7.
High Head, 87, 162, 337, 459, 474.
Hilton Flecan, 227.
Hobson, Thomas, 340.
Hodgson, family, 346; Alice, 154; Hugh, 200; John, 294; Mr. and Mrs. T. H., 418.

Hoff, 99.
Holker, 262.
Holm Cultram Abbey, 6, 12, 42; industries, 27-8, 35, 36, 37; in Scots wars, 43, 64, 70, 75, 98; abbot, 45-6, 55, 131, 170-1; income, 69n; dissolution, 177-81; and Pilgrimage of Grace, 184-5; appropr. churches, 471, 472.
    manor and parish, 344, 407; tenures, 21, 22, 31; chapels, 160, 162; parish church, 276, 337, 358, 467, 472; clergy, 180, 215; George Fox at, 268.
Holm St. Cuthbert, 400, 401; St. Paul, see Silloth.
Holme (Burton), 398, 461; Eden, 399, 401.
Holy Communion, ceremonial, 255, 257, 274, 278, 457;
    frequency of reception, 15th c., 127; 16th c., 207, 209, 216; 17th c., 246, 255, 257, 274, 280; 18th c., 388-9; 19th c., 383, 387, 391, 394, 432, 439; 20th c., 457.
    numbers, 245, 382; test of admittance, 209, 216, 255; Lady Anne Clifford and, 271.
Holy Days, 278, 280, 329, 389.
Honister crag, 351-2.
Horncastle, 48, 67, 107, 108, 195; John de, 85.
Horneby, Thomas, 152.
Hospitals, dissolution of, 191; see St. Nicholas.
Hothfield, Lord, 226.
Houghton, 398, 401.
Houses, 230, 232, 343-4, 351, 386; see benefices.
Household utensils, 228-9.
Housing estates, 406.
Howard, earl of Carlisle, 205, 226; of Greystoke, 205, 226n; of of Corby, 226n; Sir Francis, 226n; Philip, 262, 340; Lord William, 226, 247, 252.
Howberry, 340.
Howgill, 87.
Hudleston, family of, 126n, 139, 167, 234; Andrew, 283; A. F. 423; Ferdinand, 109-10; Isabel, 119; John, 19, 282; Joseph, 282; Margaret, 118; Sir Richard, 118; Sir William, ob. 1483, 119; ob. 1669, 261 (2), 264.
Hudson, Percival, 186-7.
Huggen, Anthony, 215; Jannet, 216.
Hugh, Bishop, 43-5.
Hugill, 165, 237, 241, 330, 338, 463, 467, 475.
Hullerbank, 250.
Hunter, John, 340.
Hutchinson, James, 227.

Huthuatyte, Thomas de, 124-5.
Hutton-in-the-Forest, 15, 24, 83, 185, 190, 235, 264, 281n, 295, 337, 461, 472.
    John, 282, 283, 423.
    Old, 153, 158, 165, 241, 330, 338, 464, 467, 475.
    New, 153, 338, 391, 397, 398.
    Roof, 164, 396, 463, 467, 475.
    Anthony, 184; Walter de, 152.
Hymnals, 440n.

Ilekirk, 46, 161, 262.
Incense, 17th c., 331.
Indentures, private, 119.
Indulgences, 153-4; cathedral, 71-2, 85, 91, 113, 116, 124; bridges, 87, 92, 172; roads, 87-8.
Industrial revolution, 342-3, 347, 405.
Inglewood Forest, 22-6, 161, 131.
Insula, Brian de, 47; Richard de, 145.
Ireby, 15, 276, 279, 360, 399, 401, 472.
Ireleth, 241, 338, 459, 461, 475.
Iron mines, 35, 234-5, 347, 404-5.
Irt, 36.
Irthington, 15, 215, 216, 236, 401, 471.
Irton, 136, 142, 150, 151, 155, 220, 397, 459, 461, 467, 473; Hall, 122.
    Bishop de, 55, 56-62, 74; Martha, 411; Nicholas, 119.
Isel, 15, 94, 176n, 208, 467, 472.
Ivegill, 459, 461.
Jackson Library, Carlisle, 357n, 417, 419; William, 417.
Jacobites, 213.
    Rising of 1715, 303-7.
    Rising of 1745, 319-27, 348, 352, 355, 357, 362.
James, Stephen, 239; William, 213.
Jedburgh Abbey, 471.
Jefferson, Catherine, 327; Robert, 327.
Johnby, 236.
Johnson, Edward, 240.

Karell, 32, 33.
Kelsick (Ambleside), 410.
    (Bromfield), 231.
Kelton races, 242.
Kemp, Archbishop, 150-2, 252n.
Kendale, barony, 2, 11, 17, 126, 137, 244, 250.
    parish, 37n, 136, 137-8, 153-4, 155-6, 157; chapelries, 137, 165, 211; clergy, 155-6, 220; church assessments, 333-4.
Kendal, town, 68, 233, 409; castle, 13, 137; woollen trade, 28-9, 37,

137, 234-5, 341, 343; market, 37, 406; grammar school, 138-9, 221-2, 241, 363n, 410; travellers at, 141 (2), 179n, 351; Pilgrimage of Grace at, 183-6; hospital, 191; alderman and recorder, 221-2; charter, 234; townsfolk, 236, 238, 257, 329, 363n, 370n, 416; in Civil war, 262-4; George Fox and Friends at, 267-8, 330; in 1688, 284; in 1745, 321, 322; as road centre, 348, 406; Wesley at, 370, 372-3, 374; girls high school, 410.

parish church, 138, 328, 336; patronage, 9, 194; stipend, 60, 175, 474; appropriation, 67, 143; churchyard, 83, 142, 148; building, 130-1; chantries, 144, 191; clergy, 148, 210, 220, 285; anchorite's house, 154; chapels, 221; rood loft, 221; organ, 221-2; seating, 221-2; R. Phillipson's ride, 262-3; 17th c. High Church movement, 331-2; 18th c. services, 389; restoration, 1850, 392-3, 401.

All Hallows chapel, 459, 461.
St. George's church, 389, 396, 399, 463, 467.
St. Thomas' church, 398, 461.
Kendal, Adam de, 45-6; Henry de, 145; Isabel, 134-5; Thomas, 145; William de, 77.
Kent sands, 70.
Kentmere, 158, 165, 463, 475.
Keswick, 234, 270, 348, 352, 353, 415, 434; market town, 37; chapel, 160, 161; school, 241, 410; George Fox at, 268; Wesley at, 369, 370 (2), 370n, 371, 374; St. John's church, 398, 429, 452, 461, 467; growth of, 411, 413-4; Convention, 429-30; school of art, 456.
Killington, 159, 164, 224, 461, 475.
Kilnhirst, John de, 145, 146.
Kingmoor, 469.
Kinmount, Will of, 214.
Kirkandrews on Eden, 15, 199, 471.
    on Esk, 236, 237, 319, 337, 364, 397.
Kirkbampton, 15, 358, 463, 467, 471.
Kirkbride, 15, 360, 463, 472.
    Family of, arms of, 167; Barnaby, 201; Richard de, 83.
Kirkby, Bishop de, 75-84, 89, 312.
Kirkby Ireleth, 136, 142, 151, 152, 155, 164, 210, 220, 240, 261, 329, 467, 473.
Kirkby Lonsdale, 37, 75n, 253, 330, 410.
    church, 138, 140, 141, 150, 151,

336, 461, 474; patronage, 9, 194; state, 131, 210 (2); clergy, 153, 155, 229, 266, 388; chapelries, 164; chantries, 190; 18th c. services, 388.
hospital, 191; school, 241; in Civil War, 261-4; 'Kirkby feight,' 284.
Kirkby Stephen, 37, 75; church, 9, 12, 78, 131, 401, 467, 473; Hartley chapel, 70n; chapelry, 157; vicar, 251, 416; organ, 314n; S.P.G. at, 385; school, 241, 410; and Pilgrimage of Grace, 184, 186, 187n; 17th c. shopkeeper, 229.
Kirkby Thore, 322; bridge, 87; church, 15, 240, 293, 461, 473; chapelries, 162.
Kirkby Underhale, 146.
Kirkcambeck (Cambok), 15, 36, 94, 464, 471.
Kirkland, 15, 77, 115, 162, 318, 396, 472; (Lamplugh), 464.
Kirklinton, 15, 176, 208, 217, 314, 340, 399, 401, 461, 471.
Kirkoswald, 13, 29n, 37, 67, 264, 340; church, 15, 87, 175, 192, 461, 467, 472; college, 59, 173, 190-1, 472.
Kirksanton (Chapel Suken), 335, 465, 468.
Kitwatling How, 185.
Kneeling, in church, 358, 439-40.
Knells, 239.
Knipe, 119, 290.
    John, 237.
Knowblow, John, 117.
Kyngescote, Bishop, 125.
Kytte, Bishop, 172-3, 175, 183, 187.

Lake District, The, 37, 137-8, 233, 339, 350, 404.
    in the middle ages, monastic estates, 7-8; fisheries, 32-4; woollen industry, 26-30; parish churches, 37n.
    church services, 215, 223, 391; and see chapels; 17th c. industries, 234-5; in early 18th c., 350-1; Daniel Defoe on, 351; mid 18th c. visitors to, 351-2; climate, 352; Thomas Gray and, 348, 352-3; discovery of, 353-6; Wesley and, 353, 369-71, 373; early maps, 353-4; highest mountain in, 354; smuggling, 355; guides, 353, 354, 355; residential settlement, 410-5, 411-3; Lake Poets, 411; 19th c. tourists, 414-5; 20th c. tourists, 415-6; H. D. Rawnsley and, 453-4.

Lamplugh, 136, 150, 151, 155, 220, 253, 461, 473; rector of, 117, 152, 210.
Family of, 242, 266; Elizabeth, 276n; George, 276n; John, 119, 234; Margaret, 154; Patrick de, 145; Robert, 191; Thomas, 154; a humourist at, 242-3.
Lancaster, Christopher de, 87; Thomas, 228; William de, 6, 11, 17, 87.
Lanercost Priory, 6, 42, 45, 57, 66; salt cotes, 36; Edward I at, 64, 66; and Scots, 64, 66, 82; income of, 69n; Lord Dacre and, 174; dissolution, 179-80; approp. churches, 471, 472.
Chronicle, 43-5, 57-8, 59, 61; parish church, 217 (2), 337, 401, 471; curate, 215; parish, 236, 239.
Langaran, 234.
Langbaine, Patience, 363n.
Langdale, 8, 223, 459, 461, 475; Pikes, 355; Sir Marmaduke, 263.
Langlands, 268.
Langley, Bishop, 113.
Langley, 142.
Langrigg, Adam de, 25.
Langstrath, 8.
Langthorne, Joseph, 297-8.
Langton, Bishop Thomas, 38n.
Langwathby, 161, 253, 322, 337, 474. Ralph de, 25.
Law, Bishop, Edmund, 363-4, 365; Bishop George Henry, 393; Edmund, 363n; Edward, Lord Ellenborough, 364; Henry, 229; Mary, 364; Patience, 363n.
Lawson, Sir Wilfred, 247, 260.
Lay readers, 431, 435.
Layburne, Bishop, 134; Lady Idonea de, 24; James, 213; John, 307; Margaret, 95; Nicholas de, 95, 192n.
Layton, family of, 126n; Dr. Richard, 176-7; William, 176n.
Lazonby, 15, 185, 363n, 459, 461, 472.
Mr., 360, 368.
Leconfield, Lord, 225.
Ledes, P. de, 13.
Leigh, arms of, 167; John, 285; Dr. Thomas, 176-7, 181; William, 167n, 176n.
Lengleys, Sir Robert, 19; Sir William, 87.
Lent, observance, 209, 270, 329.
Leprosy, 87.
Letters Dimissory, 145-6.
Leven, 32, 347.
Levens, 70, 154, 398, 462; Hall, 230.
Levington, barony, 10.

Lewyn, John, 97.
Lezestones, 34.
Liddell, barony, 2, 20, 21, 22, 29n.
Lindal, 405, 464 (2), 467; Close, battle of, 261.
Lindale, 267, 330, 338, 398, 461, 475.
Linstock, 45, 67, 88, 132; castle, 61, 66, 141; hermit of, 108.
Linton, Mrs. Lynn, 414.
Livingstone, Sir William, 264.
Lobenham, William de, 148.
Lollardry, 134-5.
Longevity, 279, 359, 368n.
Long Marton, 15, 198, 276, 467, 473.
Longmire, George, 236.
Longsleddale, 223, 338, 475.
Lonsdale, 11; 1st Viscount, 284, see Sir John Lowther; 3rd Viscount, 304; 1st Earl, 365-7, 390; 2nd Earl, 342, 350, 366n, 393.
Lorton, 29n; chapel, 155, 160, 163, 210, 220, 462, 475; school, 241; Wesley at, 369, 371, 373.
Loughrigg, 29n.
Loweswater, 8, 29n, 330, 353, 414; chapel, 141, 150, 156, 163, 210, 220n, 335, 398, 467, 475; fishery, 32, 33; coal mine, 34.
Lowholme, 284.
Lowick, 164, 464, 467, 475.
Lowther, 15, 141, 184, 253, 283, 293, 461, 473; rector, 25, 245-6, 290n, 366; Hall, 304, 337; school, 241; park, 322.
Family of, 233, 346; arms of, 168; of Rose and Great Orton, 112n.
Gerard, 204, 294; Governor, 359; Henry, 365-6n; Hugh de, 85; Sir James, of Whitehaven, 234, 346, 366n; Sir John (1535), 185, 189; Sir John (1644), 261; Sir John, 1st Viscount Lonsdale, 282, 283, 284; Sir John, of Whitehaven, 284n; John, 250, 270; Leonard, 245-6; Sir Richard, 189n, 202-3, 204, 245n; Richard, 287n; Sir Robert, 108; Robert, 152; Sir William, 365-6n; William, 112n, 119, 366.
Low Wray, 453n, 459, 461, 467.
Lucy, arms of, 118n, 167; Anthony de, 76; Richard de, 8; Sir Thomas, 80, 81, 89; Maud, 118n.
Lumley, Bishop, 114-6; Ralph, 1st Lord, 114; Eleanor, 114.
Lupton, 459, 461.
Lyth, 416.
Lyttleton, Bishop, 362-3.

Machell, family of, 235; John, 122; Thomas, his MSS., 262n.
McIntire, W. T., 418.

Mallerstang, 187n, 215, 272, 337, 340, 474.
Maltby, Dr., 379.
Man, Isle of, 142, 355, 420.
Manners, Society for the Reformation of, 286-7, 308.
Manorial system, 17-22, 29-30.
Mansergh, 396, 464, 467.
Manton, Rev. —., 285.
Maps, 353-4, 348.
Marches, laws of, 51, 309; government of, 205; warden of, 115, 121, 202.
Mardale, 163, 337, 462, 474.
Market towns, 36-7.
Marriage, in the middle ages, dissolution, 87, 92; breach of promise, 87; clerical, 143; Marian deprivation, 194; first married bishop, 205; irregular and clandestine, 215, 239-40; handfast, 238-9.
Marron, tarn, 32; water, 33.
Marshall, George, 216; Margaret, 240.
Martindale, 163, 276, 337, 464, 474. William, 119.
Martineau, H., 412-4.
Martyrs, 194, 213, 282.
Mary, Queen, 194-5.
Maryport, 112n, 403, 409; origin of, 346; St. Mary's church, 375, 396, 398, 462, 467; Christ church, 464, 467.
Matheson, F. W., 455.
Matterdale, 214-5, 245, 462, 474.
Mauclerk, Bishop, 46-50, 53, 157.
Mayne, Sir John, 261 (2).
Meaburn, King's, 187n; Mauld's, 119, 228, 359n.
Measures, medieval, 34.
Mechanics institutes, 409.
Melmerby, 15, 211, 338, 461, 472; proposed college of, 79, 96; vicar of, 185, 208.
Melton, Archbishop, 72, 143-6; William de, 118n.
Merke, Bishop, 63, 101-6, 108, 117.
Mester, William, 216.
Meye, Bishop, 212, 214, 217, 236.
Michaelshaw, 153.
Middleton, 338, 467, 475. Ambrose, 192n; John, 192n; William, 190.
Midgholme, 459.
Milburn, 162, 340, 474.
Milburne, Bishop, 250-2; Leonard, 252.
Mill, Dr. John, 317.
Millom, 1, 11, 29n, 37, 234, 253, 369, 404, 410; church and parish, 37, 136, 142, 147, 150, 152, 211, 335, 452, 456, 463, 467, 473; clergy, 155, 220; castle, 139, 263; in

Civil war, 261, 263; George Fox at, 267; iron works, 347; St. George's church, 464, 468; The Hill chapel, 464, 467; Henry, Lord of, 7.
Milner, Isaac, 374-5, 377, 378, 384.
Milnthorpe, 398, 406, 468.
Missions, overseas, 422-3, 427n, 432n, 435; see under Carlisle diocese and Societies; preaching, 246.
Mitchell, Edward, 241.
Monk, William, 213.
Montague, John Neville, marquis of, 119, 121.
Montrose, James Graham, marquis of, 261.
Moon, George, 294-5, 312.
Moore, George, 420n, 421, 430; Education Trust, 421n.
Moresby, 137, 151 (2), 155, 220, 397, 468, 474; rector of, 146, 152; coal mines at, 233. Hugh de, 81.
Morland, 236, 253, 322; church, 9, 12, 15, 131, 199, 275, 463, 473; brass, 207n; vicar, 276; chapelry, 162; school, 241.
Mosdalebeck, 33.
Mosstroopers, 214, 247n, 264, 270.
Mosser, 163, 191, 396, 465, 468.
Motherby, Godytha de, 87; Nicholas de, 87.
Motor cars, 406, 415.
Multon, Margaret de, 118n; Thomas de, 47, 118n.
Mummers, 131.
Muncaster, 122, 137, 140, 147, 150, 151, 155, 163, 220, 261, 369, 461, 468, 474; 1st Lord, 123n.
Mungrisdale, 29n, 215, 228, 245, 396, 474.
Murton, 459, 461.
Musgrave, 15, 364, 399, 401, 473; Little, 187n.
Agnes, Lady, 200; Sir Christopher, 291; Sir Edward, 184; Nicholas, 184; Sir Philip, 260, 262-4; Sir Richard, 191.

Nab Scar, 350.
Nateby, 187n.
National Trust, The, 415, 453.
Natland, 165, 338, 463, 469, 476.
Naworth castle, 118n, 121, 226, 230, 247, 263.
Nelson, Jeremiah, 279.
Nenthead, 369.
Netherby, 342.
Netherhall, 112n, 133, 253.
Netherton, 464, 466, 469.
Neubolde, Thomas de, 148.
Neville, arms of, 166, 167, 168; Alexander, archbishop, 148-9; Alice, 126n; Eleanor, 114,

117; George, archbishop, 126n;
George, 198n; Isabel, 119;
Margaret, 118, 125; Ralph, 2nd
Lord, 76.
Newbiggin (Temple Sowerby), 15,
131, 199, 229, 253, 322, 401, 473.
(on Lune), 469.
Newby (Morland), 322.
Newland, 347, 391.
Newlands, 215, 319, 399, 463, 474;
copper mine at, 35, 202, 234.
Newleathes, 230n.
Newspapers, early, 345.
Newton (Cartmel), 267.
(Dalton), 261.
Arlosh, 65, 157, 160, 162, 176, 400,
401, 421.
Reigny, 88, 162, 187n, 463, 468,
474.
Nicholforest, 231, 276, 319, 337 (2),
397, 459, 461, 474.
Nichols, Roland, 277-8.
Nicholson, Elizabeth, 395n; Mungo,
239.
Nicolson, Bishop William, 233, 236,
266, 313, 315, 318, 332, 385, 391;
archdeacon of Carlisle, 284,
285-7, 290n, 292; Miscellany
accounts of first visitation, 292-
4, 358, 444; ordination and
confirmation, 294-7; quarrels
with Todd, 285-6, 297-8; with
Tullie, 286-7; with Atterbury
and Todd, 296-302; political
opinions, 291, 302-3, 307-9; in
1715, 303-7; historian, 262n,
290, 309-10; diarist, 311;
character, 280-1, 312, 446.
John, 312; Joseph, 125, 289, 311,
312; Mary, 289.
Nicknames, 216, 247.
Nith, fishery of, 32.
Nonconformity, 235, 240, 307-8,
377, 450.
Nonjurors, The, 284-5.
Nonresidence, 145, 278, 390.
Norfolk, 3rd duke, 181, 185; 4th
duke, 203, 226; 5th duke, 226n;
10th duke, 365.
Northscales, 262.
Northumberland, 1st earl, 118n;
2nd earl, 34, 117, 120; 3rd earl,
121; 4th earl, 35; 6th earl, 182,
187; earl, 191; 7th earl, 202-5;
11th earl, 225; 1st duke, 379.
Norsemen (Vikings), 17-21, 26, 30.
Nostell, 6, 11.
Nunclose, 218n.

Ogle, Robert, 80.
Oglethorpe, Bishop, 195-7, 201.
Option, archbishop's, 376-7.
Ordinands, standard of, 209, 214,
294, 423; numbers of, 209, 214.

Ordinations, frequency of, 313, 363-4,
375, 378.
Orfeur, William, 234.
Organs, 221-2, 259, 281, 314n, 440n.
Ormside, 9, 12, 15, 131, 468, 473;
rector of, 194, 198, 380.
Orton, Great, 15, 112n, 240, 463, 468,
471; rector of, 245, 289, 421.
Orton, 15, 37, 131, 141, 264, 281,
322, 340, 453, 468, 473.
Osbaldeston, Bishop, 357, 361-2, 391.
Osmotherley, 464, 468.
Otley, Jonathan, 356.
Oughterside, 234.
Oulton, 342.
Ousby, 15, 108, 252n, 318, 461, 472.
Oxenholme, 311.
Oxford Movement, 441-2; Univer-
sity, Bishop Merke and, 104-5;
Bishop Strickland and, 108-9.

Paley, William 364-5.
Papcastle, 34, 160.
Pardshaw, 134-5, 187n; crag, 268 (2).
Parish, chests, 276, 329; clerks, 237,
335-6; histories, 444-5; regis-
ters, 199, 211, 235, 266, 275,
327n, 328, 418.
Parishes, creation of, 10, 157; lists of
oldest, 15, 136-7.
Parker, Alexander, 213.
Parliamentary   boroughs,   36;
elections, 291, 302.
Parton, 233n.
Parving, arms of, 211n; Sir Robert,
79-80, 96.
Patrickson, family of, 248; Bridget,
265n; Richard, 234; Thomas,
234, 265n.
Patten, Robert, 307.
Patterdale, 163, 276, 400, 401, 413,
474.
Pattinson, Alderman, 323n.
Paxton, Sir Joseph, 385.
Pearl Industry, 36.
Peel, William, 237.
Pele towers, 40.
Penance, public, 217, 279-80.
Penitentiaries, 146, 148.
Pennington, 17, 136, 138, 147, 150,
151, 155, 329, 389, 398, 474.
Adam, 39; Gamel de, 6; Sir John
de, 39n, 122; William, 261.
Penny, Bishop, 169-72.
Penrith, 29n, 37, 114, 230, 233, 279,
282, 343, 385, 409.
church, 15, 93, 162, 192, 207n, 322,
381, 461, 468, 472; chantry,
110-1, 189; vicar, 288, see
Hugh Todd; clerical church-
warden, 297-8; curate, 297-8,
307, 362; rebuilding, 313,
337.

grammar school, 38, 110-1, 189,n 240, 297, 410; friars at, 49, 88, 179n; Scots and, 80, 246-7; Bishop Strickland and, 109-11; castle, 109-10, 112, 121, 129, 130; water supply, 110-11; Pilgrimage of Grace at, 184-6. 187n. suffragan bishop of, error of, 219-20, 434; plague at, 252-3; in civil war, 263; in 1715, 304; in 1745, 321, 322; in 18th c., 348; Wesley and, 369, 374; in 19th c., 406, 407 (2); Christ Church, 400, 401; St. Saviour, 464, 468; All Hallows, 464, 468.
    Edward, 187n; Lawrence de, 113; Robert de, 113.

Perambulation (parochial), 211, 256, 257.

Penruddock, 228, 469.

Percy, arms of, 166-7; Algernon Charles, 386; Henry, 2nd Lord, 76; Sir Henry (Hotspur), 99; Sir Ralph, 120-1; Bishop Hugh, 379-87, 393, 403, 420 (2); Bishop William, 117, 120-1, 123-5, 166.
    Manors in West Cumb., 118n, 159-60, 225; customs, 21-2, 204; survey, 1578, 231; industries, 29, 32-5.

Phillipson, Hudleston, 262; Robert, 262-3.

Pickering, William, 191.

Piel harbour, 28, 123, 261.

Pilgrimages, 91-2, 116, 458.

Pilgrimage of Grace, 178, 181-8, 193, 202.

Pillar Rock, 414.

Pitt, Thomas, Lord Camelford, 363.

Plagues, 217, 248, 252-3, see Black Death.

Plumbland, 15, 25, 276, 289n, 360, 462, 472.

Plumpton, 24, 25, 207n, 396, 463, 469.

Pluralism, medieval, 144-5; 17th c., 245; 18th c., 318, 360, 363n, 364-5, 366n, 368, 390; 19th c., 378, 380.

Poaching, 24-6, 79, 95.

Ponsonby, 137, 144, 147, 150, 151, 155, 210, 220, 329 (2), 399, 401, 468, 474.

Pooley Bridge, 459, 460.

Portland, duke of, 322.

Porteous, Bishop, 388.

Porter, Lancelot, 284.

Potter, Bishop, 257-9, 265, 315.

Powsfoot, 233n.

Prayer Book, 193, 198-9.

Prayers for the dead, 207, 258.

Prescott, J. E., 442, 451-3.

Preston, 154.
    Family of, 144; Jacobina, 154;

Richard, 154; Walter, 236.
    Patrick, 7, 144, 164, 267, 400, 402, 462, 468, 476.

Prices, 31-2, 32-5, 227-30, 340.

Processions, 92, 425, see Perambulations.

Pullen, Robert, 184.

Quakers, see Friends.

Quarries, 34.

Queen Anne's Bounty, 318-9, 333.

Queen's College, Oxford, 230n, 249, 289, 290n, 315, 368, 473; foundation, 112-3; provosts, 112, 218, 257; Bishop Smith and, 281n, 282, 288.

Quincey, Thomas de, 411.

Quick, O. C., 455.

Raby Cote, 36.

Railways, 403-4, 405-7, 453.

Rainbow, Bishop, 271, 273-81, 285, 290, 312, 446; Elizabeth, 281.

Rampside, 338, 476.

Ranerdale, 160, 163.

Rashdall, Hastings, 455, 456.

Ratcliffe, family of, arms of, 168.

Raughton Head, 304n, 337, 344, 449, 462, 468, 474.

Ravenglass, 37, 233n, 353, 369.

Ravenstonedale, 15, 240 (2), 253, 337, 359, 473.

Rawes, Lancelot, 340.

Rawlinson, William, 235.

Rawnsley, H. D., 453-5; Edith, 453; Eleanor, 453.

Reade, Bishop, 100.

Readers, Order of, 223, 319.

Reagill, 322.

Redman, Bishop, 131.

Reformation, The, 134, 160; and the North, 169-70; local hostility to, 193-4; Marian reaction, 194-5; Elizabethan settlement, 197-201.

Renwick, 15, 337, 359, 399, 463, 472.

Ribton, 276.

Richardson, Henry, 362; John, 29.

Richmond, archdeacon of, 136, registers of, 115, 152-4.
    archdeaconry of (beyond the moors), 473; monastic houses, 5-8; extent, 136-7; deaneries, 136; visitations of, archiepiscopal, 139-41, 144, 148-52, 209-11, 221-3, 224, 241; episcopal, 220, 330-1, 388-92; by commissioners, 141, 143, 147, 237-8, 267, 328-30.
    Thomas, 135.

Rickerby, 92, 239.

Rickman, Thomas, 385.

Rigby, Colonel, 260-1.

Ringsfield, 276.

Ritson, 'auld Willie,' 414; Robert, 279.
Roads, in middle ages, 87-8; in 17th c. 179n, 232n; in 18th c., 345 (2), 348-9, 350, 354.
Robinson, Bishop, 193, 214, 217-8, 244-9, 315, 441; Bernard, 278-9; Christopher, 213.
Robson, Edward, 237; James, 368n; Robert, 368.
Rocliffe, 15, 266, 276, 400, 402, 468, 471.
Rogation Days, 256, see Perambulation.
Roman Catholicism, in Elizabethan days, 200-1, 203, 208, 244, 250; 'relics of popery,' 206, 209-10, 216.
Romeyn, Archbishop le, 139-41.
Rose Castle, 47,52, 273, 457; in Scots wars, 64, 67, 70, 76, 81; building of, 65, 76, 88-9, 110, 173; towers of, 110, 132, 173, 362, 376; chapel, 131-2, 270, 288, 316; in wars of Roses, 118, 119, 121; park, 95, 121; manor, 58, 70, 81; in civil war, 263, 269; restorations of, 280, 282, 362, 367, 376, 385-6; private life at, 254, 281, 292, 314, 374, 376, 448; in 1715, 304-7; in 1745, 326-7.
Rosedale priory, 67, 472.
Roses, wars of the, 117-23.
Rosley, 398.
Ross, Bishop de, 73-5.
Rothbury, 54, 67, 98, 109, 376.
Rothelfield, William de, 56.
Rowtanbek, 35.
Rusland, 338, 390, 462.
Rydal, 268, 315, 336, 350, 397, 423, 463, 468; Water, 34.

Saddleback, 354.
St. Agatha, Robert de, 52.
St. Bees priory, 5, 18, 27, 68; industries, 8, 32, 35, 36; income, 69n; visitations, 140, 147, 148-9, 151; dissolution, 179-81; appropr. churches, 474.
   parish, 136, 138, 150, 157, 204, 253, 417; church, 60, 143, 391, 393, 460, 468, 474; chapelries, 137, 151, 152, 156, 163; clergy, 155, 156, 220; assessments, 334-5; parish clerk, 336 (2).
   Grammar school, 201n, 241 (2), 410; Theological college, 393-5.
St. Cuthbert, 8n, 38n, 54, 129.
St. Edmund Hall, Oxford, 113, 277n, 315-7, 455.
St. John's in the Vale, 161, 352 (2), 399, 463, 474.
St. Malachy, 12.

St. Mary's Abbey, York, 5, 9, 12, 54, 67, 78, 132-4, 143, 144, 148-9, 471, 472, 473, 474.
St. Nicholas Hospital, Carlisle, 25, 76, 79, 128.
St. Peter's Hospital, York, 8.
Salisbury, Richard Neville, earl of, arms of, 124, 166.
Salkeld, Great, 15, 54, 65, 67, 77, 87, 199, 262, 381, 463, 468, 472; incumbent, 24, 198n, 211, 290n, 318, 360, 363n, 364.
   John, 86; Lancelot, 180, 194, 198; Richard, 87; Thomas, 192.
Salt cotes, 36.
Sanctuary, right of, 26.
Sanderson, Bartholomew, 228, 229; Robert, 216; Thomas, 304n; 'Herioc Ballad' by, 304-7.
Sandford, Thomas, 119, 120.
Sandys, Archbishop, 198, 199, 224; family of, 235.
Satterthwaite, 7, 210, 224, 338, 462, 468, 469, 476.
Saunders, Canon T. B. A., 453, 455.
Sawcott, Agnes, 239.
Sawrey, 459, 462, 468.
Scafell, 354-6, 370, 410, 414.
Scaleby, 15, 19, 234, 239, 263 (2), 276, 384n, 462, 471.
Scalescleugh, 218n.
Scattergate, 314.
Schools, schoolmasters, in middle ages, 37-9, 58; 16th c., 198n, 201n, 211, 240-1; 17th c., 235, 241-2, 282, 285, 288, 289, 329; 18th c., 344; 19th c., 407-10, 412, 432; in church, 213-4, 293, 329, 358; Church, 377, 408, 442-3, 450; Sunday, 365, 432.
Scotby, 400, 402, 462.
Scots and Scotland, raids and invasions, by, 36, 43, 64, 66-70, 76, 80-2, 98-9, 111, 171, 188, 214, 247, 263; effect on daily life, 39-41, 64-5, 68-9, 81, 100, 114-5; and Religious houses, 64, 67, 68, 70, 75, 82, 98, 114, 127; into, 64, 76, 171; and England in 18th c., 303.
Scott, Gregory, 201; John, 236; Sir Walter, 238, 350; Lamb and Co., 346.
Scrogonhegge, 34.
Scrope, Bishop, 125-6; (of Bolton), Margaret, 125; 3rd Lord, 125; 9th Lord, 204, 205; (of Masam), Geoffrey le, 76.
Sea Bathing, 349, 405.
Seakale, 378.
Seascale, 133, 464, 465, 467.
Seathwaite, 338, 351, 353, 462, 464, 468, 476.
Seaton (Seton), Nunnery, 7, 69n,

138; appropriations, 142-3, 473; dissolution, 179.

(Workington), 32, 37, 346, 347, 371, 464, 466, 469.

Sebergham, 15, 157, 237, 315, 368, 463, 471.

Selside, 165, 210, 328, 330, 338, 398, 463, 476.

Senhouse, family of, 112n; arms of, 133.
   Bishop Richard, 253, 254n; Bishop William, 132-4; Prior Simon, 133, 171; Humphrey, 346, 375; John, 253; Mary, 346; Thomas, 133.

Sermons, in middle ages, 95; 16th c., 198, 207, 211, 222; 17th c., 246, 256; 18th c., 364, 375, 388; 19th c., 382, 383.

Setmurthy, 32, 33, 163, 390, 397, 463, 476.

Seven bishops, The, 283.

Sevill cote, 36.

Sevisyke, 34.

Shap Abbey, 7, 8, 51, 127, 130; wool trade, 27; income, 69n; dissolution, 179; appropriations, 473.
   church, 15, 37, 127, 163, 199, 280, 319, 473; parish, 227, 321, 322, 384; spa, 350.

Sharpe, Archbishop, 286.

Share, John, 340.

Shaw, Joseph, 340.

Shawk, 132.

Shepherd, Edmund, 240.

Silloth, 349, 403; Christ Church, 464, 468; St. Paul, 400, 402, 468.

Silverbeke, 34.

Silver mines, 35.

Simnel, Lambert, 123.

Simpson, Elizabeth, 315; F. G., 418; Rev. James, 416.

Singleton, John, 237.

Sizergh, 107, 119, 230, 284.

Skawsely, Alice, 154.

Skelsmergh, 21, 210, 213, 224, 463, 468.

Skelton, 15, 25, 185, 192, 199, 337, 463, 468, 472; chantry of, 79-80; rector of, 200, 252n.
   Family of, arms of, 168; John de, 77; Sir Thomas, 113.

Skiddaw, 354, 355, 414.

Skinburness, 37, 160, 233n.

Skirpenbeck, 149.

Skirwith, 459, 462.

Slee, Christopher, 174.

Smardale, 187n.

Smith, Bishop, 274, 280, 281-8, 290, 295, 315, 316-8; Elizabeth, 281; George, 351n, 354n; Dr. Henry, 281; John, 281, 290n; Sir Thomas, 205; William, 290n; Sydney, 379.

Smoke money, 336.

Smuggling, 355, 370.

Snoden, Bishop, 232, 249-50, 265; Mrs., 249n, 250.

S.P.C.K., 378.

S.P.G., 384-5, 422, 432n.

Sodor, and Man, bishop of, 142, 393, 420, 447.

Solway, Firth, 371; Moss, 188.

Soulby, 187n, 337, 463, 475.

Southey, Robert, 411.

Spas, 349-50.

Spedding, Thomas, 237.

Spenclay, Christopher, 213; Richard, 213.

Stainburn, 68.

Staindrop College, 473.

Stainmore, 13, 67, 163, 187n, 241, 264, 337, 399, 475; North, 459, 462.

Stainton, 110, 468.

Stake Green, 184.

Stanley, William, 133.

Stanwix, 87, 239, 319; church, 15, 276, 399, 402, 471; vicar, 279, 318, 327n, 357, 364, 365; parish registers, 321, 327n; vicarage, 360.

Stapleton, 15, 108, 176, 192, 200, 208, 293, 398, 471.
   William de, 87.

Statesmen, condition of, 227-9, 230-2, 342-3, 368n, 409.

Staveley (Cartmel), 338, 363n, 476.
   (Kendale), 29a, 158, 165, 224, 251, 329, 459, 462, 476.

Stegdall, Thomas, 237.

Sterne, Bishop, 266, 269-71, 280, 385.

Stipends, see benefices.

Stokdale, Alice de, 87; John de, 87.

Stonegarthside, 319.

Storey, Bishop, 124, 126-8; Thomas, 274.

Stramongate, 92.

Stratford, William, 333.

Strensal, John de, 149.

Stricket, John, 216.

Strickland, Great, 228, 463, 468; Head, 268; Ketel, 91n, 237.
   Family of, arms of, 107-8, 166; Bishop, 38, 100, 103, 107-12, 189; Cecilia, 108n; Dowce, 154; Isabel, 108; Sir Robert, 264; Sir Thomas (1366), 107n; (1688), 284; Sir Walter (1448), 119; (1552), 192n; (1569), 230; Walter, 154.

Styhead, 353, 355, 414.

Subsidy, clerical, 94.

Sunday observance, 93, 209, 216, 236-7, 258, 426, 451.

Surnames, 32n.

Surplice, use of, 211, 255, 257, 293, 329, 425, 432, 441.

Swan, Jenkin, 216.

Swarthmoor, 123n, 267 (2), 268, 464.
Swayne, Emma de, 87; Nicholas de, 87.
Swinburne, arms of, 167; John, 119.
Swindale, 337 (2), 475.
Synods, 53-4, 127.

Tait, A. C., 382, 386n, 420n.
Tallentire, 187n.
Talkin, 250, 400.
Taxatio of 1291, 59-61, 69n, 470-4.
    of 1318, 68-9, 470-4.
Tarnmeryn, 32, 33.
Taxation assessment for, 226.
Taylor, John, 216, 340; Rev. S., 122, 242.
Tebay, 464, 468.
Temple Sowerby, 162, 187n, 322, 396, 468, 475.
Tennison, Archbishop, 301, 302.
Thanet, earl of, 226.
Thirlmere, 353.
Thompson, A. Hamilton, 90, 124, 135, 145n, 258n; Alice, 216; Robert, 184, 185, 200.
Thomson, John, 237.
Thoresby, Archbishop, 148.
Thornburgh, family of, 165; William, 119.
Thornthwaite, 158, 161, 340, 398, 400, 402, 468, 475.
Threlkeld, 96, 161, 396, 463, 475.
    Family of, arms of, 211n; Edward, 211; Sir Henry, 114, 119.
Thrimby, 276, 322, 337, 397, 475.
Thursby, 15, 80, 399, 471.
Thwaites, 267, 335, 338, 397, 400, 402.
    Edward, 290n.
Thweng, Sir William, 158.
Tindal fell, 34.
Tithes, 92-3, 186.
Tobacco, 238, 345, 428.
Todd, Anthony, 237; Dr. Hugh, 38, 110-1, 252, 265, 291, 312; his Histories, 262n, 277, 289-90, 307, 308; his quarrels, see Bishop Nicolson.
    Thomas, 264.
Todhunter, Thomas, 228.
Toppin, Isabel, 235.
Torpenhow, 186-7; church, 15, 67, 293, 381, 468, 472; chantry, 58-9, 190; vicar, 278-9, 290.
Torver, 164, 210, 463, 464, 468, 476.
Towneley, Dr. 185.
Tractarianism, 387, 425.
Travel, Travellers, in middle ages, 140-1, 143-4, 150-2, 211; 17th c., 179n, 261, 330, 336; 18th c., 292, 330-1, 336, 349n, 365-6n, 369-72; 19th c., 379, 387, 403, 405-6.
Trierman, 9.

Trokell, William, 152.
Troutbeck (West.), 29n, 165, 223, 230, 236, 241, 462, 476.
Tuffen, Edward, 159.
Tullie House, see Carlisle museum.
    Isaac, 260, Thomas, 287n, 300, 357.
Tunstall, Bishop, 176n, 183, 196; Thomas, 126n.
Turner, Bartholomew, 236.
Tynworth, Robert, 149.

Ukmanby, 162.
Uldale, 15, 160, 268, 276, 360, 396, 398, 459, 462, 472.
Ullswater, 8, 348, 353.
Ulpha, 224, 234, 333n, 335, 476.
Ulverston, 6, 37, 123n, 261, 349n, 374; church, 136, 138, 147, 150, 151, 211, 459, 462, 474; chapels, 147, 164; clergy, 155, 220, 449n; school, 241 (2), 410; George Fox at, 267; St. Jude's, 464; Holy Trinity, 398, 468.
Underbarrow, 165, 267, 462, 476.
Undermilbeck, 29n.
Upperby, 384, 399, 402, 462.
Urswick, 136, 138, 142, 146, 147, 150, 151, 155, 210, 237, 241, 336, 463, 474.
Usher, Archbishop, 259-60.
Usury, 216-7.

Valor Ecclesiasticus, 175-6, 470-4.
Vernon, Bishop, 374-7; Lady Anne, 374n, 376.
Vicarages, ordination of, 44, 58, 127, 142, 176.
Villiers, Bishop, 387, 420-2, 426 (2).
Vipont, family of, 8; Bishop de, 52; Isabel de, 118n; Robert de, 118n.
Visitations, Heraldic, 233, 287n, and see under Carlisle cathedral and diocese and archdeaconry of Richmond.

Wake of Liddell, Thomas, Lord, 76; Baldwin, 20.
Wardle, Robert, 324.
Waldegrave, Bishop, 387, 422-6, 430, 440.
Walker, Anthony, 235; Henry, 119; Janet, 217.
Walking silver, 29.
Walney, 224, 262, 400, 402, 469, 476.
Walton, 15, 230, 276, 459, 462, 471.
Waberthwaite, 122, 137, 140, 150, 151, 155, 211, 220, 474.
Warcop, 15, 127, 199, 235, 253, 402, 473; Isabel, 108; Margaret, 108; Robert, 146; Thomas, 108.
Ward, Sir Simon, 143; Nathaniel, 263.

Ware, Bishop, 408, 417, 418, 434.
Warin, John, 238.
Warwick, 12, 15, 78, 145, 162, 462, 475.
   Richard Neville, earl of, 118, 121.
Wastdale, 156, 353-4, 370, 414-5; Head, 163, 354, 391, 476; Nether, 163, 192, 211, 456, 476; (Shap), 227.
Wastwater, 33, 137.
Watendlath, 8.
Watermillock, 240, 253; chapel of, 96, 161, 196, 245, 246, 463, 464, 468, 475.
Wateruse, 33.
Watre Priory, 472.
Watson, Bishop, 365, 366, 391; Agnes, 216.
Watton, Priory, 473.
Waugh, Bishop, 314-5, 357; Chancellor John, 321, 323-4, 327n, 357-61; his 'Notes' on the diocese, 357-61, 368, 470-4. John, 314.
Waverton, 160, 229, 459, 462.
Weary Hall, 234.
Weather, the local, 92, 150, 352, 391.
Weaving, home, 227, 342.
Wellinton, 58.
Wells, Cecilia, 108n.
Wellyng, 213.
Welton, 464, 468; Bishop de, 53, 85-91, 96, 111; John de, 88.
Wesley, John, 353, 368-74.
Westmorland, archdeaconry of, 421, 434, 449n; county of, 21, 76, 226; 1st earl of, 114, 117, 125; 4th earl of, 182; 6th earl of, 202-4; Bernard, 235.
Westnewton, 237, 459, 462.
Westward, 34, 161, 239, 241, 344, 397, 468, 475.
Wetheral, priory, 5, 18, 54, 88; sanctuary at, 26; industries, 32, 36; income, 69n; Bishop Kirkby and, 78; dissolution, 179.
   church and parish, 12, 15, 78, 145, 174n, 360, 368, 441, 462, 469, 471; Anthony, 251.
Wharton, Sir Thomas, 184; 1st Lord, 200; 2nd Lord, 204.
Whelpdale, Bishop, 112-3; Gilbert, 184.
Wheyrigg, 231.
Whicham, 136, 145, 150, 151, 155, 220, 463, 474.
Whinfell, 24, 35.
Whinlatter, 369.
Whitbeck, 137, 144, 147, 150, 151, 155, 210, 220, 469, 474.
Whitby abbey, 12, 42, 473.
White, Bishop, 253-6, 257, 258.

Whitehaven, 283-4n, 349n, 354, 360, 365n; in middle ages, 32, 34, 36; in 16th and 17th c., 233, 234, 348; in 18th c., 345, 347, 348; in the 19th c., 347, 404 (2), 409, 410; Christ Church, 399, Holy Trinity, 338, 389, 391, 462; St. James, 391, 396, 462, 469; St. Nicholas, 233, 333n, 338, 389, 464, 465n, 469; St. Peter, 458, 469; Wesley at, 369, 370, 371, 372, 374; Weekly Courant, 345.
Whitewall, 281.
Whytefield, Alice, 87; Richard, 87.
Whytehead, William, 87.
Wickewane, Archbishop, 139-40.
Widowhood, vows of, 154.
Wigs, 378-9.
Wigton, 29n, 114, 213, 235, 267, 342, 409; church of, 15, 75, 397, 463, 469, 472; market town, 37, 407; chapels near, 159, 160; hospital at, 191; schools, 344 (2), 410 (2); Wesley at, 373.
   Lady Dyonisia de, 24; Lady Margaret de, 75.
Wilkinson, John, 268.
Williams, Bishop, 379, 455; Mrs. M., 379, 385.
Williamson, Sir Joseph, 287n, 289-90; Joseph, 289n.
Wills, inventories to, 226-30, 339-40.
Wilson, Canon James, 53n, 418-9, and in passim; James, 329; Robert, 430; Thomas, 323-4; Titus, 416.
Windermere, 29n, 365n, 391, 410, 415, 453; 19th c. growth of, 411-4; St. Martin's church, 83, 131, 136, 137, 146, 147, 150, 151, 157, 165, 211, 462, 474; clergy of, 148, 155, 220; St. Mary's church, 399, 402, 413, 459, 462, 469; St. Mary's College, 412-3; St. John's church, 452, 464, 469; Lake, 34, 353, 423; Belle island, 262, 341.
Winster, 165, 464, 469, 476.
Winter, Elizabeth, 236; Robert, 217.
Winton, 228.
Witchcraft, 126, 215-6, 236, 242.
Witherslack, 123, 224, 338, 338n, 452, 469, 476.
Wolsty, 160.
Woodburn, Thomas, 237.
Woodend (Egremont), 234.
Woodland, 164, 425, 459, 462, 476.
Woodside (Wigton), 213.
Wool Pack Inn (Eskdale), 370.
Wool trade, 26-30, 37, 233, 234-5, 341, 345, see Weaving.
Woolthorpe, 171.
Wordsworth, William, 30, 123, 343, 356, 393, 410, 411.

Workington, 138, 202, 341, 374; St. Michael's church, 137, 143, 150, 151, 163, 389, 396, 462, 469, 474; destruction, 390-1; clergy, 145, 153, 155, 201n, 220; parish clerk of, 336; chapel of 'le Gill' in, 153-4; in 17th c., 233, 283, 348; in 18th c., 346, 347; in 19th c., 347, 404, 409, 410; St. John's church, 397, 456; Westfield chapel, 465.
Gospatric de, 17; Patrick, son of Thomas de, 158; Thomas de, 7, 143; William de, 143.
Wragmire, 88, 291.
Wreay, 276, 337 (2), 399, 402, 475.

Wrynose, 354, 370.
Wybergh, Mrs., 385.
Wycliff, John, 134.
Wyndham, Sir William, 225.
Wyse, Agnes, 216; John, 216.
Wysenholes, 34.
Wythburn, 161, 337, 463, 475.
Wythop, 163, 187n, 421, 459, 462, 476.

York, archbishop, 3, 14, 52, 115, 296-7.
York, 132, 204, 261, 262; dean and chapter of, 473.

Zouche, Archbishop, 83, 146-7.

Titus Wilson & Son, Limited, Printers, 28, Highgate, Kendal.